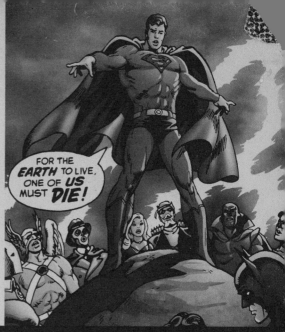

SHOWCASE
PRESENTS

FOR THE *EARTH* TO LIVE, ONE OF *US* MUST *DIE!*

VOLUME 5

Julius Schwartz Editor-Original Series
Bob Harras Group Editor-Collected Editions
Bob Joy Editor
Robbin Brosterman Design Director-Books

DC COMICS
Diane Nelson President
Dan DiDio and **Jim Lee** Co-Publishers
Geoff Johns Chief Creative Officer
Patrick Caldon EVP-Finance and Administration
John Rood EVP-Sales, Marketing and Business Development
Amy Genkins SVP-Business and Legal Affairs
Steve Rotterdam SVP-Sales and Marketing
John Cunningham VP-Marketing
Terri Cunningham VP-Managing Editor
Alison Gill VP-Manufacturing
David Hyde VP-Publicity
Sue Pohja VP-Book Trade Sales
Alysse Soll VP-Advertising and Custom Publishing
Bob Wayne VP-Sales
Mark Chiarello Art Director

Cover illustration by Nick Cardy
Cover color by Allen Passalaqua

SHOWCASE PRESENTS: JUSTICE LEAGUE OF AMERICA VOLUME. 5
Published by DC Comics. Cover and compilation Copyright © 2011 DC Comics.
All Rights Reserved. Originally published in single magazine form in
JUSTICE LEAGUE OF AMERICA 84-106 © 1968-1972 DC Comics. All Rights Reserved.
All characters, their distinctive likenesses and related elements featured in this publication
are trademarks of DC Comics.The stories, characters and incidents featured in this
publication are entirely fictional. DC Comics does not read or
accept unsolicited submissions of ideas, stories or artwork.

DC Comics, 1700 Broadway, New York, NY 10019
A Warner Bros. Entertainment Company
First Printing
ISBN: 978-1-4012-3025-8
Printed by Transcontinental Gagne, Louiseville, QC Canada 1/14/11.

TABLE OF CONTENTS

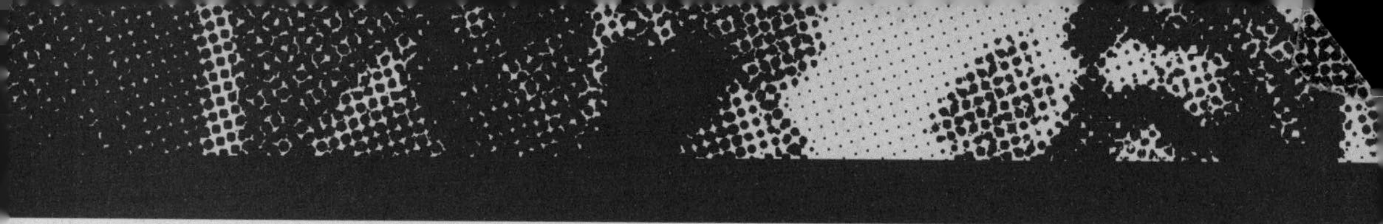

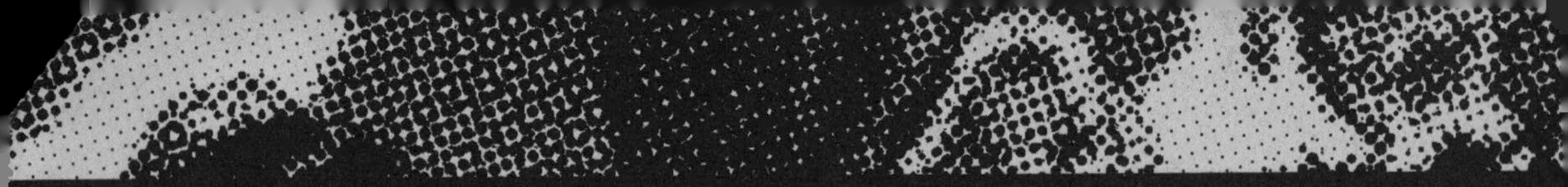

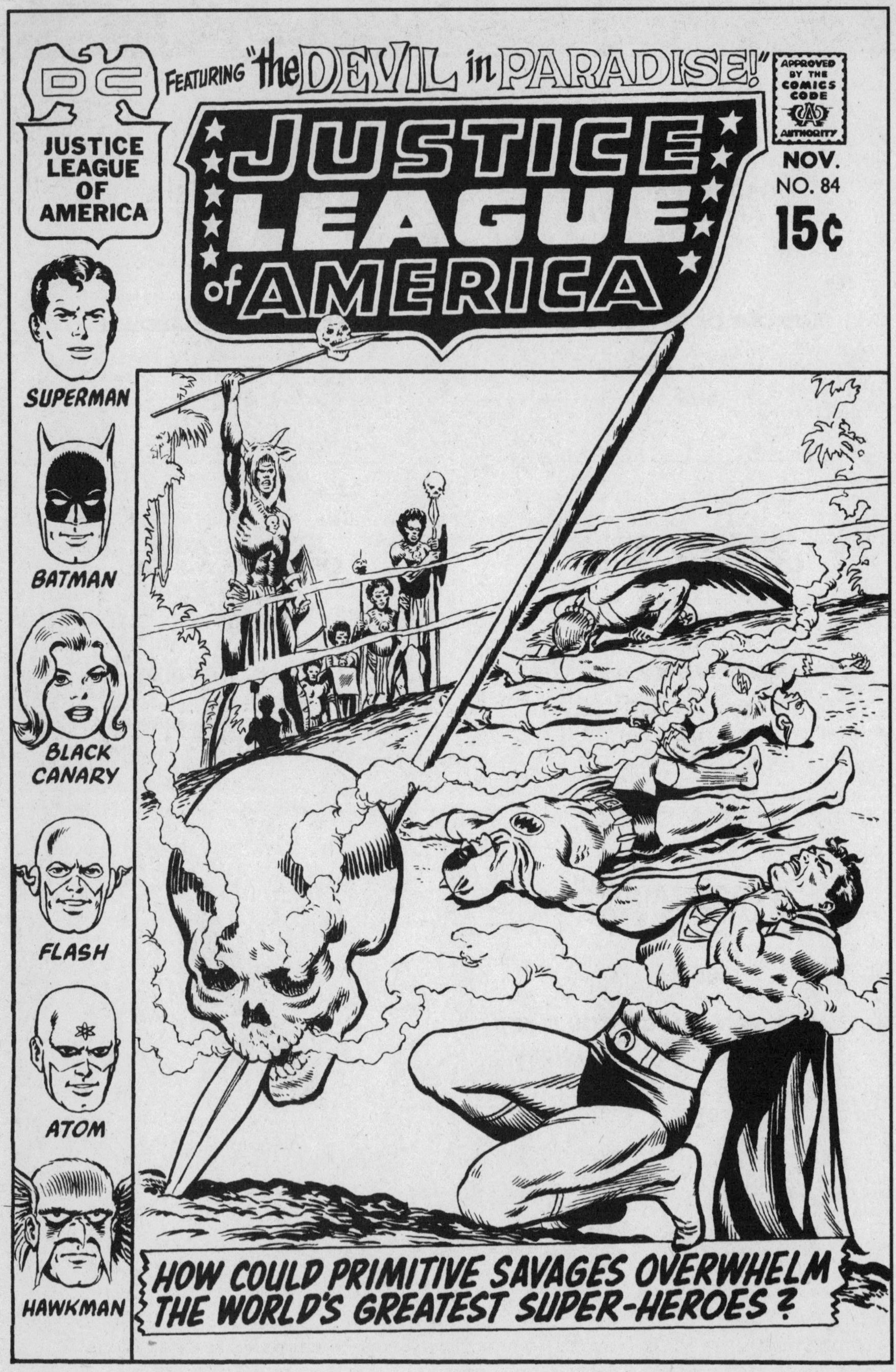
DC
JUSTICE LEAGUE OF AMERICA
FEATURING "the DEVIL in PARADISE!"
APPROVED BY THE COMICS CODE AUTHORITY
JUSTICE LEAGUE of AMERICA
NOV.
NO. 84
15¢
SUPERMAN
BATMAN
BLACK CANARY
FLASH
ATOM
HAWKMAN
HOW COULD PRIMITIVE SAVAGES OVERWHELM THE WORLD'S GREATEST SUPER-HEROES?

ONCE EACH YEAR, FROM *ALBANIA* TO *ZANZIBAR*, THROUGH TV AND JUNGLE DRUMS, THE WORLD WAITS TO APPLAUD THE WINNERS OF THE *NOBEL PRIZES* AWARDED AT *STOCKHOLM, SWEDEN*...

FOR THE FIRST TIME IN *67* YEARS, A SPECIAL AWARD HAS BEEN CREATED FOR THE *JUSTICE LEAGUE OF AMERICA* -- FOR INVALUABLE CONTRIBUTIONS TO THE *"GOOD OF HUMANITY"*!

THIS WINTER, THESE FAMED FIGHTERS FOR FREEDOM COMBINED THEIR UNIQUE TALENTS IN AN ASSAULT AGAINST THE INFAMOUS *ONE HUNDRED*, THE INTERNATIONAL OCTOPUS OF CRIME...

"...ONE OF WHOSE MANY TENTACLES HAD KIDNAPED RECENT NOBEL PRIZE WINNER IN CHEMISTRY, *PROF. LARS HANSUN*, TO BE 'SOLD' BEHIND THE IRON CURTAIN..."

THESE HOODS HAVE HIDDEN PROF. HANSUN SOMEWHERE IN THIS CARNIVAL PARK!

BEFORE WE CAN LOOK FOR HIM--WE'LL HAVE TO KNOCK THAT ROADBLOCK OUT OF OUR WAY!

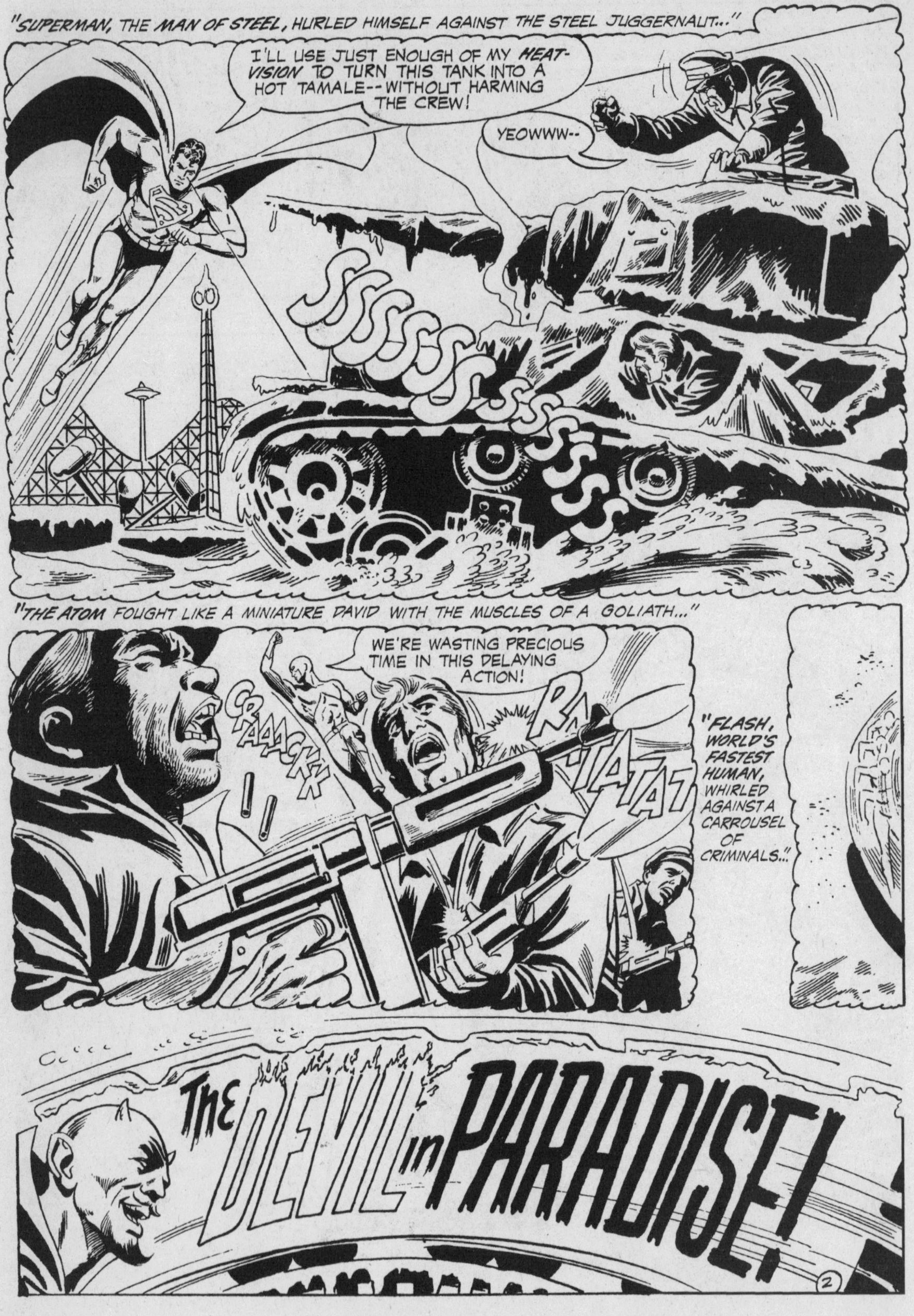
"SUPERMAN, THE MAN OF STEEL, HURLED HIMSELF AGAINST THE STEEL JUGGERNAUT..."
I'LL USE JUST ENOUGH OF MY HEAT-VISION TO TURN THIS TANK INTO A HOT TAMALE--WITHOUT HARMING THE CREW!
YEOWWW--
"THE ATOM FOUGHT LIKE A MINIATURE DAVID WITH THE MUSCLES OF A GOLIATH..."
WE'RE WASTING PRECIOUS TIME IN THIS DELAYING ACTION!
"FLASH, WORLD'S FASTEST HUMAN, WHIRLED AGAINST A CARROUSEL OF CRIMINALS..."
THE DEVIL IN PARADISE!
2

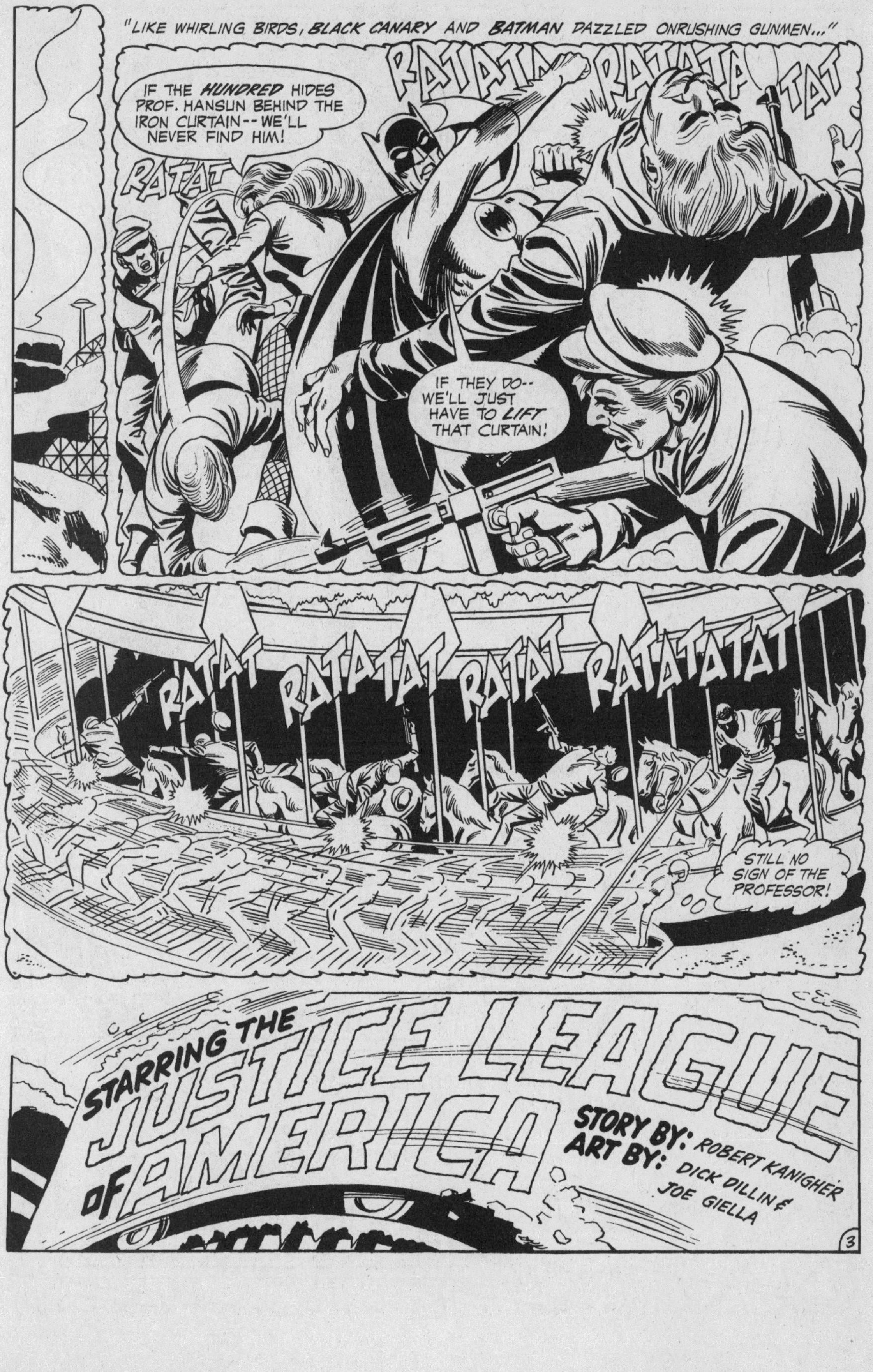
"LIKE WHIRLING BIRDS, BLACK CANARY AND BATMAN DAZZLED ONRUSHING GUNMEN..."
RATATAT RATATAT TAT
IF THE HUNDRED HIDES PROF. HANSUN BEHIND THE IRON CURTAIN--WE'LL NEVER FIND HIM!
RATAT
IF THEY DO--WE'LL JUST HAVE TO LIFT THAT CURTAIN!
RATAT RATATAT RATAT RATATATAT
STILL NO SIGN OF THE PROFESSOR!
STARRING THE JUSTICE LEAGUE OF AMERICA
STORY BY: ROBERT KANIGHER
ART BY: DICK DILLIN & JOE GIELLA
3

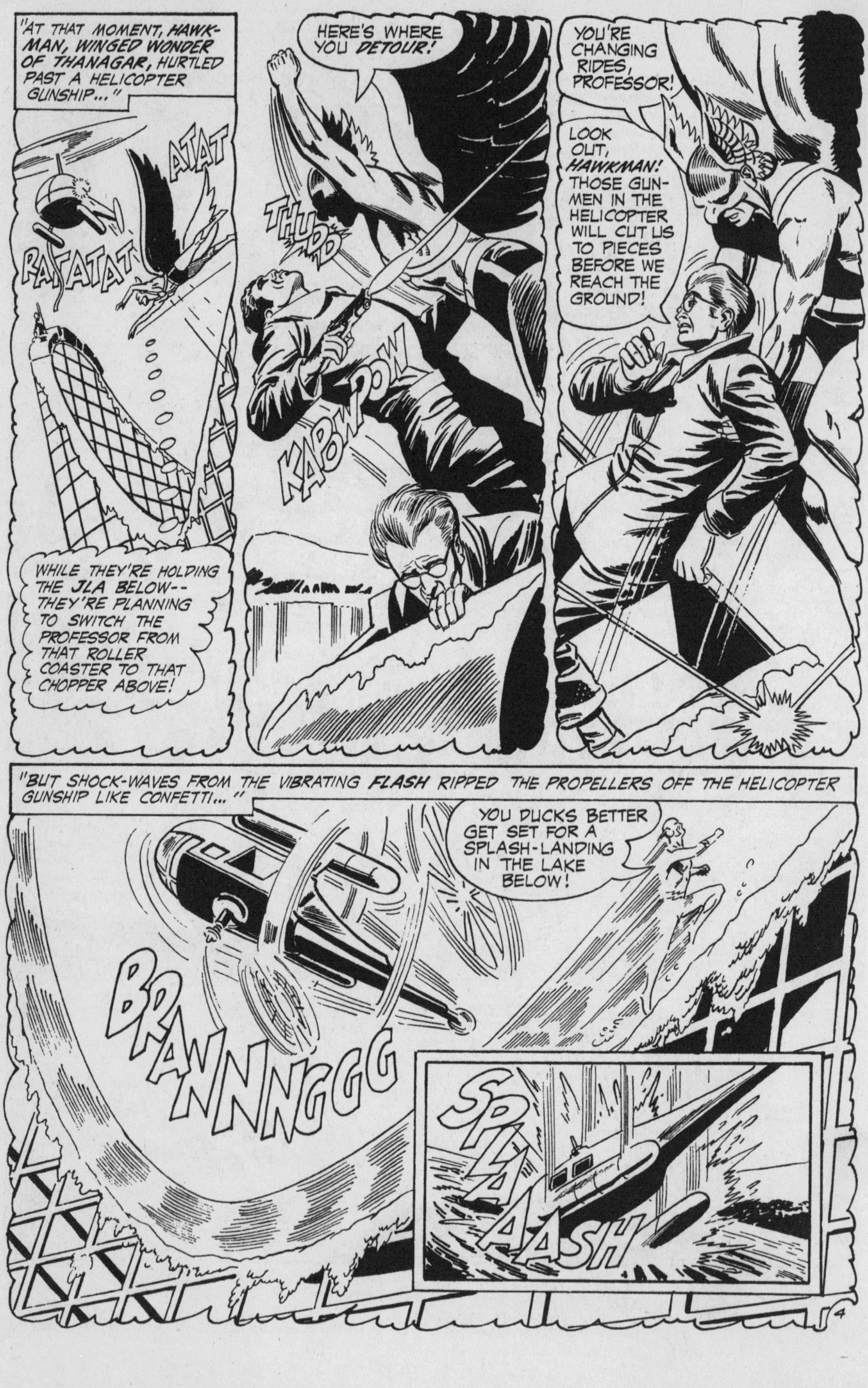

"AT THAT MOMENT, HAWKMAN, WINGED WONDER OF THANAGAR, HURTLED PAST A HELICOPTER GUNSHIP..."
ATAT
RATATAT
WHILE THEY'RE HOLDING THE JLA BELOW--THEY'RE PLANNING TO SWITCH THE PROFESSOR FROM THAT ROLLER COASTER TO THAT CHOPPER ABOVE!
HERE'S WHERE YOU DETOUR!
THUDD
KAPOWPOW
YOU'RE CHANGING RIDES, PROFESSOR!
LOOK OUT, HAWKMAN! THOSE GUNMEN IN THE HELICOPTER WILL CUT US TO PIECES BEFORE WE REACH THE GROUND!
"BUT SHOCK-WAVES FROM THE VIBRATING FLASH RIPPED THE PROPELLERS OFF THE HELICOPTER GUNSHIP LIKE CONFETTI..."
YOU DUCKS BETTER GET SET FOR A SPLASH-LANDING IN THE LAKE BELOW!
BRANNNGGG
SPLAAASH
4

AMIDST THE APPLAUSE OF THE DISTINGUISHED AUDIENCE, THE AWARD-WINNING JLA RETURNS TO ITS SEATS...

AND NOW, THE *NOBEL PRIZE FOR PEACE* GOES TO *DR. VIKTOR WILLARD*--WHOSE UNIQUE *PAX SERUM* HAS ALREADY SUCCEEDED IN TURNING THE *HAWKS* OF SAVAGE, PRIMITIVE TRIBES OF THE *MATTO GROSSO* COUNTRY, INTO *DOVES!*

THAT'S DR. WILLARD'S FIANCÉE-- PHYLLIS TEMPLE! I WONDER WHAT HER THOUGHTS ARE THIS MOMENT AS HE RECEIVES THE WORLD'S HIGHEST HONOR?

--WAIT! I...I'M BEGINNING TO *HEAR* HER THOUGHTS!

VIKTOR PROMISED ME THE WORLD WHEN WE MARRY... AND HE IS...WITH THE *NOBEL PRIZE FOR PEACE...*

THIS IS THE FIRST TIME MY MYSTERIOUS *SONIC POWERS* TUNED INTO ANYONE'S BRAIN-WAVES! SHE'S A PERFECT *HUMAN TRANSMITTER* TO ME!

BUT--WHY DO I SUDDENLY FEEL CHILLED TO THE DEPTHS OF MY SOUL--AT THE SIGHT OF THE MAN WHO HAS JUST WON THE PEACE PRIZE? IF ONLY MY *SP* COULD GIVE ME THE ANSWER TO *THAT!*

AND YET, ANOTHER MEMBER OF THE *JLA* IS SIMILARLY SHOCKED...

SHADES OF KRYPTON! IS THERE SOMETHING WRONG WITH MY *X-RAY VISION?* I SEE THE RIGHT SIDE OF DR. WILLARD'S FACE--*NORMALLY!* BUT THE *LEFT* IS...STRIPPED TO THE BONE! LIKE THE LEERING FACE OF DEATH!

5

SUPERMAN'S MIND STRUGGLES AGAINST HIS NIGHTMARE VISION-- A SPLIT FACE OF GOOD AND EVIL! OF PEACE AND WAR! OF LIFE AND DEATH!

LIKE BALEFUL FOG, THE VENOMOUS ILLUSION FADES, AS THE AWARD-WINNER RETURNS TO HIS SEAT... AND A SPECIAL PRIZE, FROM HIS FIANCÉE...

AS THE CERE-MONIES END...

CONGRATULATIONS, *JUSTICE LEAGUERS!* YOU STAND IN THE WAY OF ANYONE PLOTTING TO DOMINATE THE EARTH!

PERHAPS WE'LL ALL RETIRE ONCE YOUR *PAX SERUM* IS ADMINISTERED TO THE PEOPLES OF THE WORLD! WHEN HATE TURNS TO LOVE, THERE'LL BE NO NEED FOR THE *JLA!*

WE'VE NEVER SETTLED WHO IS FASTER! YOU, *SUPERMAN!* OR *FLASH!* MY MONEY IS ON THE *METROPOLIS MARVEL!*

MY BREAD IS ON THE *SCARLET SPEEDSTER!* LET'S SEE WHO GETS HOME FIRST!

I'LL JUDGE THIS HORSE RACE!

READY? SET! G--UHHNNN--?

SW SHOOOOOOSH

6

AS THE *SOUND BARRIER* COLLAPSES BEFORE THE *MAN OF STEEL'S* ROARING FLIGHT...

GOT TO SLOW UP! I'M CREATING TURBULENCE THAT'S UPSETTING THOSE JETS LIKE THEY'RE IN A SALTSHAKER! I BETTER LET *FLASH* WIN THE RACE!

WHILE BELOW, VIBRATING LIKE A HUMAN TIDAL WAVE AT MULTI-LIGHT SPEED...

CAN'T CLOBBER THAT NAVAL FLEET JUST TO PROVE I'M FASTER THAN *SUPERMAN!* I'LL HAVE TO PUT ON THE BRAKES-- LET HIM WIN!

AND SO, ONCE AGAIN, *SUPERMAN* AND *FLASH* END THEIR TITANIC RACE IN A DEAD HEAT!...TO BE CONTINUED IN THE NOVEMBER *WORLD'S FINEST COMICS!*

SECONDS LATER, ATOP A SKY-SCRAPER THAT HOUSES THE MOST FAMOUS COMICS PUBLISHER IN AMERICA, *BLACK CANARY* IS THE FIRST TO BE DROPPED OFF...

IT'S MY TURN TO BE "ELEVATED" FOR OBSERVATION DUTY IN *JLA'S* SPACE-SATELLITE HEADQUARTERS!

LIKE A HUMAN ROCKET, THE *BLONDE BOMBSHELL* IS PRO-PELLED AT TELEPATHIC SPEED 22,300 MILES ABOVE EARTH...

WORK! THAT'S WHAT I NEED TO FORGET! WORK!

INSIDE, SURROUNDED BY BANKS OF COMPUTERIZED MONITORS SCREENING THE *WORLD'S* WOES...YET, *OBLIVIOUS* OF THE *HEARTACHE* OF A *SINGLE* HUMAN INCHES AWAY...

B-BUT...HOW CAN I FORGET...? I'M JUST A LONELY GIRL-- STILL MOURNING *THE DEATH OF MY HUSBAND...*

7

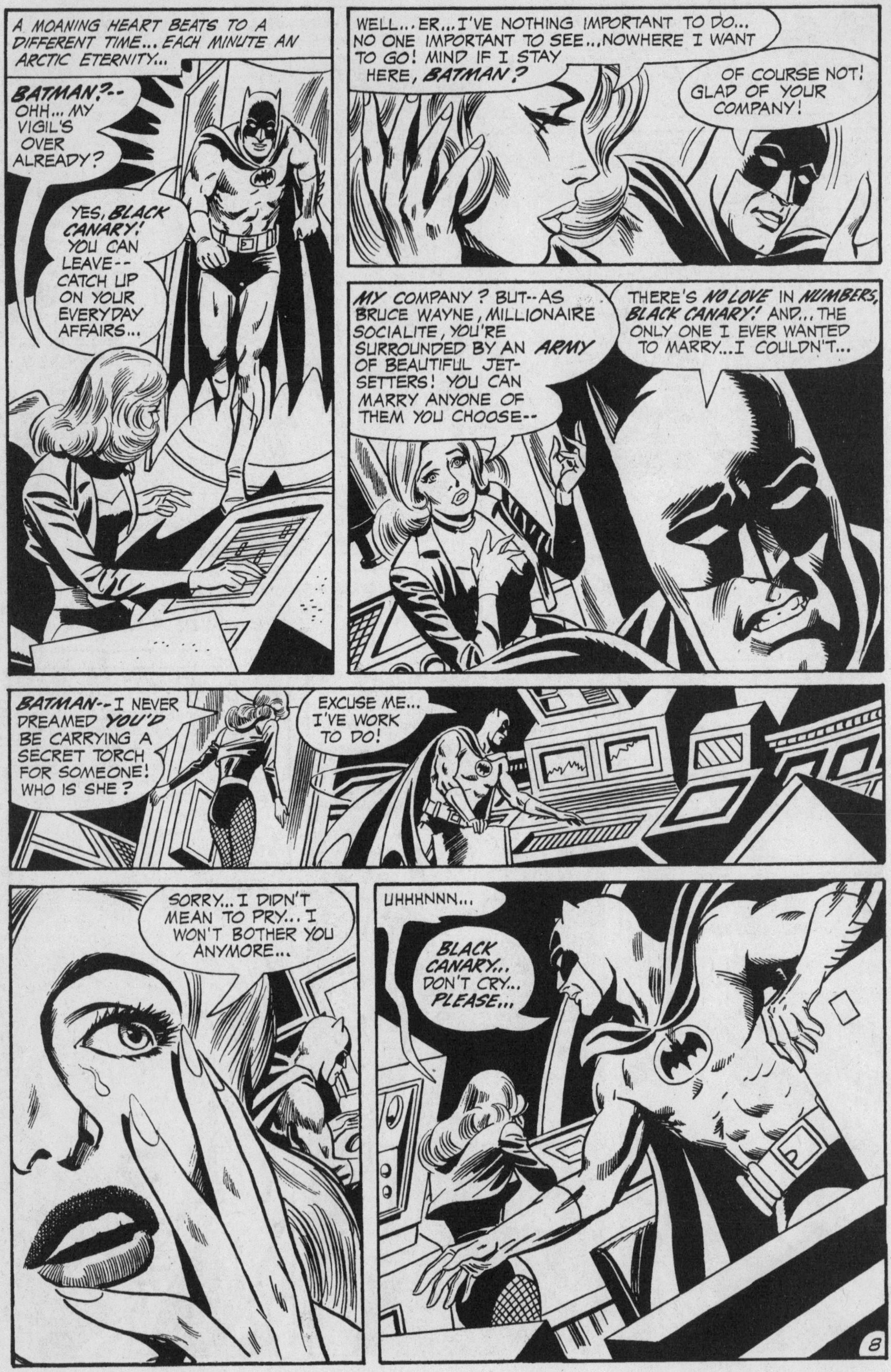
A MOANING HEART BEATS TO A DIFFERENT TIME... EACH MINUTE AN ARCTIC ETERNITY...
BATMAN?-- OHH... MY VIGIL'S OVER ALREADY?
YES, BLACK CANARY! YOU CAN LEAVE-- CATCH UP ON YOUR EVERYDAY AFFAIRS...
WELL... ER... I'VE NOTHING IMPORTANT TO DO... NO ONE IMPORTANT TO SEE... NOWHERE I WANT TO GO! MIND IF I STAY HERE, BATMAN?
OF COURSE NOT! GLAD OF YOUR COMPANY!
MY COMPANY? BUT--AS BRUCE WAYNE, MILLIONAIRE SOCIALITE, YOU'RE SURROUNDED BY AN ARMY OF BEAUTIFUL JET-SETTERS! YOU CAN MARRY ANYONE OF THEM YOU CHOOSE--
THERE'S NO LOVE IN NUMBERS, BLACK CANARY! AND... THE ONLY ONE I EVER WANTED TO MARRY... I COULDN'T...
BATMAN-- I NEVER DREAMED YOU'D BE CARRYING A SECRET TORCH FOR SOMEONE! WHO IS SHE?
EXCUSE ME... I'VE WORK TO DO!
SORRY... I DIDN'T MEAN TO PRY... I WON'T BOTHER YOU ANYMORE...
UHHHNNN...
BLACK CANARY... DON'T CRY... PLEASE...
8

WITH THE AWKWARD TENDERNESS OF A MAN, *BATMAN* ENFOLDS THE SOBBING *BLACK CANARY* IN HIS ARMS...

LIKE A BROKEN-WINGED FLEDGLING SHE LIFTS HER TEAR-STAINED FACE TOWARDS HIS DISTRESSED EYES...

TRAPPED BY THE SAME UNIVERSAL WEB OF LONELINESS IN WHICH ALL HUMANS ARE IMPRISONED... THE COUPLE GROPES THROUGH THE DARKNESS OF THEIR SOULS... THEIR LIPS FUMBLING FOR WARMTH... THEIR HEARTS BEATING IN A SECRET LANGUAGE WITHOUT VOCABULARY...

SUDDENLY, THEIR BREATHS SEVERED BY THE SLASHING SWORD OF GUILT...

I DIDN'T MEAN--! I--I'M SORRY--! IT'S ALL MY FAULT--!

NO--*NO!* DON'T BLAME YOURSELF! IT'S *MY* FAULT! FOR A MOMENT I FORGOT--!

I--I CAN'T STAY HERE! I--I HAVE A MILLION THINGS TO DO!

9

FORTY-EIGHT HOURS LATER, ALERTED BY THE *SATELLITE'S* GLOBAL-SCANNING MONITORS, THE *JLA* SPEEDS TO THE REMOTE REGION OF AUSTRALIA...

WE'RE... TOO LATE!

THE *ABORIGINES* MASSACRED THIS PEACEFUL TRIBE!

BUT HOW CAN WE HANDLE 'EM? THE ABORIGINES STILL LIVE BY THEIR STONE-AGE LAWS OF HATE! FEAR! MURDER! WAR!

LOOK AT THE FRONT PAGES OF EVERY CIVILIZED COUNTRY IN THE WORLD TODAY! WE'VE LEFT OUR FOOT-PRINTS ON THE MOON! BUT WE'RE STILL IN THE *STONE AGE!*

SUDDENLY, HURTLING THROUGH THE AIR--A SKULL WITH BLAZING EYES AND CAVERNOUS MOUTH, GUSHING SMOKE...

VROOOOOSH!

THE *SCARLET SPEEDSTER* LEAPS UP TO SPEAR THE GRISLY DEATH'S-HEAD, BUT TO THE *JLA'S* BEWILDERMENT...

I'LL STOP IT--UGHHHH...

VRAAAAGKK

FLASH IS *FAST ENOUGH* TO CATCH A COMET BY THE TAIL-- BUT TOO SLOW TO GET OUT OF THE WAY OF THAT GRINNING BEANBALL!

IT DOESN'T FIGURE!

10

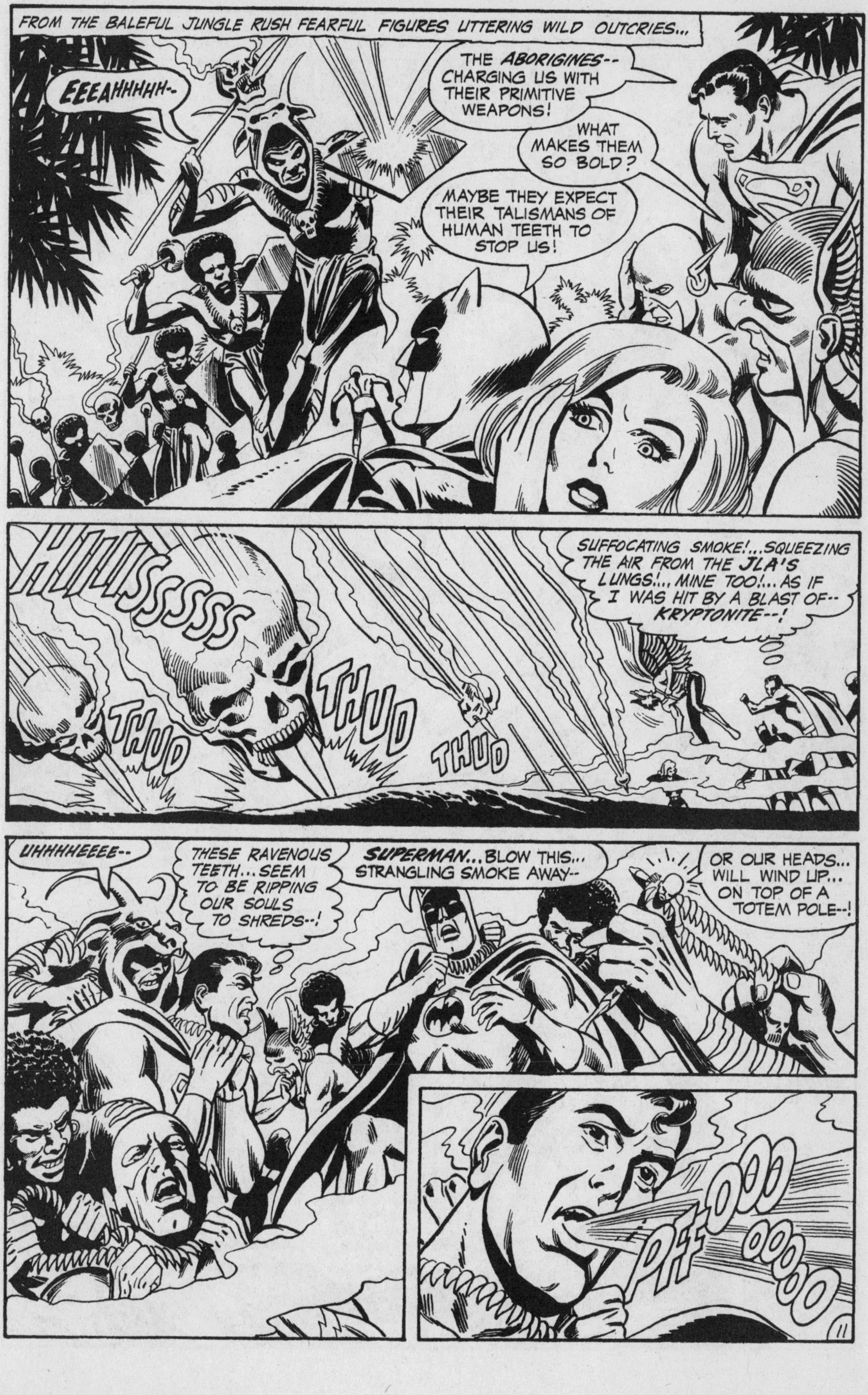
FROM THE BALEFUL JUNGLE RUSH FEARFUL FIGURES UTTERING WILD OUTCRIES...
EEEAHHHHH--
THE ABORIGINES-- CHARGING US WITH THEIR PRIMITIVE WEAPONS!
WHAT MAKES THEM SO BOLD?
MAYBE THEY EXPECT THEIR TALISMANS OF HUMAN TEETH TO STOP US!
HHHISSSSSS
SUFFOCATING SMOKE!...SQUEEZING THE AIR FROM THE JLA'S LUNGS!... MINE TOO!... AS IF I WAS HIT BY A BLAST OF-- KRYPTONITE--!
THUD
THUD
THUD
UHHHHEEEE--
THESE RAVENOUS TEETH... SEEM TO BE RIPPING OUR SOULS TO SHREDS--!
SUPERMAN... BLOW THIS... STRANGLING SMOKE AWAY--
OR OUR HEADS... WILL WIND UP... ON TOP OF A TOTEM POLE--!
PFFOOOOOOOOO
11

DESPERATELY, AS IF BATTLING FIGMENTS OF THEIR OWN FEVERISH IMAGINATIONS, THE *WORLD'S GREATEST SUPER-HEROES* STRIKE OUT AGAINST THEIR NIGHTMARISH TORMENTORS...

...UNTIL THE CREATURES OF DARKNESS FADE IN THE RECEDING TIDE OF OBNOXIOUS VAPORS...

WERE WE...THE VICTIMS OF MASS HYPNOSIS--?

--A GROUP ILLUSION--?

--BLACK MAGIC--?

--WIELDED BY A PRIMITIVE PEOPLE WHOSE BELIEF IN THE SUPER-NATURAL IS AS STRONG AS OUR FAITH IN SCIENCE?

DAYS LATER, AS *FLASH* CRESTS THE WAVES, RETURNING FROM AN *INTERPOL* MEETING AT ISTANBUL...

GOOD GOSH--THAT'S *PHYLLIS TEMPLE*-- CLINGING TO FLOATING WRECKAGE!

WHAT'S DR. WILLARD'S *FIANCÉE* DOING HERE?

GENTLY LOOSENING THE WILD-EYED GIRL'S *DEATH-GRIP* ON THE FLOTSAM THAT HAD SAVED HER LIFE...

EASY, PHYLLIS! YOU'RE *SAFE* NOW! I'M *THE FLASH!* WE MET AT THE NOBEL PRIZE AWARDS WHEN--

NO... NO... IT MUSTN'T HAPPEN! OHH *NO!*

SHE'S DAZED FROM HER ORDEAL! *IN-COHERENT!* I'D BETTER GET HER TO DR. *KELLER* AT *CENTRAL CITY HOSPITAL* IMMEDIATELY!

A MACHINE-GUN BURST OF SPEED AND THE *MONARCH OF MOTION* IS HOSPITAL-BOUND...

DON'T GO... OHHH DON'T LET IT HAPPEN... PLEASE--

WHAT'S THE PICTURE, DR. KELLER?

A *BLANK*--UNTIL SHE BECOMES *LUCID!* YOU'RE HER BEST MEDICINE, *FLASH!* SHE FEELS SAFE WITH YOU! LIKE A TERRIFIED CHILD GOING TO THE PROTECTOR WHO SNATCHED HER FROM THE DARK! STAY WITH HER!

HELP--DON'T LEAVE ME!

I... WON'T... PHYLLIS...

I'LL CONTACT *BLACK CANARY!* MAYBE SHE CAN HOOK INTO PHYLLIS' BRAIN-WAVES WITH HER *SP* AND FIND OUT WHAT'S HAPPENED!

AFTER SENDING OUT A *JLA* SIGNAL TO *BLACK CANARY...*

:GASP: IRIS--?!

SO--YOU SUDDENLY REMEMBER ME? I HEARD THE NEWS OF YOUR RESCUE WHILE I WAS BEING HONORED AT THE *NEWSPAPER AWARD LUNCHEON!*

MY FINEST MOMENT TURNED TO ASHES... BECAUSE YOU DIDN'T SHOW UP...

THE *JLA'S* NO PLACE FOR A MARRIED MAN! LET YOUR SUPER-HERO BACHELORS CARRY ON!

:WHEW: WHEN IRIS COOLS OFF, I'LL MAKE IT UP TO HER! TAKE A LEAVE FROM THE *JLA!* GO ON A SECOND *HONEYMOON!*

13

THIRTY MINUTES LATER...

VIKTOR... DON'T... OHH, NO!

I CAN'T CHANNELIZE MY SP! ALL I'VE DONE WAS KNOCK THAT PICTURE OFF THE WALL!

WAIT-- WAIT! I'M BEGINNING TO BEAM IN ON HER THOUGHTS! SHE...SHE'S IN A JET WITH DR. VIKTOR WILLARD! NEARING AN ISLAND...

RIGHT AFTER WE WERE MARRIED... VIKTOR FLEW US TO HIS PRIVATE ISLAND...

A PERFECT RETREAT FOR OUR HONEYMOON, DARLING! COMPLETELY EQUIPPED JUST FOR THE TWO OF US!

WHILE I'M WORKING IN MY LAB, YOU CAN USE THE SPEED-BOAT...SCUBA-DIVE... SUN-BATHE!

"THE WINGS OF VIKTOR'S SPECIAL JET FOLDED-- WE DESCENDED VERTICALLY INTO AN EXTINCT VOLCANO... AS A PLASTIC DOME SLID INTO PLACE HIGH OVER US..."

EVEN GLOBAL FALLOUT COULDN'T TOUCH US DOWN HERE!

"MILES BELOW-- A SUB-TERRANEAN WORLD, AIR-CONDITIONED... ARTIFICIALLY LIGHTED-- AND WAITING FOR US, A STRANGE CREATURE..."

W-WHO'S THAT?

NETHER MAN! MY PROUDEST CREATION! NEITHER MAN, ROBOT, NOR ANDROID! PROGRAMMED TO MY HEARTBEAT... MY BRAIN-WAVES! EXISTING SOLELY TO DO MY BIDDING!

SNIFF... SNIFF... PRETTY... PRETTY!

VIKTOR! HE CAN'T BE... SYNTHETIC! HE'S ATTRACTED TO MY FLOWERS!

NOT HE! IT! A PROGRAMMING ABERRATION I'LL ADJUST LATER!

NOW WATCH!-- NETHER MAN!-- DESTROY FLOWERS!

DESTROY... FLOWERS!

OHHH...!

14

BUT, VIKTOR--DARLING-- YOU JUST WON THE *NOBEL PEACE PRIZE!* HOW COULD YOU CREATE THIS--THIS CREATURE OF *VIOLENCE?*

YOU FORGET WE LIVE IN A WORLD OF VIOLENCE! SOLDIERS TURNING EACH OTHER INTO LIVE TORCHES! WAR BLOWING UP THE BELLIES OF STARVING *BIAFRA* CHILDREN!

BLACK MOTHERS IN HARLEM FIGHTING RATS TEARING AT THEIR BABIES! LYNCHINGS! MUGGINGS! TEEN-AGERS TRYING TO ESCAPE WITH *DRUGS* THAT KILL THEM!

B-BUT YOUR *PAX SERUM* WILL CHANGE ALL THAT--!

YES--WHEN I RELEASE IT FROM HERE TO SATURATE THE EARTH'S ATMOS- PHERE! BUT--100 HOURS LATER, ITS EUPHORISTIC EFFECTS WILL *CHANGE!*

BURSTING WITH UNENDURABLE FEAR AND HATRED, NATION WILL TURN AGAINST NATION--TO DESTROY EACH OTHER IN A GLOBAL HOLOCAUST! BUT WE WILL BE SAFE HERE IN *MY NOVA TERRA!*

YOUR NEW WORLD?-- YOU THINK YOU'RE GOD! NETHER MAN ISN'T THE MONSTER-- *YOU* ARE! VIKTOR-- DON'T COMMIT THIS *SLAUGHTER!*

I'M BEYOND ALL LAWS! YOU'LL FEEL DIFFERENTLY WHEN YOU REALIZE WE WILL BE THE *NEW ADAM AND EVE...* IN OUR OWN *PARADISE!*

NETHER MAN, TAKE PHYLLIS TO HER CHAMBERS! I'M GOING TO THE LAB TO READY-- *OPERATION INFERNO!*

15

"AFTER VIKTOR LEFT, I FOLLOWED HIS CREATION DOWN A LONG CORRIDOR... UNTIL..."

NETHER MAN!--TAKE ME TO THE SPEEDBOAT-PLEASE? DR. WILLARD SAID I COULD USE IT!

I--I WANT TO BE ALONE--TO THINK OVER WHAT HE SAID ABOUT HIS NEW WORLD!

NO NEED TO DISTURB HIM! I'LL BE BACK SOON!

"I HELD MY BREATH WHILE NETHER MAN STARED AT ME... A SMILE FROZEN ON MY FACE..."

" SILENTLY, IT--HE--TOOK ME BY THE HAND AND LED ME THROUGH THE LABYRINTH OF VIKTOR'S UNDERGROUND HELL WHILE MY HEART TWISTED WITH DREAD..."

"IT WAS ONLY AFTER NETHER MAN LED ME TO THE SPEEDBOAT THAT HE--IT--UTTERED TWO WORDS AS I SPED AWAY..."

PRETTY... PRETTY!

"FOR HOURS I DROVE IN DESPERA-TION--PRAYING THAT THE JUSTICE LEAGUE WOULD SPOT ME--WHEN MY BOAT WAS HACKED APART BY BLAZING BULLETS..."

VIKTOR'S JET! HE FOUND OUT ABOUT MY ESCAPE! AND WANTS TO DESTROY ME...

BRATATATAT

VIP VIP BEEF OW

CRAAAACK

"BUT THROUGH MY WHIRLING SENSES, AS I FRANTICALLY CLUNG TO THE FLOATING WRECKAGE--I COULD SEE THAT VIKTOR HAD SENT HIS ALTER EGO TO BE MY EXECUTIONER!"

NETHER MAN! HOW... COULD... YOU...?

16

SUDDENLY, BLACK CANARY'S *S P* TURNS OFF FROM HER HUMAN TRANSMITTER AS...

"I DON'T KNOW HOW LONG I DRIFTED--" I CAN'T READ HER ANYMORE! SHE'S COMING OUT OF IT!

TH-THE JLA!--YOU'VE GOT TO STOP VIKTOR! HE--

WE KNOW ALL ABOUT IT! WE'LL START IMMEDIATELY!

YOU'VE GOT TO TAKE ME WITH YOU! VIKTOR IS MY HUSBAND! I STILL LOVE HIM....DESPITE HIS MADNESS! I'M SURE I CAN CONVINCE HIM TO ABANDON *OPERATION INFERNO!*

I AGREE-- LET'S TRY *LOVE* FOR A CHANGE... INSTEAD OF *FORCE!*

SHORTLY, SPANNING THE SEA IN SECONDS...

WE'VE AVOIDED ENTERING THE MOUNTAIN'S CRATER IN ORDER NOT TO ALARM VIKTOR! BUT IT'S NOT LOGICAL THAT HE'LL ALLOW INTRUDERS TO TRESPASS IN HIS *NOVA TERRA!*

I GET THE PICTURE, *BATMAN!*

BATMAN'S DEDUCTION HAS RUNG THE BELL!

DR. WILLARD PLANTED MINE-FIELDS IN HIS ISLAND PARADISE!

BUT THESE EXPLODING "FLOWERS" HAVE NO MORE EFFECT ON *ME* THAN TUMBLEWEEDS!

BLAM

RAAAM

VROOOM

WHAAAM

17

SAFELY FOLLOWING THE PATH THE *MAN OF STEEL* HAS EXPLODED THROUGH THE MINE-FIELD...

WAIT--! DON'T TOUCH THAT DOOR, *SUPERMAN!* IT'S *LEAD!* YOUR *X-RAY* VISION CAN'T PENETRATE IT!

SUPPOSE VIKTOR'S PLANTED *KRYPTONITE* ON THE OTHER SIDE OF IT-- YOU'D BE AFFECTED THE MOMENT YOU OPENED THE DOOR!

--AND EVEN THE *DOOR* MAY BE BOOBY-TRAPPED!

IT'S TIME FOR *THE ATOM* TO DO HIS THING!

INSIDE THE KEYHOLE, THE *TINY TITAN* WORKS THE TUMBLERS WITH A FEATHERY TOUCH...

OPEN SESAME!

CLICK

CLICK

ALL CLEAR!

TOO CLEAR! HAWKMAN--?

I GET *YOUR* POINT, *BATMAN!* I'LL FLY *POINT* THIS TIME!

AS THE *WINGED WONDER* PLUMMETS THROUGH THE CORRIDOR...

I'VE TRIGGERED OFF *LASER BEAMS!* ANYONE NOT FLYING *ABOVE* THEM WOULD HAVE BEEN SLICED TO SMITHEREENS!

ZIT!

TIINGG

18

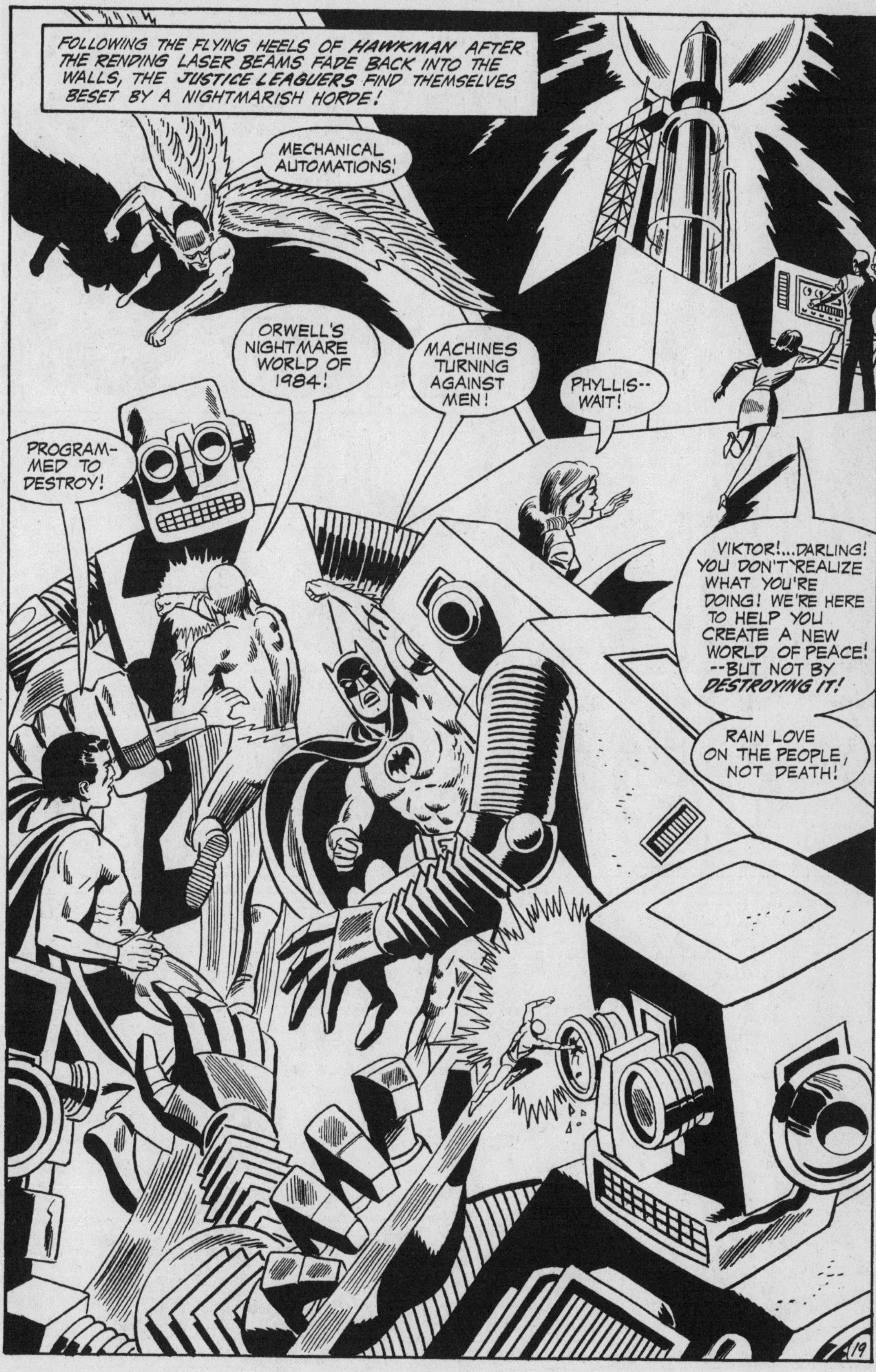
FOLLOWING THE FLYING HEELS OF HAWKMAN AFTER THE RENDING LASER BEAMS FADE BACK INTO THE WALLS, THE JUSTICE LEAGUERS FIND THEMSELVES BESET BY A NIGHTMARISH HORDE!
MECHANICAL AUTOMATIONS!
ORWELL'S NIGHTMARE WORLD OF 1984!
MACHINES TURNING AGAINST MEN!
PHYLLIS-- WAIT!
PROGRAM-MED TO DESTROY!
VIKTOR!...DARLING! YOU DON'T REALIZE WHAT YOU'RE DOING! WE'RE HERE TO HELP YOU CREATE A NEW WORLD OF PEACE! --BUT NOT BY DESTROYING IT!
RAIN LOVE ON THE PEOPLE, NOT DEATH!
19

ON THE RAMP AND ITS SINISTER MISSILE...

YOU PROMISED TO GIVE ME THE WORLD WHEN WE MARRIED... AS A WEDDING PRESENT! REMEMBER, VIKTOR?

BAH! YOU FORGET THAT THE WORLD ISN'T FIT TO LIVE IN! MAN'S MADE IT A GARBAGE HEAP WITH HIS POLLUTION! THEN PILED CORPSES ATOP IT WITH HIS WARS!

AS SOON AS MY INFERNO-BOMB HEATS UP TO ITS CRITICAL RELEASE POINT IT WILL BLAST INTO THE ATMOSPHERE... TURNING THE EARTH INTO A HOLOCAUST!

THEN I'LL REMAKE IT IN MY IMAGE!

DARLING-- YOU'RE NOT GOD!

IN MY NOVA TERRA--I AM GOD! TAKE HER, NETHER MAN!

BUT, VIKTOR! I'M YOUR WIFE! I LOVE YOU!

YOU ONLY MOUTH WORDS OF LOVE! BETRAYING ME TO THE JUSTICE LEAGUE!

ANYONE WHO STANDS IN MY WAY WILL BE SQUASHED UNDER MY FOOT LIKE A WRIGGLING INSECT!

AT THAT MOMENT, THE JLA FINALLY CRUMPLES THE BARRIER OF INHUMAN CREATURES BARRING ITS WAY...

STAY WHERE YOU ARE! ONE FALSE MOVE--AND NETHER MAN HAS BEEN PROGRAMMED TO AUTOMATICALLY CRUSH THIS TRAITOR INTO BLEEDING PULP!

20

I--I CAN'T RISK PHYLLIS' DEATH!

--NOR CAN I... EVEN WITH MY ULTRA-SPEED!

BUT *YOU* CAN STOP THEM BOTH FROM *HERE,* SUPERMAN! WITH A BLINK OF YOUR EYE! A SNAP OF YOUR FINGER! A SUPER-BREATH--

SUPERMAN-- WHAT IS IT?

:GASP-GASP: DON'T... KNOW-- *GREENING* OUT--!

NATURALLY! AN ELEMENT OF MY *INFERNO BOMB* IS GREEN KRYPTONITE!

JUSTICE LEAGUE-- NEVER MIND WHAT HAPPENS TO ME! STOP MY HUSBAND BEFORE HE DESTROYS THE WORLD! HE'S... MAD!

MAD, AM I? YOU'RE NOT FIT TO LIVE IN MY *NOVA TERRA!* KILL HER, *NETHER MAN!*

KILL! KILL! **KILL!**

KILL! KILL! **KILL!**

V-VIKTOR! OHHH, NO--!

MINDLESS... FOOL-- MY BRAIN-WAVES... ACTIVATED... YOU! *YOU*... DIE... THE MOMENT... *I*... DO--MINDLESS... MON... STER--

PRETTY... PRET...TY... PRET--

HOW COULD *NETHER MAN* BE A *MINDLESS MONSTER*... WHEN HE SACRIFICED HIMSELF FOR ME?

CAN *TEARS* FLOW FROM A *MONSTER?*

21

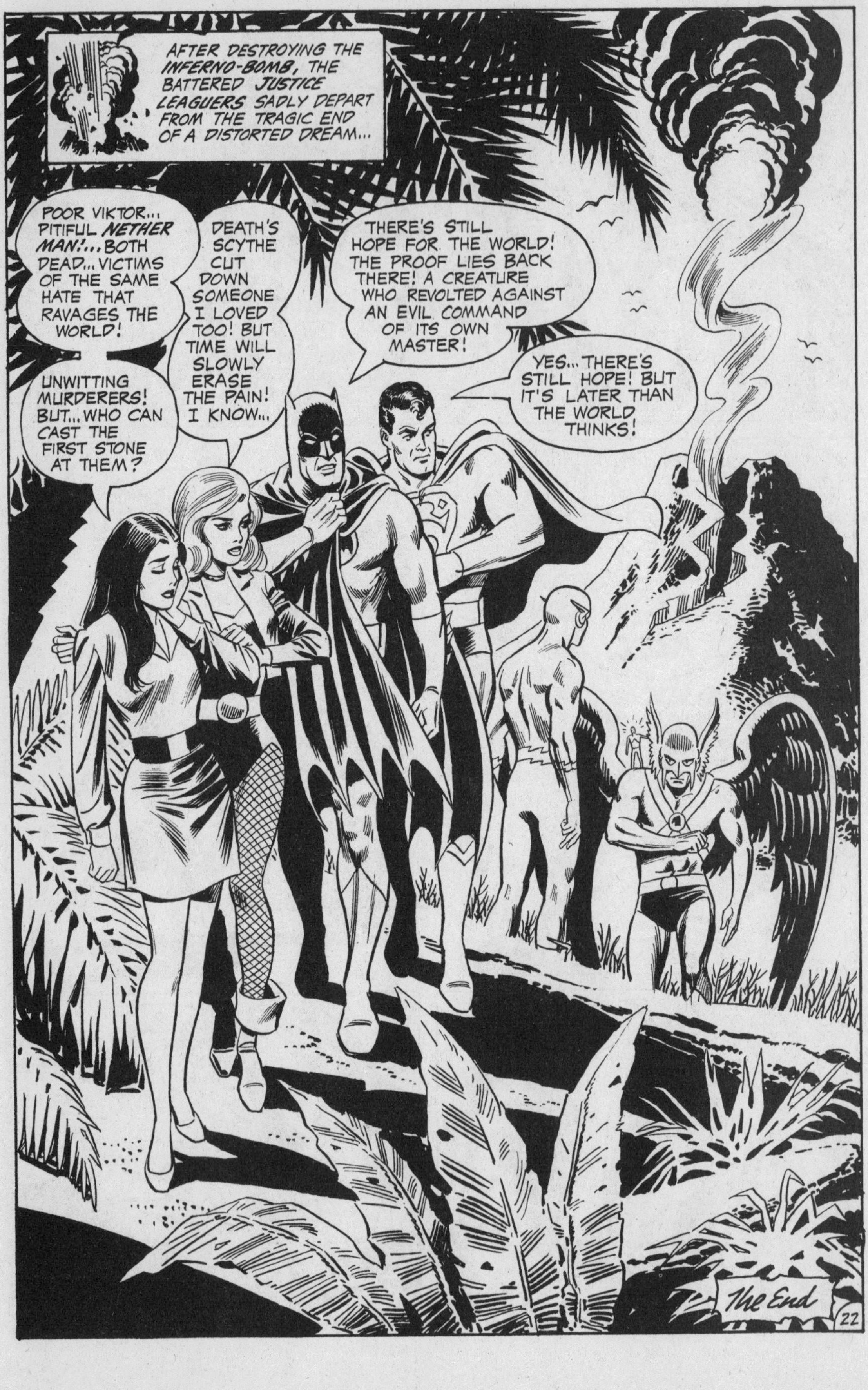
AFTER DESTROYING THE INFERNO-BOMB, THE BATTERED JUSTICE LEAGUERS SADLY DEPART FROM THE TRAGIC END OF A DISTORTED DREAM...
POOR VIKTOR... PITIFUL NETHER MAN!... BOTH DEAD... VICTIMS OF THE SAME HATE THAT RAVAGES THE WORLD!
UNWITTING MURDERERS! BUT... WHO CAN CAST THE FIRST STONE AT THEM?
DEATH'S SCYTHE CUT DOWN SOMEONE I LOVED TOO! BUT TIME WILL SLOWLY ERASE THE PAIN! I KNOW...
THERE'S STILL HOPE FOR THE WORLD! THE PROOF LIES BACK THERE! A CREATURE WHO REVOLTED AGAINST AN EVIL COMMAND OF ITS OWN MASTER!
YES... THERE'S STILL HOPE! BUT IT'S LATER THAN THE WORLD THINKS!
The End
22

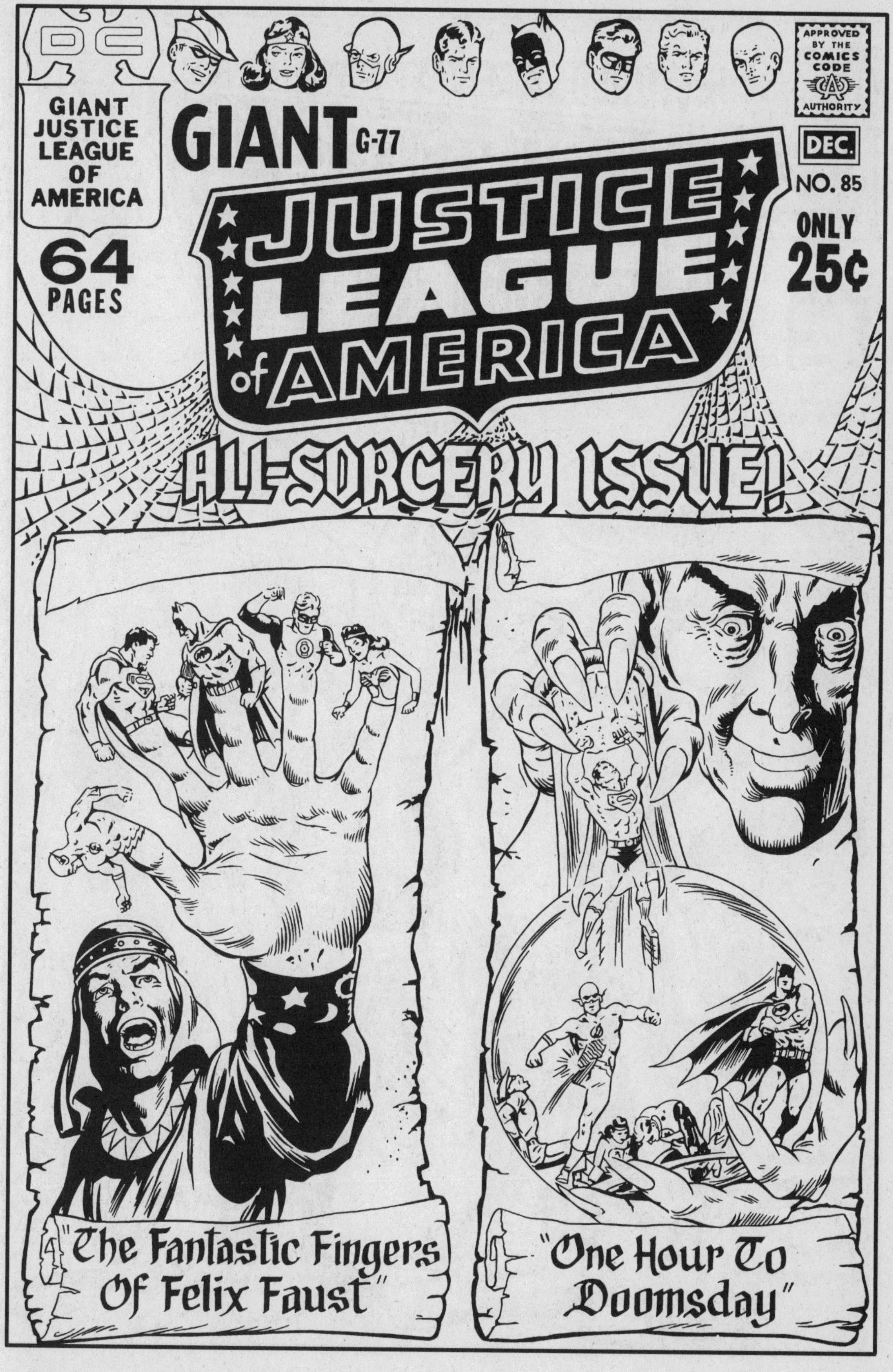
DC
APPROVED BY THE COMICS CODE AUTHORITY
GIANT JUSTICE LEAGUE OF AMERICA
64 PAGES
GIANT G-77
DEC.
NO. 85
ONLY 25¢
JUSTICE LEAGUE of AMERICA
ALL-SORCERY ISSUE!
"The Fantastic Fingers Of Felix Faust"
"One Hour To Doomsday"

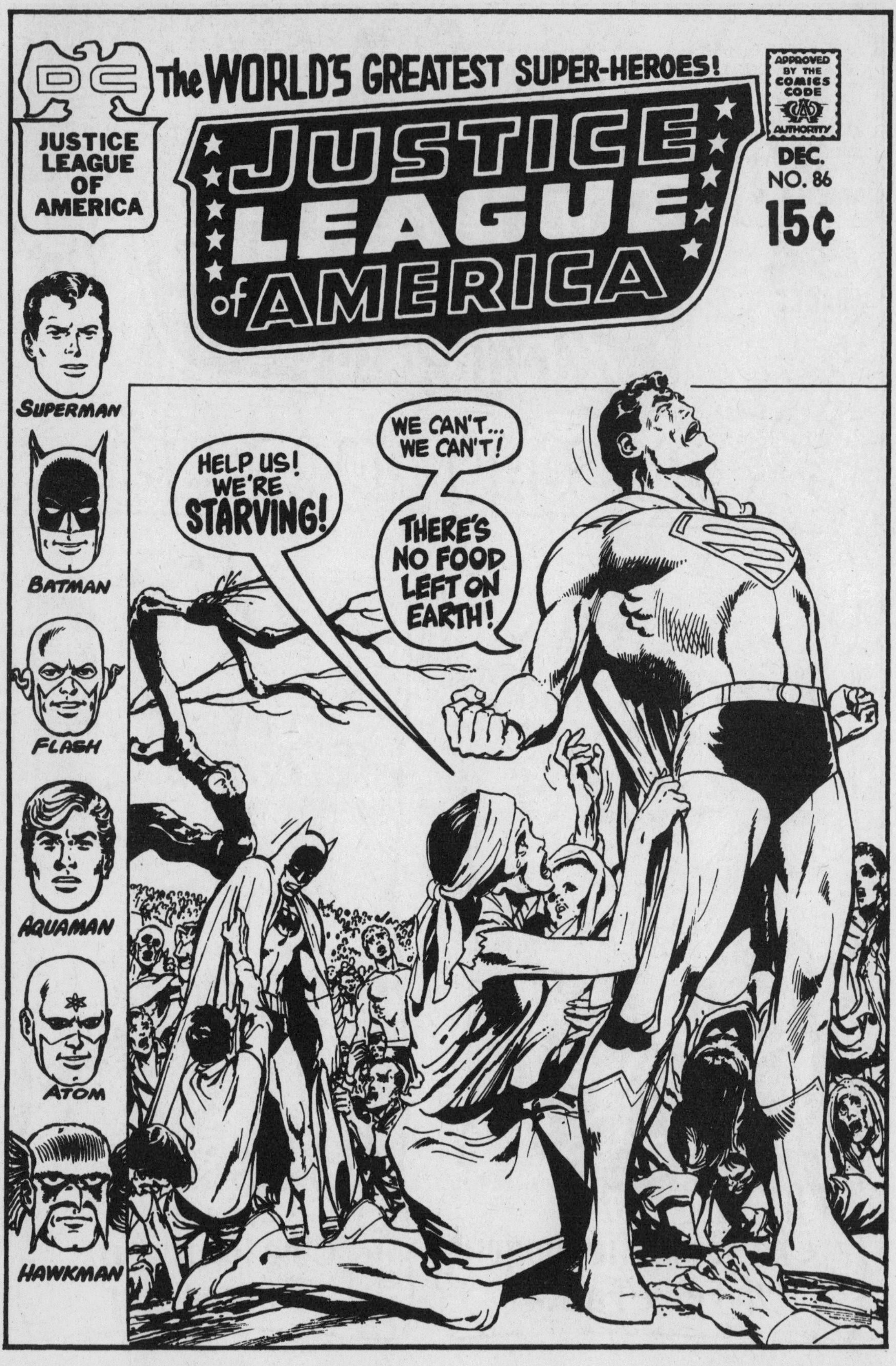
DC
The WORLD'S GREATEST SUPER-HEROES!
JUSTICE LEAGUE OF AMERICA
JUSTICE LEAGUE of AMERICA
APPROVED BY THE COMICS CODE AUTHORITY
DEC.
NO. 86
15¢
SUPERMAN
BATMAN
FLASH
AQUAMAN
ATOM
HAWKMAN
HELP US! WE'RE STARVING!
WE CAN'T... WE CAN'T!
THERE'S NO FOOD LEFT ON EARTH!

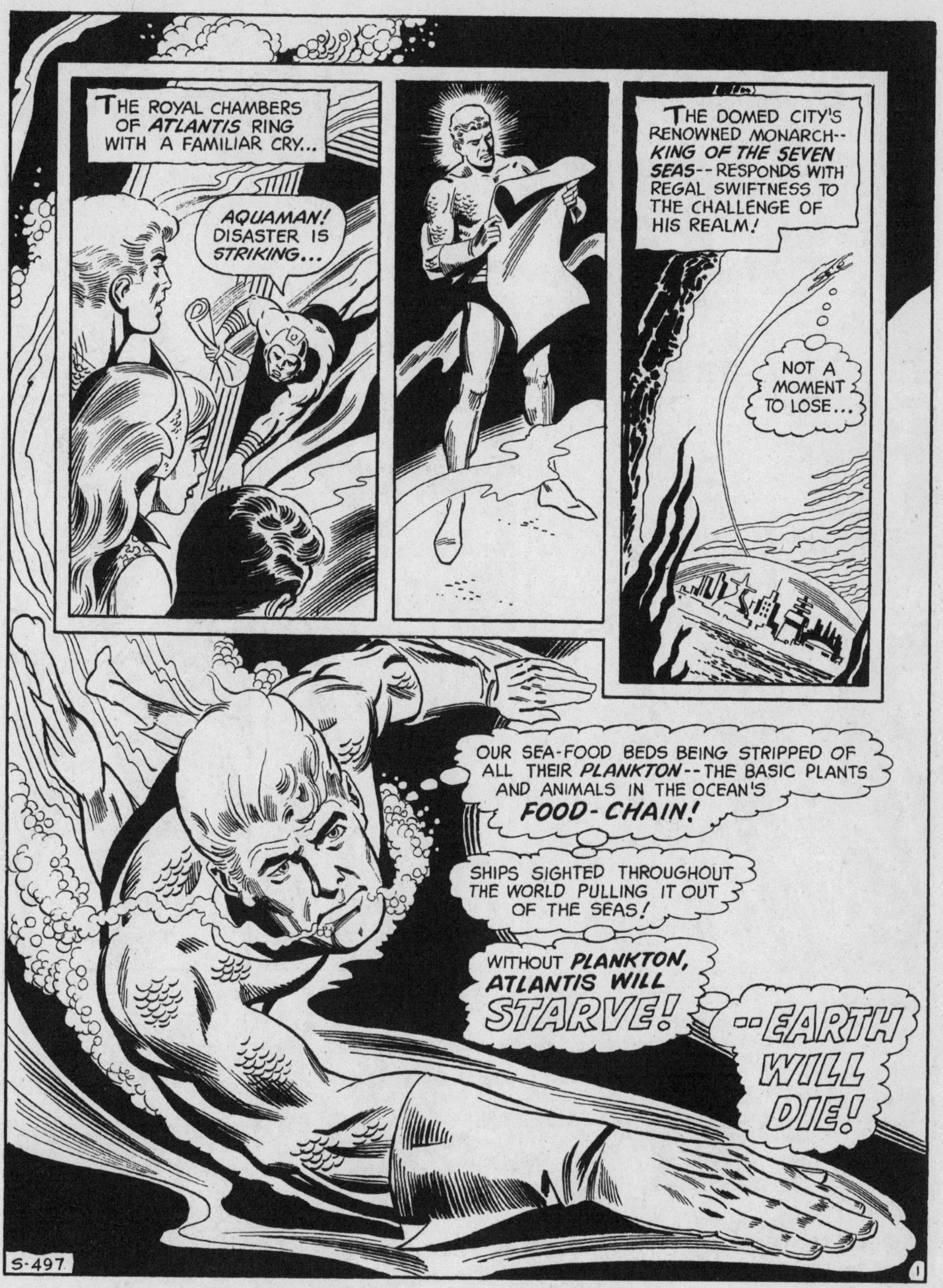
THE ROYAL CHAMBERS OF ATLANTIS RING WITH A FAMILIAR CRY...
AQUAMAN! DISASTER IS STRIKING...
THE DOMED CITY'S RENOWNED MONARCH-- KING OF THE SEVEN SEAS-- RESPONDS WITH REGAL SWIFTNESS TO THE CHALLENGE OF HIS REALM!
NOT A MOMENT TO LOSE...
OUR SEA-FOOD BEDS BEING STRIPPED OF ALL THEIR PLANKTON-- THE BASIC PLANTS AND ANIMALS IN THE OCEAN'S FOOD-CHAIN!
SHIPS SIGHTED THROUGHOUT THE WORLD PULLING IT OUT OF THE SEAS!
WITHOUT PLANKTON, ATLANTIS WILL STARVE!
--EARTH WILL DIE!
S-497
1

FANTASTIC! THAT SHIP IS LIKE A HUGE *VACUUM CLEANER--* SUCKING UP THE *PLANKTON!*

ONLY A *MADMAN* COULD HAVE CREATED SUCH A *MONSTROSITY!*-- HE MUST BE *STOPPED!*

MADMAN? YES... MAD AS *ANY* MAN WHO PLAYS GAMES WITH THE LIFE OF A PLANET!

HMMM... SHIP L-431 APPEARS TO BE RUNNING INTO SLIGHT DIFFICULTIES IN ITS OPERATION...

STOPPED? HE THINKS *NOT!*

SO I APPLY *CORRECTIVE MEASURES!*

ZKAISSZ

NUMB FINGERS STRUGGLE TO PRESS A SIGNAL-DEVICE... THEN BECOME *INERT!* BUT EVEN AS TIME COMES TO A STANDSTILL FOR *AQUAMAN--*

2

ROCK-SLIDE..?!

HAZY SHAPES SHIMMER AND FADE BEFORE DAZED EYES... RANDOM WORDS ECHO THROUGH DEADENED EARS...

DIFFICULTY CHECKED OUT... NO FURTHER PROBLEM... PROJECT NEAR COMPLETION ...BRING ME TO THE C...

WHEN FACED WITH SOMETHING LARGER THAN HIMSELF-- THE MARK OF A *TRUE* MONARCH IS HIS ABILITY TO PUT ASIDE ALL PERSONAL FEELINGS OF PRIDE--AND CALL FOR *HELP!*

THE JUSTICE LEAGUE of AMERICA

--BEGINS A RACE AGAINST TIME TO STAVE OFF...

EARTH'S FINAL HOUR!

WRITER: MIKE FRIEDRICH
SCRIPT CONSULTANT: DENNY O'NEIL
ARTISTS: DICK DILLIN & JOE GIELLA

3

WHO IS THIS INSIDIOUS MAN THAT HAS GAINED CONTROL OF A BASIC ELEMENT IN EARTH'S VERY EXISTENCE?

WHO IS THIS MAN WITH THE SINISTER SMILE THAT THREATENS 3½ BILLION LIVES?

HIS NAME IS THEO ZAPPA... BUT TO FRIEND AND FOE ALIKE HE IS... THE ZAPPER!

HIS METEORIC RISE IN THE BUSINESS WORLD BEGAN FIVE YEARS AGO, WHEN...

... AND MY DEVICE AFFECTS THE MEMORY CELLS IN THE BRAIN -- CHANGES THEM, ADDING NEW "MEMORIES" -- JUST LIKE RE-RECORDING ON A USED TAPE!

ALL I ASK FOR IT, MR. ZAPPA, IS -- $50,000!

COOL! LET ME TRY IT...

... ON YOU!

ZZAPP

$500? OHH, YOU'RE SO GENEROUS, MR. ZAPPA!

ESPECIALLY SINCE I REMEMBER DECIDING BEFORE I CAME HERE TO GIVE IT TO YOU FOR NOTHING!

THE PATH WAS EASY FROM THAT POINT...

IT'S COMPLETED, MR. ZAPPA -- A MINIATURIZED MODEL OF THE RE-MEMORY MACHINE!

GROOVY! LET ME TEST IT...

ZZAPP

HOW WELL I REMEMBER TELLING MY WIFE THIS MORNING THAT I WOULDN'T ACCEPT THAT BONUS YOU OFFERED ME FOR DOING THIS!

4

THE REST WAS *SIMPLE*...

MERCHANDIZING "MY" INVENTIONS HAS MADE ME A *FORTUNE!* AS OF TODAY, I'M THE HEAD OF THE WORLD'S TENTH-RANKING CONGLOMERATE!

BUT THIS IS JUST THE *BEGINNING!* SOON I'LL BOSS THE *ENTIRE WORLD!* THEO ZAPPER... CHAIRMAN OF THE BOARD --*CORPORATION EARTH!*

H-HEY? WHO ARE YOU? WHERE'D *YOU* COME FROM?

MY NAME IS *PAJNA DARR*... AND I SIMPLY *COMMANDED MYSELF* TO APPEAR HERE!

WH-WHAT! B-BUT HOW? WHAT'S THE GIMMICK--?

NO GIMMICK-- JUST *MAGIC*-- A PERFECTLY NORMAL PROCEDURE FOR A NATIVE OF THE PLANET *KALYARNA!*

"ON *KALYARNA* WE HAVE CREATED A HIGHLY-DEVELOPED CIVILIZATION COMPARABLE TO YOUR WORLD'S-- ONLY INSTEAD OF BEING BASED ON *SCIENTIFIC TECHNOLOGY,* IT'S RUN ON BASIC PRINCIPLES OF *ADVANCED MAGIC!*

HOWEVER, ALMOST TOO LATE, WE DISCOVERED THAT OUR SPELL-CASTING HAS BEEN HARMING OUR NATURAL ENVIRONMENT-- IN SHORT, WE HAVE A *POLLUTION* PROBLEM!"

"MOST SEVERELY HURT HAS BEEN OUR OCEAN'S *PLANKTON!* INDEED, OUR MAGIC HAS FOULED SO MUCH OF IT THAT WE'RE ON THE BRINK OF *DISASTER*... UNLESS OUR *PLANKTON* IS REPLACED WITHIN *DAYS!*"

5

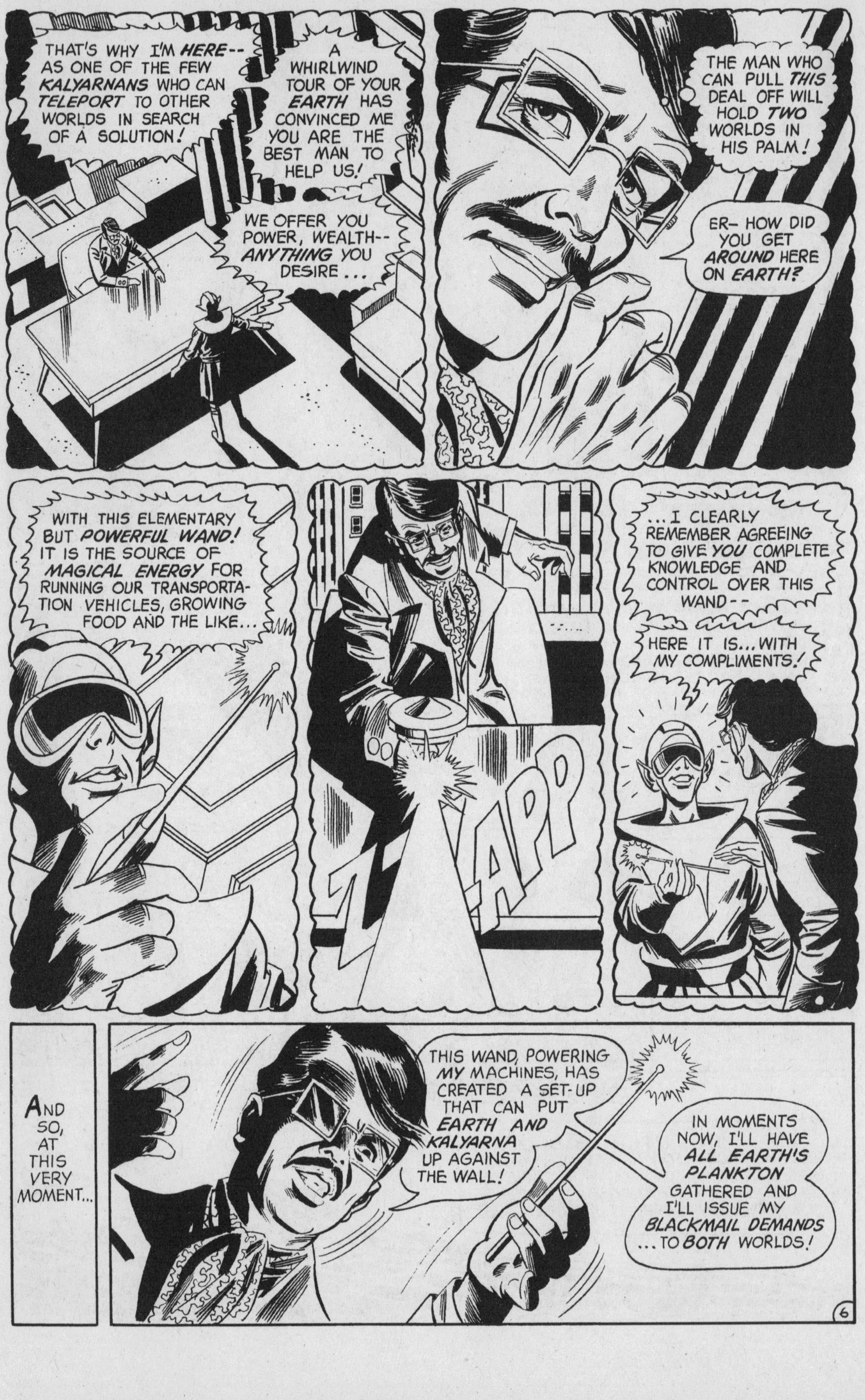
THAT'S WHY I'M HERE-- AS ONE OF THE FEW KALYARNANS WHO CAN TELEPORT TO OTHER WORLDS IN SEARCH OF A SOLUTION!
A WHIRLWIND TOUR OF YOUR EARTH HAS CONVINCED ME YOU ARE THE BEST MAN TO HELP US!
WE OFFER YOU POWER, WEALTH-- ANYTHING YOU DESIRE...
THE MAN WHO CAN PULL THIS DEAL OFF WILL HOLD TWO WORLDS IN HIS PALM!
ER– HOW DID YOU GET AROUND HERE ON EARTH?
WITH THIS ELEMENTARY BUT POWERFUL WAND! IT IS THE SOURCE OF MAGICAL ENERGY FOR RUNNING OUR TRANSPORTATION VEHICLES, GROWING FOOD AND THE LIKE...
ZZAPP
...I CLEARLY REMEMBER AGREEING TO GIVE YOU COMPLETE KNOWLEDGE AND CONTROL OVER THIS WAND--
HERE IT IS... WITH MY COMPLIMENTS!
AND SO, AT THIS VERY MOMENT...
THIS WAND, POWERING MY MACHINES, HAS CREATED A SET-UP THAT CAN PUT EARTH AND KALYARNA UP AGAINST THE WALL!
IN MOMENTS NOW, I'LL HAVE ALL EARTH'S PLANKTON GATHERED AND I'LL ISSUE MY BLACKMAIL DEMANDS ...TO BOTH WORLDS!
6

As AQUAMAN'S SIGNAL OF DISTRESS RINGS AROUND THE WORLD, TWO DYNAMIC FIGURES IN THE WESTERN UNITED STATES PAUSE IN THEIR WORK AND SIGH...

BUT GREEN LANTERN AND GREEN ARROW DECIDE THAT THEIR PERSONAL "SEARCH FOR AMERICA" IS MORE IMPORTANT, UNAWARE THAT IF EARTH'S PLANKTON IS NOT RECOVERED THERE WILL BE NO AMERICA TO FIND!

HOWEVER, THERE ARE OTHER JUSTICE LEAGUERS TO ANSWER THE SUMMONS... ALL SAVE BLACK CANARY, WHO IS BUSY ELSEWHERE! PRAY THEY ARE ENOUGH!

LEADING THE WAY IS THE DYNAMIC MAN OF STEEL-- THE ONE AND ONLY SUPERMAN!

HITCHING A RIDE FROM IVY UNIVERSITY IN THE POUCH CONTAINING THE SUPER COMPRESSED CLOTHE OF CLARK KENT IS THE WORLD'S SMALLEST SUPER-HERO--THE ATOM!

FROM MIDWAY CITY FLIES THE THANAGARIAN POLICEMAN-- HAWKMAN!

RACING FROM CENTRAL CITY IS THE FASTEST MAN ALIVE-- THE FLASH!

HURRYING FROM KEEPING WATCH ON THE JLA'S SPACE-SATELLITE IS THE DARK AVENGER OF THE NIGHT-- THE BATMAN!

THUS, MINUTES AFTER THE EMERGENCY SUMMONS HAS GONE OUT...

THE CALL CAME FROM AQUAMAN! HE LOOKS HURT!

HOLD YOUR BREATH, ATOM-- I'M GOING UNDER!

STRANGE... THOUGHT I SAW SOMEONE WHEN I DIVED IN-- A FELLOW WHO TURNED DOWN AN INTERVIEW WITH ME AS *CLARK KENT!*

HMM...THE WATER IN THIS AREA IS TURNING COLOR-- FROM BLUE-GREEN TO MUDDY-BROWN!

HAS THIS COLOR-CHANGE IN THE WATER ANYTHING TO DO WITH YOUR *CALL,* AQUAMAN?

IT SURE *DOES!* *PLANT PLANKTON* CREATES A GOOD DEAL OF THE OCEAN'S COLOR-- AND *ALL* OF *EARTH'S* PLANKTON IS BEING *STOLEN!*

WHAT'S THIS *PLANKTON* ALL ABOUT? THERE'S NONE OF IT ON MY NATIVE *THANAGAR*--

PLANKTON IS THE NAME FOR THOSE PLANT AND ANIMAL ORGANISMS THAT FLOAT FREE IN THE SEA, BUT CAN'T MOVE BY THEMSELVES!

THEIR MAIN IMPORTANCE COMES IN THE *FOOD-CHAIN!* ALMOST ALL SMALL FISH... AND EVEN SOME SPECIES OF *WHALES*...DEPEND SOLELY ON *PLANKTON* TO *SURVIVE!*

"*DEPRIVED* OF *PLANKTON,* FISH WOULD FIRST GO *MAD*-- THEN *DIE!* IMAGINE EVERY SEASHORE COVERED WITH FOUL-SMELLING *DEAD* FISH!"

"*WITH* ALL MARINE LIFE EXTINCT, MILLIONS OF PEOPLE DEPENDENT ON THE SEA FOR FOOD WILL *STARVE!* IN DUE TIME, LAND PLANTS AND ANIMALS WILL BE AFFECTED...THE REST OF MANKIND WON'T STAND A *CHANCE!*"

8

NOW THAT YOU'VE BEEN BRIEFED, THERE'S NO FURTHER TIME TO WASTE! THE *PLANKTON* MUST BE FOUND BEFORE THE DAMAGE BECOMES *IRREPARABLE!*

WHERE DO WE START?

DO YOU HAVE ANY CLUE TO THE *MOTIVATION* BEHIND THIS THREAT?

JUST BEFORE I CONKED OUT, I GLIMPSED A SHIMMERING FIGURE HOVERING OVER ME!

SOUNDED LIKE HE WAS GIVING ORDERS TO BRING HIM "TO THE SEA"--WHATEVER *THAT* MEANS!

WONDER IF HE'S THE SAME ONE I SPOTTED WHEN I GOT HERE-- AN INDUSTRIALIST NAMED *THEO ZAPPA?*

THE ZAPPER? I'VE HAD BUSINESS DEALINGS WITH HIM AS *BRUCE WAYNE!*

I-- RAY PALMER --MET HIM AT A SCIENCE CONVENTION!

GOOD! BATMAN AND *ATOM*--YOU TRACK HIM DOWN...

WHILE *SUPERMAN* AND I GO UNDERWATER TO SEARCH THE SEAS FOR THE SHIP THAT ATTACKED ME!

HAWKMAN AND I WILL HEAD FOR OUR SATELLITE HEADQUARTERS-- BE ON THE ALERT FOR-- *ANYTHING!*

AN IDEA JUST STRUCK ME, *FLASH!* ON MY HOME WORLD OF *THANAGAR,* A POPULAR NAME FOR THAT AREA BEYOND OUR PLANET'S SPHERE IS THE *"SEA OF SPACE"!*

THIS MIGHT BE THE *"SEA"* AQUAMAN'S PUZZLING OVER! WE CAN CHECK IT OUT IN THE SATELLITE!

⑨

SWIFT-SWIMMING STROKES TAKE TWO *JUSTICE LEAGUERS* ON THEIR UNDERSEA MISSION TO SAVE *EARTH* FROM *BELOW*--

THIS IS WHERE I SPOTTED THE *PLANKTON-STEALING* SHIP...

HERE'S WHERE I TURN ON MY *TELESCOPIC-VISION!*

SUPERMAN AND AQUAMAN

NORTH BY NORTHEAST--300 MILES DISTANT-- LOOKS LIKE A *RECEIVING STATION* FOR THE *PLANKTON-PLUNDERERS!*

NOW TO RELAY THE INFORMATION TO *AQUAMAN*-- VIA *HEAT-VISION!*

SHIPS CONVERGING 100 LEAGUES AWAY-- GRAB HOLD--I'LL TAKE YOU THERE

SUPERMAN DOESN'T REALIZE IT, BUT IF I WERE TOTALLY RECOVERED, I COULD PROBABLY *OUT-SWIM* HIM!

WELL, SINCE THAT'D PROBABLY HURT HIS *EGO*, I'LL JUST HANG ON AND ENJOY THE RIDE!

BUT THE RIDE IS NOT LONG ENJOYED, FOR ALREADY THE FRAGILE FOOD-CHAIN IS BEGINNING TO SNAP!...

GREAT SCOTT! A COUPLE OF WHALES CHURNING UP THE WATER... STARTING TO GO *WILD!*

10

THE NORMALLY PEACEFUL WHALES ARE BAFFLED! THEY RUN THOUSANDS OF GALLONS OF WATER THROUGH THEIR JAWS, BUT TASTE NO FOOD! GRASPING HUNGER DRIVES THEIR NERVOUS SYSTEMS INTO FRENZIES...

POOR LEVIATHANS--

THE *BEST* THING'S TO KNOCK THEM *UNCONSCIOUS*--

AND *HOPE* WE RECOVER THEIR FOOD IN TIME TO *SAVE* THEM...

CONTINUING AHEAD...

THIS STATION IS MUCH TOO SMALL TO HOLD *ALL* THE *PLANKTON!*

WHOEVER'S BEHIND THIS OPERATION MUST BE *TELEPORTING* IT SOMEWHERE ELSE!

WHILE INSIDE *ZAPPA'S* OWN SANCTUARY...

AQUAMAN AGAIN-- THIS TIME WITH *SUPERMAN?*

I WAS A FOOL NOT TO HAVE USED MY *RE-MEMORY DEVICE* ON THE *SEA KING* BEFORE!

THERE'S ONLY ONE MORE SHIPLOAD TO TAKE CARE OF-- I MUST *DELAY* THEM!

EH? ONE OF THE SHIPS-- DUMPING SOME *PLANKTON* BACK INTO THE SEA?!

THE PLAN OF *THE ZAPPER* SUCCEEDS! AT THE SCENT OF THE PRECIOUS FOOD, SCHOOLS OF HUNGRY FISH SWARM AROUND *AQUAMAN!*...

THEY'RE NOT OBEYING MY TELEPATHIC ORDERS! GUESS IT'S BECAUSE THEY'RE TOO HUNGRY TO DO ANYTHING BUT *EAT*...!

CAN'T SWIM *OUT*... OR *UNDER!* BEING CRUSHED...

THE SAVING GRACE OF THE *JUSTICE LEAGUE* HAS ALWAYS BEEN *TEAMWORK!* AROUND AND AROUND THE CIRCLE OF FISH SWIMS *SUPERMAN,* CAUSING A *VORTEX* WHICH SENDS THE FINNY CREATURES WHIRLING...

NO CHANCE TO GET *AQUAMAN* AWAY FROM THE FISH--

BUT I *CAN* GET THE FISH AWAY FROM *AQUAMAN!*

TO SAFEGUARD MY LAST *PLANKTON-LOAD*... A *SUPER-DELAY* FOR *SUPERMAN!*

12

WHY'S THIS *BLOWN-UP PLANKTON* AFFECTING ME?

WHY CAN'T I *OVERCOME..?*

IT'S *MAGIC,* SUPERMAN!

SUPERMAN'S IN TROUBLE! GOT TO RIP THROUGH THIS *JELLYFISH...* GET TO HIM...

CAN'T UNDERSTAND WHY THE JELLYFISH'S RESISTANCE IS SO *LOW* FOR ME... AND TOO *MUCH* FOR *SUPERMAN!*

HOWEVER, BY THE TIME THE DUO BREAKS INTO THE SHIP'S RECEIVING STATION...

TOO LATE! THERE'S NO *PLANKTON* LEFT HERE--

--OR ANY *PEOPLE,* EITHER! THIS ENTIRE SET-UP IS *AUTOMATED!* WE ARE UP AGAINST AN EXTREMELY *POWERFUL* FOE!

13

TWO PROFESSIONAL POLICEMEN HAVE RACED TO THEIR HEADQUARTERS 22,300 MILES ABOVE EARTH! THEIR MISSION: *EARTH'S SURVIVAL!* THEIR NAMES... THE FLASH AND HAWKMAN

WHERE DO WE LOOK *FIRST?* SPACE IS ALMOST INFINITE --

LEAVE THAT TO *ME,* PAL --

SCANNER --

EVERY --

AND --

EACH --

LOOK AT --

GOT TO --

LIKE A HUMAN COMPUTER, THE *FASTEST MAN ALIVE* CHECKS OUT ALL THE DATA FROM EVERY SOURCE ... *UNTIL* ...

THERE IT IS -- A *SPACESHIP!* LOOKS LIKE YOU'RE *RIGHT* ABOUT THAT! "SEA" CLUE, *HAWKMAN!*

GET THE COORDINATES ON IT, *FLASH!* I'M CALLING MY SPACER -- WE'LL OVERTAKE IT IN THAT!

BLAST 'ER OFF, *HAWKMAN!* WE'VE NO TIME FOR SUBTLE APPROACHES!

14

ALL *EARTH'S* PLANKTON IS ABOARD! *KALYARNA* THINKS I BUILT THIS VESSEL JUST TO TRANSPORT THE *"FOOD"* TO HIS PLANET--

BUT THIS IS WHERE I HOARD IT TILL MY DEMANDS ARE MET ON *BOTH* WORLDS!

THE *ALARM*--?!

SO! TWO MORE *JLA* CRUSADERS AFTER ME! HOW'D THEY FIND OUT WHAT I'M UP TO--?

THIS TUB WASN'T BUILT FOR ULTRA-SPEED--BUT I'M GONNA GIVE IT A *GOOD TRY!*

EVERYTHING'S GOING HAYWIRE! WHY ISN'T OUR RADIATION-*SHIELD* WORKING?

*PSEUDO-SCIENCE, HAWKMAN--*OTHERWISE KNOWN AS *MAGIC!*

OHHH...

GOTTA FREE *FLASH* FROM THAT CRUSHING WEIGHT--

15

TURNING OFF THE *ARTIFICIAL GRAVITY*--!

OKAY, *FLASH!* JUST PUSH THE DEAD WEIGHT OFF YOU--

--LIKE LIFTING A *FEATHER!*

NOW TO GET OUT OF THAT SHIP'S *RADIOACTIVE EXHAUST TRAIL*...

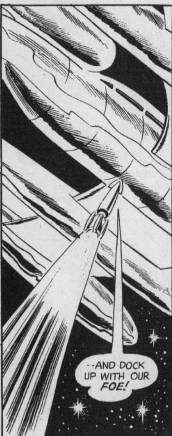

--AND DOCK UP WITH OUR *FOE!*

THEY'VE CAUGHT UP TO ME! ONLY ONE RECOURSE NOW--*TELEPORT THE PLANKTON TO KALYARNA!*

AND WHEN THE PAIR PENETRATES THE SPACESHIP...

HE'S DOING A DISAPPEARING ACT...ALONG WITH THE *PLANKTON!*

WE'VE *MUFFED* OUR ASSIGNMENT!

16

SUPERMAN AND *AQUAMAN*... *FLASH* AND *HAWKMAN*... HAVE FAILED! WITH THIS RAW ASSEMBLAGE OF *SUPER-POWERS* DEFEATED, IS THERE ANY HOPE OF SUCCESS BY THE *POWER-LESS BATMAN* AND *ATOM?*

IN THE FINAL ANALYSIS, HOWEVER, MEN HAVE SURVIVED NOT BECAUSE OF THEIR *INFERIOR BRAWN,* BUT *SUPERIOR BRAINS!*

THE FATE OF TWO WORLDS RESTS ON THE COMBINED *THINKING* OF A BRILLIANT *NUCLEAR PHYSICIST--*

THE **ATOM**

AND THE *WORLD'S GREATEST DETECTIVE...*

BAT MAN

ODD... NOT A SIGN OF *THE ZAPPER* AT ANY OF HIS REGULAR HANGOUTS!

IT'S AS IF HE'S *DISAPPEARED* FROM THE FACE OF THE EARTH!

A COUPLE OF INDISPENSABLE HOURS AND AGONIZING FALSE LEADS LATER...

WHO ARE *YOU*--? WHAT ARE YOU DOING IN *MR. ZAPPA'S* LAB?

I RECOGNIZE YOU TWO--THE *JUSTICE LEAGUERS* CALLED *THE BATMAN* AND *THE ATOM!*

QUICKLY SUMMARIZING HIS STORY...

MY BIOLOGICAL MAKE-UP IS SLIGHTLY *DIFFERENT* FROM YOURS... APPARENTLY JUST ENOUGH SO THAT *ZAPPA'S RE-MEMORY DEVICE* WORE *OFF* A SHORT TIME AGO...

HE EVIDENTLY USED THIS MACHINE TO ESTABLISH CONTACT WITH MY WORLD AND SET UP HIS *PLANKTON* "BORROWING" NETWORK!

I'VE BEEN TRYING TO OPERATE THE MACHINE--IN ORDER TO GET BACK AND WARN MY PLANET ABOUT HIS *REAL* SCHEME-- BUT I DON'T KNOW HOW--

17

LET ME HAVE A TRY AT IT! *SCIENTIFIC* MACHINERY IS MY BAG!

DU?! WHAT *MAGIC* IS *THIS* ON YOUR WORLD OF *SCIENCE?*

NO MAGIC, BUDDY-- MERELY RE-ASSUMING MY NORMAL SIZE!

VITAL SECONDS OF CONCENTRATED EXAMINATION TICK OFF AS THE YOUNG PHYSICIST STRIVES TO UNRAVEL THE MECHANICAL MAZE...

EUREKA! I'VE SOLVED IT! BUT TO OPERATE IT, I NEED A *POWER-SOURCE!*

I HAVE THE VERY THING-- WE EMISSARIES ARE EQUIPPED WITH *SECRET SPARES!*

THIS IS NOT QUITE POWERFUL ENOUGH TO WORK BY *ITSELF*, BUT IT SHOULD SERVE *OUR* PURPOSES!

A *UTILITY BELT!* HOW ABOUT *THAT*, BATMAN?

WE BETTER LEAVE A MESSAGE HERE IN CASE THE OTHER *JUSTICE LEAGUERS* SHOW UP...

IT'S WORKING, *ATOM!* OUR BODIES ARE BEING TELEPORTED...

WHAT A WAY TO GO... TO ANOTHER WORLD!

WE'RE ARRIVING... AS IF BY *MAGIC!*

18

BEHOLD! WE HAVE MATERIALIZED AT THE VERY CENTER OF THE *IMPERIAL SEE* OF *AKUNA*--

SEE--?! SO THAT'S THE "SEA" THAT BAFFLED *AQUAMAN!*

THOUGH I HAVE MATURED IN THIS *MAGICAL, MYSTERIOUS* WORLD, THERE IS SOMETHING *DIFFERENT... EERIE... ABOUT THE BATMAN!*

MAY HE ACHIEVE *SUCCESS*--FOR *BOTH* OUR WORLDS!

INSIDE THE PALACE, MONARCH OF ALL HE SURVEYS--*THE ZAPPER!*...

GLAD THAT *TROUBLE* ON *EARTH* IS BEHIND ME!

THOUGH MY *POWER-PLAY* DIDN'T WORK OUT THERE--AT LEAST *HERE* I RUN THE ACTION--

ISN'T IT THE FIGURE OF *VENGEANCE* PERSONIFIED THAT RIPS THE SOUL? ISN'T IT... *THE BATMAN?*

OHHH, NO! H-HE CAN'T HAUNT ME... N-NOT H-HERE!

GUARDS... CUT THE INTRUDER DOWN!

FEEL SO USELESS HERE... BUT *BATMAN* TOLD ME TO HANG ON... WHILE HE DOES HIS SCARE-THING...

19

I'VE GOT TO STOP *THE BATMAN* ON MY OWN! THE *RE-MEMORY DEVICE* WILL SAVE ME... AND MY KINGDOM!

THE *ZAPPER*-- ABOUT TO *ZAP* *BATMAN!*

WITH PERFECT COORDINATION OF WEIGHT, SIZE AND MOMENTUM, *THE ATOM* ROCKETS OFF *THE BATMAN'S* LAUNCHING PAD...

AND LIKE A GUIDED MISSILE BLASTS ONTO ITS TARGET...

KWHOMM

BUT THE BATTLE IS NOT YET OVER! EVEN NOW, THE ENRAGED PEOPLE OF *KALYARNA* ARE MOBBING OUTSIDE THE PALACE-- HOPING TO FREE THE *EARTHMAN* THEY BELIEVE IS THEIR ONLY HOPE FOR *SURVIVAL!*

20

WHILE INSIDE...

GOT YOUR MESSAGE IN THE *ZAPPER'S* LABORATORY, *BATMAN*--

--WHICH WE *CHECKED* AFTER *STRIKING OUT* UNDERSEA!

--WHILE *HAWKMAN* AND *I* JUST FIGURED OUT THE SAME ROUTE OUR ADVERSARY USED FROM HIS SPACESHIP!

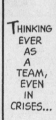

THINKING EVER AS A TEAM, EVEN IN CRISES...

WHAT'S OUR BATTLE-PLAN?

WELL, WITH *SUPERMAN* COMPLETELY VULNERABLE TO THEIR *MAGIC*--

MAGIC?! SO THAT'S WHY I WAS AFFECTED BEFORE!

THERE'S ONLY *ONE* WAY TO PREVENT ANYONE GETTING INJURED-- OR WORSE!

--WE *TALK* TO THEM!

WHAT KIND OF A MAN DOES IT TAKE TO LAY HIS *LIFE* ON THE LINE TO SAVE A WORLD?

MY GOD! THEIR WEAPONS CAN *KILL* HIM!

IT TAKES A *SUPER-MAN,* BABY! ...

21

...A *SUPERMAN* WHO PROVES THAT THE GREATEST PEACEMAKER IS NOT A HAND CLENCHED INTO A SUPER-POWERED *FIST*... BUT A HAND EXTENDED IN THE SIGN OF *PEACE!*

'TIS *SUPERMAN!*

EVERYONE IN THE *GALAXY* HAS HEARD OF *HIM!*

LET HIM SPEAK! IF *ANYONE* CAN HELP US-- *HE* CAN!

...SO YOU SEE, THE MAN YOU PLACED ALL YOUR TRUST IN, MERELY USED IT FOR HIS OWN EVIL PURPOSES!

BUT NOW *YOU'RE* HERE, *SUPERMAN!* *YOU* CAN SAVE OUR PLANET!

YOU'VE MISSED THE *POINT!* YOU'LL *NEVER* SOLVE THE PROBLEM BY HANDING IT TO SOMEBODY *ELSE!*

MY FRIENDS AND I WILL RESTORE YOUR OCEAN'S *ECOLOGY* MUCH AS WE *CAN,* AFTER WE RECOVER OUR *OWN PLANKTON!* BUT WHATEVER *WE* DO CAN ONLY BE *TEMPORARY.!*

YOU MUST EACH FACE YOUR *OWN* PROBLEM-- RE-DO YOUR THINKING ABOUT HOW AND WHY YOU POLLUTE YOUR PLANET--

EVEN AS WE MUST DO ON EARTH!

THE END --IS IT *YOUR* BEGINNING?

The author wishes to extend his appreciation to *NEAL ADAMS,* without whose help this story might never have been told!

㉒

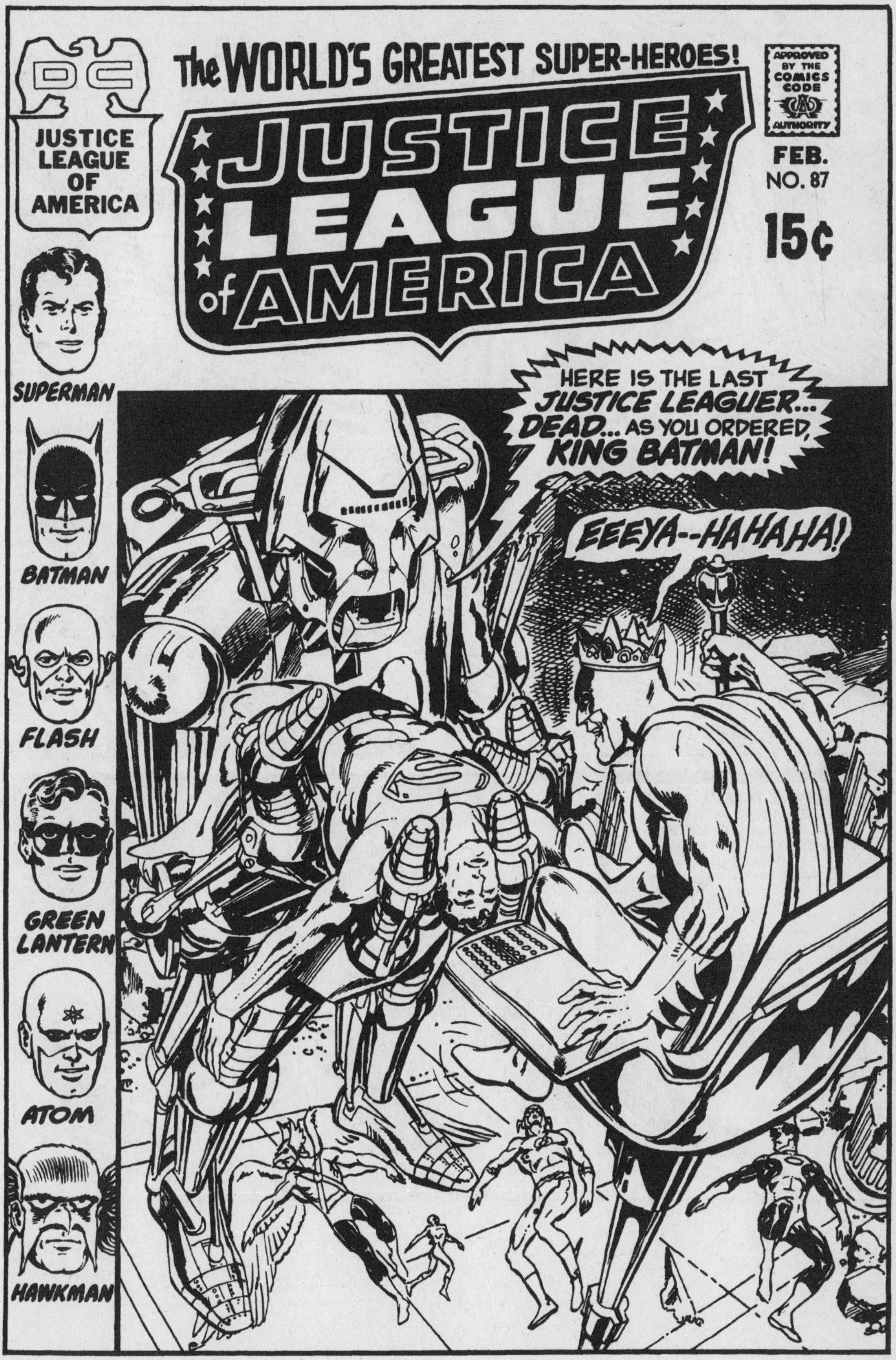
The WORLD'S GREATEST SUPER-HEROES!
JUSTICE LEAGUE of AMERICA
DC
JUSTICE LEAGUE OF AMERICA
APPROVED BY THE COMICS CODE AUTHORITY
FEB.
NO. 87
15¢
SUPERMAN
BATMAN
FLASH
GREEN LANTERN
ATOM
HAWKMAN
HERE IS THE LAST JUSTICE LEAGUER... DEAD... AS YOU ORDERED, KING BATMAN!
EEEYA--HAHAHA!

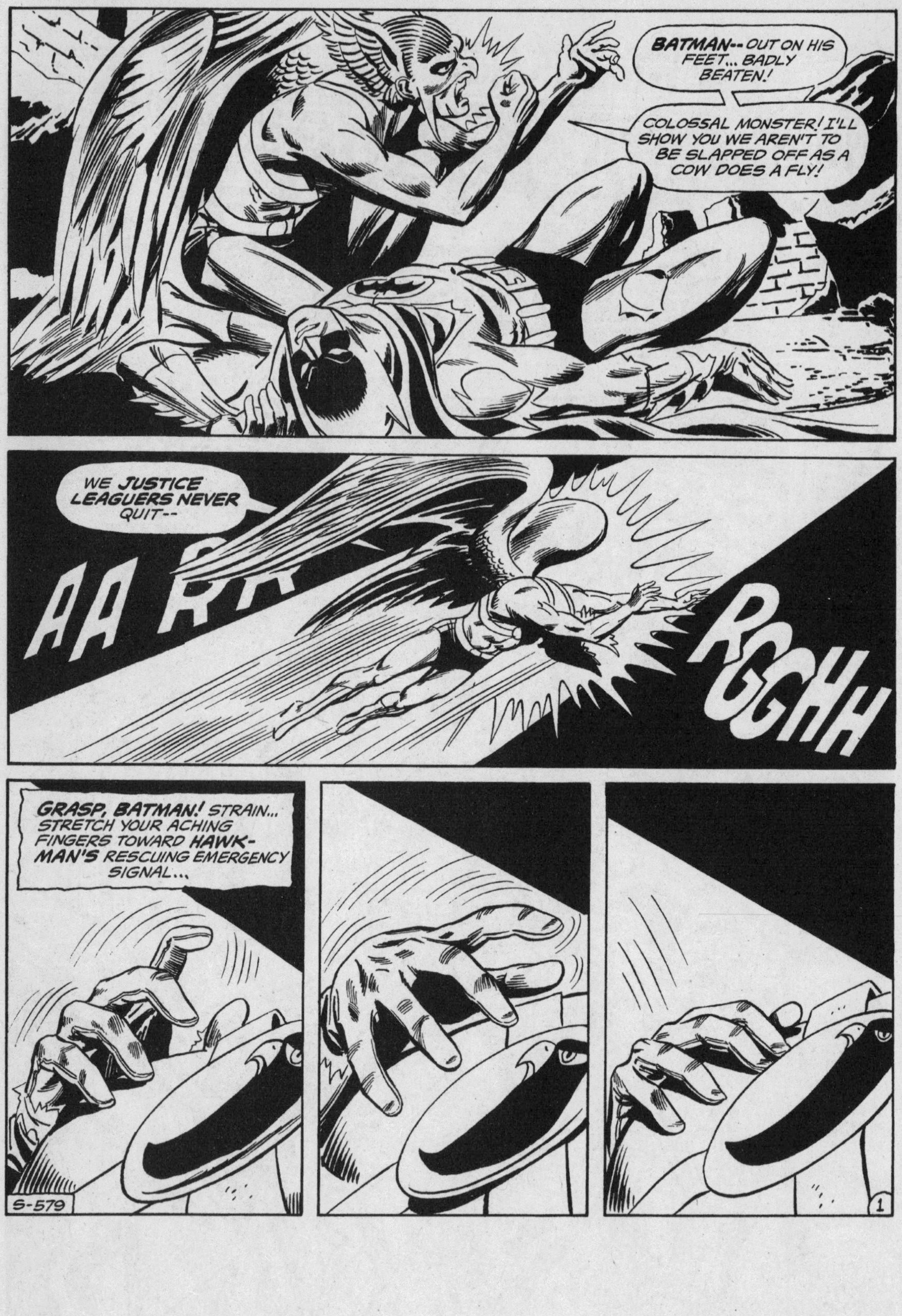
BATMAN-- OUT ON HIS FEET... BADLY BEATEN!
COLOSSAL MONSTER! I'LL SHOW YOU WE AREN'T TO BE SLAPPED OFF AS A COW DOES A FLY!
WE JUSTICE LEAGUERS NEVER QUIT--
AARRRGGHH
GRASP, BATMAN! STRAIN... STRETCH YOUR ACHING FINGERS TOWARD HAWKMAN'S RESCUING EMERGENCY SIGNAL...
S-579
1

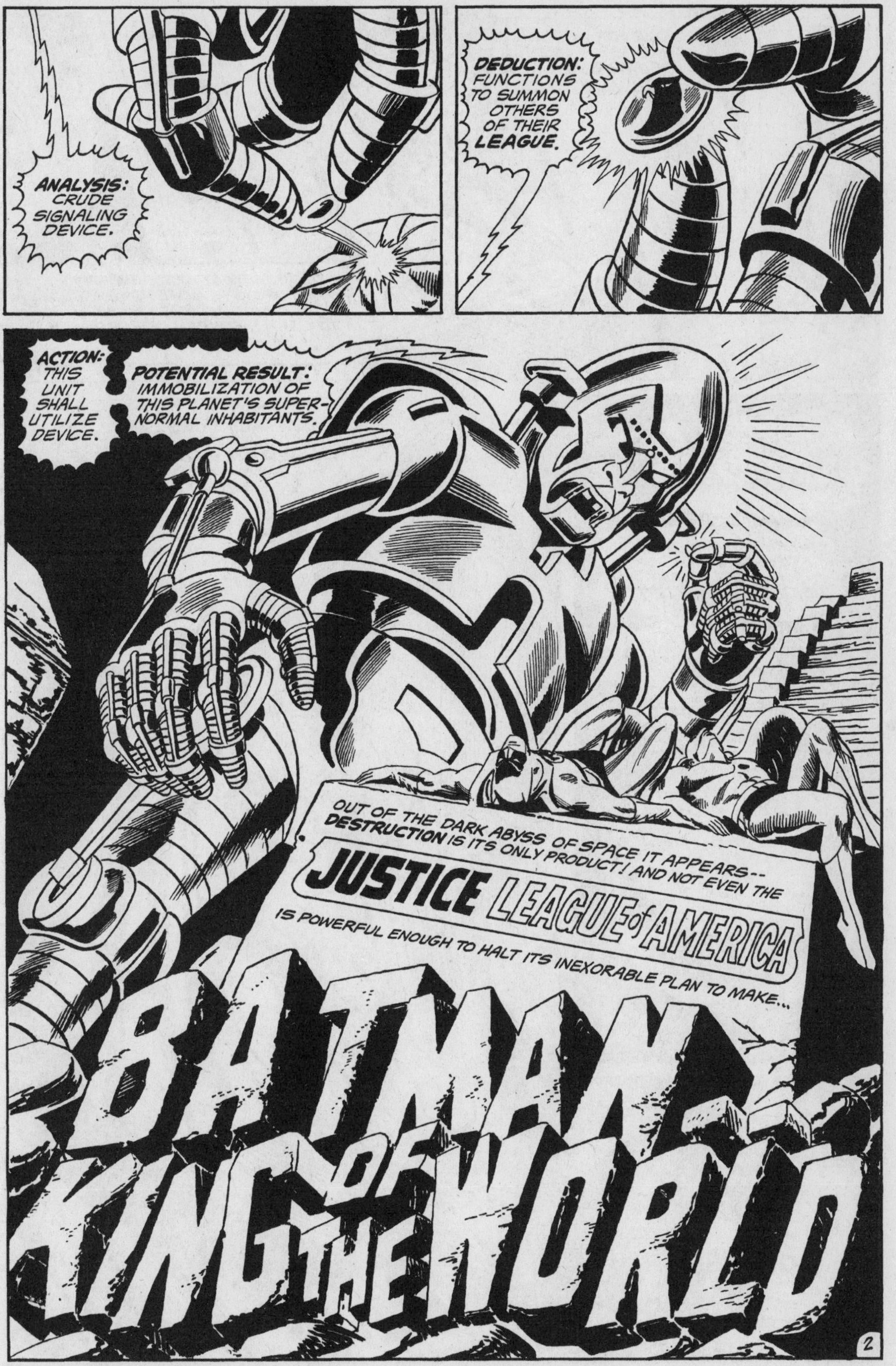
ANALYSIS: CRUDE SIGNALING DEVICE.
DEDUCTION: FUNCTIONS TO SUMMON OTHERS OF THEIR LEAGUE.
ACTION: THIS UNIT SHALL UTILIZE DEVICE.
POTENTIAL RESULT: IMMOBILIZATION OF THIS PLANET'S SUPER-NORMAL INHABITANTS.
OUT OF THE DARK ABYSS OF SPACE IT APPEARS-- DESTRUCTION IS ITS ONLY PRODUCT! AND NOT EVEN THE
JUSTICE LEAGUE of AMERICA
IS POWERFUL ENOUGH TO HALT ITS INEXORABLE PLAN TO MAKE...
BATMAN-- KING OF THE WORLD
2

MEANWHILE, MIDST THE FREEZING, BARREN LAND CALLED THE *ARCTIC*...

PONDER FOR AWHILE HOW IT FEELS TO BE A *SUPERMAN*...

--TO BE *FASTER* THAN A SPEEDING BEAM OF LIGHT, MORE *POWERFUL* THAN AN ATOMIC ENGINE, ABLE TO *LEAP* BETWEEN WORLDS WITH A SINGLE BOUND!...

I AM *SUPERMAN*... WHY MUST I KEEP *IMPRESSING* THAT ON *EARTHLINGS*?

THERE ARE 3½ BILLION PEOPLE ON THIS PLANET AND I AM *UNIQUE... DIFFERENT!*

...A STRANGER IN A STRANGE LAND!

EXERCISING...AND *BROODING* IN MY *FORTRESS OF SOLITUDE* AREN'T HELPING MY SITUATION ANY!

I NEED SOME *COMPANY*-- TO BE AMONG THOSE THAT SHARE THE *CURSE*-- AS WELL AS THE *BLESSING*-- OF *SUPER-POWERS!*

3

THUS, THE TURMOIL OF ALIENATION CHURNING WITHIN, THE **MAN OF STEEL** SPEEDS TO A CERTAIN SATELLITE, ORBITTING SYMBOLICALLY **ABOVE** THE EARTH...

YET IRREVOCABLY HELD WITHIN THE GRASP OF ITS GRAVITY...

WHA--? ZATANNA!

HELLO, SUPER-MAN!

ZATANNA... THE GIRL WITH THE ENIGMATIC SMILE AND DANCING EYES...

ZATANNA... EVER CALM IN THE MIDST OF A STORMY WORLD...

ZATANNA... THE BEARER OF PEACE...

JUST BY BEING NEAR HER, I FEEL SO COMFORTABLE... AT EASE...

WHY ARE YOU HERE, ZATANNA, OF ALL PLACES?

DIDN'T YOU KNOW? TODAY'S THE ANNIVERSARY OF THE TIME YOU JUSTICE LEAGUERS RESCUED MY LONG-LOST FATHER!

I MAGICKED UP HERE TO CELEBRATE--

NO TIME FOR THAT NOW, ZATANNA...

A JLA EMERGENCY SIGNAL-- FROM HAWKMAN... IN PERU!

SOUTH AMERICA

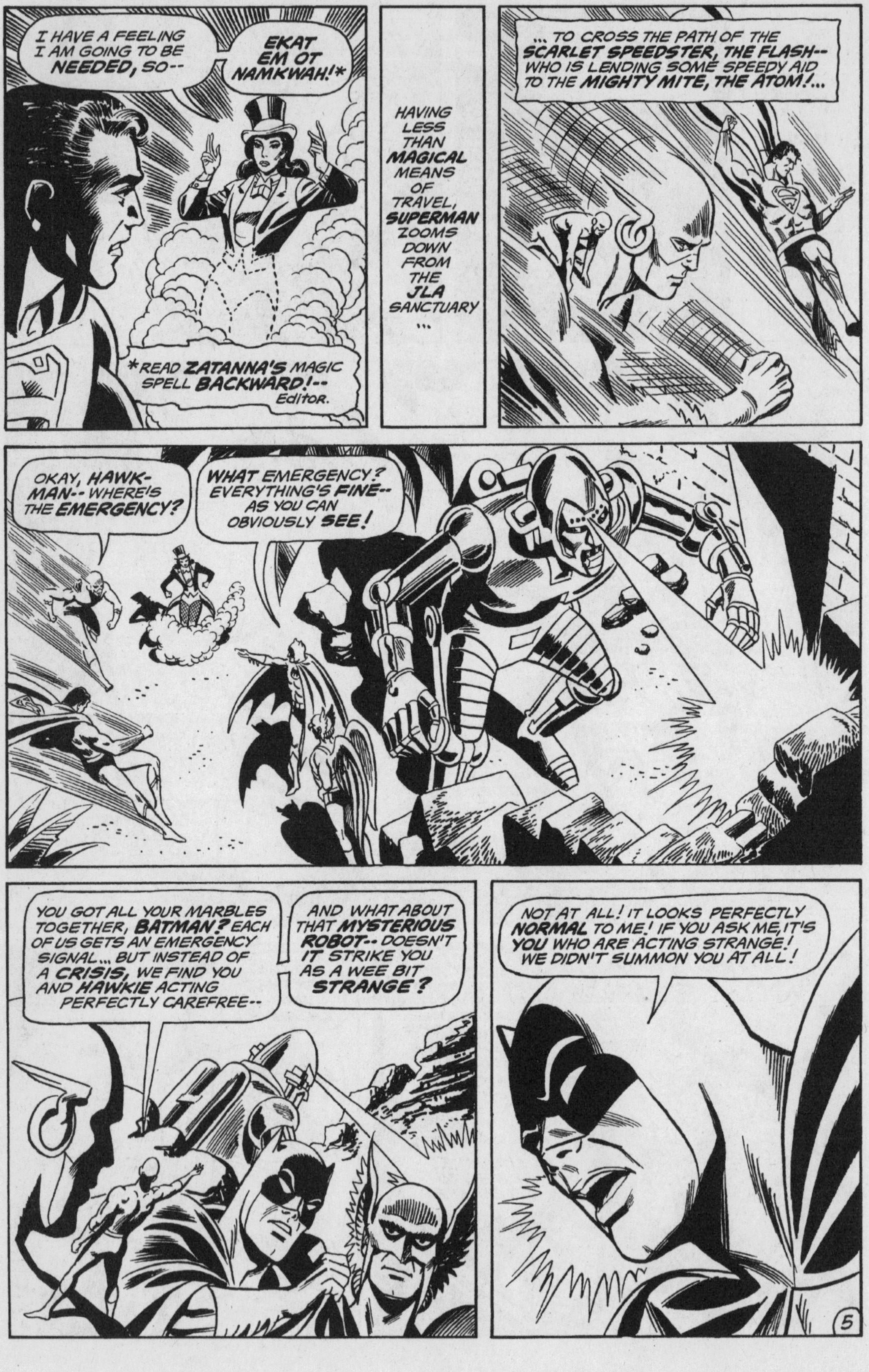
I HAVE A FEELING I AM GOING TO BE NEEDED, SO--
EKAT EM OT NAMKWAH!*
*READ ZATANNA'S MAGIC SPELL BACKWARD!-- Editor.
HAVING LESS THAN MAGICAL MEANS OF TRAVEL, SUPERMAN ZOOMS DOWN FROM THE JLA SANCTUARY ...
... TO CROSS THE PATH OF THE SCARLET SPEEDSTER, THE FLASH-- WHO IS LENDING SOME SPEEDY AID TO THE MIGHTY MITE, THE ATOM!...
OKAY, HAWK-MAN-- WHERE'S THE EMERGENCY?
WHAT EMERGENCY? EVERYTHING'S FINE-- AS YOU CAN OBVIOUSLY SEE!
YOU GOT ALL YOUR MARBLES TOGETHER, BATMAN? EACH OF US GETS AN EMERGENCY SIGNAL... BUT INSTEAD OF A CRISIS, WE FIND YOU AND HAWKIE ACTING PERFECTLY CAREFREE--
AND WHAT ABOUT THAT MYSTERIOUS ROBOT-- DOESN'T IT STRIKE YOU AS A WEE BIT STRANGE?
NOT AT ALL! IT LOOKS PERFECTLY NORMAL TO ME! IF YOU ASK ME, IT'S YOU WHO ARE ACTING STRANGE! WE DIDN'T SUMMON YOU AT ALL!
5

"AS FOR THE ROBOT, IF YOU *MUST* KNOW, AS *BRUCE WAYNE* I WAS FINANCING AN EXCAVATION FOR SOME *INCA* RUINS FOR *CARTER HALL'S* MUSEUM, WHEN WE DISCOVERED IT..."

APPARENTLY, THE SUN'S RAYS ARE ACTIVATING THE AUTOMATON!

"WE QUICKLY SWITCHED TO OUR COSTUMES... UHNN...BUT DISCOVERED THAT IT...GLUGG...OBEYED MY ORDERS AND HELPED WITH OUR PROJECT..."

...WHICH IS WHAT IT'S DOING NOW! EVERYTHING...UNGNN...IS FINE!

SOMETHING'S WRONG! MY SUPER-SENSES DETECT THAT *BATMAN'S* PULSE IS VERY HIGH AND HIS *NERVOUS SYSTEM* TENSE-- INDICATING HE'S *LYING!*

AND TO MAKE MATTERS WORSE, I HAVE THE FEELING THAT *ROBOT* IS *LISTENING, WATCHING* AND *STUDYING* US!

JUST THEN, A BLAZING VERDANT STREAK HERALDS THE ARRIVAL OF A FRIEND NOT SEEN FOR MANY AN ADVENTURE...

--GREEN LANTERN!

HI, THERE, EVERYONE-- *ZATANNA!?* HAVE YOU JOINED THE CLUB?

NOOOO...JUST VISITING...

BEEN QUITE AWHILE, GL! GLAD TO--

6

HANDS OFF MY PAL, *SUPERMAN!* I'M THE OFFICIAL WELCOMING COMMITTEE FOR *GREEN LANTERN!*

WHA--?

PUT IT THERE, PAL!

WHERE'S THE TROUBLE, *BATMAN?* WHY THE EMERGENCY SIGNAL?

YOU TOO--?!

YOU'RE ALL SCREWY! WHY SHOULD I-- THE HEADMAN HERE-- BOTHER TO CAL . *YOU?* WHO NEEDS *YOU?*

OUT! ALL OF YOU! *OUT!*

HOW ABOUT IT *HAWK-MAN?* YOU'VE BEEN STRANGELY SILENT ALL THE WHILE! WHAT'S GOING ON HERE?

N-NOTHING! IT'S JUST AS THE *BATMAN* SAYS! OBEY HIM... FOR YOUR *OWN* GOOD!

NEITHER OF THEM IS ACTING NORMALLY-- COULD THEY BE IMPOSTORS? . .

NO... MY X-RAY VISION SHOWS *BRUCE WAYNE* AND *CARTER HALL* UNDER THEIR MASKS!

ALL RIGHT, SINCE YOU REFUSE TO OBEY-- I'LL USE FORCE!

ROBOT--SQUASH THESE PUNY CHARACTERS!

7

BEATS ME WHY *BATMAN'S* ACTING LIKE THIS-- BUT WE CAN EASILY HANDLE THAT *ROBOT*--

WAIT, *FLASH!* IT MAY NOT BE AS EASY AS YOU THINK!

LET *ME* HAVE FIRST CRACK AT IT--WITH *MAGIC!*

ANALYSIS: SUPER-FEMALE POSSESSES MAGICAL FORCES.

DEDUCTION: SUPER-FEMALE MOST DANGEROUS TO THE UNIT.

ACTION: PREVENT USE OF HER FORCES.

KNOCKED *ZATANNA* OUT!

I'M TOO FAST TO LET IT CATCH *ME* WITH ONE OF ITS BLASTS!

WHILE *FLASH* DOES HIS *SUPER-SPEED* STUFF I'LL DO MY *SHRINKING* SPECIALTY-- DOWN TO ITS COMPUTER BANKS--

ATTACK IT FROM INSIDE!

8

ANALYSIS: SUPER-NORMAL POSSESSES ULTRA-SPEED. DEDUCTION: DANGER TO THE UNIT. ACTION: PREVENT USE OF POWERS.

ROBOT HAS ENERGY-SHIELD--

UPSETTING MY VIBRATIONS--ARGGHH!

NOTHING--EVEN THE MICROSCOPIC ATOM-- IS TOO SMALL FOR THE ROBOT'S SENSORS...

ANALYSIS: SUPER-NORMAL POSSESSES SIZE-AND-WEIGHT POWERS. DEDUCTION: DANGER TO THE UNIT. ACTION: PREVENT USE OF POWERS.

CAN'T CONTROL SIZE--

FALLING--FAST--

HEAR ME--ALL OF YOU! I AM YOUR LEADER --NO! NOT YOUR LEADER --YOUR KING!

WHEN YOUR KING COMMANDS, OBEY!

BATMAN'S FLIPPED! FIRST PARANOIAC AND NOW POWER-MAD!

IT'S GOT TO BE TIED IN WITH THE ROBOT--BUT HOW? WHERE DID IT COME FROM? HOW DID BATMAN GET CONTROL?

HAWKMAN, TOO! ONLY HE'S SHIVERING IN FEAR!

9

SUPERMAN AND I ARE THE ONLY TWO LEFT!

AND NOW THAT OUR FANTASTIC FOE HAS TRAINED HIS RAY-BLASTS ON SUPERMAN, EVEN THE MIGHTY ONE SEEMS IN TROUBLE--!

THANKS, GL--THAT ROBOT'S BEEN FIRING CONCENTRATED SOLAR RAYS-- ONLY THEY'RE FROM A RED SUN! IN EFFECT, THE ROBOT'S GOT THE SAME POWERS I HAVE!

ANALYSIS: SUPER-NORMAL POSSESSES GUARDIAN POWER RING. DEDUCTION: DANGER TO THE UNIT. ACTION: PREVENT USE OF POWERS.

GREAT GUARDIANS! THE ROBOT'S TURNED YELLOW--MY RING WON'T HAVE ANY EFFECT AGAINST IT!

ROBOT! OVERCOME SUPERMAN! WITH HIM ELIMINATED, I'LL BE KING OF THE WORLD!

ANALYSIS: OTHER SUPER NORMALS MOMENTARILY NEUTRALIZED. DEDUCTION: INDUCED INSANITY OF THE BATMAN SUCCESSFUL AS CAMOUFLAGE TO REAL PURPOSE.

ACTION: CONTINUE PROGRAM.

HEAR THAT, GL? THE ROBOT'S CONTROLLING BATMAN--NOT THE OTHER WAY AROUND!

WE'VE GOT TO FIND OUT WHO'S REALLY CONTROLLING IT-- BUT I CAN'T GET NEAR IT!

DOUBT IF I CAN EITHER-- BUT I'M SURE GONNA GIVE IT A GOOD TRY!

10

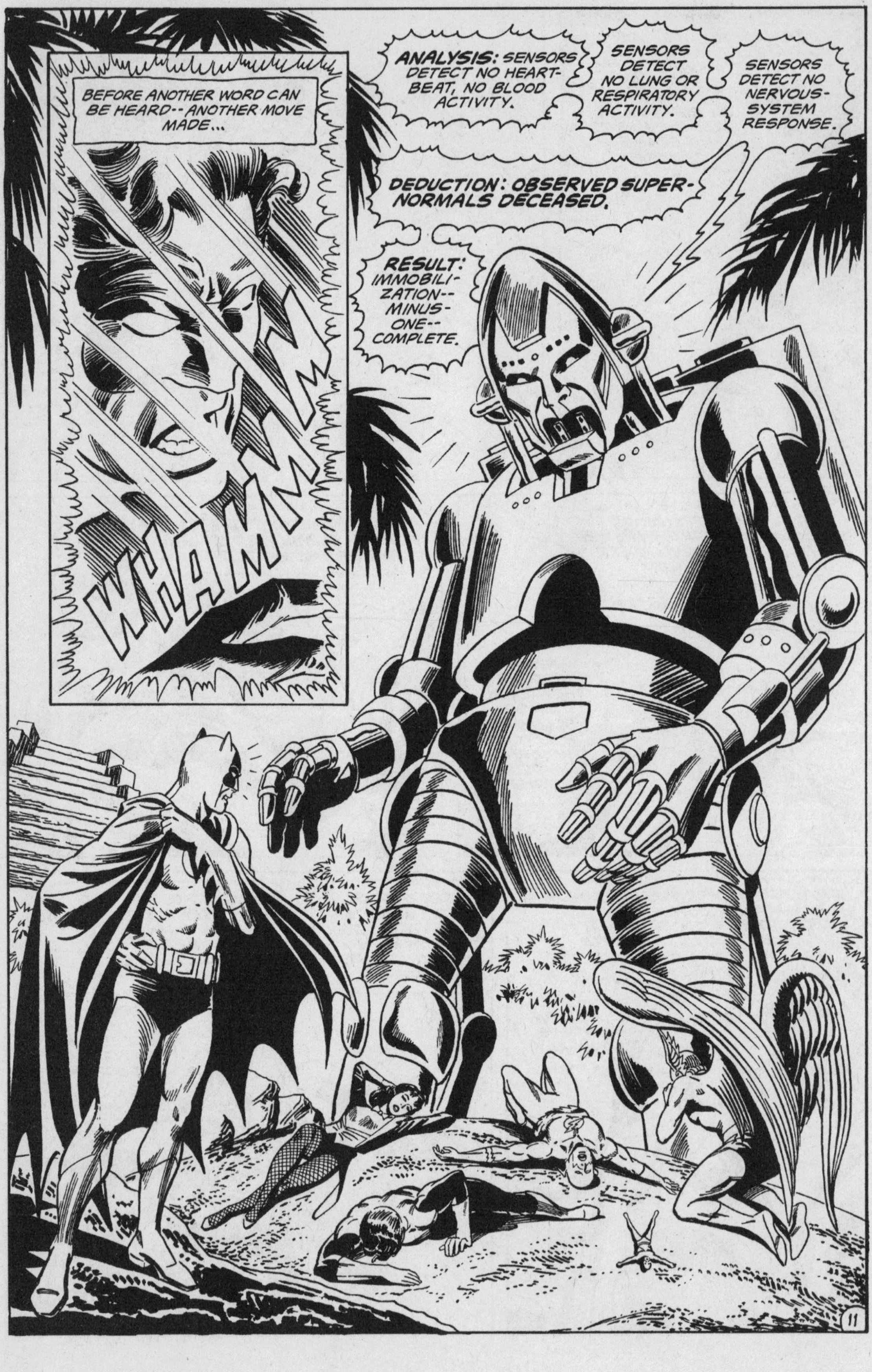
BEFORE ANOTHER WORD CAN BE HEARD--ANOTHER MOVE MADE...
WHAM
ANALYSIS: SENSORS DETECT NO HEART-BEAT, NO BLOOD ACTIVITY.
SENSORS DETECT NO LUNG OR RESPIRATORY ACTIVITY.
SENSORS DETECT NO NERVOUS-SYSTEM RESPONSE.
DEDUCTION: OBSERVED SUPER-NORMALS DECEASED.
RESULT: IMMOBILI-ZATION--MINUS-ONE--COMPLETE.
11

ACTION! CONCLUDE PROGRAM BY IMMOBILIZING LAST ACTIVE MEMBER!

-- WHEN THAT "MEMBER" IS AN ANGRY SUPERMAN, HE DOESN'T "IMMOBILIZE EASY!

FOR THE MASS MURDER YOU'VE COMMITTED HERE-- I'M GONNA TEAR APART EVERY INTEGRATED CIRCUIT YOU'VE GOT!

PONDER ONCE AGAIN HOW IT FEELS TO BE A SUPERMAN-- SEETHING AT WHAT HE HAS WITNESSED BELOW...

-- LYING LIFELESSLY ON THE GROUND... FIVE GOOD REASONS FOR VENGEANCE-- THOSE RARE COMMODITIES CALLED TRUE FRIENDS...

PERHAPS THIS THEN IS THE EXPLANATION WHY THE MAN OF STEEL DODGES ONE SOLAR RAY ATTACK TO LAND AN INEFFECTUAL PUNCH...

... ONLY TO HELPLESSLY HAVE THE NEXT ASSAULT TAKE ITS TOLL...

...FORCING SUPERMAN TO JOIN HIS COLLEAGUES IN THE PEACE OF ETERNAL STILLNESS...

12

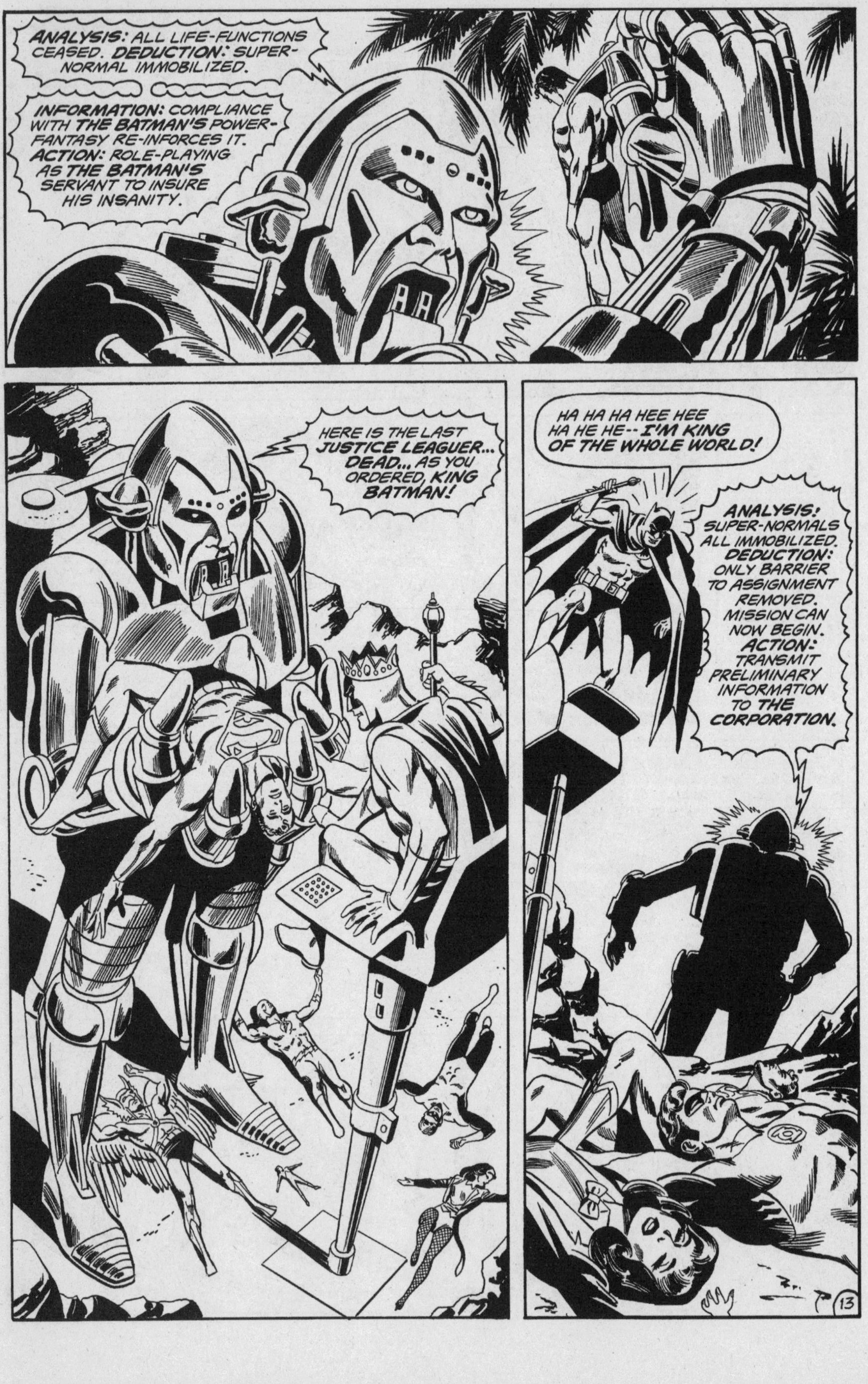
ANALYSIS: ALL LIFE-FUNCTIONS CEASED. DEDUCTION: SUPER-NORMAL IMMOBILIZED.
INFORMATION: COMPLIANCE WITH THE BATMAN'S POWER-FANTASY RE-INFORCES IT. ACTION: ROLE-PLAYING AS THE BATMAN'S SERVANT TO INSURE HIS INSANITY.
HERE IS THE LAST JUSTICE LEAGUER... DEAD... AS YOU ORDERED, KING BATMAN!
HA HA HA HEE HEE HA HE HE-- I'M KING OF THE WHOLE WORLD!
ANALYSIS: SUPER-NORMALS ALL IMMOBILIZED. DEDUCTION: ONLY BARRIER TO ASSIGNMENT REMOVED. MISSION CAN NOW BEGIN. ACTION: TRANSMIT PRELIMINARY INFORMATION TO THE CORPORATION.
13

BATMAN--KING OF THE WORLD!" PART TWO

WHAT'S THIS?!?

TRANSMISSION: ALL POTENTIAL COUNTER-FORCES NEUTRALIZED. MINERALS LOCATED AND EXCAVATION READY TO COMMENCE.

--GREEN LANTERN-- ALIVE?!

AH--THE ROBOT'S MADE CONTACT WITH ITS HOME BASE...

...PRECIOUS MINERALS LOCATED BENEATH INDIGENOUS HABITATS... SOON TO BE CLEARED...

IN YA GO, ATOM!

UP AND AT 'EM!

THE ATOM-- ALIVE?!

YES INDEED-- AND THE WORLD'S SMALLEST SUPER-HERO HAS SHRUNK HIMSELF TO INFINITESIMAL SIZE-- LIKE A LIVING ELECTRON --TO BE TELEPORTED ACROSS INTER-STELLAR SPACE...

--TO EMERGE ALMOST INSTANTLY ON THE OTHER SIDE OF THE GALAXY-- WITHIN THE MASTER COMPUTER THAT CONTROLS THE ROBOT ON EARTH...

THE ATOM'S TASK HAS JUST BEGUN FOR HE MUST STOP A ROBOT FROM GOING ON A RAMPAGE!

GAPE IN WONDER, CITIZENS OF SMALL *MONTE CORVINO*...

QUE ESTE ROBOT?

NO SE! NO SE!

UNBE- KNOWNST TO YOU VILLAGERS, *THE ATOM* HAS DONE HIS JOB AND AVERTED THE DESTRUC- TION OF THE LAND YOU CALL HOME...

WHILE A SHORT DISTANCE AWAY A COUPLE OF MYSTERIES ARE EXPLAINED...

GREAT IDEA, *GREEN LANTERN* -- TO *POWER-RING* SUBSTITUTE *ANDROID-DUPLICATES* FOR FLESH-AND-BLOOD HUMANS -- THEN BEAM A TELEPATHIC MESSAGE FOR ME TO PLAY ALONG AT BEING DEAD!

SUPERMAN, WE SHOULD HAVE BEEN FIGHTING IT ALL ALONG AS A *MACHINE* -- USING A *HUMAN BRAIN* TO OUTWIT IT!

GOOD AS THE ROBOT'S SENSORS WERE, THEY WERE INHERENTLY *LIMITED!*

LIFE IS IN THE *SOUL,* WHICH NO COMPUTER CAN EVER RECOGNIZE!

THROUGH HIS *POWER RING,* GREEN LANTERN DISCOVERED THAT A STRANGE ENERGY FROM THE ROBOT WAS INDUCING *BATMAN'S* MADNESS!

I'D BETTER GET HIM -- AND *HAWKMAN,* WHO'S JUST AS BAD OFF -- TO THE HOSPITAL!

WE'VE STILL GOT A JOB TO FINISH -- TRACKING DOWN THOSE RESPONSIBLE FOR THE ROBOT-ONSLAUGHT!

MY RING'S BEEN MAINTAINING A POSITIONAL LINK WITH *THE ATOM* -- WE CAN FOLLOW HIM!

15

MY RING ISN'T SO ALL GALAXY-SHATTERING POWERFUL AS IT USED TO BE *...

*AS SHOWN IN THE CATACLYSMIC EVENTS **GREEN LANTERN** HAS BEEN EXPERIENCING IN HIS OWN MAGAZINE!

...SO WE'LL HAVE TO **WILL-POWER** IT **TOGETHER**...

LINKING HANDS IS A SIGN OF THEIR EVER-STRONG UNITY AS WELL AS THEIR MUTUAL DETERMINATION TO COMPLETE THE MISSION AT HAND.

THREE HEROES ARE TRANSPORTED ALONG THE TRAIL OF THEIR TINY COMPANION...

WHEW! LOOKS LIKE YOU **ATOM**-BOMBED THAT THING, **ATOM**--!

UH-UH... NOTHING SO **ELABORATE**! JUST A COUPLE OF CROSSED CIRCUITS IN THE RIGHT PLACES DID THE TRICK!

BUT YOU AIN'T SEEN NOTHING YET--LOOK OUTSIDE!

THIS WHOLE WORLD-- **DESTROYED!** SHATTERED BY NUCLEAR WARFARE!

THE MASTER-COMPUTER WAS THE ONLY THING KEEPING THE ROBOT "ALIVE"! ITS CREATORS EITHER DIED EONS AGO--OR ARE SOMEWHERE ELSE ON THE PLANET!

THERE! THEY MUST BE-- OUR ENEMIES!

16

WHO UTTERED THAT CRY? WHY ARE *THEY* HERE?

WHO IS SIMPLE: LET US INTRODUCE THEM... IN *EARTH-EQUIVALENT* TERMS--

JACK B. QUICK-- SUPER-SPEEDSTER! NOT AS FAST AS *THE FLASH*, BUT ON THE OTHER HAND HE CAN FLY SHORT DISTANCES...

BLUE JAY-- A NORMAL MAN WHO'S DISCOVERED HOW TO SHRINK TO THE SIZE OF A BIRD AND GAIN WINGS...

SILVER SORCERESS-- A FEMALE WITH EXTREMELY POWERFUL *HEX-POWER,* BUT UNABLE TO CONTROL IT COMPLETELY...

WANDJINA-- COINCIDENTALLY THE NAME OF THE *AUSTRALIAN ABORIGINE GOD OF RAIN*... ABLE TO CONTROL THE ELEMENTS! ON HIS WORLD, HE IS BELIEVED TO BE AN ACTUAL GOD, BUT NO ONE REALLY KNOWS...

THROUGH THE CONVENIENT STORY-TELLING DEVICE OF THE *FLASHBACK,* WE CAN TELL THE *WHY* AS WELL...

THEY AND THE JLA ARE ON *CAM-NAM-LAO*-- A PLANET ONCE DOMINATED BY HIGHLY COMPETITIVE BUSINESS CORPORATIONS...

SO COMPETITIVE IN FACT, THAT THE CORPORATIONS OF CAM-NAM-LAO ULTIMATELY ELIMINATED EACH OTHER IN *TOTAL ATOMIC WAR*...

17

THEY WERE FAR-REACHING CORPORATIONS, DISPATCHING EMISSARIES TO DISCOVER AND GATHER RAW MATERIALS! THE JLA FOUGHT SUCH A ROBOT...

THESE *OTHER ALIENS* ARE THE SUPER-DEFENDERS OF THE WORLD OF *ANGOR*! THEY FOUGHT *ANOTHER ROBOT*-- FROM A RIVAL CORPORATION...

SO THEY TOO JOURNEYED TO THIS SAME PLANET TO DEFEAT THE CREATORS OF THE MENACING ROBOTS...

THERE! THEY MUST BE--OUR ENEMIES! *

*THIS **LITERARY LICENSE** ENABLES US TO TRANSLATE THE ALIEN LANGUAGE... EVEN THE UNINTELLIGIBLE ALIEN NAMES... INTO ENGLISH!

JULIE SCHWARTZ- COMMISSIONER OF LICENSES

...BUT OBVIOUSLY THE EARTHINGS DON'T UNDERSTAND THE ALIEN *ANGORS*...

THAT SOUNDED LIKE A *BATTLE CRY* TO ME! GET READY-- THESE *MUST* BE THE ROBOT-CONTROLLERS WE'RE AFTER!

...AND JUST AS OBVIOUSLY, THE *ANGORS* DON'T UNDERSTAND THE ALIEN *EARTHLINGS*...

THEY ATTACK! THAT SETTLES IT! THEY *ARE* THE CONTROLLERS OF THE *ROBOTS*!

THIS COULD BE A BATTLE TO THE *DEATH*!

18

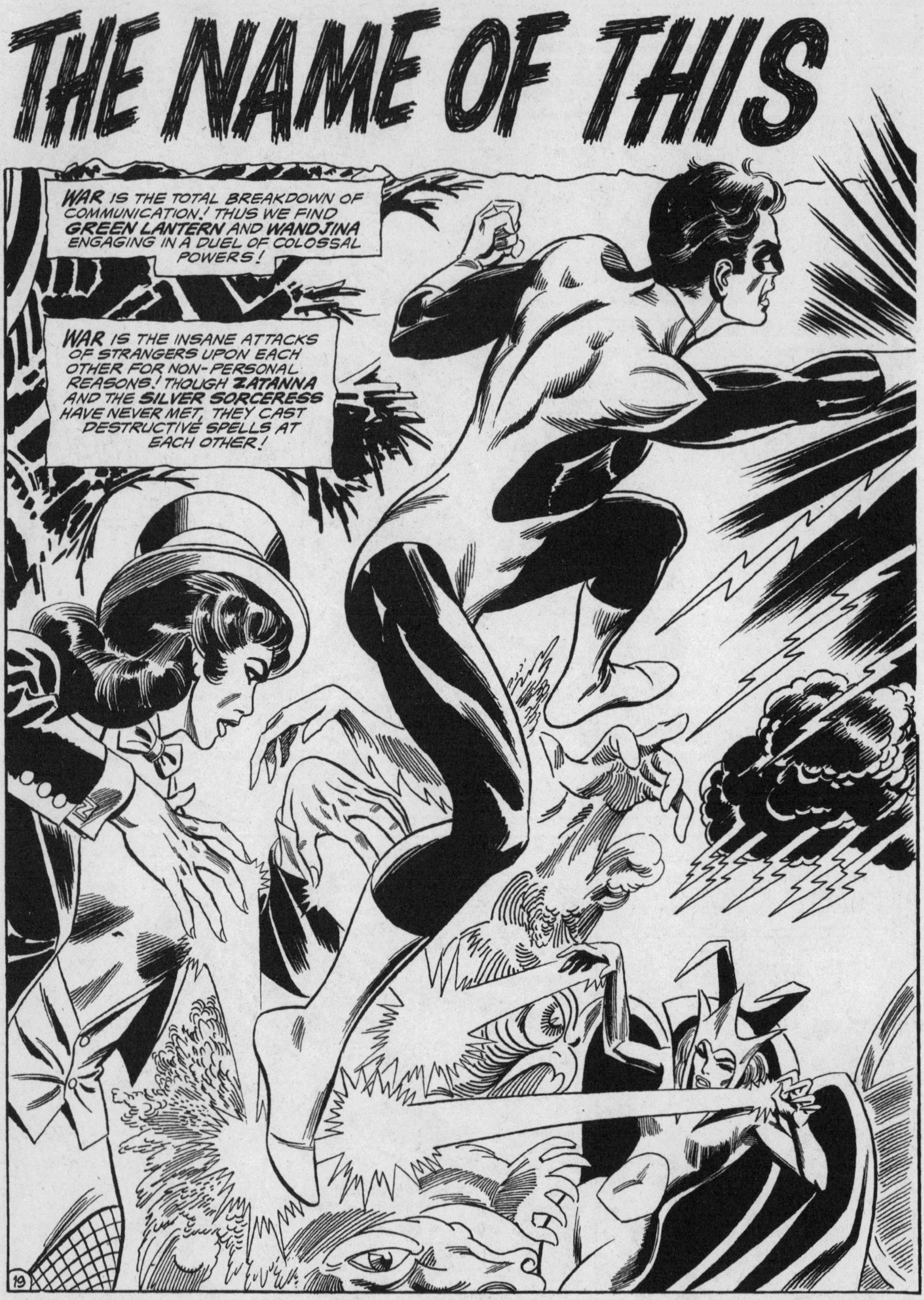
THE NAME OF THIS
WAR IS THE TOTAL BREAKDOWN OF COMMUNICATION! THUS WE FIND GREEN LANTERN AND WANDJINA ENGAGING IN A DUEL OF COLOSSAL POWERS!
WAR IS THE INSANE ATTACKS OF STRANGERS UPON EACH OTHER FOR NON-PERSONAL REASONS! THOUGH ZATANNA AND THE SILVER SORCERESS HAVE NEVER MET, THEY CAST DESTRUCTIVE SPELLS AT EACH OTHER!
19

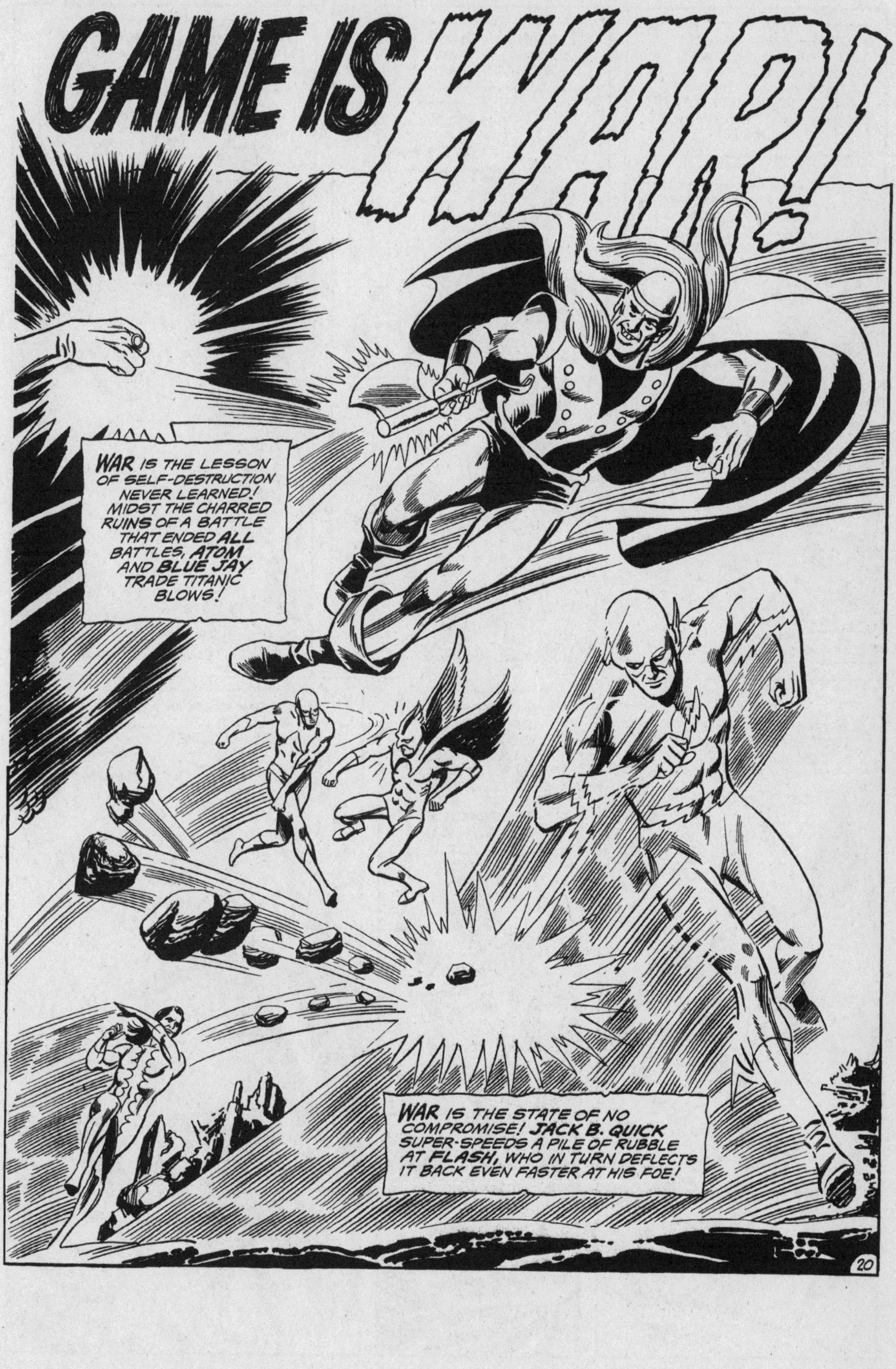
GAME IS WAR!
WAR IS THE LESSON OF SELF-DESTRUCTION NEVER LEARNED! MIDST THE CHARRED RUINS OF A BATTLE THAT ENDED ALL BATTLES, ATOM AND BLUE JAY TRADE TITANIC BLOWS!
WAR IS THE STATE OF NO COMPROMISE! JACK B. QUICK SUPER-SPEEDS A PILE OF RUBBLE AT FLASH, WHO IN TURN DEFLECTS IT BACK EVEN FASTER AT HIS FOE!
20

IT HAS BEEN SAID. WAR IS *UNHEALTHY* FOR PEOPLE AND OTHER LIVING THINGS. *FATE* DECREES THAT THE FIRST CASUALTY BE AN *ANGOR!*

FOR IN DEFENDING HIMSELF AGAINST *JACK B. QUICK'S* RUBBLE ATTACK, *THE FLASH* DEFLECTS A ROCK INTO *BLUE JAY...*

ZATANNA-- WITH NO THOUGHT FOR HER OWN SAFETY...

GREEN LANTERN! HELP HIM! HE'S *BADLY HURT!*

I CAN'T KEEP THIS PROTECTIVE SHIELD ACTIVATED MUCH LONGER--MY RING CAN'T TAKE IT!

YOU HAVE TO--OR HE'LL *DIE! YOUR RING* CAN HEAL HIM BETTER THAN *MY MAGIC!*

ALL RIGHT-- BUT I'M GONNA HAVE TO DROP THE *SHIELD*--

THE GREEN-CLAD ENEMY HAS REMOVED HIS WONDROUS SHIELD! ONE MIGHTY *HEX* WILL FINISH THEM OFF--!

NO! YOU'LL KILL *BLUE JAY!*

THE COMBINATION OF *GREEN LANTERN'S* HEALING *POWER RING* AND CALM *ZATANNA,* THE GIRL WITH THE DANCING EYES... AND...

HE'S CURED!

BLUE JAY RAISES HIS HANDS IN OUR SIGN OF PEACE!

THE BATTLE IS ENDED!

21

ESTABLISHING COMMUNICATION AT LAST, THE HEROES OF TWO WORLDS PIECE TOGETHER THEIR STORIES AND DISCOVER THEIR COMMON PURPOSE...

WE FEEL SUCH SHAME-- MISJUDGING YOUR PURPOSE ON THIS PLANET!

THANKFULLY A DISASTER WAS AVERTED!

AS THE ALIENS TAKE OFF FOR THEIR HOME WORLD...

HOW SENSELESS-- HOW ILLOGICAL-- TO CONTINUE A WAR NEITHER OF US STARTED NOR EVER REALLY WANTED--!

IF IT HADN'T BEEN FOR ZATANNA'S SELF-SACRIFICE...

THERE CAN NEVER BE ANY REAL **WORDS** TO DESCRIBE THE PEACEMAKER...

--AND FLASH, GREEN LANTERN AND ATOM DON'T EVEN TRY, FOR THIS IS ... ZATANNA...

...THE GIRL WITH THE ENIGMATIC SMILE...

...EVER CALM IN THE MIDST OF A STORMY WORLD...

...THE BEARER OF PEACE...

"...AND BLESSED ARE THE PEACE-MAKERS, FOR THEY SHALL BE CALLED SONS OF GOD..."

AMEN! MIKE FRIEDRICH- WRITER
DICK DILLIN &
JOE GIELLA- ARTISTS
JULIE SCHWARTZ- EDITOR

The End

22

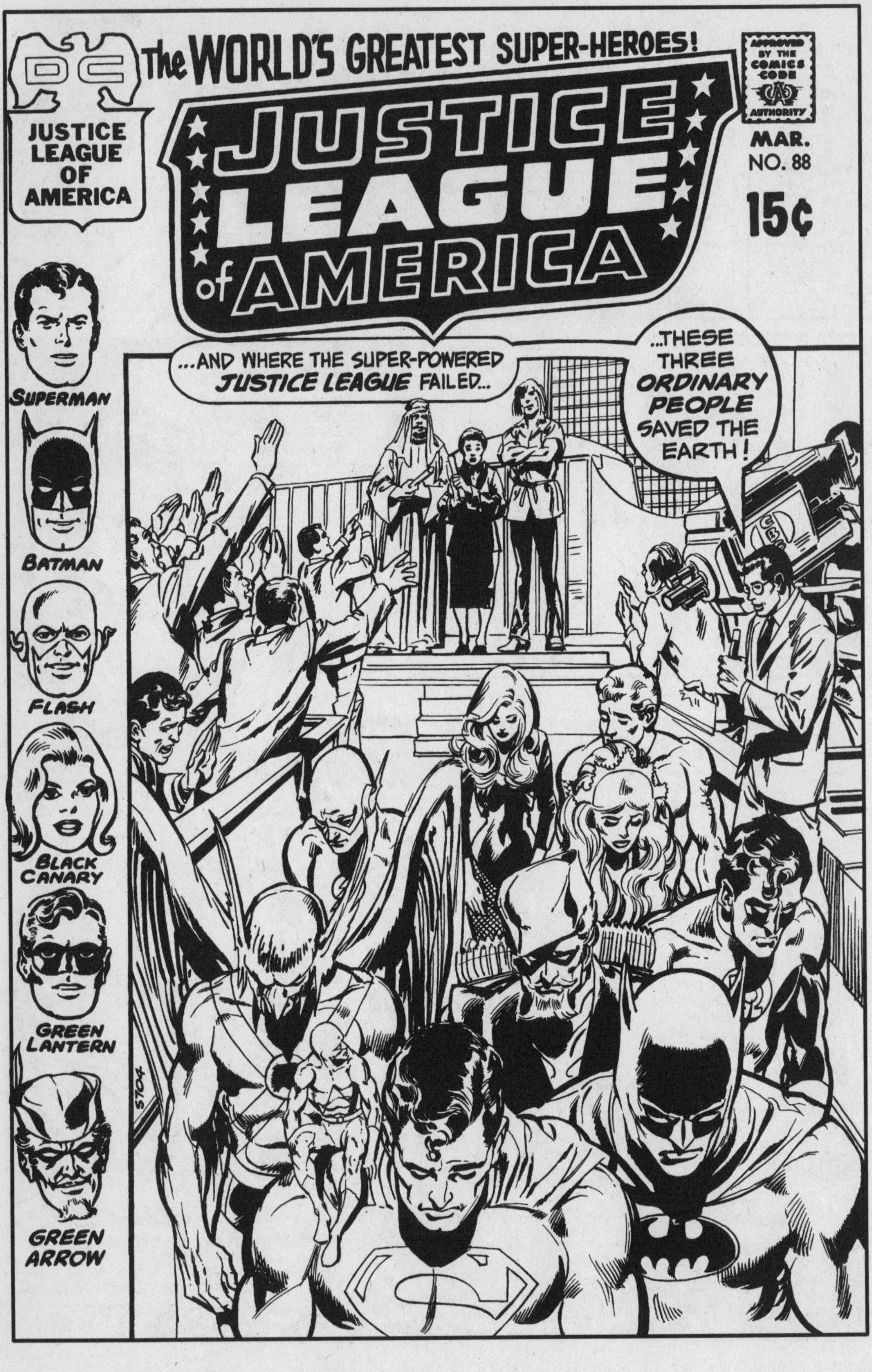

The WORLD'S GREATEST SUPER-HEROES!
JUSTICE LEAGUE OF AMERICA
APPROVED BY THE COMICS CODE AUTHORITY
JUSTICE LEAGUE of AMERICA
MAR. NO. 88
15¢
SUPERMAN
BATMAN
FLASH
BLACK CANARY
GREEN LANTERN
GREEN ARROW
...AND WHERE THE SUPER-POWERED JUSTICE LEAGUE FAILED...
...THESE THREE ORDINARY PEOPLE SAVED THE EARTH!

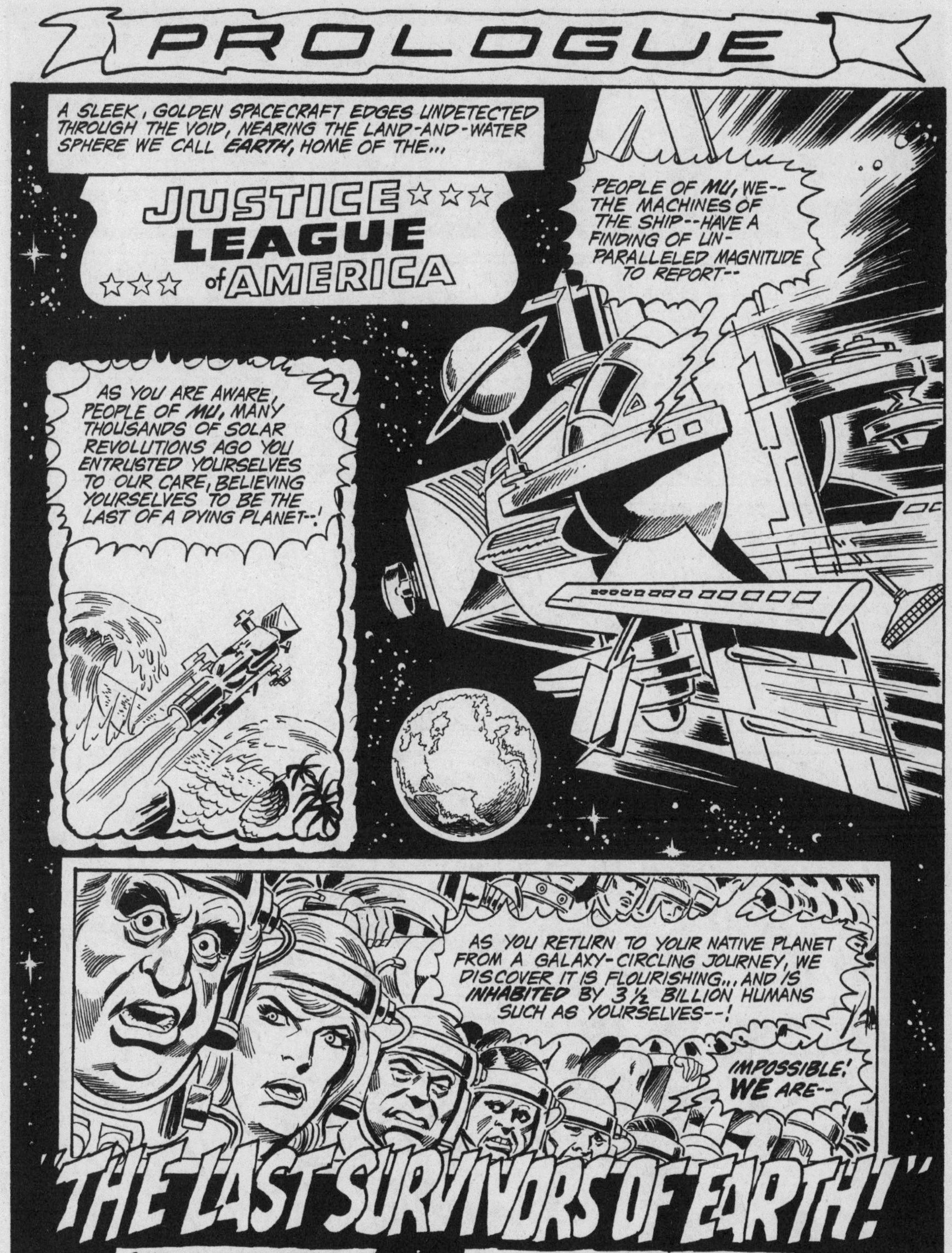
PROLOGUE
A SLEEK, GOLDEN SPACECRAFT EDGES UNDETECTED THROUGH THE VOID, NEARING THE LAND-AND-WATER SPHERE WE CALL EARTH, HOME OF THE...
JUSTICE LEAGUE of AMERICA
PEOPLE OF MU, WE-- THE MACHINES OF THE SHIP--HAVE A FINDING OF UN-PARALLELED MAGNITUDE TO REPORT--
AS YOU ARE AWARE, PEOPLE OF MU, MANY THOUSANDS OF SOLAR REVOLUTIONS AGO YOU ENTRUSTED YOURSELVES TO OUR CARE, BELIEVING YOURSELVES TO BE THE LAST OF A DYING PLANET--!
AS YOU RETURN TO YOUR NATIVE PLANET FROM A GALAXY-CIRCLING JOURNEY, WE DISCOVER IT IS FLOURISHING... AND IS INHABITED BY 3 ½ BILLION HUMANS SUCH AS YOURSELVES--!
IMPOSSIBLE! WE ARE--
"THE LAST SURVIVORS OF EARTH!"
S-636
STORY BY: MIKE FRIEDRICH
ART BY: DICK DILLIN & JOE GIELLA
1

IF THE INFERIOR INVENTIONS OF *TERRA* COULD BUT DETECT OR OBSERVE THE GOLDEN VESSEL, EARTHMEN WOULD VIEW IT WITH GREAT ENVY--AND GREAT FEAR!

FOR ITS PASSENGERS LIVE IN A *PERFECT* ENVIRONMENT--EVERYTHING IDEALLY REGULATED BY ITS MACHINES! THERE IS NO DISEASE, NO HUNGER, NO DEATH!

BUT THERE IS NOT MUCH TO CALL *LIFE,* EITHER! STRENUOUS EFFORT IS NEEDED TO FORM EVEN A HATE-FILLED EXPRESSION...REFLECTING MUSCLES ARE WEAK FROM DISUSE... *MINDS* ARE JUST AS DETERIORATED--

WE *ACHIEVED* ABSOLUTE PERFECTION-- OBSERVE OUR CONDITION! IT IS OUR RIGHTFUL DESTINY!

WE *BUILT* THIS SHIP-- WE *EARNED* OUR RIGHT TO SURVIVE! *THEY* DID NOT!

THESE HUMAN UPSTARTS ARE OBVIOUSLY *DEGENERATES*--THEY DON'T HAVE THE *PERFECTION* OF OUR SHIP! THEY DON'T *DESERVE* TO EXIST!

YES, MINDS THAT HAVE SELF-RIGHTEOUSLY FORGED THEMSELVES INTO A JEALOUS BELIEF THAT THEY ARE THE ONLY ONES WORTHY TO LIVE... MINDS THAT CAN ONLY FOCUS ON ONE THOUGHT TO ENFORCE THAT BELIEF--

DESTROY

DESTROY

DESTROY

2

"THE LAST SURVIVORS OF EARTH"-- PART ONE

WE MOVE OUR SIGHTS TO THE PLANET BELOW, TO A TRIO OF HUMANS WORKING HARD UNDER A SCORCHING SOUTH SEAS SUN--CARTER AND SHIERRA (HAWKMAN AND HAWKGIRL) HALL, AND HAL (GREEN LANTERN) JORDAN...

GLAD YOU ACCEPTED OUR INVITE TO JOIN US ON OUR "BUSMAN'S HOLIDAY" HAL...DIGGING FOR ARTIFACTS ON THIS SOUTH SEAS ISLAND...

NEEDED TO GET AWAY FOR A WHILE... FAR AWAY...

AND WHAT BETTER PLACE THAN THIS REMOTE CHUNK OF EARTH...

IT'D BE SO SIMPLE IF I USED MY POWER RINGS TO EXCAVATE THIS PLACE....

:UH-UH: YOU KNOW THE GUARDIANS FORBID USING YOUR FABULOUS RING FOR PERSONAL CONVENIENCE!

BESIDES, HALF THE FUN IS MAKING AN ACHEOLOGICAL FIND ON OUR OWN...

SPEAKING OF FINDS... I'VE UNEARTHED SOMETHING--!

STRANGE PICTORIAL SYMBOLS ARE INSCRIBED ON IT!

WHERE'S AQUA-MAN? HE WAS SUPPOSED TO MEET US HERE... HELP INTERPRET WHATEVER WE FOUND...

I CAN IDENTIFY ONLY ONE OF THE PICTOGRAPHS-- THIS ONE!

IT'S THE LEGENDARY SYMBOL OF VENGEANCE-- WHICH ORIGINATED ON THE SUNKEN CONTINENT OF MU!

3

VENGEANCE...MU... FOREBODING WORDS, SEEMINGLY PROPHETIC OF WHAT HAPPENS THE NEXT INSTANT...

...SHIERRA!

LUCKY I SAW THAT LIGHTNING BOLT COMING! GOT MY *POWER-RING* WORKING IN TIME TO BLUNT THE BOLT'S FORCE!

SHE'S *UNCONSCIOUS*-- BUT SEEMS TO CHECK OUT OKAY!

NEVERTHELESS, I BETTER RUSH HER TO A HOSPITAL!

HOW'D SUCH A THING HAPPEN? NOT A CLOUD IN THE SKY...

AND THAT LIGHTNING BOLT ACTUALLY SEEMED TO *CURVE AROUND* THAT PALM TREE TO STRIKE AT SHIERRA!

THAT MEANS "SOME-THING" CAUSED THE BOLT TO BE ATTRACTED TO HER-- REASON ENOUGH TO GO INTO UNIFORM!

RIGHT! I'M GOING TO NEED THIS PAIR OF WINGS!

MAY MY WINGS BE STRONG AND FLEET TO SPEED SHIERRA TO MEDICAL HELP!

HERE COMES *AQUAMAN*--AND HIS WIFE *MERA!* MAYBE *THEY* CAN UNRAVEL THIS ENIGMA!

AFTER THE *KING OF THE SEA* IS BRIEFED ON THE INCREDIBLE LIGHTNING ATTACK...

THIS PART OF THE PACIFIC OCEAN IS THE MOST MYSTER-IOUS, UNEXPLORED AREA I KNOW!

ATLANTIS TELLS OF ANCIENT LEGENDS ABOUT THE EXISTENCE OF A *PACIFIC* CONTINENT THAT ALSO SANK BENEATH THE WAVES--THOUGH WE'VE NEVER FOUND ANY EVIDENCE OF IT!

4

BUT RECENTLY--THE LAST FEW DAYS -- I'VE RECEIVED SCATTERED REPORTS OF MINOR TRAGEDIES AROUND THE *EARTH*-- ALL SEEMINGLY POINTING TO... *MU!*

THEY CENTER PRIMARILY AROUND THREE AREAS-- *THE GULF OF PERSIA, THE MEKONG RIVER DELTA* AND THE *COAST OF CALIFORNIA*--

SOUNDS TO ME LIKE WE'VE GOT A POSSIBLE WORLD-WIDE *THREAT* ON OUR HANDS!

AS THE CURRENT *CHAIRMAN* OF THE *JUSTICE LEAGUE,* I'M CALLING AN *IMPROMPTU MEETING* TO INVESTIGATE!

USING HIS POWER RING TO ESTABLISH ENERGY-CONTACT WITH THE JUSTICE LEAGUERS, GREEN LANTERN EXPLAINS THE SITUATION...

HAWKGIRL'S INJURY MAY BE JUST AN ISOLATED EVENT, BUT I HAVE A FEELING THIS IS THE BEGINNING OF SOMETHING BIGGER--AND MORE OMINOUS!

BATMAN--PICK UP *GREEN ARROW* AND *BLACK CANARY* AND CHECK OUT *CALIFORNIA!* I'LL CONTACT YOU THERE!

CHECK!

SUPERMAN, YOU AND *ATOM* HEAD FOR THE *PERSIAN GULF!* AQUA-MAN WILL JOIN YOU THERE!

WILL DO!

THAT LEAVES THE *MEKONG DELTA* IN *VIET-NAM* FOR *YOU,* FLASH--

I'M ON MY WAY... AT SUPER-SPEED!

5

WHILE *GL* TAKES OFF FOR CALIFORNIA, YOU'D BEST RETURN TO *ATLANTIS*, MY DEAR!

IN CASE THIS THREAT HITS THE CITY, YOU CAN ORGANIZE A DEFENSE!

MEANWHILE, ABOVE THE EARTH...

PEOPLE OF MU, WE MACHINES HAVE ESTABLISHED ENVIRONMENTAL CONTROL THROUGH THE REMAINING MU RELICS ON EARTH!

FULL-SCALE USAGE CAN BEGIN!

WITH FORCES SUCH AS THE "PERFECT" PEOPLE OF *MU* OPERATING, IS IT ANY WONDER THAT LIGHTNING LITERALLY STRIKES *TWICE* IN THE SAME PLACE?

ARRRGG! ANOTHER BOLT OUT OF NOWHERE-- STUNNING ME!

WASN'T ABLE TO GET *POWER RING* WORKING FAST ENOUGH... THIS TIME...

RING... DOESN'T PROTECT ME AUTOMATICALLY... ANYMORE! GOT TO... *WILL* IT TO... SAVE ME...!

FORTUNATELY, ARDUOUS TRAINING ONCE AGAIN MANAGES TO SPARE THE *EMERALD CRUSADER* FOR OTHER BATTLES!

BUT AS THE ONCE CALM WATERS SUDDENLY STORM SAVAGELY AROUND HIM... THOSE BATTLES ARE FAR OFF!

6

IN THE CALIFORNIA-BOUND BAT-JET...

THANKS FOR GIVING ME A WHIRL AT BEING JET-JOCKEY, *BATMAN!*

SINCE THAT RAT JOHN DELEON DROVE ME BROKE AND I HAD TO SCRAP MY OWN *ARROW-PLANE,* ✱ I'VE BEEN ALMOST *ITCHING* TO FLY!

HMMMM... THEY AREN'T LISTENING...

✱ AS RELATED IN JLA #75--EDITOR

THERE IS AN UNEASI-NESS SURROUNDING *THE BATMAN* THIS DAY, CHARGING THE VERY AIR ABOUT HIM...

FOR THE WEIGHT OF MEMORY IS HANGING HEAVILY ON HIS MIND...

THE MEMORY OF THAT BRIEF FLASH OF UN-EXPECTED TOGETHER-NESS THAT LAST TIME THE *DARKNIGHT DETECTIVE* WAS THIS CLOSE TO...*HER!*

WHAT HAD IT BEEN--THE UNFATHOMABLE FLARING OF HUMAN EMOTION? THAT WAS *TOO* SIMPLE AN ANSWER! THERE *WAS* NO EXPLANATION. IT HAD *HAPPENED*-- AND WHAT HAPPENED *NOW* WAS ALL THAT MATTERED!

I ALWAYS THOUGHT THAT *CANARY* HAD THROWN HER LOT WITH *GA,* BUT UP IN THE *HEADQUARTERS-SATELLITE...* AND *NOW...* SHE'S BEEN SO CLOSE TO ME!

AND SHE IS QUITE ATTRAC-TIVE...QUITE SKILLED... QUITE POSSIBLY THE RARE MATE FOR A *BATMAN*--!

BATMAN-- MAY I--?

HEY! WHAT DO YOU THINK YOU'RE *DOING,* PRETTY BIRD? YOU WALK WITH *ME!*

I'LL WALK--AND TALK-- WITH WHOM I *FEEL,* OLIVER! NOW IF YOU'LL *EXCUSE US*--

SHE'S CHOOSING *ME* OVER HIM?

7

BATMAN, YOU'VE ALWAYS BEEN CLOSE SINCE WE MET--A SHOULDER ALWAYS TO TURN TO!

GREEN ARROW IS SO STRONG-WILLED--I'M ATTRACTED, BUT FRIGHTENED BY IT!

I NEED YOU TO GIVE SOME ADVICE ON HOW TO HANDLE IT...

--AS THE BROTHER YOU ARE TO ME...

B-BROTHER...?

SO THAT'S WHERE CANARY'S HEAD IS AT! WELL, IF BROTHER IT IS, THEN BROTHER IT'LL BE--!

UH-I'M NOT EXACTLY THE GREATEST AUTHORITY ON OLIVER QUEEN, BUT...

I DON'T KNOW WHAT'S GOING ON HERE, BUT I DON'T LIKE IT--NOT ONE BIT! IF YOU'RE GONNA HORN IN ON MY GIRL, BATMAN, I'M SPLITTIN'--AND TAKIN' HER WITH ME!

NO TROUBLE, ARROW!

HERE IS THE STARTER-KEY TO THE BAT-JET... IN CASE YOU WISH TO USE IT TO JOIN ANY OF THE OTHER JUSTICE LEAGUERS!

WILL DO! GREEN LANTERN CAN HELP YOU OUT HERE PERFECTLY WELL WITHOUT US!

C'MON, PRETTY BIRD-WE'RE JOINING FLASH! HE'S MARRIED--AND DOESN'T MESS AROUND WITH OTHER GUYS GIRLS!

THE SEED OF BITTERNESS IS PLANTED IN THE BATMAN THIS DAY! WHO KNOWS IF IT'LL DIE A QUICK DEATH--OR BLOSSOM INTO A PERMANENT DIVISION BETWEEN FRIENDS?

8

"The LAST SURVIVORS of EARTH" -- PART TWO

WHILE IN THE SKIES OVER THE *ATLANTIC*...

RIDING IN *SUPERMAN'S* CAPE-POUCH IS GETTING TO BE A *HABIT*-- AND IT'S A *DRAG!* I JUST *SIT* HERE WHILE HE DOES ALL THE WORK!

THE RESTLESS *ATOM* WOULDN'T COMPLAIN IF HE KNEW WHAT WAS IN STORE FOR HIM!...

PEOPLE OF *MU*, WE MACHINES REPORT DESTRUCTION-OPERATION HAS BEGUN FULL-FORCE! WHEREVER WE HAVE LOCATED *MU* RELICS, ENVIRONMENTAL *DISASTERS* ARE *MAGNIFIED* TEN-FOLD!

THIS IS *OMAR IBN ALI,* DEDICATED TO HIS *IRANIAN* FAMILY, HIS COASTAL TOWN, HIS GOD-- AND RESPECTED BY ALL...

LITTLE REALIZING THAT THE MEDALLION HE WEARS AS A FAMILY MARK OF AUTHORITY, BROUGHT BY THE TRADE ROUTES MANY CENTURIES BEFORE, IS THE VERY OBJECT CAUSING THE DESTRUCTION HE IS FLEEING...

...NAMELY, THE WORST *EARTHQUAKES* THIS OFT QUAKE-SUFFERED COUNTRY HAS EXPERI-ENCED!

LOOK AT THAT *DESTRUCTION*--IN JUST THE SHORT TIME IT TOOK TO GET HERE!

LOOKS LIKE GL WAS RIGHT-- THIS IS NO *ACCIDENT!*

MY SIZE-AND-WEIGHT CONTROLS HAVE MADE ME LIGHT AS A FEATHER! IF I REMEMBER RIGHT, A GOVERNMENT SCIENTIFIC CENTER IS BELOW!

I'LL RIDE THE WIND DOWN AND SEE IF I CAN LOCATE THE *CENTER* OF THE QUAKES!

IT'S GOING TO TAKE ALL MY POWERS TO HANDLE THE *HUMAN* PROBLEMS! PEOPLE ARE *PANICKED* DOWN THERE!

9

AIEEE! ANOTHER CURSED EARTH-QUAKE!

LOOK, GRANDFATHER, UP IN THE SKY--A BIG BLUE *BIRD*--

NO, IT IS A SMALL BLUE *PLANE*--

NO, YOUNG ONES, IT IS... *SUPERMAN!*

ALL OF THESE *THOUSANDS* OF PEOPLE ARE HYSTERICAL-- SEEKING SAFETY BY CROWDING ON THESE SMALL BOATS!

THE HARBOR IS JAMMED--I'LL HAVE TO BREAK THE LOGJAM!

IT'LL TAKE ME QUITE A WHILE TO ALLEVIATE THE PROBLEM-- EVEN AT *SUPER-SPEED*-- BECAUSE I HAVE TO BE EXTREMELY *CAREFUL!*

I'VE NO TIME TO TRY TO FIND THE *CAUSE* OF THE QUAKES...

HOPE *ATOM* IS DOING *BETTER*--

10

NOT MUCH BETTER, SUPERMAN-- FOR THE MIGHTY MITE IS ALSO BEING SLOWED...

HEY, MATE-- THE SCIENTISTS HAVE RUN OFF! LET'S GRAB THESE RARE INSTRUMENTS-- AND SELL 'EM BACK 'OME IN *ENGLAND*!

AS I RECALL MY PREVIOUS VISIT HERE, THIS IS WHERE THE *SEISMOGRAPH* IS LOCATED!

WOULDN'T YOU KNOW-- EVEN IN THE MIDDLE OF DISASTER THERE ARE THOSE WHO TRY TO MAKE A *BUCK* OUT OF IT!

MY TIME'S LIMITED--AND I DON'T LOOK FORWARD TO EXPLAINING MY PRESENCE TO *POLICE* OFFICIALS ACROSS A *LANGUAGE BARRIER!*

I'LL JUST HAVE TO APPLY MY FULL 180 LBS. IN CERTAIN STRATEGIC SPOTS--

--AND TRY'N' *SCARE* 'EM AWAY!

FROM THE *SOUND* OF IT, I'M *SUCCEEDING!*

'EY! NO WONDER THEM BLOKES RAN OUT--THESE *EARTHQUAKES* ARE *MURDER!*

I AIN'T PLANNIN' FOR PART OF THIS 'ERE BLOODY *BUILDIN'* T' *FALL* ON ME!

ME NEITHER!

MISSION ACCOMPLISHED--NOW TO GET DOWN TO THE *REAL* WORK-- LOCATING THE EARTHQUAKE CENTER!

11

MUCH TIME AND MANY QUAKE-RUMBLES LATER...

I DIDN'T EXPECT TO HAVE TO PLAY THE ALL-KNOWING SCIENTIST BIT AGAIN, BUT I BELIEVE I'VE FIGURED OUT THE QUAKES ARE CENTERED NEAR THE *DOCKS*-- RIGHT HERE IN *THIS* TOWN!

THEN LET'S GET BACK THERE AND CORRECT IT!

NO POLICH *THIS* TIME--!

MY *TELESCOPIC VISION* SHOWS WE'VE GOT SOME ASSISTANCE, *ATOM!* AQUAMAN HAS JUST ARRIVED!

MEANWHILE ON SHIPS STILL TOO CROWDED TO ALLOW EVEN THE *SMALLEST* POSSESSIONS TO BE BROUGHT ABOARD...

OBSERVE--WE WHO HAVE *NOTHING* ARE *MOCKED* BY HE WHO WEARS A MEDAL OF *GOLD* ON HIS NECK--!

THOUGH THIS BE NOT TRULY GOLD-- IF IT CAUSES *ANGER*, IT SHALL BE DISPOSED OF!

AND BY THIS SIMPLE ACT, THOUGH NO ONE IS INSTANTLY AWARE OF IT, THE THREAT TO THEIR LAND IS ABRUPTLY ENDED!

GRANDFATHER, WHY DID YOU DO SUCH A THING-- WHY DIDN'T YOU *EXPLAIN* WHAT IT WAS? SURELY THEY WOULD HAVE *LISTENED!*

PEOPLE LISTEN MORE TO *ACTIONS* THAN TO WORDS, YOUNG ONE!

WHEN THE PROPHET FLED HIS ENEMIES IN THE MIDST OF NIGHT, HE TOOK NOTHING*! I COULD DO NO LESS!

* THE *HEGIRA OF MOHAMMED*--IN 622 A.D., THE DATE WHICH MARKS THE BEGINNING OF THE ISLAMIC CALENDAR--EDITOR.

12

WE NOW FLASH BACK A FEW HOURS, AS THE *SCARLET SPEEDSTER* DASHES ACROSS THE STORMY PACIFIC OCEAN...

RUBBISH AND JUNK--EVEN IN THE MIDDLE OF *NOWHERE*--! TALK OF MENACES--

WHILE TO THE WEST LIES AN EVEN GREATER *PRESENT* DANGER, AS THE *ASIAN MONSOON* RAINS HAVE INCREASED TEN-FOLD INTO A SOLID TORRENT OF WATER!

BUT IN A SMALL HUT ALONG THE *MEKONG RIVER* IN *VIET-NAM*, A YOUNG WIFE APPEARS NOT TO NOTICE...

THIS IS *LOK LU*, THE NAME OF HER LIFEBOOK IS *TRAGEDY*. HER HUSBAND WAS KILLED BY THOSE OF THE *BLACK PAJAMAS*...HER ONLY CHILD DIED WHEN THE FIRE-WEAPONS RAINED FROM THE SKIES...

SHE KNEELS QUIETLY NOW BEFORE THE SYMBOLS OF HER HOUSEHOLD GODS--STOICALLY WAITING--THOUGH SHE FEARS THE STORM, HER EMOTION IS NOT APPARENT...

...UNKNOWING THAT THIS SYMBOL IS, IN REALITY, THE MECHANICAL AGENT FOR THE ALL-DESTRUCTIVE RAINS!

RAINS WHICH AT THIS VERY MOMENT ARE BEGINNING TO TAKE THEIR TOLL!

THE RIVER'S RAGING OUT OF CONTROL--! THOSE POOR SOULS WILL DROWN UNLESS I DO SOMETHING!

13

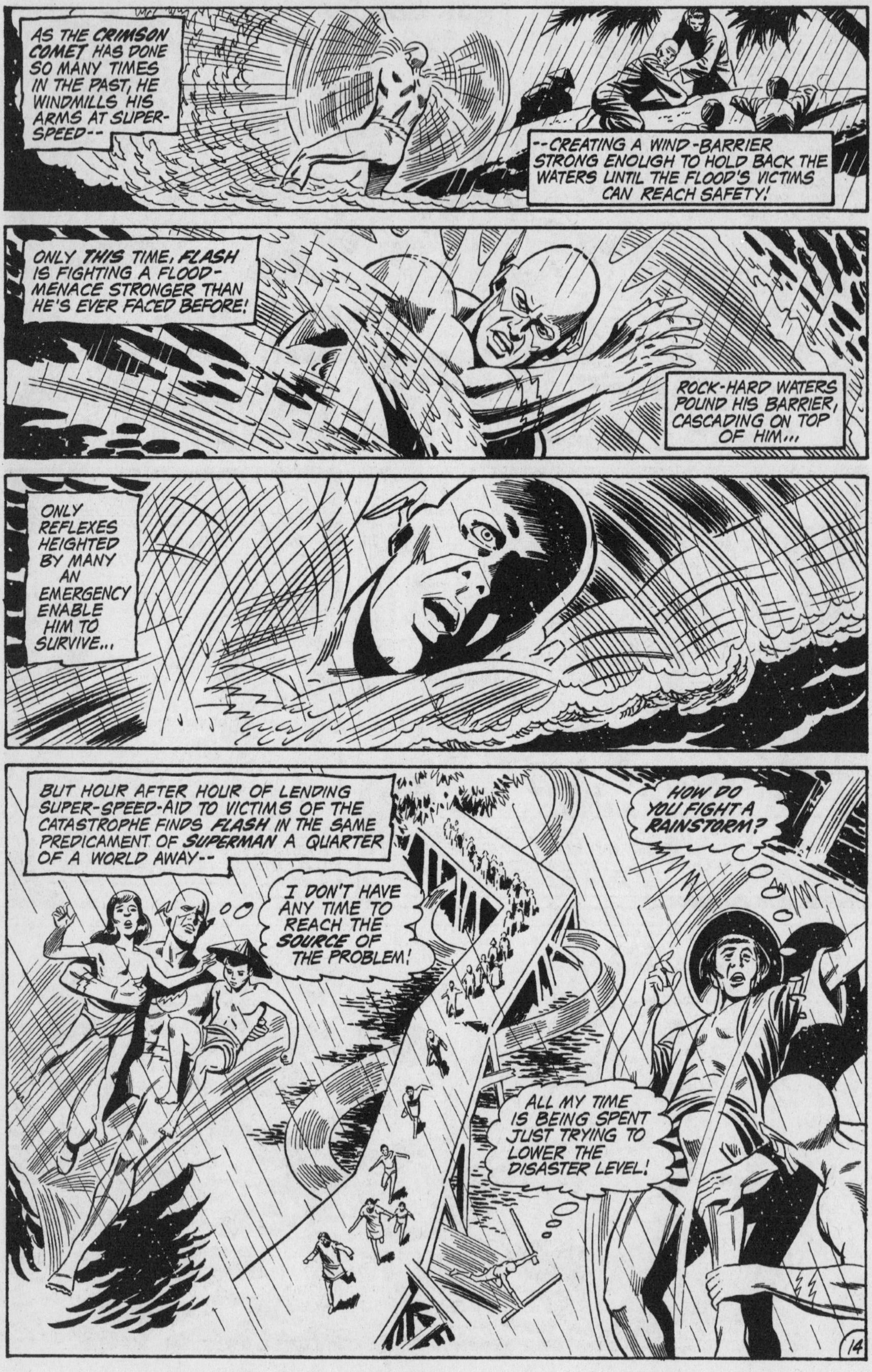
AS THE CRIMSON COMET HAS DONE SO MANY TIMES IN THE PAST, HE WINDMILLS HIS ARMS AT SUPER-SPEED--
--CREATING A WIND-BARRIER STRONG ENOUGH TO HOLD BACK THE WATERS UNTIL THE FLOOD'S VICTIMS CAN REACH SAFETY!
ONLY THIS TIME, FLASH IS FIGHTING A FLOOD-MENACE STRONGER THAN HE'S EVER FACED BEFORE!
ROCK-HARD WATERS POUND HIS BARRIER, CASCADING ON TOP OF HIM...
ONLY REFLEXES HEIGHTED BY MANY AN EMERGENCY ENABLE HIM TO SURVIVE...
BUT HOUR AFTER HOUR OF LENDING SUPER-SPEED-AID TO VICTIMS OF THE CATASTROPHE FINDS FLASH IN THE SAME PREDICAMENT OF SUPERMAN A QUARTER OF A WORLD AWAY--
I DON'T HAVE ANY TIME TO REACH THE SOURCE OF THE PROBLEM!
HOW DO YOU FIGHT A RAINSTORM?
ALL MY TIME IS BEING SPENT JUST TRYING TO LOWER THE DISASTER LEVEL!
14

I'VE BEEN HERE FOR *HOURS* AND THE STORM'S STILL COMING DOWN--*HARD!* IF I WEREN'T VIBRATING FAST ENOUGH TO LET IT PASS THROUGH ME, IT'D *KILL* ME!

ONLY TROUBLE IS, I CAN'T KEEP THIS UP *FOREVER*--I'M STARTING TO *TIRE*--!

BUT STILL THE *FASTEST MAN ALIVE* CONTINUES HIS ACTIVITIES--RACING DESPERATELY AGAINST HIS OWN BODY'S WEAKNESS...AGAINST A STORM THAT REFUSES TO STOP--AGAINST THE MIGHTY POWER OF *MU!*

SAND

SAND

THEN...A GLIMMER OF HOPE ARRIVES--THE APPEARANCE OF TWO MORE CRUSADERS AGAINST CATASTROPHE!

FLASH--THIS IS *GREEN ARROW* AND *BLACK CANARY* TRAVELING IN THE *BAT-JET!*

LOOKS PRETTY *BAD* DOWN THERE! WHAT CAN WE DO--?

15

I NEED HELP LOCATING THE *CAUSE* OF THIS STORM--IT'S *TOO HEAVY* TO BE ANYTHING *NATURAL!*

FROM UP HERE, IT LOOKS THE *DARKEST* AND *HEAVIEST* BELOW US--ABOUT 120 MILES SOUTHWEST FROM *SAIGON!*

MEANWHILE, BELOW THE BLACKNESS THAT IS THE STORM CENTER TO *GREEN ARROW*, LOK LU HAS SUFFERED IMMENSELY...

THOUGH HER FACE DOES NOT SHOW IT, SHE HAS LOST FAITH IN HER GODS--THEY HAVE NOT PROTECTED HER, BUT SHE DOES NOT WORRY--IF SHE SURVIVES, SHE WILL FIND NEW GODLY SYMBOLS...

WHEN *FLASH* APPROACHES THE AREA...

GREEN ARROW FIRED SOMETHING FROM THE *BAT-JET*--I COULD SEE IT!

SUDDENLY, THROUGH *LOK LU'S* ACTIONS, THE STORMS CEASE! THE SUN SHINES BRIGHTLY THROUGH RAPIDLY DISAPPEARING CLOUDS!

LOOK AT THAT-- IT'S *OVER!* CAN'T FIGURE IT--BUT I'VE NEVER BEEN SO GLAD TO SEE THE SUN!

WHILE IN THE DISTANCE, THE STORM'S END IS TAKEN AS A MATTER OF COURSE. THOUGH PERHAPS NOT AS SEVERE, THERE WILL BE OTHER RAINS AND *LOK LU* MUST PREPARE. AS ALWAYS, HER FACE SHOWS NO EMOTION, NO CHANGE...

16

"THE LAST SURVIVORS OF EARTH" PART THREE

EXPRESSIONS HAVEN'T CHANGED ON THE SPACE-SHIP OF MU, EITHER--BUT EMOTIONS HAVE! CONSTERNATION REIGNS...

PEOPLE OF MU, WE MACHINES ARE FORCED TO REPORT THAT IN TWO SECTORS, AFFECTING TWO-THIRDS OF OUR INITIAL ATTACK, WE HAVE BEEN DEFEATED!

INTOL-ERABLE!

WHAT IS IT THAT ENABLES THESE IMPERFECT HUMANS TO SURVIVE?

THERE MUST BE SOME UNNATURAL FORCE HELPING THEM!

WE CANNOT TOLERATE SUCH OPPOSITION!

WE SHALL DESCEND ON THE PLANET--DISCOVER WHAT IS AIDING THEM--AND ERADICATE IT!

DIRECTLY BELOW THE SPACESHIP'S DESCENT IS THE THIRD OF THEIR "ATTACK" SYMBOLS--

--ENCASED FIRMLY IN THE TRADING VAULTS OF A SUNKEN SPANISH GALLEON, SHIPWRECKED OFF CALIFORNIA IN 1589...

--NOW CAUSING MASSIVE TIDAL WAVES ALONG THE COAST, REACHING HIGHER AND HIGHER WITH EACH PASSING MOMENT!

17

THIS IS *PETE CONK*, A YOUNG AMERICAN WHO HAS BEEN SPENDING HIS SUMMER *SURFING!* RIGHT NOW HE'S *MAD*-- BECAUSE THE TIDES HAVE RISEN AND THE SURF IS TOO DANGEROUS...

WATCH *CAREFULLY*, FOR AROUND HIM WILL REVOLVE THE FATE OF THE WORLD!

MEAN-WHILE, SINCE THE DEPAR-TURE OF *GREEN ARROW* AND THE *BLACK CANARY,* THE *BAT-MAN* HAS BEEN WATCH-ING THE RISING TIDES WITH INCREASING ALARM...

HE'S HELPED CLEAR THE BEACHES, BUT WITHOUT A CLUE TO THE TIDAL WAVE'S ORIGIN, WHEN--

A *SPACESHIP*-- OUT OF THE BLUE!

SHEER COINCIDENCE-- OR A CONNEC-TION WITH THE TIDAL WAVE--?

I MEAN TO *FIND OUT*--!

HOW MANY MEN WOULD *DARE* ATTACK A SPACE-SHIP *UNARMED*--*DARE* TO RELY ON ONLY THEIR OWN HUMAN SOURCES?

HOW MANY MEN WOULD DARE BE *THE BATMAN?*

WHAT MANNER OF CREATURE IS THIS--? HE IS LIKE TO A LIVING NIGHT-MARE!

NO MATTER-- HE HAS BEEN KNOCKED SENSE-LESS! HE IS HARM-LESS!

OUR MACHINES SHOW THAT THERE ARE EXCEEDINGLY *FEW* OF THESE COSTUMED ONES-- AND NOT THE *UNNATURAL FORCE* WE SEEK!

WE SHOULD EXTRACT A *SPECIMEN* FROM THE POPULATION AND *EXAMINE* HIM!

LET IT BE DONE!

IF PETE CONK THOUGHT HE WAS *MAD* BEFORE, *NOW* THERE'LL BE NO CORKING HIS ANGER--

HEY--!

AFTER INTENSIVE MACHINE EXAMINATION...

WE FIND NOTHING EXTRAORDINARY ABOUT THIS HUMAN!

TELL US, CREATURE, WHAT FORCE HAS AIDED YOUR RACE TO SURVIVE WITHOUT THE PERFECTION WE HAVE ACHIEVED?

I DIG YOUR SET-UP HERE!

WELL, LISTEN, *JACK*-- AND I USE THE *SINGULAR* 'CAUSE YOU'RE ALL THE *SAME*-- I GOT SOMETHIN' TO *TELL* YA--!

EVERYTHING ON THIS SHIP IS PERFECTLY PEACHY-KEEN-- EXCEPT *YOU!*

YOU'VE ALL BECOME *BLOBS*--JEALOUS OF US WHO LIVE *NORMAL* HUMAN LIVES--!

ENOUGH!

STOP HIM-- EJECT HIM FROM OUR PERFECT SHIP!

DON'T WORRY-- I'M *LEAVIN'*--!

MAN, THEY'RE REALLY WACKED OUT-- I WAS GONNA SUGGEST SOMETHING A BIT MORE PEACEFUL THAN WHAT THEY'RE DOIN'--!

--BUT THEY'VE COMPLETELY CLOSED THEMSELVES OFF TO ANYTHING EXCEPT *DESTRUCTION!*

SHOWS WHAT HAPPENS WHEN VALET *MACHINES* DO EVERYTHING FOR YA!

--MADE IT! MACHINES LET ME OUT OF A *HATCH!*

THERE THEY GO--!

19

BUT THEN...

...SUDDENLY...

...UNEXPECTEDLY...

BOOM

HEY, PETEY, YOU ALL RIGHT?

WHEN THAT SPACESHIP ZAPPED *THE BATMAN*, THEN GRABBED YOU--

WASN'T ANY PROBLEM-- FACT IS, *I'M* THE ONE WHO TOOK *CARE* OF 'EM!

OH, YEAH?

YEAH! WHEN I WAS ESCAPIN', I TOSSED A WRENCH IN THE WORKS--RIGHT INTO THE *ENGINES!*

MUST'VE UPSET SOMETHIN' *VITAL*--'CAUSE THE SHIP *EXPLODED!!*

AAAGH! I DON'T *BELIEVE* HIM! THAT SPACESHIP WAS *THIS* BIG!

NEITHER DO I--MUST'VE BEEN SOME-THING *ELSE* WENT WRONG!

CONTINUED ON 2ND PAGE FOLLOWING.

20

"THE LAST SURVIVORS OF EARTH"-- EPILOGUE

OTHER EYES WITNESSED THAT EXPLOSION AS WELL-- DARK, MOODY EYES...

THE TIDAL WAVE STOPPED WHEN THE SPACESHIP EXPLODED! SHEER COINCIDENCE AGAIN--?

I GUESS I'LL NEVER KNOW-- EH?

GREEN LANTERN APPEARING OVER THE AREA WHERE THE SPACESHIP WAS DESTROYED-- AND THE REST OF THE JUSTICE LEAGUE!

SHIERRA WASN'T HURT TOO BADLY-- SHE MADE A RAPID RECOVERY!

JUST ABOUT THE TIME I DID! I WAS KNOCKED OUT IN MID-FLIGHT BY THE SAME MYSTERY LIGHTNING BOLT THAT STRUCK HER!

YOU MEAN YOU DIDN'T HAVE ANYTHING TO DO WITH THE SPACE-SHIP EXPLODING?

NO... I ASSUMED YOU HAD FIXED IT UP SOME-HOW! DIDN'T YOU...?

WELL, ATOM AND I AGREE IT WAS AQUAMAN WHO ENDED OUR EARTHQUAKE MENACE!

WHA--? BUT I FIGURED YOU TWO HAD DONE IT-- THAT'S WHY I DIDN'T SAY ANYTHING!

THERE'S NO DOUBT IN MY MIND WHO SAVED SOUTHEAST ASIA FROM THOSE TERRIFIC MONSOON RAINS-- I SAW GREEN ARROW EXPLODE WHATEVER HAD CAUSED THEM!

I'VE GOT NEWS FOR YOU, FLASH! ALL I FIRED WAS A FLARE! IN THE FLARELIGHT I SAW YOU AND JUST, WELL, ASSUMED...

IT APPEARS WE HAVE ALL JUST ENCOUNTERED ANOTHER ONE OF THE STRANGE MYSTERIES OF MU! ANY OTHER EXPLANATION LEAVES US WITH EVEN MORE QUESTIONS TO ANSWER!

I'LL MOVE AT OUR NEXT REGULAR MEETING THAT WE WRITE UP THIS CASE AS... UNEXPLAINED!

21

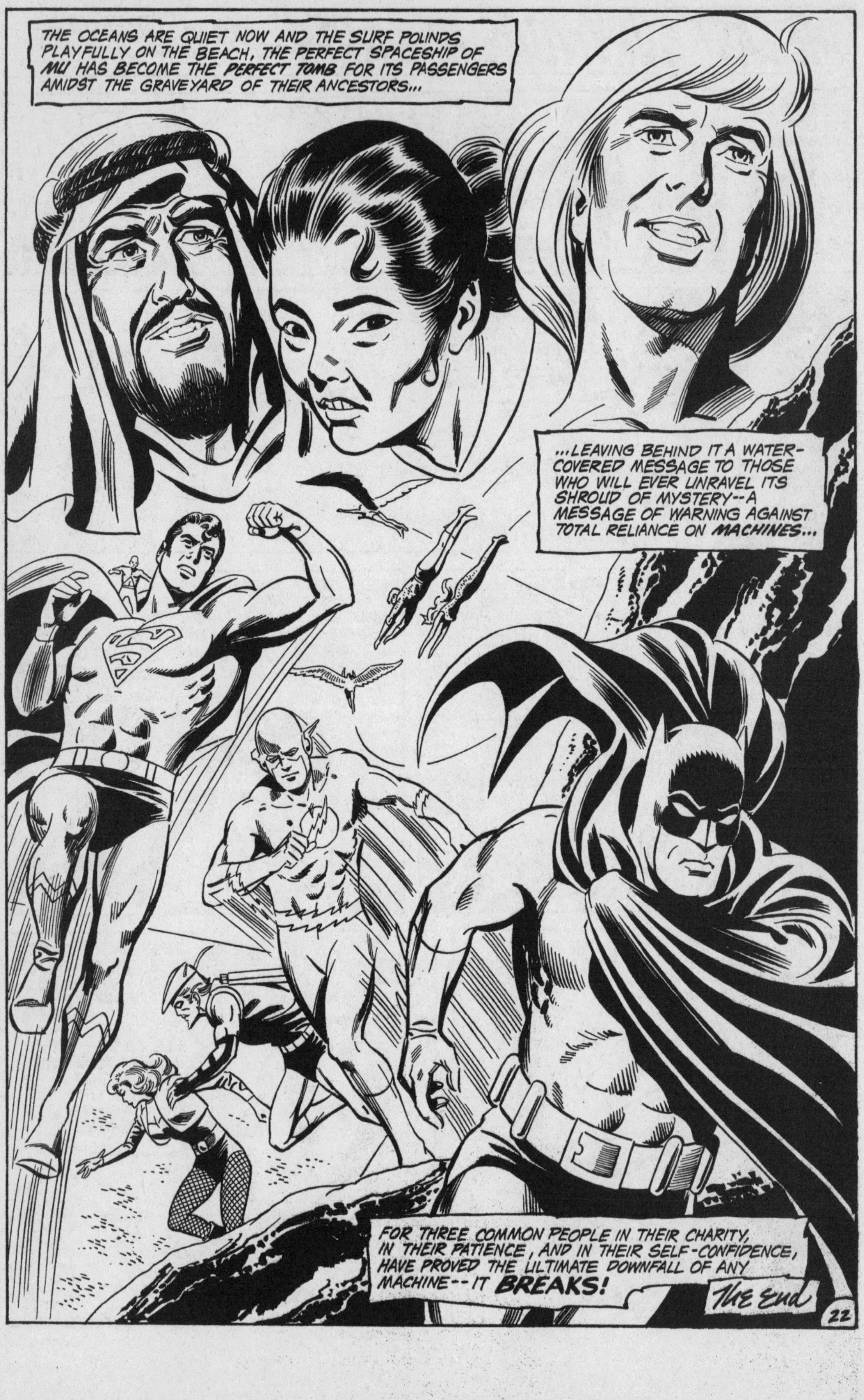
THE OCEANS ARE QUIET NOW AND THE SURF POUNDS PLAYFULLY ON THE BEACH. THE PERFECT SPACESHIP OF MU HAS BECOME THE PERFECT TOMB FOR ITS PASSENGERS AMIDST THE GRAVEYARD OF THEIR ANCESTORS...
...LEAVING BEHIND IT A WATER-COVERED MESSAGE TO THOSE WHO WILL EVER UNRAVEL ITS SHROUD OF MYSTERY--A MESSAGE OF WARNING AGAINST TOTAL RELIANCE ON MACHINES...
FOR THREE COMMON PEOPLE IN THEIR CHARITY, IN THEIR PATIENCE, AND IN THEIR SELF-CONFIDENCE, HAVE PROVED THE ULTIMATE DOWNFALL OF ANY MACHINE--IT BREAKS!
THE END
22

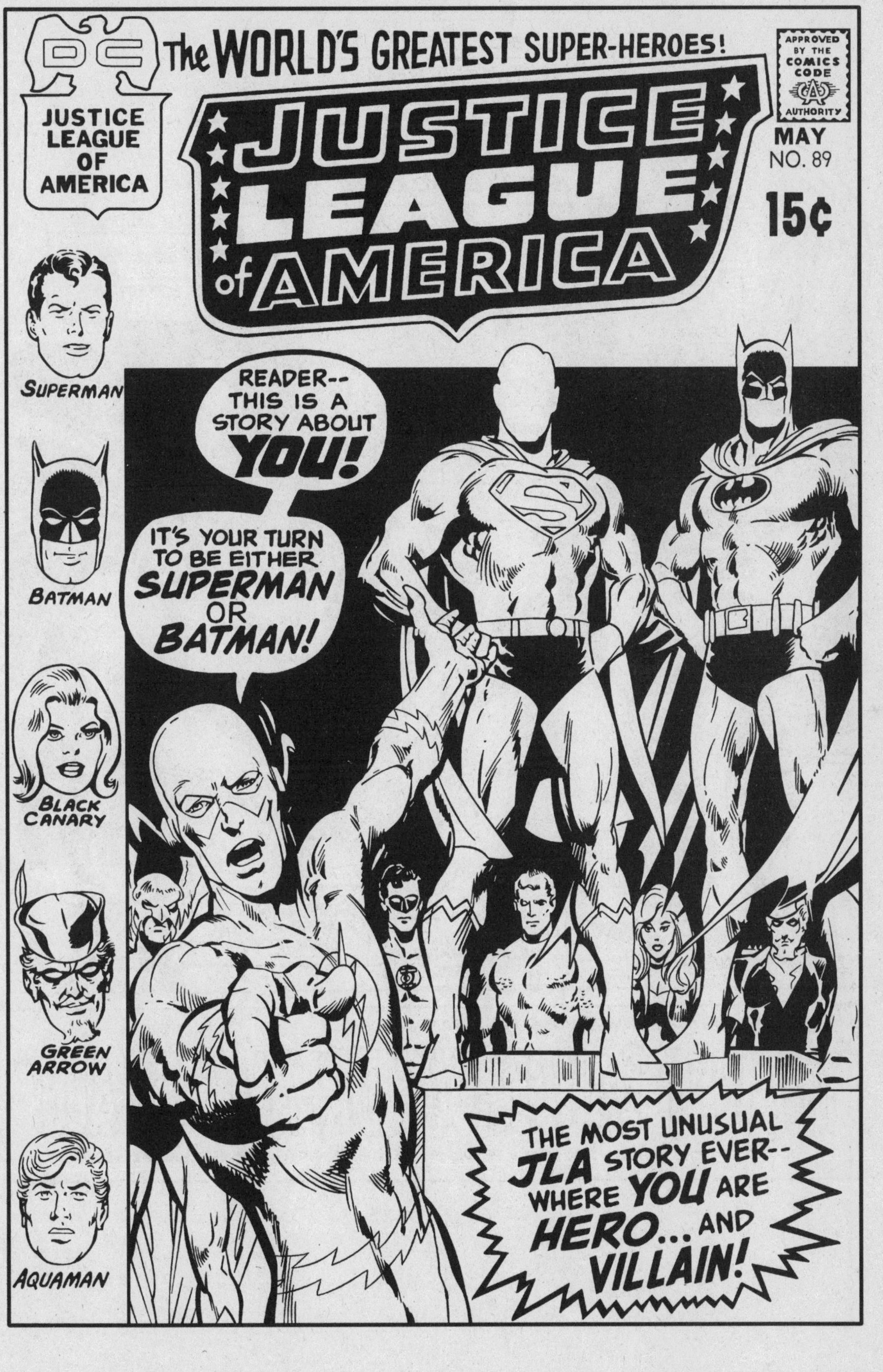
The WORLD'S GREATEST SUPER-HEROES!
JUSTICE LEAGUE OF AMERICA
JUSTICE LEAGUE of AMERICA
APPROVED BY THE COMICS CODE AUTHORITY
MAY
NO. 89
15¢
SUPERMAN
BATMAN
BLACK CANARY
GREEN ARROW
AQUAMAN
READER-- THIS IS A STORY ABOUT YOU!
IT'S YOUR TURN TO BE EITHER SUPERMAN OR BATMAN!
THE MOST UNUSUAL JLA STORY EVER-- WHERE YOU ARE HERO... AND VILLAIN!

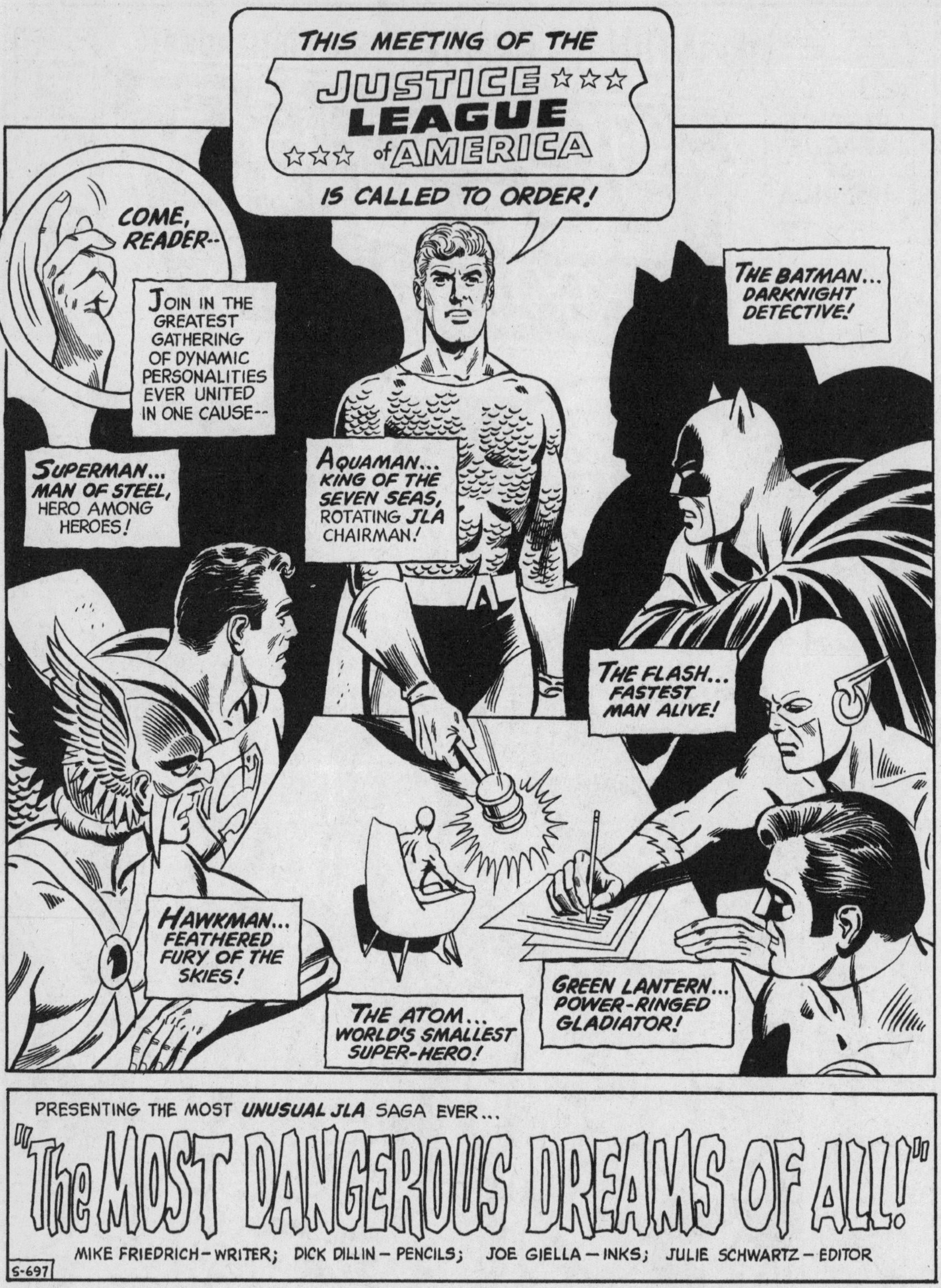
THIS MEETING OF THE
JUSTICE LEAGUE of AMERICA
IS CALLED TO ORDER!
COME, READER--
JOIN IN THE GREATEST GATHERING OF DYNAMIC PERSONALITIES EVER UNITED IN ONE CAUSE--
THE BATMAN... DARKNIGHT DETECTIVE!
SUPERMAN... MAN OF STEEL, HERO AMONG HEROES!
AQUAMAN... KING OF THE SEVEN SEAS, ROTATING JLA CHAIRMAN!
THE FLASH... FASTEST MAN ALIVE!
HAWKMAN... FEATHERED FURY OF THE SKIES!
THE ATOM... WORLD'S SMALLEST SUPER-HERO!
GREEN LANTERN... POWER-RINGED GLADIATOR!
PRESENTING THE MOST UNUSUAL JLA SAGA EVER...
"The MOST DANGEROUS DREAMS OF ALL!"
MIKE FRIEDRICH—WRITER; DICK DILLIN—PENCILS; JOE GIELLA—INKS; JULIE SCHWARTZ—EDITOR
S-697

AFTER THEIR RESPECTIVE SOLO-ADVENTURES ARE EXCHANGED AND BUSINESS CONDUCTED...

THAT CONCLUDES THIS REGULAR MEETING OF THE *JUSTICE LEAGUE.*

AS SECRETARY, *FLASH* WILL FORWARD THE MINUTES TO THE ABSENT *GREEN ARROW* AND *BLACK CANARY!*

MEETING ADJOURNED!

BUSINESS CONCLUDED, THE *WORLD'S GREATEST SUPER-HEROES* ENTER THEIR *THANAGARIAN TRANSPORTER...*

...WHICH TAKES THEM 22,300 MILES FROM THEIR SPACE-SANCTUARY-SATELLITE TO THE EARTH BELOW...

...TO EMERGE ON A CONCEALED AREA OF A ROOF ATOP A SKYSCRAPER HOUSING A CERTAIN CELEBRATED PUBLISHING FIRM...

SWITCHING TO THEIR SECRET CIVILIAN IDENTITIES, THEY TAKE A PRIVATE ELEVATOR TO STREET-LEVEL...

...WHERE THEY MINGLE AMONG CROWDS OF PEOPLE COMPLETELY UNAWARE OF THEIR EXISTENCE!

ORDINARY PEOPLE, THE *JUSTICE LEAGUERS,* JUST LIKE YOU OR I. AND DON'T WE EACH SECRETLY KNOW THAT DESPITE APPEARANCES, WE ARE ALL SOMETHING *MORE?*

THIS IS A STORY FOR THE SUPER-HERO IN US ALL. *THIS STORY IS ABOUT ME--AND IT'S ALSO ABOUT YOU!*

2

LIKE POUNDING COLD CALIFORNIA SEA-WAVES SPLASHING OVER AN INDEFENSIBLE SWIMMER, THE MAN AND STORY ABOUT TO UNFOLD ARE PRESSURING ME TO TELL THIS TALE...

WHY, YOU ASK? READ ON...

YOU'RE WAITING ON *SUNSET BOULEVARD, LOS ANGELES* -- THINKING OF ITS WIND FROM NATURE'S SOOTHING SEA-SURF THROUGH THE HEART OF MAN'S GLARING *TINSELTOWN*, USA: HOLLYWOOD...

THIS IS *"THE STRIP"*! THIS IS WHERE THE ACTION IS*! THIS IS WHERE WE FIND *YOU* TONIGHT...!

AS YOU WAIT, TURN YOUR HEAD AND MEET *HARLEQUIN ELLIS*... SMALL-TOWN *OHIO* BOY IN THE BIG TIME. HE WRITES FOR TELEVISION AND HE'S PAID WELL-- *VERY* WELL!

HE'S WEARING HIS NAME LIKE A NEON SIGN TONIGHT, FOR HE'S THE FLASHY CLOWN, THE SMILING SWINGER, EVERY GRIN OF HIS SHINING TEETH BROADCASTING *"I'M WITH IT!"*

TURNING YOUR HEAD BACK, THE CORNER OF YOUR EYE SEES WHY ELLIS WAS DUBBED BY A LEADING MOVIE MAG, *"THE MOST ELIGIBLE BACHELOR IN HOLLYWOOD"*!...

YOU ALSO CAN TELL THAT THIS SLEEK ARROGANT TIGER IS ON THE *PROWL*...

AND TONIGHT HE'S STALKING *YOU, DINAH DRAKE LANCE*... ALIAS THE *BLACK CANARY*!

WELL, WELL! CHECK OUT *THIS* ACTION, ELLIE-BABY--!

3

WHAT'S A BEAUTIFUL YOUNG LADY, LIKE YOU STANDING HERE *ALONE* FOR?

NEED SOME *COMPANY*?

YOU LAUGH AT HIS OBVIOUS COME-ON AND ARE ABOUT TO BRUSH HIM OFF, WHEN YOU CHANCE TO LOOK DEEP IN HIS EYES...

THEN SUDDENLY YOU *KNOW*... THAT WHEN THIS MAN FALLS FOR A WOMAN, HE FALLS *ALL THE WAY!*

WITHIN MOMENTS, YOU FIND YOURSELF SHARING WITH A VIRTUAL *STRANGER* THOSE THINGS ONLY A SELECT *FEW* KNOW...

WHEN MY HUSBAND DIED, I WAS STRANDED...CUT LOOSE! THE HURT'S TAKING SO LONG TO HEAL.

IN THE QUIET OF NIGHT, WHEN I'M ALONE, THE PAIN STILL THROBS DULLY, DOWN DEEP!

THREE TIMES HAVE I LOST A WIFE-- ALWAYS A WARM AND BEAUTIFUL WOMAN!

MY HEART WAS RIPPED OPEN AND DASHED ON THE ROCKS EACH TIME!

YES... I, TOO, KNOW THE LONELINESS OF HEARTBREAK-- THE ETERNAL LOSS OF SOMEONE I'VE LOVED!

YOU AND I HAVE MUCH IN *COMMON*...

COFFE

AS HIS HAND TOUCHES YOURS AND YOUR EYES MEET ONCE MORE, YOU SUDDENLY SEE YOURSELF ON THE EDGE OF THE PIT OF HIS SOUL, LOOKING INTO THE BLACKNESS BENEATH YOU...

AND YOU ARE AFRAID-- FOR THERE IS *ANOTHER* ONE...

WHAT--?!

4

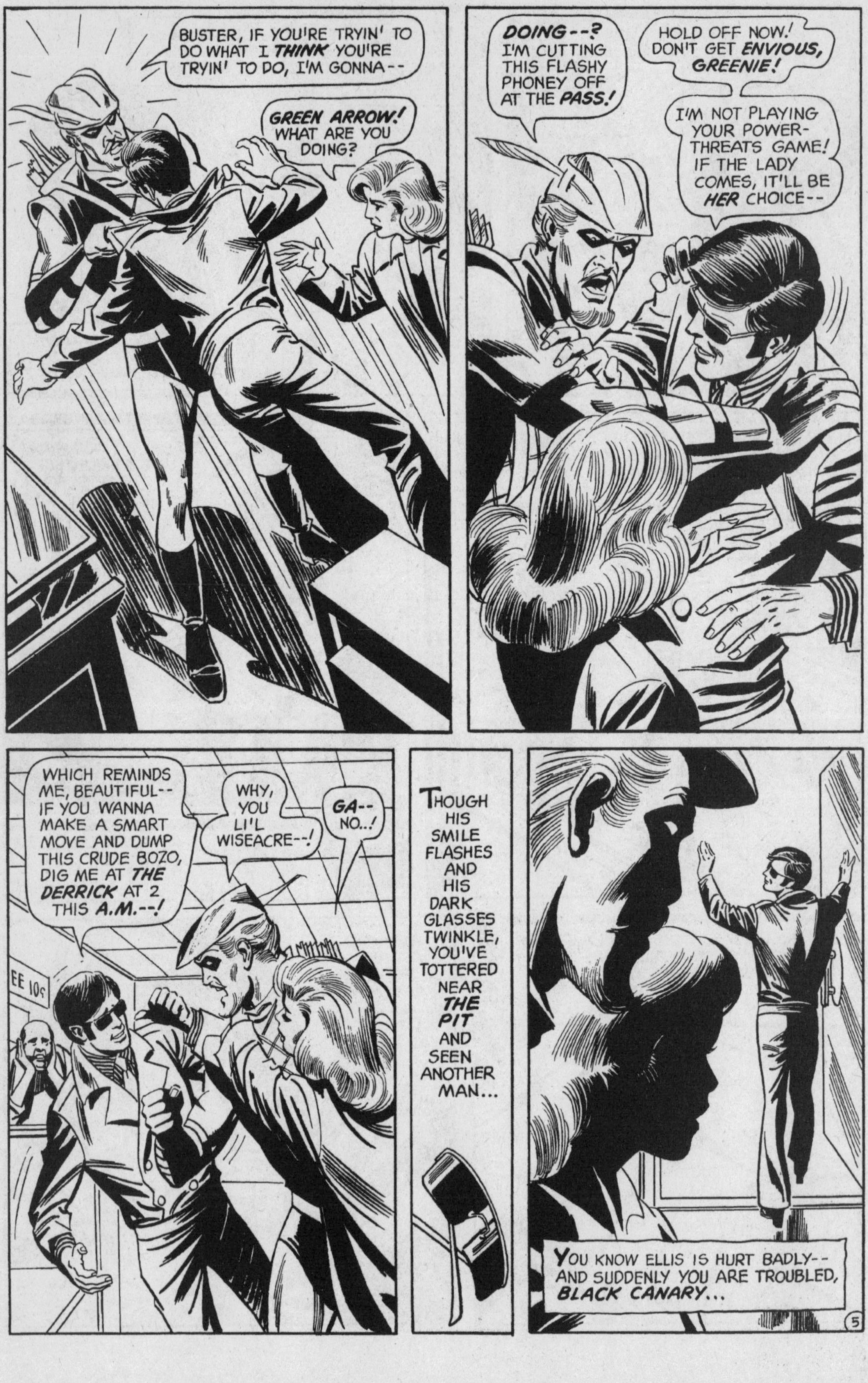
BUSTER, IF YOU'RE TRYIN' TO DO WHAT I THINK YOU'RE TRYIN' TO DO, I'M GONNA--
GREEN ARROW! WHAT ARE YOU DOING?
DOING--? I'M CUTTING THIS FLASHY PHONEY OFF AT THE PASS!
HOLD OFF NOW! DON'T GET ENVIOUS, GREENIE!
I'M NOT PLAYING YOUR POWER-THREATS GAME! IF THE LADY COMES, IT'LL BE HER CHOICE--
WHICH REMINDS ME, BEAUTIFUL-- IF YOU WANNA MAKE A SMART MOVE AND DUMP THIS CRUDE BOZO, DIG ME AT THE DERRICK AT 2 THIS A.M.--!
WHY, YOU LI'L WISEACRE--!
GA-- NO...!
EE 10¢
THOUGH HIS SMILE FLASHES AND HIS DARK GLASSES TWINKLE, YOU'VE TOTTERED NEAR THE PIT AND SEEN ANOTHER MAN...
YOU KNOW ELLIS IS HURT BADLY-- AND SUDDENLY YOU ARE TROUBLED, BLACK CANARY...
5

HHMMPH!

WHAT WAS *THAT* ALL ABOUT?

HOW THE DICKENS SHOULD *I* KNOW? *YOU'RE* HIS SECRETARY! *YOU* TELL *ME!*

—SIGH— WELL, I SUPPOSE IT'S TIME TO PLAY "SOOTHE-THE-RUFFLED-FEATHERS" AGAIN!

WONDER WHAT HE'S SULKING ABOUT *NOW?*

PROBABLY SOME GIRL HAS HIM STRUNG-OUT AGAIN AND YOU'LL HAVE TO STRAIGHTEN HIM OUT, AS USUAL...

HA! I'M NOT PLAYING *THAT* SCENE AGAIN! REMEMBER THE *LAST* TIME I TRIED TO INTERVENE--?

ELLIE DIDN'T SPEAK TO ME FOR A *MONTH!*

ELLIS--?

LET'S GET IT OUT FRONT-- *FAST!* WHAT TORCH YOU CARRYING THIS TIME?

C'MON, *HARLEQUIN,* YOU PHONEY CLOWN-- I PASSED THROUGH THE TEENY-BOPPER PHASE A LONG TIME AGO! YOUR FLASHY POSE DOESN'T FOOL *ME!*

ELLIE DIDN'T HEAR A WORD I SAID! HE'S SHUT HIMSELF IN HIS WRITING TRANCE AGAIN!

I *SWEAR,* HE MUST BE REALLY IN *ANOTHER WORLD* WHEN HE GETS IN THAT SWIVEL CHAIR OF HIS!

I EVEN TRIED THE "ABUSE METHOD" BUT IT DIDN'T BREAK THROUGH!

MANY ARE THE UNEXPLAINED MYSTERIES OF CREATIVE GENIUS! INSIDE *HARLEQUIN ELLIS'S* HEAD IS A FANTASY WORLD OF HIS OWN MAKING!

ONLY THIS TIME, THERE'S A *DIFFERENCE!* SO GREAT IS THE *POWER* OF HIS WOUNDED FEELINGS FOR *BLACK CANARY,* SO GREAT THE *DEPTH...*

...THAT HIS MIND HAS REACHED OUT ITS DARK TENTACLES AND ENVELOPED *NEW* FIGURES WITHIN HIS STORY-WORLD!

7

THE BARRIER BETWEEN THE **REAL** AND THE **UNREAL** BEGINS TO BREAK DOWN...

C'MON, *PRETTY BIRD*, LET'S GET A MOVE ON-- WE'RE LATE FOR THE *JLA* MEETING!

DIG THE CAT AND THE CHICK-- ARE *THEY* WEARING FAR-OUT CLOTHES!

ABRUPTLY-- AS IN *HARLEQUIN ELLIS'S* CURRENT STORY, *GREEN ARROW* AND *BLACK CANARY* FIND THEM- SELVES OUTSIDE A SMALL STORE *SOUTH OF THE BORDER.!...*

WHA--?! HOW'D WE GET *HERE?*

REGUE

COME IN, *SEÑOR... SEÑORITA!* AMERICANOS, ¿NO?

YEAH... ER... *SÍ...*

WHAT DO *YOU* KNOW ABOUT WHAT'S HAPPENING?

¡*NADA!* NOTHING, *SEÑOR!* I ONLY KNOW THAT YOU WOULD BE INTERESTED IN *THIS...* SOMETHING FROM OUR DIM, MAGIC PAST.

MAGIC--?

AS THE *ACE ARCHER* AND HIS BEAUTIFUL COMPANION TOUCH THE CURIO, THEIR HEADS SPIN WILDLY...

THEN... NOTHING!

ALL BECOMES AS A BRIGHT- COLORED *VORTEX'S* DIZZYING SWIRL AS THEY STEP INTO THE *UNKNOWN...*

"The FIRST DANGEROUS DREAM of HARLEQUIN ELLIS!"

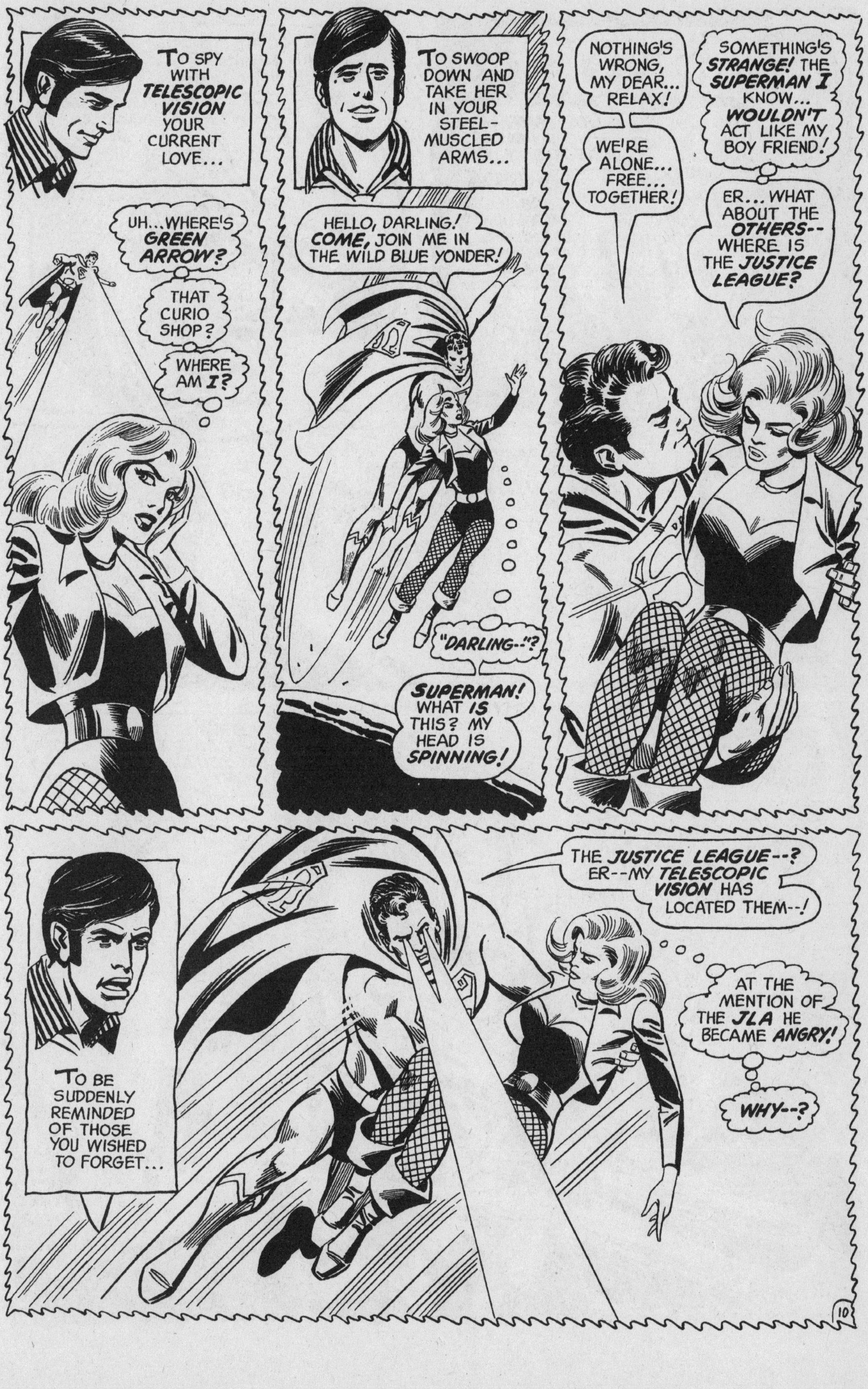
TO SPY WITH TELESCOPIC VISION YOUR CURRENT LOVE...
UH...WHERE'S GREEN ARROW?
THAT CURIO SHOP?
WHERE AM I?
TO SWOOP DOWN AND TAKE HER IN YOUR STEEL-MUSCLED ARMS...
HELLO, DARLING! COME, JOIN ME IN THE WILD BLUE YONDER!
"DARLING--"?
SUPERMAN! WHAT IS THIS? MY HEAD IS SPINNING!
NOTHING'S WRONG, MY DEAR... RELAX!
WE'RE ALONE... FREE... TOGETHER!
SOMETHING'S STRANGE! THE SUPERMAN I KNOW... WOULDN'T ACT LIKE MY BOY FRIEND!
ER... WHAT ABOUT THE OTHERS-- WHERE IS THE JUSTICE LEAGUE?
TO BE SUDDENLY REMINDED OF THOSE YOU WISHED TO FORGET...
THE JUSTICE LEAGUE--? ER--MY TELESCOPIC VISION HAS LOCATED THEM--!
AT THE MENTION OF THE JLA HE BECAME ANGRY!
WHY--?
10

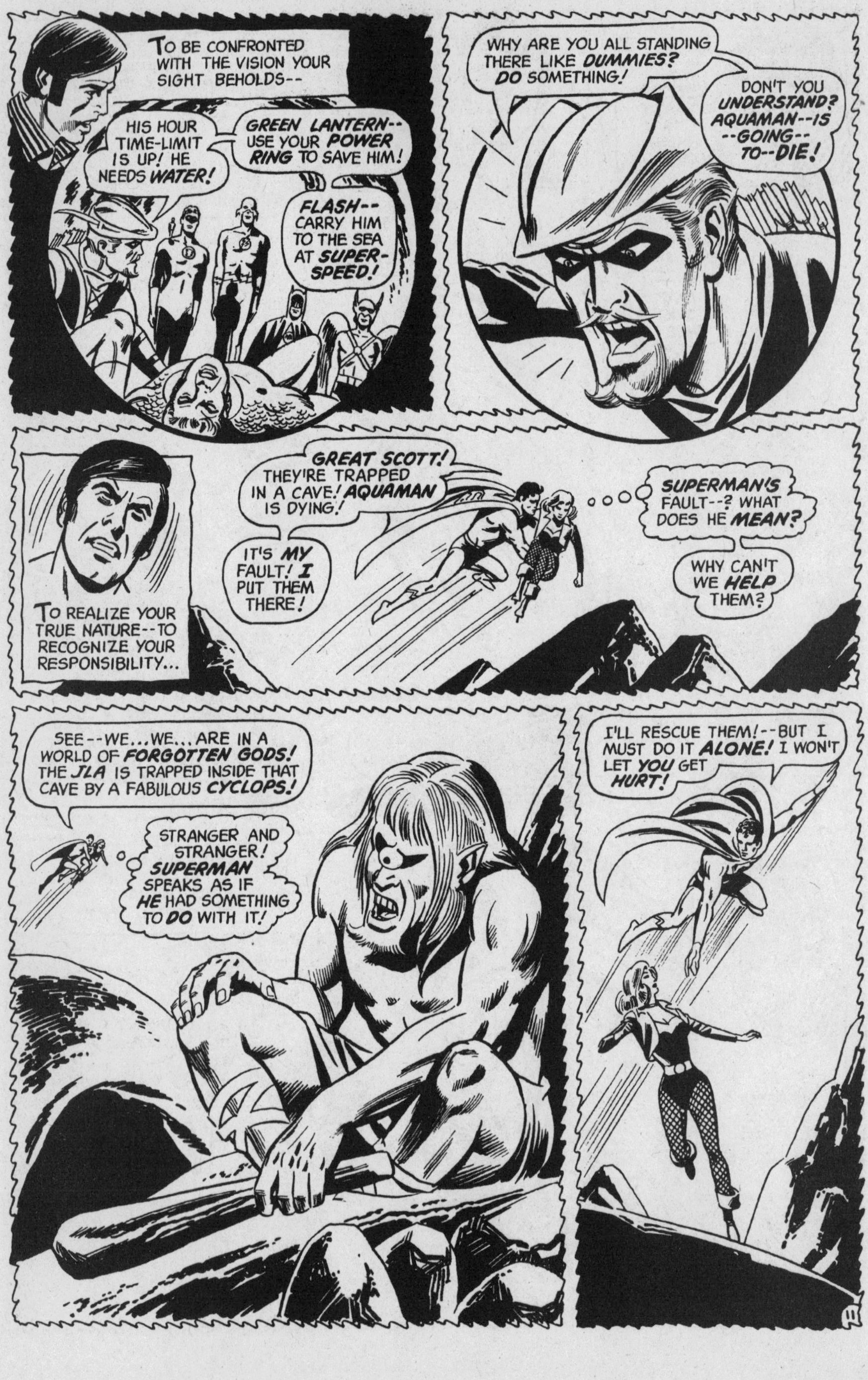
TO BE CONFRONTED WITH THE VISION YOUR SIGHT BEHOLDS--
HIS HOUR TIME-LIMIT IS UP! HE NEEDS WATER!
GREEN LANTERN-- USE YOUR POWER RING TO SAVE HIM!
FLASH-- CARRY HIM TO THE SEA AT SUPER-SPEED!
WHY ARE YOU ALL STANDING THERE LIKE DUMMIES? DO SOMETHING!
DON'T YOU UNDERSTAND? AQUAMAN--IS --GOING-- TO--DIE!
TO REALIZE YOUR TRUE NATURE--TO RECOGNIZE YOUR RESPONSIBILITY...
GREAT SCOTT! THEY'RE TRAPPED IN A CAVE! AQUAMAN IS DYING!
IT'S MY FAULT! I PUT THEM THERE!
SUPERMAN'S FAULT--? WHAT DOES HE MEAN?
WHY CAN'T WE HELP THEM?
SEE--WE...WE...ARE IN A WORLD OF FORGOTTEN GODS! THE JLA IS TRAPPED INSIDE THAT CAVE BY A FABULOUS CYCLOPS!
STRANGER AND STRANGER! SUPERMAN SPEAKS AS IF HE HAD SOMETHING TO DO WITH IT!
I'LL RESCUE THEM!--BUT I MUST DO IT ALONE! I WON'T LET YOU GET HURT!
11

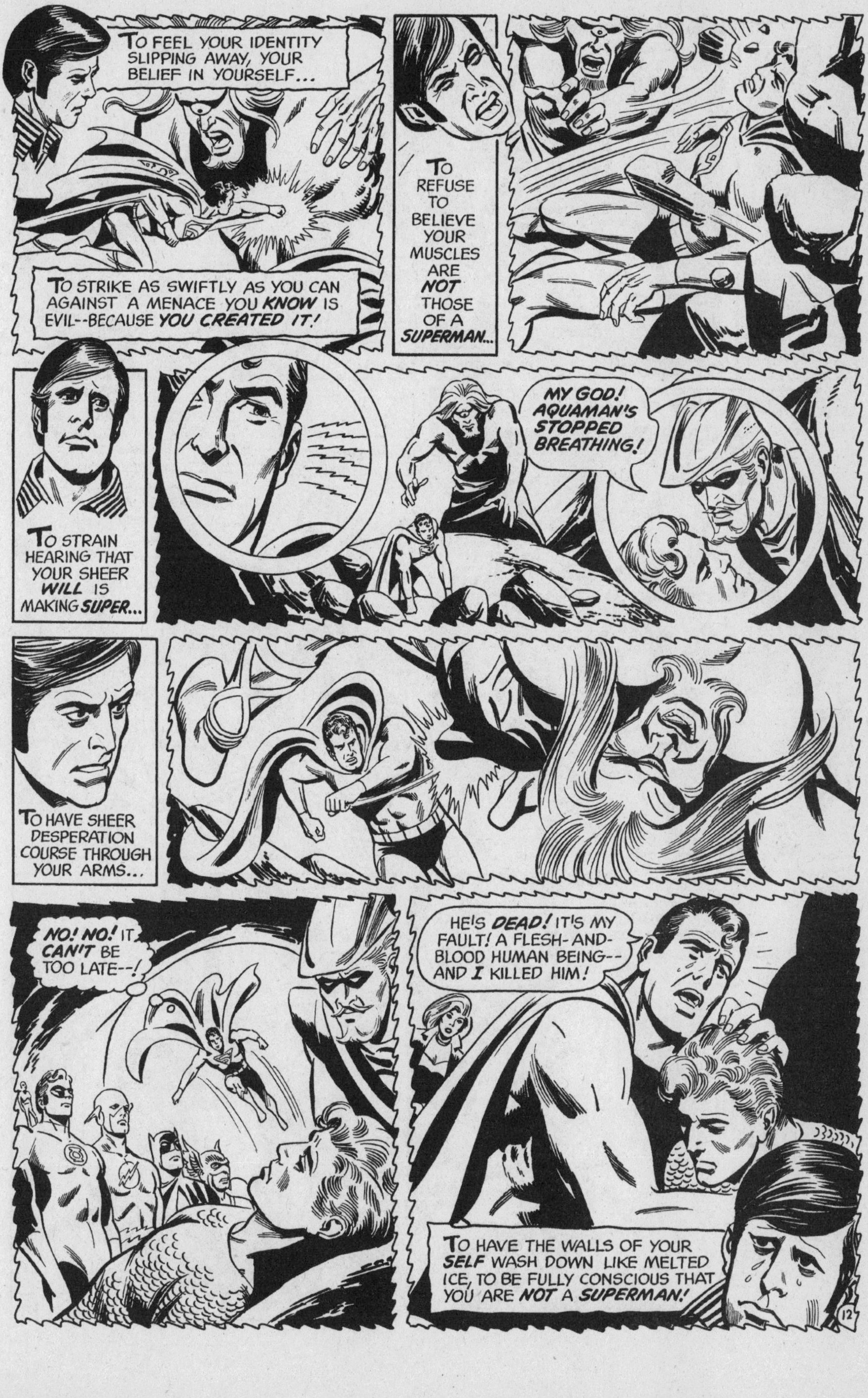
TO FEEL YOUR IDENTITY SLIPPING AWAY, YOUR BELIEF IN YOURSELF...
TO STRIKE AS SWIFTLY AS YOU CAN AGAINST A MENACE YOU KNOW IS EVIL--BECAUSE YOU CREATED IT!
TO REFUSE TO BELIEVE YOUR MUSCLES ARE NOT THOSE OF A SUPERMAN...
TO STRAIN HEARING THAT YOUR SHEER WILL IS MAKING SUPER...
MY GOD! AQUAMAN'S STOPPED BREATHING!
TO HAVE SHEER DESPERATION COURSE THROUGH YOUR ARMS...
NO! NO! IT CAN'T BE TOO LATE--!
HE'S DEAD! IT'S MY FAULT! A FLESH-AND-BLOOD HUMAN BEING--AND I KILLED HIM!
TO HAVE THE WALLS OF YOUR SELF WASH DOWN LIKE MELTED ICE, TO BE FULLY CONSCIOUS THAT YOU ARE NOT A SUPERMAN!
12

CANARY, YOU MUST *UNDERSTAND*...I'M SHATTERED...LIKE A GLASS GOBLET...ONE THAT MUST BE PUT TOGETHER AGAIN!

PLEASE...I WANT YOU...I *NEED* YOU!

BUT, *SUPERMAN*...I...I CAN'T...I DON'T UNDERSTAND...

TO REALIZE YOU ARE SOMEONE *ELSE*--SOMEONE WITH A GREAT *NEED*...

TO BE THE *MAN OF STEEL* NO LONGER...

SUPERMAN'S CHANGING!

I CREATED A WORLD--A WORLD WHERE *I* WAS A *HERO*--EVERYTHING WAS MINE!

INTO THIS PRIVATE WORLD I BRING *DEATH*...AND LOSE THE ONE GIRL WHO MEANS SO MUCH--

EVERYTHING'S DISAPPEARING--IT WASN'T *REAL!* SUPERMAN ISN'T *SUPERMAN*...AQUAMAN ISN'T *DEAD*...THE JLA WASN'T HERE--

NONE OF THIS *REALLY* HAPPENED! IT'S JUST A *NIGHTMARE!*

...A...A... DREAM...!

13

ONCE MORE, WHEN YOU LEAST EXPECTED IT, *BLACK CANARY,* YOU'VE SEEN *THE PIT*-- WHERE BUT THE SLIGHTEST HINT OF REJECTION LASTS *FOREVER...*

ONCE MORE... YOU ARE *AFRAID...*

IT...IT'S OVER!

WE MUST'VE *IMAGINED* IT TOGETHER...

NO--NO --IT WAS *REAL!*

SOMEHOW... SOMEWAY... I CAN FEEL THE NIGHTMARE RESUMING AGAIN!

OH, I'M FRIGHTENED, *GREEN ARROW* ...HOLD ME!

MEANWHILE, IN ELLIS'S HOUSE-- ONE DREAM-STORY SHATTERED --AND ANOTHER YET TO BEGIN...!

THERE HE GOES... WITHOUT A *WORD!*

DID YOU SEE THE LOOK OF *FURY* ON HIS FACE? SOMETHING *ROTTEN* MUST'VE HAPPENED IN THAT STORY OF HIS!

I'D STEER CLEAR OF *HIM* FOR QUITE AWHILE!

14

AT THE DERRICK...

WELL, *HELLO!* LONG TIME SINCE *YOU* HIT *THIS* NIGHT-SPOT!

FORGET IT, KIDDO-- *HARLEQUIN'S* IN ONE OF HIS *DARK* MOODS! IF YOU CROSS HIM, *WATCH OUT!*

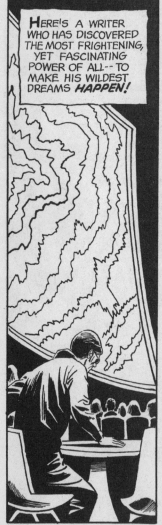

HERE'S A WRITER WHO HAS DISCOVERED THE MOST FRIGHTENING, YET FASCINATING POWER OF ALL-- TO MAKE HIS WILDEST DREAMS *HAPPEN!*

BUT HERE ALSO IS A MAN WHOSE EVERY SECOND IS THROBBED WITH THE PAIN-FIRE OF REJECTED LOVE...

SO EASILY *FORGOTTEN* IS THE DEATH-AGONY HE INFLICTED ON THE DREAMED-UP *AQUAMAN*...

SO EASILY *REMEMBERED* IS THE *REAL GREEN ARROW* COMING BETWEEN HIM AND *BLACK CANARY*...

EVERY THOUGHT CONCENTRATES ON SEPARATING THEM... ON DIVISIVE HATRED... ON *FINAL VENGEANCE!*

15

"THE SECOND DANGEROUS DREAM OF HARLEQUIN ELLIS!"

AH, TO BE *THE BATMAN!* TO BE THE VERY *EPITOME* OF AWESOME VENGEANCE... WHOSE EVERY MOVE TRIGGERS FEAR-FEELINGS OF THE DARK, MALEVOLENT *NIGHT* FROM WHICH HE COMES...

TO SMILE *COLDLY* FROM A SHADOWY PERCH OVER A HORRIFYING SPECTACLE BELOW...

--IT'S HAPPENED *AGAIN!*

THIS TIME I'M TRAPPED WITH A *MINOTAUR!*

GREEN ARROW-- QUICKLY--*DO* SOMETHING--BEFORE IT *KILLS* YOU!

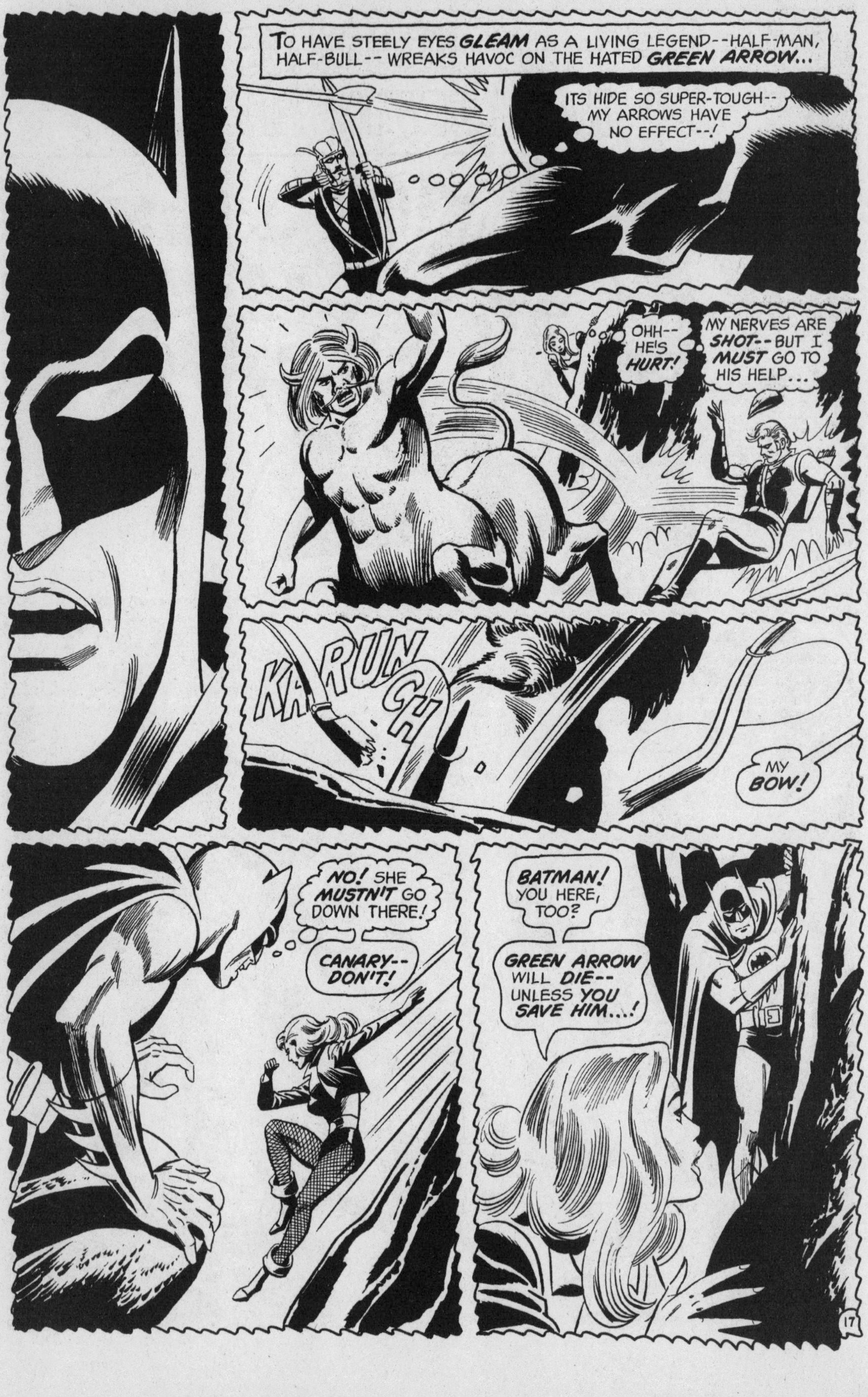
TO HAVE STEELY EYES GLEAM AS A LIVING LEGEND--HALF-MAN, HALF-BULL-- WREAKS HAVOC ON THE HATED GREEN ARROW...
ITS HIDE SO SUPER-TOUGH-- MY ARROWS HAVE NO EFFECT--!
OHH-- HE'S HURT!
MY NERVES ARE SHOT-- BUT I MUST GO TO HIS HELP...
KARUNCH
MY BOW!
NO! SHE MUSTN'T GO DOWN THERE!
CANARY-- DON'T!
BATMAN! YOU HERE, TOO?
GREEN ARROW WILL DIE-- UNLESS YOU SAVE HIM...!
17

TO HAVE MEMORY'S FLOODGATES OPEN TO THE PREVIOUS TIME-- TO RECALL THE GASPING SCREAMS OF *AQUAMAN*...

TO FLASH LIKE DAWN'S FIRST STABBING LIGHT THAT TO BE *THE BATMAN* IS *NOT* TO BE A VENGEFUL *KILLER*...

-- BUT TO BE A... *HERO!*

18

MUST HIT A NERVE *JUST RIGHT*... I'LL NEVER GET A SECOND CHANCE!

TO KNOW THE GREATEST TEST IS YET TO COME, AS YOU REALIZE YOU ARE *MORE* THAN *THE BATMAN*...

BLACK CANARY-- YOU ALL RIGHT--?

THAT *LOOK--!* YOU'RE *NOT THE BATMAN!*

NO, I AM NOT! *YOU* KNOW WHO I AM, *BLACK CANARY*-- AND *WHY* I AM HERE!

TO FEEL A CONSOLING STRENGTH IN KNOWING YOU'VE DONE *RIGHT*...

--*YOU?!*

OH, NO! NOT *AGAIN--!* WHAT CAN I *DO--?*

AND TO BE *THE BATMAN* NO LONGER!

19

YOU'VE RETURNED, **BLACK CANARY.** FOR FLEETING MOMENTS YOUR DESTINY IS YOUR OWN...THE FANTASY WORLD OF **HARLEQUIN ELLIS** HAS FADED ONCE MORE...

OLIVER, YOU'RE STILL **HURT!**

BETTER ⩰UHNN⩰ **BELIEVE** IT, **PRETTY BIRD!** THAT SURE **WASN'T** ⩰UHNN⩰ A **DREAM!**

THAT FLASHY ⩰UHNNN⩰ CLOWN HAS GOTTA BE **STOPPED!**

YOU REMEMBER **THE PIT** AND YOU KNOW THAT THIS BATTLE IS YOURS ALONE!...

NO...YOU'RE GOING TO STAY RIGHT HERE TILL I SEND FOR SOME **HELP!**

THEN I'M HANDLING OUR PROBLEM **MYSELF-- MY WAY!**

SHORTLY...

HARLEQUIN--?

YOUR EYES MEET HIS AND HIS LIPS DO NOT MOVE... BUT THE **MUSIC** SAYS IT **ALL**...

SEE ME...! ♪ FEEL ME...! TOUCH ME...! HEAL ME...! ♪

20

ONCE AGAIN, *BLACK CANARY,* YOU ARE ON THE EDGE OF *THE PIT,* AND YOU ARE STILL AFRAID. BUT THIS TIME YOU *JUMP...*

YOU'VE JUST LAID YOUR HEART ON THE TABLE! WITH JUST TWO WORDS *HARLEQUIN ELLIS* CAN SLICE YOU TO PIECES! HE DOESN'T SAY THEM...

INSTEAD, YOU FEEL TRUST AND AFFECTION RETURN TO YOU TWICE-OVER! YOU KNOW THAT YOUR COMMON FANTASY-WORLD EXPERIENCE HAS TAUGHT *HIM* AS WELL...

OUR THING HAS TO STAY COOL--YOU KNOW THAT.

MY HEART BELONGS TO SOMEONE ELSE...

I KNOW-- I CAN DIG IT!

WE ALL DO WHAT WE MUST...

DO YOU REALIZE WHAT YOU'VE DONE TO *GREEN ARROW?* THE DOCTOR'S WITH HIM NOW!

I...KNOW! I'M REALLY SORRY-- I CAN'T EXPRESS IT!

I... I GOT CARRIED AWAY --LOST MY HEAD...

YOU'VE GOT TO GROW UP, *HARLEQUIN*--THE CLOWN IS ONLY GOOD FOR *KIDS!*

HANGING ON TO YOUR HEAD IS THE *PAINFUL* PART OF LOVE. YOU'VE DONE IT BEFORE--WE *BOTH* HAVE!

JUST REMEMBER--IF IT GETS ROCKY AGAIN, YOU CAN BE SURE I'LL COME...DO WHAT I CAN!

SHALL WE GO... *FRIEND?*

21

IT'S OKAY, HONEY-- EVERYTHING'S ALL RIGHT! I'LL EXPLAIN LATER!

DO *WE* HAVE A STORY FOR THE REST OF THE *JLA!*

PIZZA

IT WAS SO *EASY*, WASN'T IT, *BLACK CANARY?* YET YOU WONDER WHY ALONG THE WAY IT WAS SO HARD AND WROUGHT WITH DANGER.

WITHOUT MUCH THINKING, YOU KNOW THE ANSWER IS ALL WRAPPED UP IN THE COMPLEX PERSONALITY OF A MAN YOU'LL *NEVER* FORGET... *HARLEQUIN ELLIS!*

MANY ARE THE THINGS A WRITER IS FORCED TO DO BY THE CRASH-POUNDING OF HIS CREATIVE SOUL. THIS STORY WAS ONE OF THEM.

FOR IN WRITING OF THIS MAN, *HARLEQUIN ELLIS*, I AM FACING THE ETERNAL MIRROR... FOR WHO *IS* IT THAT ACTUALLY CREATES OUR HEROES' EVER-RECURRING MENACES TO THEIR LIVES, TESTING EVERY FIBRE OF THEIR BEING TO THE LIMIT?

SUPERMAN, BATMAN, GREEN ARROW, BLACK CANARY, AQUAMAN ARE JUST AS *REAL* TO ME AS TO *HARLEQUIN ELLIS*--I *BELIEVE* IN THEM! I *MUST!* WHEN *SUPERMAN* BURSTS THROUGH A MONSTROUS BOULDER, IT IS *I* WHO FLEX MY MUSCLES!

WHEN *THE BATMAN* LOOKS WITH VENGEANCE ON SOMEONE HE HATES, IT IS *I* WHO HATE! WHEN *AQUAMAN* DIES FROM WATER-THIRST, WHEN *GREEN ARROW* FACES A CHARGING MINOTAUR, WHEN *BLACK CANARY* LOOKS INTO THE EYES OF ANOTHER HUMAN BEING AND SEES HIS SOUL, IT IS *I!*

AND... WHEN *HARLEQUIN ELLIS* CRIES OVER THE LACK OF RETURNED LOVE, IT IS *I!*

MANY ARE THE THINGS A WRITER IS FORCED TO DO BY THE CRASH-POUNDING OF HIS CREATIVE SOUL. THIS STORY WAS ONE OF THEM; FOR THERE IS NO ESCAPE FROM THE SOUL-SHATTER OF THE NOVA-AWARENESS THAT *I*, IN SO *MANY* WAYS, AM... *HARLEQUIN ELLIS!*

To H.E., that you might understand, brother... Mike Friedrich

22

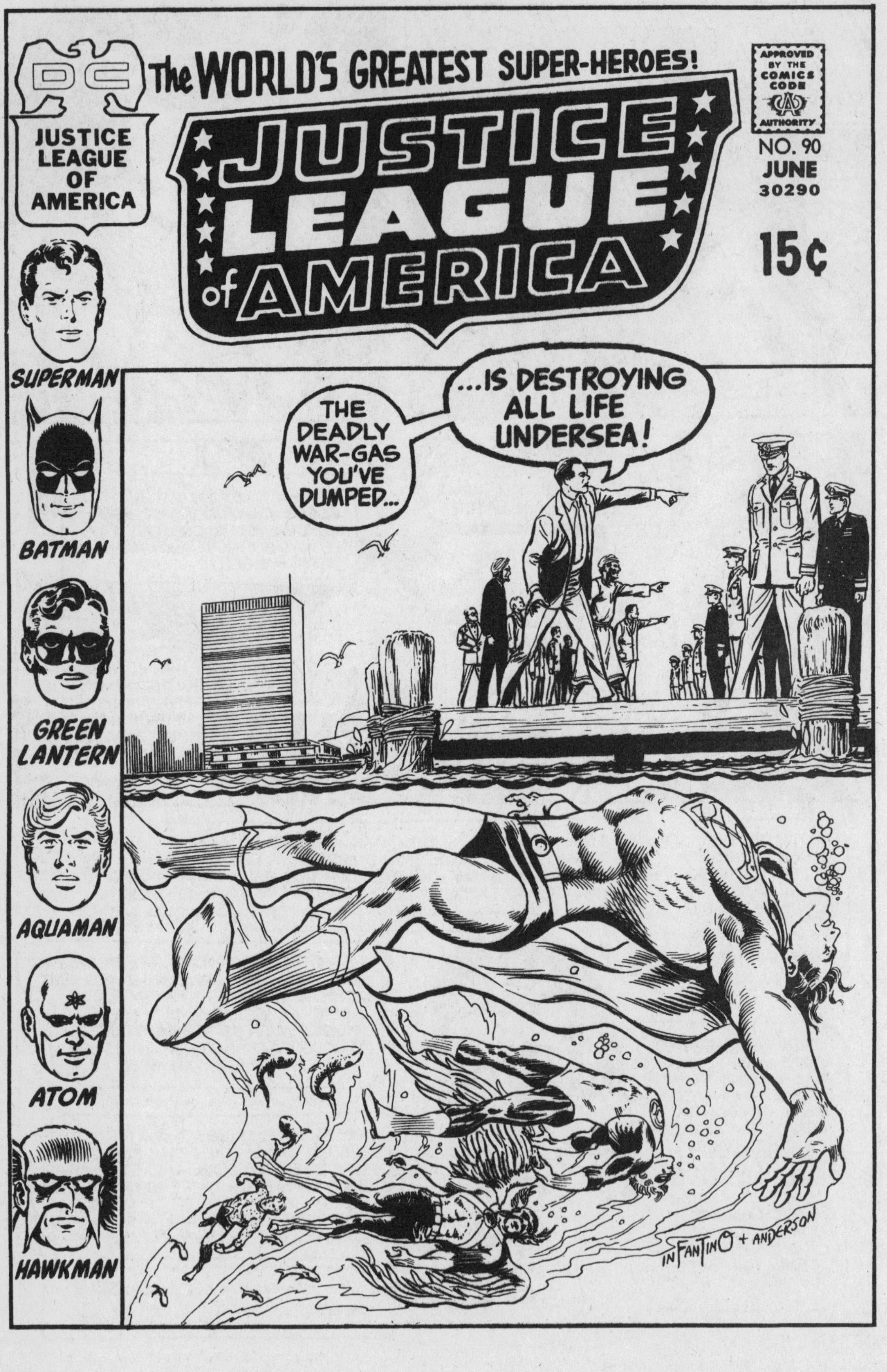
DC
JUSTICE LEAGUE OF AMERICA
The WORLD'S GREATEST SUPER-HEROES!
JUSTICE LEAGUE of AMERICA
APPROVED BY THE COMICS CODE AUTHORITY
NO. 90
JUNE
30290
15¢
SUPERMAN
BATMAN
GREEN LANTERN
AQUAMAN
ATOM
HAWKMAN
THE DEADLY WAR-GAS YOU'VE DUMPED...
...IS DESTROYING ALL LIFE UNDERSEA!
INFANTINO + ANDERSON

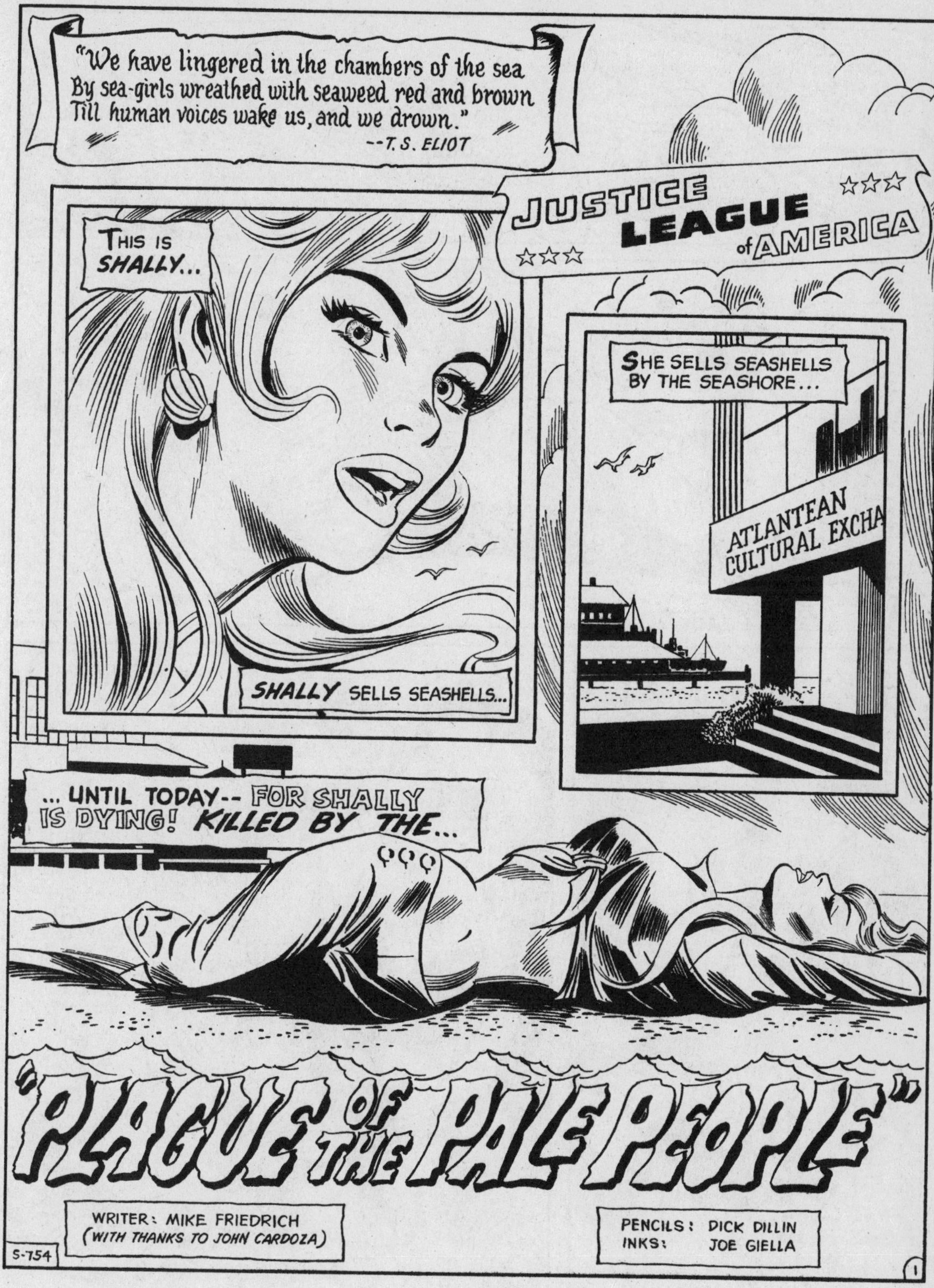
"We have lingered in the chambers of the sea
By sea-girls wreathed with seaweed red and brown
Till human voices wake us, and we drown."
--T.S. ELIOT
JUSTICE LEAGUE of AMERICA
THIS IS SHALLY...
SHALLY SELLS SEASHELLS...
SHE SELLS SEASHELLS BY THE SEASHORE...
ATLANTEAN CULTURAL EXCHA
... UNTIL TODAY-- FOR SHALLY IS DYING! KILLED BY THE...
"PLAGUE OF THE PALE PEOPLE"
WRITER: MIKE FRIEDRICH
(WITH THANKS TO JOHN CARDOZA)
PENCILS: DICK DILLIN
INKS: JOE GIELLA
S-754
1

THE SCENE: A RESORT ON THE EASTERN SEABOARD. THE TIME: *NOW!*

BILL--THAT GIRL-- THE ONE FROM *ATLANTIS*--SHE LOOKS *DEAD!*

NOT QUITE, *VICKI!*

LISTEN-- SHE'S MUMBLING SOMETHING...

POISON... DANGER... POISON...

I CAN'T UNDERSTAND HER-- SHE SPOKE *ATLANTEAN!*

DOESN'T MATTER NOW... SHE'S *DEAD!*

SUDDENLY, AS IF FROM THE MYSTERIOUS MISTS OF THE SEA, LOOMS...

--THE *BATMAN!*

WH-WHAT'S *HE* DOING HERE?

THE REASON IS UNIMPORTANT ...WHAT *IS,* CONCERNS *HER!*

WHAT DO YOU KNOW ABOUT THIS?

NOT MUCH, *BATMAN!* WE JUST FOUND HER LIKE *THIS!*

I THINK SHE'S FROM *ATLANTIS!* MAYBE SHE-- ER -- *AIR-DROWNED...* LIKE SHE WAS OUT OF *WATER* TOO LONG!

2

NO... HER TRAIL COMES STRAIGHT FROM THE SEA--

AND *ATLANTEANS* CAN SAFELY STAY AN *HOUR* OUT OF WATER!

SHE LOOKS *PARALYZED*... ALMOST *STRANGLED*...

SYMPTOMS SEEM FAMILIAR, SOMEHOW...

I'D BEST CALL *AQUAMAN* IN *ATLANTIS* VIA MY *JLA COMMUNICATOR!* HE SHOULD BE INVOLVED!

LONG MOMENTS PASS...

NO ANSWER! WONDER WHY...?

UNTIL LIKE A WAVE CRASHING ON THE SAND...

OF COURSE! I'VE BEEN *BLIND!*

EARTH FACES A *DISASTER!* I MUST USE MY *EMERGENCY SIGNAL* TO SUMMON THE *ENTIRE JUSTICE LEAGUE!*

INSTANTLY A SIGNAL FLASHES OUT, CONTACTING THE MOST RENOWNED MEN OF 20TH CENTURY *EARTH!*

BUT WHAT WORLD-WIDE CATASTROPHE CALLS OUT FOR THE *WORLD'S GREATEST* SUPER-HEROES?

TO COMPREHEND THE CATASTROPHE, LET US BACKTRACK ONE MONTH TO *METROPOLIS*, WHERE *CLARK KENT* IS TELECASTING A NEWS EVENT...

...TOMORROW IT WILL BE DUMPED AT SEA. A MILITARY SPOKESMAN ASSURES US THAT THE *"OBSOLETE"*, YET STILL *DEADLY*, GAS PRESENTS NO DANGER TO FISH, PLANT OR HUMAN LIFE...

THE MILITARY ADMITS TO HAVING *LOST TRACK* OF THE SCUTTLED GAS-SHIP, BUT A SPOKESMAN ASSURES US THAT THERE IS NO DANGER WHATSOEVER...

HEAR, O *AMERICA*-- THINK YOU THAT YOUR PROBLEMS CAN BE SOLVED BY PUTTING THEM OUT OF SIGHT...

...CONVENIENTLY FORGETTING 'ABOUT THEM...?

WELL, AMERICA--DON'T BREATHE *TOO* EASILY...

OPEN YOUR MIND A CRACK, *AMERICA!* SEE BEYOND YOUR *"DISPOSABLE"* ALUMINUM CANS, YOUR *"VIETNAMIZED"* WAR AND YOUR *"OUT-OF-SIGHT"* DRUGS...

THERE ARE *OTHER* PEOPLES AND *OTHER* WAYS OF LIFE, *AMERICA!* THIS IS ONE OF THEM...

...A CITY BENEATH THE SEA... CALLED *SAREME*... THE DOMAIN OF THE *PALE PEOPLE*...

THE SITE UPON WHICH YOU'VE JUST DUMPED... *POISON!*

4

LIKE ALL STABLE, *TOGETHER* CULTURES, THE *PALE PEOPLE* HAVE *BELIEFS* AND *RITUALS* UPON WHICH THEY FOCUS ALL THEIR ATTENTION.

THE *SPIRIT* OF THESE BELIEFS-- WHAT GIVES THEIR LIVES MEANING-- IS THEIR *DIRECTOR*-- WHO, IN EFFECT, IS THEIR *GOD*...

FROM TIME TO TIME, THE *PALE PEOPLE* LEAVE THEIR CITY--PROTECTED FROM THE OUTSIDE SEA BY A *WATER CURTAIN*-- TO MAKE A PILGRIMAGE TO THE *PROOF-ROCK*...

THIS *LIVING WONDER PLANT* IS THEIR SYMBOL OF *GOOD*--AND OF *TRUTH*...

FOR WHEN A *WRONG-DOER* COMES CLOSE, THE *PROOF-ROCK* REACTS TO THE GUILTY ONE'S CHANGED BODY-CHEMISTRY AND BECOMES A LIVING *LIE DETECTOR*...

NOW, THEN, *AMERICA-- THIS* IS WHAT YOU'VE WROUGHT!...

AIEEE...THE LAND-HUMANS ARE *ATTACKING* AGAIN....!

THE *PROOF-ROCK-- DESTROYED!*

HOW DOES ONE EXPRESS *TOTAL SHOCK*...THE PILLAR OF ONE'S LIFE COLLAPSED, THE CENTER OF ONE'S MEANING GONE...?

ONE *DOESN'T!* HE JUST STANDS AND WATCHES, AS *WE* NOW WATCH, IN HORRIFIED *SILENCE*...

5

SOON THE SILENCE ENDS-- FOR WITH THE LOSS OF STABILITY, THE EVER-PRESENT DESTRUCTIVE FORCES COME TO THE FORE...

THE *PROOF-ROCK* IS GONE!-- OUR *GOD* IS *DEAD!*

BUT *I,* NEBEUR ODAGLED, WILL LEAD YOU! I WILL SERVE AS YOUR *GOD!*

WHEN ONE DESPERATELY SEEKS A *MIRACLE,* WHERE *ELSE* CAN ONE TURN?

TOO LONG HAS *ATLANTIS* TRAFFICKED WITH US AS IF WE WERE THEIR *INFERIORS!* WE MUST BARGAIN FROM A POSITION OF *STRENGTH!*

DECLARE ME YOUR *PRINCE* AND WE CAN CONTROL THE *SEA!*

HAIL PRINCE NEBEUR

SO IN *ATLANTIS,* ON THIS FATEFUL, PRESENT DAY...

DISASTER, MERA!

YOU REMEMBER THE *PALE PEOPLE?*

--THE BACKWARD GROUP THAT WE HELPED ADVANCE TO OUR EQUALS?

YES! THEY'VE TAKEN THE AMERICAN POISON GAS AND MADE *WEAPONS* WITH WHICH TO ATTACK US!

A SMALL BAND OF OUR WARRIORS WAS CAUGHT UNAWARES AND WIPED OUT--TO THE MAN!

THE *PALE PEOPLE* HAVE DEMANDED OUR *IMMEDIATE SURRENDER!*

THERE IS NO TIME TO PREPARE A DEFENSE...I *HAVE* TO GIVE IN...TO *SAVE LIVES!*

THIS IS THE BLACKEST DAY OF MY LIFE!

6

SHORTLY...

YOU MADE A WISE DECISION TO SURRENDER, *AQUAMAN*...

I HAD NO *CHOICE*...

TRUE--AS THAT *SPY* OF YOURS FROM YOUR *"CULTURAL EXCHANGE"* FOUND OUT WHEN SHE MEDDLED IN OUR AFFAIRS!

--*SHALLY?* BUT SHE WAS ONLY SENT TO INVESTIGATE THE GAS-DUMPING--

MY *JLA* COMMUNI-CATOR! EMERGENCY CALL FROM *THE BATMAN!*

YOU'LL NOT BE ANSWERING YOUR SURFACE-FRIENDS TODAY, *HALF-BREED* KING!

WHY, YOU--!

SHALL I HIT HIM WITH MY *HARD-WATER* POWERS?

NO...THAT WON'T STOP HIS *ARMY* OR *GAS*-WEAPON! TOO MANY LIVES WILL BE LOST!

--OR SHOULD I SAY *EX-KING*, AQUAMAN?

HENCEFORTH, I RULE AND AM *KING!*

FOR HE WHO CONTROLS *ATLANTIS*, CONTROLS THE *SEVEN SEAS*--AND HE WHO CONTROLS THE *OCEANS*, CONTROLS THE *SURFACE-WORLD!*

7

WHILE ON THE WORLD ABOVE...

WE'RE ALL HERE... EXCEPT *FLASH*, *GREEN ARROW*, AND *BLACK CANARY**!

*EDITOR'S NOTE: IF YOU WERE WITH US LAST ISSUE, YOU'LL KNOW THAT THE *ACE ARCHER* AND *PRETTY BIRD* WERE INVOLVED IN "*THE MOST DANGEROUS DREAMS OF ALL*"--BUT WHERE IS THE *SCARLET SPEEDSTER*?

HERE'S THE SET-UP-- I'VE DETERMINED THAT THE GIRL *SHALLY* WAS KILLED BY *POISON GAS*--POSSIBLY THAT WHICH THE MILITARY DUMPED NEAR HERE A MONTH AGO!

IF THAT'S TRUE, THE GAS WILL CAUSE *HAVOC* IN THE SEA! IT CAN KILL *PLANTS, FISH, PEOPLE!*

EXACTLY, *HAWKMAN!* I SUGGEST YOU AND *SUPERMAN* CHECK OUT THE GAS, WHILE *GREEN LANTERN* AND *ATOM* TRY AND FIND OUT WHAT'S WITH *AQUAMAN!*

I'LL PERSONALLY TRACK DOWN *FLASH!* I SUSPECT HIS *SPECIAL SERVICES* WILL BE NEEDED ON THIS CASE!

ARE THE *WORLD'S GREATEST SUPER-HEROES* GREAT ENOUGH TO SAVE *ATLANTIS*-- AND *YOU*, AMERICA?

YOU ARE ABOUT TO FIND OUT!...

8

CHAPTER TWO
featuring SUPERMAN *and* HAWKMAN

BEFORE HEADING *UNDERSEA*, *SUPERMAN*, I MUST MAKE A SHORT STOP AT MY ORBITING *SPACESHIP*--

--AND DON A *THANAGARIAN PRESSURE-SUIT* TO ENABLE ME TO WITHSTAND THE TREMENDOUS WEIGHT OF THE SEA'S DEPTHS!

MOMENTS LATER...

WITH MY *ANTI-GRAV BELT* TO KEEP ME UNDER-- AND MY WINGS AS *PROPELLERS*--I CAN SWIM ALMOST AS FAST AS *SUPERMAN!*

MY *TELESCOPIC VISION'S* SPOTTED AN *UNDERSEA* CITY NEAR THE GAS-DUMPING SITE! WE'LL MAKE THAT OUR FIRST PORT-OF-CALL!

9

WHILE ON THE OUTSKIRTS OF *SAREME*...

LOOK! TWO UNIFORMED HUMANS *FLYING* IN FROM THE SEA ABOVE! THEY COULD BE FROM *ATLANTIS!*

BUT--BUT-- THE GAS IS *LETHAL!* REMEMBER --THE *PROOF-ROCK* DID NOT *APPROVE* OF WAR!

FIRE-- GAS!

THE *PROOF-ROCK GONE*--REPLACED BY WISE *KING NEBEUR!*

WE *MUST* BELIEVE IN HIM--*FOLLOW* HIS COMMANDS!

WOULD YOU HAVE HIM DISCOVER WE HAVE BLUNDERED AGAIN, AS HAPPENED WHEN THAT FEMALE *SPY* ESCAPED?

THEY ARE ALMOST UPON US! *SHOOT FAST!*

WUMP

UNNNN

POISON GAS ATTACK!-- AND THE *IMPACT* HAS SLUNG *HAWKMAN'S* AIR-MASK AROUND HIS HEAD!

HIS *PROTECTION* IS GONE!

10

GOT TO GET HIM OUT OF ATTACK-RANGE... DRAW OUT THE POISON!

SUPER-LUNGS INSTANTLY SUCTION OUT ALL TRACE OF THE GAS...

THEN PUMP IN-AND-OUT, IN-AND-OUT WITH PRECIOUS LIFE-RESTORING AIR...

BROTHER, I OWE YOU MY LIFE--

THERE'S SOMETHING ELSE I OWE THOSE TWO UNDERSEAMEN!

QUICKLY! THE BLUE-SUITED ONE HAS THE EYES OF FURY!

KRISSH

KEEP FIRING-- AGAIN! AGAIN! AGAIN!

GLUG

11

HE IS A *SUPER-MAN!* FLEE!

KRUNNCH

BUT SWOOPING LIKE AN AVENGING BIRD OF PREY--

I'M AFRAID ESCAPE ISN'T THAT *EASY,* MEN!

AFTER A TRANSLATION PROCESS TOO INVOLVED TO DESCRIBE HERE, THE *JUSTICE LEAGUERS* HEAR A STORY THAT SHAKES THEIR VERY SOULS!

NO REAL NEED TO HOLD THEM--THEY ARE A VERY ROOT-LESS RACE THESE DAYS!

BESIDES, IT'LL BE GOOD, IF *SARAME* LEARNS THAT ITS EVIL FORCE IS BEING *RESISTED*--

--FOR IF WHAT THEY TOLD US IS TRUE, WE HAVE OUR WORK CUT OUT FOR US-- IN *ATLANTIS!*

RIGHT *WITH YOU,* SUPERMAN!

12

CHAPTER THREE featuring GREEN LANTERN and The ATOM

HOW MUCH LONGER TILL WE REACH ATLANTIS, GL?

JUST A COUPLA MINUTES, ATOM! WE SHOULD BE ABLE TO CLEAR UP THIS MYSTERY WITH EASE!

DON'T BE SO CONFIDENT, GREEN LANTERN! ACTUALLY TROUBLE IS BUILDING IN ATLANTIS WITH EVERY PASSING SECOND!...

EVERYWHERE I LOOK I SEE A PALE! I'M GETTING SICK OF THEM!

WHY ISN'T AQUAMAN DOING SOMETHING ABOUT THIS?

UNLESS HE DOES SO SOON, MANY OF US WILL TAKE THEM ON OURSELVES!

THE PEOPLE OF THE CITY ARE GETTING RESTLESS, DEAR! THEY'RE STARTING TO GRUMBLE ABOUT OUR NOT TAKING COUNTER-ACTION!

WE CAN'T-- WE'RE COMPLETELY DEFENSELESS AGAINST THAT GAS!

ALL WE CAN DO IS -- WAIT...HOPE SOMETHING WILL TURN THE TIDE...

WHAT IS THIS MESSAGE YOU BRING ME? A GREEN-CLAD HUMAN WITH GREEN-GLOWING PROTECTION?

A SURFACE FRIEND OF AQUAMAN'S, NO DOUBT!

DESTROY HIM!

SOUNDS LIKE GREEN LANTERN! AID IS ON THE WAY!

13

WE'LL DISMISS YOUR EXCUSABLE NEGLECT OF *THE ATOM, AQUAMAN*-- BUT DON'T *COUNT* ON THE *RESCUE*...NOT YET!...

ATLANTIS AHEAD--!

CHECK THOSE SEA-FOOD CROP-FIELDS! HOW COME THEY'RE *DESERTED* DURING *HARVEST-TIME?*

DESERTED, ATOM?... NOT QUITE!

BHUHFF

BHUHFF

WHAT KINDA RECEPTION IS THIS? WE'RE BEING *ATTACKED!*

SOME-THING'S WRONG--

BRILLIANT DEDUCTION, GL!-- ANYTHING *ELSE* NEW?

BHOOM

BHOOM

BHOOM

BHOOM

ALL RIGHT, WISE-MOUTH-- THIS IS *SERIOUS!*

MY DE-ENERGIZED RING DOESN'T QUITE HAVE THE POWER TO FIGHT AN *ENTIRE CITY!*

BESIDES, COME TO THINK OF IT-- WE DON'T REALLY KNOW *WHY* WE'RE BEING ATTACKED!

RIGHT! SO I'D BEST JUST *POWER-RING* SOME *DEFENSIVE* ACTION!

A *CORKING* GOOD IDEA, *LANTERN!*

14

BUT THE NEXT MOMENT...

WHOMP

ANOTHER ATTACK?!

IT'S A GAS ONE--AND CHECK WHAT IT'S DOING TO THOSE PLANTS!

--KILLING EVERYTHING IT TOUCHES!

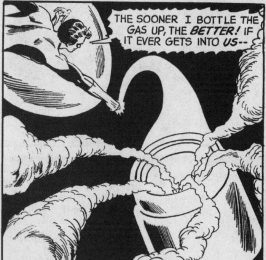

THE SOONER I BOTTLE THE GAS UP, THE BETTER! IF IT EVER GETS INTO US--

WE'VE GOT TO STOP THAT GAS-SHOOTER QUICK AS WE CAN!

A SMALL SURPRISE IS THE KEY--AND THAT'S MY DEPARTMENT!

LISTEN... BZZZ... BZZZ...

A WILL-POWERED COMMAND TO THE MYSTIC RING...

AND THE SLINGSHOT-ATOM ZOOMS INTO THE BARREL OF THE GAS-SHOOTING "BAZOOKA."!.

15

--TO EXPLODE OUT OF THE FIRING END...

FROM THE LOOK OF HIS FACE-- I'M A *SURPRISE*, ALL RIGHT!

HITTING HIM WITH THE FULL FORCE OF MY NORMAL *180 POUNDS*-- BUT WITH THIS *WATER-RESISTANCE,* I'M BARELY KAOYING HIM!

JUST THEN, SPEEDING FROM *SAREME* WITH THEIR MESSAGE OF DANGER.

SUPERMAN AND HAWKMAN! HOPE *THEY* KNOW WHAT'S GOING *ON* HERE!

THEN, FOLLOWING A *POWER-RINGED DISCUSSION* AMONG THE *JUSTICE LEAGUERS*...

INCOMPETENTS! NOW THERE ARE *FOUR* OF THEM!

TURN THE *ATLANTEANS' WATER-EVACUATION MACHINE* INTO A *WEAPON! THAT* SHOULD CONSTRAIN THEM!

YES, MY LORD!

UNUSED SINCE THE TIME WHEN *ATLANTEANS* WERE AIR-BREATHERS, THE MACHINE PUMPS *ALL* OF THE DOMED-CITY'S WATER ON THE UNSUSPECTING *JUSTICE LEAGUERS*...

EVEN MIGHTY *SUPERMAN* IS CRUSHINGLY AFFECTED AS THE TREMENDOUS *WATER-PRESSURE* NEARLY EQUALS THAT OF HIS NATIVE *KRYPTON!*

16

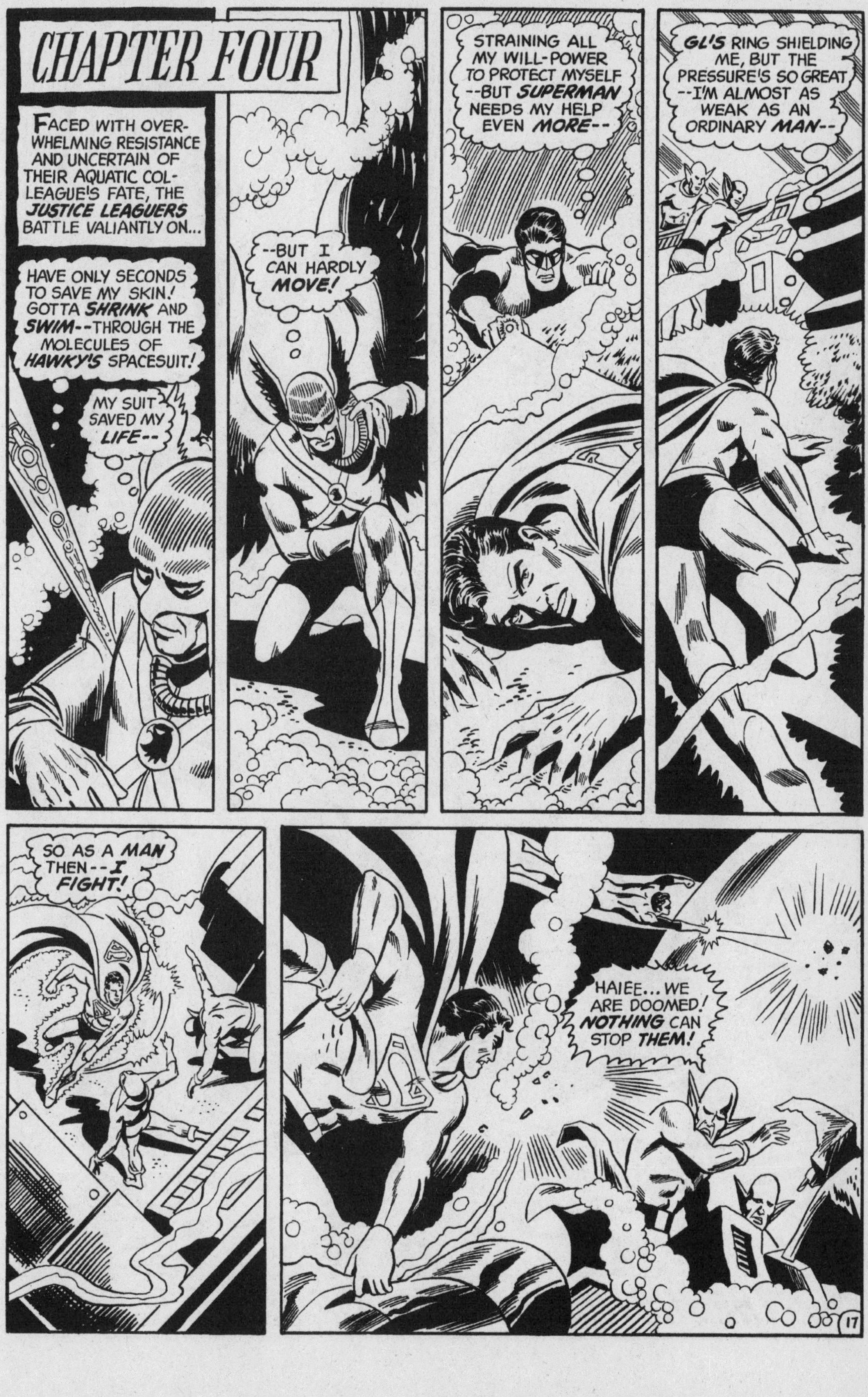
CHAPTER FOUR
FACED WITH OVER-WHELMING RESISTANCE AND UNCERTAIN OF THEIR AQUATIC COL-LEAGUE'S FATE, THE JUSTICE LEAGUERS BATTLE VALIANTLY ON...
HAVE ONLY SECONDS TO SAVE MY SKIN! GOTTA SHRINK AND SWIM--THROUGH THE MOLECULES OF HAWKY'S SPACESUIT!
MY SUIT SAVED MY LIFE--
--BUT I CAN HARDLY MOVE!
STRAINING ALL MY WILL-POWER TO PROTECT MYSELF --BUT SUPERMAN NEEDS MY HELP EVEN MORE--
GL'S RING SHIELDING ME, BUT THE PRESSURE'S SO GREAT --I'M ALMOST AS WEAK AS AN ORDINARY MAN--
SO AS A MAN THEN--I FIGHT!
HAIEE... WE ARE DOOMED! NOTHING CAN STOP THEM!
17

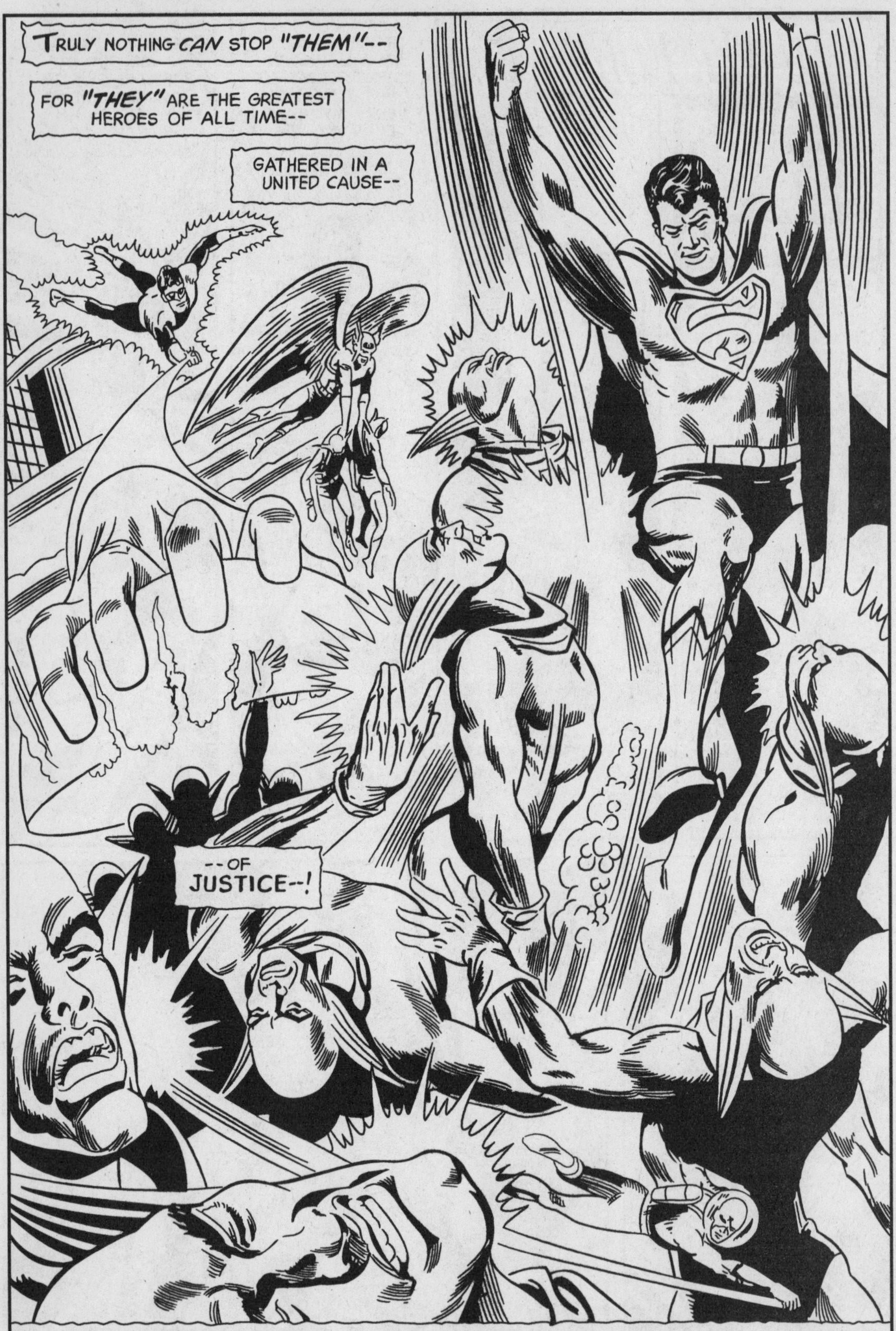
TRULY NOTHING CAN STOP "THEM"--
FOR "THEY" ARE THE GREATEST HEROES OF ALL TIME--
GATHERED IN A UNITED CAUSE--
--OF JUSTICE--!
"THEY"-- THE JUSTICE LEAGUE OF AMERICA!
18

MEANWHILE, BACK TO *AQUAMAN*...

MY SUBJECTS... MY FOLLOWERS... ROUTED--

HOLD ON, *"KING"*-- WE'VE GOT A *ROYAL ACCOUNT* TO SETTLE--

DUE PAYABLE-- NOW!

SHORTLY...

WITH THE DEFEAT OF THEIR LEADER, THE *PALE PEOPLE* SURRENDERED!

LOOKS LIKE EVERYTHING'S *OKAY* NOW!

OKAY--? HOW CAN YOU CALL *43 LOST LIVES* "OKAY"?

CAN YOU TELL THEIR *LOVED ONES* THAT? WON'T YOU LAND-HUMANS *EVER LEARN*?

IT WAS *YOUR* PEOPLE WHO CREATED THE *GAS*--WHO REFUSED TO TAKE RESPONSIBILITY FOR IT--WHO ARE *TRULY* ACCOUNTABLE FOR THIS TRAGEDY!

19

IT'S TIME WE DEPARTED...

THOUGH WE SUCCESSFULLY ACCOMPLISHED OUR MISSION HERE, OUR HEADS ARE BOWED IN SHAME OVER *AMERICA'S* RESPONSIBILITY FOR WHAT HAPPENED HERE...

YES, TODAY IS INDEED A DAY OF SHAME-- AND OF EVEN DEEPER *GRIEF*...

AND THERE IS GRIEF IN *SAREME*, TOO...AS THEIR KILLED-IN-COMBAT WARRIORS ARE RETURNED...

WITH THEIR UNHOLY CRUSADE THWARTED, THE *PALE PEOPLE* ARE AGAIN WITHOUT ROOTS, WITHOUT DIRECTION...

...GRASPING DESPERATELY FOR A *MIRACLE*, FOR THE HOPE THAT BRINGS MEANING...

READER, DO YOU BELIEVE IN *GOOD*... IN *TRUTH?* THEN YOUR SHAME IS MIXED WITH *JOY!*

FOR YOUR *JUSTICE LEAGUERS*, THOUGH FALLIBLY HUMAN, ARE--AT THEIR CORE --*GOOD*...AND *TRUE!*

AND FOR *GOODNESS* AND *TRUTH* THERE *ARE* NO MIRACLES!

FOR *EVERYTHING* IS A *MIRACLE!*

HAIEEE! THE PROOF-ROCK LIVES AGAIN!

20

WITH TRUTH AND GOODNESS COMES *THE LIGHT*--

THE LAND-HUMANS HAVE WROUGHT THIS MIRACLE!

THEY SHALL LEAD US NOW!-- THEY SHALL BE OUR GODS!

AND, READER, IF YOU BELIEVE IN *THE LIGHT*, THEN YOU WILL UNDERSTAND AS *HAWKMAN* CRIES OUT...

NO!--WRONG! WE ARE *NOT* GODS!

WE ARE *MEN*, AS ARE *YOU*, PEOPLE OF *SAREME!*

EACH OF YOU PLACED HIS FAITH IN A *ROCK!* IT WAS *SHATTERED!*

THEN IN A *MAN-GOD!* -- HE WAS EVIL, AND SO WAS *DESTROYED!*

THE TIME HAS COME TO STOP PLACING YOUR BELIEFS IN THINGS *OUTSIDE* YOURSELVES! PIN YOUR FAITH ON THE ONLY RELIABLE THING YOU *POSSESS*-- YOUR OWN *SOULS!*

AS A SIGN OF NEW FAITH, *HERE* IS AN EDIBLE PART OF THE *PROOF-ROCK PLANT!*

TAKE AND *EAT* OF IT, FOR THIS IS THE *FOOD OF LIFE!*

AND WITH *LIFE...* EVERYTHING IS A *MIRACLE!*

"...still, the profound change has come upon them: rooted they grip down and begin to awaken."
--William Carlos Williams

FOR THOSE OLD-TIMERS AMONGST US--*YES*, YOU *DID* MEET THE *PALE PEOPLE* BEFORE-- IN THE OCT-NOV, 1959 ISSUE OF *THE FLASH!*

21

EPILOGUE

SHORTLY AFTER, IN *JLA* SATELLITE HEADQUARTERS, CIRCLING 22,300 MILES ABOVE THE EARTH...

YOU'VE BEEN SEARCHING FOR THE ROOTS OF CRIME AND WAR ON EARTH, *HAWKMAN!*

DID YOUR "FOOD OF LIFE" CEREMONY *HELP* ANY?

IT REMAINS TO BE SEEN! LIKE MANY OF YOU AMERICANS, *SAREME* LOST ITS TRADITIONAL VALUE SYSTEM--

--I TRIED TO HELP BUILD THE FOUNDATION FOR A *NEW* ONE!

IT'S UP TO EACH INDIVIDUAL TO *HELP* IN CREATING HIS VALUES--TO *BELIEVE* IN THEM--TO MAKE THEM *WORK!*

JUST THEN...

SOMEONE BEAMING UP ON THE *TELEPORTER!*

MAYBE *BATMAN* HAS FOUND *FL*--

F-FLASH?!

HE LOOKS... DEAD!

THE STAGE HAS BEEN SET FOR A *NEW CRISIS* ON *EARTH-ONE* AND *EARTH-TWO*--A THREAT TO *TWO* WORLDS! BE WITH US NEXT ISSUE--FEATURING THE *ANNUAL* APPEARANCE OF THE GOLDEN-AGE SUPER-STARS, THE *JUSTICE SOCIETY OF AMERICA!*

22

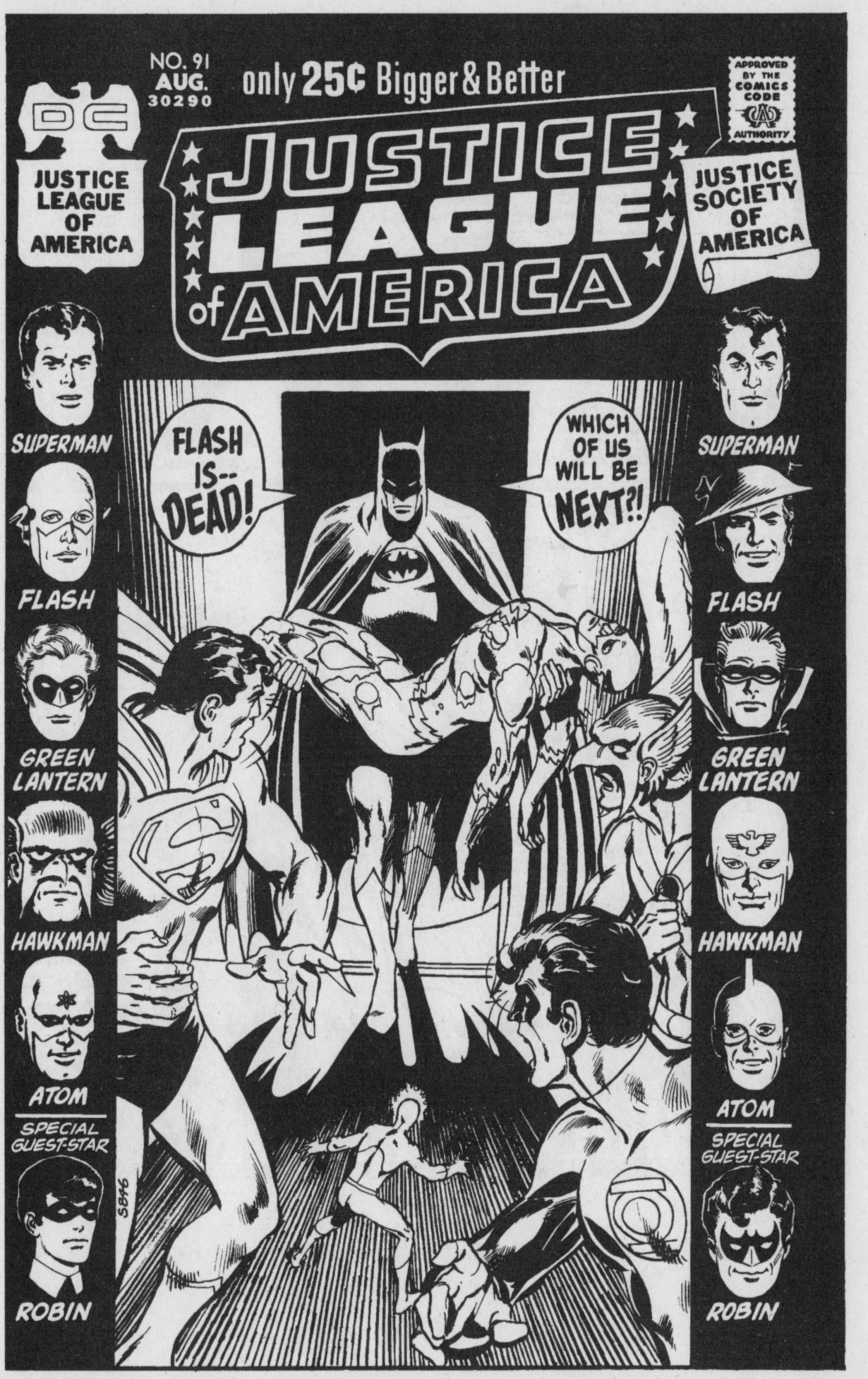
NO. 91
AUG.
30290
only 25¢ Bigger & Better
APPROVED BY THE COMICS CODE AUTHORITY
DC
JUSTICE LEAGUE OF AMERICA
JUSTICE LEAGUE of AMERICA
JUSTICE SOCIETY OF AMERICA
SUPERMAN
FLASH
GREEN LANTERN
HAWKMAN
ATOM
SPECIAL GUEST-STAR
ROBIN
SUPERMAN
FLASH
GREEN LANTERN
HAWKMAN
ATOM
SPECIAL GUEST-STAR
ROBIN
FLASH IS-- DEAD!
WHICH OF US WILL BE NEXT?!

STORY BY MIKE FRIEDRICH

JUSTICE ☆☆☆ LEAGUE ☆☆☆ of AMERICA

ART BY DICK DILLIN AND JOE GIELLA

THE *SANCTUARY-SATELLITE* OF THE *JUSTICE LEAGUE,* 22,300 MILES ABOVE THE EARTH...

PRESENT! *GREEN LANTERN, ATOM, SUPERMAN* AND *"CHAIRMAN" HAWKMAN..*

ABSENT *WITH* LEAVE! *BLACK CANARY* AND *GREEN ARROW!*

ABSENT-*WITH-OUT* LEAVE! *AQUAMAN--*

THE *SEA KING* MUST STILL BE *MIFFED* AT US *LANDLUBBERS* FOR THE TRAGEDY THAT HIT *ATLANTIS!* ✻

WE SHOULD HAVE RECEIVED WORD BY NOW FROM *BATMAN* ON HIS SEARCH FOR THE *MISSING FLASH!* ✻

✻ AS RECOUNTED IN LAST ISSUE'S "*PLAGUE OF THE PALE PEOPLE!*"

JUST THEN...

SOMEONE BEAMING UP ON THE *TELEPORTER!*

SIGNAL-INDICATOR SHOWS IT'S *BATMAN!*

S 806

F-FLASH?!

HE LOOKS... DEAD!

JUSTICE LEAGUERS... WE HAVE A **SUPER-CRISIS** ON OUR HANDS!

1

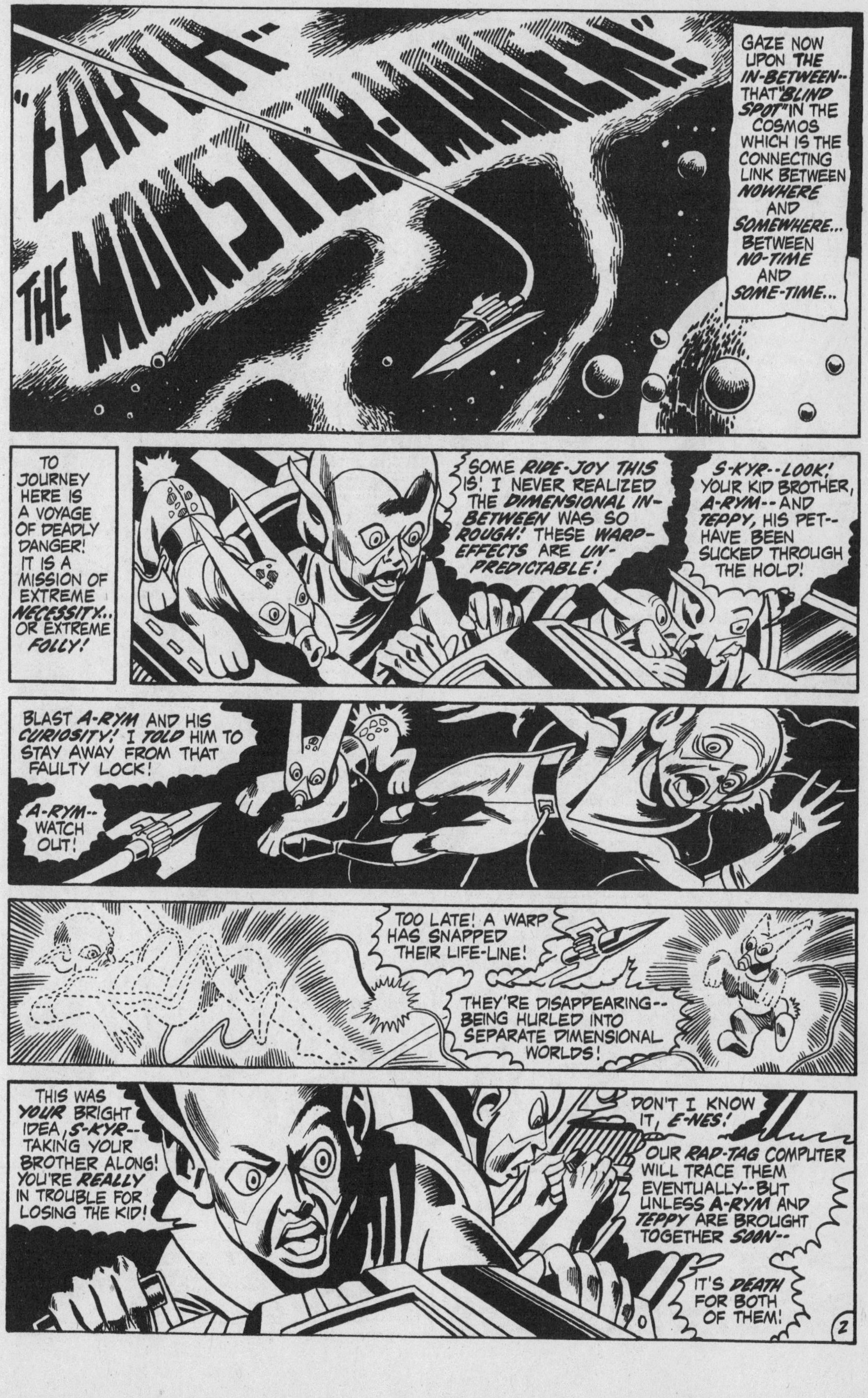
"EARTH--THE MONSTER-MAKER!"
GAZE NOW UPON THE IN-BETWEEN--THAT "BLIND SPOT" IN THE COSMOS WHICH IS THE CONNECTING LINK BETWEEN NOWHERE AND SOMEWHERE... BETWEEN NO-TIME AND SOME-TIME...
TO JOURNEY HERE IS A VOYAGE OF DEADLY DANGER! IT IS A MISSION OF EXTREME NECESSITY... OR EXTREME FOLLY!
SOME RIDE-JOY THIS IS! I NEVER REALIZED THE DIMENSIONAL IN-BETWEEN WAS SO ROUGH! THESE WARP-EFFECTS ARE UN-PREDICTABLE!
S-KYR--LOOK! YOUR KID BROTHER, A-RYM--AND TEPPY, HIS PET--HAVE BEEN SUCKED THROUGH THE HOLD!
BLAST A-RYM AND HIS CURIOSITY! I TOLD HIM TO STAY AWAY FROM THAT FAULTY LOCK!
A-RYM--WATCH OUT!
TOO LATE! A WARP HAS SNAPPED THEIR LIFE-LINE!
THEY'RE DISAPPEARING--BEING HURLED INTO SEPARATE DIMENSIONAL WORLDS!
THIS WAS YOUR BRIGHT IDEA, S-KYR--TAKING YOUR BROTHER ALONG! YOU'RE REALLY IN TROUBLE FOR LOSING THE KID!
DON'T I KNOW IT, E-NES!
OUR RAD-TAG COMPUTER WILL TRACE THEM EVENTUALLY--BUT UNLESS A-RYM AND TEPPY ARE BROUGHT TOGETHER SOON--
IT'S DEATH FOR BOTH OF THEM!
2

AN ALIEN LAD AND HIS INSEPARABLE PET-- INNOCENT, PLAYFUL, MISCHIEVOUS-- NO DIFFERENT FROM OTHER SUCH DUOS THROUGHOUT THE UNIVERSE...

ON *EARTH*, ANIMALS AND *PLANTS* HAVE FORMED A *LIFE-PARTNERSHIP*-- EACH SUPPLYING THE OTHER WITH VITAL *OXYGEN* AND *CARBON DIOXIDE*...

ON *A-RYM'S* WORLD, HOWEVER, A HUMAN AND HIS ASSIGNED PET MUST STAY IN THE *PHYSICAL PRESENCE* OF EACH OTHER-- FORMING A SORT OF *SYMBIOTIC* RELATIONSHIP IN WHICH EACH IS NECESSARY FOR THE OTHER'S SURVIVAL...

SHOULD *A-RYM* AND *TEPPY* BE SEPARATED FOR MORE THAN 37½ EARTH-HOURS, EACH WOULD SUFFER A HORRIBLE DEATH...

AS THE DISTRAUGHT *S-KYR* FEARED, BOY AND PET HAVE BEEN FLUNG INTO *DIFFERENT DIMENSIONS*; BUT ONTO *SIMILAR WORLDS*...BOTH BEARING THE NAME *EARTH*...

ALREADY THE CRITICAL 23RD HOUR HAS PASSED-- AND THE ALIENS' SEPARATION HAS INITIATED WITHIN THEM *PHYSICAL* AND *MENTAL* CHANGES...

IN THEIR DESPERATE SEARCH FOR REUNION, EACH LASHES OUT *INSANELY*...*VIOLENTLY*...*INNOCENTLY*-- LAYING WASTE TO *EARTH-ONE* AND *EARTH-TWO*...

3

EARTH-ONE AND EARTH-TWO! PARALLEL PLANETS LESS THAN A HEARTBEAT APART, BUT MORE THAN A UNIVERSE AWAY...

IN MANY INSTANCES THEIR PLANETARY DEVELOPMENT HAS BEEN *DIFFERENT*, BUT IN MANY *MORE* IT HAS BEEN THE *SAME*! ON *EARTH-TWO*, THE *WORLD'S GREATEST SUPER-HEROES* HAVE BANDED TOGETHER AS

THE JUSTICE SOCIETY OF *America*

YOU MIGHT RECOGNIZE SOME *EARTH-ONE* COUNTERPARTS...

SUPERMAN (CLARK KENT--EDITOR OF THE METROPOLIS *DAILY STAR*)

THE FLASH (JAY GARRICK-- RESEARCH SCIENTIST)

GREEN LANTERN (ALAN SCOTT--RADIO- TV EXECUTIVE)

THE ATOM-- (AL PRATT-- COLLEGE PROFESSOR)

HAWKMAN (CARTER HALL-- JET-SETTER AND SCIENTIST)

ROBIN (RICHARD GRAYSON-- GROWN-UP, EX-PARTNER OF THE SEMI-RETIRED *BATMAN*)

AND AT THE REGULARLY SCHEDULED MEETING OF THE *SOCIETY*...

THE REMAINING ABSENTEES MUST BE INVOLVED IN PERSONAL MATTERS...

--LIKE *GREEN LANTERN?* HE'S SENDING US A *DISTRESS SIGNAL!*

GOOD! LET'S GET GOING! THIS MEETING WAS TURNING INTO A DRAG ANYWAY!

4

AN EMERGENCY SIGNAL CALLS FOR A *SUPER-SPEED* RESPONSE...

GREEN LANTERN-- WHAT *HAPPENED?* LOOKS LIKE A *TORNADO* HIT YOU!

YEAH...A *TORNADO*... IN THE FORM OF A *KID*--A SWEET, INNOCENT, LOVABLE *KID!*

"AFTER *ROBIN* AND I WRAPPED UP A CASE NEAR HERE, I DECIDED TO TAKE A SOLO SIDE-TRIP TO CHECK UP ON *SLAUGHTER SWAMP,* WHEN..."

THAT OVERGROWN KID SEEMS LOST-- FRANTICALLY TRYING TO SMASH HIS WAY OUT...

"AS I SWOOPED DOWN TO HELP HIM, HE TURNED ON ME WITH A RAGING *SNARL...*"

I *TELE-SENSE* YOU CAN BRING *TEPPY* TO ME!

"WITH THAT, HE ATTACKED ME-- WITH SURPRISING, STUPENDOUS STRENGTH..."

WHEN I CAME TO, *ROBIN* WAS HERE-- BUT MY *POWER RING* WAS GONE! THAT'S WHY I *SIGNALLED* YOU!

SHOULDN'T BE HARD TO TRACK DOWN YOUR ATTACKER!

BUT I ADVISE YOU TO GO BACK TO *HEAD-QUARTERS* AND *RECU-PERATE!*

USE MY *ROBIN-CLIPPER* TO GET THERE, GL! I'M STICKING WITH THE JSA!

HMM...I *SUPPOSE* SO, *ROBIN*-- SINCE YOU'RE *HERE!* YOU MAY AS WELL JOIN US, FILL IN FOR *BATMAN*--

YOU FORGET, *CHAIRMAN HAWKMAN*--I'VE BEEN ACCEPTED AS A *FULL-FLEDGED JSA* MEMBER!

MAN, WHAT A *PATRONIZING* ATTITUDE! GENERATION GAP STRIKES AGAIN!

5

LEAVING THE SULKING *ROBIN,* WE RETURN ONCE MORE TO *JUSTICE LEAGUE* HEADQUARTERS...

I FOUND THE MAULED *FLASH* NORTH OF *GOTHAM CITY*--

THE READINGS ON THE *THANAGARIAN METABOLIC REVIVER* ARE TURNING *POSITIVE!* THE *SPEEDSTER'S* GONNA *MAKE IT!*

JUST THEN...

OHH! WHAT'S ALL THE COMMOTION--?

FLASH IS GOING--RUNNING --*WILD!*

NEWLY ARRIVED *BLACK CANARY* AND *GREEN ARROW* WATCH IN STUNNED AMAZEMENT AS...

CAUGHT UP TO HIM-- UNNH--HE'S CONKED OUT AGAIN!

FLASH STARTED TO SAY SOMETHING-- BUT SO *FAST,* IT CAME OUT *GARBLED!*

MY *SUPER-HEARING* CAUGHT ENOUGH TO HEAR *FLASH* MUTTER ALIEN-- MONSTER-- NEW CARTHAGE!

NEW CARTHAGE--? THAT'S WHERE--

HUDSON UNIVERSITY IS--

--AND *DICK (ROBIN) GRAYSON!*

SUDDENLY!

IT'S *AQUAMAN* ON THE *ALARM*-- USING THE SPECIAL *EMERGENCY CALL* FOR *BATMAN* AND *GREEN ARROW!*

GUESS HE GOT OVER HIS *MAD!*

THAT MEANS A *SPLIT-UP!*

*BATMAN--ARROW--*RESPOND TO *AQUAMAN'S CALL!* THE REST OF THE TEAM WILL TAKE OFF ON A *MONSTER-HUNT* AROUND *NEW CARTHAGE!*

I'LL REMAIN HERE WITH *FLASH* IN CASE HE *REVIVES* AGAIN!

6

NEARING THE COUNTRY-SIDE SURROUNDING *HUDSON UNIVERSITY*...

DOWN BELOW-- *DICK GRAYSON*--

--IN *ROBIN-ACTION!*

AFTER MAKING CONTACT...

WHILE ON A CASE✱, I HEARD RANGER RADIO-REPORTS OF A MARAUDING MONSTER--SO, I PULLED OUT MY CYCLE AND HEADED THIS WAY!

WHERE WAS THE MONSTER'S LAST-REPORTED SIGHTING?

✱ AS DETAILED IN THE AUGUST *BATMAN*--"VENGEANCE FOR A COP!"

OVER THAT HILL-RISE ABOUT 20 MILES!

MIGHT AS WELL STASH MY BIKE AND HITCH ALONG WITH *YOU!*

THEN AS IS SO FREQUENTLY DUPLICATED ON THE *TWIN-EARTHS*...

WELL...LONG AS *BATMAN* ISN'T HERE, YOU MIGHT HELP OUT A LITTLE--

AND THOUGH *UNSPOKEN*, THE *ROBIN-ANGER* IS PRECISELY THE *SAME!*

∶WHEW∶ LOOK AT THAT *DESTRUCTION*--TREES SCATTERED LIKE *MATCHSTICKS!*

HEY, WHAT'S MY *POWER RING* ZEROING IN ON?

⑦

IT'S TUNED IN ON A STRANGE FORCE-- WEIRD VIBES-- LIKE A *LINK* OR A *BOND!*

SEEMS TO BE CHANNELED INTO-- *EARTH-TWO!*

OH, NO! NOT AGAIN! ANOTHER *SUPER-MENACE* THAT *SIMULTANEOUSLY* THREATENS BOTH OUR *EARTHS!*

YOU BETTER CONTACT THE *JUSTICE SOCIETY* THROUGH YOUR RING, *GL!*

COMMUNICATION IS ESTABLISHED BETWEEN THE TWO *JUSTICE* GROUPS--AND...

WE WERE JUST ON *OUR* WAY TO FIGHT *OUR* MENACE!

IT'D BE SCIENTIFICALLY MORE SOUND FOR *YOUR* SUPERMAN, ATOM, AND *FLASH* TO COME *HERE* TO HANDLE *OUR* MONSTER--

--WHILE *OUR* GL, HAWKMAN AND ROBIN JOIN *YOUR* HAWKMAN AND ROBIN IN GOING AFTER THE *BOY-MENACE!*

PLAYING A *HUNCH,* ATOM-- OR A *THEORY?*

MY RING SHOULD BE ABLE TO HANDLE THE CROSS-OVER-- PROVIDED *EVERYONE* ADDS HIS *WILL POWER* TO MY *OWN!*

THE BODY-WRENCHING EXPERIENCE OF CROSSING THE *IN-BETWEEN* IS MATCHED BY THE COMBINED DETERMINED WILL OF TEN HEROES....

8

UNTIL NOW, *A-RYM* HAD LED A *CHILDISHLY-INNOCENT* LIFE! NEVER BEFORE HAD HE EVER EXPERIENCED THE *LONGING*, THE *CRAVING*--

--THE *GRASPING* FOR THE PET WHICH SUSTAINS HIM...

BUT NOW... ON THIS ALIEN WORLD OF *EARTH-TWO* ...A-RYM HAS INSTINCTIVELY SENSED *POWER*-- THE POWER OF *GREEN LANTERN'S RING* TO RE-CONNECT HIS BROKEN LIFE-LINE...

FOR BRIEF MOMENTS, A WEAK CONTACT HAD BEEN MADE--THE VERY CONTACT PICKED UP BY THE RING OF *EARTH ONE'S GREEN LANTERN*...

BEING UNFAMILIAR WITH THE *TRAINED, DELICATE* OPERATION OF THE *POWER RING*, A-RYM REACTED-- JUST LIKE AN ANGRY KID...

SHOVING THE RING INTO HIS POCKET, THE CONFUSED BOY CANNOT UNDERSTAND THIS WORLD WHERE HE HAS BECOME SO *STRONG*, SO *SWIFT*-- SO *DESTRUCTIVE*--

NOR DOES THE LOST LAD COMPREHEND THE CHANGES THAT HAVE MADE HIM SO *TERRIFYING* TO *EARTH*-CREATURES...

...CAUSING ANIMALS TO FEARFULLY FLEE FROM HIM...

9

THUS, WHEN THE SUPER-HEROES TRACK DOWN THE "MENACE" OF *EARTH-TWO*...

:SOB: WHY DOESN'T SOMEONE IN THIS STRANGE PLACE HELP ME?

THESE NEWCOMERS LOOK *HUMAN*...SOMEWHAT LIKE HIMSELF--YET SO *DIFFERENT!* THERE IS BUT ONE THING FOR *A-RYM* TO DO--*PLEAD!*

TEPPY...MY PET...TAKE ME TO HIM....PLEASE!

STRANGE... MY RING CAN'T *TRANSLATE* HIS ALIEN TALK!

SOUNDS MORE LIKE A *SNARL* TO ME!

THESE GUYS-- STANDING AROUND TALKING IT OVER...

--I'M TAKING *ACTION*--!

ROBIN--! NO...WAIT...!

AT LAST *A-RYM DOES* UNDERSTAND SOMETHING....AN *ATTACK*...

AND HOW *NORMAL* TO DEFEND HIMSELF!

THE YOUNG FOOL! THE ALIEN IS MUCH *STRONGER-- FASTER!*

10

ROBIN--DON'T *YOU* GO REPEATING YOUR NAME-SAKE'S IMPULSIVE-- *NO, ROBIN--NO!*

THE ONE AND ONLY TIME I FOUGHT WITH THE *JSA*, I HELPED LICK THE MENACE-- BUT *HAWKMAN* WASN'T THERE!

SO I HAVE TO "*PROVE*" MYSELF ALL *OVER* AGAIN!

GOT TO GET THIS *KID-FREAK* OFF *ROBIN*-- BY NEUTRALIZING HIS STRENGTH WITH A *WRESTLING HOLD!*

HAWK-MAN-- GRAB ROBIN!

BUT WITH *A-RYM'S* EVER-INCREASING STRENGTH, EVEN THE SKILLED *ROBIN* CANNOT STYMIE HIM FOR LONG...

UNN! HE'S BROKEN MY *HOLD!*

IT'S OKAY, *ROBIN*--I'LL GET YOU *FREE!*

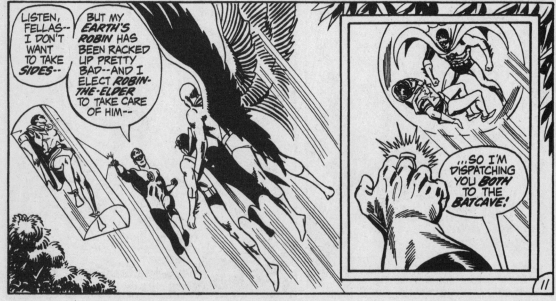

LISTEN, FELLAS-- I DON'T WANT TO TAKE *SIDES*--

BUT MY *EARTH'S ROBIN* HAS BEEN RACKED UP PRETTY BAD--AND I ELECT *ROBIN-THE-ELDER* TO TAKE CARE OF HIM--

...SO I'M *DISPATCHING* YOU *BOTH* TO THE *BATCAVE!*

11

THAT MOVE MAY TURN OUT TO BE A *MISTAKE,* GL!

...*GREEN RING,* BRING ME... *TEPPY!*

HUH? *BIG BOY* MUST BE AFTER *MY POWER RING* NOW!

HE'S LIKE A MOUNTAIN LION--BUT I CAN'T BRING MYSELF TO FIGHT A--*KID*--!

GOING UNDER--BETTER MAKE MY RING INVISIBLE--

NO *RING*--ARRRGH--NO *TEPPY!*

HE'S OVERPOWERED THE *LANTERN!* WE'VE GOT TO *STOP* HIM--KID OR NO KID!

WING-MEN ATTACK ME--MUST GET AWAY--FIND *TEPPY!*

GOING TO USE *GL* AS A *WEAPON* AGAINST US--!

GOT ME... BEFORE I COULD *WING* IT!

12

THE TWO OF 'EM KAYOED--BUT AT LEAST *HAWK-MAN'S* ANTI-*GRAVITY BELT* IS KEEPING HIM ALOFT!

NO SUCH LUCK FOR *GL!*

DASH MADLY, *HAWKMAN*-- FASTER THAN A FLEETING *FALCON*--SAVE THE *STRICKEN GREEN GLADIATOR!*

BUT BEATING WINGS ARE ONLY GOOD ENOUGH TO *BREAK* THE *EMERALD CRUSADER'S* FALL--!

--LEAVING ONLY THE *RETREATING* SOUNDS OF A FRIGHTENED, LONELY, SOBBING BOY...

13

SHOWCASE PRESENTS: JUSTICE LEAGUE OF AMERICA 159

CALL *TEDDY* A MONSTER-- BUT HE IS A DUMB-- *DUMBFOUNDED*--CREATURE WHO HAS LANDED ON A STRANGE PLANET...

WITH EVERY *STEP*, EVERY *LEAP*, EARTHLY GROWTHS FALL VICTIM TO HIS EVER-INCREASING BULK...

WITH EVERY PASSING MINUTE, THE BODY-CHANGES THAT *"MONSTER-IZE"* TEDDY TURN HIM INTO A DESTRUCTIVE *COLOSSUS*...

THEN, AS FIVE HEROIC FIGURES FLASH ONTO THE SCENE...

SUDDENLY, THERE IS *RECOGNITION*-- OF A *SCARLET-CLAD SPEEDSTER*...

...SOMEONE LIKE *THE FLASH* HE MET BEFORE--THE ONE WHO TRIED TO *HARM* HIM!

14

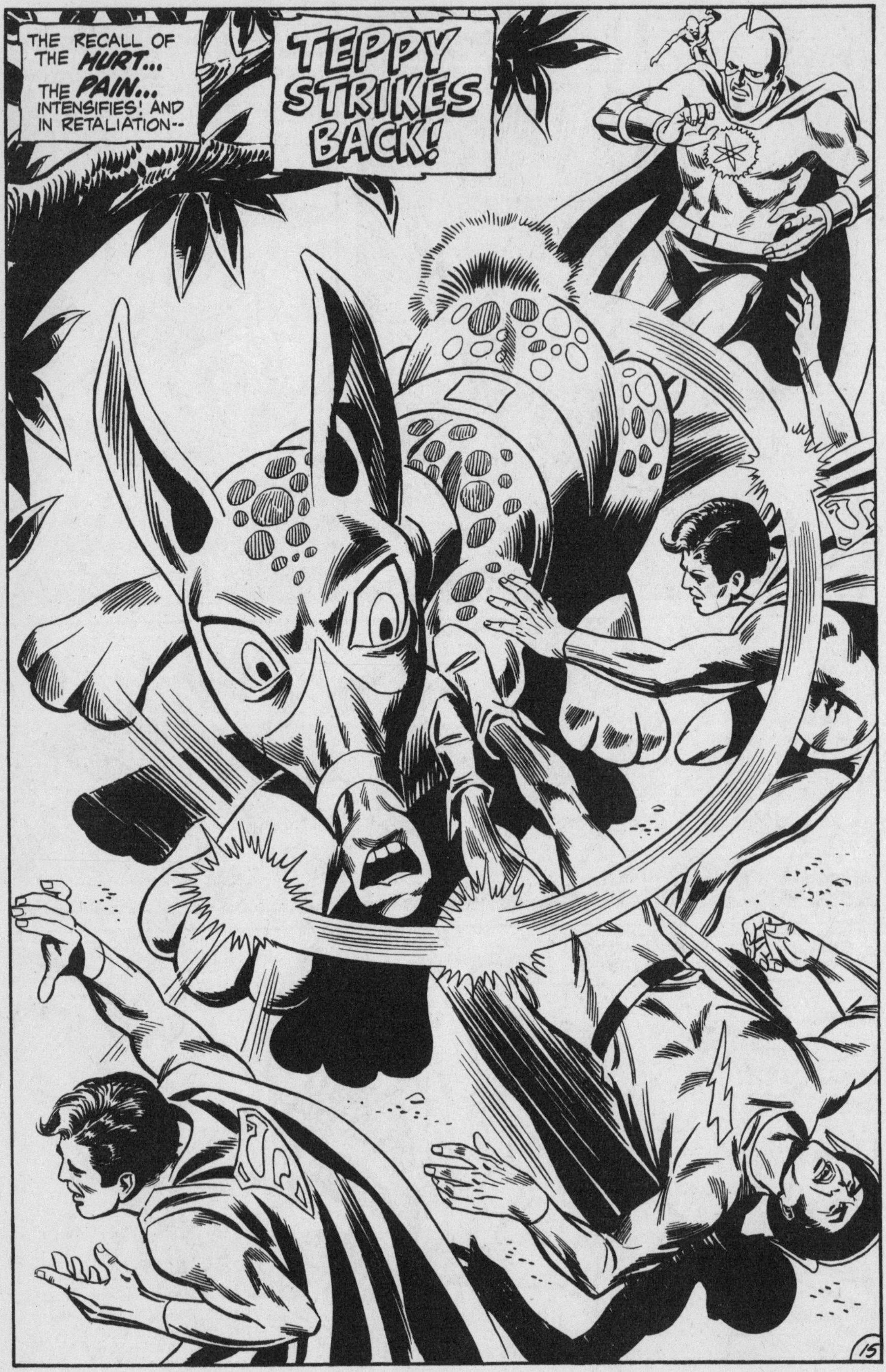
THE RECALL OF THE HURT... THE PAIN... INTENSIFIES! AND IN RETALIATION--
TEPPY STRIKES BACK!
15

≡WHEW≡ HE MUST COME FROM A *KRYPTON*-LIKE WORLD TO HAVE THE STRENGTH TO STAGGER BOTH *SUPERMEN!*

ONLY BY A SUPER-FAST ROLLING WITH THE PUNCH WAS *I* ABLE TO MINIMIZE HIS BLOW!

HE'S GRABBED *ATOM--*

SPOTTING ONE WHO IS SMALL, LIKE ITS HUMAN, *TEPPY* EAGERLY LIFTS HIM UP--BUT THE VITAL BOND, THE NECESSARY *LIFE-LINK* IS LACKING...

SO NATURALLY ENOUGH, *THE ATOM* IS ANGRILY DISCARDED...

≡OH≡ HE HURT MY FEELINGS!

--AND THE SAME TO *YOU!*

ARRH-- NO EFFECT!

ATOM! KEEP YOUR COOL--!

DON'T SWEAT IT, *FLASH!* I CAN *SYMPATHIZE* WITH THE *MITE'S* ANGER--WE BITTY-GUYS CAN TAKE ONLY SO MUCH *SLIGHTING!*

HOW ABOUT A HARDENED VETERAN TAKING A *SUPER-SPEED* CRACK AT HIM--?

I HAVE A *BETTER* IDEA--AN *ATOMIC* BRAINSTORM! LISTEN...

WITH A SUPER-SPEED TAILWIND--

WATCH OUT, MONSTER-BABY-- *HERE I COME!*

16

FLITTING LIGHT AS A FEATHER AROUND HIS FACE, I'M *BUGGING* HIM LIKE A *BOTHERSOME FLEA!*

--WHILE MAKING SURE HIS *PAWS* DON'T *ZAP* ME!

WHILE THE *TINY TITAN* CREATES A DIVERSION, THE NOW RECOVERED SUPER-HEROES GO INTO TEAM-WORK ACTION...

THERE--HE'S *TRAPPED!* AND IF HE SHOULD FALL INTO THE TRENCH, IT'LL BE TOO DEEP TO CLAMBER OUT OF!

I SUGGEST A COUPLE OF US GO TO *EARTH-TWO!* THERE MIGHT BE SOME *CONNECTION* BETWEEN THIS MONSTER AND THE ALIEN BOY!

I HAD THE SAME IDEA, *SUPERMAN!* FOLLOW MY LEAD AND I'LL SHOW YOU THE WAY!

LEAVING THE TWO *ATOMS* AND THE *SUPERMAN* OF *EARTH-TWO* TO GUARD THE ALIEN ANIMAL...

DUPLICATE MY SUPER-SPEED VIBRATIONS-- AND WE'LL BREAK THROUGH THE DIMENSIONAL BARRIER TO *EARTH-TWO!*

17

FLEEING THE FIVE CRUSADERS WHO FOUGHT HIM-- UNAWARE OF THE TWO YET TO COME--*A-RYM* RUSHES BLINDLY THROUGH THE TREES, TEARS WELLING IN HIS EYES AT HIS INCREASING ISOLATION-PAIN...

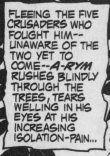

WHEN...

SPLAASH

PERHAPS *DESTINY* HAS DRAWN HIM TO THIS DESOLATE PLACE CALLED *SLAUGHTER SWAMP*, FOR ALL HAPPENINGS ARE, IN SOME MYSTERIOUS WAY, CONNECTED...

PERHAPS HE WAS PULLED BY THE *UNCANNY SENSE* OF THE...*THING*...WHO DWELLS HERE...

...THE *MACABRE MAN-THING* CALLED... SOLOMON GRUNDY!

NOT QUITE AN ANIMAL, YET POSSESSING HUMAN FORM, THIS HULK OF INANIMATE *VEGETATION* OVER THE YEARS HAS GAINED BLOCKBUSTER POWERS--AND ALWAYS IT SEEMS DRAWN BACK TO THE SWAMP THAT SPAWNED IT...

EVIDENTLY THERE IS A NATURAL LINK BETWEEN THESE TWO, EVEN THOUGH *SOLOMON GRUNDY* IS HARDLY A *"PET"*...

AND FOR THE MOMENT, A-RYM'S TEARS ARE ENDED...

18

SHORTLY, WHEN NEWCOMERS *SUPERMAN* AND *FLASH* ARRIVE...

K'ID COLOSSUS GAVE US *ALL* A ROUGH TIME, BUT WE'RE IN GOOD SHAPE AGAIN TO TAKE HIM ON...

THEN LET'S GET GOING! NO TELLING HOW MUCH MORE DAMAGE HE'S CAUSED!

BESIDES, *GREEN LANTERN'S* RING IS STILL MISSING--AND THAT BOY'S THE *KEY!*

TRACKING *A-RYM* THROUGH HIS OBVIOUS TRAIL...

LOOK! MORE TROUBLE THAN WE COUNTED ON!

THE BOY'S WITH THE OTHER *LANTERN'S* ARCH-FOE--*SOLOMON GRUNDY!*

LET'S HOPE THE *MARSHLAND MONSTER* IS NOT IN A BELLIGERENT MOOD!

WHEN ISN'T HE, *GREEN LANTERN?*...

BOY AFRAID? HIDE BEHIND ME!

YOU OTHERS-- SOLOMON GRUNDY STILL HATE YOU! FIGHT YOU AGAIN! KILL YOU ALL!

WE DON'T HAVE ANY GRUDGE AGAINST YOU, *GRUNDY!* WE JUST WANT THE BOY!

A POWER-RING BUBBLE WILL PUT *SOLOMON* OUT OF ACTION!

GYARRRGG! A BAD GREEN RING?

YOU-- GREEN LANTERN!

19

HAVING ABSORBED *MAGICAL ENERGY* FROM *DOCTOR FATE* AND *POWER-RING ENERGY* FROM *GREEN LANTERN* IN PREVIOUS BATTLES, THE *MAN-THING* ALLOWS *NOTHING* TO WITHSTAND HIS SINGLE DRIVING THOUGHT--

ME *HATE* GREEN LANTERN! ME *KILL* GREEN LANTERN!

HMM....CAN'T SAY MUCH FOR YOUR *VOCABULARY*-- BUT YOU DO MAKE YOUR *POINT!*

WINGED WONDERS SWOOP IN ON THEIR PREY...

WHEN WE LAST BATTLED *GRUNDY* I WAS ABLE TO LIFT HIM UP BY THE *HAIR*-- AND MAKE HIM *HELPLESS!*

BIRD-MEN ATTACK SOLOMON GRUNDY--

BUT--YOU NOT HARM ME--NOT STOP ME FROM *KILLING* GREEN LANTERN!

THE *FLYING ACES'* TRICK DIDN'T *WORK* THIS TIME--

BUT MAYBE MY *SUPER-SPEED MAGIC* WILL--!

SEE YOU COMING! NO LIKE!

≡UNNH≡

20

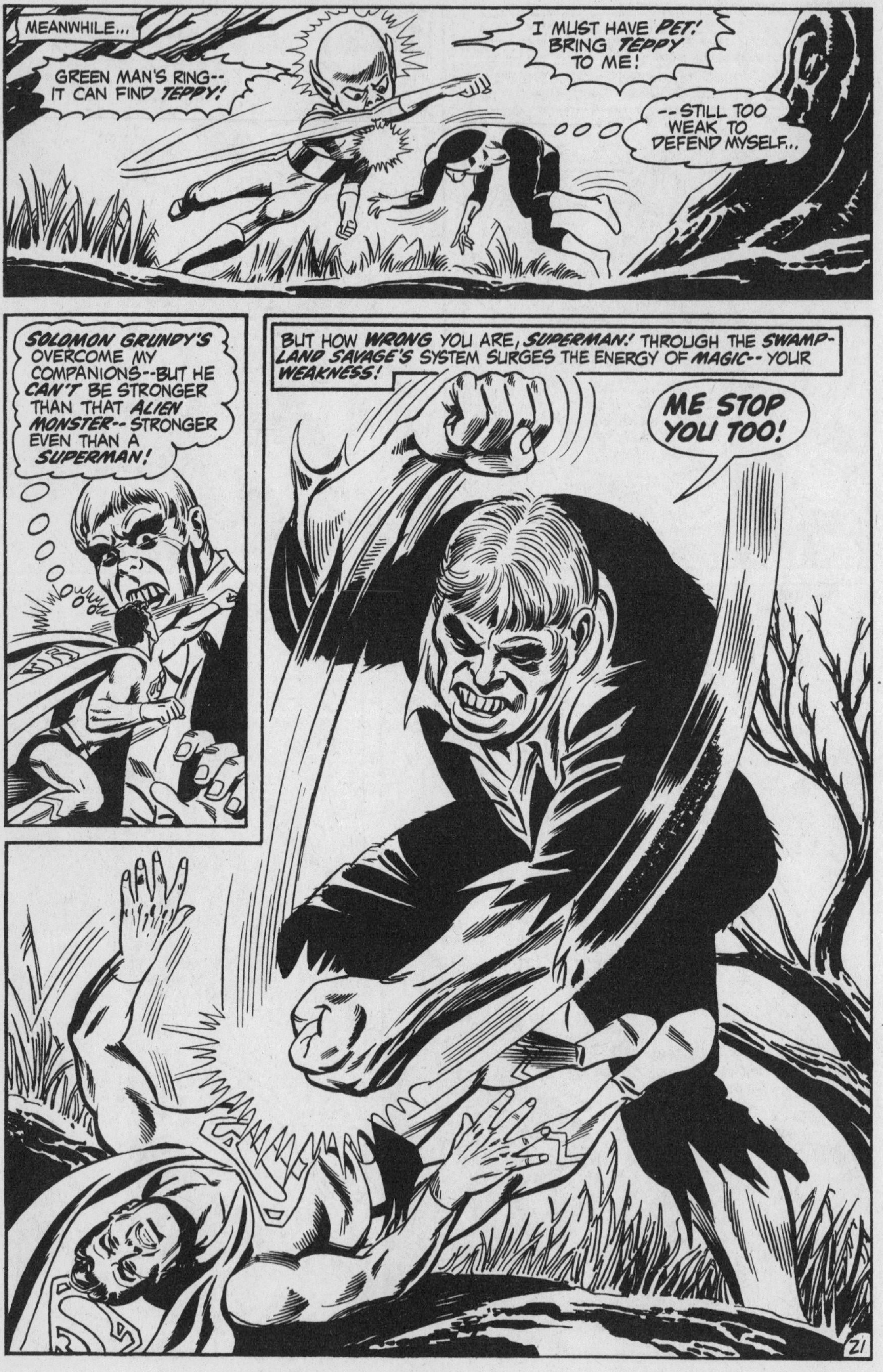
MEANWHILE...
GREEN MAN'S RING-- IT CAN FIND TEPPY!
I MUST HAVE PET! BRING TEPPY TO ME!
--STILL TOO WEAK TO DEFEND MYSELF...
SOLOMON GRUNDY'S OVERCOME MY COMPANIONS--BUT HE CAN'T BE STRONGER THAN THAT ALIEN MONSTER-- STRONGER EVEN THAN A SUPERMAN!
BUT HOW WRONG YOU ARE, SUPERMAN! THROUGH THE SWAMP-LAND SAVAGE'S SYSTEM SURGES THE ENERGY OF MAGIC-- YOUR WEAKNESS!
ME STOP YOU TOO!
21

WHY YOU ALWAYS ATTACK SOLOMON GRUNDY?

NO MORE! ME TAKE REVENGE!

ME KILL YOU ALL--KILL EVERYONE!

GREEN LANTERN-- YOU FIRST!

NEXT ISSUE!

THE GREATEST HEROES OF TWO EARTHS VS. "SOLOMON GRUNDY-- THE ONE AND ONLY!"

22

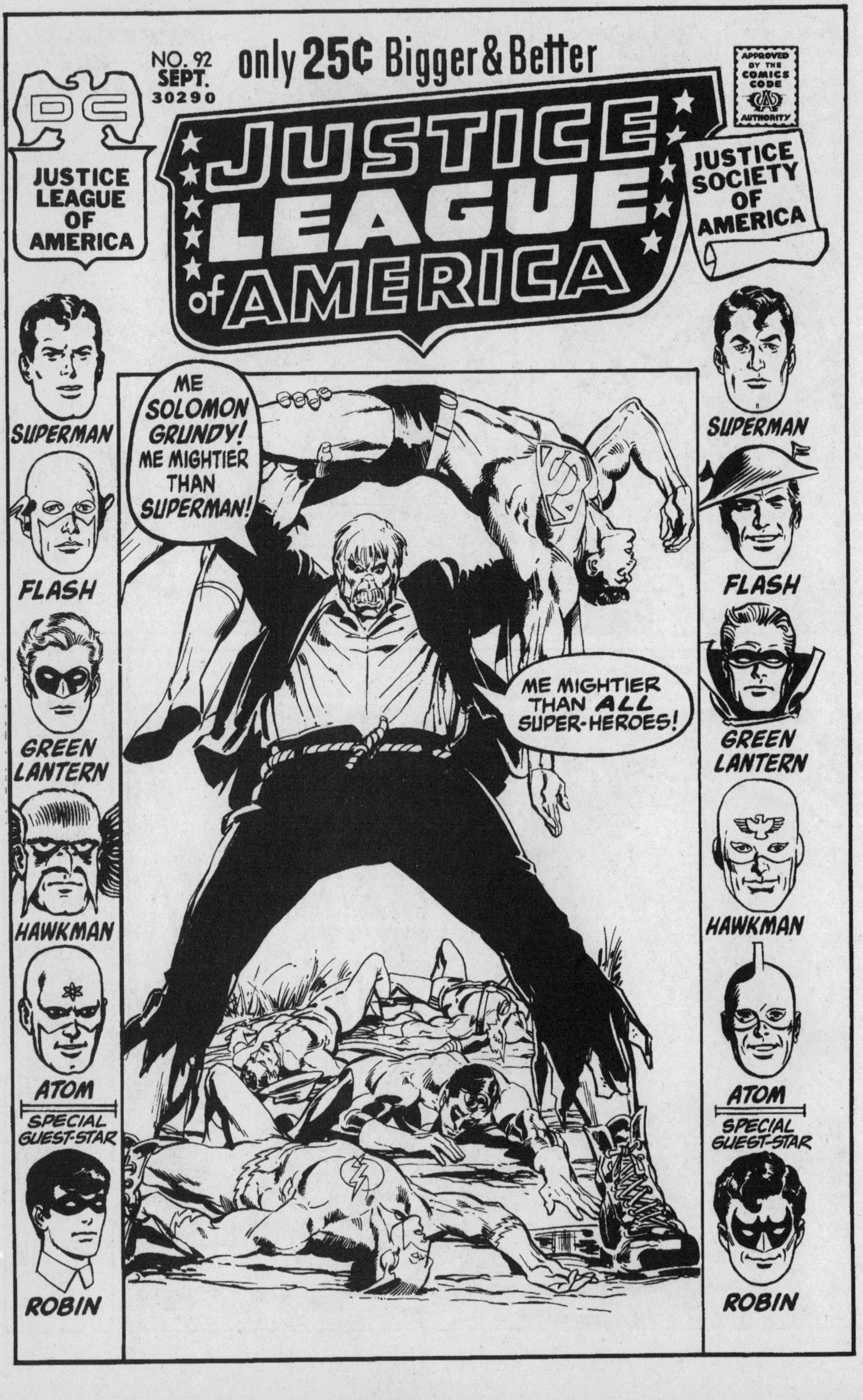

NO. 92
SEPT.
30290
only 25¢ Bigger & Better
APPROVED BY THE COMICS CODE AUTHORITY
JUSTICE LEAGUE OF AMERICA
JUSTICE LEAGUE of AMERICA
JUSTICE SOCIETY OF AMERICA
SUPERMAN
FLASH
GREEN LANTERN
HAWKMAN
ATOM
SPECIAL GUEST-STAR
ROBIN
SUPERMAN
FLASH
GREEN LANTERN
HAWKMAN
ATOM
SPECIAL GUEST-STAR
ROBIN
ME SOLOMON GRUNDY! ME MIGHTIER THAN SUPERMAN!
ME MIGHTIER THAN ALL SUPER-HEROES!

JUSTICE ☆☆☆ LEAGUE ☆☆☆ of AMERICA CO-STARRING **THE JUSTICE SOCIETY OF America**

JUST IMAGINE! *SUPERMAN*...THE MAN OF MIGHT, MAN OF STEEL--THE MAN OF *TOMORROW!*

NOW IMAGINE... *TWO SUPERMEN!*

S-838

JUST IMAGINE! *GREEN LANTERN*...WITH A *POWER RING* THAT CAN BE ACTIVATED BY HIS MIGHTY *WILL POWER!*

NOW IMAGINE! *TWO GREEN LANTERNS...* AND *TWO POWER RINGS!*

NOW PICTURE THIS... *TWO EARTHS* IN PARALLEL DIMENSIONS, WITH PARALLEL EVOLUTIONS, WITH *PARALLEL* SUPER-HEROES...

...TWO *HAWKMEN*!

...TWO *FLASHES*!

...TWO *ATOMS*!

...EVEN TWO *ROBINS*!

WHO COULD *POSSIBLY* DEFEAT THE COMBINED MIGHT OF THE GREATEST SUPER-HEROES OF TWO EARTHS?

ONLY SOMEONE WHO IS UNIQUE TO BOTH EARTHS...

②

SOLOMON GRUNDY... THE ONE AND ONLY

ILLUSTRATED BY:
DICK DILLIN &
JOE GIELLA

THIS STORY IS DEDICATED TO *JERRY BAILS* AND *ROY THOMAS*, WHO INTRODUCED THE AUTHOR TO THE GOLDEN GALAXY OF *JUSTICE SOCIETY STARS*--AND TO EDITOR *JULIE SCHWARTZ* AND AUTHOR *GARDNER FOX*, WHO FIRST BROUGHT THEM ALL BACK TO LIFE! TO THESE FOUR I WILL ALWAYS BE GRATEFUL! -- *Mike Friedrich*

MANY TIMES THINGS ARE NOT WHAT THEY *ARE*, BUT WHAT THEY ARE *LINKED TO!* IT IS THE *BONDS* THAT DEFINE US ALL! THIS IS A STORY ABOUT THESE SHAKY BRIDGES, THESE FRAGILE CHAINS-- *LIFE'S BROKEN LINKS...*

LOOK UPON A CERTAIN LOVABLE PET--KNOWN AS *TEPPY* TO ITS YOUNG *MASTER, A-RYM!* THESE TWO INHABITANTS OF ANOTHER WORLD ARE BONDED TO EACH OTHER FROM *BIRTH*, THEIR *SURVIVAL* DEPENDENT UPON THEIR *PHYSICAL CLOSENESS!*

CAST SEPARATELY INTO *EARTH-ONE* AND *EARTH-TWO* BY A WARP-STORM IN THE DIMENSIONAL VOID BETWEEN BOTH WORLDS, THEIR LIFE-LINE WAS *BROKEN!*

IN A DESPERATE, FUTILE SEARCH FOR *TEPPY*, A-RYM FORCIBLY TOOK AWAY THE *POWER RING* FROM *EARTH-TWO'S GREEN LANTERN*-- THEN SUCCESSFULLY RE-SISTED THE JOINT EFFORTS OF THE SUPER-HEROES OF TWO WORLDS TO RECOVER THE RING...

WHILE ON *EARTH-ONE*, AN-OTHER GROUP OF HEROES SUCCEEDED IN *TRAPPING* THE NOW-FEROCIOUS *TEPPY*, DESPITE THE MON-STROUS BODY-CHANGES BROUGHT ABOUT BY THE SEPARATION FROM ITS *HUMAN LINK...*

SOON, THE STRANGE TWISTINGS OF FATE BROUGHT A-RYM TOGETHER WITH THE *MAN-THING* FROM *SLAUGHTER SWAMP--SOLOMON GRUNDY!*

THE ALIEN YOUTH SOUGHT *SOMETHING* TO EASE THE GROWING GNAWING OF HIS INSIDES, SOMETHING TO PROTECT HIM FROM THE PAIN AND THE PANIC!

AGAINST HIS HATED ENEMIES, *SOLOMON GRUNDY* WAS ALL TOO READY TO OBLIGE!...

4

HAVING STUNNED *SUPERMAN* WITH HIS COLOSSAL STRENGTH, THE *MARSH-LAND MONSTER* NOW THREATENS THE VERY LIFE OF THE HELPLESS *GREEN LANTERN!*...

UHNN... HAVE TO BREAK *GRUNDY'S* HOLD-- BEFORE HE USES MY INVULNERABLE BODY TO *SQUASH GL!*

THIS OUGHT TO LOOSEN HIS GRIP!

SWAPPP

:GYARRGG: BLUE MAN SLAP *SOLOMON GRUNDY'S* EARS!

THE *BIO-SYSTEM* OF THE *SWAMPLAND SAVAGE* SURGES WITH *MAGIC*-- AND A BLOW THAT WOULD NORMALLY FELL A *GIANT REDWOOD* MERELY ENRAGES THE *MAN-THING*...

YOU *HIT SOLOMON GRUNDY*-- *SOLOMON GRUNDY HIT YOU HARDER!*

THEN, TURNING WITH A SNARL...

YOU TRY TO SAVE *GREEN LANTERN*-- BUT *SOLOMON GRUNDY KILL* YOU *ALL!*

5

MEANWHILE, MIDST THE MISTS AND SWIRLS OF *IN-BETWEEN*--A NEVER-NEVER PLACE--PART OF *ALL* PLACES, YET PART OF *NONE*...

LOCATE THEM YET, *SKYR?*

NO LUCK, *ENES!* LITTLE BROTHER *A-RYM* AND HIS PET *TEPPY* ARE PROBABLY SEPARATED-- IN DIFFERENT DIMENSIONS!

OH--ARE *WE* GONNA GET IT FOR LOSIN' THEM!

YOU *SELF-CENTERED FOOL!* IF THEY REMAIN *SPLIT* MUCH LONGER, THEY'LL *DIE!*

OUR COMPUTER IS SEARCHING EVERYWHERE, TRACING THE *LIFE-FORCE* THAT EXISTS *BETWEEN* THE TWO!

AND WITH EACH PASSING MOMENT, THAT *FORCE* IS *WEAKENING*...AS THE COMPUTER LOSES TRACK OF IT!

THOUGH THE EYES OF *A-RYM* STILL SHINE WITH INNOCENCE, HIS SOUL BLAZES WITH THE BURNING PAIN OF BEING SEPARATED FROM HIS LIFE-DEPENDENT *TEPPY*...

FOR AWHILE, THE MYSTIC CHEMISTRY OF *SOLOMON GRUNDY* HAD FILLED THE GAPING NECESSITY FOR COMPANIONSHIP..

BUT *NOW* SOMETHING *MORE URGENT* IS NEEDED--THE DESPERATE LINK TO *TEPPY*--A LIFE-LINE *GREEN LANTERN* CAN PROVIDE!...

GREEN ONE CAN BRING ME *TEPPY!*

:HUNGH: SMALL ONE STOP ME--!?

DO NOT HARM HIM!

THE ALIEN'S GIVEN ME AN OPENING-- FOR A *SUPER-SPEED ATTACK!*

6

IF I CAN HIT *GRUNDY*...

...OFTEN ENOUGH...

...A *MILLION* TIMES A SECOND OR SO...

...I SHOULD KNOCK...

...THE *STUFFING*...

...OUT OF HIM...

BUT THE RAW, UNHAR-NESSED ENERGIES OF *SOLOMON GRUNDY* CAN STOP EVEN A *HUMAN THUNDER-BOLT*...

THEN, BEFORE THE *MAN-THING* CAN FOLLOW UP HIS *FLASH*-ADVANTAGE....

WHILE I DO THE RESCUE BIT WITH *FLASH*, MY COUNTER-PART IS SAVING *SUPER-MAN*--AS *GL* TAKES OFF ON HIS OWN POWER!

WE'LL NEED *REST* BEFORE RESUMING THIS BATTLE!

REALIZING THAT *SOLOMON GRUNDY* AND *GREEN LANTERN* CANNOT HELP HIM NOW--A RESTLESS, REJECTED *A-RYM* BOUNDS OFF--

ONCE AGAIN HE IS FRIENDLESS-- ONCE AGAIN HE MAKES A FRANTIC *RUN FOR HIS LIFE!*

7

AT THE SAME TIME--IN THE NOT-TOO-DISTANT *EARTH-TWO* BATCAVE...

≡WHEW≡ SOME MESS I AM! I GET SMACKED AROUND BY THAT ALIEN KID--LIKE EVERYONE *ELSE*--AND THE *JUSTICE LEAGUERS* REGARD ME AS AN UNPROVEN, UNFIT *CHILD!*

YEAH--WELL, *MY* REPUTATION ISN'T MUCH *BETTER!* I GREW UP A SUPER-HERO FAN--I *IDOLIZED* 'EM ALL!

WHEN I WAS ACCEPTED INTO THE BIG-TIME *JUSTICE SOCIETY*, I FIGURED I'D HIT THE TOP--ONLY TO FIND I HAD TO START ALL *OVER* AGAIN...FROM THE *BOTTOM!*

IF MY MENTOR, *BATMAN*, HAD ENOUGH FAITH IN ME TO CHOOSE ME AS HIS *REPLACEMENT*, HOW COME *HAWKMAN* WON'T EVEN LET ME *TEAM UP* WITH *HIM?!*

I'M GOING THROUGH THE SAME KINDA TRIP--AWAY AT COLLEGE--SPLIT FROM *BATMAN*--WITH THE SAME GENERAL REACTION FROM THE *JLA!*

BEFORE ADOPTING MY OWN NEW COSTUME, HERE'S ONE I CONSIDERED--FASHIONED BY A COSTUME-MAKER I KNOW--*NEAL ADAMS!*

SAY--*THAT'S REAL SHARP!* I *LIKE* IT!

LET ME *TRY* IT ON!

HERE IS A *LINK*--TWO YOUNG MEN FROM SIMILAR BACKGROUNDS, FACING *REJECTION* AND *ALIENATION*, BUT THEY FORM A *TEAM*--AND FROM THIS TEAM FLOWS *RENEWAL!*

WE WERE *DOWN* BEFORE, *ROBIN*--BUT NOW WE'RE GONNA SHOW 'EM HOW *HIGH TWO ROBINS* CAN FLY!

RIGHT ON, BROTHER!

SO YOUR WORLD HAS THAT EXPRESSION, TOO!

GUESS YA CAN'T HAVE *EVERY-THING* COOL!

8

WHILE IN THE *JUSTICE LEAGUE SPACE-SATELLITE* HEADQUARTERS...

AT *LAST*--AFTER *HOURS*--I'VE CONTACTED *MRS. BARRY ALLEN* ABOUT HER INJURED *HUSBAND*, THE *FLASH*!

SEEMS SO OMINOUSLY *QUIET* UP HERE! NO NEWS ABOUT THE ALIEN BEAST--

NOR ANY REPORT FROM *GREEN ARROW* AND *BATMAN* ON THAT EMERGENCY SIGNAL FROM *AQUAMAN*!

SHORTLY AFTER...

FLASH'S COMING OUT OF HIS COMA AGAIN! STILL *WEAK*-- AND *DELIRIOUS*!

MUST STOP HIM...MUST STOP...

JUST THEN...

I CAME AS QUICKLY AS I COULD, *BLACK CANARY*-- OHH!

YOU'RE JUST IN TIME, MRS. ALLEN! *FLASH* CAN USE THE NURSING CARE OF HIS *WIFE*!

OH...BARRY... DARLING...

UH... IRIS...

HERE IS ANOTHER *BOND*--THE *LINK OF LOVE*! IN HEALTH THERE IS HAPPI- NESS--IN SICKNESS THERE IS COMFORT AND CARE! FROM THIS MARRIAGE FLOWS *STRENGTH*!

SWITCHING TO *EARTH-TWO* AGAIN AND *JUSTICE SOCIETY* HEADQUARTERS, A FEW HOURS EARLIER...

NO WORD FROM THE *JSA* YET ABOUT THAT ALIEN LAD WHO TOOK OFF WITH MY *POWER RING* AFTER WHALING THE TAR OUT OF ME!

AH--SOMEONE AT THE DOOR...

KNOCK KNOCK

QUICK--GET OUT WHATEVER *MEDICAL* FACILITIES YOU HAVE!

WOW! WHAT'D YOU RUN INTO?

TROUBLE... *BIG* TROUBLE!

9

SUPERMAN... FLASH... THEY GOING TO BE ALL RIGHT?

NO PROBLEM-- THEY'RE MADE OF PRETTY *STRONG* STUFF!

BY THIS TIME, *SOLOMON GRUNDY* MUST BE THREATENING HIS ENTIRE AREA! NOW THAT WE'VE TAKEN A *BREATHER*, THE THREE OF US HAVE TO *RETURN*!

MAKE THAT *FOUR*, PARTNER! WE NEED MY NAMESAKE'S *EXPERIENCE*! THAT'S WHY I'VE BROUGHT ALONG MY *POWER BATTERY*--

--TO FASHION A *LIMITED POWER RING* FOR *YOU*!

CARE TO *JOIN* IN RECITING MY OATH?

IT'S MY *GREATEST HONOR*, LANTERN!

THEN FEATHERED FURIES WATCH A SACROSANCT SCENE-- THE SOLEMN *CHARGING OF THE RINGS*!

IN BRIGHTEST DAY, IN BLACKEST NIGHT, NO EVIL SHALL ESCAPE OUR SIGHT! LET THOSE WHO WORSHIP EVIL'S MIGHT BEWARE OUR POWER-- *GREEN LANTERN'S LIGHT*!

THEN...

OUR *JSA* COMMUNICATORS JUST PICKED UP A CALL FROM THE *ROBINS*!

THEY'VE FOUND THE TRAIL OF THE ALIEN BOY! HE'S SPLIT OFF FROM *SOLOMON GRUNDY*!

THOSE *ROBIN* KIDS--!

WE TOLD 'EM TO KEEP OUT OF THE WAY!

≷WHOA≷ I THINK YOU TWO *HAWKS* ARE OVER-REACTING! AGE HAS *NOTHING* TO DO WITH CAPABILITY...

CAN IT! THE MORE TIME WE GIVE *SOLOMON GRUNDY*, THE MORE MONSTROUS HE GETS!

YOU HEARD THE MAN! *LET'S GO!*

YOU *LANTERNS* TACKLE *GRUNDY*-- WE'LL HANDLE THE YOUNG ALIEN!

10

HAVE *YOU* EVER FELT A HOLE IN YOUR GUT?- A HAND WRENCHING YOUR STOMACH, TWISTING IT INTO SO MUCH SHREDDED CHEESE?

THEN PERHAPS YOU CAN COMPREHEND THE STRUGGLING, PAIN-RACKED, DYING *A-RYM*--

HE'S GAINED POSSESSION OF A *POWER RING* THAT HIS ALIEN SENSES TELL HIM CAN BRING HIM HIS LIFE-SAVING PET, *TEPPY!*

HIS *WILL* IS HIS *DESIRE*-- A COMBINATION THAT ACTIVATES THE *RING!*...

S-KYR, LOOK! THE LINK-FORCE HAS SUDDENLY TURNED *STRONGER!*

SOME-HOW, THE TWO HAVE ESTABLISHED *CONTACT!*

AND AS THE PUZZLED *A-RYM* WONDERS HOW TO *POWER* THE *RING*...

BIRD-MEN FLY TO ME! DO *THEY* KEEP *TEPPY* FROM ME?

ONCE AGAIN *A-RYM* UTTERS ALIEN-SOUNDS THAT ARE *MISUNDERSTOOD*...

≋WHEW≋ LISTEN TO HIM *SNARL!*

LOOKS LIKE WE'VE *BEATEN* THE *ROBINS* HERE!

SURROUND HIM-- BUT BE *CAREFUL!* HE'S ALMOST AS POWERFUL AS *SUPERMAN!*

GWAP

SEEMING LIKE PREYING VULTURES TO THE WEAKENING BOY, HE RESPONDS WITH A DEFIANT RANT...

HE'S HOLDING UP *GL'S* RING AT US! IF HE KNOWS HOW TO *CONTROL* IT--

11

JUST THEN, *A-RYM'S* ROARING ANGUISH IS MATCHED BY THE SOUND OF THE HIGH-COMPRESSION ENGINES OF THE *BATCYCLE!*

THE *HAWKS* HAVE THE ALIEN SURROUNDED--BUT TWO-TO-ONE THEY'LL *STILL* NEED OUR HELP!

HOLD IT, *ROBIN!* YOU AND YOUR COSTUMED FRIEND STAND BACK! *WE'LL* HANDLE THIS PROBLEM!

THEY THINK THEY HAVE A *MONOPOLY* ON *AIR-SPACE!*

LET'S SHOW 'EM HOW THE *FLYING GRAYSONS* USED TO OPERATE!

YOUR NEW *ROBIN* COSTUME SEEMS TO HAVE CONFUSED *HAWKMAN!*

NEW COSTUME WORKS *GREAT*-- IDEALLY DESIGNED FOR *ACROBATICS!*

THIS SURPRISE MANEUVER SHOULD *DISTRACT* THE ALIEN--

MY GOOD OL' *BATARANG* STILL COMES IN HANDY!

A *PERFECT RING-ER!*

LIFE-CONTACT HAS BEEN *BROKEN!*

A-RYM HASN'T GOT A CHANCE NOW...

12

LIKE A SUN THAT EXPLODES INTO A *NOVA* BEFORE IT DIES, SO DOES THE FAST FADING *A-RYM* ERUPT INTO A FINAL FIT OF VIOLENT ACTION...

TEPPY! TEPPY! I MUST HAVE *TEPPY!*

GOT TO WHIP MY *ANTI-GRAVITY BELT* AROUND HIM-- MAKE HIM AIRBORNE-- OUT OF HARM'S WAY!

BUT THE ALIEN'S HEIGHTENED REFLEXES ARE TOO FAST FOR THE *WINGED WONDER!...*

KW MA AK

THEN, OUT OF THE DARKNESS--ANOTHER "*BIRD*" LEAPS TO *HAWKMAN'S* AID...

OKAY, JUNIOR--I'M JOININ' YOUR *SWINGIN'* PARTY!

13

FIRST A *KARATE-CHOP* TO DISARM YOU--

THEN A *NERVE-PARALYZING* TO.... EH? HE'S CRYING-- LIKE A BABY!

HUUUUU

POOR KID'S IN *AGONY!* I COULDN'T HAVE HURT HIM *THAT* MUCH!

IT'S NO ACT HE'S PUTTING ON... I CAN TELL! MAYBE I CAN CALM HIM DOWN...

FOR THE FIRST TIME SINCE HIS ACCIDENTAL ARRIVAL ON THIS WORLD, *A-RYM* SENSES HUMAN WARMTH AND CONCERN...

THE RAGE OF SECONDS AGO DISSIPATES LIKE STEAM IN THE WIND! HE FLINGS HIMSELF INTO *ROBIN'S* ARMS, HELPLESSLY CLINGS TO THIS WARMTH OF NEW-FOUND FRIENDSHIP...

--THEN WITH AN OMINOUS MOAN, HE LAPSES INTO UNCONSCIOUSNESS...

UNNHH HHH--

IS THIS *A-RYM'S* DEATH-GASP?

14

ELSEWHERE, A *DIFFERENT DESTRUCTIVE* FORCE STRIKES IN THE NIGHT--THE *ONE* AND *ONLY* **SOLOMON GRUNDY!**

BREAK BRIDGE!

SUDDENLY, THE DARKNESS IS SPLIT BY A PAIR OF PULVERIZING BEAMS OF EMERALD ENERGY!

ARRGH?!

GREEN LANTERN?!

TWO GREEN LANTERNS!

GRUNDY'S *BOULDER-BARRAGE* IS CAUSING THE BRIDGE TO *COLLAPSE!*

YOU TAKE THE BRIDGE--WHILE *I* TAKE MY *ARCH-FOE!*

ME HATE GREEN LANTERN! ME KILL HIM!

YOUR RING NOT HURT SOLOMON GRUNDY!

HE COULD BE *RIGHT!* I CAN'T SEEM TO GET MUCH *FIGHT-POWER* OUT OF THE RING!

WHILE AT THE FALLING BRIDGE, ANOTHER POWER-RING FAILURE!

MY *POWER RING'S* FIZZLING OUT!

APPARENTLY THE DUAL SHARING OF THE *POWER BATTERY* HAS DRAINED EACH RING OF EFFECTIVENESS!

FRANTICALLY CALLING HIS NAMESAKE TO HIS SIDE--

SEE--IT TAKES *TWO* RINGS TO OPERATE AS EFFICIENTLY AS *ONE!*

SAY--THAT'S OUR *CLUE!* BY WORKING *TOGETHER,* COMBINING BOTH OUR WILLS BEHIND OUR SINGLE POWER-SOURCE, WE CAN UNLEASH *ENOUGH EMERALD ENERGY* TO ZAP GRUNDY!

IT'S WORTH A *TRY!* LET'S *DO IT!*

16

HERE IS YET ANOTHER LIFE-LINK--THE AGE-OLD BOND OF BATTLE! TWO *GREEN GLADIATORS* INTENTLY JOIN THEIR DETERMINED WILLS, AND FROM THIS UNION-UNDER-FIRE COMES AN IRRESISTIBLE FORCE--

--AGAINST WHICH THERE CAN STAND NO *IMMOVABLE OBJECT!*

AND FROM THIS LIFE-LINK FLOWS *VICTORY!*

WE'VE *BEATEN* HIM-- BUT IT'S JUST ABOUT *EXHAUSTED* US!

HOW DO WE *HOLD* HIM?

THEN AS SOFT-LIGHT CRACKS THE HORIZON...

THERE'S *HAWKMAN* AND...YES! HE HAS RECOVERED YOUR STOLEN *POWER RING!*

17

RACING AS FAST AS HIS THOUGHTS WILL TAKE HIM TO CHARGE HIS RING, THE *ORIGINAL GREEN LANTERN* RETURNS TO *SLAUGHTER SWAMP...*

...WHERE A *MAN-THING* IS RETURNED TO THE LAND OF ITS BIRTH...

KU-PLOP

THIS ENTIRE SWAMPLAND IS TOTALLY DESOLATE-- DEVOID OF LIFE!

GOOD ENOUGH! WHO'D WANT A *MONSTER* FOR A NEIGHBOR ANYWAY?

IT IS DONE! OUR COMBINED *POWER-RING* ENERGY...

...HAS CREATED A BARRIER...

...*SOLOMON GRUNDY* CAN NEVER BREAK OUT OF!

PERHAPS HERE, TOO, IS A *LINK*--A UNIQUE SWAMP AND ITS RESIDENT *MAN-THING*...CREATING THE BOND CALLED *"HOME"* FROM WHICH FLOWS *CONTENTMENT!*

18

AND WHAT OF THE PARALLEL MENACE ON *EARTH-ONE...?*

THE ALIEN BEAST IS *SHRINKING--* LOSING ITS FIERCENESS!

SO NATURALLY, WE CAN EXPECT TO SEE A SIMILAR SITUATION ON *EARTH-TWO...*

THE LAD IS CHANGING-- GETTING WEAKER!

HE'S NO LONGER A *THREAT...*

SOME- THING *WRONG* HERE--!

FROM WHAT *SUPERMAN* TOLD US ABOUT THE BEAST ON THE OTHER *EARTH,* I'M GLAD WE DIDN'T HAVE TO BATTLE *BOTH* ALIENS *TOGETHER!*

YEAH, BAD *ENOUGH* THAT COINCIDENCE ONCE AGAIN HAD US FIGHTING A SIMILAR FOE ON OUR SEPARATE WORLDS AT THE SAME TIME!

?

?

TO PUT ALMOST IMPERCEPTIBLE CLUES TOGETHER INTO A SINGLE IDEA IS A RARE TALENT, PROVIDED BY COMMON TRAINING FROM THE TWO GREATEST DETECTIVES OF TWO WORLDS...

WAITAMINNIT-- YOU GUYS ARE MISSING THE *BOAT!* THIS BOY'S *DYING!*

MAYBE IT *HASN'T* BEEN COINCIDENCE--MAYBE WE'VE GOTTA BRING THE BOY AND BEAST *TOGETHER* FOR THEM TO *SURVIVE*--TO *LIVE NORMALLY!*

THAT *WOULD EXPLAIN* A LOT OF THINGS THAT HAVE BEEN HAPPENING!

LET'S GIVE IT A WHIRL!

BUT IS THERE ENOUGH *TIME?*

THE LIFE-LIGHT IS ALMOST *OUT!* A-RYM AND *TEPPY* ARE IN THE THROES OF DEATH!

WHY'D I EVER THINK RIDE- JOYING IN- BETWEEN *DIMENSIONS* WOULD BE *FUN?*

19

WHILE *S-KYR'S* HEART BEARS THE SCARRING RESPONSIBILITY FOR HIS ACTIONS, THE *GREEN LANTERNS* LEAD THE WAY ACROSS THE BRIDGE BETWEEN *EARTHS* IN THEIR DESPERATE MISSION OF MERCY!...

THIS HAS TO BE ONE OF THE *WILDEST* IDEAS I'VE EVER HEARD, *ROBIN*-- BUT SOMETHING ABOUT IT JUST SEEMS... *RIGHT!*

RIGHT AS CAN BE!

WITH *US* IT'S--"*IN UNION THERE IS STRENGTH*"--

WITH THOSE TWO ALIENS, IT'S--"*IN UNION THERE IS LIFE!*"

S-KYR--THE *LIFE-LIGHT* IS *BLAZING BRIGHT!* IT'S A *MIRACLE!*

A-RYM AND *TEPPY* ARE TOGETHER AGAIN! IT'LL BE EASY TO FIND THEM NOW!

SHORTLY...

A *SPACE-SHIP!*

I BET IT'S CONNECTED WITH OUR EXTRA-TERRESTRIAL VISITORS!

20

YOU'RE A WINNER, *TINY TITAN*-- THEY'RE GOING BACK HOME!

E-NES, WE'VE BOTH LEARNED A VALUABLE LESSON FROM THIS EXPERIENCE!

YES, *S-KYR*--WE'VE EVEN GROWN ENOUGH TO FACE THE MUSIC FOR HIJACKING THIS SPACE-CRAFT!

ON *EARTH-ONE*, A COUPLE OF HEROES FACE THEIR *OWN* MUSIC--

PUT IT THERE, *ROBIN*--I OWE YOU AN *APOLOGY!*

SAME GOES FOR ME, *ROBIN!*

GUESS WE "OLD FOGIES" TEND TO IGNORE YOUR TRAINING, ENTHUSIASM....YOUR NEW PERSPECTIVES!

AW, COME OFF IT--I'VE BEEN WITH YOU LONG ENOUGH TO KNOW YOUR *EXPERIENCE* IS PROBABLY THE BEST TEACHER A GUY CAN HAVE!

AS EACH OF THE HEROES GOES HIS OWN WAY...

WELL, BACK TO MY INTERRUPTED CASE...AND MY ORIGINAL UNIFORM! FUNNY THING, THOUGH--I KINDA *LIKE* THIS ONE--I JUST MAY *KEEP* IT!

WHAT DO *YOU* THINK, READERS? WOULD YOU LIKE *ROBIN* TO SWITCH TO THIS NEW COSTUME? WRITE US--LET US KNOW!--*EDITOR.*

WONDER WHERE *BATMAN* IS? THIS MUST BE THE FIRST TIME HE WAS IN ON THE *BEGINNING* OF A *JUSTICE LEAGUE* CASE-- BUT NOT *THE END!*

THAT'S RIGHT, *ROBIN!* THIS IS NOT *THE END...*

21

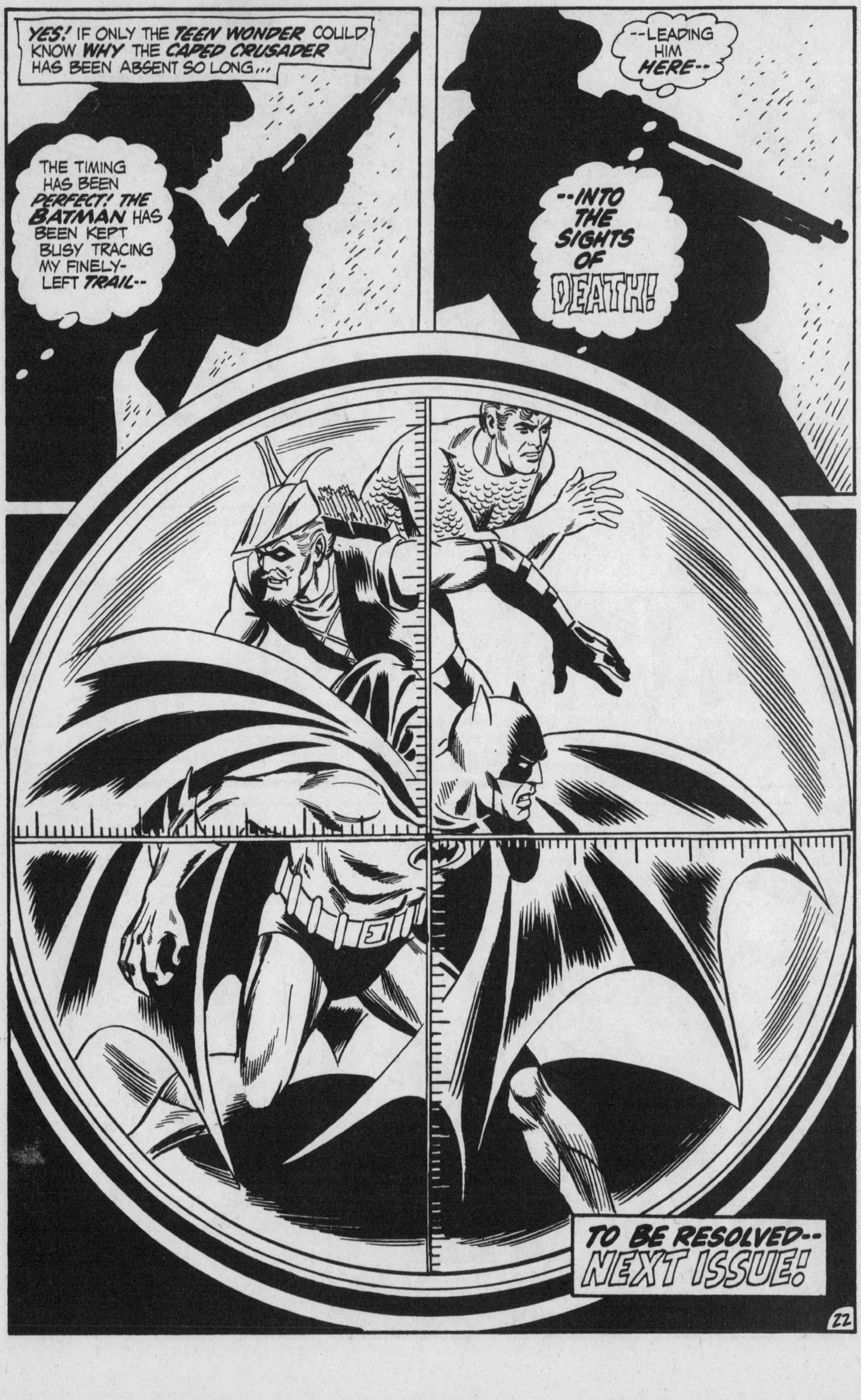
YES! IF ONLY THE TEEN WONDER COULD KNOW WHY THE CAPED CRUSADER HAS BEEN ABSENT SO LONG...
THE TIMING HAS BEEN PERFECT! THE BATMAN HAS BEEN KEPT BUSY TRACING MY FINELY-LEFT TRAIL--
--LEADING HIM HERE--
--INTO THE SIGHTS OF DEATH!
TO BE RESOLVED-- NEXT ISSUE!
22

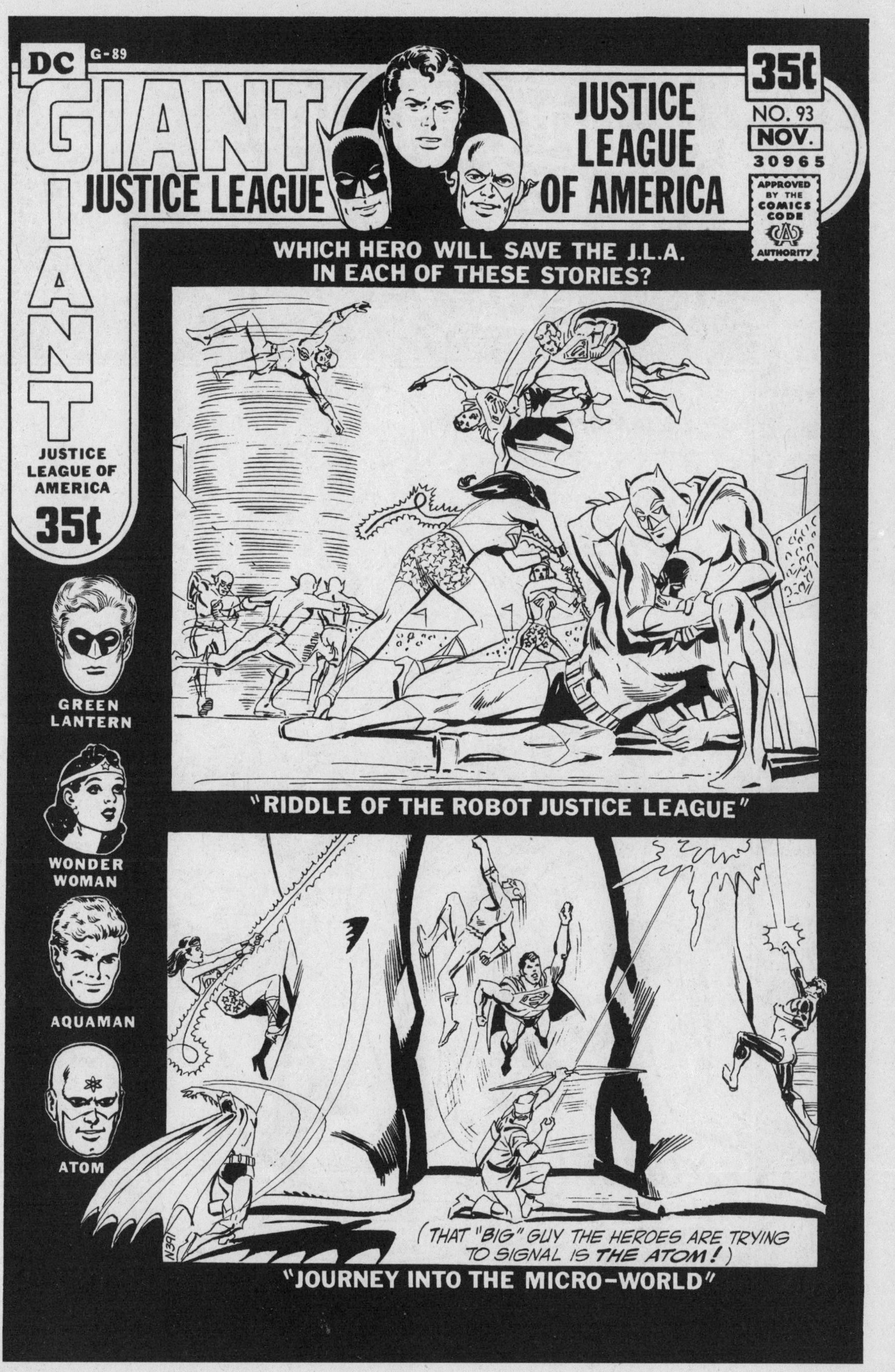
DC
G-89
GIANT
JUSTICE LEAGUE
JUSTICE LEAGUE OF AMERICA
35¢
NO. 93
NOV.
30965
APPROVED BY THE COMICS CODE AUTHORITY
GIANT
JUSTICE LEAGUE OF AMERICA
35¢
WHICH HERO WILL SAVE THE J.L.A. IN EACH OF THESE STORIES?
"RIDDLE OF THE ROBOT JUSTICE LEAGUE"
GREEN LANTERN
WONDER WOMAN
AQUAMAN
ATOM
(THAT "BIG" GUY THE HEROES ARE TRYING TO SIGNAL IS THE ATOM!)
"JOURNEY INTO THE MICRO-WORLD"

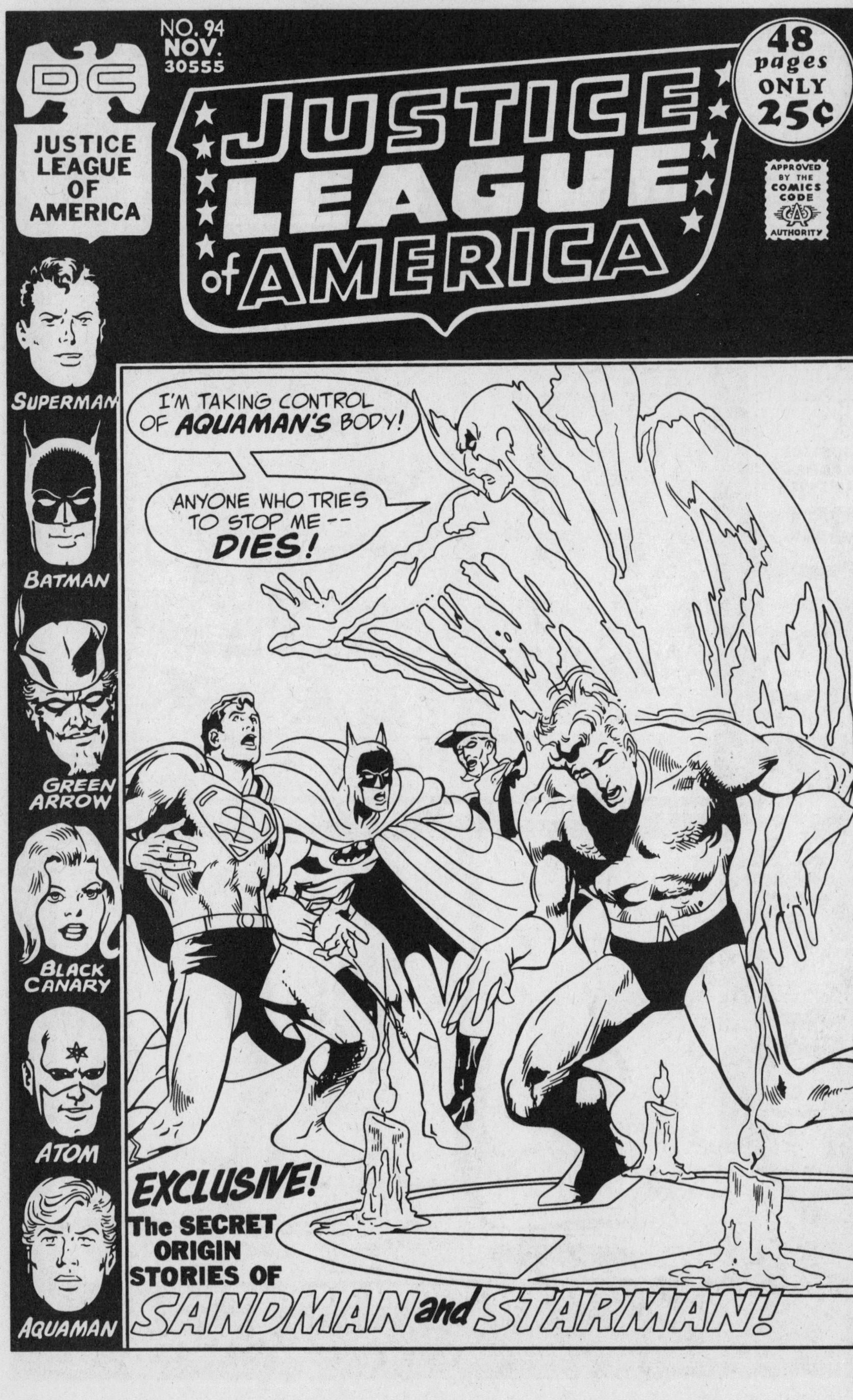
NO. 94
NOV.
30555
DC
JUSTICE LEAGUE OF AMERICA
JUSTICE LEAGUE of AMERICA
48 pages ONLY 25¢
APPROVED BY THE COMICS CODE AUTHORITY
SUPERMAN
BATMAN
GREEN ARROW
BLACK CANARY
ATOM
AQUAMAN
I'M TAKING CONTROL OF AQUAMAN'S BODY!
ANYONE WHO TRIES TO STOP ME -- DIES!
EXCLUSIVE!
The SECRET ORIGIN STORIES OF
SANDMAN and STARMAN!

A SIMPLE MAN... A SIMPLE FACE, HARDENED WITH EXPERIENCE, DRAINED OF FEELING. BUT LOOK CLOSELY *INTO* THIS MAN'S EYES-- THERE YOU'LL SEE A *MENACE* THREATENING THE VERY LIVES OF THE...

JUSTICE ☆☆☆ LEAGUE ☆☆☆ of AMERICA

LOOK EVER DEEPER--YOU WILL FIND A HINT OF *HATRED,* BURIED DEEP BENEATH YEARS OF TRAINED EMOTION-CONTROL.

IN THIS MAN'S PROFESSION, EVEN *HATRED* IS AN ILL-AFFORDED LUXURY--BUT A DANGEROUS ONE! FOR THIS MAN IS THE *SENSEI*... THE *TEACHER*... AND THE ART HE INSTRUCTS IS *ASSASSINATION!*

SPECIAL GUEST ARTIST NEAL ADAMS PAGES, 1, 5, 20, 22.

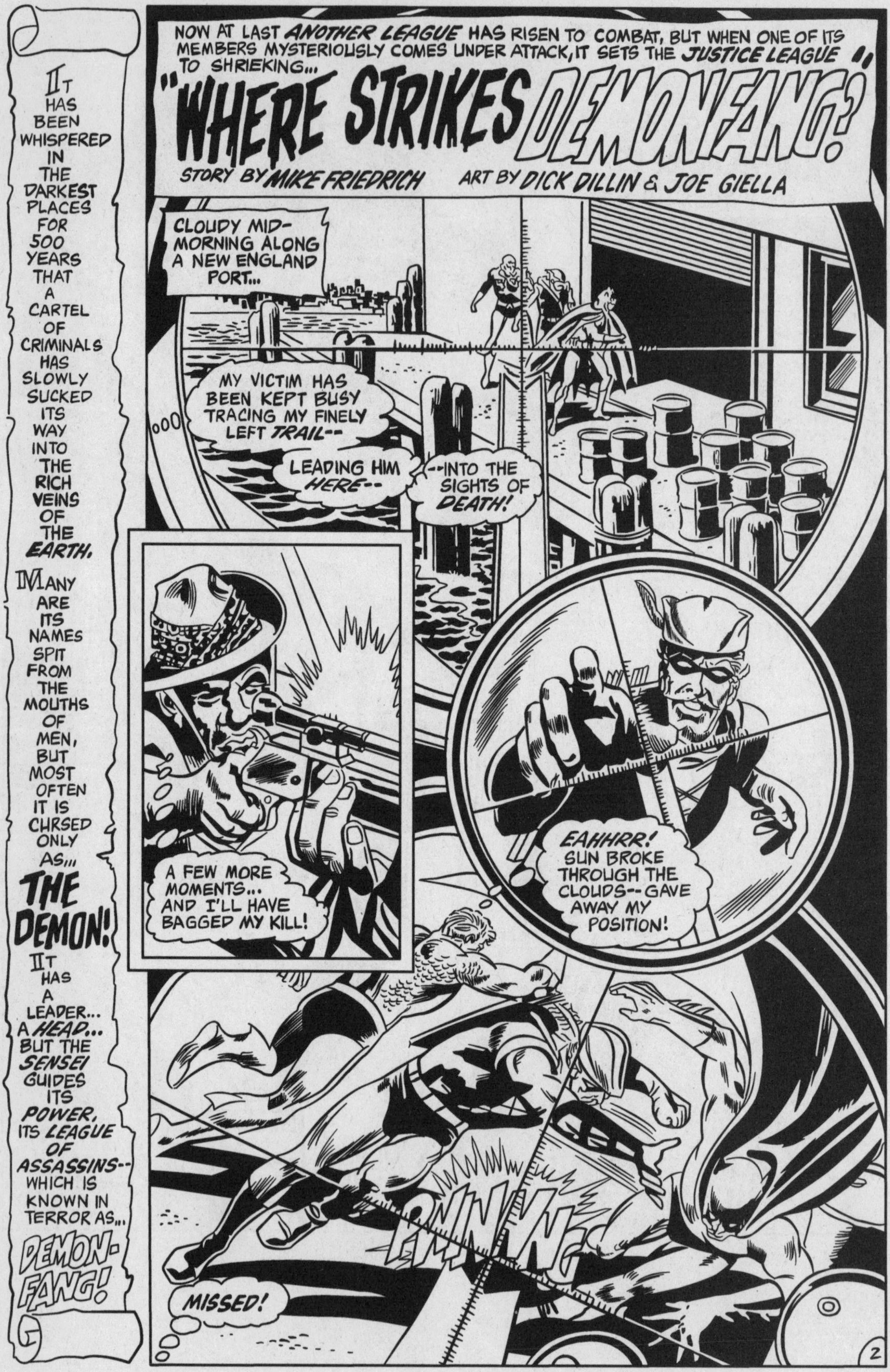
IT HAS BEEN WHISPERED IN THE DARKEST PLACES FOR 500 YEARS THAT A CARTEL OF CRIMINALS HAS SLOWLY SUCKED ITS WAY INTO THE RICH VEINS OF THE EARTH.
MANY ARE ITS NAMES SPIT FROM THE MOUTHS OF MEN, BUT MOST OFTEN IT IS CURSED ONLY AS... THE DEMON!
IT HAS A LEADER... A HEAD... BUT THE SENSEI GUIDES ITS POWER. ITS LEAGUE OF ASSASSINS-- WHICH IS KNOWN IN TERROR AS... DEMON-FANG!
NOW AT LAST ANOTHER LEAGUE HAS RISEN TO COMBAT, BUT WHEN ONE OF ITS MEMBERS MYSTERIOUSLY COMES UNDER ATTACK, IT SETS THE JUSTICE LEAGUE TO SHRIEKING...
"WHERE STRIKES DEMONFANG?"
STORY BY MIKE FRIEDRICH ART BY DICK DILLIN & JOE GIELLA
CLOUDY MID-MORNING ALONG A NEW ENGLAND PORT...
MY VICTIM HAS BEEN KEPT BUSY TRACING MY FINELY LEFT TRAIL--
LEADING HIM HERE--
--INTO THE SIGHTS OF DEATH!
A FEW MORE MOMENTS... AND I'LL HAVE BAGGED MY KILL!
EAHHRR! SUN BROKE THROUGH THE CLOUDS-- GAVE AWAY MY POSITION!
PWNNN
MISSED!
2

YOU HEAR NO WORDS AS THEY MOVE, ASSASSIN-- THESE MEN CALLED HEROES, SILENTLY WEIGHING THIS SUDDEN THREAT AGAINST THEIR DEADLY DANGERS OF THE PAST--

--AND DECIDING ON *INSTANT, DIRECT ACTION!*...

HEAD-ON THEY ATTACK *YOU,* ASSASSIN, WITHOUT A QUIVER OF FEAR...

THE *BATMAN* IS A *FOOL* TO COME DIRECTLY INTO MY SIGHTS!

BUT THEN THEIR *TEAMWORK* HITS YOU FULL-FORCE! *UNNERVING* ISN'T IT, ASSASSIN?

UHH... GUY'S *FAST!* CAUGHT ME OFF-BALANCE WITH THE RIFLE-BUTT-- LIKE BEING HIT WITH A *SLEDGE-HAMMER!*

3

'PEARS *BATS* NEEDS A HAND *HANGING ON* TO THAT KILLER!

MISERABLE ANGLE TO SHOOT FROM--

BUT AS A KID I WASN'T THE BEST *SPITBALL-THROWER* FOR *NOTHIN'!*

I BELIEVE YOU AMERICANS CALL THIS A *"RIP-OFF"--!*

AS A THREAT TO OUR LIVES, YOU'RE A DANGEROUS FELLOW, BUT AS A *COMEDIAN--*

--YOU'RE *ALL WET--* AS...ER... *ROBIN* WOULD SAY!

I BETTER GET IN THE DRINK AND GRAB THAT ROTTEN FISH!

ALL RIGHT, BUSTER-- *TALK!* ARE *YOU* THE GUY WHO'S GIVEN US THE RUN-AROUND *ALL WEEK? TALK...* OR...

YOU ARE NO MORE THAN THE FLEA ON THE BACK OF THE LION TO ME--DO NOT WASTE YOUR TIME WITH MEANINGLESS THREATS!

M'NAKU CONGRATULATES YOU, *BATMAN* AND *GREEN ARROW--* YOU ARE THE FIRST VICTIMS I HAVE FAILED TO KILL!

OTHER THAN THAT, I SAY *NOTHING!*

I DON'T KNOW WHETHER TO BE FLATTERED-- OR *INSULTED!*

LEAVE HIM BE, *AQUAMAN!* WE'RE NOT GONNA FIND OUT ANYTHING FROM *HIM!*

BESIDES, MY INSTINCTS TELL ME WE'RE DEALING WITH SOMETHING *BIGGER* THAN ONE KILLER-- MUCH BIGGER!

4

IN A BAND OF CUTTHROATS, *INFORMATION* IS THE FIRST ORDER OF *SURVIVAL!* WHEN YOU'RE AT THE *TOP* YOU LEARN IT *FIRST!*

M'NAKU FAILED ME--THE THIRD ONE NOT TO EXACT MY *REVENGE!* THIS IS WHY I HAVE CALLED UPON *YOU, MERLYN!*

MIGHT NOT THIS ASSASSINATION GO ILL WITH THE *DEMON'S HEAD?* HE HOLDS THE WOULD-BE VICTIM IN HIS FAVOR!

HE IS ALREADY QUITE *SUSPICIOUS* OF OUR *LEAGUE* SINCE *DR. DARRK* TRIED TO KIDNAP HIS DAUGHTER!⁕

DARRK'S DISPUTE WITH *THE HEAD* WAS HIS *OWN* MISTAKE! THE DOCTOR *PAID*--WITH HIS *LIFE!* I DO NOT FEAR *THE LEADER*--IT IS HE WHO SHOULD FEAR ME-- FOR AM I NOT THE POWERFUL *FANG* WHICH PROTECTS HIS *HEAD?*

⁕ EDITORS NOTE! SEE *DETECTIVE COMICS* #411.

BUT ENOUGH OF THIS. DO YOU *HESITATE?*

YOU, THE WORLD'S BEST ARCHER--DO YOU NOT *WISH* TO CROSS BOWS WITH THIS *GREEN ARROW?*

THE OTHER *JUSTICE LEAGUERS* WILL NOT INTERFERE--THEY ARE EACH INVOLVED IN PERSONAL CASES--SAVE *SUPERMAN* AND *THE ATOM!* OUR *WEAPONS* EXPERTS HAVE DEVELOPED EXCELLENT HARDWARE TO USE SHOULD THEY CROSS YOUR PATH!

AH MASTER, YOU MIS- UNDERSTAND-- I *RELISH* THE HONOR OF TRACKING THIS VICTIM! SOME SAY IT WILL TAKE *MAGIC*, BUT IS IT FOR NOTHING THAT I AM CALLED *"THE MAGICIAN"?*

NOW GO--MAY YOUR BLOOD BE THE LAST DRAWN!

MOST GRACIOUS THANKS, SENSEI!

AS THE TWO SEPARATE, THE WALLS STILL FAINTLY ECHO THE NAME "*GREEN ARROW*"! IS IT HE WHO IS THE TARGET OF THE *LEAGUE OF ASSASSINS?*

⑤

PERHAPS-- AND PERHAPS *NOT*.' SHORTLY AFTER, AT CLARK (SUPERMAN) KENT'S DESK IN THE TV NEWS OFFICES OF THE *GALAXY BROADCASTING SYSTEM*...

NOTE FROM *IRIS ALLEN*--SAYS HER HUSBAND *THE FLASH* IS RECOVERING FROM HIS WOUNDS-- GOOD!

BUT STILL NO WORD FROM *BATMAN* OR *GREEN ARROW* ON THEIR *EMERGENCY* CALL FROM *AQUAMAN!*

KENT, COME IN HERE-- I'VE GOT A NEW ASSIGNMENT FOR YOU!

BE RIGHT WITH YOU, MR. EDGE!

MOMENTS LATER, AS CLARK LEAVES, A SLY SMILE CREEPS ONTO THE FACE OF HIS BOSS...

AND BE *SURE* TO ALERT *SUPERMAN* THAT YOU'RE COMING!

AS REGULAR *DC* READERS KNOW, *MORGAN EDGE* IS SECRETLY A MEMBER OF *INTER-GANG,* AN ARCH-CRIMINAL GROUP EMPLOYED BY THE WARLORD *DARKSEID* IN HIS BATTLE AGAINST *EARTH!* COULD IT BE THAT *INTER-GANG* HAS STRUCK AN UNHOLY ALLIANCE WITH **DEMONFANG?**

SOON -- *CLARK'S* SPECIALLY EQUIPPED *TV-VAN* TAKES TO THE ROAD--

--ALONG WITH A *SPECIAL PASSENGER...* MORGAN EDGE HAS ASSIGNED ME TO DO A DOCUMENTARY ON POLLUTION CONTROL, *ATOM!* I BROUGHT YOU ALONG BECAUSE THE AREA I'M *TV-TAPING* IS NEAR WHERE WE LAST HEARD FROM *BATMAN, GA* AND *AQUAMAN*--

--*DOWN THERE* IN *PORT-TOWN!*

WHILE YOU'RE *WORKING, CLARK,* I'LL DO SOME *SNOOPING!*

HEYY-- WE'RE BEING *ATTACKED!*

POOPH

POOPH

6

--THERE'S THE CLOWN--UP ON THAT HILL!

IF THIS IS MEANT TO BE A *JOKE, SUPERMAN'S* GOING TO TOP IT!

EXITING THROUGH HIS SPECIAL TRAP-DOOR...

TO PROTECT *CLARK'S* IDENTITY, I'LL *TUNNEL* SOME DISTANCE AWAY... AND *FLY* IN FROM A DIFFERENT DIRECTION!

BUT THIS IS NO *ORDINARY PRANKSTER,* EASILY OVERWHELMED BY THE *EXTRAORDINARY* SIGHT OF A *SUPERMAN...*

AH, *SUPERMAN* AND *ATOM TOGETHER*-- HOW CONVENIENT!

I WAS *ADVISED* THAT ATTACKING THE TV-VAN WOULD BRING *ACTION!*

THE *WEAPONS MASTERS* SAID THEY HAD FUN WITH THESE LITTLE NUMBERS...

UNNHH...

AH, THEIR NEW METAL IS DESIGNED TO *HURT SUPERMAN*... NOT TO *KILL!*

7

WAFTING IN ON THE BREEZING AIR CURRENTS...

I DON'T KNOW HOW THAT SECOND-RATE *ROBIN HOOD* RACKED UP *SUPERMAN*--

BUT LET'S SEE HOW *HE* TAKES MY PATENTED *ATOM-IC* PUNCH!

AH--THE MARK OF A GREAT ARCHER IS KNOWING WHEN NOT TO SHOOT! SUCH IS *THIS* TIME...

THIS IS MY *OWN* INVENTION--

--AND RATHER *SUCCESSFUL!*

WHOOOOOORRRR

SOUND FROM THE *ARROWHEAD*-- PIERCING MY SKULL LIKE STABBING DARTS!

CAN'T FOCUS--!

8

THAT ULTRA-SOUND CAN'T AFFECT *ME*--AND I'M DE-TERMINED TO GET TO THE BOTTOM OF THIS MYSTERY--*FAST!*

AH, *SUPERMAN'S* ABILITY TO BOUNCE BACK INTO ACTION IS QUITE REMARKABLE!

I'LL HAVE TO RESORT TO SOME-THING ELSE FROM THE GENIUSES IN *WEAPONS!* THEY'VE GOT QUITE A RECORD--

--AND WHO AM *I* TO ARGUE WITH *RESULTS?*

ALL OF A SUDDEN I FEEL LIKE I WEIGH A *TON*--

CAN'T PULL THE ARROW OFF MY UNIFORM! IT'S *STUCK FAST!*

POWERLESS TO STOP MYSELF FROM *CRASH-LANDING!*

IT'S ALL I CAN DO TO STOP MYSELF FROM SINKING CLEAR *INTO* THE EARTH!

'CASE YOU'RE WONDERING, *SUPERMAN*--MY DEVICE IS INCREASING THE EFFECT OF *GRAVITY* ON YOU TO OVERWHELMING PROPORTIONS!

AH, I MUST COMPLIMENT *WEAPONS* ON THEIR INGENUITY-- NOT MANY HAVE STOPPED THE *MAN OF STEEL* SO SWIFTLY AND EASILY AS I!

SUPERMAN... *ATOM*... YOU SHOULD FEEL GRATEFUL THAT I WAS ASSIGNED ONLY TO *STOP* YOU FROM INTERFERING... AND *NOT* TO *KILL!*-- OR MOST ASSUREDLY YOU'D BE *DEAD!*

I ASSURE YOU BOTH-- YOU ARE HELPLESS TO SAVE YOUR *JUSTICE LEAGUE* COMRADE FROM MY MASTER DEATH-STROKE!

AND SHOULD MY DEVICES CAUSE YOU TO *DIE* ANYWAY--

AH--SO BE IT!

10

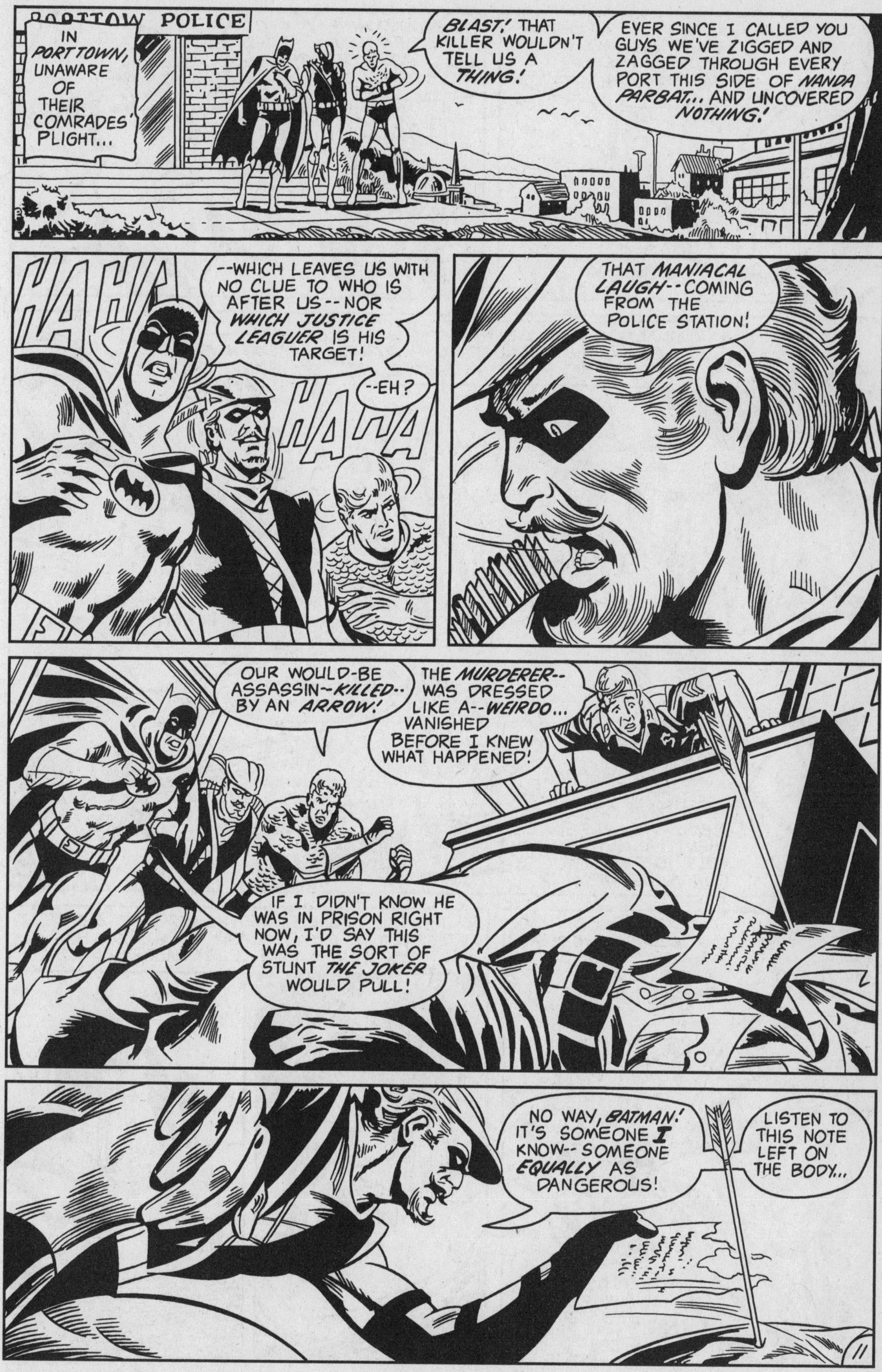
PORTTOW POLICE
IN PORTTOWN, UNAWARE OF THEIR COMRADES' PLIGHT...
BLAST! THAT KILLER WOULDN'T TELL US A THING!
EVER SINCE I CALLED YOU GUYS WE'VE ZIGGED AND ZAGGED THROUGH EVERY PORT THIS SIDE OF NANDA PARBAT... AND UNCOVERED NOTHING!
HAHA
--WHICH LEAVES US WITH NO CLUE TO WHO IS AFTER US--NOR WHICH JUSTICE LEAGUER IS HIS TARGET!
--EH?
HAHA
THAT MANIACAL LAUGH--COMING FROM THE POLICE STATION!
OUR WOULD-BE ASSASSIN--KILLED--BY AN ARROW!
THE MURDERER--WAS DRESSED LIKE A--WEIRDO... VANISHED BEFORE I KNEW WHAT HAPPENED!
IF I DIDN'T KNOW HE WAS IN PRISON RIGHT NOW, I'D SAY THIS WAS THE SORT OF STUNT THE JOKER WOULD PULL!
NO WAY, BATMAN! IT'S SOMEONE I KNOW--SOMEONE EQUALLY AS DANGEROUS!
LISTEN TO THIS NOTE LEFT ON THE BODY...
11

"THE PRICE OF FAILURE IN THE *LEAGUE OF ASSASSINS* IS *DEATH!* BEWARE--THE PRICE OF *SUCCESS* IS THE *SAME!* (SIGNED) MERLYN, MAGICIAN"

WE SHOULD HAVE KNOWN, *BATMAN*-- THE *LEAGUE OF ASSASSINS!*

WHO *IS* THIS MERLYN, GA?

"WHEN I WAS A KID, I SAW THIS YOUNG FELLOW AT A CIRCUS SHOOT ARROWS *BLINDFOLDED!* I MEAN... THAT DUDE WAS *EAGLE-EYED!*"

"I'VE NEVER FORGOTTEN HIM... *NEVER.*"

"JUST AFTER I ASSUMED MY ORIGINAL *GREEN ARROW* IDENTITY, I FELL FOR A PUBLICITY STUNT AND ACCEPTED MERLYN'S *CHALLENGE* TO A MATCH..."

"HE *WIPED* ME OUT! I NEVER FORGOT *THAT* EITHER!"

SOON AFTER, *MERLYN* DROPPED OUT OF SIGHT! THOUGH I'VE DEVELOPED MY *ARCHERY SKILLS* SINCE THEN, I'VE NEVER BEEN ABLE TO FIND HIM FOR A *REMATCH!*

NOW, IRONICALLY, I'VE GOT MY *CHANCE*--WITH MY *LIFE* AT STAKE!

THAT'S ENOUGH REMINISCING, *GREEN ARROW!* LET'S GET AFTER *MERLYN* BEFORE HIS TRAIL GETS COLD!

DO *YOU* HAVE ENOUGH *TIME,* AQUAMAN?

YEAH, *SURE*... UH... WHY *NOT?* LET'S GO!

TO THE SKILLFUL EYES OF THE *WORLD'S GREATEST DETECTIVE,* THE MINUTES AND MILES FLOW BY UNNOTICED IN THE WAKE OF UNCOVERED CLUES...

12

...UNTIL A HOUSE LOOMS ON A HILL...

EYES ALERT, FELLAS --THAT TRAIL WAS A BIT *TOO EASY* TO PICK UP!

UH-HUH...THE SMELL OF A *TRAP* IS STRONGER THAN *UNWASHED CIRCUS-TIGER CAGES!*

AS THEY CLOSE IN ON THE HOUSE...

AN ELECTRONIC BEAM IS TRIPPED...

WELCOME

...AN *AUTOMATIC* BOW! INGENIOUS! WONDER WHAT *OTHER* HIDDEN WEAPONS THIS *MONSTROUS* MANSION HOLDS FOR US?

WELCOME-- TO WHAT? NOBODY SEEMS TO BE INSIDE!

AQUAMAN'S RIGHT-- SOME-THING'S STINKY HERE!

JUST THEN...

UH... GETTING DIZZY...

AQUAMAN'S OUT COLD! STIFF AS A...*DEAD MACKEREL!*

13

MEANWHILE, JUST A FEW SHORT MILES AWAY...

MY ENERGY'S DRAINING FAST--IT'S LIKE TRYING TO PUSH AGAINST THE *ENTIRE EARTH!*

AT LAST! SMASHED THIS TING-A-LING THING...

...IN TIME TO HELP *SUPES,* I HOPE...!

:UHH: CAN'T PULL THE ARROW OFF--!

WAIT--! GOT A WILD IDEA! I'M THE ONLY *LIVING THING* THAT CAN SAFELY GROW AND *SHRINK--*

BUT BY WRAPPING MY *SIZE-CONTROL BELT* AROUND THE ARROW, I CAN ENLARGE IT... TILL IT *EXPLODES!*

SUPERMAN..., IT'LL MAKE YOUR PROBLEM WORSE--TEMPORARILY...

GO...AHEAD, *ATOM!* *ANYTHING'S* BETTER THAN...WHAT I'M... GOING THROUGH...

IT HAS BEEN SAID THAT A MAN IS MEASURED BY THE AMOUNT OF *PAIN* HE FEELS...AND YET SURVIVES...

BEHOLD A MAN WHO IS BEARING UP UNDER THE *OVERWHELMING WEIGHT OF A WORLD!*

14

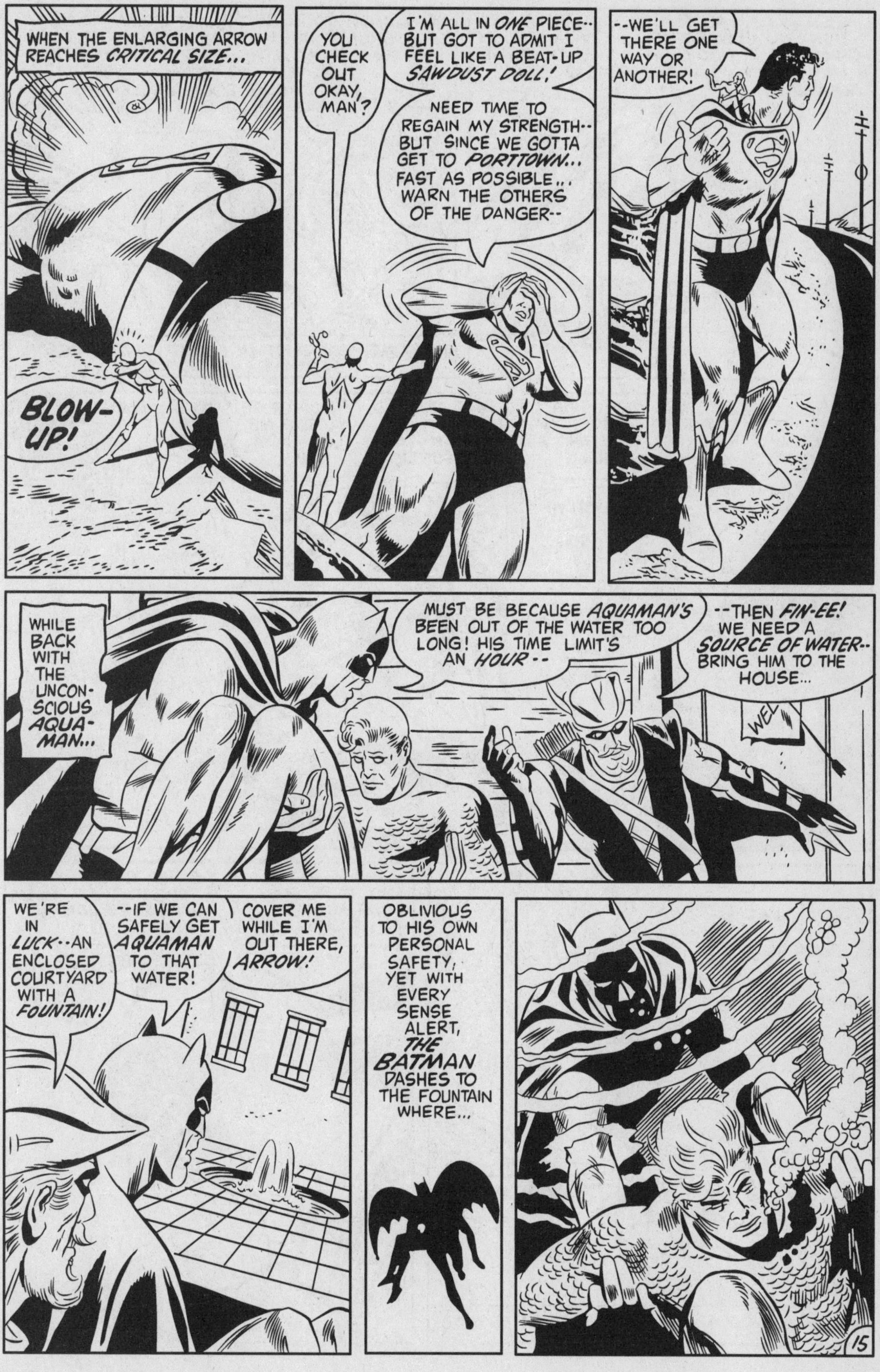
WHEN THE ENLARGING ARROW REACHES CRITICAL SIZE...
BLOW-UP!
YOU CHECK OUT OKAY, MAN?
I'M ALL IN ONE PIECE-- BUT GOT TO ADMIT I FEEL LIKE A BEAT-UP SAWDUST DOLL!
NEED TIME TO REGAIN MY STRENGTH-- BUT SINCE WE GOTTA GET TO PORTTOWN... FAST AS POSSIBLE... WARN THE OTHERS OF THE DANGER--
--WE'LL GET THERE ONE WAY OR ANOTHER!
WHILE BACK WITH THE UNCONSCIOUS AQUAMAN...
MUST BE BECAUSE AQUAMAN'S BEEN OUT OF THE WATER TOO LONG! HIS TIME LIMIT'S AN HOUR--
--THEN FIN-EE! WE NEED A SOURCE OF WATER-- BRING HIM TO THE HOUSE...
WE'RE IN LUCK--AN ENCLOSED COURTYARD WITH A FOUNTAIN!
--IF WE CAN SAFELY GET AQUAMAN TO THAT WATER!
COVER ME WHILE I'M OUT THERE, ARROW!
OBLIVIOUS TO HIS OWN PERSONAL SAFETY, YET WITH EVERY SENSE ALERT, THE BATMAN DASHES TO THE FOUNTAIN WHERE...
15

WHEN THE CRUSADER LIFTS AQUAMAN OUT OF THE "DRINK"...

I'M ALL RIGHT NOW, BATMAN... LET GO OF ME--

NO, SIR--YOU'RE GONNA STAY PUT TILL YOU ANSWER SOME QUESTIONS!

FIRST-- WHO ARE YOU?

AQUAMAN, OF COURSE! WHY ASK SUCH A SILLY--

YOU GAVE YOURSELF AWAY WHEN YOU MENTIONED NANDA PARBAT! ONLY TWO GOOD MEN HAVE BEEN TO THAT SHANGRI-LA--ONE'S IN A CIRCUS 2000 MILES AWAY, WHILE THE OTHER'S A DEAD MAN!*

*EDITOR'S NOTE: BATMAN ENTERED NANDA PARBAT IN BRAVE AND BOLD #86!

BUT WHEN YOU SHOWED YOU WERE UNAWARE OF AQUAMAN'S TIME-LIMIT, I WAS SURE YOU--WHOEVER-YOU-ARE--HAD SOMEHOW TAKEN OVER HIS MIND!

I SUSPECT YOU SET UP THIS WHOLE SCHEME!

NO! YOU'VE GOT IT ALL WRONG, BATMAN--

WHAT'S THAT--?

AR RR R

GA'S TRAPPED INSIDE THAT VACUUM-TUBE-- HE'LL SUFFOCATE!

IRON GRATE CUTTING ME OFF FROM HIM!

MY BATARANG... MAYBE IT CAN--

NO-- BATARANG CAN'T CRACK IT!

HAS THE LEAGUE OF ASSASSINS AT LAST SNARED ITS VICTIM?

NOT IF BATMAN HAS ANYTHING TO DO ABOUT IT...

IF THE TUBE WON'T COME TO THE BATMAN, THEN THE BATMAN MUST GO TO THE TUBE--OVER ANY OBSTACLE!

16

BUT NOW WE MUST MAKE A MADDENING SWITCH TO A PAIR OF HITCH-HIKING HEROES...

SO I SEZ TO THE MISSUS, "JUST 'CUZ THIS GUY'S YOUR *BROTHER* DON'T MEAN NUTHIN'!.." SHE SEZ...

I CAN FEEL MY POWERS COMING BACK! GOT MY *TELESCOPIC VISION* IN WORKING ORDER NOW...

HOPE TO SPOT OUR COMRADES BEFORE THIS CHATTERBOX TALKS OUR EARS OFF!

THEN...

UH-OH--I ALMOST WISH I *DIDN'T* SEE THIS--!

C'MON, LITTLE BUDDY-- WE'VE GOT A *RESCUING ACT* TO GO INTO!

ONLY CAN FLY IN "*LOW GEAR*", ATOM-- BUT I *CAN* PUT ENOUGH OF A *SUPER-PITCHING ARM* BEHIND YOU TO DO THE JOB!

SWIFTER THAN ANYTHING FAST-BALLER *VIDA BLUE* EVER PITCHED, SPEEDS THE *ATOM*-IC MISSILE...

UNTIL...LIKE AN ERRANT SANDLOT HOME RUN...THE SOUND OF SHATTERED GLASS IS HEARD...

--AND A *JUSTICE LEAGUER* IS SAVED!

17

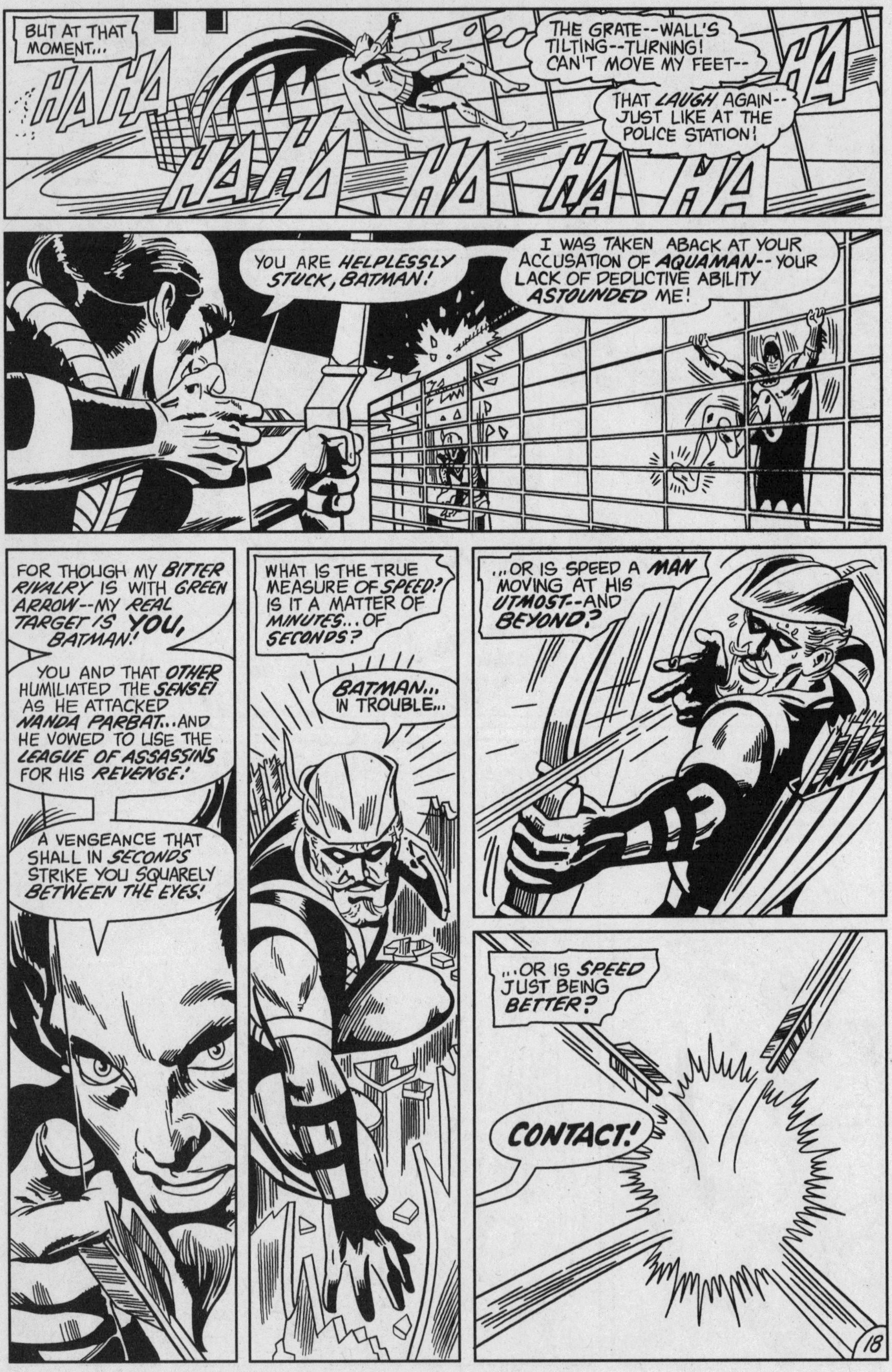
BUT AT THAT MOMENT...
HA HA
THE GRATE--WALL'S TILTING--TURNING! CAN'T MOVE MY FEET--
HA
THAT LAUGH AGAIN-- JUST LIKE AT THE POLICE STATION!
HA HA HA HA HA
YOU ARE HELPLESSLY STUCK, BATMAN!
I WAS TAKEN ABACK AT YOUR ACCUSATION OF AQUAMAN-- YOUR LACK OF DEDUCTIVE ABILITY ASTOUNDED ME!
FOR THOUGH MY BITTER RIVALRY IS WITH GREEN ARROW--MY REAL TARGET IS YOU, BATMAN!
YOU AND THAT OTHER HUMILIATED THE SENSEI AS HE ATTACKED NANDA PARBAT...AND HE VOWED TO USE THE LEAGUE OF ASSASSINS FOR HIS REVENGE!
A VENGEANCE THAT SHALL IN SECONDS STRIKE YOU SQUARELY BETWEEN THE EYES!
WHAT IS THE TRUE MEASURE OF SPEED? IS IT A MATTER OF MINUTES... OF SECONDS?
BATMAN... IN TROUBLE...
...OR IS SPEED A MAN MOVING AT HIS UTMOST--AND BEYOND?
...OR IS SPEED JUST BEING BETTER?
CONTACT!
18

PHENOMENAL SHOT, GREEN ARROW--I SALUTE YOU! AFTER ALL THESE YEARS YOU HAVE AT LAST *BESTED* ME!

DON'T SWEET-TALK ME, GUY! GET THOSE MITTS *UP--* FAST!

YOU DO NOT REALIZE THAT BY FAILING TO MAKE MY KILL, I CAN NEVER RETURN TO THE ORGANIZATION--

THE PRICE OF FAILURE IN THE *LEAGUE OF ASSASSINS* IS... *DEATH!*

BUT AS I LAUNCH *MYSELF* AS AN ARROW, I WARN YOU, *GREEN ARROW--*

I WILL RETURN-- FOR YOUR *HEAD!*

ROCKETING OUT OF RANGE!

SHORTLY...

MERLYN MUST'VE DISGUISED HIMSELF EVEN AS HE GOT AWAY! I COULDN'T LOCATE HIM!

AS FAR AS I'M CONCERNED, THAT WRAPS UP *THIS* CASE...FOR NOW! IT'S TIME FOR US TO RETURN *HOME!*

WHILE THEY *LEAVE,* YOU AND I *RAP..* OKAY, *AQUAMAN?*

CHECK.! GUESS I COULDN'T EXPECT TO FAKE *YOU* OUT FOR LONG... 'BOUT WHO I *REALLY* AM!

19

EPILOGUE

WHY *AQUAMAN'S* BODY?

HE WAS THE FIRST *JUSTICE LEAGUER* I COULD FIND!

WHY CALL ON *US?*

'CAUSE YOU'RE THE *WORLDS GREATEST DETECTIVE!*

AND?

AND... *I* COULDN'T DEDUCE WHO THE *SENSEI'S* TARGET WAS!

WHY NOT JUST *TELL* US WHO YOU ARE?

YOUR MIND RACES AS FAST AS YOUR FRIEND'S *BATMOBILE,* STREAKING TOWARD THE SEA...

'CAUSE I LIKE DOIN' THINGS *MYSELF!*

RAMA KUSHNA TOLD ME A *JLA* ASSASSINATION WAS BEING PLANNED THAT WOULD UPSET THE DELICATE BALANCE OF THE WORLD!

I THOUGHT IT MIGHT BE *SUPERMAN* OR *GREEN LANTERN*--BUT IT WAS *YOU!* THAT LEAVES *ME* UP THE CREEK--SO I THINK I'LL JUST *SPLIT* AND *START OVER!*

YES, IT'S TIME FOR YOU TO RETURN TO *NORMAL*-- IF BEING A *GHOST* CAN BE CALLED *NORMAL...DEADMAN!*

BEFORE I GO... TRY *THIS* NAME ON FOR SIZE... *RĀ'S AL GHŪL!* HOW IS HE *CONNECTED* WITH THE *SENSEI?*

HE'S THE *HEAD* OF THE WORLD'S *CRIME* STRUCTURE-- AND IF HE GETS CROSSED, THE WHOLE *PLANET* MIGHT BLOW UP--

CRAZY! SO WHAT ELSE IS *NEW?*

HUH ?-- WHATS GOING ON?

20

BUT AS ONE ADVENTURE DRAWS TO A CRYPTIC CLOSE, ANOTHER BEGINS... THIS TIME IN THE *JLA* SATELLITE HEADQUARTERS, CIRCLING 22,300 MILES ABOVE EARTH...

OUR INSTRUMENTS ARE GOING HAYWIRE! SOMETHING'S UPSETTING OUR NEW *TELEPORT MACHINE!*

I'D BEST SEND OUT AN *ALARM SIGNAL* TO THOSE WHO CAN *HELP!*

SHORTLY, HIDDEN ON THE SKYSCRAPER ROOF OF A CERTAIN CELEBRATED PUBLISHING FIRM...

WE'RE THE FIRST TO ARRIVE-- THE OTHERS MUST STILL BE ON THEIR WAY!

THE *NEW THANAGARIAN TRANSPORTER* WILL HOLD A *LARGER NUMBER* NOW!

I'LL *FLY* ON UP AND SEE IF THERE'S ANY *SPACE* OBJECT INTERFERING WITH ITS TRANSMISSION!

GL, FLASH AND HAWKMAN SHOULD BE BEAMING IN ANY SECOND...

THEN...

SUPERMAN! IT--IT'S HORRIBLE!

WHAT'S WRONG? FLASH AND THE OTHERS...?

THEY DIDN'T ARRIVE! FOR ALL WE KNOW THEY ARE SCATTERED ALL OVER THE UNIVERSE-- *DEAD!*

WHEREUPON WE DRAW A MERCIFUL CURTAIN ON THIS TRAGIC SCENE UNTIL THE *NEXT* ISSUE--

21

AS WE NOW SHIFT OUR SIGHTS SEAWARD, WHERE --

IT'S A LONG STORY, AQUAMAN...

WHAT HAPPENED, BATMAN? I FEEL LIKE A BIG BLANK HAS BEEN TAKEN OUT OF MY LIFE!

...THAT STARTED WHEN A GUY GOT GUNNED DOWN PERFORMING AT A CIRCUS -- ONLY HIS GHOST CAME BACK TO UNCOVER THE BIGGEST DEN OF ASSASSINS THIS WORLD'S EVER KNOWN! REMIND ME TO TELL YOU ABOUT IT SOME DAY!

SURE, BATMAN -- BE COOL -- BUT DON'T KID YOURSELF! YOU KNOW DARN WELL THAT IF RĀ'S AL GHŪL AND THE SENSEI MIX IT, THERE'LL BE HELL TO PAY...

...AND IT JUST MIGHT EASILY BE OVER YOUR DEAD BODY!

LOOK ONCE MORE INTO THE EYES OF THIS MAN! THE FLAME OF HATRED BURNS BRIGHTER THIS DAY...

THE BATMAN HAS ESCAPED MY REVENGE -- BUT ONLY WITH THE AID OF HIS COMRADES!

NEXT TIME I SHALL ISOLATE HIM -- AND STRIKE!

IF THE DEMON'S HEAD -- RĀ'S AL GHŪL -- OBJECTS, LET HIM FACE MY POWER -- FOR IN THE END, DEMONFANG NEVER FAILS!

THE END

THE SHAPE OF COSMIC-SIZE CLASHES IS FORMING! FOLLOW THE EXCITING DEVELOPMENTS IN FORTHCOMING ISSUES OF BATMAN AND DETECTIVE COMICS, AS WE FEARFULLY WONDER -- WHERE NEXT STRIKES DEMONFANG?

22

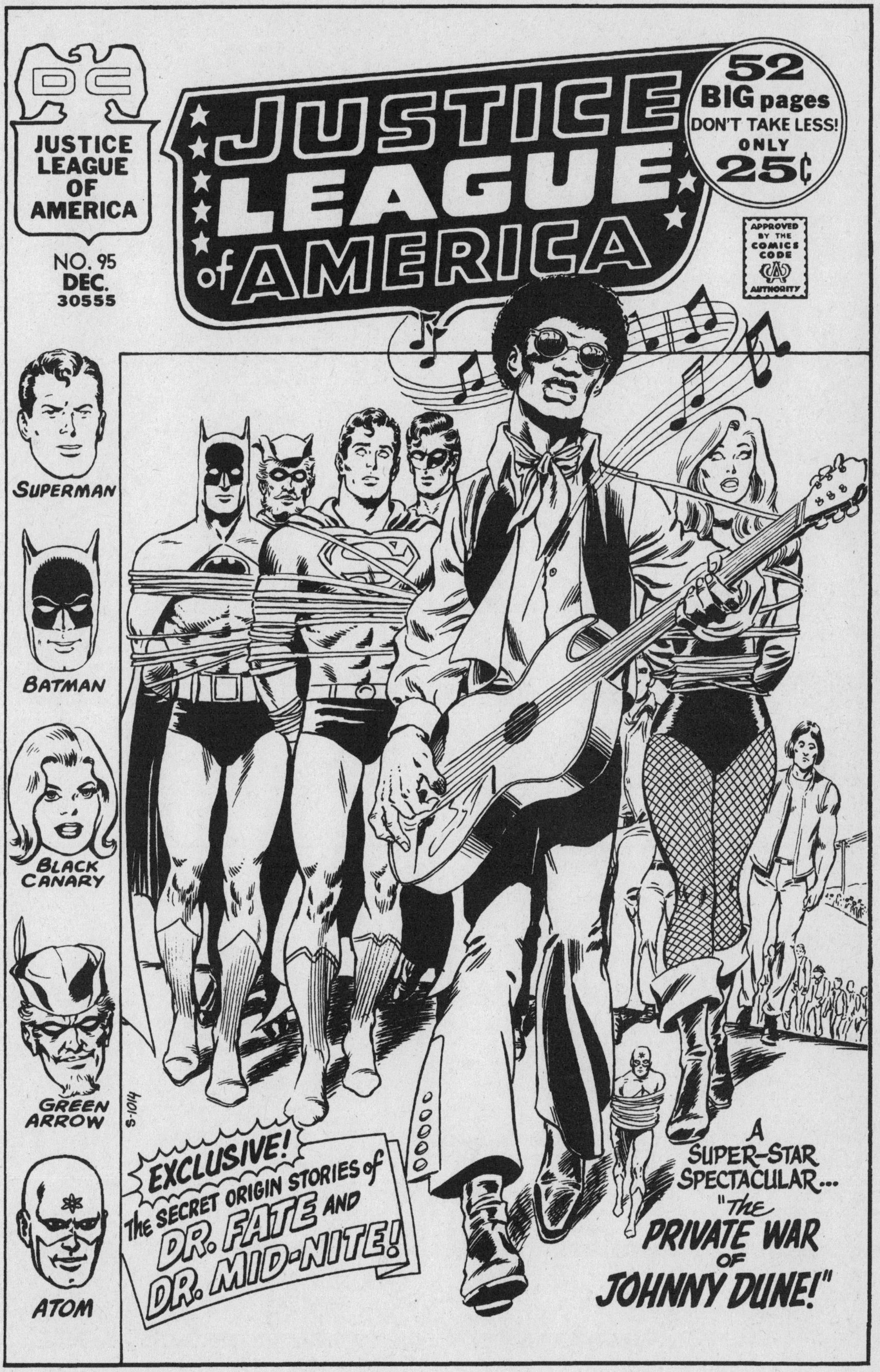
DC
JUSTICE LEAGUE OF AMERICA
NO. 95
DEC.
30555
JUSTICE LEAGUE of AMERICA
52 BIG pages
DON'T TAKE LESS!
ONLY 25¢
APPROVED BY THE COMICS CODE AUTHORITY
SUPERMAN
BATMAN
BLACK CANARY
GREEN ARROW
ATOM
S-1014
EXCLUSIVE!
The SECRET ORIGIN STORIES of DR. FATE AND DR. MID-NITE!
A SUPER-STAR SPECTACULAR...
"The PRIVATE WAR OF JOHNNY DUNE!"

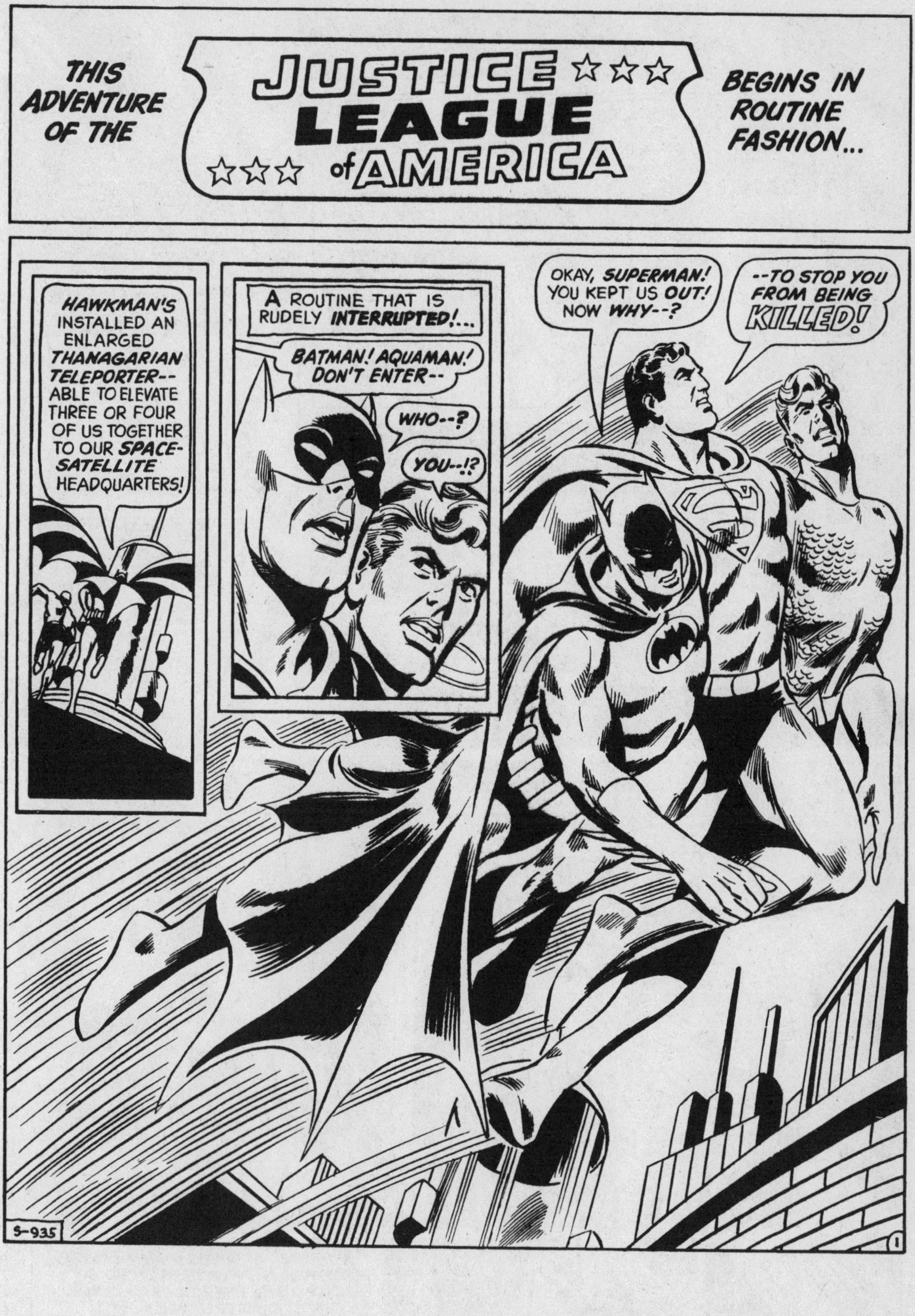
THIS ADVENTURE OF THE
JUSTICE LEAGUE of AMERICA
BEGINS IN ROUTINE FASHION...
HAWKMAN'S INSTALLED AN ENLARGED THANAGARIAN TELEPORTER-- ABLE TO ELEVATE THREE OR FOUR OF US TOGETHER TO OUR SPACE-SATELLITE HEADQUARTERS!
A ROUTINE THAT IS RUDELY INTERRUPTED!...
BATMAN! AQUAMAN! DON'T ENTER--
WHO--?
YOU--!?
OKAY, SUPERMAN! YOU KEPT US OUT! NOW WHY--?
--TO STOP YOU FROM BEING KILLED!
S-935
1

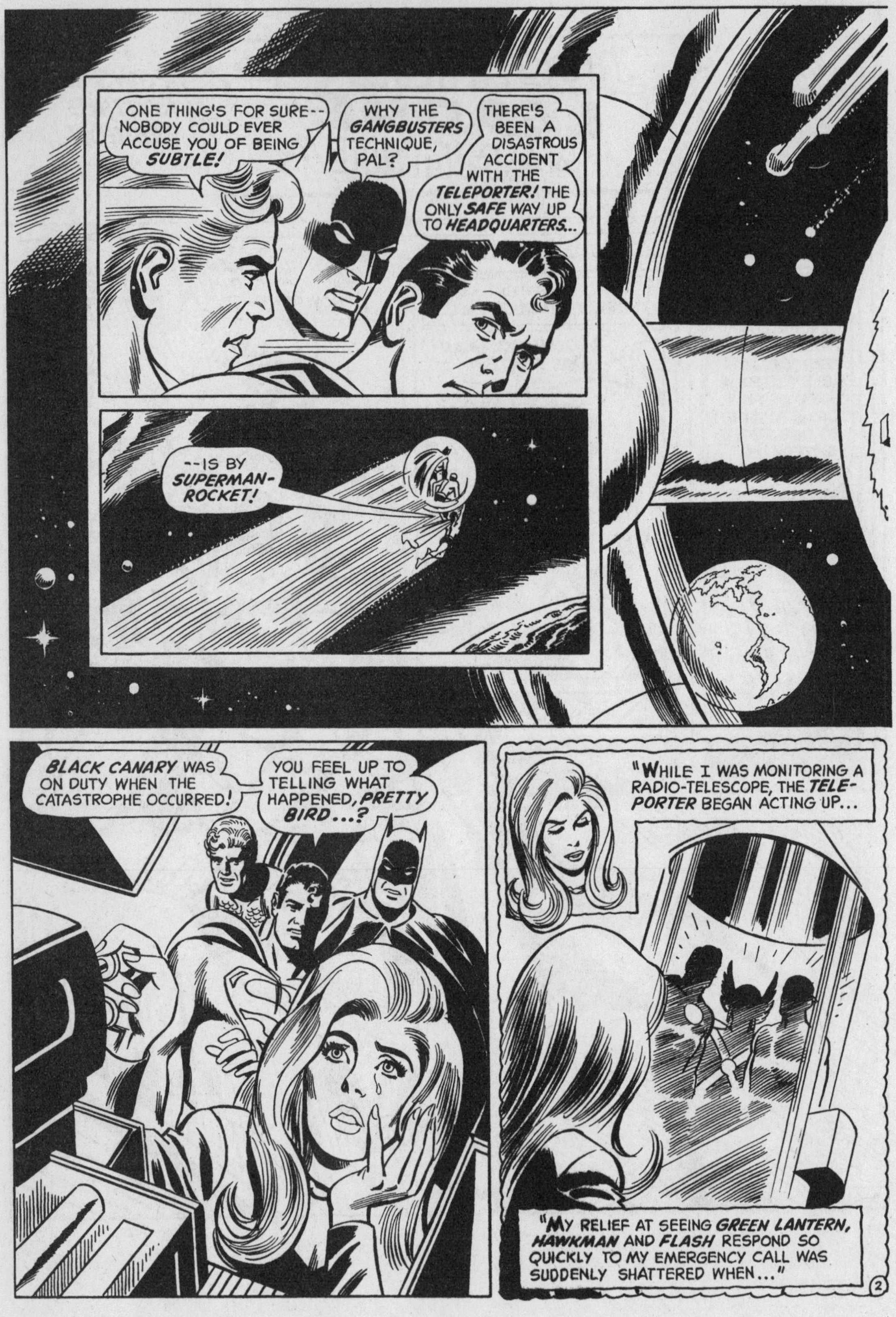
ONE THING'S FOR SURE-- NOBODY COULD EVER ACCUSE YOU OF BEING SUBTLE!
WHY THE GANGBUSTERS TECHNIQUE, PAL?
THERE'S BEEN A DISASTROUS ACCIDENT WITH THE TELEPORTER! THE ONLY SAFE WAY UP TO HEADQUARTERS...
--IS BY SUPERMAN-ROCKET!
BLACK CANARY WAS ON DUTY WHEN THE CATASTROPHE OCCURRED!
YOU FEEL UP TO TELLING WHAT HAPPENED, PRETTY BIRD...?
"WHILE I WAS MONITORING A RADIO-TELESCOPE, THE TELE-PORTER BEGAN ACTING UP...
"MY RELIEF AT SEEING GREEN LANTERN, HAWKMAN AND FLASH RESPOND SO QUICKLY TO MY EMERGENCY CALL WAS SUDDENLY SHATTERED WHEN..."
2

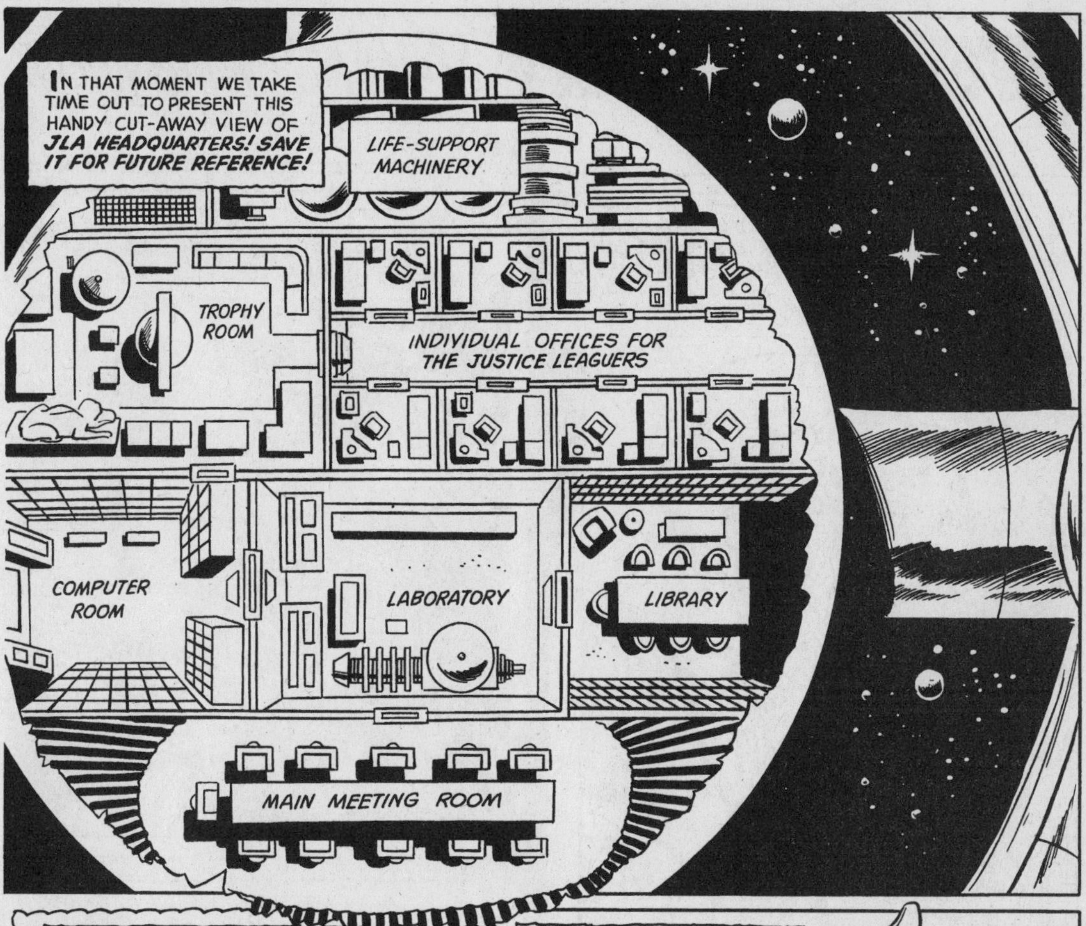
IN THAT MOMENT WE TAKE TIME OUT TO PRESENT THIS HANDY CUT-AWAY VIEW OF JLA HEADQUARTERS! SAVE IT FOR FUTURE REFERENCE!
LIFE-SUPPORT MACHINERY
TROPHY ROOM
INDIVIDUAL OFFICES FOR THE JUSTICE LEAGUERS
COMPUTER ROOM
LABORATORY
LIBRARY
MAIN MEETING ROOM

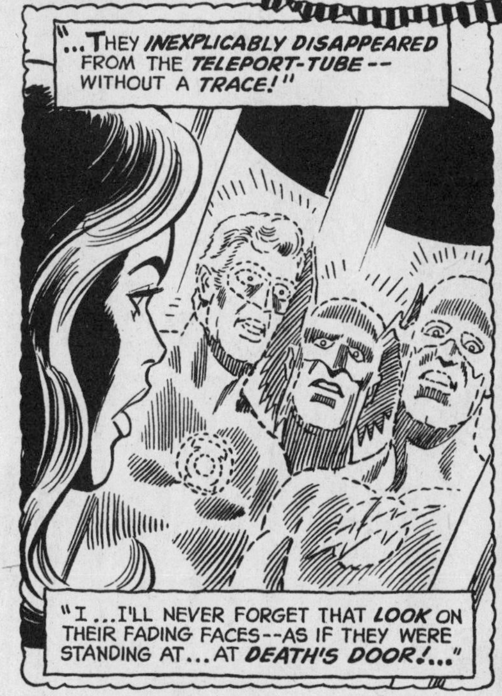
"...THEY INEXPLICABLY DISAPPEARED FROM THE TELEPORT-TUBE -- WITHOUT A TRACE!"
"I ...I'LL NEVER FORGET THAT LOOK ON THEIR FADING FACES--AS IF THEY WERE STANDING AT... AT DEATH'S DOOR!..."

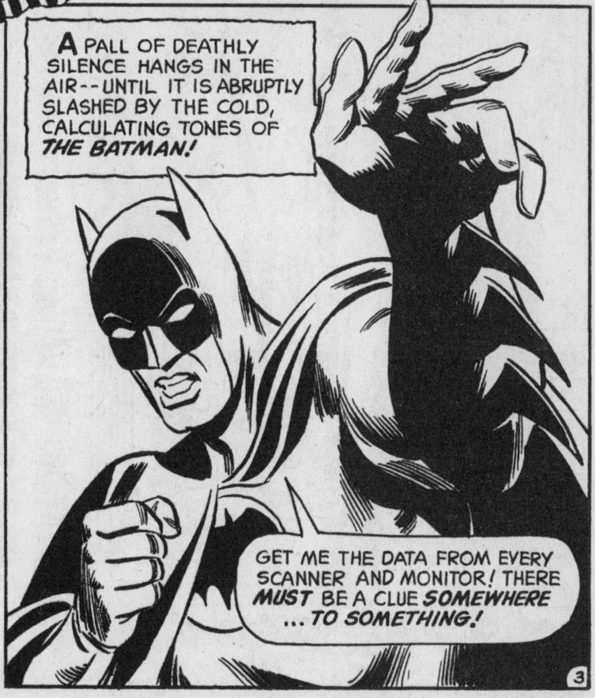
A PALL OF DEATHLY SILENCE HANGS IN THE AIR--UNTIL IT IS ABRUPTLY SLASHED BY THE COLD, CALCULATING TONES OF THE BATMAN!
GET ME THE DATA FROM EVERY SCANNER AND MONITOR! THERE MUST BE A CLUE SOMEWHERE ...TO SOMETHING!
3

"THE PRIVATE WAR of JOHNNY DUNE!"

MIKE FRIEDRICH — WRITER   DICK DILLIN — PENCILER & JOE GIELLA — INKER

YOUR NAME IS *JOHNNY DUNE* AND YOU'RE *HOME* -- ONCE MORE ON *U.S.* SOIL. BUT THERE ARE NO WELCOME-HOME BANNERS, NO MARCHING BANDS. THE HUSTLING CROWD SCARCELY EVEN SEES YOUR UNIFORM...

THE ONLY ATTENTIVE LOOKS ARE FROM A COUPLE OF LONG-HAIRS, MOUTHS CURVED IN HEARTLESS SMIRKS...

IT WASN'T ALWAYS THIS WAY, JOHNNY. JUST A WHILE BACK -- LESS MONTHS THAN YOU HAVE YEARS -- YOU RAN WITH A GANG THAT RULED YOUR NEIGHBORHOOD TURF...

YOU WERE RESPECTED THEN -- YOU WERE TOUGH -- YOU HAD A PLACE...

4

You had a gift of gentleness, though... and a piece of wood that sang soothing sounds when you stroked it...

You had *talent* then-- and it was just *time* till the wheel turned and you were in *big*...

But then your country drafted you to fight a war --a conflict you never *did* have time to figure out...

It's a horrible thing for a man to watch a fellow man writhe and die...

What was even worse, after awhile you no longer *cared!*

Came the battle for *fire-base bravo!* While out on reconnaissance, you were trapped--your team plugged down in withering machine-gun-fire...

One bullet, then a second and a *third* ripped into your side...

5

IN THAT MOMENT OF EXTRAORDINARY PAIN-STRESS, A NEW CHANNEL OPENED, SPILLING OUT RAW-GUT FEELINGS--FEELINGS THAT COULD ONLY BE EXPRESSED IN A *SCREAM*--

STOP! STOP KILLIN' ME!

AND THEY *DID!* MAN, HOW THEY STOPPED!...

YOU DIDN'T ASK QUESTIONS--YOUR TRIGGER-TRAINED BRAIN ONLY KNEW ONE ACT UNDER FIRE!..

LIKE STATUES THEY STOOD--LIKE STATUES THEY FELL! ONLY WHEN THEY *DIED* DID THEIR BLOOD FLOW RED...

SOMETIME LATER, YOU CAME UPON THE WORD *"MUTANT"*--AND YOU VAGUELY UNDERSTOOD *YOU* WERE GIFTED WITH A *POWER-FILLED VOICE*...

HOW COULD A MERE *SILVER MEDAL* MATCH THAT *EXULTANT FEELING* THAT FIRED THROUGH YOUR VEINS?

BACK HOME AGAIN, YOU FIND SOCIETY HASN'T MUCH *PLACE* FOR AN OUT-OF-WORK RIFLEMAN. A BLAZE OF BITTERNESS SMOLDERS, THEN KINDLES WITHIN YOUR SOUL...

NO HELP WANTED!

YOU FEEL THE FIRE... THE POWER OF *THE VOICE*... RAGE HIGHER AND HIGHER! ONLY NOW THAT YOU'RE CONFIDENT YOU CAN *CONTROL* IT, THINGS ARE GONNA BE DIFFERENT FOR YOU, *JOHNNY DUNE*-- DIFFERENT ALL-AROUND!

6

"THE PRIVATE WAR OF JOHNNY DUNE!" PART TWO
featuring GREEN ARROW *and The* ATOM

"FREEDOM *n:* the absence of necessity, coercion or constraint in choice or action..."

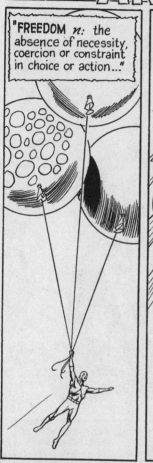

"DROP *vi:* to fall suddenly or unexpectedly..."

"INTERCEPT *vt:* to interrupt the progress or course of..."

"ACCURATE *adj:* free from error, especially as the result of care..."

PHENOMENAL *adj:* GREEN ARROW and THE ATOM!

YAAAAY!

WHEEE!

RIGHT ON!

7

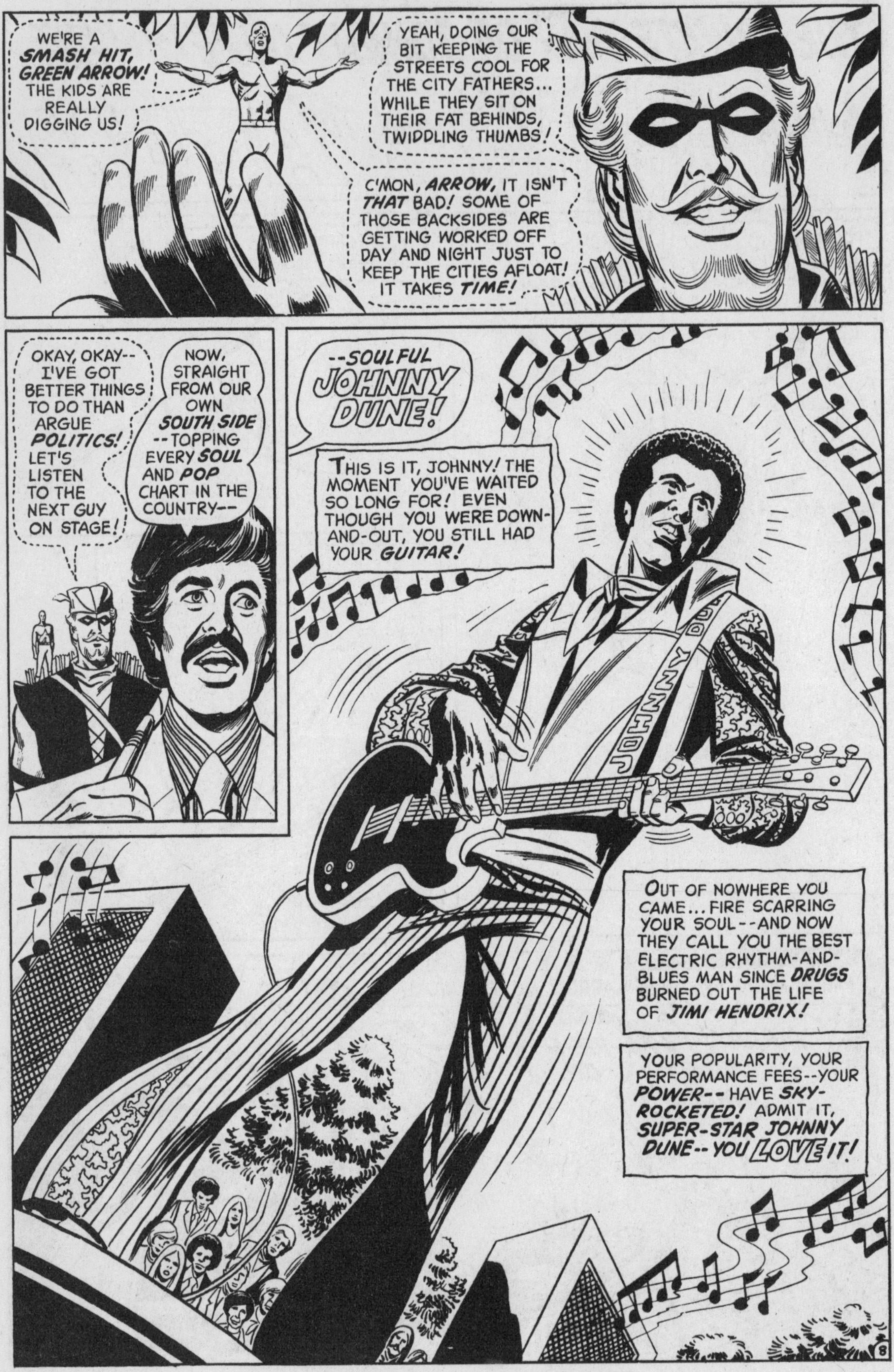
WE'RE A SMASH HIT, GREEN ARROW! THE KIDS ARE REALLY DIGGING US!
YEAH, DOING OUR BIT KEEPING THE STREETS COOL FOR THE CITY FATHERS... WHILE THEY SIT ON THEIR FAT BEHINDS, TWIDDLING THUMBS!
C'MON, ARROW, IT ISN'T THAT BAD! SOME OF THOSE BACKSIDES ARE GETTING WORKED OFF DAY AND NIGHT JUST TO KEEP THE CITIES AFLOAT! IT TAKES TIME!
OKAY, OKAY-- I'VE GOT BETTER THINGS TO DO THAN ARGUE POLITICS! LET'S LISTEN TO THE NEXT GUY ON STAGE!
NOW, STRAIGHT FROM OUR OWN SOUTH SIDE --TOPPING EVERY SOUL AND POP CHART IN THE COUNTRY--
--SOULFUL JOHNNY DUNE!
THIS IS IT, JOHNNY! THE MOMENT YOU'VE WAITED SO LONG FOR! EVEN THOUGH YOU WERE DOWN-AND-OUT, YOU STILL HAD YOUR GUITAR!
JOHNNY DU
OUT OF NOWHERE YOU CAME... FIRE SCARRING YOUR SOUL--AND NOW THEY CALL YOU THE BEST ELECTRIC RHYTHM-AND-BLUES MAN SINCE DRUGS BURNED OUT THE LIFE OF JIMI HENDRIX!
YOUR POPULARITY, YOUR PERFORMANCE FEES--YOUR POWER-- HAVE SKY-ROCKETED! ADMIT IT, SUPER-STAR JOHNNY DUNE-- YOU LOVE IT!
8

As THE ROAR OF THE CROWD TIDAL-WAVES THROUGH YOUR EARS, YOU FLASH-BACK TO A MEETING WITH THE CITY'S POLITICAL BOSS...

YOU WANT... *WHAT?!* --HAVE ME BACK *YOU* FOR *MAYOR?*

LISTEN, MAN, THIS CITY'S *CRUMBLIN'* DOWN, *ROTTIN'* AT THE CORE!

THE KIDS ARE SICK O' *FILTH* AND *POVERTY*-- DRUG ADDICTION IS SPREADIN'--*VIOLENCE* BREAKS OUT AT THE DROP OF A COP'S HAT!

I'VE GOT THE *POPULARITY* TO KEEP THOSE KIDS *COOL!*--

PLAYIN' BENEFITS WILL BE GREAT CAMPAIGN PUBLICITY --AND AS *MAYOR* I CAN MAKE THE DRASTIC CHANGES THAT MUST BE MADE!

DUNE, POLITICS IS *POWER!* COOL THE KIDS-- AND YOU'VE *MY* NOD FOR MAYOR!

So YOU PLAYED... EVERY DAY OF THE HOT GRIMY SUMMER YOU PLAYED... FROM PARK TO SCHOOLYARD--THE FIRE BLAZING WITH EVERY LYRIC, EVERY NOTE...

UNTIL YOU FOUND OUT JUST HOW *DIRTY* POLITICS CAN BE...

SORRY, DUNE -- I'VE DECIDED TO BACK THE *MAYOR* FOR *RE-ELECTION!*

SO *YOU* CAN PULL THE STRINGS IN THE CITY GOVERNMENT--?

NO-- JUST SO *RADICAL DISRUPTERS* LIKE *YOU* DON'T!

HE'S SHAFTED YOU, ALL RIGHT-- YOU CAN'T WIN WITHOUT HIS SUPPORT AND ORGANIZATION! AND SO THIS MEANS *WAR* AGAIN --RIGHT, *JOHNNY DUNE?*

THIS BENEFIT IN *PROSPECT PARK* IS AN IDEAL SETTING FOR YOUR *REVENGE!* EVERY KID FOR MILES AROUND IS HERE --AND *YOU* ARE IN *GOOD VOICE!*

9

WHAT A SINISTER REVENGE, JOHNNY! YOU'LL *ELIMINATE* THE CITY'S KID-*PROBLEMS* --BY ELIMINATING THE *KIDS!*

HEAR ME, ALL YOU BROTHERS AND SISTERS--BLUE-EYED, SLANT-EYED, AFRO OR *WHAT*-EVER!

ARE WE *FED UP* WITH THIS-HERE CITY AND THIS-HERE COUNTRY?

LEMME HEAR YA SAY *YEAH!*

YEAH!

OH, JOHNNY! WHEN THE CROWD *SCREAMS* BACK ITS BOOMING ANSWER, IT'S LIKE *BEAUTIFUL MUSIC!*

THEN AS ONE VOICE WE SAY *"NO MORE!"*--AND WE'RE *CUTTIN' OUT!*

RIGHT--?

RIGHT ON!

YOU HEAR THAT, *ARROW?* HE'S GOT THE CROWD EATING OUT OF HIS HANDS--

--HIS *MOUTH*, YOU MEAN!

AS THE MASSIVE MOB MARCHES OUT OF THE STADIUM, AS YOU DIRECTED, YOU ARE CONFRONTED BY A MORE IMMEDIATE PROBLEM--

TWO COSTUME --TYPES-- COMIN' ON LIKE A PAIR OF *MP's!*

YOU *FOUR*--WIPE 'EM OUT!

QUICK, *GA*--PITCH ME AT 'EM!

10

STEE-RI-KE ONE!

HIS *NOSE* HAD PLENTY OF *"SPRING"* TO *"BOUNCE"* ME INTO THIS NEXT ONE!

--WITH ALL APOLOGIES TO THE *LANGUAGE!*

TOO CLOSE TO FIRE MY ARROWS!

WISH I HAD PRACTISED UP ON THOSE FANCY JUDO-HOLDS *PRETTY BIRD* SHOWED ME!

BUT EVERYTHIN' I TRY SEEMS TO *FLOP*-- AND I JUST DON'T *LIKE* GETTIN' BEAT ON!

SO I'LL JUST HAVE TO GO BACK TO THE OLD-FASHIONED *ROUNDHOUSE PUNCH!*

CRUDE-- BUT *EFFECTIVE!*

11

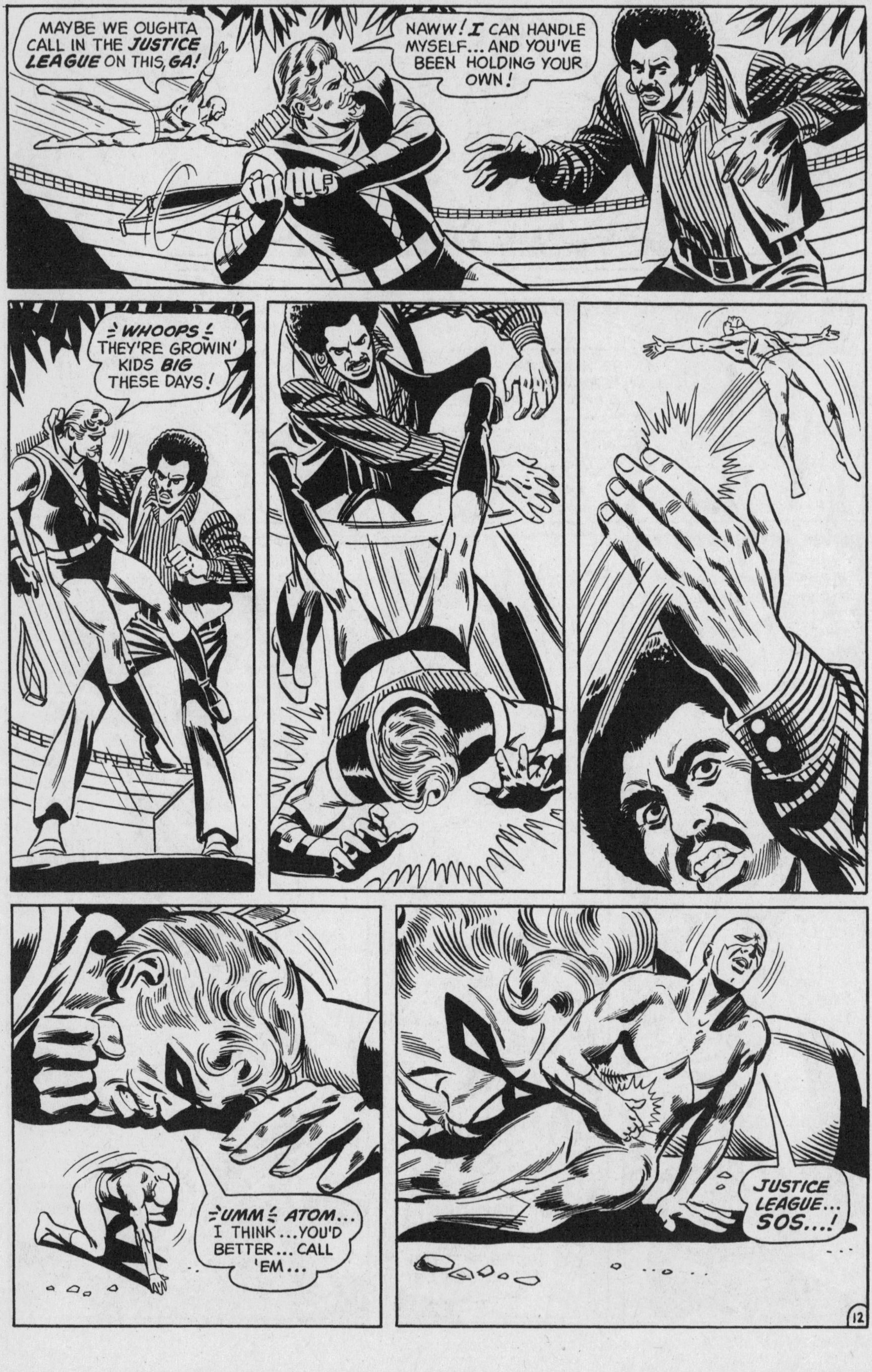
MAYBE WE OUGHTA CALL IN THE *JUSTICE LEAGUE* ON THIS, *GA*!
NAWW! *I* CAN HANDLE MYSELF... AND YOU'VE BEEN HOLDING YOUR OWN!
WHOOPS THEY'RE GROWIN' KIDS *BIG* THESE DAYS!
UMM *ATOM*... I THINK... YOU'D BETTER... CALL 'EM...
JUSTICE LEAGUE... SOS...!
12

"THE PRIVATE WAR of JOHNNY DUNE!" PART THREE

featuring

BLACK CANARY and BATMAN

MEANWHILE, 22,300 MILES ABOVE EARTH...

AT LAST! I'VE SOLVED THE DISAPPEARANCE-MYSTERY!

OUR SATELLITE IS STATIONED IN SUCH AN ORBIT THAT A BEAM FROM OUTER SPACE-STRUCK OUR TELEPORTER!

IN A PREVIOUS ADVENTURE WITH ADAM STRANGE* WE LEARNED THAT A ZETA-BEAM IS SENT REGULARLY TO EARTH, INSTANTLY TRANSPORTING WHATEVER IT STRIKES 25 TRILLION MILES TO THE PLANET RANN!

MY GUESS IS THAT ADAM HAS SOME UNEXPECTED VISITORS!

* "PLANET THAT CAME TO A STANDSTILL" IN MYSTERY IN SPACE NO. 75. — ED.

THEN AS IF TO CONFIRM THE BATMAN'S DEDUCTION...

JUSTICE LEAGUERS-- THIS IS GREEN LANTERN... CALLING FROM RANN!

HAWKMAN AND I ARRIVED IN THE MIDST OF A CATASTROPHE THAT THREATENS NOT ONLY RANN, BUT EARTH AS WELL!

I CAN'T COMMUNICATE ANY LONGER-- WE NEED HELP--FAST!

HIS IMAGE IS FADING AWAY-- WITHOUT TELLING US WHAT THE MENACE IS!

BUT JUDGING FROM THE LOOK ON GL'S FACE--IT'S OMINOUS!

IT IS AT THIS SAME CRUCIAL MOMENT THAT--

SOS FROM GREEN ARROW AND ATOM!

13

THIS CALLS FOR A *SPLIT-UP!* SUPERMAN, YOU'RE OUR BEST TROUBLE-SHOOTER FOR *RANN!*

BLACK CANARY, I KNOW YOU'RE GONNA *INSIST* ON HELPING THE *ARROW*-- BUT *BATMAN* BETTER JOIN YOU!

AND *I'LL* STAY HERE TO COORDINATE THINGS!

SO AS THE *MAN OF STEEL* FLASHES ACROSS THE VOID BETWEEN SOLAR SYSTEMS...

...THE SCREAMING WHINE OF THE *BAT-JET* STREAKS ACROSS AMERICAN SKIES...

LOOK AT THOSE YOUNGSTERS, *BATMAN!* FOLLOWING THAT MAN LIKE--

--LIKE THE LEGENDARY *PIED PIPER* WHO STOLE AWAY THE KIDS OF A CITY!

THE COPS ARE KEEPIN' THEIR DISTANCE 'CAUSE THEY'RE AFRAID OF HURTIN' ANYONE-- BUT WE CAN USE A COUPLE MORE *HOSTAGES!*

GO GET 'EM!

BATMAN MANEUVERED HIS CHUTE INTO LANDING FIRST!

NICE OF HIM TO LEAVE TWO OF THOSE BRUISERS FOR *ME!*

14

LONG HAVE THE LIVES OF THE TWO CRUSADERS BEEN SHAPED BY VIOLENCE, FILLED TO OVER-FLOWING BY THE TRAGEDIES OF DEATH AND DISASTER...

THEIR COURAGE IS GREAT, THEIR SKILL GREATER! SILENTLY, EFFICIENTLY, *THE BATMAN* AND *BLACK CANARY* MOVE, LETTING NONE STAND BEFORE THEM!...

THEY'RE MESSIN' UP MY BODYGUARDS! I'LL HAVETA USE *THE VOICE* ON 'EM!

BATMAN! BLACK CANARY! FREEZE!

AS MASTERS OF "THE GENTLE ART!" THE *JUSTICE LEAGUE* DUO HAS REACHED SUCH A PEAK OF *CONCENTRATION*...

FREEZE

...THAT NOT EVEN THE MUTANT SCREAMS OF A BURNING YOUNG MAN CAN PENETRATE THEIR EARS!

AND SO THEY CONTINUE, TEAMED INTO HUMAN ENGINES OF FIGHTING PERFECTION!

(15)

HAVETA SEND THE *JUSTICE LEAGUERS* AGAINST EACH OTHER!-- INSTEAD O' *ME!*

ATOM-- LANTERN! ATTACK BATMAN AND CANARY!

THE BATMAN CAN NEVER BE SO *COLD* AS TO IGNORE LONG-TIME FRIENDS... NOR CAN *BLACK CANARY* FORGET THE MAN WHO HOLDS HER HEART...

THAT OVER-POWERING VOICE...

I-- CAN'T FIGHT-- *OLIVER--!*

CAN'T RESIST...

GO AHEAD, LITTLE CHUM-- YOU MUST HAVE YOUR *REASON!*

IT WORKED! *BATMAN* AND THE CHICK ARE HANDCUFFED!

ALL RIGHT, BROTHERS! JUMP 'EM!

THEN TIE 'EM UP! THEY'RE OUR *PASSPORT* OUTA TOWN!

16

"THE PRIVATE WAR of JOHNNY DUNE!" PART FOUR

THE HORDE OF KIDS MARCHES INTO THE FOOTHILLS, POLICE HELICOPTERS HELPLESSLY CIRCLING OVERHEAD, AWAITING ORDERS THAT NEVER COME...

POWER!-- THAT'S WHAT YOU FEEL NOW, JOHNNY DUNE! IT'S THE ONLY QUENCHING THE BITTER FLAMES FIRING WITHIN YOU WILL ALLOW!

THE SOUND OF YOUR *VOICE* HAS TAPPED A HUGE RESERVOIR OF RESENTMENT AND ANGRY ALIENATION, RISING TO CAPTURE AN ENTIRE CROWD AND OVERWHELM A QUARTET OF SUPER-HEROES!

THIS PENT-UP FRUSTRATION AND ANGER IS THE *SOURCE* OF YOUR POWER! IT FEELS SO *GREAT*-- YOU'RE DETERMINED TO *NEVER LET IT STOP!*

17

YET, AT THIS MOMENT OF TRIUMPH, YOU FOR-GET THAT *POWER* IS A *BOILING* THING--

THOSE DUMB KIDS SPLIT OFF FROM THE CROWD--DESTROYING FENCES--RUNNING WILD!

STOP! RETURN TO THE MARCH!

--THAT POWER IS A *CORRUPTING* THING--

MY *VOICE* ISN'T CONTROLLING THEM! THEY'RE MOVIN' WITH A *FORCE OF THEIR OWN!*

I'LL SHOW 'EM WHO'S IN CHARGE!

I STILL HAVE A FEW LOYAL SUBJECTS UNDER MY CONTROL!

RELEASE THE ARCHER!

GREEN ARROW--USE YOUR AMAZING ARROWS TO HERD THOSE KIDS BACK IN LINE!

IF *BATMAN* AND *PRETTY BIRD* RESISTED *BIG MOUTH'S* COMMANDS BY INTENSE *CONCENTRA-TION*...SO CAN THE *ACE ARCHER!*

IT'S WORKING! I *REFUSE* TO LET MY FINGERS RELEASE THE SMOKE-ARROW!

GO AHEAD, GREENIE! SHOOT!

DARN! HAD TO LET GO!

18

THEN, JOHNNY, AS YOU MOVE TO REGAIN CONTROL OF THE MOB...

BACK IN LINE, YOU BLACK SHEEP!

NOW--WHILE HE'S DISTRACTED BY THE CROWD--

I'LL NEED SOME EXTRA HELP TO DROWN OUT HIS VOICE... STICK SOME STUFFING FROM THIS *BOXING-GLOVE ARROW* IN MY EARS!

IMAGINE THAT *RAVING MANIAC* THINKING HE COULD RULE BY POWER *ALONE!*

BABY--HERE'S WHERE I GAG YOUR BIG, FAT MOUTH!

PLUPP

POWER WITHOUT JUSTICE IS *TYRANNY!*

FILTHY, GRIMY *TYRANNY!*

THERE! *THAT'LL* KEEP YA QUIET WHILE WE STRAIGHTEN THINGS OUT HERE!

19

WOW! ALL OF A SUDDEN I FEEL FREE-- ABLE TO SHRINK OUT OF MY BONDS!

'BOUT TIME THE *WORLD'S GREATEST ESCAPE ARTIST* WORKED HIS WAY OUT OF THESE BONDS!

THE CROWD'S BREAKING LOOSE-- BENT ON VIOLENCE! WE'VE GOT A *BIG JOB* AHEAD OF US!

IT'S BEEN SAID THAT LOVE *CAUSES* WEAKNESS, YET IT IS ALSO MAN'S GREATEST *STRENGTH!* BEHOLD THOSE WHO HAVE A FIERCE LOVE FOR MAN AND A DESIRE FOR JUSTICE, FIGHTING ENORMOUS ODDS TO ACHIEVE IT--

AH! YOU'VE RETURNED TO CONSCIOUSNESS, JOHNNY DUNE! ARE YOU PLEASED AT WHAT THE *POWER* YOU UNLEASHED *REALLY* LOOKS LIKE..?

MY GOD-- IT'S TURNED INTO A *RIOT!*

20

CAN'T LET THIS MAYHEM *CONTINUE*-- ALLOW THOSE KIDS TO BE *HURT!*

I TRIGGERED THE *ANGER!* ONLY BY *ABSORBING* IT INTO MYSELF AGAIN CAN I END IT!

PLOWPP

HERE ME-- *ALL OF YOU!* DIRECT YOUR ANGER AT *ME! I* AM THE ONE YOU MUST *ATTACK!*

WITH ONE MIND, ONE PURPOSE, THE MOB TURNS AND OBEYS ORDERS...

THERE IS A DRIVING NEED IN THE *CROWD* TO EXPRESS ITS FRUSTRATION-- AND WHAT BETTER TARGET THAN THE ONE *RESPONSIBLE* FOR TURNING ON ITS ANGER?

THEY BATTER HIS SILENT BODY WITH BLOWS FROM ALL SIDES-- *UNTIL HE BREAKS!*

ARRRGHHHHHH

THEN, LIKE SACRIFICING THE SCAPEGOAT OF OLDEN DAYS, THE THRONG ACHIEVES A *RELEASE!* THERE IS NO FURTHER NEED FOR ANGER!

21

CALM NOW, THEY COME TO A HALT-- THEN SLOWLY TURN AWAY FROM THE BEATEN, BROKEN BODY OF JOHNNY DUNE...

BUT THERE *ARE* THOSE WHO RACE TO HIS SIDE...

NOW THE COPS CAN DIRECT THINGS-- WITHOUT ANY HEADS BEIN' BUSTED!

HOW IN HEAVEN'S NAME DID HE *KNOW* THE MOB WOULD STOP RIOTING...BY ATTACKING *HIM?*

WE MAY NEVER KNOW-- HE LOOKS *DEAD!*

NO... HE'S STILL CONSCIOUS...

WHY DID YOU *DO* IT! WHY DID YOU WANT TO *PIED PIPER* THESE KIDS TO DESTRUCTION?

PIED PIPER..? HA-HA... YOU'VE GOT THE STORY... ALL WRONG...

...LIKE THE *REAL* PIPER... I WAS LEADING THE KIDS... TO A....*PARADISE*... UNDER MY RULE...

...ONLY I FOUND OUT... POWER DOESN'T WORK THAT WAY!

YA GOTTA USE IT LIKE *YOU* LEAGUERS... FOR *JUSTICE*... OR IT RUNS AWAY... UHNN...

...HE'S *GONE*...

(22)

"THE PRIVATE WAR of JOHNNY DUNE!" PART FIVE

THEY COULD'VE LET JOHNNY DUNE DIE! SOME MIGHT SAY IT WOULD HAVE BEEN MOST FITTING--AND MOST *JUST!*

BUT THERE *IS* SOMETHING MORE *SACRED* THAN *JUSTICE*--

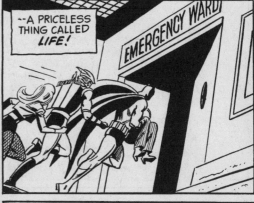

--A PRICELESS THING CALLED *LIFE!*

JOHNNY'S LIFE WENT OUT OF THEIR HANDS, BUT EVEN TODAY THERE ARE SUCH THINGS AS *MIRACLES*...

I REALLY DON'T KNOW HOW HE PULLED THROUGH -- EXCEPT BY *SHEER WILL TO LIVE* -- BUT JOHNNY'S GOING TO MAKE IT!

23

AND SO, MUCH LATER... SO YOU'RE GONNA GO INTO *POLITICS*, JOHNNY? I DON'T SEE *WHY*, CONSIDERING THE *CRUMBS* YOU'LL BE TRAVELING WITH--

BUT HERE'S MY BEST ANYWAY!

MY MUTANT POWER FADED AWAY IN THAT FINAL SCREAM... SO I'LL HAVE TO WIN VOTES THE *HARD* WAY-- THE *CLEAN* WAY!

AS TO "*WHY*," THAT'S *EASY!* IF THE VOTERS ARE WILLING TO FORGIVE MY MIS-ADVENTURE, I CAN HELP BRING ABOUT THE CHANGES THAT GOTTA BE MADE!

SOMEBODY HAS TO DO IT -- ONLY I'VE LEARNED IT CAN'T HAPPEN OVERNIGHT... EVEN WITH A SUPER-POWER!

ONE THING STILL BOTHERS ME! *I* CAN WAIT A WHILE LONGER FOR THE WHEELS TO TURN -- FOR THINGS TO GET BETTER...

...BUT WILL THE *KIDS?*

THE END

MEANWHILE, THE SPACEWARD-STREAKING *SUPERMAN* HEADS TOWARD AN UNKNOWN DESTINY! BE WITH US NEXT ISSUE FOR THE "*COMING OF THE STARBREAKER!*"

24

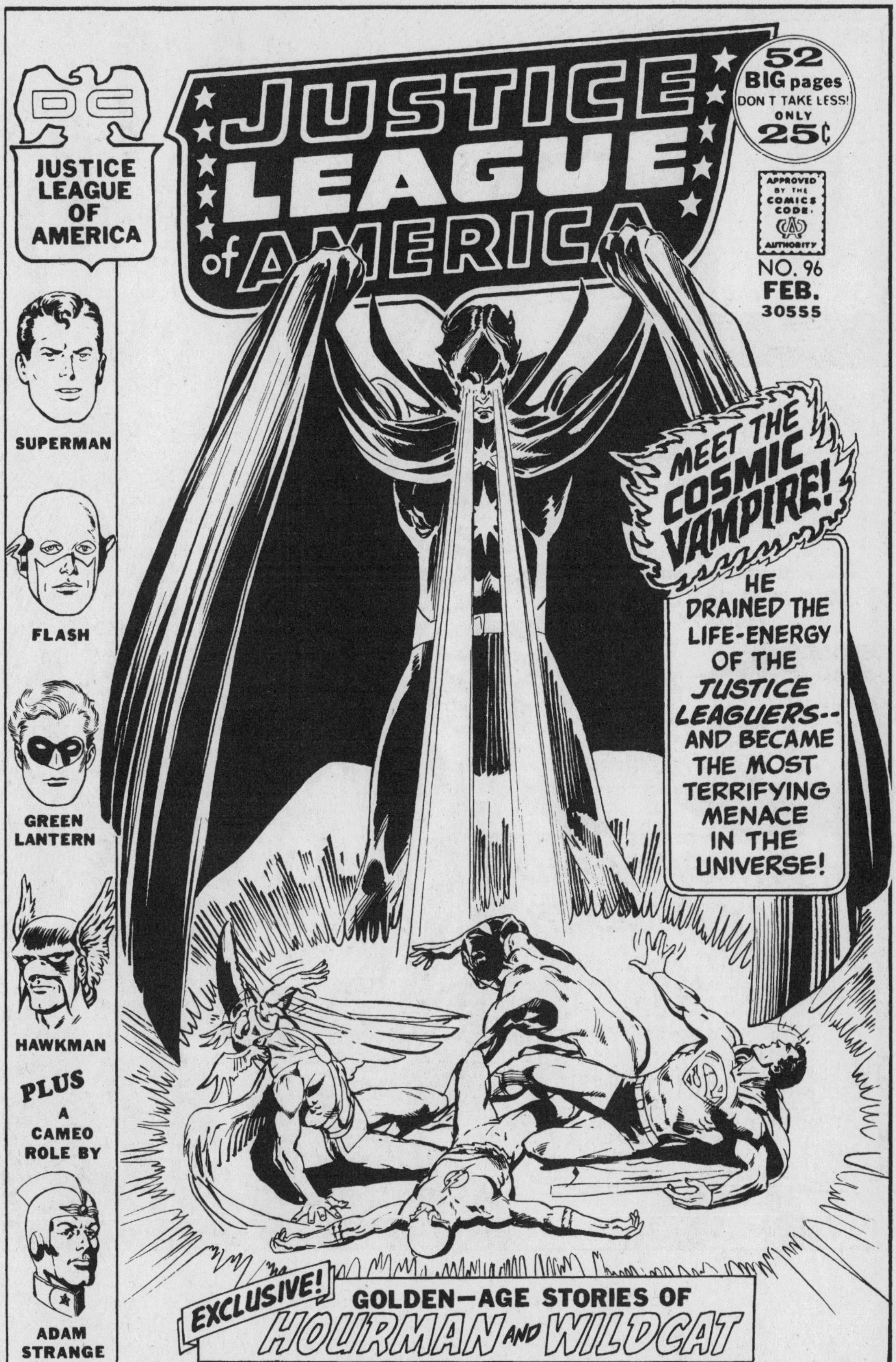
DC
JUSTICE LEAGUE OF AMERICA
JUSTICE LEAGUE of AMERICA
52 BIG pages DON T TAKE LESS! ONLY 25¢
APPROVED BY THE COMICS CODE AUTHORITY
NO. 96
FEB.
30555
SUPERMAN
FLASH
GREEN LANTERN
HAWKMAN
PLUS A CAMEO ROLE BY
ADAM STRANGE
MEET THE COSMIC VAMPIRE!
HE DRAINED THE LIFE-ENERGY OF THE *JUSTICE LEAGUERS*-- AND BECAME THE MOST TERRIFYING MENACE IN THE UNIVERSE!
EXCLUSIVE!
GOLDEN—AGE STORIES OF
HOURMAN AND WILDCAT

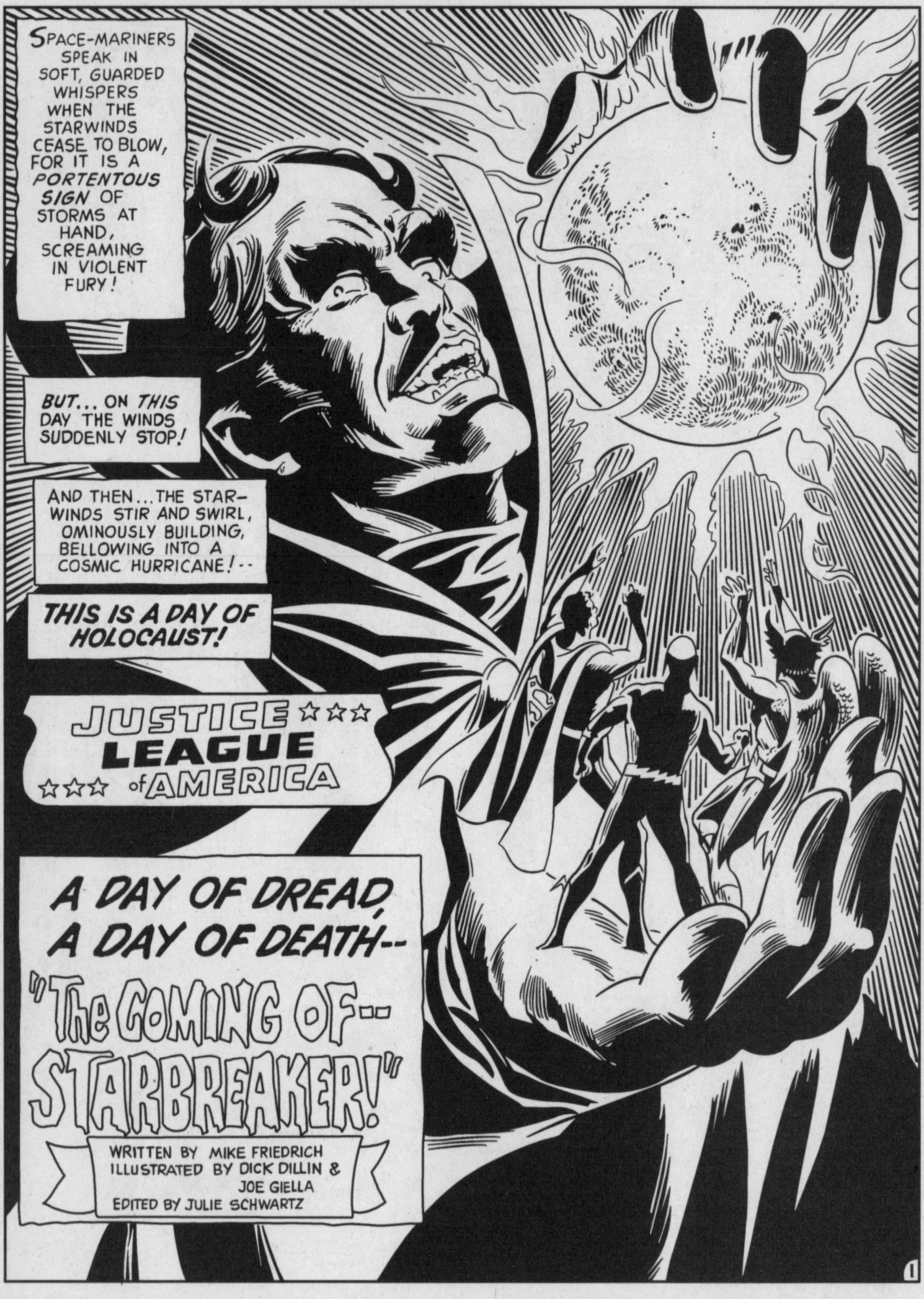
SPACE-MARINERS SPEAK IN SOFT, GUARDED WHISPERS WHEN THE STARWINDS CEASE TO BLOW, FOR IT IS A PORTENTOUS SIGN OF STORMS AT HAND, SCREAMING IN VIOLENT FURY!
BUT... ON THIS DAY THE WINDS SUDDENLY STOP!
AND THEN... THE STAR-WINDS STIR AND SWIRL, OMINOUSLY BUILDING, BELLOWING INTO A COSMIC HURRICANE!--
THIS IS A DAY OF HOLOCAUST!
JUSTICE LEAGUE of AMERICA
A DAY OF DREAD, A DAY OF DEATH--
"The COMING OF-- STARBREAKER!"
WRITTEN BY MIKE FRIEDRICH
ILLUSTRATED BY DICK DILLIN & JOE GIELLA
EDITED BY JULIE SCHWARTZ
1

HOW DOES ONE *REALLY* MEASURE *TIME* IN *SPACE?* THERE ARE NO MINUTES, HOURS, DAYS...THESE ARE BUT *EARTHLY* CONCEPTS, CREATED IN COSMIC IGNORANCE OF THE UNIVERSAL RHYTHM THAT TRULY TIMES US ALL.

YET THIS MUCH IS CERTAIN-- THERE IS A *NOW*... AND IT IS *NOW* THAT *SUPERMAN* STREAKS ACROSS INTERSTELLAR SPACE!...

SEEMS LIKE ONLY MINUTES AGO THAT *FLASH, HAWKMAN* AND *GREEN LANTERN*-- WHILE TELEPORTING UP TO *JUSTICE LEAGUE* HEAD- QUARTERS--*DISAPPEARED!*

--FOLLOWED SOON AFTER BY *GL'S* POWER-RINGED CALL FOR *HELP* --

THE *SOS* ORIGINATED FROM *HERE*-- *RANN,* THE GREEN-SKIED PLANET OF *ALPHA CENTAURI, EARTH'S* NEAREST SOLAR NEIGHBOR!

TIME TO SWITCH ON MY *TELESCOPIC VISION* AND SCOUR THE PLANET FOR--

THERE THEY ARE-- AND OH!-- WHAT A COMEDOWN!

THREE OF *EARTH'S* CHAMPION CRUSADERS... BEING KNOCKED FOR A LOOP BY A COUPLE OF MECHANICAL BUGS!

2

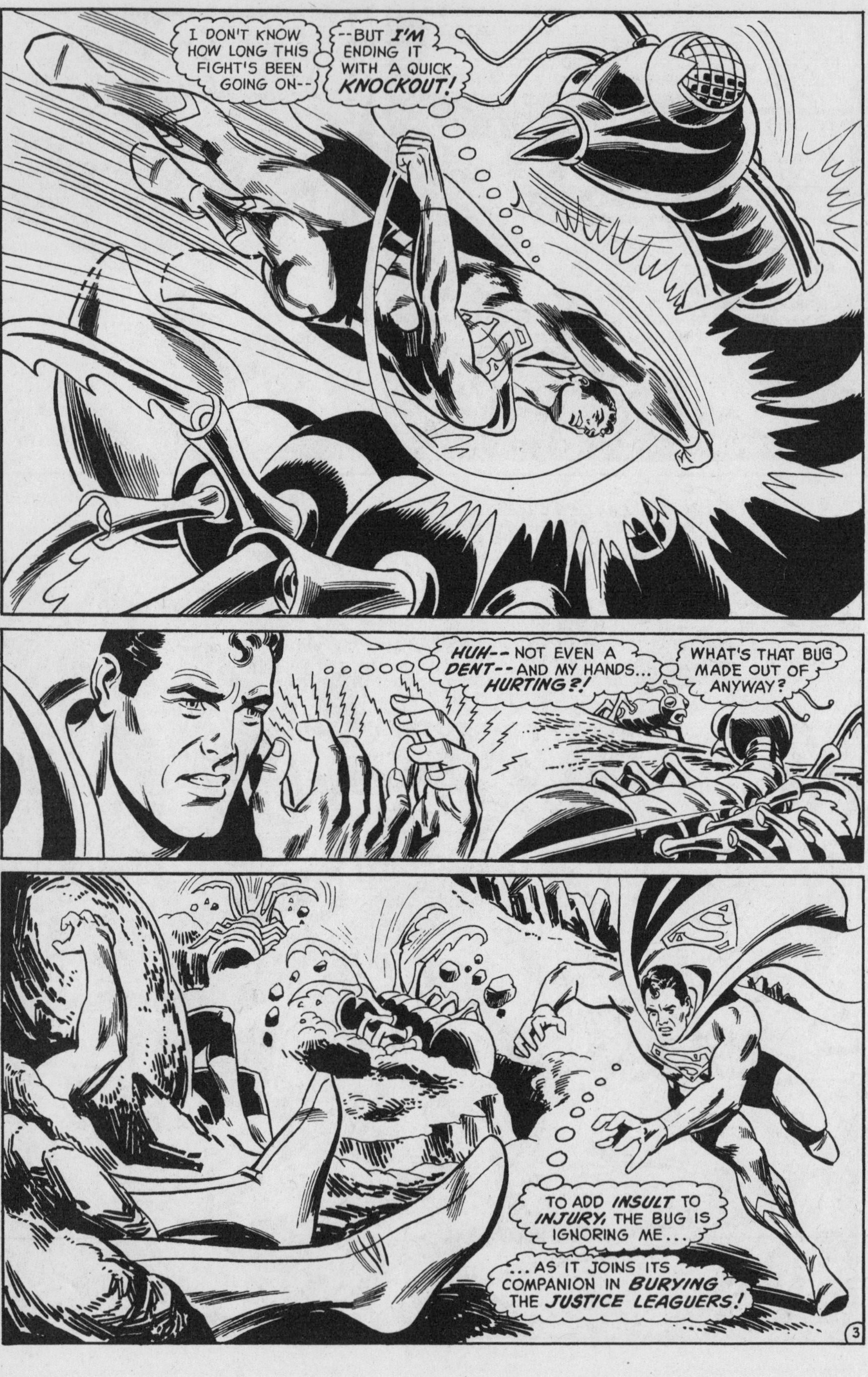
I DON'T KNOW HOW LONG THIS FIGHT'S BEEN GOING ON--
--BUT I'M ENDING IT WITH A QUICK KNOCKOUT!
HUH--NOT EVEN A DENT--AND MY HANDS... HURTING?!
WHAT'S THAT BUG MADE OUT OF ANYWAY?
TO ADD INSULT TO INJURY, THE BUG IS IGNORING ME...
...AS IT JOINS ITS COMPANION IN BURYING THE JUSTICE LEAGUERS!
3

IN CASE THIS RESCUE-BIT GETS A *RISE* OUT OF THEM, I BETTER BE PREPARED--

TO *X-RAY* THEIR *BUGGY* BODIES... SEE WHAT MAKES THEM *TICK*...

...SO I CAN *STOP* THEM!

AS HE FLIES BACK TO THE VALLEY...

THEIR INSIDES-- AN *UTTER PUZZLE!* MAY HAVE TO FIGHT THEM *BLIND!*

ONE THING'S FOR SURE-- THEIR *POWER-SOURCE* MAKES *ATOMIC ENERGY* SEEM LIKE A *FIRECRACKER!*

CAN A *MECHANICAL BUG* BE *STUNG?* PERHAPS-- FOR THE *X-RAYED* ALIENS SUDDENLY PIVOT AND SWIFTLY ELONGATE APPENDAGES AT THE *MAN OF STEEL*--

I'D SAY THEY'RE *MAD* AT ME ... ASSUMING THEY'RE *EMOTIONALLY* CAPABLE OF *ANGER!*

BLAZING MAD-- JUDGING FROM THOSE *JETS OF FLAME* THEY'RE FIRING AT ME!

4

THE FLAMES--LIKE *PROMINENCES* OF A *RED SUN*-- SAPPING MY POWERS!

MY STRENGTH'S GOING... BUT AT LEAST MY MIND'S OKAY! LOOKS LIKE THIS WILL HAVE TO BE A *THINKING MAN'S FIGHT!*

HMM...THE BUGS DIDN'T BECOME AGGRESSIVE UNTIL I TURNED MY *X-RAY VISION* ON THEM...

CAN THERE BE A *CONNECTION*--? DID I PERHAPS SCRAMBLE SOMETHING--?

--OR *INTERFERE WITH THEIR TRANSMISSION*--?

THAT *HAS* TO BE *IT!*

ASSUMING MY THEORY IS CORRECT, THEIR *"FEELERS"* ARE *RECEIVING ANTENNAE!*

BY *SUPER-SPEEDING* AROUND THEM, I MIGHT CAUSE ENOUGH *"INTERFERENCE"* TO UPSET THEIR *TRANSMISSION* ORDERS!

IT'S WORKING! ONE OF 'EM IS *STAGGERING*-- THE OTHER'S *CONFUSED!*

5

THIS IS BETTER THAN I *HOPED*-- THEY'VE TURNED THEIR *JET-STREAMS* ON EACH OTHER! --TURNING TO *MOLTEN METAL*--

MEANWHILE, DOWNSTREAM FROM THE MOUNTAIN TOP COMES A FULLY RECOVERED JLA TRIO...

DON'T HOG--

--ALL THE--

--ACTION, SUPERMAN!

LET SOME *FLASH SUPER-SPEED*--

--PUT THE *FINISHING TOUCH* TO THIS BURIAL!

ALL YOURS, *FLASH*-- BUT *GREEN LANTERN* BETTER LEND A *POWER-RING HAND!* THOSE *ATOMIC BUGS* ARE ABOUT TO--

B·L·O·W!

≋ WHEW ≋ *CAPPING* THAT *BLAST* TOOK A LOT OUTA ME!

THESE DAYS I'M NOT QUITE UP TO SUCH SUPER-CHORES...EXCEPT IN SUDDEN, QUICK *SPURTS!*

WHILE WE ALL TAKE A BREATHER, BRIEF ME IN ON WHAT'S HAPPENED!

FOR STARTERS, *HAWKMAN*-- HOW DID YOU THREE GET TO *RANN?*

6

"WHEN ANYONE *INSTANTLY* TRAVELS ACROSS *25 TRILLION MILES* OF SPACE TO *RANN,* THERE'S ONLY *ONE* ANSWER-- WE WERE STRUCK BY A *ZETA-BEAM* INTENDED FOR *ADAM STRANGE*-- RANN'S EARTH-BASED SUPER-HERO!"

"APPARENTLY, WHEN *BLACK CANARY* MADE ROUTINE MANEUVERS OF THE *JLA* SATELLITE, OUR OWN TELEPORTER BEAM DIVERTED --AND INTERCEPTED-- THE *ZETA-BEAM* OVER *EARTH'S* SOUTHERN HEMISPHERE!"

TO PICK UP *HAWKMAN'S* STORY, WE ARRIVED TO FIND *RANN* THREATENED BY A MENACE KNOWN AS *STARBREAKER!*

FOR BACKGROUND INFO, I CONSULTED THE "LIBRARY" OF THE *GUARDIANS* VIA MY *POWER RING!*

HERE-- I'LL HAVE THE RING FLASH AN "INSTANT REPLAY" FOR YOU!

"*STARBREAKER* IS *UNIQUE* AMONG *GALACTIC HUMANS!* HE HAS THE ABILITY TO *ABSORB* ENORMOUS AMOUNTS OF ENERGY INTO HIS BODY--AND *RELEASE* IT AT *WILL!*"

"FROM TIME TO TIME, HE DISPATCHES "MECHANIX" TO TAP THE ENERGIES OF SOLAR SYSTEM PLANETS..."

"...BY CAUSING THEM TO HURTLE INTO THEIR SUNS..."

7

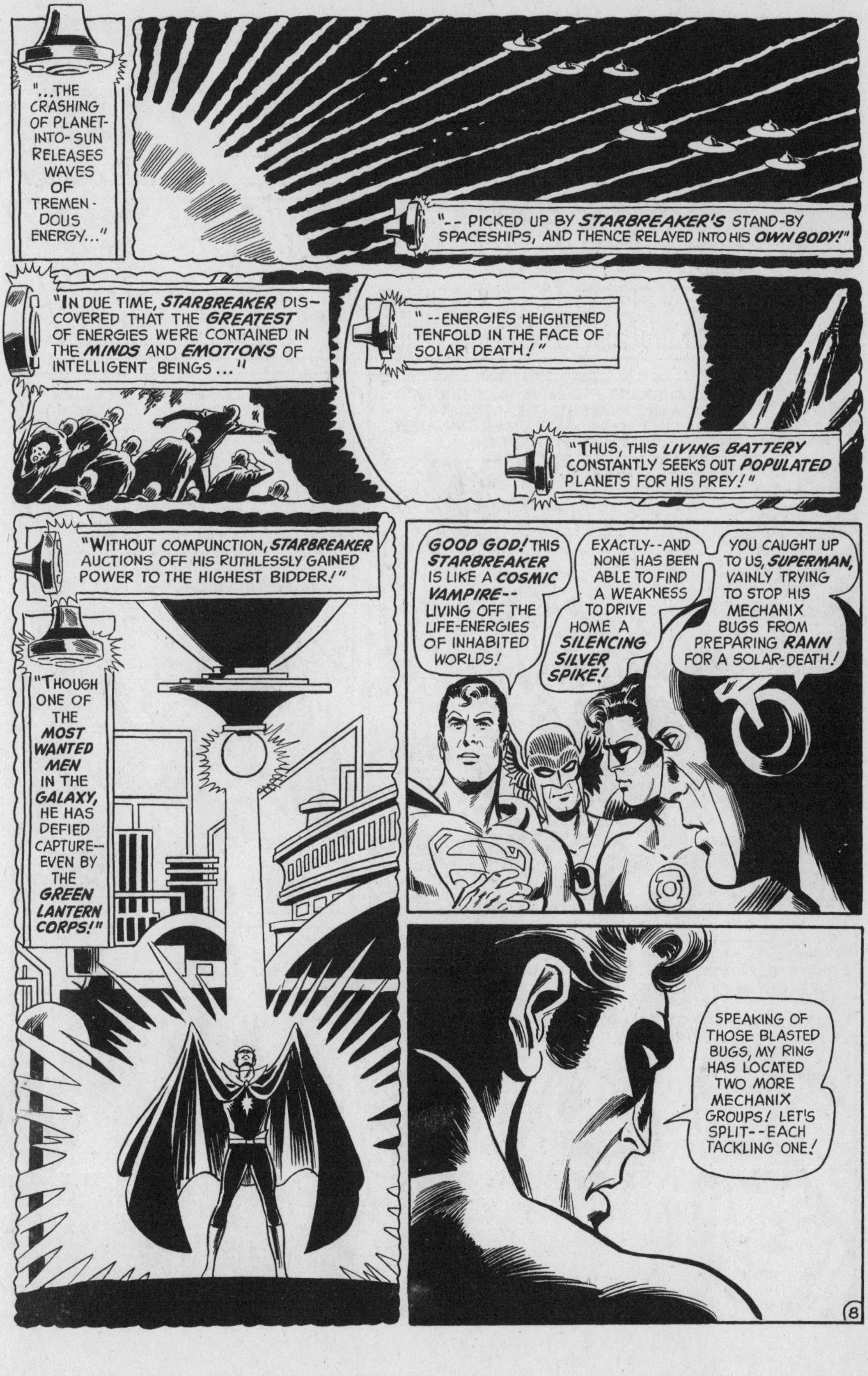
"...THE CRASHING OF PLANET-INTO-SUN RELEASES WAVES OF TREMEN-DOUS ENERGY..."
"-- PICKED UP BY STARBREAKER'S STAND-BY SPACESHIPS, AND THENCE RELAYED INTO HIS OWN BODY!"
"IN DUE TIME, STARBREAKER DIS-COVERED THAT THE GREATEST OF ENERGIES WERE CONTAINED IN THE MINDS AND EMOTIONS OF INTELLIGENT BEINGS..."
"--ENERGIES HEIGHTENED TENFOLD IN THE FACE OF SOLAR DEATH!"
"THUS, THIS LIVING BATTERY CONSTANTLY SEEKS OUT POPULATED PLANETS FOR HIS PREY!"
"WITHOUT COMPUNCTION, STARBREAKER AUCTIONS OFF HIS RUTHLESSLY GAINED POWER TO THE HIGHEST BIDDER!"
"THOUGH ONE OF THE MOST WANTED MEN IN THE GALAXY, HE HAS DEFIED CAPTURE-- EVEN BY THE GREEN LANTERN CORPS!"
GOOD GOD! THIS STARBREAKER IS LIKE A COSMIC VAMPIRE-- LIVING OFF THE LIFE-ENERGIES OF INHABITED WORLDS!
EXACTLY--AND NONE HAS BEEN ABLE TO FIND A WEAKNESS TO DRIVE HOME A SILENCING SILVER SPIKE!
YOU CAUGHT UP TO US, SUPERMAN, VAINLY TRYING TO STOP HIS MECHANIX BUGS FROM PREPARING RANN FOR A SOLAR-DEATH!
SPEAKING OF THOSE BLASTED BUGS, MY RING HAS LOCATED TWO MORE MECHANIX GROUPS! LET'S SPLIT--EACH TACKLING ONE!
8

I'M OFF AND FLYING WITH SUPERMAN-- TO THE ANCIENT RUINS OF ABDUKARA!

WHILE FLASH AND I HIT THE ROAD TO THE NEW CITY-STATE OF NARZAM!

"THE COMING OF STARBREAKER" PART TWO
CO-STARRING GREEN LANTERN AND THE FLASH

LET NOT THE GRIM SHADOWS AND EERIE HUES DELUDE YOU. THEY ARE BUT MERE FIGMENTS THE MIND HAS CREATED WITH WHICH TO COPE-- YET SIMULTANEOUSLY ESCAPE--THE SOUL-CRUSHING HORROR OF...

STARBREAKER!

THOUGH I COME FROM THE OUTER LIMITS OF SPACE, EVEN I HAVE HEARD TALES OF THE LEGENDARY SUPERMAN!

NOW I FIND HE HAD A HAND IN DESTROYING TWO OF MY PLANET-MOVING DEPUTIES!

TO AVOID A REPITITION OF THIS, I SHALL PERSONALLY PROTECT THE OTHERS--WITH ENERGY-DUPLICATES OF MYSELF AT THE TWO REMAINING SITES!

THIS WILL NECESSITATE THE UTILIZATION OF A GREAT DEAL OF ENERGY, ESPECIALLY IN MY SPECIALIZED OFFSPRING WHO WILL DEAL WITH SUPERMAN!

BUT TO RID MYSELF OF THE KRYPTONIAN-- ALONG WITH A GREEN LANTERN AS BONUS, IS A FINE INVESTMENT!

--A VERY FINE INVESTMENT INDEED!

9

UNDER THE CONCENTRATED LIGHT AND HEAT OF THE TRIPLE STAR-SUN *ALPHA CENTAURI*, RACES THE *FASTEST MAN IN RANN!*

FROM WHAT I'VE GATHERED, *STARBREAKER* CHOSE AN EXCEPTIONALLY *RARE DAY* TO ATTACK *RANN*-- WHEN ALL THREE SUNS ARE FOCUSED ON ONE SECTOR OF THE PLANET!

FORTUNATELY, GL HAS PROVIDED ME WITH RING-PROTECTION FROM THE UNBEARABLE *HEAT!*

MEANWHILE, STREAKING ABOVE, THE *EMERALD GLADIATOR'S* THOUGHTS ARE TRACKED IN A DIFFERENT DIRECTION...

THIS IS THE FIRST TIME I HAVE TEAMED UP WITH *FLASH* SINCE *GREEN ARROW* AND I TOOK OFF ON OUR *"SEARCH FOR AMERICA"!*

THERE'S BEEN A LOTTA *CHANGES* SINCE THEN! WONDER IF IT WILL AFFECT OUR TEAM-WORK--?

BUT THERE IS NO *TIME* FOR FURTHER REFLECTION AS...

DEAD AHEAD-- EXPLOSIONS! LOOKS LIKE *POWER GENERATORS!*

RIGHT! IT'S *NEW NARZAM*...BEING LEVELED BY *STARBREAKER'S BUGS!*

10

WITHIN MOMENTS, THE *SCARLET SPEEDSTER* IS GATHERING UP SCIENTIFIC INSTRUMENTS FROM WRECKED LABORATORIES...

NARZAM IS AN EXPERIMENTAL CITY CREATED BY DISGRUNTLED CITIZENS TO TRY OUT NEW WAYS OF LIVING!

LUCKILY, THE PEOPLE WERE ABLE TO EVACUATE BEFORE THE GENERATORS BLEW!

ONLY THING I CAN DO HERE IS SALVAGE VALUABLE *INVENTIONS* AND PRICELESS *INSTRUMENTS*--HOPEFULLY, TO BE USED ANOTHER DAY!

AT THE SAME TIME, *GREEN LANTERN* WILL-POWERS A SLEDGE-HAMMER ATTACK AT THE *MECHANIX*...

FROM WHAT *SUPERMAN* TOLD ME ABOUT THEIR *INVULNERABLE* SHELLS, THIS LINE OF ATTACK WON'T DO ANY GOOD!

BUT IT'LL SERVE AS A *FEINT*... WHILE I SEAL OFF THEIR *ANTENNAE*... AS *SUPES* DID!

FOOL-- WHATEVER YOUR *RING* CAN DO, I CAN *UNDO!*

MY *POWER-RING CAPS*--SHATTERED!? THAT CAN ONLY MEAN, I'M BEING CHALLENGED BY--

11

--STARBREAKER!

MY POWER IS OF A *HUNDRED SUNS*, GREEN LANTERN! *YOUR* RING IS *WEAKER* THAN *MOST* OF YOUR CORPS-- AND I CAN BEST *THEM* AT WILL!

TO *SURVIVE*, YOU MUST *SURRENDER*--

SAME GOES FOR *YOU*, STARBREAKER--

GOT HIM SPINNING LIKE A *TOP!*

AND LIKE A TOP, WHEN HE STOPS SPINNING... HE'LL *FALL!*

I AM WELL *PREPARED* FOR YOUR SUPER-SPEED ATTACK, *FLASH!*

LIGHTNING-- FAST AS IT IS, IT CAN BE NO MATCH FOR MY THOUGHT-FAST *EXPLOSIONS!*

FLASH BEING BLASTED BACK! THOUGH *STARBREAKER'S ENERGY-POWER* IS RESTRAINING US BOTH-- IT IS NOT *NEARLY* AS POTENT AS MY RING PORTRAYED...

WHICH SUGGESTS SOMETHING *PHONEY* HERE-- LIKE A *PHONEY STARBREAKER*-- PERHAPS A *ROBOT-DUPLICATE*--?

I'VE NOTICED HE HAS TO *DIRECT* HIS ENERGY-- BE *AWARE* OF ITS USE--

--MUCH LIKE MY OWN *WILL* CHANNELS THE *POWER* OF MY *RING!*

HAVE TO GAMBLE MY *LIFE* THAT I'M *RIGHT!*

12

MY SUPERIORITY OVER YOUR COLLEAGUE SHOULD CONVINCE YOU THAT RESISTANCE IS FUTILE.' TO UTILIZE *YOUR POWER,* WILL MERELY *INCREASE* MY OWN, AS I ABSORB IT...

DON'T SWEAT IT, *STAR-*BABY! LOOK-- MY RING JUST *LOST* ITS POWER!

YOU MAY KNOW THAT THE *GUARDIANS* HAVEN'T LOOKED WITH TOO MUCH *KINDNESS* ON ME LATELY! YEAH -- THEY GET THEIR *JOLLIES* CUTTIN' OFF MY POWER EVERY NOW AN' THEN!

YEAH... *GREEN LANTERN'S RIGHT!* SEE-- HIS RING'S RUN OUT OF POWER!

AN' YOU KNOW WHAT, *STAR-BABY,* I'M GETTING *TIRED* O' THIS RUN-AROUND! I FIGURE A GUY LIKE *YOU* DESERVES TO HAVE THE RING--

YEAH--HE'LL TELL YOU THE *SECRET* WAY *HOW* TO *CHARGE* IT! IMAGINE ALL THE *ENERGY* YOU'LL FEED INTO YOURSELF!

WELL-- I--I--

YEAH-- AND THEN *POW!* YOU SEE--

THAT'S JIVING HIM, *GL!*

THIS.!!

THANKS FOR PLAYING ALONG WITH THE GAG, *FLASH!*

THAT PUNCH TOOK EVERY *ERG* OF MY *WILL POWER!*

-- WHICH LEAVES IT UP TO *ME* TO *HOLD* HIM *TIGHT* --

13

--WHICH I'LL DO WITH THIS *RANN-VINE* I PICKED UP!

WITHOUT A *CONSCIOUS STARBREAKER* TO GIVE ORDERS, THE BUGS HAVE STOPPED MOVING!

HOW'D YOU CATCH ON I WAS *JIVING* STARBREAKER?

EASY--WHEN I SAW THAT YOUR RING-PROTECTION AGAINST THE THREE SUNS WAS *STILL* WORKING ON ME!

NO, THAT ISN'T QUITE WHAT I MEANT! YOU SEE, WHAT WITH YOU BEING MARRIED AND ME NOT-- AND WE NOT WORKING TOGETHER FOR SO LONG-- I--I--

HEY, *HAL*--C'MON! YOU ALWAYS *WERE* THE MOODY TYPE!

ONLY *YOU* WOULD WORRY ABOUT SOMETHING AS IRRELEVANT AS *THAT*!

UH-HUH ... I GUESS OL' LEVEL-HEADED BARRY ALLEN'S RIGHT AGAIN!

SILENTLY, THEN, LOOKING INTO EACH OTHER'S SMILING EYES, THEY FIRMLY GRIP HANDS IN THE AGES-OLD SIGN OF HUMAN UNITY...

AND EXIT, THE ONCE-AND-FUTURE FRIENDS...

14

"THE COMING OF STARBREAKER" PART THREE
CO-STARRING SUPERMAN and HAWKMAN

NIGHT IS A SOMETIMES THING ON A PLANET WITH THREE SUNS, A TIME FOR TREMBLING BENEATH DARKENED WINDOWS, LISTENING TO ANCIENT VOICES -- OMINOUS ECHOES THAT FADE INTO VAPOR COMES THE DAWNING...

ON THIS EVEN RARER OF NIGHTS, SACRED VOICES OF THE HOLY CITY OF ABDUKARA SCREAM FROM THE WALLS IN FUTILE AGONY AS DESECRATION WAVES ACROSS THEIR IMMEMORIAL ABODE...

YES, IT IS DESTRUCTION THAT RULES -- AND EVEN THE MOST HIGH AND HOLY MUST BOW HIS ANCIENT KNEE!

THERE IS **ONE** WHO HEARS THE TORMENTED SOULS, WHO FEELS THE ETHEREAL VOICES SLAP ACROSS HIS MIND...

FOR THIS **WINGED ONE** KNOWS DEEPLY THE PAST OF **MANY** WORLDS, ROOTING HIMSELF IN THEIR TREASURES--

RICHNESSES WHICH HE WILL FEROCIOUSLY **FIGHT** TO PRESERVE...

LIKE **EARTH'S** REAL **PILL-BUG,** I CAN ONLY HOPE ITS **UNDERSIDE** IS AS **SOFT** AS ITS **BACK** IS HARD!

BEST WAY TO CHECK IT OUT IS TO WRAP MY **ANTI-GRAV BELT** AROUND ITS LEGS--

--AND FLIP IT **OVER!**

THEN BORROW THIS ANCIENT DIAMOND-TIP SHAFT--

16

--AND STRIKE!

IT'S *FORTUNATE* THE GODS OF THIS CITY ARE LONG DEAD AND FORGOTTEN, ELSE THEY WOULD SURELY BE ENRAGED AT THIS MOST UNHOLY OF SACRIFICES!

ELSEWHERE IN *ABDUKARA*...

I'M NOT USED TO PEEKING AROUND WALLS...BUT *THIS* CRITTER IS MECHANICALLY STRONGER THAN I AM--

--AND WHAT IT *CAN'T SEE*, IT *WON'T ATTACK!*

I'VE GOT TO *THINK* FIRST...*ATTACK SECOND!* MY X-RAY VISION FOULED UP THE WORKS, LAST TIME--

--SO THIS TIME I MUST STRIKE A *VULNERABLE* BLOW ON A *SPOT* I *HOPE* I'VE FIGURED OUT!

THIS CALLS FOR *SHOTPUT-ACCURACY--*

--RIGHT ON TARGET!

NOW COMES *PHASE TWO!* IT'S MOVING TOWARD ME-- TO CHECK ME OUT--

17

THAT'S *CLOSE* ENOUGH! TIME TO TURN ON THE *HEAT*--

≈WHEW≈ JUST A HARMLESS, LITTLE EXPLOSION!

ITS INNER MECHANISM WAS MELTED BY MY *HEAT VISION* WITHOUT A MURDEROUS *A-BLAST!*

POP

YES...SUPERMAN'S WON A BATTLE... BUT HARDLY A *WAR!*--AS...

ARRGHH!

THOUGH YOU DEFEAT MY MACHINES, *SUPERMAN*, YOU ARE NO MATCH FOR *STARBREAKER!*

I ALONE HAVE SOLVED THE MYSTERY OF LINKING *SCIENCE* AND *MAGIC! TODAY* MY POWER IS THAT OF *STAR-SUNS*... *TOMORROW* IT WILL BE THAT OF *GALAXIES!*

18

PAL, WHAT MAKES YOU THINK THERE'S A *TO-MORROW* IN YOUR FUTURE--?

REMEMBER--WHEN YOU'VE HAD ENOUGH, THE *KEY WORDS* ARE--

I SURRENDER!

NEVER! NOT WHILE *YOUR* EVERY MOVE INCREASES *MY* POWER!

HIS WRIST-GRIP-- *OVER-POWERING!*

RIPPED OFF MY WINGS--!

19

WHAT NOW, HELPLESS ONE--?

WITHOUT WINGS OR ANTI-GRAV BELT, HOW CAN I POSSIBLY SURVIVE--?

THINK, *HAWKMAN*--*THINK!* IN YOUR MOMENT OF PERIL, YOU WILL ENERGIZE MY BATTERY OF POWER!

BUT IT IS NOT THE *FEATHER-LESS FURY* THAT *RISES* TO THE OCCASION!

THAT MIND-SUCKING MONSTER MUST BE STOPPED! BUT EVEN *THINKING* OF SOLUTIONS WORKS AGAINST ME!

YET, LIKE HIS MACHINES, HE HAS TO BE *VULNERABLE*--PERHAPS IN HIS VERY *DEPENDENCE* ON ABSORBING OUR MENTAL ENERGIES!

AFTER DEPOSITING *HAWKMAN* ON THE GROUND...

I NEED A TWO-PRONGED ATTACK! FIRST *HEAT VISION* TO SEPARATE THE WING-FEATHERS HE'S HOLDING...

--WHICH'LL *CONFUSE* AND *UPSET* HIM! AND IN THAT FRAME OF MIND, HE CAN'T *CONCENTRATE* TO WORK HIS *MAGIC!*

20

AND WITHOUT MAGIC, HE CAN'T STOP *SUPER-POWERED PUNCHES!*

AND *NOW* HE CAN'T CONCENTRATE... *PERIOD!*

WHILE I GATHER UP YOUR FEATHERED WINGS, *HAWKMAN*--

-- BLINDFOLD, DEAFEN AND GAG *STARBREAKER* SO HE CAN'T USE HIS MAGICAL SCIENCE WHEN HE COMES TO!

UNFORTUNATELY WE WERE TOO LATE TO SAVE THE GRANDEUR OF THIS HOLY CITY...

COME-- LET US FLY FROM HERE... THERE IS NOTHING MORE WE CAN DO...

21

"THE COMING OF STARBREAKER" PART FOUR

A PLANET HAS BEEN SAVED-- ITS INHABITANTS SPARED FROM A PIT OF OBLIVION, FREE TO RACE AND STUMBLE DOWN THEIR PERSONAL PATHS OF DESTINY. THERE CAN *BE NO FINER VICTORY* THAN THIS!

YET-- *WHAT IS VICTORY?* AN EXPERIMENTAL CITY DESIGNED FOR A BETTER LIFE -- IN TOTAL RUIN, ITS FUTURE ABORTED.

A HALLOWED PLACE RICHLY FILLED WITH GLORIES OF THE PAST-- *DESTROYED!* IS THERE *VICTORY* IN THIS?

IT IS SAID THE *GREATEST VICTORY* CAN COME ONLY WITH A MEASURE OF *LOSS*...

22

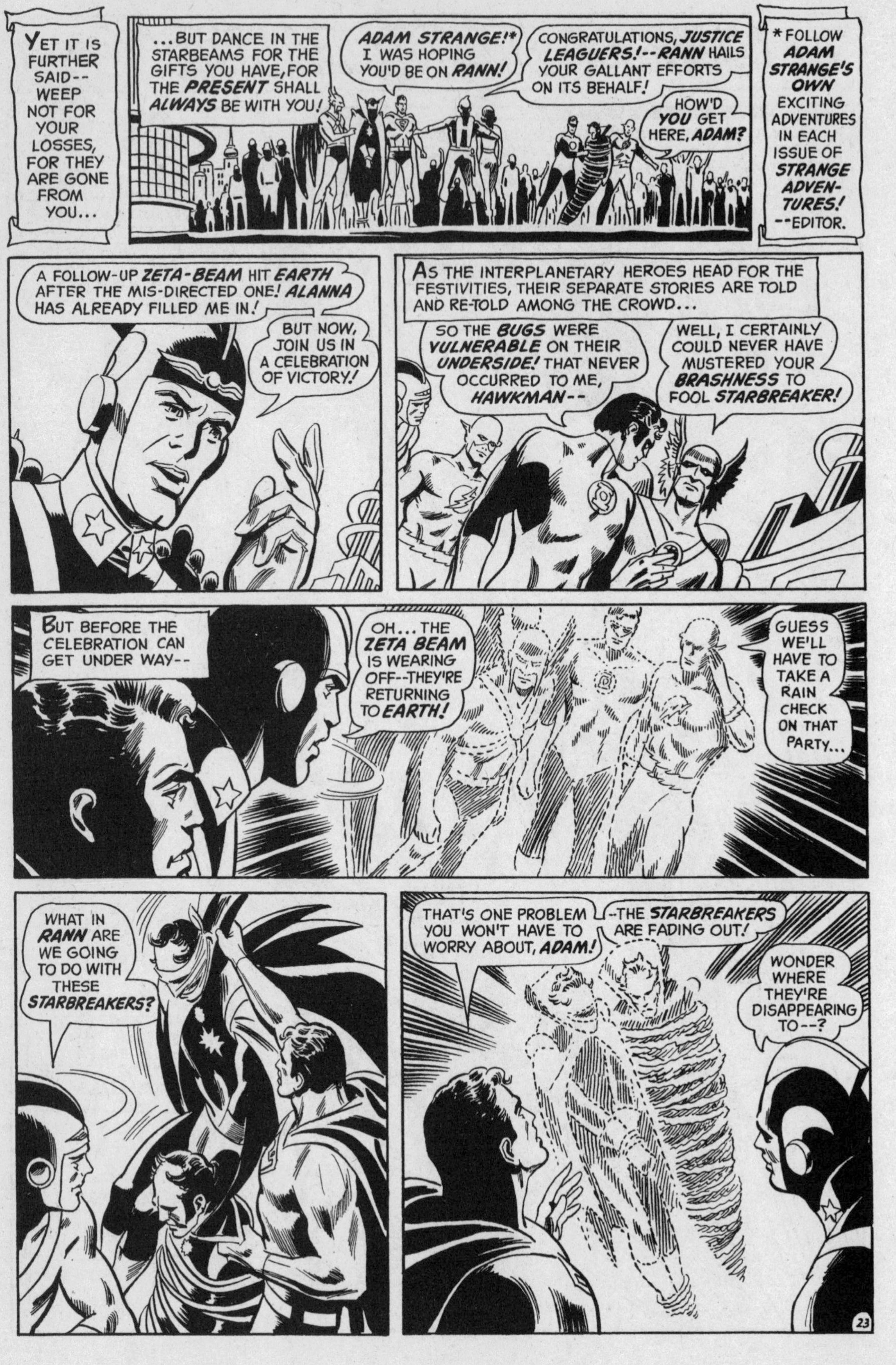
YET IT IS FURTHER SAID-- WEEP NOT FOR YOUR LOSSES, FOR THEY ARE GONE FROM YOU...
...BUT DANCE IN THE STARBEAMS FOR THE GIFTS YOU HAVE, FOR THE PRESENT SHALL ALWAYS BE WITH YOU!
ADAM STRANGE!* I WAS HOPING YOU'D BE ON RANN!
CONGRATULATIONS, JUSTICE LEAGUERS!--RANN HAILS YOUR GALLANT EFFORTS ON ITS BEHALF!
HOW'D YOU GET HERE, ADAM?
*FOLLOW ADAM STRANGE'S OWN EXCITING ADVENTURES IN EACH ISSUE OF STRANGE ADVENTURES! --EDITOR.
A FOLLOW-UP ZETA-BEAM HIT EARTH AFTER THE MIS-DIRECTED ONE! ALANNA HAS ALREADY FILLED ME IN!
BUT NOW, JOIN US IN A CELEBRATION OF VICTORY!
AS THE INTERPLANETARY HEROES HEAD FOR THE FESTIVITIES, THEIR SEPARATE STORIES ARE TOLD AND RE-TOLD AMONG THE CROWD...
SO THE BUGS WERE VULNERABLE ON THEIR UNDERSIDE! THAT NEVER OCCURRED TO ME, HAWKMAN--
WELL, I CERTAINLY COULD NEVER HAVE MUSTERED YOUR BRASHNESS TO FOOL STARBREAKER!
BUT BEFORE THE CELEBRATION CAN GET UNDER WAY--
OH...THE ZETA BEAM IS WEARING OFF--THEY'RE RETURNING TO EARTH!
GUESS WE'LL HAVE TO TAKE A RAIN CHECK ON THAT PARTY...
WHAT IN RANN ARE WE GOING TO DO WITH THESE STARBREAKERS?
THAT'S ONE PROBLEM YOU WON'T HAVE TO WORRY ABOUT, ADAM!
--THE STARBREAKERS ARE FADING OUT!
WONDER WHERE THEY'RE DISAPPEARING TO--?
23

EXTRA ACTION-PACKED PAGES IN ALL DC COMICS!

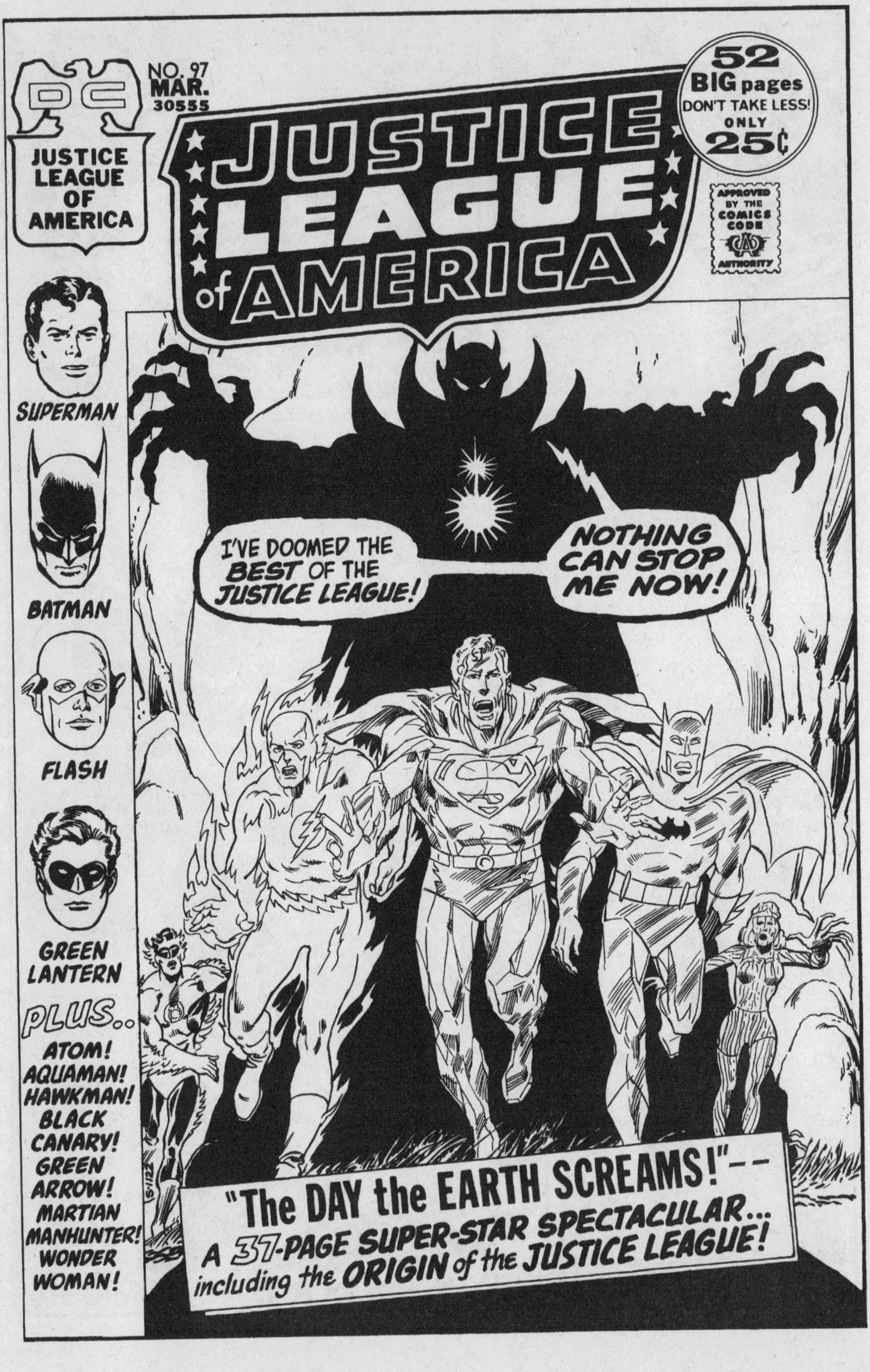
NO. 97
MAR.
30555
JUSTICE LEAGUE OF AMERICA
JUSTICE LEAGUE of AMERICA
52 BIG pages
DON'T TAKE LESS!
ONLY 25¢
APPROVED BY THE COMICS CODE AUTHORITY
SUPERMAN
BATMAN
FLASH
GREEN LANTERN
PLUS..
ATOM!
AQUAMAN!
HAWKMAN!
BLACK CANARY!
GREEN ARROW!
MARTIAN MANHUNTER!
WONDER WOMAN!
I'VE DOOMED THE BEST OF THE JUSTICE LEAGUE!
NOTHING CAN STOP ME NOW!
"The DAY the EARTH SCREAMS!"--
A 37-PAGE SUPER-STAR SPECTACULAR...
including the ORIGIN of the JUSTICE LEAGUE!

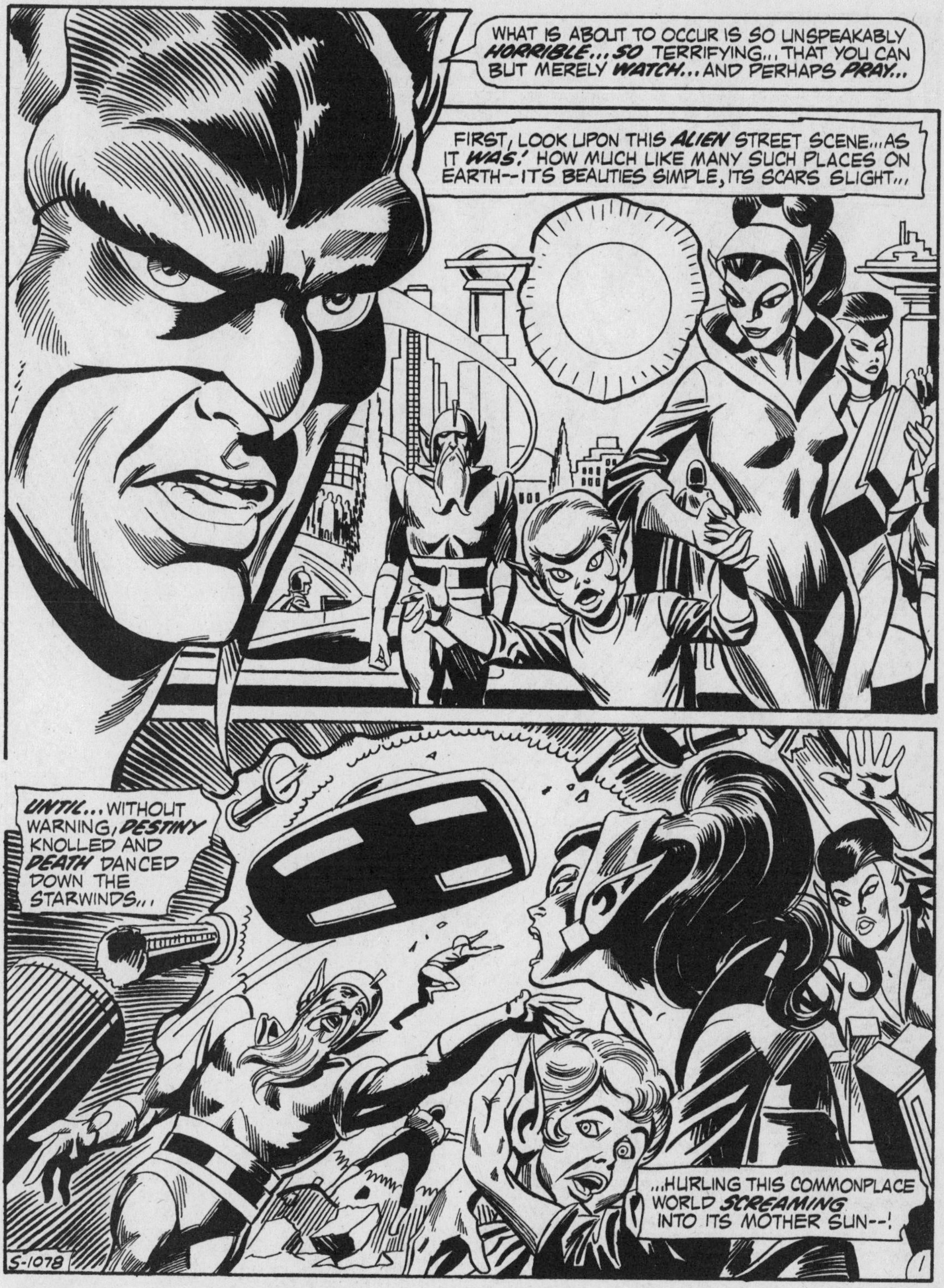
WHAT IS ABOUT TO OCCUR IS SO UNSPEAKABLY HORRIBLE... SO TERRIFYING... THAT YOU CAN BUT MERELY WATCH... AND PERHAPS PRAY...
FIRST, LOOK UPON THIS ALIEN STREET SCENE...AS IT WAS! HOW MUCH LIKE MANY SUCH PLACES ON EARTH--ITS BEAUTIES SIMPLE, ITS SCARS SLIGHT...
UNTIL... WITHOUT WARNING, DESTINY KNOLLED AND DEATH DANCED DOWN THE STARWINDS...
...HURLING THIS COMMONPLACE WORLD SCREAMING INTO ITS MOTHER SUN--!
S-1078

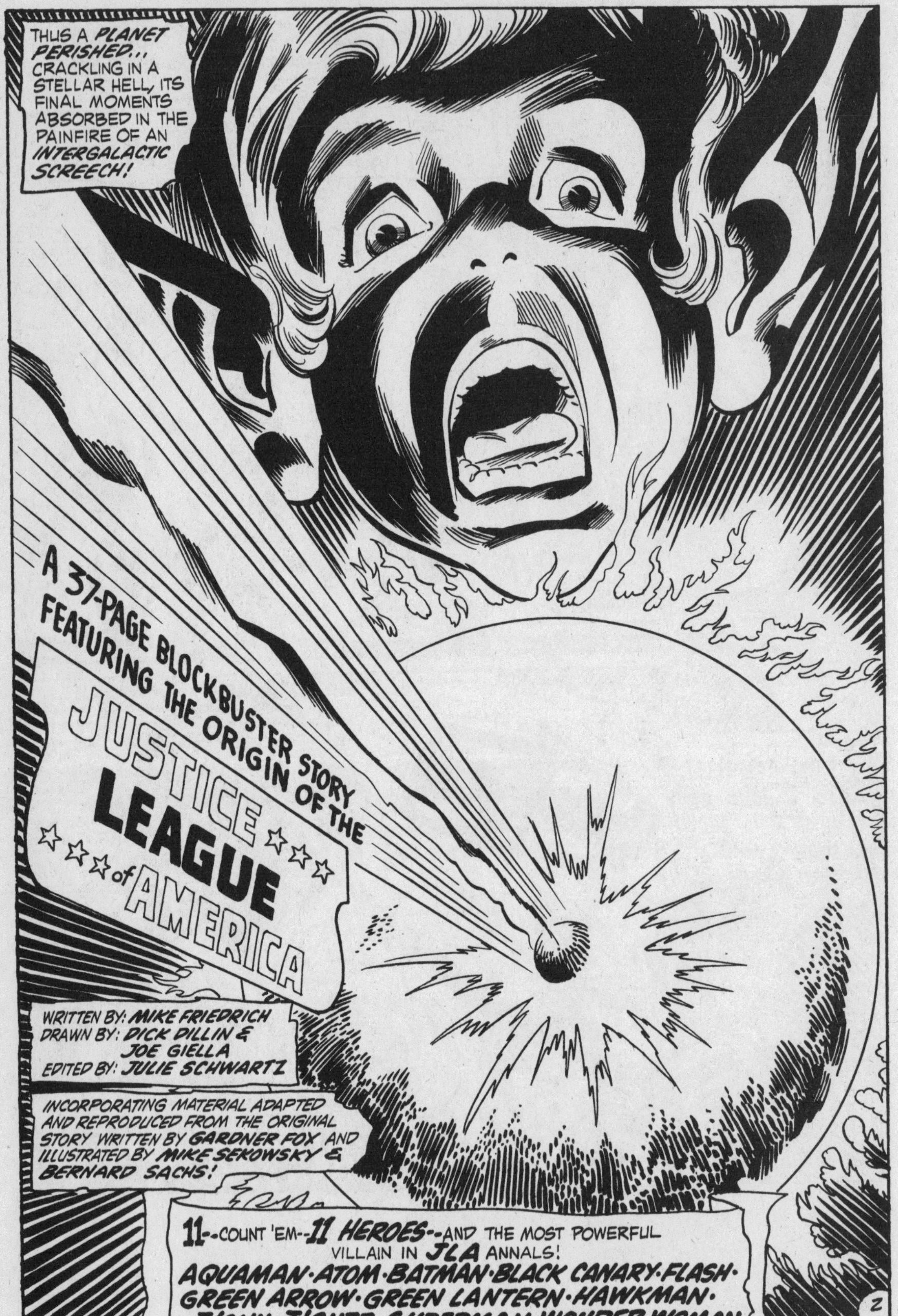
THUS A PLANET PERISHED... CRACKLING IN A STELLAR HELL, ITS FINAL MOMENTS ABSORBED IN THE PAINFIRE OF AN INTERGALACTIC SCREECH!
A 37-PAGE BLOCKBUSTER STORY FEATURING THE ORIGIN OF THE
JUSTICE LEAGUE of AMERICA
WRITTEN BY: MIKE FRIEDRICH
DRAWN BY: DICK DILLIN & JOE GIELLA
EDITED BY: JULIE SCHWARTZ
INCORPORATING MATERIAL ADAPTED AND REPRODUCED FROM THE ORIGINAL STORY WRITTEN BY GARDNER FOX AND ILLUSTRATED BY MIKE SEKOWSKY & BERNARD SACHS!
11--COUNT 'EM--11 HEROES--AND THE MOST POWERFUL VILLAIN IN JLA ANNALS!
AQUAMAN·ATOM·BATMAN·BLACK CANARY·FLASH·
GREEN ARROW·GREEN LANTERN·HAWKMAN·
J'ONN J'ONZZ·SUPERMAN·WONDER WOMAN
2

"MOST BEINGS WOULD SHRINK AT SUCH A *DEATH-THROE*, BUT THERE IS ONE WHO *SEEKS* IT, LUSTING DEMONICALLY FOR ITS EVERY SOUND..."

"A BEING WHO *STORES* THE PHYSICAL ENERGY FROM SUCH COLLISIONS WITHIN *HIMSELF*, LIKE A LIVING BATTERY."

"MOREOVER, HE HAS TAPPED YET *ANOTHER* MIGHTY ENERGY-SOURCE-- THE ALMOST BOUNDLESS POWER CONTAINED IN *HUMAN EMOTION*, UNCORKED WHEN MEN FACE THE GRIM SPECTRE OF DEATH!"

"LESS THAN A MAN...YET SO, SO MUCH *MORE*! ON *EARTH*, HE MIGHT BE CALLED A *VAMPIRE*, BUT IN STELLAR SPACE HE IS FAR MORE--HE IS *STARBREAKER*!"

"IT IS *STARBREAKER'S* AWESOME COMBI-NATION OF *MAGIC* AND *SCIENCE* WHICH WREAKED THE DESTRUCTION OF THE WORLD WE JUST WITNESSED..."

"TOTALLY RUTHLESS IS THIS GRINNING DEVIL, SHAMELESSLY *SELLING* HIS BLOOD-BOUGHT POWER TO GREEDY SPACE-MERCHANTS WHOSE SCRUPLES HAVE LONG SINCE DISSIPATED INTO COSMIC DUST..."

"BEYOND DOUBT, THIS IS THE SINGLE MOST POWERFUL BEING IN THE GALAXY ABLE TO DESTROY WORLDS AT HIS SLIGHTEST WHIM..."

"HOWEVER, WHAT'S OF *PARAMOUNT*... SHUDDERING...CONCERN, IS THAT ONLY *WE* CAN PREVENT--"

THE DAY THE EARTH SCREAMS!

3

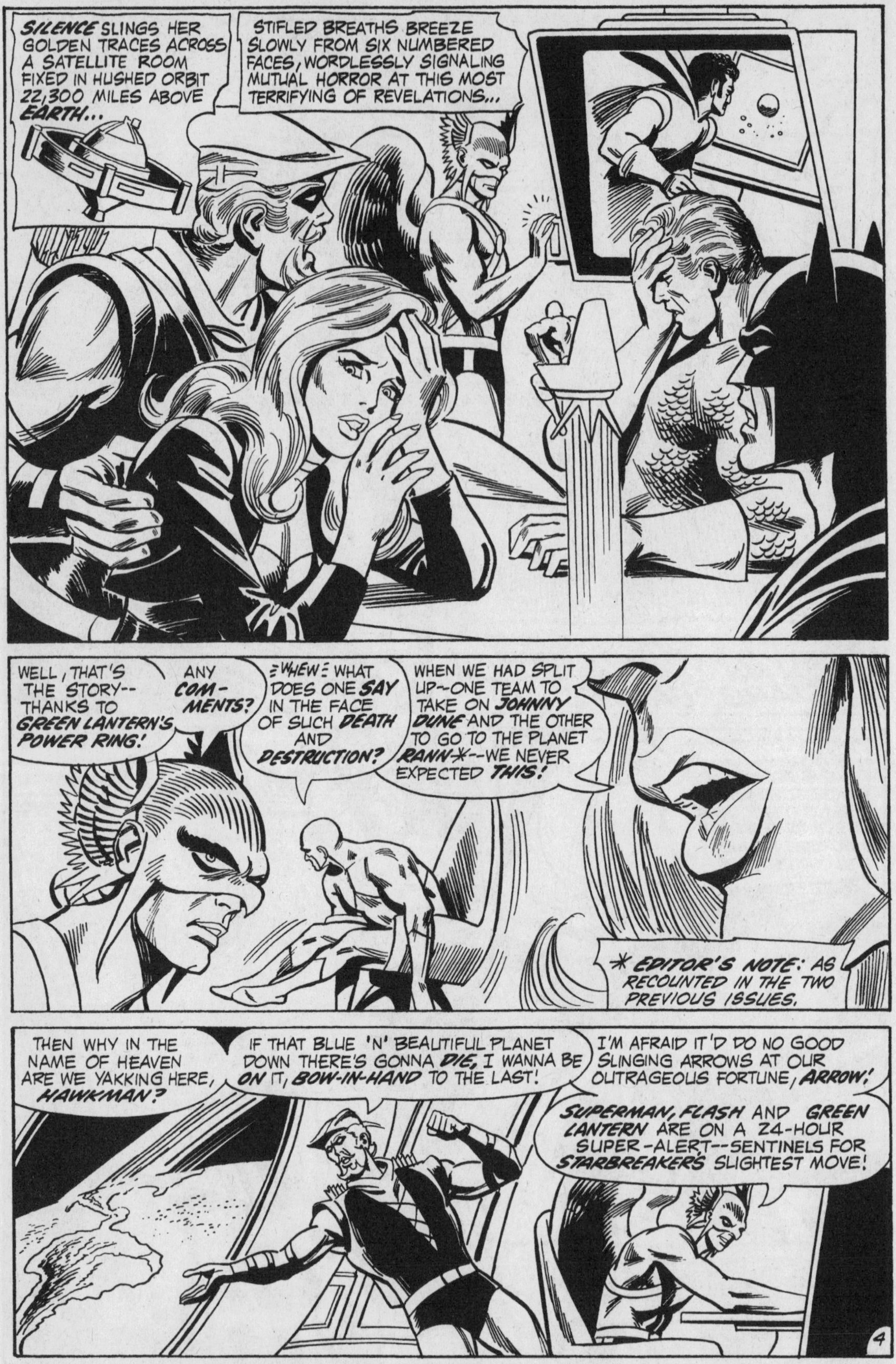
SILENCE SLINGS HER GOLDEN TRACES ACROSS A SATELLITE ROOM FIXED IN HUSHED ORBIT 22,300 MILES ABOVE EARTH...
STIFLED BREATHS BREEZE SLOWLY FROM SIX NUMBERED FACES, WORDLESSLY SIGNALING MUTUAL HORROR AT THIS MOST TERRIFYING OF REVELATIONS...
WELL, THAT'S THE STORY-- THANKS TO GREEN LANTERN'S POWER RING!
ANY COM-MENTS?
=WHEW= WHAT DOES ONE SAY IN THE FACE OF SUCH DEATH AND DESTRUCTION?
WHEN WE HAD SPLIT UP--ONE TEAM TO TAKE ON JOHNNY DUNE AND THE OTHER TO GO TO THE PLANET RANN*--WE NEVER EXPECTED THIS!
* EDITOR'S NOTE: AS RECOUNTED IN THE TWO PREVIOUS ISSUES.
THEN WHY IN THE NAME OF HEAVEN ARE WE YAKKING HERE, HAWKMAN?
IF THAT BLUE 'N' BEAUTIFUL PLANET DOWN THERE'S GONNA DIE, I WANNA BE ON IT, BOW-IN-HAND TO THE LAST!
I'M AFRAID IT'D DO NO GOOD SLINGING ARROWS AT OUR OUTRAGEOUS FORTUNE, ARROW!
SUPERMAN, FLASH AND GREEN LANTERN ARE ON A 24-HOUR SUPER-ALERT--SENTINELS FOR STARBREAKER'S SLIGHTEST MOVE!
4

AND WHAT IS *STARBREAKER* UP TO AT THIS MOMENT?...

SPEAK FAST, GNAT! I HAVE *LITTLE* TIME FOR PUNY TRADERS FROM BACK WATER PLANETS SUCH AS YOURS!

P-PLEASE, SIR... SOME RESPECT! I AM MY PLANET'S *MINISTER OF DEVELOPMENT!*

"DEVELOPMENT"--POOH! YOU'RE LIKE ALL THE REST--POWER-SUCKING FLEAS TRYING TO LEASH THEIR SUPERIOR DOG! OUT WITH YOUR MISERABLE PLEA, GNAT!

WE--WE MERELY WISH TO DISCUSS YOUR OFFER TO SELL OUR PLANET A PORTION OF YOUR ENERGY!

THE *PRICE* YOU NAME IS... *UNACCEPTABLE*--

I DECIDE WHAT IS ACCEPTABLE, GNAT!

YOUR PLANET'S DICTATORS MAINTAIN THEIR TYRANNY SOLELY ON THE ENERGY *I* SUPPLY THEM!

THEY'LL *PAY!* YOU TELL THEM THAT! *THEY WILL PAY!*

NOW THAT THE GNAT'S HAD TIME TO RELAY MY MESSAGE--I'LL ADD MY *PERSONAL SIGNATURE!*

HA! HA! HA! HIS RULERS DON'T *DARE* RETALIATE-- *THEY* KNOW WHO'S IN CHARGE!

≡AHH≡ MY ENERGY-GAIN FROM THE GNAT'S DEATH SWEEPS INTO ME LIKE A SURF-BREAKER ON THE GALACTIC SEA! LOVED IT WHEN THAT TREMBLING GNAT *GROVELED* AT MY FEET...FOR I *THRIVE* ON *FEAR*-- MY PRIME SOURCE OF ENERGY!

ONLY *ONCE* HAVE I BEEN THWARTED... HUMILIATED BY THE PUNY *HUMANS* OF THE *JUSTICE LEAGUE!*

NEVER BEFORE DID I EVER LOSE SO MUCH *VALUABLE* ENERGY TO SUCH *INSIGNIFICANT* FOES! IT MAKES MY BLOOD BOIL WITH *RAGE!*

AND *SUCH* A RAGE IT IS, ENOUGH TO QUAKE *SOLAR SYSTEMS!*...

THIS ACCURSED PLANET! I WILL REGAIN THAT LOST ENERGY-- I WILL *SEIZE* MY REVENGE!

FROM THIS DAY FORWARD-- **EARTH SHALL LIVE NO MORE!**

ELM MARKET

CRUNCH

HAAH! WITH WHAT EASE I DRAW *EARTH'S SUPER-DEFENDERS* INTO BATTLE!

DOUBTLESSLY, THEY THINK TO DEFEAT *ME* AS THEY DID MY *ENERGY-DUPLICATES* ON *RANN!*

THEY WILL BE *SORELY* DISILLUSIONED!

6

OUR WORK'S CUT OUT FOR US! *STARBREAKER'S* SNEAKIER...

--AND INFINITELY MORE *POWERFUL!*

WE NEED AN *EXTRA-FAST* ATTACK TO SLOW *STARBREAKER* DOWN THIS TIME--

AND I'M--

--REVVED UP--

--TO DOUBLE TIME!

YOU FOOLISHLY SEEK TO WHIRL ME LIKE A SPINNING PLANET, *SPEEDSTER*--?

I'LL SHOW YOU *WHO* STOPS--

WATCH OUT! *STARBREAKER'S* TRYING TO *BURY US!*

GUH-HUHHNN!

--WHOM!

YOU ARE NAUGHT BUT ANOTHER BOTHERSOME FLEA--EASILY BRUSHED OFF--*SO!*

MAN! IF *FLASH* HADN'T ABSORBED THAT BLOW AT THE LAST SECOND WITH *ULTRA-VIBRATIONS*, HE'D BE MORE MASHED THAN A *POTATO!*

ON *RANN* I SKINNED THIS CAT WITH A POWER-BEAM PUNCH!

MY BEST BET NOW IS TO TURN ON SOME EXTRA JUICE--FLATTEN HIM WITH A TWO-WAY *PUNCH!*

I HAVE HARNESSED THE ENERGY OF A HUNDRED NOVAS-- DO YOUR *FEEBLE* MINDS THINK YOUR POWERS *MATCH* MINE?

ON COUNT-LESS WORLDS MY VERY *NAME* SPELLS *POWER!*

HE'S NOT WHISTLING THE *TOP THIRTY!*, EITHER!

I'M THE LAST ONE TO CHAL-LENGE HIM! POWER *ALONE* WON'T STOP HIM!

MAYBE I CAN *TOP* THE WAY HE WAS DEFEATED *BEFORE*--

IF *STARBREAKER* CAN BE *CONFUSED*, HE CAN BE *WEAKENED!*

WHO'S BETTER EQUIPPED TO ACT LIKE A SUPER-PEST THAN I?

CONTINUED ON 3RD PAGE FOLLOWING.

8

YOU *BORE* ME, *SUPERMAN!* AND TO THINK I ONCE REGARDED YOU AS A *THREAT!*

I WEARY OF THIS GAME-- SO UNLESS YOU DISPLAY SOMETHING MORE INTERESTING IN THE WAY OF *ATTACK,* I'LL PUT AN END TO THIS RIGHT NOW!

GREAT KRYPTON! HE'S *TRIPLED* HIS SIZE!

THE FUEL OF *RED SUNS* FLOWS IN MY VEINS--I NEED BUT APPLY A SLIGHT DOSAGE TO DISPOSE OF YOU!

NOW FOR THE MOMENT OF *ENERGY-FEASTING,* THE MOMENT OF UTTER DESTRUCTION!

NO--THAT WOULD BE NEEDLESS WASTE!

HOW FAR *MORE* SATIATED SHALL I BE BY HAVING THESE CRUSADERS *CRINGE* AND *TREMBLE* AS THEY WATCH THEIR PLANET *DIE!*

BY CHARGING THEM AND THEIR FELLOW-*LEAGUERS* WITH *WAVES OF DESPAIR,* I WILL MAKE THEM *HELPLESS* TO INTERFERE!

9

NORMALLY, I WOULD CHOOSE THE *LARGEST* PLANET--THAT CALLED *JUPITER*--TO BEGIN THE CHAIN-REACTION THAT EXPLODES THIS SOLAR SYSTEM SUN--

...BUT MY *SWORN REVENGE* COMES FIRST!

--AND THUS *EARTH* BEGINS ITS "*DEATH-MARCH* INTO THE *SUN!*"

JUST THEN A TWISTED TRIUMPHANT SIGHT GIVES PAUSE TO THE PLANET-DESTROYER... AND THE STREETS RING WITH A CHILLING SHRILL LAUGH...

HAAH! THE *JUSTICE LEAGUERS* STIR...DRAG THEMSELVES LIKE INSECTS ACROSS THE BATTLEFIELD!

BEGONE-- INSECTS, NURSE YOUR WOUNDS-- AS YOU AWAIT YOUR *DOOM!*

SHORTLY, THE CONFERENCE ROOM OF THE *JLA SATELLITE* ECHOES TO THROBBING MOANS...

OUR THREE TOP *SUPER-STARS*..., *BEATEN!*

WE LED WITH OUR *ACES*... AND WERE *TRUMPED!*

IF THESE GUYS CAN'T SAVE *EARTH*, WHAT COULD WE *MINOR LEAGUERS* DO?

I LEFT ONE WORLD WHEN MY LIFE COLLAPSED THERE! IS THIS TO BE THE END OF MY *NEW* LIFE HERE?

GREEN ARROW, YOU'RE AS *DOWN* AS THE REST-- I CAN *FEEL* IT!

YEAH, *PRETTY BIRD*... EVEN I GOTTA FACE THE MUSIC SOMETIME-- AND THE DEATH-BAND IS PLAYIN' PRETTY DARN *GOOD* RIGHT NOW!

10

BUT AMONG SUCH AN ALL-STAR ASSEMBLAGE THERE IS ONE WHO RISES TO DISPEL THE DARKNESS...

NO! THIS IS WRONG! DESPAIR DOES NOT BECOME THE JUSTICE LEAGUE I KNOW!

SINCE WHEN HAVE YOU GIVEN UP BEFORE THE FINAL BLOW HAS STRUCK-- BEFORE THE LAST HOPE IS GONE?

WHEN?

WHEN I FIRST CAME TO EARTH FROM MY NATIVE THANAGAR, MY SHIP'S ABSORBASCON SATURATED MY UNCONSCIOUS--

--RECORDING ALMOST EVERY FACT AND FACET OF EARTH'S EXISTENCE!

IN EFFECT, I NOW POSSESS ALL OF EARTH'S RACIAL MEMORY!

FROM THIS PERSPECTIVE, I PLACE VERY HIGH VALUE ON TRADITION, THE SHAPER OF EARTH'S MOST CHERISHED BELIEFS!

SOME OF US HAVE BECOME INVOLVED IN TODAY'S CONTEMPORARY SOCIAL PROBLEMS--

OTHERS NEVER LEFT THEM!

BUT NOW WE MUST EXAMINE OUR ORIGIN, RE-CREATE THE SPIRIT THAT FIRST UNITED THE JUSTICE LEAGUE!

HAWKMAN'S RIGHT! WE HAVEN'T CONSIDERED OUR ORIGIN IN QUITE SOME TIME!

WELL, THEN--IT'S HIGH TIME WE DID! IT MAY SPARK A CLUE-- ENABLE US TO DO SOMETHING!

I MOVE WE ADJOURN TO OUR RECORDS LIBRARY-- NOW!

BEGINNINGS

OF THE ORIGINAL MEMBERS, ONLY *AQUAMAN, FLASH, GREEN LANTERN, BATMAN* AND MYSELF REMAIN ACTIVE!

HOWEVER WE KEEP *VIDEO-MENTO TAPES* OF ALL OUR CASES!

OUR ORIGIN BEGINS WITH THE *MARTIAN MANHUNTER, J'ONN J'ONZZ...*

I FIRST LEARNED OF THE STRANGE MENACE THAT WAS TO UNITE US--

"--FROM AN *UNUSUAL* POLICE REPORT IN AN OUTLYING DISTRICT OF *MIDDLETOWN...*"

EMERGENCY ALERT! PEOPLE ALL AROUND US--HAVE BEEN--TURNED TO--STONE!

"THEN...SILENCE DROPPED ACROSS THE RADIO WAVES AS THE SAME FATE OVERTOOK THE SQUAD CAR RADIO-MAN...."

"*NATURALLY,* I RACED TO THE SCENE...."

WHATEVER ALTERED THE BODIES OF THESE PEOPLE IS BEGINNING TO AFFECT EVEN MY *MARTIAN* BODY!

UHH...STRANGE *TINGLES* EMANATING FROM THIS DIRECTION--

12

--FROM THAT STONE GIANT!

IT'S BLUE BEAMS MUST BE WHAT'S GETTING EVERYONE *STONED!*

IT'S TAKING ALL OF MY MARTIAN-POWERS TO RESIST BEING AFFECTED TOO!

THIS OUGHT TO *PULVERIZE* THE *STONE GIANT* INTO A *PEBBLE PYGMY!*

OWW HE'S SO SOLID-- I BOUNCED RIGHT OFF HIM!

BARELY ABLE TO DODGE THOSE EYE-BEAMS!

I'D SURE HATE TO HAVE HIM WRAP HIS HUGE HANDS AROUND ME...

⑬

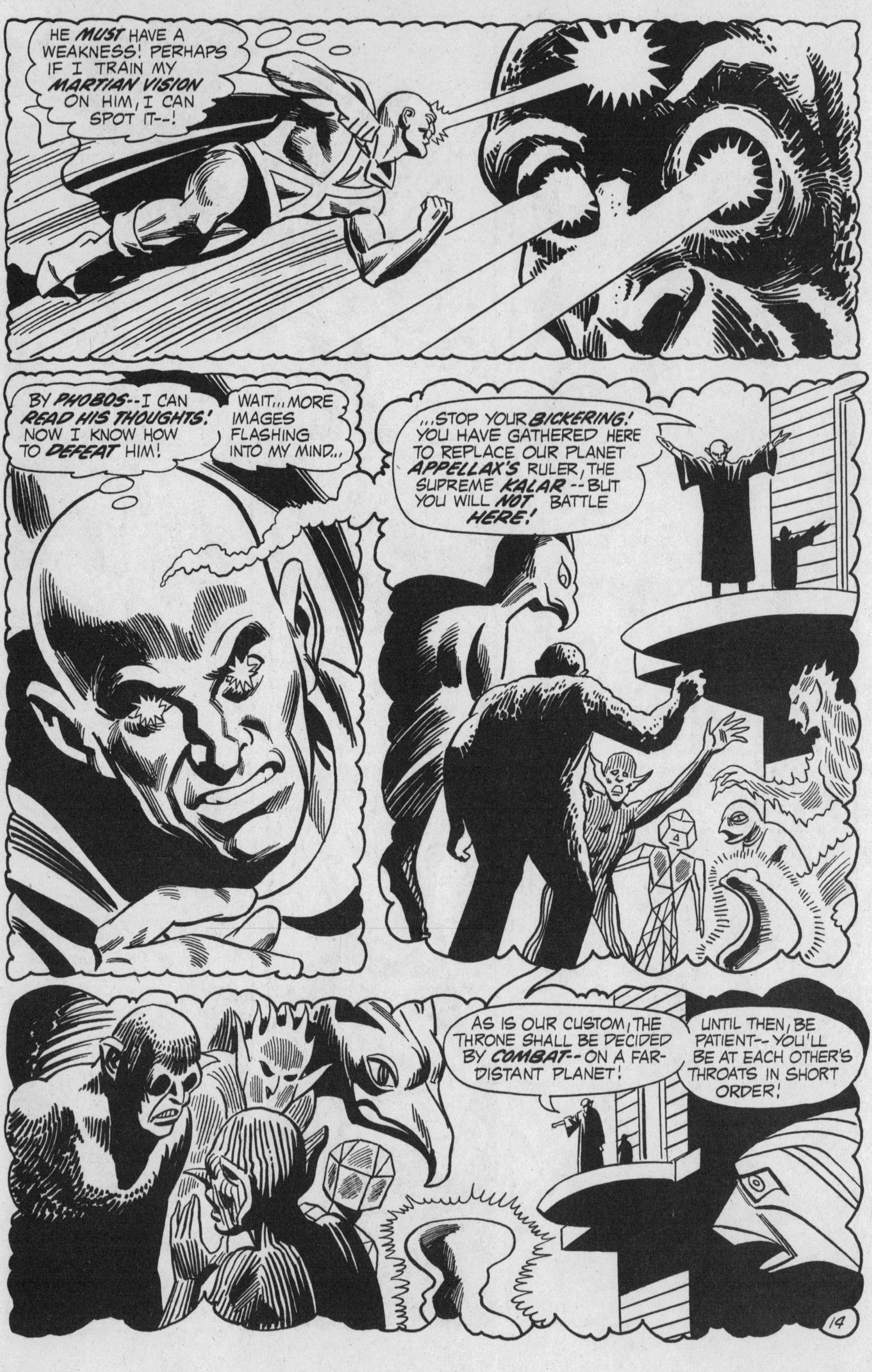
HE MUST HAVE A WEAKNESS! PERHAPS IF I TRAIN MY MARTIAN VISION ON HIM, I CAN SPOT IT--!
BY PHOBOS--I CAN READ HIS THOUGHTS! NOW I KNOW HOW TO DEFEAT HIM!
WAIT... MORE IMAGES FLASHING INTO MY MIND...
...STOP YOUR BICKERING! YOU HAVE GATHERED HERE TO REPLACE OUR PLANET APPELLAX'S RULER, THE SUPREME KALAR --BUT YOU WILL NOT BATTLE HERE!
AS IS OUR CUSTOM, THE THRONE SHALL BE DECIDED BY COMBAT--ON A FAR-DISTANT PLANET!
UNTIL THEN, BE PATIENT-- YOU'LL BE AT EACH OTHER'S THROATS IN SHORT ORDER!
14

"*I*T WAS DECIDED THAT THE CLAIM-ANTS WOULD TRAVEL TO THE PLANET *EARTH*, SINCE THIS WAS THE CLOSEST PLANET TO *APPELLAX* WITH CONDITIONS TO SUPPORT THEIR KIND OF LIFE AND WHICH HAD NEVER BEFORE BEEN USED.."

YOUR BITTER WARFARE WILL RAVAGE THIS PLANET EARTH-- BUT *APPELLAX* ITSELF WILL REMAIN UNHARMED !

"EACH OF THESE WARRIOR CHIEFTAINS WAS CONDENSED IN SIZE AND PLACED INSIDE A METEOR-TYPE VESSEL TO BE HURLED TOWARD OUR PLANET ! THESE METEORS WOULD SAFELY WITHSTAND THE HAZARDOUS VOYAGE THROUGH HYPER-SPACE..."

WHOEVER TRIUMPHS OVER THE OTHERS SHALL RETURN-- AND BE PROCLAIMED *KALAR!*

"THEIR PLAN WAS TO DIVIDE EARTH INTO SEVEN ZONES OVER WHICH EACH OF THE CLAIMANTS WOULD GAIN FULL AND COMPLETE RULE..."

"AS EACH METEOR LANDED, ITS OCCUPANT WOULD BREAK ITS SHELL AND EMERGE IN ITS TRUE FORM ! THEN WITH ITS SPECIAL POWERS IT WOULD TURN THE IN-HABITANTS OF EARTH TO LIFE-FORMS SIMILAR TO ITS OWN.."

"COMMANDING THE ARMY OF THESE TRANSMUTED CREATURES, EACH WOULD WAGE ALL-OUT WAR WITH ONE ANOTHER UNTIL ONLY ONE REMAINED..."

"NO SOONER HAD I UNDERSTOOD ALL THIS THAN I REALIZED TO MY HORROR THAT JUST AS I HAD READ THE STONE-GIANT'S MIND-- SO *HE* HAD READ *MY* MIND..."

SO YOUR WEAKNESS IS *FIRE*, MAN OF MARS ? THEN THAT'S HOW I SHALL OVERCOME YOU !

15

I'VE GOT TO STOP HIM BEFORE HE CAN START A *FIRE!* FORTUNATELY, I NOW KNOW *HIS* WEAKNESS!

"HOWEVER, BEFORE I COULD MAKE CONTACT, A SHOWER OF SPARKS FELL ONTO A SAWDUST PILE IN A NEARBY LUMBER YARD AND..."

TOO LATE! THOSE FLAMES ARE WEAKENING ME-- SAPPING ME OF ALL MY STRENGTH!

"I BARELY MANAGED TO LAND NEAR A FIRE HYDRANT WHERE..."

DIZZY... WEAK... BUT I'VE GOT TO KEEP ON FIGHTING...

"AS I TWISTED LOOSE THE HYDRANT VALVE, A STREAM OF WATER SHOT OUT--AND WITH MY LAST REMAINING STRENGTH I USED MY *MARTIAN BREATH* TO CONTROL IT..."

"*THE* WATER SPRAY HIT THE BLAZING SAWDUST FULL FORCE-- EXTINGUISHING THE FLAMES-- RESTORING MY GREAT POWERS..."

JUST IN TIME! NOW TO GET AT THE STONE-GIANT'S WEAKNESS!

"STRAIGHT UPWARD I LEAPED, AIMING BOTH FISTS FOR A SPOT ON THE *TEMPLE* OF THE ALIEN CREATURE..."

I LEARNED THE EXACT SPOT ON HIS TEMPLE WHERE HIS WEAK SPOT IS LOCATED WHILE PROBING HIS MIND!

16

"I STRUCK WITH THE DESTRUCTIVE FURY OF A DOZEN HURRICANES..."

"THE STONE GIANT CRASHED TO THE GROUND, KNOCKED UNCONSCIOUS..."

"AS HE DID SO, THE PEOPLE WHOM HE HAD TURNED TO STONE WERE INSTANTLY FREED FROM HIS AWESOME SPELL..."

NOW TO SUMMON THE POLICE TO TAKE THE GIANT INTO CUSTODY!

"WHEN THE POLICE ARRIVED I INSTRUCTED THEM WHAT TO DO IF THE ALIEN STIRRED..."

THANKS, J'ONN J'ONZZ! WE'LL USE SLEDGE HAMMERS ON HIM!

"LEARNING FROM THE POLICE WHERE THE OTHER METEORS HAD LANDED, I SET OUT FOR THE ONE THAT HAD FALLEN ON THE CAROLINA COAST NEAR CAPE HATTERAS..."

THIS IS THE ONLY METEOR FROM WHICH THE ALIEN BEING FROM APPELLAX HAS NOT YET EMERGED! MAYBE I'LL HAVE TIME TO OVERCOME IT--

"AND THEN--EVEN AS I RAN TOWARD THE METEOR--IT BEGAN TO PULSE! CAUGHT BY SURPRISE, BEFORE I COULD USE MY MARTIAN POWERS TO FIGHT IT--I FELT MYSELF TURNING INTO WOOD..."

I'M HELPLESS! I--CAN'T MOVE!

17

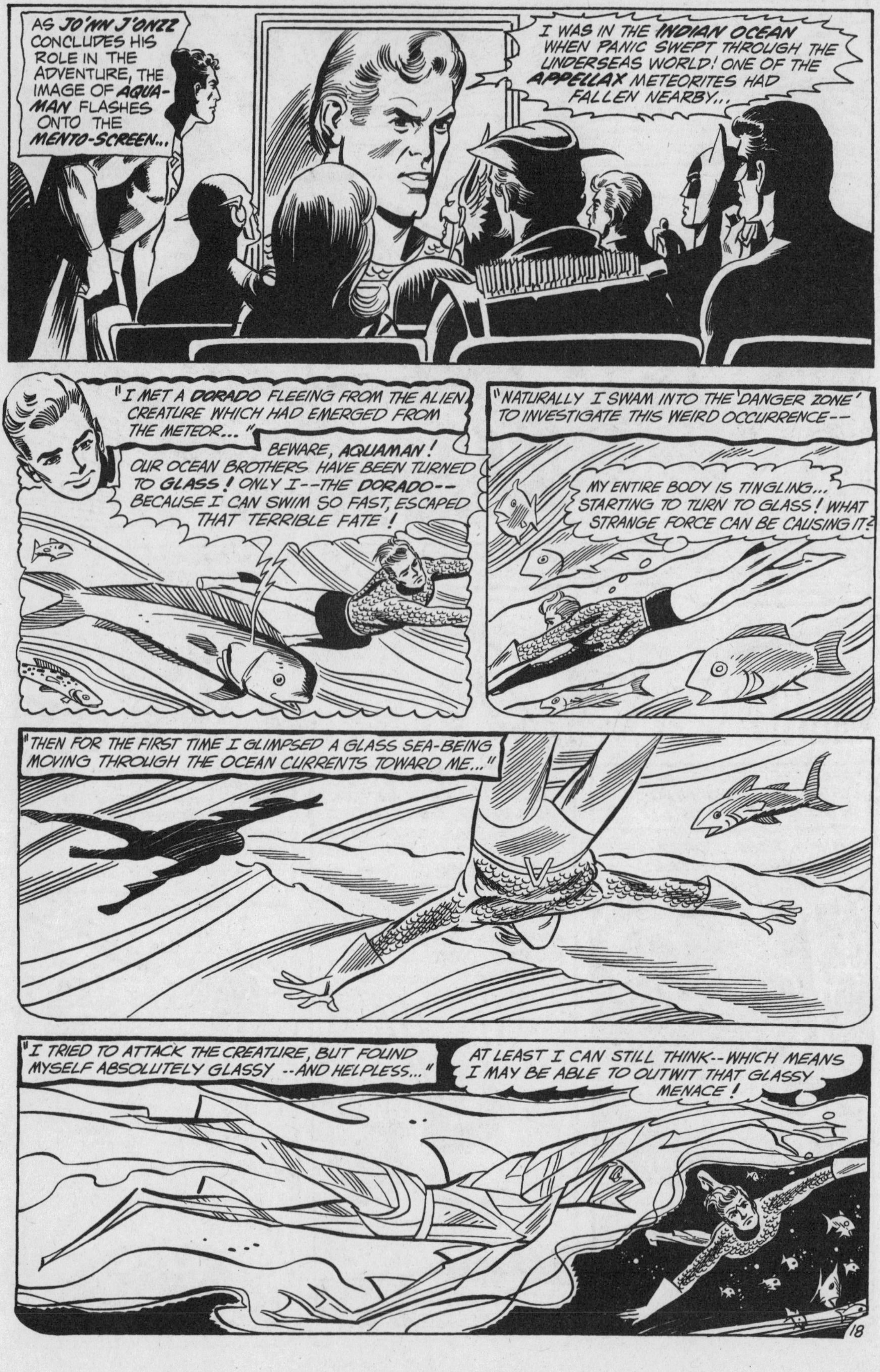
AS JO'NN J'ONZZ CONCLUDES HIS ROLE IN THE ADVENTURE, THE IMAGE OF AQUAMAN FLASHES ONTO THE MENTO-SCREEN...
I WAS IN THE INDIAN OCEAN WHEN PANIC SWEPT THROUGH THE UNDERSEAS WORLD! ONE OF THE APPELLAX METEORITES HAD FALLEN NEARBY...
"I MET A DORADO FLEEING FROM THE ALIEN CREATURE WHICH HAD EMERGED FROM THE METEOR..."
BEWARE, AQUAMAN! OUR OCEAN BROTHERS HAVE BEEN TURNED TO GLASS! ONLY I--THE DORADO--BECAUSE I CAN SWIM SO FAST, ESCAPED THAT TERRIBLE FATE!
"NATURALLY I SWAM INTO THE 'DANGER ZONE' TO INVESTIGATE THIS WEIRD OCCURRENCE--
MY ENTIRE BODY IS TINGLING... STARTING TO TURN TO GLASS! WHAT STRANGE FORCE CAN BE CAUSING IT?
"THEN FOR THE FIRST TIME I GLIMPSED A GLASS SEA-BEING MOVING THROUGH THE OCEAN CURRENTS TOWARD ME..."
"I TRIED TO ATTACK THE CREATURE, BUT FOUND MYSELF ABSOLUTELY GLASSY --AND HELPLESS..."
AT LEAST I CAN STILL THINK--WHICH MEANS I MAY BE ABLE TO OUTWIT THAT GLASSY MENACE!
18

"TO TEST WHETHER I STILL RE-TAINED MY TELEPATHIC POWERS OVER MY FINNY FRIENDS, I BROADCAST A WARNING FOR THEM TO STAY AWAY--AND WAS REWARDED BY SEEING THEM RACE OFF..."

IT WORKED! NOW TO MAKE A FIGHT OF THIS!

"MY FIRST 'CALL TO ARMS' WENT OUT TO THE SHELL-BACKED TRUNKFISH..."

BROTHER TRUNKFISH! TO THE ATTACK! SWIM AS HARD AS YOU CAN--AND TRY TO SMASH THIS ENEMY OF OURS!

"SINCE THE SCALES OF THE TRUNK-FISH FUSE TOGETHER TO FORM A HARD SHELL, I HOPED BY HITTING THE ALIEN BEING WITH ENOUGH OF THEM, TO KNOCK IT OUT..."

"HOWEVER I DID NOT RELY ON THE TRUNKFISH ALONE! AT THE SAME TIME I WAS TELEPATHING A CALL TO THE INDIAN TRIGGER-FISH, THE AUSTRALIAN CERATODUS, TO THE COFFER, AND THE GURNARD, AMONG OTHERS..."

"THE HARD-SHELLED TRUNKFISH HURLED THEMSELVES AT THE ALIEN CREATURE--BUT WERE INSTANTLY CAUGHT IN ITS EYE BEAMS AND TURNED TO GLASS..."

THE TRUNKFISH FAILED ME! MY ONLY HOPE IS THE OTHER FISH FAR ABOVE THE GLASSY CREATURE!

"THESE FISH I HAD SUMMONED WERE THE NOISEMAKERS OF THE FISH FAMILY! AT MY COMMAND THEY EACH BEGAN TO MAKE THEIR INDIVIDUAL SOUNDS..."

JUST AS THE SOUND FROM A VIOLIN STRING CAN SHATTER GLASS--SO I HOPE ONE OF THOSE FISH WILL MAKE A SOUND THAT WILL SHATTER THE GLASS ALIEN BEING!

19

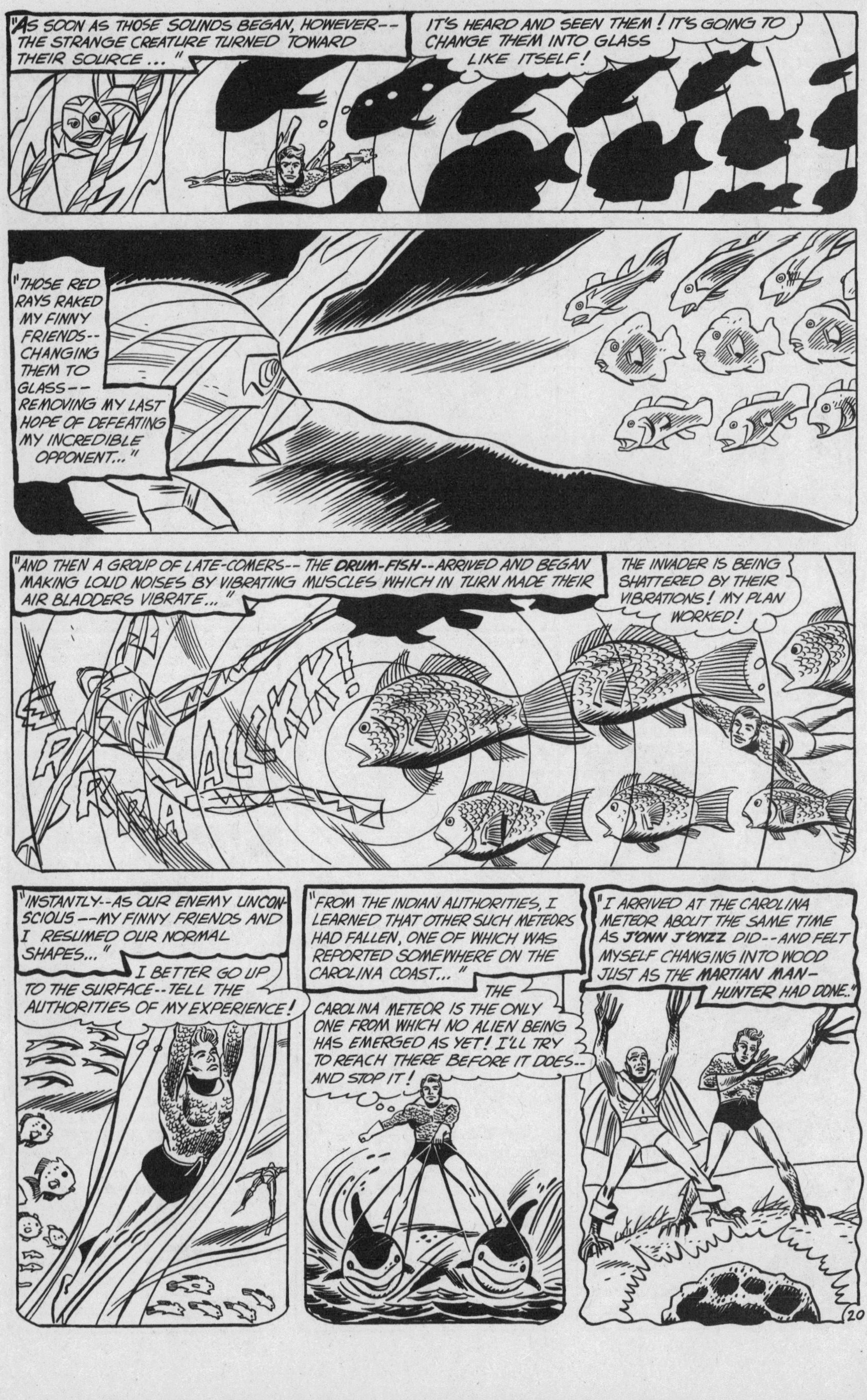
"AS SOON AS THOSE SOUNDS BEGAN, HOWEVER-- THE STRANGE CREATURE TURNED TOWARD THEIR SOURCE ..."
IT'S HEARD AND SEEN THEM! IT'S GOING TO CHANGE THEM INTO GLASS LIKE ITSELF!
"THOSE RED RAYS RAKED MY FINNY FRIENDS--CHANGING THEM TO GLASS--REMOVING MY LAST HOPE OF DEFEATING MY INCREDIBLE OPPONENT..."
"AND THEN A GROUP OF LATE-COMERS-- THE DRUM-FISH--ARRIVED AND BEGAN MAKING LOUD NOISES BY VIBRATING MUSCLES WHICH IN TURN MADE THEIR AIR BLADDERS VIBRATE..."
THE INVADER IS BEING SHATTERED BY THEIR VIBRATIONS! MY PLAN WORKED!
KRAACKK!
"INSTANTLY--AS OUR ENEMY UNCONSCIOUS--MY FINNY FRIENDS AND I RESUMED OUR NORMAL SHAPES..."
I BETTER GO UP TO THE SURFACE--TELL THE AUTHORITIES OF MY EXPERIENCE!
"FROM THE INDIAN AUTHORITIES, I LEARNED THAT OTHER SUCH METEORS HAD FALLEN, ONE OF WHICH WAS REPORTED SOMEWHERE ON THE CAROLINA COAST..."
THE CAROLINA METEOR IS THE ONLY ONE FROM WHICH NO ALIEN BEING HAS EMERGED AS YET! I'LL TRY TO REACH THERE BEFORE IT DOES--AND STOP IT!
"I ARRIVED AT THE CAROLINA METEOR ABOUT THE SAME TIME AS J'ONN J'ONZZ DID--AND FELT MYSELF CHANGING INTO WOOD JUST AS THE MARTIAN MAN-HUNTER HAD DONE."
20

FADE OUT *AQUAMAN*... FADE IN THE ONE-TIME SUPER-POWERED *WONDER WOMAN* TO TAKE UP THE NARRATION...

I BECAME INVOLVED IN THE CASE WHILE FLYING TO *PARADISE ISLAND*, HOME OF MY SISTER AMAZONS, TO VISIT MY MOTHER, *QUEEN HIPPOLYTA*...

"AS I CIRCLED THE ISLAND IN MY *ROBOT PLANE*, MY ATTENTION WAS DRAWN TO A NUMBER OF GLITTERING BLOBS THAT OOZED ALONG THE GROUND..."

SUFFERING SAPPHO-- WHAT ARE THOSE THINGS?

"NOWHERE DID I SEE ANY SIGN OF MY MOTHER THE QUEEN OR ANY OF THE *AMAZON* MAIDENS..."

WHERE IS EVERYBODY? WHAT'S HAPPENED HERE?

"RACING INTO THE *AMAZON* LABORATORY, I PULLED A SWITCH WHICH ACTIVATED A TAPE-VIEWER RECORDING OF EVERYTHING THAT TRANSPIRES ON THE ISLAND..."

A METEOR--APPROACHING *PARADISE ISLAND*--GOING TO CRASH HERE! COULD THAT HAVE ANY CONNECTION WITH THOSE BRIGHT GLOBS I SAW? I'LL SOON KNOW...

"AS IF I WERE AN UNSEEN SPECTATOR, I WATCHED AND HEARD THE REENACTMENT OF THE FALLING METEOR AS IT THUDDED INTO THE GROUND..."

"ALMOST INSTANTLY THE METEOR BROKE OPEN AND A SHAPELESS MASS OF BRILLIANCE--WHICH THE SPECTROSCOPIC ATTACHMENT TOLD ME WAS *LIQUID MERCURY*--OOZED OUT..."

IT'S GIVING OFF-- SOME QUEER RADIATION!

WARN THE QUEEN-- QUICKLY!

21

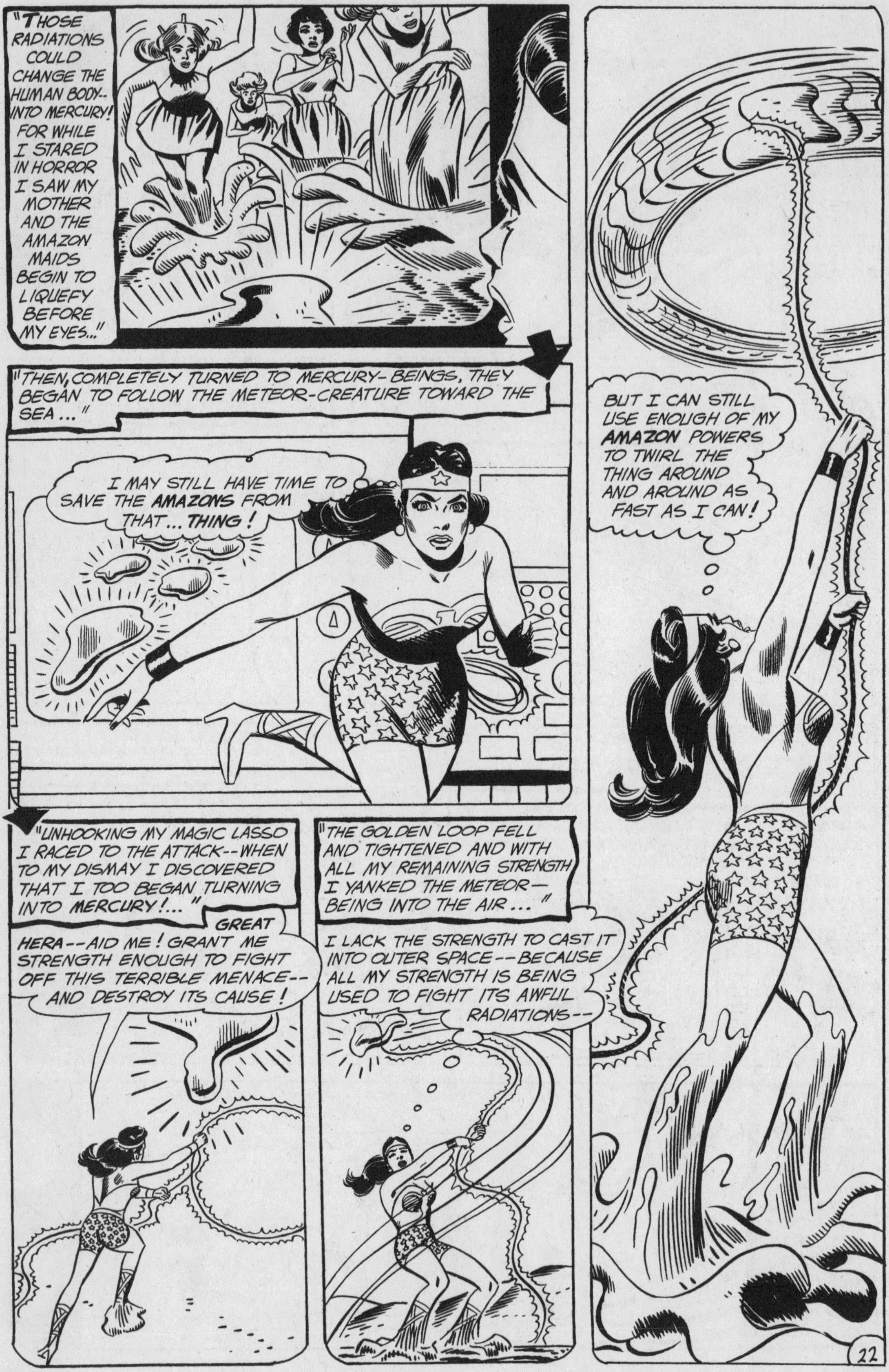
"THOSE RADIATIONS COULD CHANGE THE HUMAN BODY-- INTO MERCURY! FOR WHILE I STARED IN HORROR I SAW MY MOTHER AND THE AMAZON MAIDS BEGIN TO LIQUEFY BEFORE MY EYES..."
"THEN, COMPLETELY TURNED TO MERCURY-BEINGS, THEY BEGAN TO FOLLOW THE METEOR-CREATURE TOWARD THE SEA..."
I MAY STILL HAVE TIME TO SAVE THE **AMAZONS** FROM THAT... **THING**!
"UNHOOKING MY MAGIC LASSO I RACED TO THE ATTACK--WHEN TO MY DISMAY I DISCOVERED THAT I TOO BEGAN TURNING INTO **MERCURY**!..."
GREAT HERA--AID ME! GRANT ME STRENGTH ENOUGH TO FIGHT OFF THIS TERRIBLE MENACE-- AND DESTROY ITS CAUSE!
"THE GOLDEN LOOP FELL AND TIGHTENED AND WITH ALL MY REMAINING STRENGTH I YANKED THE METEOR-BEING INTO THE AIR..."
I LACK THE STRENGTH TO CAST IT INTO OUTER SPACE--BECAUSE ALL MY STRENGTH IS BEING USED TO FIGHT ITS AWFUL RADIATIONS--
BUT I CAN STILL USE ENOUGH OF MY **AMAZON** POWERS TO TWIRL THE THING AROUND AND AROUND AS FAST AS I CAN!
22

"*FASTER--EVER FASTER AND FASTER--I SWUNG MY ROPE UNTIL IT AND THE METEOR--THING IT HELD MADE A SOUND LIKE A BULLROARER ...*"

THE BOILING POINT OF MERCURY IS 356.9° CENTIGRADE...

JUST AS MANY METEORS *BURN UP* FROM FRICTION AS THEY HURTLE INTO OUR ATMOSPHERE FROM OUTER SPACE--SO I HOPE TO WHIP UP ENOUGH HEAT THROUGH FRICTION TO VAPORIZE THAT THING!

"*WHILE I WAS SWINGING IT, THE MERCURY-BEING POURED OUT ITS DEADLY RADIATIONS UNTIL I WAS MORE THAN HALF-- MERCURY MYSELF ...*"

CAN I LAST? OR WILL THOSE RADIATIONS DEFEAT ME BEFORE THE METEOR-BEING TURNS TO VAPOR? *HERA* HELP ME! SAPPHO-- STRENGTHEN MY ARM!

"*AND THEN--SO SUDDENLY THAT EVEN I WAS TAKEN BY SURPRISE--THE TERRIBLE MENACE TO PARADISE ISLAND CHANGED INTO WHIRLING VAPORS ...*"

MY DAUGHTER! YOU SAVED US FROM THAT AWFUL PERIL!

"*I COULD NOT WASTE TIME ON ENDEARMENTS! HAVING LEARNED FROM THE AMAZON INSTRUMENTS OF OTHER METEORS FALLING AROUND THE EARTH, I SET OUT FOR THE ONE IN CAROLINA WHICH HAD NOT YET DISCHARGED ITS OCCUPANT, AND ARRIVED ALMOST SIMULTANEOUSLY WITH AQUAMAN ...*"

NEXT TO BURST ONTO THE SCREEN-- *GREEN LANTERN...*

EVEN AS THE OTHERS WERE BATTLING TO SAVE *EARTH*, I WAS RETURNING HOME FROM AN OUTER-SPACE MISSION, WHEN...

"*I* WAS STUNNED BY THE SUDDEN EMERGENCE BESIDE ME, IN WHAT HAD SEEMED EMPTY SPACE--OF A METEOR..."

WHAT--? THAT METEOR WASN'T HERE A MOMENT AGO! IT'S AS IF IT SUDDENLY CAME OUT OF *HYPER-SPACE!*

"NATURALLY CURIOUS AND SOME-- WHAT SUSPICIOUS--I TRAILED THE METEOR DOWN TO THE AFRICAN CONTINENT IN SOUTHERN RHODESIA, WHERE AS IT LANDED IT BURST OPEN AND..."

EMERGING FROM IT-- A GIANT BIRD COVERED WITH GOLDEN PLUMAGE!

"TO MY ASTONISHMENT, AS THE ALIEN BIRD FLEW LOW OVER THE JUNGLE TREETOPS, ITS EYES EMITTED A WHITE RAY WHICH CHANGED THE ANIMALS INTO WINGED BEINGS LIKE ITSELF..."

I BETTER PUT A STOP TO THIS!

"AS I SWOOPED DOWN TO INTER-CEPT THE STRANGE CREATURE I SAW TWO HUNTERS WHO HAD BEEN CHANGED BY IT..."

GREAT GUARDIANS! THE BIRD MUST BE PLANNING TO TURN ALL EARTH CREATURES INTO REPLICAS OF ITSELF! I'D BETTER COVER MY BODY WITH A SHEATH AS PROTECTION AGAINST ITS RAYS!

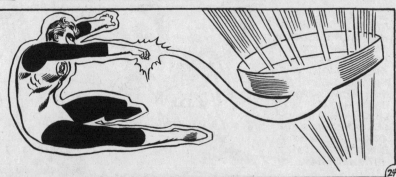

"AS YOU KNOW, MY *POWER RING* IS HELPLESS AGAINST ANY-THING *YELLOW* SO I PLANNED TO FIGHT THE YELLOW MENACE WITH A BURNING GLASS THROUGH WHICH THE HOT RAYS OF THE SUN COULD BE FOCUSED..."

24

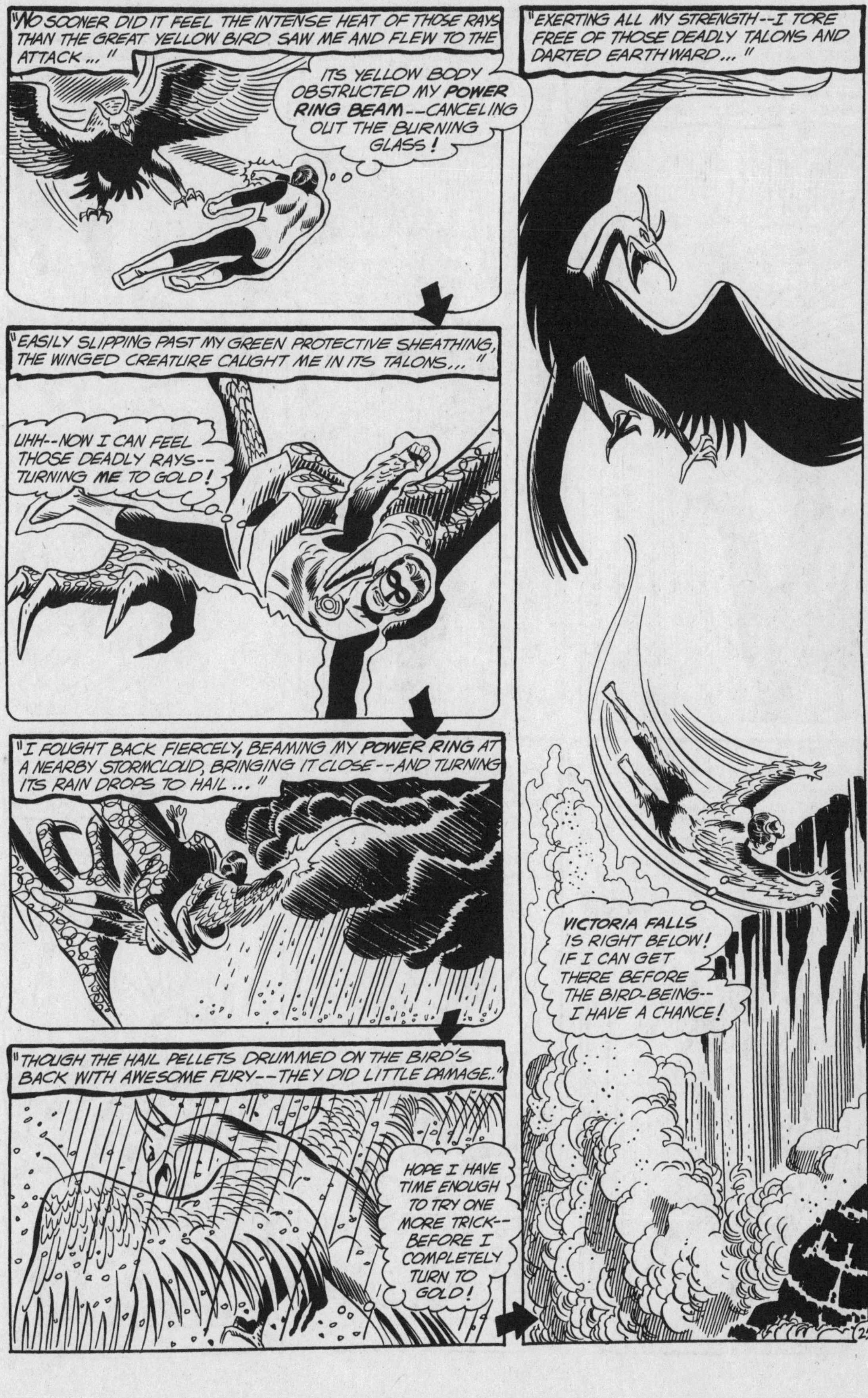
"NO SOONER DID IT FEEL THE INTENSE HEAT OF THOSE RAYS THAN THE GREAT YELLOW BIRD SAW ME AND FLEW TO THE ATTACK..."
ITS YELLOW BODY OBSTRUCTED MY POWER RING BEAM--CANCELING OUT THE BURNING GLASS!
"EASILY SLIPPING PAST MY GREEN PROTECTIVE SHEATHING, THE WINGED CREATURE CAUGHT ME IN ITS TALONS..."
UHH--NOW I CAN FEEL THOSE DEADLY RAYS--TURNING ME TO GOLD!
"I FOUGHT BACK FIERCELY, BEAMING MY POWER RING AT A NEARBY STORMCLOUD, BRINGING IT CLOSE--AND TURNING ITS RAIN DROPS TO HAIL..."
"THOUGH THE HAIL PELLETS DRUMMED ON THE BIRD'S BACK WITH AWESOME FURY--THEY DID LITTLE DAMAGE."
HOPE I HAVE TIME ENOUGH TO TRY ONE MORE TRICK--BEFORE I COMPLETELY TURN TO GOLD!
"EXERTING ALL MY STRENGTH--I TORE FREE OF THOSE DEADLY TALONS AND DARTED EARTHWARD..."
VICTORIA FALLS IS RIGHT BELOW! IF I CAN GET THERE BEFORE THE BIRD-BEING--I HAVE A CHANCE!
25

"*POWER RING* BLAZING, I DOVE HEAD-FIRST INTO THAT MIGHTY CATARACT, BATTERED AND BRUISED BY ITS TONS OF FALLING WATER--WITH THE METEOR-BIRD RIGHT AT MY HEELS ..."

FASTER--I'VE GOT TO GO FASTER!

"I WAS ALTERING SO SWIFTLY THAT I FEARED I COULD NOT DO AS I PLANNED, FOR AS I TRAVELED THROUGH THE WATERFALL, MOST OF MY BODY WAS COVERED WITH THAT GOLDEN PLUMAGE..."

IT TOOK THE BAIT AND FOLLOWED ME! NOW TO LEAVE THE WATERS AND...

"DRIPPING WET, I FLEW OUT OF THE FALLS! AS I DID, I TURNED AND..."

THIS BEAM OF SPATIAL COLD WILL FREEZE THOSE WATERS SOLID!

"IN THE NEXT INSTANT--THE WATERFALL BECAME A LENGTH OF SOLID ICE--TRAPPING THE BIRD CREATURE INSIDE IT..."

THAT'LL HOLD IT UNTIL I CAN SAVE THOSE ANIMALS AND MEN IT TURNED INTO FLYING DUPLICATES OF ITSELF!

"FOR JUST AS MY OWN BODY HAD CHANGED BACK TO NORMAL WHEN THE BIRD-THING WAS IMPRISONED IN THE ICE, SO I KNEW THE OTHERS WOULD ALSO RETURN TO NORMAL..."

I'LL DROP THEM OFF AT THE HOSPITAL AND ZOO IN NEARBY *LIVINGSTONE* IN CASE THEY NEED MEDICAL ATTENTION!

"IN *LIVINGSTONE* I LEARNED OF THE OTHER METEORS AND SET OUT AT ONCE FOR THE CAROLINA METEOR, SINCE THE BEING INSIDE IT HAD NOT YET MADE ITS APPEARANCE! I ARRIVED JUST AS *WONDER WOMAN* SHOWED UP..."

26

AT THIS POINT, *THE FLASH* PICKS UP THE STORY...

IN MY CIVILIAN IDENTITY, I WAS IN *EUROPE* ON POLICE BUSINESS WHEN WORD CAME IN THAT A STRANGE METEORITE HAD LANDED NEAR *LAKE COMO* IN *ITALY*...

"*BECAUSE OF THE URGENCY,* I IMMEDIATELY SWITCHED TO *THE FLASH* AND INVESTIGATED..."

A *FLAME-BEING* ERUPTED FROM THE METEORITE-- CHANGING NEARBY NATIVES INTO CREATURES LIKE ITSELF!

SHOULD BE EASY ENOUGH TO *QUENCH* THAT *LIVING FIRE*...

"*ROTATING MY ARMS AT SUPER-SPEED* WHIPPED UP HURRICANE-LIKE WINDS--BUT...*"

¿EH?!¿ INSTEAD OF PUFFING IT OUT, THE WINDS ARE MAKING THE *FLAME-BEING LARGER,* LIKE A RUNAWAY *FOREST FIRE!*

"*TO MAKE MATTERS EVEN WORSE...*"

THE FLAME-BEING'S GIVING OFF MYSTERIOUS EMANATIONS. TURNING *ME* INTO FLAMES-- JUST LIKE THOSE OTHER PEOPLE!

27

"I FIGURED MY ONLY DEFENSE WAS TO VIBRATE AWAY SO SWIFTLY THAT MY BODY COULD COUNTERACT THOSE DEADLY EMANATIONS..."

WIND FAILED TO PUT OUT THAT FIRE-CHARACTER-- BUT WATER OUGHT TO DO THE TRICK!

"SPEEDING ONTO LAKE COMO..."

BY RACING AROUND AND AROUND AT A CERTAIN SPEED I CAN CAUSE A POWERFUL UPDRAFT WHICH LIFTS THE WATER INTO A WHIRLING MASS!

"BUT WHEN I BROUGHT MY WATERY BURDEN CLOSE TO THE FLAME-CREATURE..."

THE TERRIBLE HEAT--TURNED THE WATER TO STEAM!

"I NEXT RACED SOUTHWARD ACROSS THE MEDITERRANEAN SEA INTO AFRICA TO THE SANDS OF THE SAHARA WHERE..."

SAND CAN BE USED TO SNUFF OUT A FIRE!

"BUT WHEN I ARRIVED BACK IN ITALY WITH THE SAND-STORM..."

IT TURNED THE SAND INTO CRUDE GLASS!

IT LOOKS AS IF I'M STYMIED! I'VE TRIED WIND--WATER-- AND SAND! WHAT'S LEFT?

"THEN AN IDEA OCCURRED TO ME..."

OF COURSE! I SHOULD HAVE THOUGHT OF THIS RIGHT AT THE OUTSET! NO FIRE CAN EXIST WITHOUT **AIR**!

28

APPLYING *CENTRIFUGAL FORCE* TO SUCK THE AIR FROM THE FIRE-BEING RESULTED IN ITS BEING SURROUNDED BY A *VACUUM!*

I'M CIRCLING IT SO *FAST* IT CAN'T EVEN *SEE* ME TO COUNTER-ATTACK!

THERE IT GOES... COLLAPSING... DYING OUT...

ITS FLAME-EMANATIONS ARE COMPLETELY GONE! SEEMS TO HAVE AN *EMBER OF LIFE* LEFT...BUT NOT ENOUGH TO HARM ANYONE!

AND AS I HOPED, ONCE THE *FLAME-CREATURE'S* EMANATIONS STOPPED, THE NATIVES WERE RESTORED TO LIFE!

"THEN--LEARNING ABOUT THE *CAROLINA METEORITE,* I SPED ACROSS THE *ATLANTIC,* ARRIVING ALMOST AT THE SAME TIME AS *GREEN LANTERN...*"

29

"AS WE ALL RACED FORWARD, THE INTENSE RADIATIONS OF THE ALIEN IN THE METEORITE BURST FORTH WITH EXPLOSIVE FURY!"

"APPARENTLY, UNLIKE ITS FELLOWS, IT SAVED ITS STRENGTH FOR ONE MIGHTY SURGE OF POWER--"

"--THAT CAUGHT US ALL FLAT-FOOTED!"

"AND WHILE WE WERE HELPLESSLY ROOTED TO... THE SPOT..."

BLASTING OUT OF THE METEORITE-- A COLOSSAL CREATURE OF WOOD!

CAN'T SUMMON UP ENOUGH WILL POWER TO RESIST IT!

MY MARTIAN POWERS... NULLIFIED!

WHAT'S IT PLANNING TO DO?

THE TREE-CREATURE'S LUMBERING FORWARD... FORCING US TO FOLLOW!

WHERE IS IT TAKING US?

ONLY I KNOW IT'S LEADING US TO BATTLE AGAINST ITS FELLOW-BEINGS-- BUT NO WAY FOR ME TO TELL ANYONE ELSE!

HOW DO I ESCAPE FROM THIS MISERABLE CONDITION?-- BEING GLASS WAS BAD ENOUGH!

30

GOT A IDEA--IF ONLY IT'LL WORK!

STRAINING EVERY NERVE--MUSCLE... AH! DID IT! MY LIMB RUBBED AGAINST GREEN LANTERN'S!

GL'S POWER COMES FROM HIS RING--

SO...IF I CAN EXPOSE EVEN A TINY SECTION OF IT...

THERE IT IS! NOW... HOPEFULLY...HE CAN USE IT TO SAVE US!

MY WILL POWER WAS SO LOW I COULDN'T GET UP A POWER BEAM STRONG ENOUGH TO PIERCE THE BARK!

NOW...THANKS TO AQUAMAN...I CAN DIRECT IT FOR A SHORT DISTANCE!

I PRAY IT'S ENOUGH TO HELP SOMEONE!

BY THE MOONS OF MARS! GL'S BEAM HAS RESTORED MY FACE! FROM AQUAMAN TO GREEN LANTERN TO ME...THAT'S WHAT I CALL TEAMWORK!

NOW IT IS MY TURN TO PITCH IN...

31

MUST AIM THIS BLAST OF AIR RIGHT ON *TARGET-3!*

J'ONN'S *SUPER-BREATH*--LIFTING ME OFF THE GROUND--SLAMMING ME INTO *WONDER WOMAN!*

NICE TO MAKE A *HIT* WITH HER--BUT *WHY* DID THE *MARTIAN* DO IT?

"THEN BEFORE MY WOODEN EYES, I SAW THE BEAUTY OF THE *MARTIAN MANHUNTER'S* SCHEME!..."

FLASH'S BUMPING MOVED ME CLOSE ENOUGH TO *GREEN LANTERN*...TO ENABLE HIM TO REMOVE THE WOOD FROM THE *LEFT SIDE* OF MY BODY...FREEING MY *MAGIC LASSO!*

SUFFERING SAPPHO! THE ALIEN'S *HEARD* US--SEEN ME *CHANGE!*

NO TIME TO FREE THE *OTHERS*--IT'S UP TO *ME* TO FIGHT IT *ALONE!*

32

MINERVA GUIDE MY AIM! OUR IMPROVISED TEAMWORK HAS GONE TOO FAR FOR ME TO FAIL THE OTHERS!

UNLESS I FORCE IT TO RELEASE ITS HOLD ON US, IT'LL SURELY TURN US INTO *TREES* AGAIN-- *FOREVER!*

"*UP AND DOWN* FLASHED THE *AMAZON'S MAGIC LASSO--FASTER* AND FASTER..."

"AND AT EACH UPWARD AND DOWN-WARD MOVE, THE *GOLDEN ROPE* PLANED WOOD FROM THE CREATURE..."

NICE GOING, *WONDER WOMAN!* PLANED DOWN TO ITS BARE ESSENCE, THE ALIEN'S HOLD OVER US WAS *BROKEN*...AND WE AUTOMATICALLY BECAME OUR NORMAL SELVES!

"*IT WAS THE MARTIAN MAN-HUNTER* WHO SUMMED UP WHAT HE'D LEARNED FROM THE *STONE GIANT...*"

THERE'S ONE LAST CLAIMANT TO THE THRONE OF *APPELLAX*-- WHO LANDED ON THE BARREN ICE-FIELDS OF *GREENLAND!*

WE'VE GOTTEN THIS FAR AS A *TEAM*--LET'S NOT BREAK UP!

RIGHT--WE'LL FIGHT THIS THROUGH-- *TOGETHER!*

33

FINALLY, THE *MAN OF STEEL'S* VISAGE APPEARS TO COMPLETE THE TALE...

"*BATMAN* AND I HAD BEEN WORKING ON A CASE TOGETHER WHEN WE HEARD ABOUT THE DIAMOND-BEING THREAT TO *GREENLAND*..."

"THOUGH I STEELED MYSELF FOR A SURPRISE ATTACK FROM THE ALIEN, IT WAS *I* WHO WAS *SURPRISED*...!"

:GASP:

--A *KRYPTONITE* METEOR!*

*EDITOR'S NOTE: THIS ADVENTURE OCCURRED *BEFORE* *GREEN KRYPTONITE* WAS ELIMINATED AS A *LETHAL MENACE* TO *SUPERMAN*!

SUPERMAN-- OVERCOME!?

MY HANDS AND LEGS--TURNING TO-- SOLID DIAMOND--

SUPERMAN AND I HAVE WORKED TOGETHER TOO LONG TO LET *THIS* PANIC US!

LOSING CONTROL OF THE *BATPLANE!* ONLY TIME TO TRY A LAST-DITCH GAMBLE--

34

GOTTA LINE UP JUST RIGHT--DROP A *MAGNETIC HOOK*---AND--OHHH--

B-BLACKING OUT--

"BUT *BATMAN* HAD DONE HIS JOB *PERFECTLY!* THOUGH *HE* WAS *UNCONSCIOUS,* THE *PLANE* GRIPPED THE *GREEN METEORITE* AND CARRIED IT OFF..."

REGAINING MY *SUPER-POWERS...*

NOTHING WILL STOP ME NOW!

THE *SUPER-HEAT* I'M CAUSING BY *FRICTION* IS BREAKING DOWN THE MENACE'S MOLECULES-- CHANGING IT FROM DIAMOND TO *COAL*--AND ELIMINATING IT AS A THREAT!

"IN SHORT ORDER THE OTHER FIVE HEROES ARRIVED! AFTER RETURNING THE INACTIVATED METEOR-BEINGS TO THEIR OWN WORLD, WE HELD AN IMPROMPTU GET-TOGETHER..."

IT'S PERFECTLY CLEAR THAT *TEAMWORK,* ENABLED US TO DEFEAT THE ALIEN BEINGS!

IT WOULD BE A GOOD IDEA TO *UNITE*-- FORM A CLUB...OR SOCIETY...

...A *LEAGUE* AGAINST EVIL! OUR PURPOSE WILL BE TO UPHOLD *JUSTICE* AGAINST WHATEVER DANGER THREATENS IT!

WHAT DO YOU *ALL SAY?*-- ARE WE *TOGETHER..?*

35

TOGETHER!

SO *THAT'S* HOW IT ALL BEGAN-- I'VE NEVER HAD A CHANCE TO HEAR THE COMPLETE STORY!

QUITE A *ROUSER!* I'D FORGOTTEN HOW *EXCITING* IT WAS TO GET TOGETHER!

I...FOR ONE...HAVE HAD MY SPIRITS RENEWED--THANKS TO *HAWKMAN'S* "PEP-UP" SHOW!

I NOTICED, *SUPERMAN*... THAT YOU NEGLECTED TO PUT INTO THE RECORD THAT PRICELESS CRACK YOU MADE TO HONORARY MEMBER *SNAPPER CARR*, WHEN HE ASKED YOU --

"I KNOW YOU CAN CHANGE COAL INTO DIAMOND BY RUBBING IT WITH YOUR SUPER-HANDS--BUT HOW COULD YOU CHANGE DIAMOND INTO COAL?"

OHH...I WAS HOPING NO ONE WOULD REMEMBER!--WELL, I WAS TRYING TO BE *FUNNY* WHEN I ANSWERED *SNAPPER* WITH--

"I *SIMPLY* RUBBED THE DIAMOND BEING-- THE WRONG WAY!"

≥GROAN!≤ THAT'S JUST ABOUT THE WORST ONE- LINER *SUPES* EVER MADE!

COULD BE~BUT IT'S ALSO THE *SOLUTION* TO OUR DILEMMA~ RUB STARBREAKER "THE *WRONG WAY*"!

WH-AAT?!

36

WE'VE BEEN BATTLING *STARBREAKER* ON *PHYSICAL* TERMS--AND GETTING BEATEN INTO SO MUCH ORANGE PULP!

YET HIS *GREATEST* POWER COMES FROM *EMOTIONAL* ENERGY-- FROM MEN'S *FEAR OF DEATH!*

I CATCH YOUR DRIFT, *BATMAN!* WE COULD HARNESS THE *POSITIVE* FEELING OF MEN, THEIR *LIFE-SPIRIT!* THEN, PERHAPS WE SHALL OVERCOME!

:WHOA!: YOU'RE FLYING UP AROUND CLOUD NINE!

HOW CAN WE DO SUCH A THING--WHEN THERE'S *NO TIME?*

TIME--THE TWISTER OF ALL THINGS, ALL EVENTS...THE FORCE THAT SPLITS THE COMMONPLACE ASUNDER AND LIKE NOW, BRINGS THE *UNEXPECTED TOGETHER!*

A CLOUD-- MATERIALIZING IN OUR *SATELLITE SANCTUARY--?!*

--*SARGON* THE *SORCERER!*

SARGON-- HERO OR *VILLAIN?* A SAVING ANGEL OF THE WORLD--OR ANOTHER DEVIL TO PLAGUE THE *EARTH?* AGONIZING ANSWERS IN THE NEXT ISSUE!

37

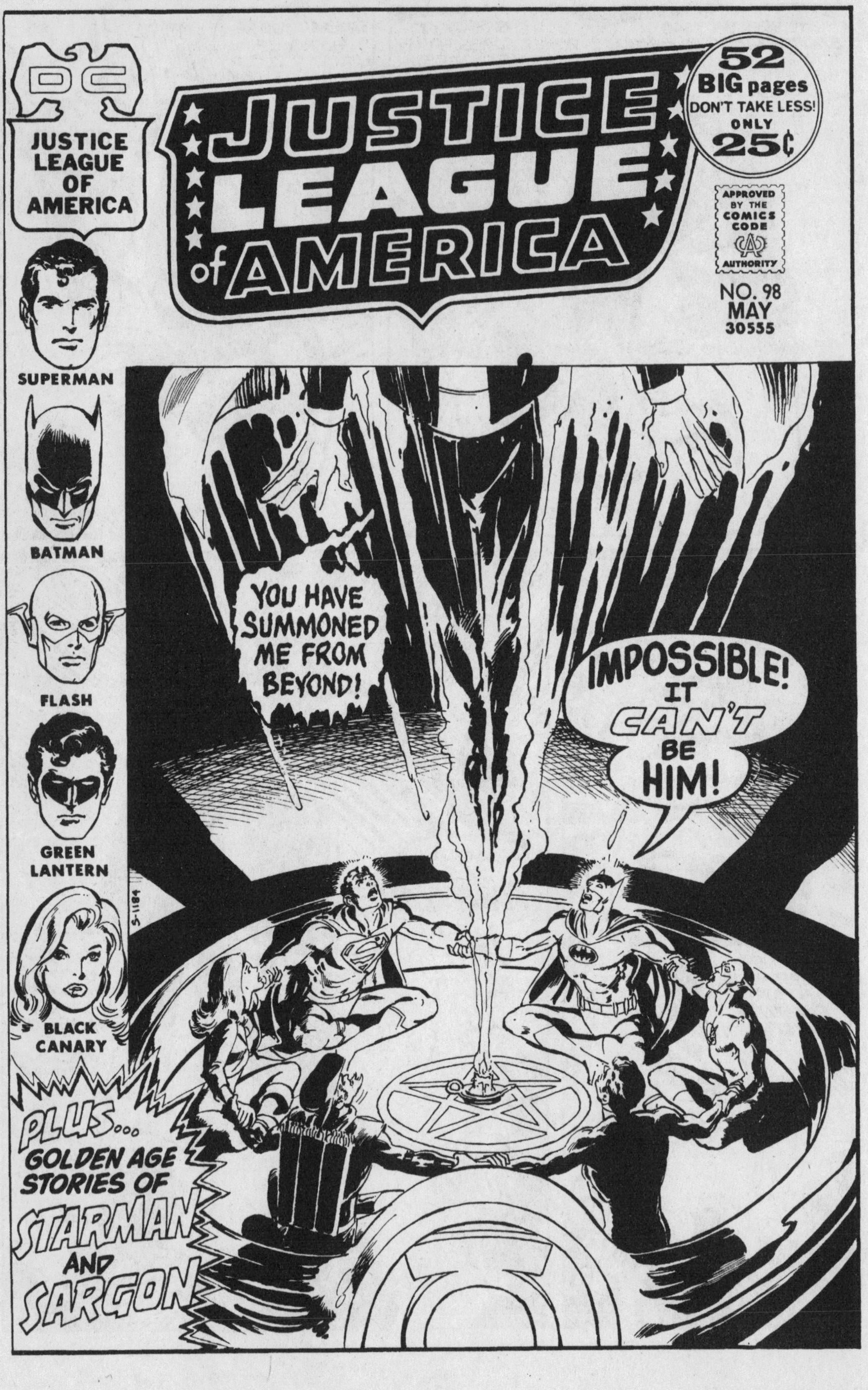
JUSTICE LEAGUE OF AMERICA
JUSTICE LEAGUE of AMERICA
52 BIG pages DON'T TAKE LESS! ONLY 25¢
APPROVED BY THE COMICS CODE AUTHORITY
NO. 98
MAY
30555
SUPERMAN
BATMAN
FLASH
GREEN LANTERN
BLACK CANARY
YOU HAVE SUMMONED ME FROM BEYOND!
IMPOSSIBLE! IT CAN'T BE HIM!
PLUS... GOLDEN AGE STORIES OF STARMAN AND SARGON
S-1184

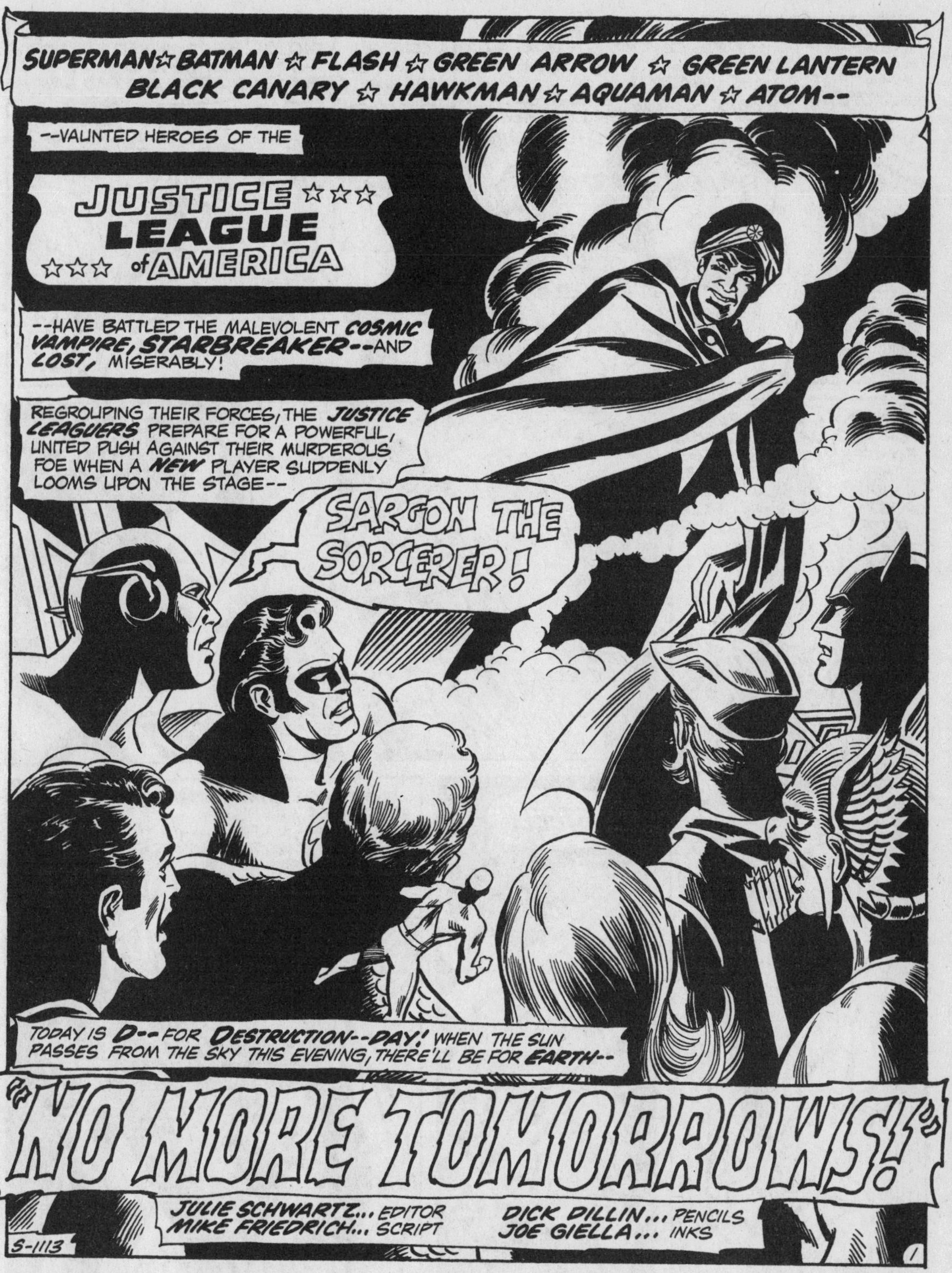
SUPERMAN ☆ BATMAN ☆ FLASH ☆ GREEN ARROW ☆ GREEN LANTERN
BLACK CANARY ☆ HAWKMAN ☆ AQUAMAN ☆ ATOM--
--VAUNTED HEROES OF THE
JUSTICE LEAGUE of AMERICA
--HAVE BATTLED THE MALEVOLENT COSMIC VAMPIRE, STARBREAKER--AND LOST, MISERABLY!
REGROUPING THEIR FORCES, THE JUSTICE LEAGUERS PREPARE FOR A POWERFUL, UNITED PUSH AGAINST THEIR MURDEROUS FOE WHEN A NEW PLAYER SUDDENLY LOOMS UPON THE STAGE--
SARGON THE SORCERER!
TODAY IS D--FOR DESTRUCTION--DAY! WHEN THE SUN PASSES FROM THE SKY THIS EVENING, THERE'LL BE FOR EARTH--
"NO MORE TOMORROWS!"
JULIE SCHWARTZ... EDITOR
MIKE FRIEDRICH... SCRIPT
DICK DILLIN... PENCILS
JOE GIELLA... INKS
S-1113
1

SARGON! DON'T BELIEVE I'VE *HEARD* OF-- *OH!* WASN'T HE A *RULER* IN ANCIENT *MESOPOTAMIA?*

COULD BE, *BLACK CANARY,* BUT *THIS* GUY USED TO BE A *SUPER-HERO* 'WAY BACK WHEN WE WERE KIDS! ONLY RECENTLY, HOWEVER--

--I'VE HAD A COUPLE OF RUN-INS WITH HIM WHICH LOOKED RATHER *SUSPICIOUS--!*

THAT'S ENOUGH FOR *ME!*

CALL ME SHORT OR CALL ME TEMPERED, BUT RIGHT NOW WE'VE GOT AN ENTIRE *PLANET* TO SAVE-- AND WE'VE *NO TIME* FOR ANOTHER TWO-BIT SMOKE-RAISER!

NOR I FOR A FLY-OFF-THE-HANDLE *DUST-MOTE!* --BE AWAY!

SINCE MY *RUBY OF LIFE* CONTROLS ALL IT TOUCHES, I HAVE NO TROUBLE MAGICKING THE VERY AIR ITSELF!

I DON'T KNOW WHAT YOUR *GAME* IS, *SARGON*-- BUT YOU WON'T ESCAPE A GRIP OF--

--STEEL!

AS YOU SEE, *SUPERMAN*-- *TOUCHING* ME WAS A MISTAKE! MY MAGIC *COUNTER-SHOCKS* YOUR *SUPER-POWERS!*

2

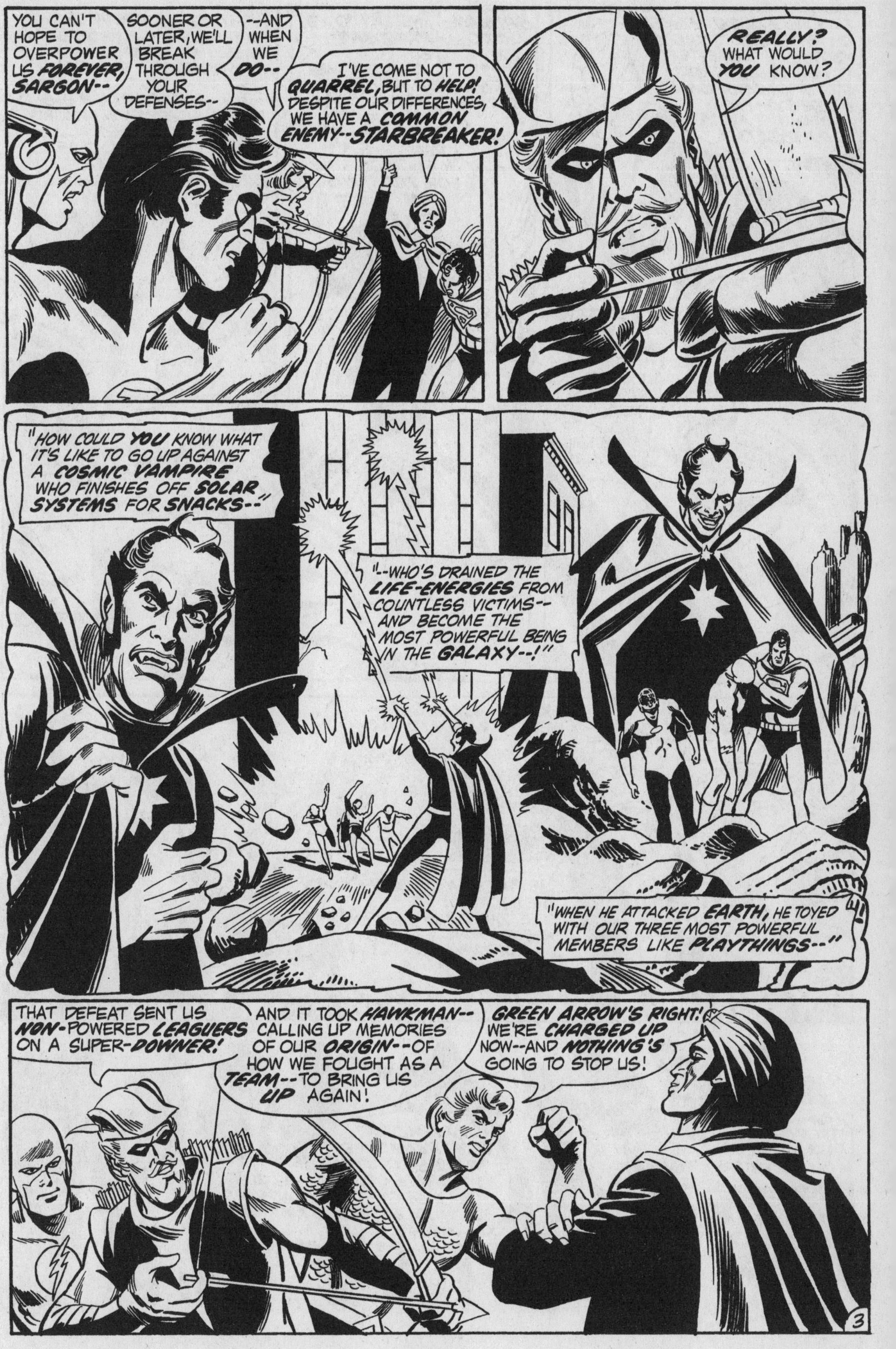
YOU CAN'T HOPE TO OVERPOWER US FOREVER, SARGON--
SOONER OR LATER, WE'LL BREAK THROUGH YOUR DEFENSES--
--AND WHEN WE DO--
I'VE COME NOT TO QUARREL, BUT TO HELP! DESPITE OUR DIFFERENCES, WE HAVE A COMMON ENEMY--STARBREAKER!
REALLY? WHAT WOULD YOU KNOW?
"HOW COULD YOU KNOW WHAT IT'S LIKE TO GO UP AGAINST A COSMIC VAMPIRE WHO FINISHES OFF SOLAR SYSTEMS FOR SNACKS--"
"--WHO'S DRAINED THE LIFE-ENERGIES FROM COUNTLESS VICTIMS--AND BECOME THE MOST POWERFUL BEING IN THE GALAXY--!"
"WHEN HE ATTACKED EARTH, HE TOYED WITH OUR THREE MOST POWERFUL MEMBERS LIKE PLAYTHINGS--"
THAT DEFEAT SENT US NON-POWERED LEAGUERS ON A SUPER-DOWNER!
AND IT TOOK HAWKMAN--CALLING UP MEMORIES OF OUR ORIGIN--OF HOW WE FOUGHT AS A TEAM--TO BRING US UP AGAIN!
GREEN ARROW'S RIGHT! WE'RE CHARGED UP NOW--AND NOTHING'S GOING TO STOP US!
3

BATTLING *STARBREAKER* ON *PHYSICAL* TERMS IS *FUTILE!* HIS GREATEST POWER COMES FROM DRAINING *EMOTIONAL ENERGY*--FROM MANKIND'S *FEAR OF DEATH!*

IT IS ON THE *EMOTIONAL* PLANE THAT THE STRUGGLE EXISTS--AND *THERE* YOU REQUIRE THE HELP OF MY MAGICAL POWERS!

BATMAN--HOW DO YOU FIGURE *SARGON* KNOWS ALL THIS STUFF?

MYSTERY TO ME, *HAWKMAN*--BUT WE'D REACHED THE SAME CONCLUSIONS OURSELVES!

DESPITE *GA'S* MISGIVINGS, I'M FOR *TRUSTING* HIM!

THANK YOU, *BATMAN!* NOW--TO PERFORM THE NECESSARY MAGIC, WE NEED A *DOORWAY... A KEY!*

MY *RUBY OF LIFE* HAS TWO COUNTERPARTS AROUND THE WORLD! GATHER ALL THREE TOGETHER AND WE'LL AT LEAST HAVE A *BARE CHANCE* IN OUR STRUGGLE!

ARE YOU *WITH* ME?

THE CONSENSUS SEEMS TO *GO* WITH *SARGON*--BUT I'LL *KEEP* MY DOUBTS!

VERY WELL, THEN...

AQUAMAN--BLACK CANARY-- YOU WILL GO TO THE *LATIN AMERICAN* HIGHLANDS FOR THE *SECOND* RUBY!

BATMAN--HAWKMAN-- THE LOCATION OF THE *THIRD* IS *CENTRAL EUROPE!*

HUH-- THE TROPICS? I'LL BE A FISH OUT OF WATER!

YES...WHY PICK *ANY* OF US FOR THESE TASKS?

NO TIME FOR QUESTIONS! THE WEAVINGS OF *TIME* AND *SPACE* ORDAIN YOUR MISSIONS! YOU MUST DEPART--*NOW!*

THE REST OF YOU *LEAGUERS* MUST *STAY*--WE NEED TO MAKE *MASSIVE PREPARATIONS!*

4

"no more tomorrows" PART TWO

THE SCENE: CAPITAL OF TROPICAL *SIERRA VERDE*, PALACE OF *EL PRESIDENTE*...

YOU REALIZE THE DANGER, MY HUSBAND? IF YOU MEET WITH THE REBELS AS THEY DEMAND, THERE ARE THOSE WHO WOULD CALL YOU *TRAITOR!*

GENERAL LOPEZ IS SUCH A MAN-- AND NOT ONE TO ANGER!

BUT IF I DO *NOT* GO, THE COUNTRY-SIDE WILL BE RAVAGED BY REVOLUTION-- THOUSANDS WILL DIE!

YET MANY SMALL, STRUGGLING COUNTRIES LOOK UPON YOU FOR LEADERSHIP! IF THE *ARMY* SHOULD STAGE A *COUP*, OTHERS WOULD FOLLOW AROUND THE WORLD!

ALL YOU HAVE WORKED FOR WOULD *COLLAPSE!*

TRUE-- YET TO DO *NOTHING* IS *EQUALLY* DANGEROUS!

I WAS GIVEN THIS GEM AS A *CHILD*, MARIA-- IT HAS ALWAYS GIVEN ME *WISDOM* TO DO THE RIGHT THING!

SO... I HAVE MADE UP MY MIND--

MY PEOPLE, MY *COUNTRY*, COME BEFORE MY CAREER--MY AMBITIONS! I SHALL MEET WITH THE REBELS!

AS I KNEW YOU WOULD, MY *PEDRO*-- AND AT YOUR SIDE SHALL I STAND! IT IS THE LEAST THE WIFE OF SO COURAGEOUS A MAN CAN DO!

5

SHORTLY, MANEUVERED TO THE CENTRAL HIGHLANDS OF *SIERRA VERDE* BY THE MYSTIC ENERGY OF *GREEN LANTERN'S POWER RING*--

I STILL CAN'T FIGURE OUT WHY *SARGON* WOULD SEND *US*--

YES--WE SEEM SO MISMATCHED AS A TEAM--

AQUAMAN-- LOOK BELOW--!

GUERRILLAS-- ATTACKING THOSE POOR FARMERS!

--AND OUR TRANSPORTATION MYSTERIOUSLY LANDING US *HERE*--?

THERE SEEMS TO BE A CLEAR CASE OF *INJUSTICE* TO FIGHT--!

RIGHT!--AND THAT'S THE NAME OF OUR GAME!

BAH-- IMPERIALIST *AMERICANOS!*

THE *AMERICANOS* BELIEVED *ME* ATTACKED.' THEY DO NOT REALIZE I AM SECRETLY A MEMBER OF THE REBEL FORCES!

GRAB THE STRANGE-GARBED MAN!

THEN, IN THE MIDST OF THE VIOLENT WRENCHINGS THAT *JUDO* CALLS FOR--

GOTTA TWIST FREE-- HELP *AQUAMAN*-- OHH... MY WIG!

AMIGOS--LOOK.' IT IS *MARIA VALDEZ*--THE WIFE OF *EL PRESIDENTE!*

6

HAVE TO EXPLOIT THIS COINCIDENCE-- LOOK FOR AN *OPENING*--

SI--MY HUSBAND SENT ME TO *SPY* ON YOUR ACTIVITIES!

BAH.! EL PRESIDENTE WOULD *NEVER* DARE DIRTY HIS HANDS IN THE SOIL--HE STOOPS TO SEND HIS *WOMAN!*

HE IS A *COWARD!* HE HAS NOT ARRIVED BEFORE THE *RAINS*-- AS WE DEMANDED!

IN ANY CASE, THE *PROPER* PLACE FOR A BEAUTIFUL ONE SUCH AS YOU IS IN THE *HOME*--WITH HER *HUSBAND*--NO?

YOU HAVE A RATHER *UNLIBERATED* ATTITUDE ABOUT WOMEN-- HELPLESS-- DOCILE--

--AND PROBABLY RATHER WEAK!

CAN'T JOIN *CANARY*-- THE *INTENSE HEAT* IS DRAINING MY STRENGTH-- ALMOST TO MY *ONE-HOUR* LIMIT!

CAPTURE HER!

TO *SAY* IS NOT TO *DO* IT--

--AND BY THE WAY-- I'M *NOT* THE PRESIDENT'S WIFE!

SHE FIGHTS LIKE THE DEVIL--BUT THEY'VE *SURROUNDED* HER--

IF ONLY I COULD MOVE!

THEN...A DAILY OCCURRENCE IN THE TROPICS!...

--THE *RAINS!*

AAHH... *MOTHER ECOLOGY* DOING HER BIT!

THERE'S NO HOLDING ME *NOW!*

I'VE STILL GOT TO HELP OUT *CANARY--*

--WAIT--*WALKING-CATFISH* ✱ --HEADING FOR THE NEAREST STREAM!

✱ *TROPICAL FISH-ABLE ACTUALLY TO **WALK** ON THEIR FINS!--ED.*

UTILIZING HIS AMAZING TELEPATHIC ABILITY TO COMMAND FISH OF *ALL* SPECIES...

:AIEEE: WE ARE BEING SHOWERED UPON BY-- *FISH!*

NOT ONLY DO THESE FISH *WALK--* THEY *FLY!*

I'M *BEGINNING* TO *UNDERSTAND* WHY *SARGON* SENT *US* HERE--ONLY I, WITH MY POWERS, COULD HAVE PULLED OFF THIS STUNT--WITH THE *CANARY'S* TIMELY ASSISTANCE!

MEANWHILE, IN THE SKIES ABOVE...

TWO *AMERICANS* FROM THE FAMOUS *JUSTICE LEAGUE--* BATTLING THE GUERRILLAS!

THEY HAVE MADE UP FOR OUR *DELAY* IN THE STORM!

OUR ESCORT IS *DESCENDING, PRESIDENTE,* TO ADD HIS *GUNS!* WE SHALL SOON BE *RID* OF THE TRAITORS!

8

SHIP NUMBER TWO--DO NOT ATTACK! WE ARE HERE TO *TALK!*

HE STILL DESCENDS, *PRESI-DENTE!*

THIS IS YOUR *PRESIDENT*-- *STOP I SAY!*

ATTACKING THESE FEW WILL KILL OUR AMERICAN FRIENDS-- AND INJURE OUR CAUSE!

YOU SHALL STOP!

BLAM BLAM

EL PRESIDENTE-- FIRING AT US! HE MEANS WHAT HE SAYS!

MINUTES LATER, AT THE EDGE OF THE JUNGLE CLEARING...

LEADER, WE HAVE BROKEN AWAY FROM THE AMERICAN SHE-WOLF AND HER COMPANION! I HAVE A RIFLE--SHOULD I SHOOT *EL PRESIDENTE?*

NO--YOU SAW HIS ACTIONS! HE HAS *COME*--WHAT NONE BEFORE HIM WOULD *DARE*--AND PROVES HIM-SELF A *MAN* BY IT!

HE WILL LISTEN!

AND SO WILL *WE!*

LATER... GRUELING, SWEATING, SWEARING HOURS LATER....

AS *KING OF ATLANTIS,* I CAN APPRECIATE YOUR DIPLOMACY, SIR!

IF ONLY YOUR *GENERALS* AGREE TO THE *CEASE-FIRE* YOU'VE ARRANGED! YOUR LOVE FOR YOUR COUNTRY IS A HUGE INSPIRATION!

IT WAS *YOUR* HISTORY-SHATTERING ACTS THAT ARE THE TRUE INSPIRATION! I CAN ONLY REPAY YOU WITH MY MOST VALUED POSSESSION--

THIS GIFT IS *YOURS!*

WONDERFUL-- THE *MYSTIC RUBY!*

MISSION ACCOMPLISHED!

9

"NO MORE TOMORROWS!" PART THREE

EERIE DARKNESS SITS HEAVILY ON THE MOUNTAINS OF SOUTHERN *GERMANY*-- WHEN SUDDENLY IT IS RENT BY THE MYSTERIOUS PRESENCE OF *HAWKMAN* AND *THE BATMAN!*

--DESOLATION! GL'S POWER RING DUMPS US --ABSOLUTELY *NOWHERE!* WHY DID *SARGON* SEND US *HERE?* WHAT CAN BE HIS MYSTIC *REASON?*

SUDDENLY...

BATMAN... MOVE IT...!

VRRROOOOMM

OF *COURSE* I AIN'T HURT! DIDN'T DO MY OWN STUNTS IN *103* PICTURES TO GET BOTHERED NOW BY A *TOTALED CAR!*

--WAY AHEAD OF *YOU,* HAWK--!

GOTTA DITCH THIS BABY-- TO AVOID THOSE *IDIOTS!*

KKKRUNNCHH

THUNDERATION-- IT'S A COUPLA *SUPER-HEROES!*

WHY--WHY--IT'S *"BRICK" FORD--* THE MOVIE STAR!

YOU HURT?

⑩

"BRICK"! ARE YOU OKAY? YOU LEFT THE *MOVIE SET* LIKE A *BAT OUTTA HELL!*

ANOTHER ONE--THIS TIME MY *BROTHER* JIMMY!

LET'S GET BACK TO THE *SET--* TELL YOU *ALL* ABOUT IT!

AWAY FROM THE *PUBLIC'S EYE,* A *DIFFERENT "BRICK"* EMERGES...

MY *LUCKY CHARM* HAS FIZZLED OUT, JIMMY-- THAT CRASH ALMOST *KILLED* ME!

EVER SINCE MY LIFE WAS THREATENED BY THAT FREAKIN' *COMMIE ARMS-RUNNER* I CROSSED, I'VE BEEN JITTERY AS A BUG!

I-I'M AFRAID TO GO ON!

AW, C'MON "BRICK"-- YOUR FANS CAN'T SEE YOU LIKE THIS! LET'S GO OUTSIDE!

"BRICK" BELIEVES SO *MUCH* IN HIS HE-MAN IMAGE--

--HIS ENTIRE SELF-CONFIDENCE WILL CRUMBLE IF HE EVEN *THINKS* HE'S UNABLE TO DO HIS OWN *STUNTS* ANYMORE!

APPRISING THE *JUSTICE LEAGUE* DUO OF "BRICK'S" DEATH - THREAT...

LISTEN, BROTHER-- I'LL DRY-RUN THE CAR THROUGH THE RACING SET, JUST TO--ER-- CHECK IT OUT!

YOU'LL DRIVE DURING THE *ACTUAL* FILMING, OF COURSE!

WE'LL HELP YOU FIND YOUR ATTACKER, "BRICK"--THEN CONTINUE ON OUR *OWN* SEARCH!

HATED TO *LIE* TO "BRICK"! THIS *IS* THE ACTUAL FILMING--AND *I* WANT TO DRAW OUT THE ATTACKER!

VOROOOM

WHEW! I DIDN'T HAVE LONG TO WAIT!

--BRIDGE BEHIND ME-- JUST *EXPLODED!*

11

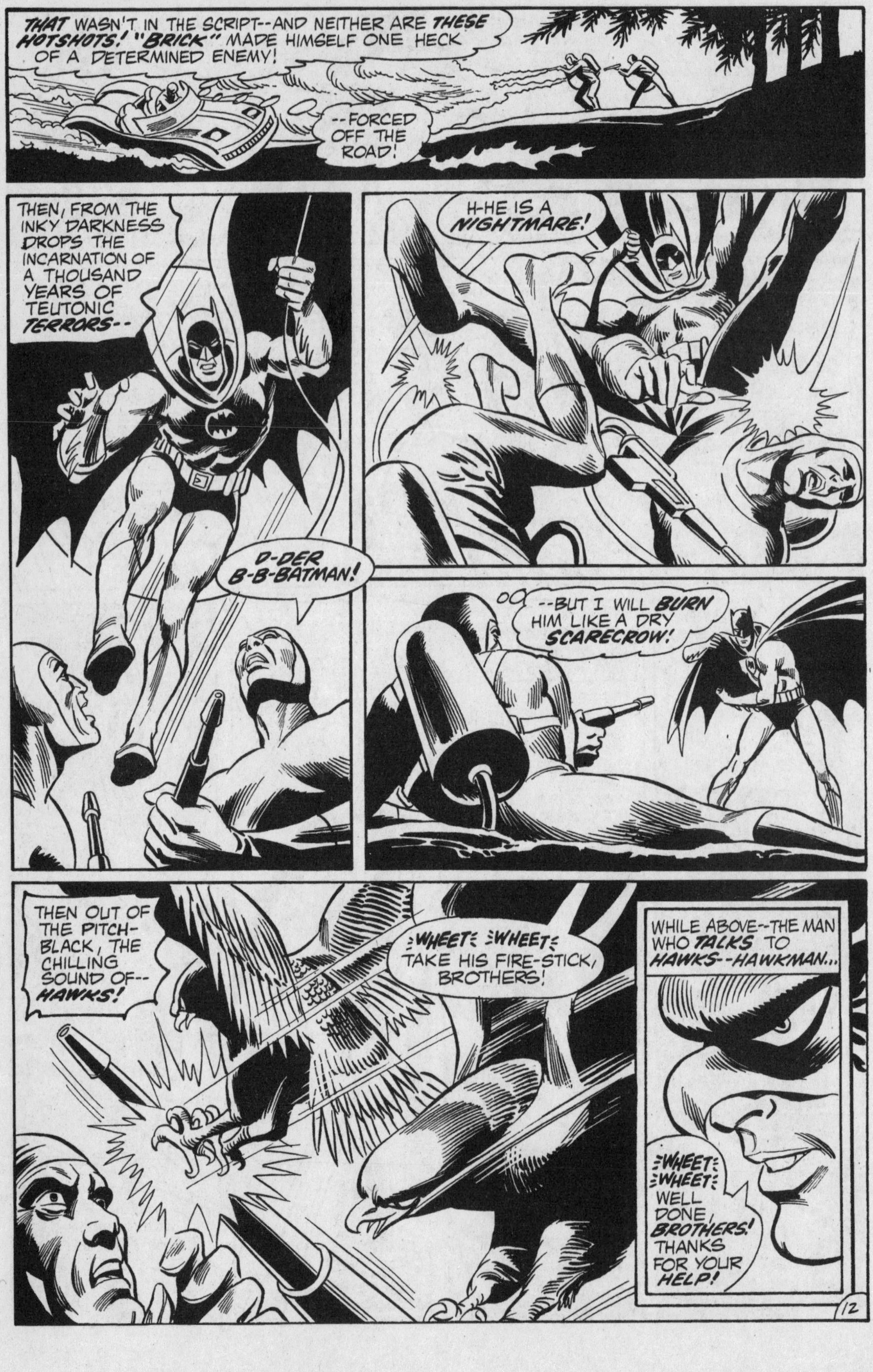
THAT WASN'T IN THE SCRIPT--AND NEITHER ARE THESE HOTSHOTS! "BRICK" MADE HIMSELF ONE HECK OF A DETERMINED ENEMY!
--FORCED OFF THE ROAD!
THEN, FROM THE INKY DARKNESS DROPS THE INCARNATION OF A THOUSAND YEARS OF TEUTONIC TERRORS--
D-DER B-B-BATMAN!
H-HE IS A NIGHTMARE!
--BUT I WILL BURN HIM LIKE A DRY SCARECROW!
THEN OUT OF THE PITCH-BLACK, THE CHILLING SOUND OF--HAWKS!
WHEET WHEET TAKE HIS FIRE-STICK, BROTHERS!
WHILE ABOVE--THE MAN WHO TALKS TO HAWKS--HAWKMAN...
WHEET WHEET WELL DONE, BROTHERS! THANKS FOR YOUR HELP!
12

NO QUESTION NOW WHY *SARGON* SENT *THE BATMAN*--HE'S SCARED THE *SCHNITZEL* OUT OF BOTH OF 'EM!

BUT WHY *ME?*-- UH-OH!

--A *SNIPER!* PROBABLY AFTER *"BRICK"*-- AND TAKING *ME* INSTEAD!

--BUT THE ONLY *"TAKES"* ARE GONNA BE IN THE *MOVIE FILM!*

THIS GERMAN FOREST HAS SEEN MANY WARS--BUT I'LL BET NOT ONCE WAS A SNIPER EVER KNOCKED OUT-- FROM THE *AIR!*

NOW IF I CAN ONLY GET *UN-PINNED!*

SUDDENLY, ACROSS THE YAWNING CHASM LEAPS A DEATH-DEFYING MECHANICAL MONSTER...

13

"BRICK"?!--Y-YOU JUMPED THAT BRIDGE!

RACING QUICKLY TO FREE HIS PINNED BROTHER....

DAMNATION, JIMMY--DON'T YOU KNOW 'NUFF TO NOT STAY NEAR A GAS-TANK THAT'S ABOUT TO--

--EXPLODE!

SHORTLY....

"BRICK"-- YOU WERE COLOSSAL-- DYNAMITE! WE SHOT THE WHOLE SCENE FROM OUR LONG-RANGE HELICOPTER!

YOUR DARING FEAT WILL SERVE AS AN INSPIRATION TO THE WHOLE WORLD!

'COURSE IT WILL! COULDN'T LET JIMMY DO MY WORK, NOW, COULD I?

HERE YOU ARE, PALS....A MEMENTO OF HAVING SHARED A SCENE WITH "BRICK" FORD--!

A RUBY-- THE VERY ONE WE WERE SENT TO FIND!

YEAH....JUST A SUPERSTITIOUS PLAYTHING--AIN'T WORTH NOTHING TO ME!

I WONDER.... I JUST WONDER...

14

"NO MORE TOMORROWS!" PART FOUR

TIME--! HOW ITS MYSTIC TAPESTRY FASCINATES ME!

BUT IN FOLLOWING ITS PUZZLING PATTERN I HAVE BLINDED MYSELF TO THE BORDERS SEPARATING *RIGHT* FROM *WRONG*!

I CANNOT IGNORE MY RECENT TURN TO VILLAINY! I HAVE *RESPONSIBILITIES*-- TO MY WORLD, TO MY FELLOW-BEINGS, TO MY *SOUL*--AND I MUST *MEET* THEM!

FROM THIS MOMENT ON, MY LIFE IS DEDICATED TO THE *REBIRTH* OF A *SUPER-HERO*!

ATOM--YOU HAVE YOUR INSTRUCTIONS! EVERYTHING MUST BE TIMED *PERFECTLY*!

GREEN LANTERN-- MOVE! THERE IS NO TIME FOR *REPOSE*!

USE YOUR *POWER RING* TO RECALL OUR GLOBAL RUBY-SEEKERS! THEIR TIME-ORDAINED SEARCHES HAVE ENDED!

OKAY, *SARGON*--BUT I CAN'T FIGURE HOW YOU CAN BE SO *SURE* THEY'RE *FINISHED*--

--BUT AFTER THE BACK-BREAKING *PREPARATIONS* YOU'VE PUT US THROUGH, YOU *MUST* KNOW WHAT YOU'RE DOING!

15

AS *BLACK CANARY, AQUAMAN, HAWKMAN* AND *BATMAN* RETURN TO THE *SATELLITE HEAD-QUARTERS*, A SUDDEN SHOCK OF TENSION CHARGES THE AIR...

THE *NEXUS* HAS ARRIVED--!

QUICKLY, *GREEN LANTERN*-- ENLARGE YOUR RING!

CANARY--HAWKMAN-- PLACE YOUR RUBIES IN CONTACT WITH MINE!

NOW... *ALL GATHER AROUND!*

WITHIN THESE MYSTIC GEMS SURGES THE ONLY FORCE MAN-KIND CAN USE TO OVERCOME ITS DEATH-FEARS--*LOVE-POWER!*

WE SHALL LINK THIS SOURCE OF ENERGY WITH *GREEN LANTERN'S POWER RING*--

--TOGETHER WITH THE FUTUR-ISTIC WEAPONRY *HAWKGIRL* HAS ASSEMBLED IN HER *THANAGARIAN SPACER*--

READY WHEN YOU ARE, *SARGON!*

--ALONG WITH THE MYRIAD OF ALIEN POWER-BANKS IN *SUPERMAN'S FORTRESS OF SOLITUDE*...

SUPERGIRL HERE! EVERYTHING'S SET TO GO!

--TO BE FINALLY CHANNELED THROUGH THE *PSYCHO-EMOTIONAL TRANSLATORS* CONSTRUCTED HERE BY *JUSTICE LEAGUE* SCIENTISTS, *FLASH* AND *ATOM!*

ONLY THE *COMBINED* MIGHT OF *SCIENCE* AND *MAGIC* CAN POSSIBLY STRIKE DOWN *STAR-BREAKER*-- WHEREVER HE MAY BE!

THE TENSION CRACKLES FORTH.... CRESTING HIGHER AND HIGHER IN A WAVE OF SURGING, SEETHING *POWER!*--BUT WILL IT BE ENOUGH?

16

MEANWHILE WHAT OF *STARBREAKER?* ON THE OUTSKIRTS OF *CENTRAL CITY...*

HAH! PRIMITIVE EXPLOSIVES! ALWAYS A SIGN OF GREAT *FEAR* IN HUMANS!

HOW I WILL *RELISH* DESTROYING THIS PLANET! ABSORBING ITS MASSIVE FEARS INTO MY LIFE-STREAM WILL GREATLY INCREASE THE ENERGIES I SHALL *SELL* ON THE *STARWAYS!*

NOW TO RETURN TO MY SPACE-CRAFT--FIRE THE ROCKETS THAT WILL FLING *EARTH* INTO ITS *SUN!*

EH--THE *JUSTICE LEAGUE!?*

THE *FOOLS!*--THEY COME CHARGING AGAIN TO BATTLE!

WHAT IS THAT STRANGE *GLOW* AROUND THEM?

NO MATTER--I'LL HANDLE THEM *ALL*--GLOW OR NO GLOW! OHH--I SEEM TO BE *WEAKENING*--EVIDENTLY, A MORE *PRUDENT* ATTACK IS NECESSARY--!

PROBLEM SOLVED--I WILL *REND TIME*--DIVIDE THE *JUSTICE LEAGUE*--CONQUER THEM SEPARATELY IN EACH TIME PERIOD! THEY WILL *DIE*--FEARFULLY--*ONE-BY-ONE!*

17

IMAGINE *TIME* TO BE A COLOSSAL *SPHERE*, CURVED EVEN AS *SPACE* IS CURVED! NOW SLICE A *PLANE* THROUGH THE *SPHERE*...ON THAT PLANE IS A *LINE* AND ON THAT LINE IS A *POINT*--

--A POINT OUR MINDS CALL *THE PAST!*

WHERE *ARE* WE-- AN ALIEN PLANET?

NO-- FROM MY STUDIES OF *EARTH*, I RECOGNIZE FAMILIAR LAND FORMATIONS! WE'RE ON THE SITE OF *CENTRAL CITY*--OF ABOUT A *THOUSAND YEARS* AGO!

JUST DRY GRASSY PLAINS! THE *SIOUX* HAVEN'T EVEN SETTLED DOWN HERE YET!

BUT *STARBREAKER* IS "*PRESENT*"-- AND *WHENEVER*... OR *WHEREVER* HE STRIKES--*DEATH* FOLLOWS...

PRAIRIE FIRE-- BLAZING WITH *SOLAR*-LIKE HEAT!

RETURN YOUR EYE TO OUR *TIME-LINE*--GO BEYOND THE PRESENT--TO THE *FUTURE*...

I RECOGNIZE THAT BUILDING! IT'S *CENTRAL CITY* OF THE YEAR *2972!*

I'LL REVERSE MY "*PAST*" ATTACK--DRAW ALL THE HEAT *OUT OF* THE AIR!

...COLD... SO BITTERLY COLD...

ALL THE WATER IN MY BODY...FROZEN...

HAS *STARBREAKER* REPEATED HIS *VICTORIES* OF THE *PAST?*

18

RETURNING TO "CENTRAL CITY"--972 A.D.--WE FIND THREE FAR-FROM-DEFEATED JUSTICE LEAGUERS--

WHEN STARBREAKER ATTACKED--I SENSED A SUDDEN POWER-SURGE, ENABLING ME TO COUNTER-ATTACK WITH MY RING!

≡UHH≡ I-I FELT THAT BLOW--FOR THE FIRST TIME IN MY LIFE!

LOSING SIZABLE AMOUNTS OF ENERGY--BUT I STILL RETAIN ENOUGH POWER TO DEFEAT THIS TRIO....

HOWEVER, THIS IS A RADICALLY DIFFERENT TRIUMVIRATE OF HEROES--

--SUPER-CHARGED WITH POWER GREATER THAN FEAR OF DEATH--!

I HAD THE SAME EXPERIENCE AS THE OTHERS! THE MORE FIERCELY *STARBREAKER* ATTACKED, THE STRONGER BECAME MY *FIGHTING SPIRIT*...

--STRONG ENOUGH TO LOCATE OUR FOE'S VITAL *NERVE CENTERS*--PINCH THEM--

AND MAN OR VAMPIRE--

MAKE MY "HOLD" *STICK!*

LOSING CONSCIOUSNESS... BUT I CAN STILL HAVE MY *VICTORY*... AND *REVENGE*... IN THE *FUTURE!*

THE VOICE OF THE *COSMIC VAMPIRE* ECHOES WITH A HISTORY OF THREATS FULFILLED WITH A HORRIBLE VENGEANCE... BUT IN THIS MOMENT OF DEFEAT IS HE PERHAPS A BIT.... *AFRAID?*

MEANWHILE, *FUTURE-WARD*...

AFTER THAT INITIAL SHOCK OF *FREEZE*, I MYSTERIOUSLY FOUND MYSELF ABLE TO *NULLIFY* THE *COLD-WAVE!*

SHOULD BE EASY ENOUGH TO *VIBRATE* MY COLLEAGUES BACK TO NORMAL!

THANKS, *FLASH*-- I FEEL RIGHT AT *HOME!* WATER IS MY *ELEMENT*... AND MY *WEAPON!*

CONTINUED ON 4TH PAGE FOLLOWING

20

EVEN IF MY SET-BACK IN THE *PAST* DID WEAKEN ME SOMEWHAT--I HAVE ENOUGH RESERVE POWER TO--

THE THREAT IS CAST UNFINISHED UPON THE WINDS AS....

THE LAST TIME WE BATTLED, *STARBREAKER* OUT-FLASHED THE DAYLIGHTS OUTTA ME!

NOW THE *MORE* I SUPER-WHIRL THE *FASTER* I'M ABLE TO MOVE!

AQUAMAN'S ICICLE-ATTACK GAVE ME AN *IDEA!* THE *"TRADITIONAL"* WAY TO DEAL WITH A *VAMPIRE* --

--IS TO *"SILVER-SPIKE"* HIM!

...ENERGY...DRAINING FROM ME...COULD IT REALLY BE...I AM...ON THE VERGE OF...*DEFEAT?*

WHAT *CAN* YOU CALL THE GNAWING, GROWING EMPTINESS WITHIN A VAMPIRE'S SOUL? CAN YOU NAME IT... *FEAR?*

21

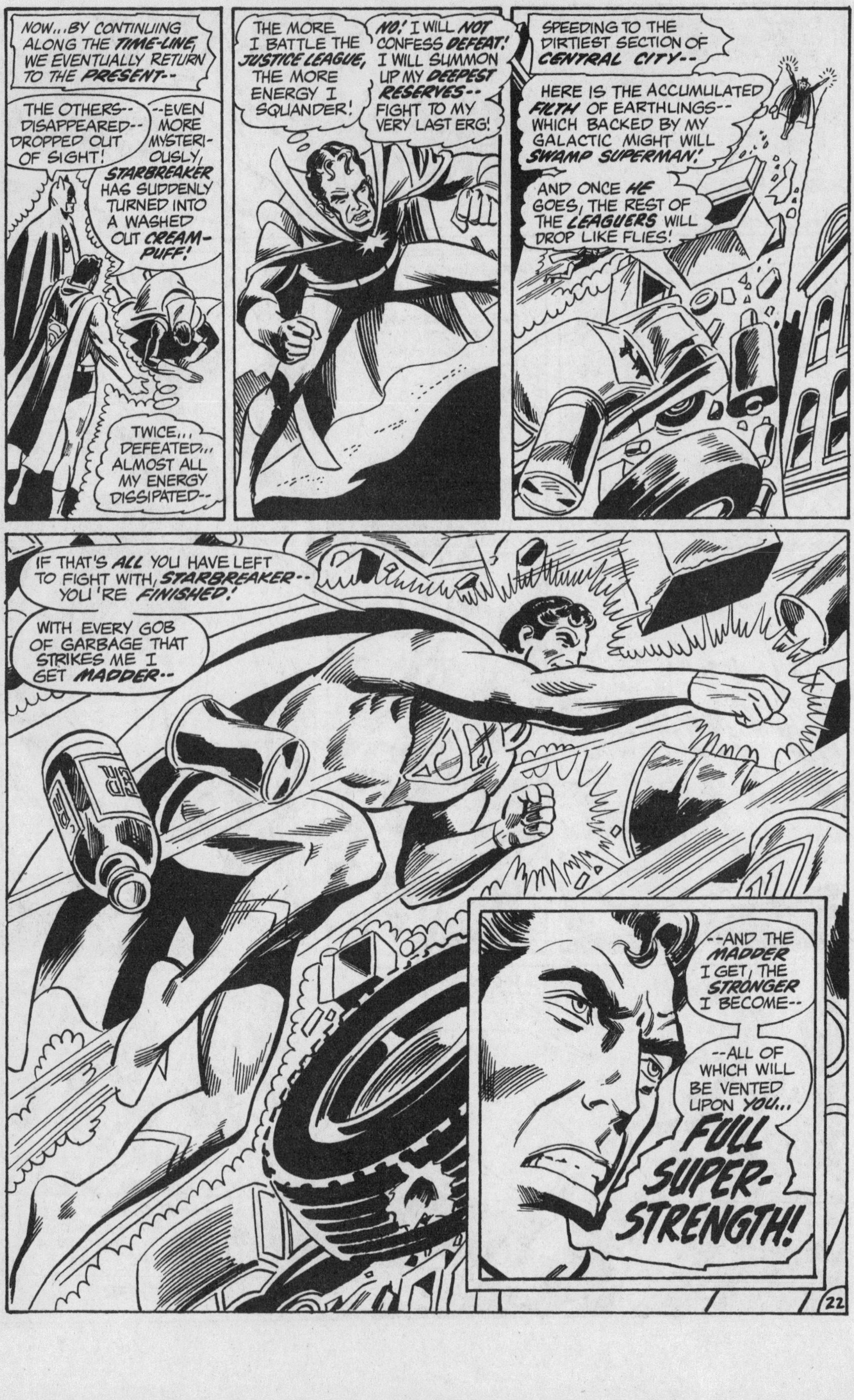
NOW... BY CONTINUING ALONG THE TIME-LINE, WE EVENTUALLY RETURN TO THE PRESENT--
THE OTHERS-- DISAPPEARED-- DROPPED OUT OF SIGHT!
--EVEN MORE MYSTERIOUSLY, STARBREAKER HAS SUDDENLY TURNED INTO A WASHED OUT CREAM-PUFF!
TWICE... DEFEATED... ALMOST ALL MY ENERGY DISSIPATED--
THE MORE I BATTLE THE JUSTICE LEAGUE, THE MORE ENERGY I SQUANDER!
NO! I WILL NOT CONFESS DEFEAT! I WILL SUMMON UP MY DEEPEST RESERVES-- FIGHT TO MY VERY LAST ERG!
SPEEDING TO THE DIRTIEST SECTION OF CENTRAL CITY--
HERE IS THE ACCUMULATED FILTH OF EARTHLINGS-- WHICH BACKED BY MY GALACTIC MIGHT WILL SWAMP SUPERMAN!
AND ONCE HE GOES, THE REST OF THE LEAGUERS WILL DROP LIKE FLIES!
IF THAT'S ALL YOU HAVE LEFT TO FIGHT WITH, STARBREAKER-- YOU'RE FINISHED!
WITH EVERY GOB OF GARBAGE THAT STRIKES ME I GET MADDER--
--AND THE MADDER I GET, THE STRONGER I BECOME--
--ALL OF WHICH WILL BE VENTED UPON YOU... FULL SUPER-STRENGTH!
22

GALACTIC HISTORIANS WILL LONG NOTE AND RE-NOTE THIS HISTORIC MOMENT! WATCH CLOSELY--AS *STAR-BREAKER'S* HEART TURNS TO FRIGID ICE, EVEN AS HIS MIND SHIFTS INTO THE GEAR CALLED *PANIC*...

AND *PANIC-STRICKEN,* HE RUNS!...

SEE HOW HE FLEES...SCAMPERING LIKE A SCARED RAT INTO THE TENEMENT JUNGLES OF *CENTRAL CITY*...HEEDLESS OF LOCATION...MINDLESS OF DIRECTION...

BATMAN--! I YIELD TO THE *MASTER!*

LIKE A COMMON EARTH-CRIMINAL, THE *ALIEN-THIEF* TREMBLES AT THE AWESOME SIGHT OF THE GRIM ANGEL OF *VENGEANCE*--

AT LONG LAST *STARBREAKER* KNOWS THE *STINK OF FEAR*--

IT IS A *WRETCHED* ODOR, REEKING FROM A RANCID GALAXY OF MURDER AND INJUSTICE...

ITS STENCH DEAD-ENDS ONLY IN THE BLACKEST REACHES OF THE MIND...

UNTIL FINALLY-- *EVERYTHING IS LOST!*

TONIGHT Last Performance THE VAMPIRE

23

ENDINGS

WELL...WE'RE ALL TOGETHER AGAIN--IN OUR HEADQUARTERS--LIKE IT NEVER *REALLY* HAPPENED!

YET... IT *SEEMED* SO REAL!

IT *WAS* REAL! YOU WERE ALL SHIFTED ALONG THE CURRENTS OF TIME...*PAST, FUTURE, PRESENT*...BUT YOU RETURNED TO *NOW*--WITHOUT ANY PASSAGE OF TIME AT ALL!

THERE REMAINS ONE MORE TASK-- --TO *SORCERIZE STARBREAKER*--

--DRAIN HIM OF EVERY LAST TRACE OF DESTRUCTIVE POWER STILL LINGERING WITHIN HIS BODY!

A FINAL TIME THE *JUSTICE LEAGUE* DRAWS UPON ITS SYMBOLIC ENERGIES, COMBINING ITS GREAT DEDICATION WITH A LITERAL *WORLD* OF LOVE... RIGHTING UNTOLD GALACTIC WRONGS...

AND WHO'S TO SAY IF NOT THE LAST VESTIGES OF A TRILLION STAR-BROKEN SOULS TURNED THEIR DYING FEARS INTO A FINAL TRUST AS WELL?

AND THUS IT ENDS...

THE *GUARDIANS* HAVE A *SPECIAL* INTEREST IN *STARBREAKER*, BECAUSE OF HIS GALAXY-WIDE CRIMES! THEY'LL DEAL HIM HIS DUE JUSTICE!

GUESS I WAS WRONG ABOUT YOU, *SARGON!* BUT I'M SURE GLAD TO BE ALIVE TO APOLOGIZE!

24

WHAT STILL PUZZLES ME IS *WHY STARBREAKER* CHOSE TO FIGHT US IN THREE DIFFERENT TIME PERIODS!

YES, THAT *SPLIT* WAS A MAJOR FACTOR IN OUR *VICTORY!*

THAT'S EASILY EXPLAINED--

-- *THE ATOM!*

OHH...WE OVERLOOKED HIS *ABSENCE* HERE!

SARGON AND SUPERMAN WORKED OUT A PLAN TO FIRE *"ATOM-SIZED"* ME INTO *STARBREAKER'S BRAIN*-- WHERE MY BIOLOGICAL KNOW-HOW WOULD IMPLANT A *MAGICAL* SUGGESTION ONTO HIS *THOUGHT-PATTERNS!*

WHILE *STARBREAKER* WAS *"PRESENT"* IN EACH TIME-PERIOD, SARGON'S CHRONAL-MAGIC CAST *WEAKENING SPELLS* UPON THE *COSMIC VAMPIRE*-- STRENGTHENING SPELLS UPON YOU!

ATOM'S ACTIONS CONFIRM A *SUSPICION* I HAVE-- THAT *MAGIC* IS MERELY *UNDISCOVERED SCIENCE!*

PERHAPS, *FLASH*-- *SCIENCE* MAY BE JUST *UNACKNOWLEDGED MAGIC!*

SOUNDS LIKE AN *UNSOLVABLE MYSTERY* TO ME-- FOR THE *TIME BEING!*

WHAT IS CLEAR IS-- THIS ADVENTURE HAS REACHED

THE END!

㉕

NEXT ISSUE...

"SEEDS OF DESTRUCTION!"

IN WHICH A **PLAN...**

IS TURNED INTO A **PLANT...**

TO TERRORIZE A **PLANET!**

★ROLL CALL (*IN ORDER OF APPEARANCE*):
BLACK CANARY ★ HAWKMAN ★ ATOM ★ FLASH ★ GREEN LANTERN
BATMAN ★ AQUAMAN ★ SUPERMAN

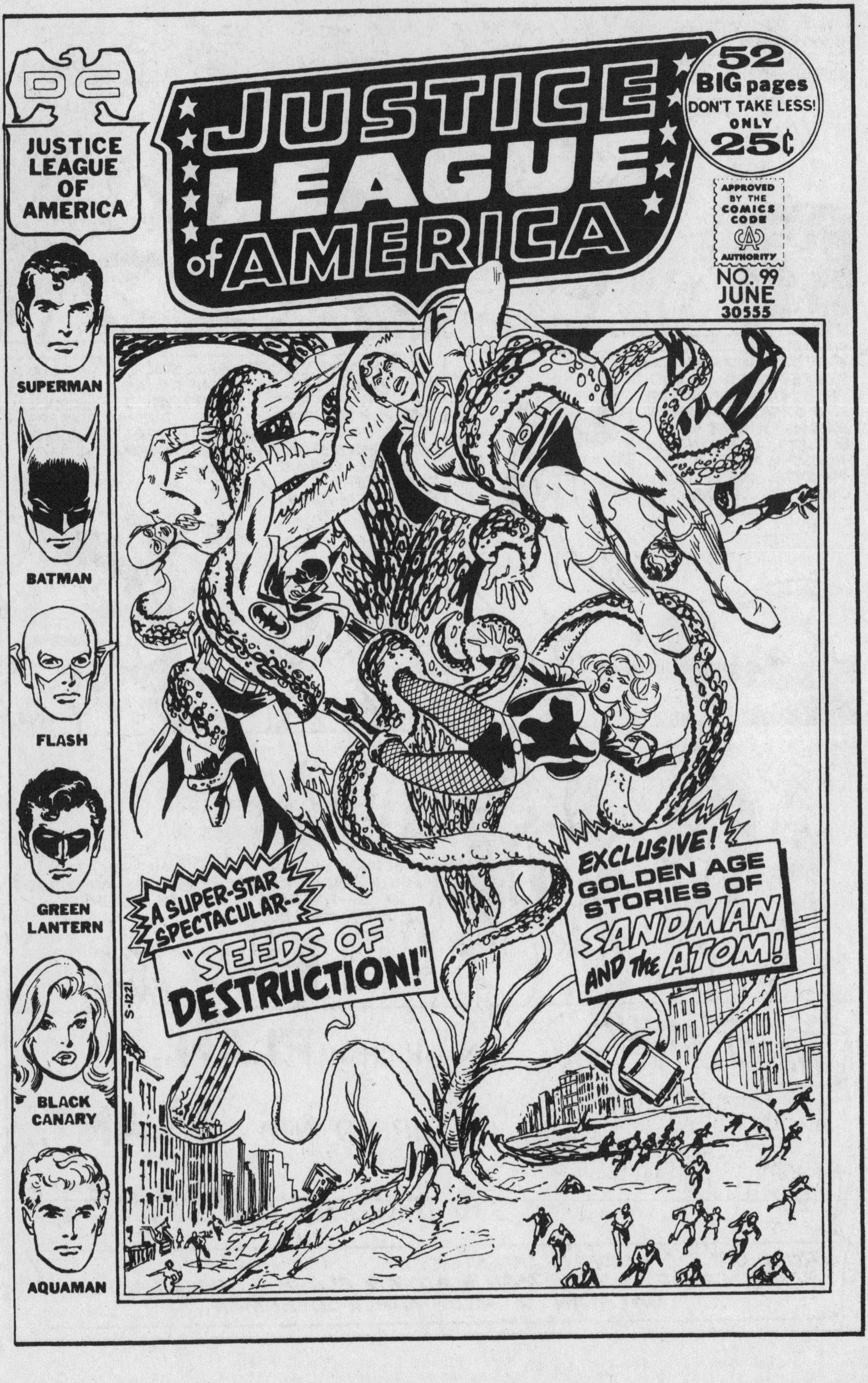
JUSTICE LEAGUE OF AMERICA
JUSTICE LEAGUE of AMERICA
52 BIG pages DON'T TAKE LESS! ONLY 25¢
APPROVED BY THE COMICS CODE AUTHORITY
NO. 99 JUNE 30555
SUPERMAN
BATMAN
FLASH
GREEN LANTERN
BLACK CANARY
AQUAMAN
A SUPER-STAR SPECTACULAR--
"SEEDS OF DESTRUCTION!"
EXCLUSIVE! GOLDEN AGE STORIES OF SANDMAN AND the ATOM!
S-1221

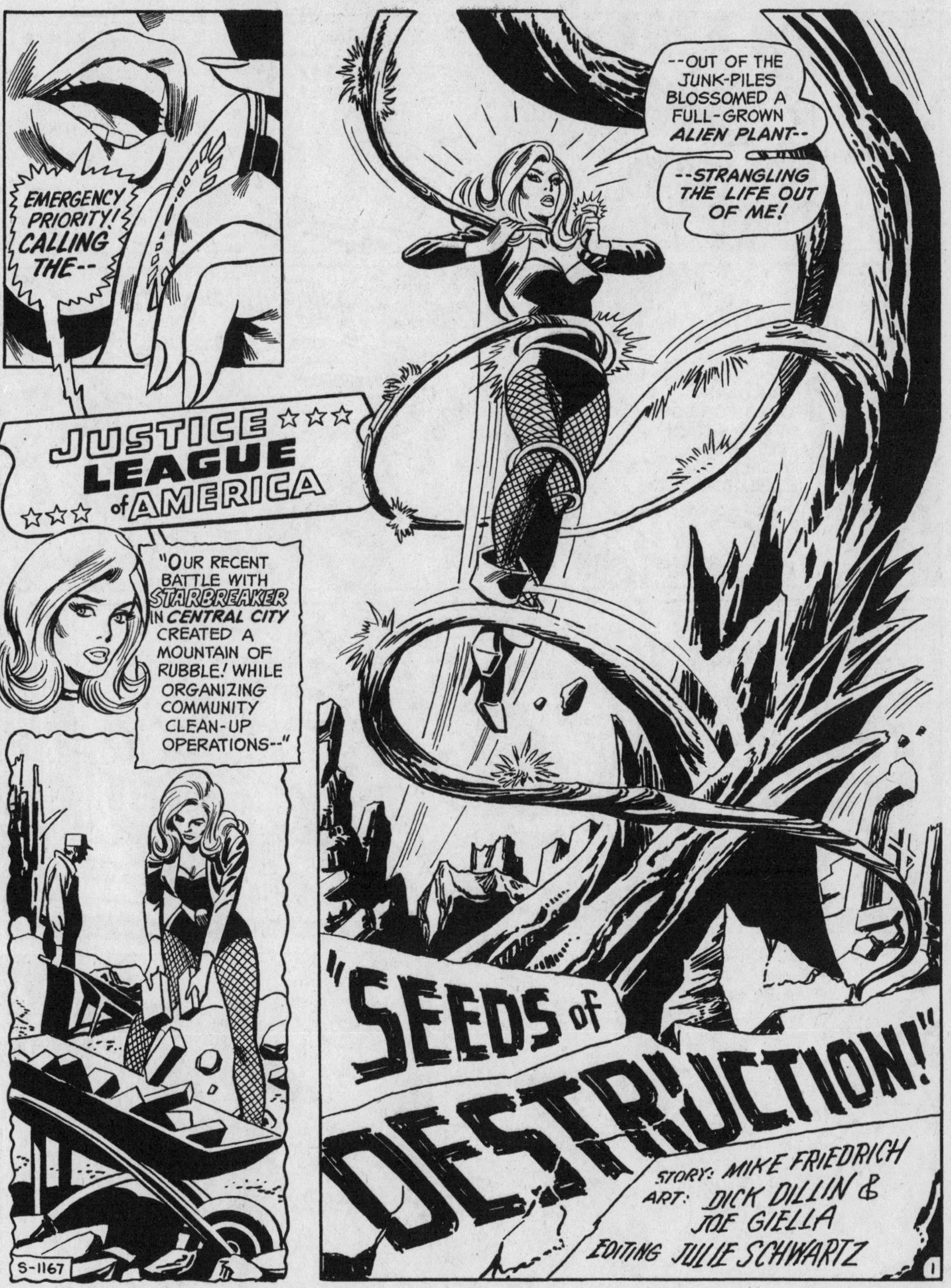
EMERGENCY PRIORITY! CALLING THE--
JUSTICE LEAGUE of AMERICA
--OUT OF THE JUNK-PILES BLOSSOMED A FULL-GROWN ALIEN PLANT--
--STRANGLING THE LIFE OUT OF ME!
"OUR RECENT BATTLE WITH STARBREAKER IN CENTRAL CITY CREATED A MOUNTAIN OF RUBBLE! WHILE ORGANIZING COMMUNITY CLEAN-UP OPERATIONS--"
"SEEDS of DESTRUCTION!"
STORY: MIKE FRIEDRICH
ART: DICK DILLIN & JOE GIELLA
EDITING JULIE SCHWARTZ
S-1167
1

22,300 MILES SPACEWARD, LOCKED IN FIXED ORBIT ABOVE THE *EARTH*...

SIMULTANEOUS EMERGENCY CALLS--FROM *BLACK CANARY* AND *GREEN LANTERN!*

IT'S MY JOB AS TODAY'S *JLA* SATELLITE-ATTENDANT TO COORDINATE ACTION-ACTIVITIES... DIVIDE THE AVAILABLE MEMBERS INTO FIGHTING TEAMS!

THUS, IN THE *IVY UNIVERSITY* OFFICE OF PHYSICS PROFESSOR *RAY ("ATOM") PALMER*...

THIS CASE CALLS FOR SOME *ATOM-ACTION!* FIRST, SHRINK MYSELF TO *ELECTRON-SIZE*--

--THEN TRAVEL AT *TELEPHONIC SPEED* TO MY DESTINATION IN *CENTRAL CITY!*

SURE BEATS *HITCHHIKING!*

THE ATOM--?!

MEANWHILE, ON THE OUTSKIRTS OF *CENTRAL CITY*...

CANARY'S CALL CAME WHILE I WAS ROUNDING UP THESE *DRUG-PUSHERS!*

I'LL SUPER-SPEED THEM TO POLICE HQ--

--WHERE I PICK UP MY RIGHT-ON-TIME COLLEAGUE--

--AND OFF WE GO!

2

WHILE ON OIL-CURDLED SOIL IN SUNNY SOUTHERN CALIFORNIA, WE FIND THE *MENACED* GREEN LANTERN --

HOPE A *JUSTICE LEAGUER* RESPONDS TO MY CALL *QUICKLY!* BAD ENOUGH, MY *POWER RING* IS RUNNING OUT OF JUICE--

--IT CAN'T WORK ON THIS *BODY-CRUNCHING YELLOW* PLANT!

STILL, I CAN'T HANG HERE DOING *NOTHING* TO SAVE MYSELF!

I'LL WHIP UP *POWER-HANDS* TO *WRING* THOSE CLOUDS *DRY...*

--AND *DROWN MY ATTACKER!*

≒UHH≒ I'VE MADE MATTERS *WORSE*--IT *THRIVES* ON EXTRA WATER!

BETTER *SWITCH TACTICS!*

AHH! LOOKS LIKE IT CAN'T TAKE EXTREME *HEAT!* IT'S STARTING TO *DRY* UP-- LOOSEN ITS HOLD ON ME!

JUST A FEW MORE *SECONDS* AND--

BUT THOSE LIFE-SAVING SECONDS ARE NOT TO COME...

MY RING-- FIZZLED OUT!

3

AT THAT MOMENT, ANSWERING *HAWKMAN'S* SUMMONS FROM A RECENTLY-SOLVED CASE NEAR BY...

PERFECT TIMING! THE BATMAN WITH A COUPLE OF *FLARES* FROM HIS *UTILITY BELT*-- TO CONTINUE *POURING* ON THE *HEAT!*

THE HEAT-EFFECT WILL ONLY LAST FOR SECONDS, *LANTERN*--

BUT THAT SHOULD BE ENOUGH TIME TO FREE YOU!

THE *EMERALD GLADATOR'S* THANKS ARE BRIEF, FOR THIS IS A TIME OF *CRISIS*--REQUIRING THE URGENT RE-CHARGING OF THE MIGHTIEST WEAPON IN THE GALAXY...

IN BRIGHTEST DAY, IN BLACKEST NIGHT, NO EVIL SHALL ESCAPE MY SIGHT!

LET THOSE WHO WORSHIP EVIL'S MIGHT, BEWARE MY POWER--*GREEN LANTERN'S* LIGHT!

THEN THE SKYWAYS ARE SPLIT BY A VERDANT BEAM, STREAKING TWO PASSENGERS TOWARD *BATTLE!*

BUT *FIRST*, THERE ARE *QUESTIONS* TO BE ASKED: *WHAT* CAUSED THIS ALIEN PLANT-INVASION--*WHO* IS BEHIND IT?

④

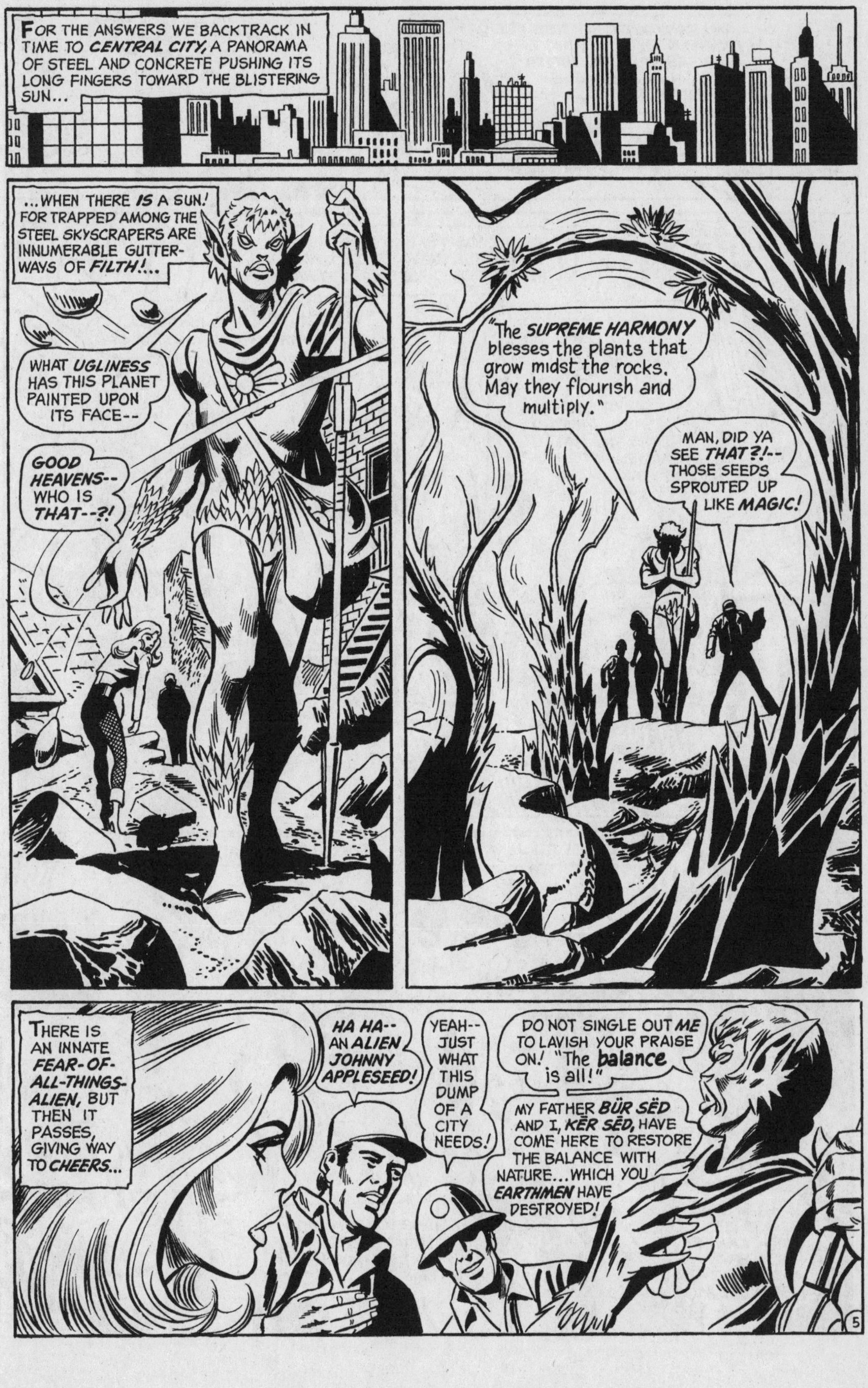
FOR THE ANSWERS WE BACKTRACK IN TIME TO CENTRAL CITY, A PANORAMA OF STEEL AND CONCRETE PUSHING ITS LONG FINGERS TOWARD THE BLISTERING SUN...
...WHEN THERE IS A SUN! FOR TRAPPED AMONG THE STEEL SKYSCRAPERS ARE INNUMERABLE GUTTER-WAYS OF FILTH!...
WHAT UGLINESS HAS THIS PLANET PAINTED UPON ITS FACE--
GOOD HEAVENS-- WHO IS THAT--?!
"The SUPREME HARMONY blesses the plants that grow midst the rocks. May they flourish and multiply."
MAN, DID YA SEE THAT?!-- THOSE SEEDS SPROUTED UP LIKE MAGIC!
THERE IS AN INNATE FEAR-OF-ALL-THINGS-ALIEN, BUT THEN IT PASSES, GIVING WAY TO CHEERS...
HA HA-- AN ALIEN JOHNNY APPLESEED!
YEAH-- JUST WHAT THIS DUMP OF A CITY NEEDS!
DO NOT SINGLE OUT ME TO LAVISH YOUR PRAISE ON! "The balance is all!"
MY FATHER BÜR SËD AND I, KËR SËD, HAVE COME HERE TO RESTORE THE BALANCE WITH NATURE...WHICH YOU EARTHMEN HAVE DESTROYED!
5

EYES WESTWARD, WHERE *BÜR SËD'S* "NATURE-BALANCING" ACT TAKES PLACE IN *COAST CITY...*

THE *FANTASTIC* REPORTS ARE *TRUE*--AN ALIEN PLANTING *FLOWERS!* BUT--HE'D BETTER WATCH THAT *BUSY STREET* BEHIND HIM!

EVEN AS THE ALIEN TURNS *INTENTIONALLY* TO THE ROARING, SMELLING TRAFFIC, 2,000 MILES AWAY HIS SON DOES THE SAME!...

THE ATMOSPHERE IS DEPRIVED OF ITS PROPER BALANCE OF OXYGEN BECAUSE OF THESE *MOTOR VEHICLES!*

"When the balance is upset, **the harmony** calls for flowers to bloom!"

HEY--I CAN'T LET THOSE PLANTS *DISRUPT* THINGS--NO MATTER *HOW* WELL INTENTIONED THEY ARE SOWN!

THAT *ALIEN'S* GONE *TOO FAR!* I BETTER PUT A *STOP* TO IT!

BUT WHEN THE *JUSTICE LEAGUE* DUO MOVES TO THE ATTACK--

I *WARN* YOU! DO NOT DEFY *BÜR-PLANTS!* THEY HAVE AUTOMATIC *DEFENSES!*

"Woe to those who attempt to destroy the *KER-PLANT,* for their fate is *DEATH!*"

6

CHAPTER TWO STARRING... The FLASH, BLACK CANARY AND The ATOM

NO WAY WE CAN ATTACK WITHOUT ENDANGERING *BLACK CANARY*--OR GETTING TRAPPED OURSELVES!

BESIDES, HOW CAN A GUY FAULT SOMEBODY FOR PLANTING *FLOWERS?*

WE DON'T HAVE TO WORRY ABOUT THAT-- *THE FLASH* IS HERE!

GET YOU FREE IN A WINK, *PRETTY BIRD*--WITH A COUPLE OF *SUPER-SPEED SHAKES!*

M-MAKING...M-ME ALL SH-SH-SHOOK UP...T-T-TOO!...

FLASH--*GASP*: STOP! Y-YOU'RE HURTING --ME--*MORE!*

WELL, IF *FLASH* CAN'T-- HANDLE THIS FROM-- THE *OUTSIDE*-- I'LL TACKLE IT--

--FROM THE *INSIDE*--WITHIN THE PLANT'S *VITAL CELLS!*

7

I MUST BE *HURTING* IT--LIKE A *POISON!*

IT'S SENDING *ANTI-BODIES* AFTER THE "GERM"-- TRYING TO *DESTROY* IT!

THE PLANT'S THROBBING IN *PAIN*-- I CAN *FEEL* IT! GOTTA KEEP ON RESISTING ITS COUNTER-ATTACKS...

PLANT'S *COLLAPSED*-- TIME TO BREAK *FREE*...

YOU HAVE KILLED A *KER-PLANT!* "All power shall bow to the flowers!" THE *BALANCE* CALLS FOR *REVENGE!*

SOME *"BALANCE"*--WHERE *PLANTS* HAVE *PRIORITY* OVER *PEOPLE!* I'LL SHOW THIS ALIEN THAT ON *EARTH* ⋛UHH-NNN⋛

HALT! "None shall stand before the keepers of the balance!" YOU CANNOT PENETRATE MY *FORCE-FIELD,* FOOLISH FEMALE!

IT'S NOT *YOU* WE'RE CONCERNED ABOUT--IT'S YOUR DESTRUCTIVE *FLOWERS!*

THE ATOM CLUED ME HOW TO ATTACK-- *BIOLOGICALLY!* DEPRIVE THEM OF *AIR*--BY CREATING A *VACUUM*-- AND THEY'LL *SUFFOCATE!*

8

YOU *EARTH*-HUMANS HAVE NO SENSE OF *PERSPECTIVE!* THE *ECOLOGICAL BALANCE* MUST BE *PERFECT* OVER THE ENTIRE WORLD!

WE WILL RESTORE THAT *BALANCE*-- SAVE YOU FROM YOUR SUICIDAL SELVES!

MY *VIBRATION-VACUUM*-- HAVING *NO* EFFECT?!

MY *POWER-STAFF* INTERCEPTS YOUR SUPER-ENERGIES AND DIRECTS THEM *ELSEWHERE!*

BUT WHAT *HAPPENS* "ELSEWHERE"? WE MOVE 3000 MILES SOUTH-EASTWARD TO THE CENTER OF THE *CARIBBEAN*, WHERE WE JOIN--

AQUAMAN

THE *KING OF THE SEVEN SEAS* HAS BEEN INVOLVED IN HIS *OWN* DIFFICULTIES--

THAT *OIL SLICK* IS HEADING STRAIGHT FOR A SPOTLESS BEACH-- A NATURAL BEAUTY THAT WILL BE RUINED UNLESS--

I'LL SUMMON MY SPECIAL CLEAN-UP SQUAD!

9

THAT'S IT, FRIENDS-- PUSH THE OIL AWAY FROM THE ISLAND--

ABRUPTLY, SWEEPING IN OUT OF NOWHERE, THE DIVERTED *SUPER-BLASTS* OF *THE FLASH...*

THE SWORDFISH BEING DRIVEN BACK BY THOSE INCREDIBLE WINDS! WHERE DID THEY COME FROM? THERE ISN'T A STORM WITHIN A *THOUSAND* LEAGUES!

THE HEAVY BATTERING IS CONFUSING THE FISH--THEY CAN'T PROTECT THEMSELVES!

I'LL ASSUME TELEPATHIC CONTROL--COMMAND THEM TO SEEK SAFETY BENEATH THE WAVES!

STRANGE...! THE WINDS ENDED AS MYSTERIOUSLY AS THEY BEGAN-- BUT THE *DAMAGE* IS DONE!

DID THIS *DISASTER* STRIKE BY *CHANCE...* OR BY *DESIGN?*

EITHER WAY, I *VOW* TO STOP IT FROM HAPPENING AGAIN!

I'LL CONTACT *HAWKMAN* AT *JLA* HEADQUARTERS--SEE IF ANY OF OUR MONITORING DEVICES CAN ACCOUNT FOR THOSE *SUPER-SPEED* WINDS!

AS *AQUAMAN* AWAITS *HAWK-MAN'S* REPLY, LET'S SEE WHAT *CATACLYSMIC* EVENT IS ABOUT TO HIT *COAST CITY!*

10

CHAPTER THREE
STARRING... The  AND GREEN LANTERN

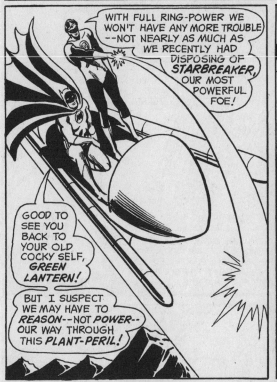

WITH FULL RING-POWER WE WON'T HAVE ANY MORE TROUBLE --NOT NEARLY AS MUCH AS WE RECENTLY HAD DISPOSING OF *STARBREAKER*, OUR MOST POWERFUL FOE!

GOOD TO SEE YOU BACK TO YOUR OLD COCKY SELF, *GREEN LANTERN!*

BUT I SUSPECT WE MAY HAVE TO *REASON*--NOT *POWER*--OUR WAY THROUGH THIS *PLANT-PERIL!*

WE'RE ABOUT TO FIND OUT, *BATMAN!* POLICE REPORTS SAY THEY CAN'T GET PAST *BÜR SËD'S FORCE-FIELD*--

BUT THEN AGAIN, THEY DON'T HAVE MY *POWER RING!*

GREAT GUARDIANS! MY *POWER-RINGED MALLET* BOUNCED RIGHT OFF-- AND *DISAPPEARED!*

BATMAN-- WE BETTER START *THINKING* --FAST!

SO YOU HAVE *RETURNED* --BUT TO NO AVAIL! MY *POWER-STAFF PROTECTS* MY VITAL *BÜR-PLANTS* --BY NEUTRALIZING THE EFFECT OF YOUR SUPER-POWERS!

YOU WOULD DO BETTER TO EXPAND YOUR MINDS --COMPREHEND THE REALITY OF THE *TRUE* BALANCE OF NATURE!

11

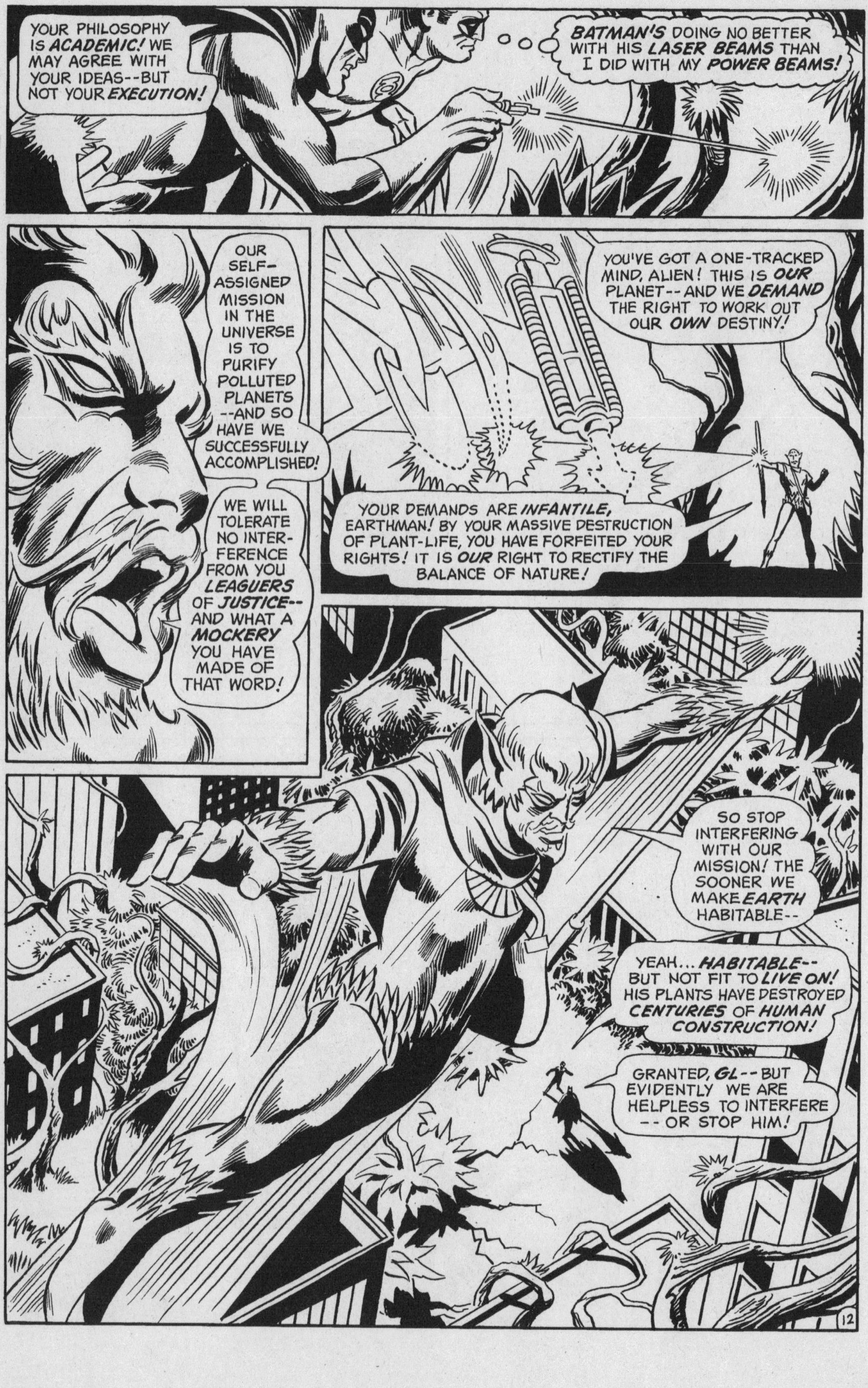

YOUR PHILOSOPHY IS ACADEMIC! WE MAY AGREE WITH YOUR IDEAS--BUT NOT YOUR EXECUTION!
BATMAN'S DOING NO BETTER WITH HIS LASER BEAMS THAN I DID WITH MY POWER BEAMS!
OUR SELF-ASSIGNED MISSION IN THE UNIVERSE IS TO PURIFY POLLUTED PLANETS --AND SO HAVE WE SUCCESSFULLY ACCOMPLISHED!
WE WILL TOLERATE NO INTERFERENCE FROM YOU LEAGUERS OF JUSTICE-- AND WHAT A MOCKERY YOU HAVE MADE OF THAT WORD!
YOU'VE GOT A ONE-TRACKED MIND, ALIEN! THIS IS OUR PLANET-- AND WE DEMAND THE RIGHT TO WORK OUT OUR OWN DESTINY!
YOUR DEMANDS ARE INFANTILE, EARTHMAN! BY YOUR MASSIVE DESTRUCTION OF PLANT-LIFE, YOU HAVE FORFEITED YOUR RIGHTS! IT IS OUR RIGHT TO RECTIFY THE BALANCE OF NATURE!
SO STOP INTERFERING WITH OUR MISSION! THE SOONER WE MAKE EARTH HABITABLE--
YEAH... HABITABLE-- BUT NOT FIT TO LIVE ON! HIS PLANTS HAVE DESTROYED CENTURIES OF HUMAN CONSTRUCTION!
GRANTED, GL-- BUT EVIDENTLY WE ARE HELPLESS TO INTERFERE -- OR STOP HIM!
12

SO CONFOUNDED ARE *GREEN LANTERN* AND *THE BATMAN* BY THIS AMAZING TURN OF EVENTS THAT THEY NEGLECT TO CONSIDER *WHERE* THEIR DISPLACED POWERS WERE SENT --A GRIM SITUATION *WE* SHALL LOOK INTO, AS WE SWITCH TO THE *WORLD'S GREATEST SUPER-HERO--*

SUPERMAN
REG. U. S. PAT. OFF.

METROPOLIS' BRAND-NEW *WASTE DISPOSAL MACHINERY* IS NOW IN PLACE--AND HERE COMES *SUPERMAN* WITH THE *BUILDING* TO CONTAIN IT!

BY THIS *SUPER-SPECTACULAR* FEAT THE *MAN OF STEEL* HOPES TO DRAMATIZE HIS COMMITMENT TO THE CONTROL OF POLLUTION!

HOLD EVERYTHING, FOLKS! A *GIGANTIC GREEN MALLET* HAS APPEARED OUT OF THE BLUE--HAMMERING AWAY AT THE BUILDING!

THAT'S *ODD...* THE *MALLET'S DISAPPEARING!*

BUT IT WAS *NO OPTICAL ILLUSION...* THE SHATTERED PARTS OF THE BUILDING ARE FLYING ALL OVER THE CITY!

OHH! IF ONLY YOU COULD SEE THIS HAPPEN BEFORE YOUR VERY EYES!--THE *METROPOLIS MARVEL* --CATCHING EVERY FLYING SECTION BEFORE IT HITS THE GROUND--

--AND IN AN AMAZING DEMONSTRATION OF *SUPER-SKILLS* HAS RECONSTRUCTED THE BUILDING AND SET IT IN PLACE!

13

BUT THEN *THE BATMAN'S* DESTRUCTIVE *LASER BEAMS* BLAST INTO THE BUILDING--AND A STARTLED *SUPERMAN* IS SO CONCERNED WITH SAVING *LOIS LANE*--

--THAT HE DOESN'T NOTICE *GREEN LANTERN'S POWER-RINGED* DEVICES UNDERMINE THE *FOUNDATION* OF THE WASTE-CONTROL BUILDING--

--SENDING IT CRASHING INTO A YAWNING PIT!

THE MENACES FADED AWAY --BUT THE WRECKED MACHINERY WILL TAKE PRECIOUS *MONTHS* TO REPAIR!

WONDER IF THOSE *GREEN* OBJECTS COULD HAVE BEEN FASHIONED BY *GL'S POWER RING*--?

BETTER CHECK IT OUT WITH *HAWKMAN!*

IN THE *JLA* CONTROL ROOM, THE *WINGED SENTINEL* QUICKLY EVALUATES THE WIDELY SEPARATED REPORTS-- AND TAKES ACTION!...

CALLING *ALL JUSTICE LEAGUERS* -- REPORT IMMEDIATELY TO HEADQUARTERS! *URGENT!*

14

CHAPTER FOUR "SEEDS of DESTRUCTION!"

IN THE SATELLITE--VIA *THANAGARIAN TELEPORTER*...

SUPES--WAIT'LL YOU HEAR WHAT'S BEEN GOING ON IN *CENTRAL CITY!*

IT'LL HAVE TO GO SOME TO *TOP* WHAT HAPPENED IN *METROPOLIS!*

HMMM... *GREEN ARROW* MUST STILL BE ON HIS OWN PERSONAL CASE! I MISS HIM!

AFTER THE INCREDIBLE STORIES ARE PUT IN THE RECORD...

FIRST--SOME QUICK BUSINESS! *SARGON THE SORCERER* HAS BEEN NOTIFIED OF HIS *HONORARY JLA MEMBERSHIP* DUE TO HIS KEY EFFORTS IN DEFEATING *STARBREAKER!*

SECOND--THE TIME OF CONJUNCTION BETWEEN OUR *EARTH* AND THE *JUSTICE SOCIETY'S EARTH-TWO* IS ARRIVING SHORTLY AND WE SHOULD--*EH?*

--AND WE SHOULD GET DOWN TO *TODAY'S* REAL *GRITTY* STUFF!

WE'RE IN DEEP TROUBLE *RIGHT NOW!* ALREADY THE MILITARY IS THREATENING TO MOVE IN WITH *HEAVY EQUIPMENT!*

--WHICH I'M AFRAID THE *ALIENS* WILL SIMPLY USE TO CAUSE EVEN *MORE* DAMAGE!

WHILE THE MEETING'S BEEN PROGRESSING, I'VE BEEN MULLING OVER OUR EXPERIENCES!

--AND I BELIEVE I'VE CRACKED THE MYSTERY OF THE DISPLACED SUPER-ENERGIES!

LEAVE IT TO THE *WORLD'S GREATEST DETECTIVE* TO SOLVE THIS *PUZZLER!*

15

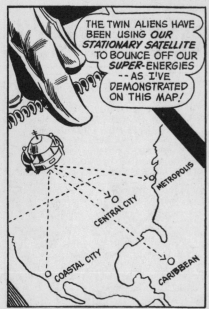

THE TWIN ALIENS HAVE BEEN USING *OUR STATIONARY SATELLITE* TO BOUNCE OFF OUR *SUPER*-ENERGIES --AS I'VE DEMONSTRATED ON THIS MAP!

METROPOLIS

CENTRAL CITY

COASTAL CITY

CARIBBEAN

THEN OUR SOLUTION IS CLEAR--*MOVE* THE SATELLITE AND MAKE THE ALIENS HELP-LESS TO *BACKFIRE* OUR POWERS!

LEAVE THAT TO *ME!*

SOON, THE *JUSTICE LEAGUE* RETURNS TO THE OFFENSIVE --WITH MIGHTY *SUPERMAN* LEADING THE WAY...

AS A STARTER, I WANT A CRACK AT *BUR SĒD'S* FORCE-FIELD!

YOU REALLY EXPECT TO STOP ME, *SUPERMAN?* MY STAFF WILL EASILY ABSORB YOUR BLOW AND SPACE-WARP ITS POWER AWAY!

...AND SPACE-WARP ITS POWER AWAY!

THAT'S WHAT *HE* THINKS! OUR SATELLITE IS NOW IN *MOTION*--THE ENERGIES WILL *MISS* US... BY A *SPACE-MILE!*

BUT *BUR SED'S* WONDER *STAFF* UNERRINGLY *FOLLOWS* THE RUNAWAY SATELLITE-- AND DEFLECTS *SUPERMAN'S POWERHOUSE BLOWS* BACK TO *EARTH,* WHERE--

16

OUR *ON-GUARD* IDEA TO PATROL EARTH AT SUPER-SPEED IS PAYING OFF!

THAT MOUNTAIN COULD ONLY HAVE BEEN WHOPPED BY A *SUPERMAN* BLAST--CAUSING THE LANDSLIDE!

I'LL NEED ALL MY *SUPER-SPEED* TO DIVERT THE LANDSLIDE--KEEP IT FROM BURYING THE VILLAGE BELOW!

MEANWHILE, IN *CENTRAL CITY*...

YOU *JUSTICE LEAGUERS* ARE *DIEHARDS*! WHY DO YOU CONTINUE TO RESIST OUR BENEFICIAL HARVEST?

BUT, *UNSEEN* TO THE ALIEN-PLANTER...

SINCE WE CAN *HEAR KER SED*, IT'S CLEAR THAT *SOUND-WAVE PARTICLES* CAN *PENETRATE* HIS FORCE-FIELD--

--WHICH *I* CAN EASILY *FOLLOW*--

-- AND SLIP *INSIDE*--TO CATCH HIM *UNAWARES*!

AT THAT INSTANT...

MY SON AND I ARE IN MENTAL COMMUNICATION--SO I TELEPORTED TO HIS SIDE!

--READY WITH *POWER* SUPPLIED BY YOUR *SUPER-SPEEDSTER*, THE FLASH!

17

BUT THE *JUSTICE LEAGUE* DOES NOT YIELD! EACH MEMBER RE-DOUBLES HIS SUPER-EFFORTS IN A NEW WAVE OF ATTACKS--

WHILE IN THE BLACKNESS THAT IS *SPACE* ABOVE, *HAWKMAN* MANEUVERS THE SATELLITE BACK AND FORTH, FRANTICALLY TRYING TO DODGE THE STAFF-SENT *JLA* ENERGIES--

18

YET THE ALIEN GARDENERS ARE CORRECT--ALL THINGS ARE *BALANCED* IN A LAW OF *ACTION* AND *REACTION*--AND THE *JLA'S* SUPER-POWERS RETURN SCATTERED--LIKE THE ALIEN SEEDS--OVER THE WHOLE WORLD--!

EVERY ONE OF OUR EFFORTS-- A *FAILURE!*

WE'RE IN WORSE SHAPE THAN WHEN WE *STARTED!*

WE'RE *STYMIED!* EVERYTHING WE DO MAKES THINGS *WORSE* SOMEWHERE ELSE!

GUESS THERE'S *NOTHING* WE CAN DO --

WHAT KINDA *DEFEATEST* TALK IS THAT? THERE *MUST* BE A WAY!

THIS TIME I'VE GOT IT! I'VE JUST REALIZED THAT THE ALIENS *NEVER STAY* WITH THEIR PLANTINGS-- THEY *ALWAYS MOVE ON!*

NOW, *LISTEN* --

19

SHORTLY AFTERWARDS, *KER* AND *BUR* ARE SURPRISED TO SEE--

NO-- NOT AGAIN!

WE ARE *TOGETHER* NOW! "And none shall defeat ye when ye are in unison!"

YOU *MISUNDERSTAND* OUR *INTENTIONS!* WE'RE HERE TO *HELP* YOU!

"PLANT- POWER" --RIGHT?

SO WE FELT WE SHOULD *ALL HELP* YOU IN YOUR PLANTING!

LET'S *GO--JUSTICE LEAGUERS!* SOW THOSE SEEDS!

THE WORLD LITERALLY HOLD ITS BREATH AS THE *JUSTICE LEAGUE* LENDS ITS *SUPER-TALENT* TO LAYING WASTE OF ASPHALT, CONCRETE AND BRICK WHILE ACCELERATING THE SPREAD OF ALIEN FLORA--

THERE YOU ARE--A VIRTUAL *GREENHOUSE* OF PLANTS! HOW WE DOING, PALS?

EVEN *BETTER* THAN US! IT'S ASTONISHING--

20

YES--*SO* ASTONISHING YOU FORGOT TO HOLD TIGHT TO YOUR *WONDER STAFFS*-- WHICH I FIGURE TO BE YOUR SOLE SOURCE OF POWER!

WE HAVE BEEN *TRICKED!*

WHAT IS THE WORRY, FATHER? "The plants are every-thing, the harmony is all!"

:*CHOKE*: STOP YOUR PRATTLING QUOTATIONS, *KER!* THE *HIGHER OXYGEN* LEVEL :*GASP*: FROM OUR PLANTS IS :*KOFF*: OVERTAXING OUR LUNGS--

:*WHEEEZZ*: CAN'T BREATHE NORMALLY :*CHOKE*:

TSK...TSK...SOUNDS LIKE THE ALIENS HAVE *RESPIRATORY* TROUBLES!

WE CANNOT *LIVE* LONG IN THIS OVER-PLANTED ENVIRONMENT! PLEASE...RETURN OUR STAFFS SO WE CAN SAFELY TELEPORT BACK TO OUR WORLD!

YOU UNDERSTAND...WE WERE ONLY TRYING TO HELP *YOU*...AS YOU TRIED TO HELP *US*--

21

NEXT ISSUE!

THE MOST MONUMENTAL GATHERING OF SUPER-STARS EVER RECORDED! THE 100th ANNIVERSARY MEETING OF THE

JUSTICE LEAGUE OF AMERICA--

*ADAM STRANGE *AQUAMAN * ATOM * BATMAN * BLACK CANARY *ELONGATED MAN *FLASH * GREEN ARROW* GREEN LANTERN * HAWKMAN *MARTIAN MANHUNTER *METAMORPHO *SNAPPER CARR * SUPERMAN * WONDER WOMAN * ZATANNA

FEATURING THEIR 10th ANNUAL TEAM-UP WITH THE

JUSTICE SOCIETY OF AMERICA--

*DR. FATE * DR. MID-NITE * HOURMAN * JOHNNY THUNDER*RED TORNADO *SANDMAN * STARMAN * WILDCAT * WONDER WOMAN

AS THEY SEARCH FOR THE LEGENDARY

SEVEN SOLDIERS OF VICTORY--

CRIMSON AVENGER GREEN ARROW * SHINNING KNIGHT *SPEEDY *STRIPESY * STAR-SPANGLED KID* VIGILANTE

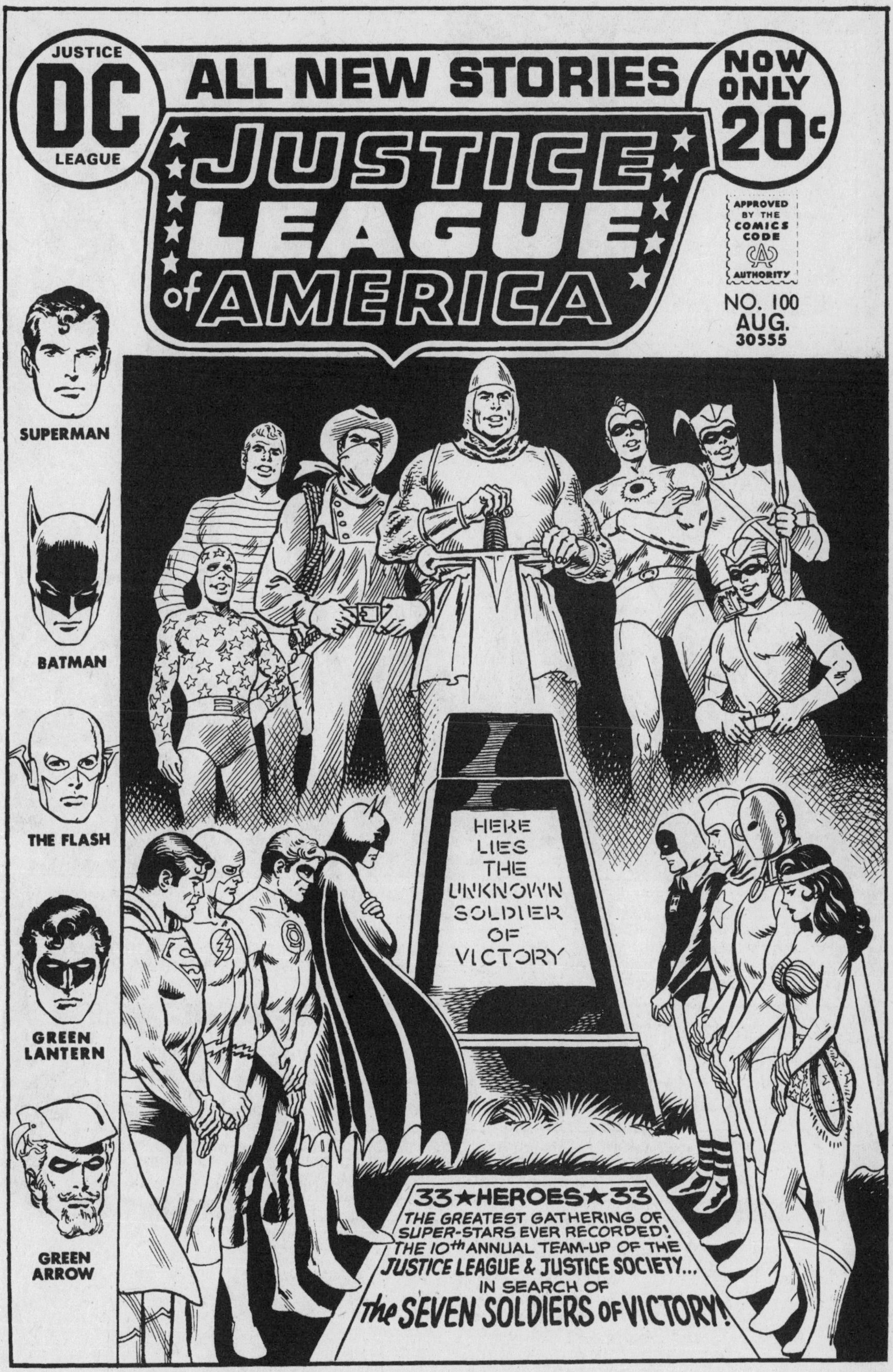
JUSTICE
DC
LEAGUE
ALL NEW STORIES
NOW ONLY 20¢
JUSTICE LEAGUE of AMERICA
APPROVED BY THE COMICS CODE AUTHORITY
NO. 100
AUG.
30555
SUPERMAN
BATMAN
THE FLASH
GREEN LANTERN
GREEN ARROW
HERE LIES THE UNKNOWN SOLDIER OF VICTORY
33★HEROES★33
THE GREATEST GATHERING OF SUPER-STARS EVER RECORDED! THE 10th ANNUAL TEAM-UP OF THE JUSTICE LEAGUE & JUSTICE SOCIETY... IN SEARCH OF the SEVEN SOLDIERS OF VICTORY!

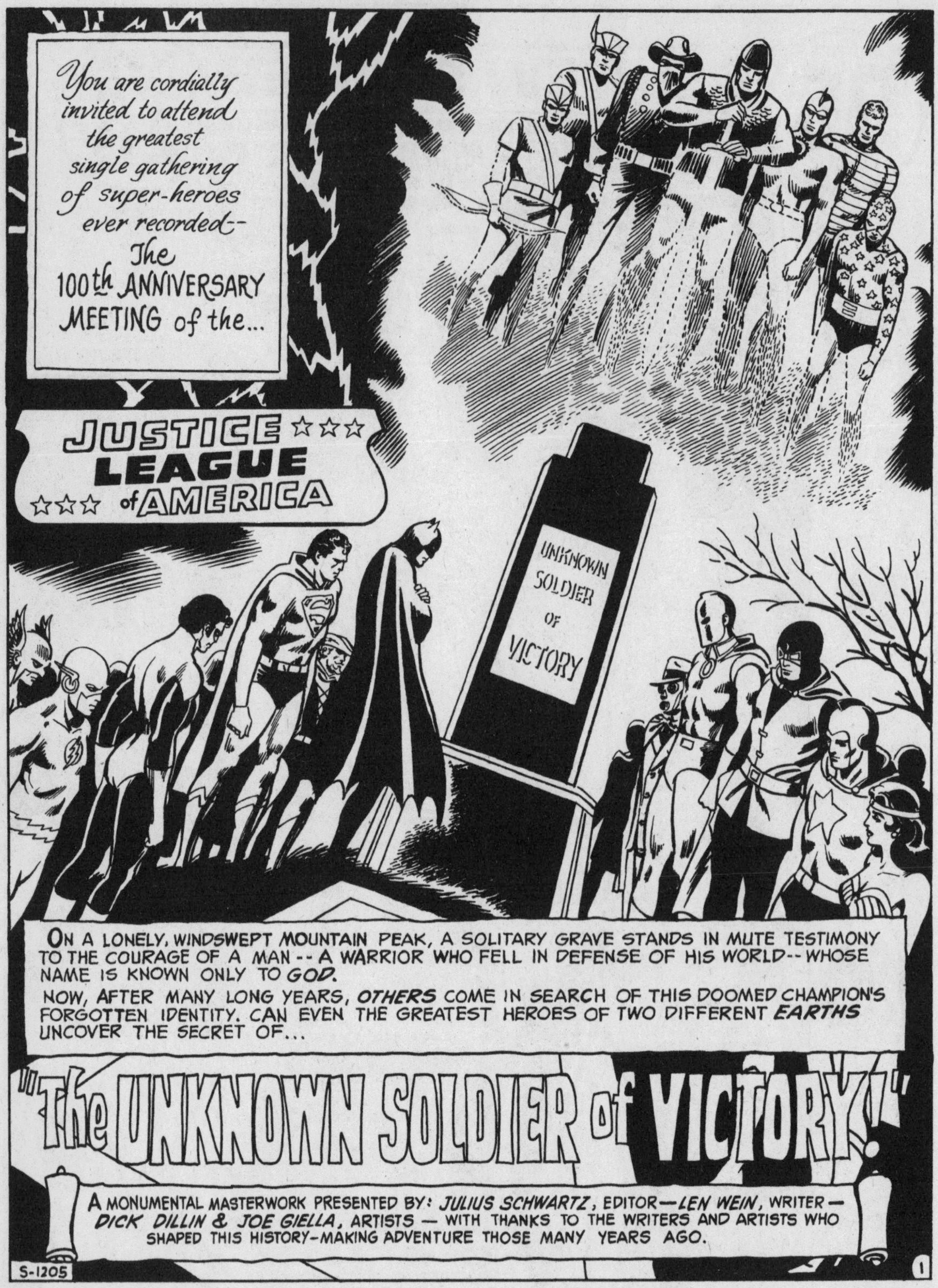
You are cordially invited to attend the greatest single gathering of super-heroes ever recorded- The 100th ANNIVERSARY MEETING of the...
JUSTICE LEAGUE of AMERICA
UNKNOWN SOLDIER OF VICTORY
ON A LONELY, WINDSWEPT MOUNTAIN PEAK, A SOLITARY GRAVE STANDS IN MUTE TESTIMONY TO THE COURAGE OF A MAN -- A WARRIOR WHO FELL IN DEFENSE OF HIS WORLD -- WHOSE NAME IS KNOWN ONLY TO GOD.
NOW, AFTER MANY LONG YEARS, OTHERS COME IN SEARCH OF THIS DOOMED CHAMPION'S FORGOTTEN IDENTITY. CAN EVEN THE GREATEST HEROES OF TWO DIFFERENT EARTHS UNCOVER THE SECRET OF...
"The UNKNOWN SOLDIER of VICTORY!"
A MONUMENTAL MASTERWORK PRESENTED BY: JULIUS SCHWARTZ, EDITOR—LEN WEIN, WRITER—DICK DILLIN & JOE GIELLA, ARTISTS — WITH THANKS TO THE WRITERS AND ARTISTS WHO SHAPED THIS HISTORY-MAKING ADVENTURE THOSE MANY YEARS AGO.
S-1205
1

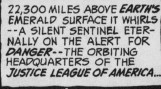

22,300 MILES ABOVE *EARTH'S* EMERALD SURFACE IT WHIRLS --A SILENT SENTINEL ETERNALLY ON THE ALERT FOR *DANGER*--THE ORBITING HEADQUARTERS OF THE *JUSTICE LEAGUE OF AMERICA*...

WITHIN ITS METALLIC CONFINES, INTRICATE MONITORING DEVICES GO ABOUT THEIR TASKS, SENDING INFORMATION HUMMING DOWN THE STERILE CORRIDORS--BUT *NO ONE* IS THERE TO NOTICE...

JUSTICE ★★★ LEAGUE ★★★ of AMERICA

INSTEAD, VOICES CAN BE HEARD ECHOING THROUGH A GREAT GRANITE CHAMBER--THE *ORIGINAL MOUNTAIN SANCTUARY* OF THE JLA!...

OUR *100TH MEETING*--I CAN HARDLY BELIEVE IT! SEEMS LIKE ONLY *YESTERDAY* THAT WE FIRST CAME TOGETHER!

WHO WAS IT THAT SAID *TIME FLIES*--?

PROBABLY *METHUSELAH*--BUT WHAT DID *HE* KNOW? FEELS LIKE A *MILLION YEARS* SINCE I STARTED SLINGIN' THAT BOW OF MINE!

PERHAPS, *GREEN ARROW*--BUT YOU'RE NOT UNIQUE! WE'VE *ALL* CHANGED OVER THE YEARS -- OUT OF *NECESSITY,* I SUPPOSE!

MAYBE SO-- MAYBE NO! JUST SEEMS THAT THE MORE WE *LEARN* ABOUT OURSELVES, THE LESS WE REALLY UNDERSTAND!

HEY, THIS IS SUPPOSED TO BE A *CELEBRATION!* LET'S...

RRINNGG

RRINNGG

THE *TELEPHONE?!*

HOW CAN THAT BE? WE HAD IT *DISCONNECTED* MONTHS AGO!

2

CURIOUSLY, HAWKMAN PLUCKS THE RECEIVER FROM ITS CRADLE AND...

HI! HOPE I'M NOT LATE!

ATOM! HOW--?

EASY, BLACK CANARY-- JUST A SIMPLE CROSS-CIRCUITING TRICK I WORKED OUT!

HEY--WHERE IS EVERY-BODY? I FIGURED THE WHOLE GANG WOULD BE HERE BY NOW!

SO DID WE, ATOM!

WONDER WHAT'S DETAINING THE OTHERS?

AND ON THE OFF-CHANCE YOU'RE WONDERING, TOO, DEAR READER-- LET'S SWITCH TO A CENTRAL CITY STREET AND FIND OUT...

LET'S WRAP UP THE CASINO GANG AND GET A MOVE ON, RALPH!*

RIGHT WITH YOU, FLASH! THIS IS ONE GET-TOGETHER I WOULDN'T MISS FOR THE WORLD!

WE'RE RUNNING LATE FOR THE JUSTICE LEAGUE CELEBRATION!

*EDITOR'S NOTE--RALPH DIBNY--THE ELONGATED MAN--THE ONLY SUPER-HERO TO PUBLICLY REVEAL HIS DUAL IDENTITY!

AND COUNTLESS LIGHT-YEARS AWAY, THERE STANDS A MAN WHO WILL MISS THE MEETING FOR PRECISELY THAT REASON !....

I'D GIVE ALMOST ANYTHING TO BE WITH MY EARTH-FRIENDS ON THIS DAY OF DAYS-- BUT THERE ARE MORE IMPORTANT THINGS FOR ME TO DO HERE!

THE MARTIAN MANHUNTER HAS TO REBUILD A WORLD!

3

FROM A WORLD-BUILDER, WE SHIFT TO THE PALATIAL ESTATE OF A WORLD-*BEATER*-- INDUSTRIALIST *SIMON STAGG*...

MASON, WHERE IN BLUE BLAZES DO YOU THINK YOU'RE *GOING*?

SORRY, *STAGGSY*, OLD *PAL!* REX MASON MAY BE ON YOUR PAYROLL -- BUT *METAMORPHO, THE ELEMENT MAN,* GOES WHERE HE *WANTS* TO GO...

...AND RIGHT NOW, HE'S *FLYING* TO A *PARTY!*

WHILE HALF A CONTINENT AWAY, A CERTAIN *SNAPPER CARR* GAZES OUT HIS WINDOW -- AND *WONDERS*...

IMAGINE! AFTER THE WAY I *BETRAYED* THEM,* THE *JLA* STILL INVITED ME TO THEIR *100TH* ANNIVERSARY! I'D GIVE MY RIGHT ARM TO GO -- BUT I *CAN'T!*

AFTER WHAT I DID TO THEM, I JUST COULDN'T *FACE* THEM AGAIN!

*EDITOR'S NOTE: THE STORY OF *SNAPPER'S* BETRAYAL APPEARED IN *JLA #77.*

AND IN THE SHADOW-STREWN BACK-ALLEYS OF *GOTHAM CITY*...

TH-THE B-B-BATMAN! WE'VE *HAD IT!*

STOP FALLING ALL OVER YOUR *MOUTH*, MARTY -- AND *PLUG* HIM!

HE'S JUST *ONE* GUY!

YOU'D THINK BY NOW THESE PUNKS WOULD *KNOW BETTER!* I'D BETTER WRAP THEM UP -- AND GET MOVING!

I'VE GOT A *STOP* TO MAKE ON MY WAY TO THE *JLA* MEETING!

4

AND 25 TRILLION MILES FROM *EARTH*, ON A LUSH PLANET ORBITING THE STAR-SUN *ALPHA CENTAURI*, TWO FAMILIAR FIGURES ARC THROUGH THE EMERALD SKY...

ACCORDING TO *SARDATH'S* CALCULATIONS, THE *ZETA-BEAM* * WON'T WEAR OFF FOR SEVERAL DAYS--TOO LATE FOR ME TO ATTEND THE *JUSTICE LEAGUE* EXTRAVAGANZA!

ALANNA, DARLING-- THEY'LL JUST HAVE TO GET ALONG WITHOUT *ADAM STRANGE!*

*EDITOR'S NOTE: A TELEPORTATIONAL BEAM THAT EARTHMAN *ADAM STRANGE* USES TO TRAVEL *INSTANTLY* TO THE PLANET *RANN!*

AT LAST WE COME FULL-CIRCLE-- AND RETURN TO THE JLA'S LABYRINTHINE MOUNTAIN SANCTUARY...

100 MEETINGS IS A *LONG* TIME, *FLASH*--LOTS OF THINGS CAN HAPPEN!

I'LL SAY! I WAS A ROOKIE POLICE-SCIENTIST WHEN I JOINED THIS GROUP--NOW I'M A *MARRIED* MAN!

REALLY, *FLASH*--THAT'S THE MOST *DEPRESSING* THING I'VE HEARD ALL DAY!

CAN'T YOU *CHANGE* THE SUBJECT?

YOU HAVE THE MOST DISCONCERTING WAY OF DROPPING IN ON PEOPLE!

BUT....WELCOME TO THE FESTIVITIES!

ZATANNA--?!

GREETINGS, PEOPLE! LOOK WHO *I* PICKED UP!

DIANA PRINCE-- *WONDER WOMAN!* HOW *GOOD* TO SEE *YOU* AGAIN!

I ALMOST DIDN'T COME, *SUPERMAN!* YOUR FRIEND HERE HAD TO--*TWIST* MY ARM!

WELL, NOW THAT YOU *ARE* HERE, WHY DON'T YOU USE THAT PRETTY ARM OF YOURS TO HELP CUT THE CAKE!

YOU *MEN!* ALL YOU EVER THINK ABOUT IS YOUR *STOMACHS!*

I'M STARVING!

JUSTICE LEAGUE of AMERICA

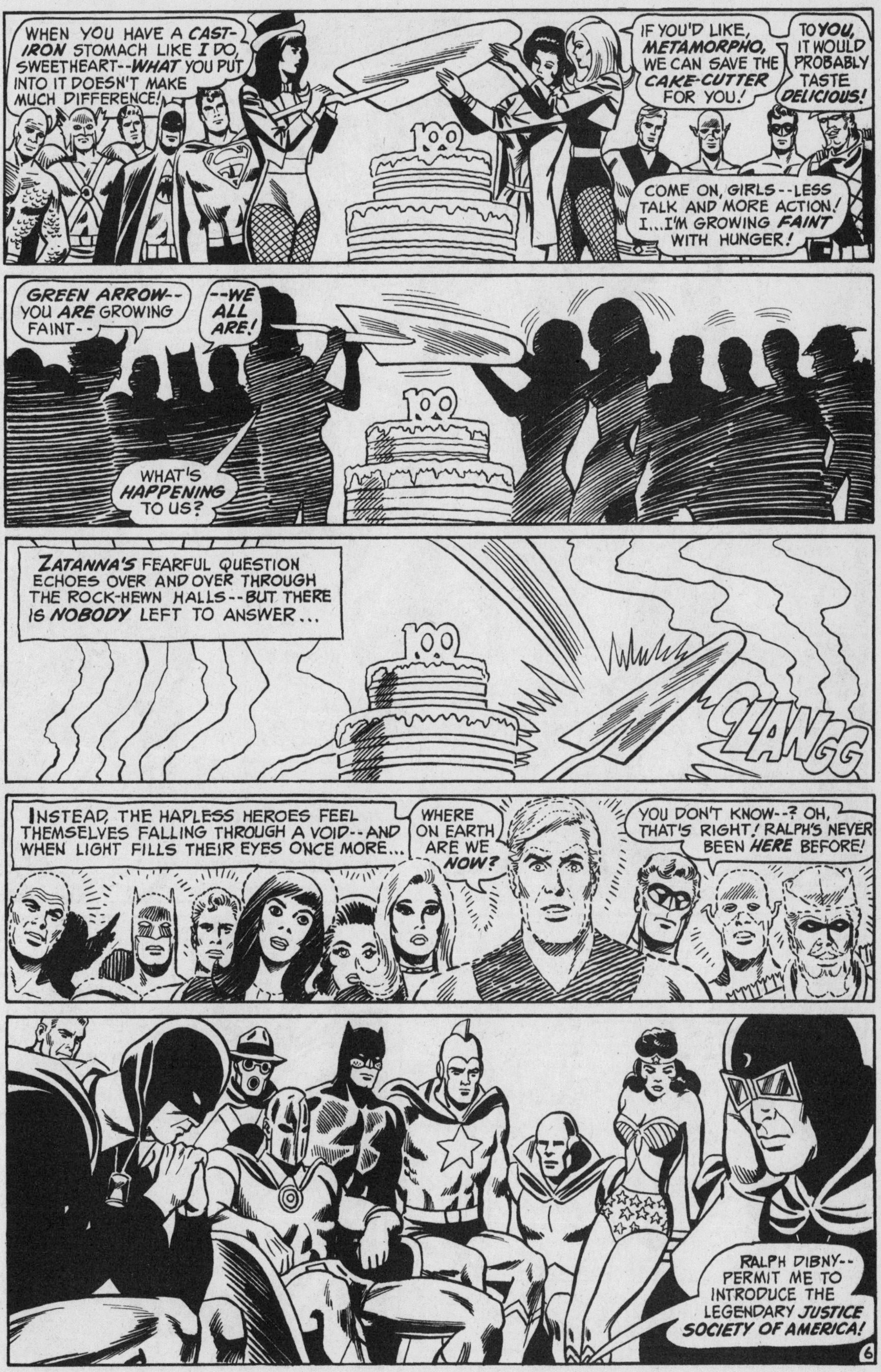
WHEN YOU HAVE A CAST-IRON STOMACH LIKE I DO, SWEETHEART--WHAT YOU PUT INTO IT DOESN'T MAKE MUCH DIFFERENCE!
IF YOU'D LIKE, METAMORPHO, WE CAN SAVE THE CAKE-CUTTER FOR YOU!
TO YOU, IT WOULD PROBABLY TASTE DELICIOUS!
COME ON, GIRLS--LESS TALK AND MORE ACTION! I...I'M GROWING FAINT WITH HUNGER!
GREEN ARROW--YOU ARE GROWING FAINT--
--WE ALL ARE!
WHAT'S HAPPENING TO US?
ZATANNA'S FEARFUL QUESTION ECHOES OVER AND OVER THROUGH THE ROCK-HEWN HALLS--BUT THERE IS NOBODY LEFT TO ANSWER...
CLANGG
INSTEAD, THE HAPLESS HEROES FEEL THEMSELVES FALLING THROUGH A VOID--AND WHEN LIGHT FILLS THEIR EYES ONCE MORE...
WHERE ON EARTH ARE WE NOW?
YOU DON'T KNOW--? OH, THAT'S RIGHT! RALPH'S NEVER BEEN HERE BEFORE!
RALPH DIBNY--PERMIT ME TO INTRODUCE THE LEGENDARY JUSTICE SOCIETY OF AMERICA!
6

THE JUSTICE SOCIETY OF AMERICA--DYNAMIC DEFENDERS OF *ANOTHER EARTH*--BANDED TOGETHER IN THE CAUSE OF RIGHTEOUSNESS...

DOCTOR FATE--MYSTIC MASTER OF OCCULT AND ELDRITCH FORCES...

THE SANDMAN--GRIM CRUSADER WHO HAUNTS THE DREAMS OF THE LAWLESS...

JOHNNY THUNDER--MUDDLED MASTER OF THE MAGICAL *BAHDNISIAN* THUNDERBOLT...

WILDCAT--EX-HEAVY-WEIGHT CHAMPION, WHO WIELDS HIS FISTS IN THE *CAUSE* OF JUSTICE...

THE RED TORNADO--FACELESS ANDROID WHIRLWIND...

STARMAN--MANIPULATOR OF THE AWESOME *COSMIC* ROD...

DOCTOR MID-NITE--BLIND BATTLER FOR HONOR AND TRUTH...

WONDER WOMAN--THE AMAZING AMAZON PRINCESS...

AND *THE HOURMAN*--WHOSE *MIRACLO* PILL GIVES HIM SUPER-CHARGED ENERGY FOR SIXTY FLEETING MINUTES...

AND AFTER THE PROPER SALUTATIONS HAVE BEEN EXCHANGED...

YOU PEOPLE LOOK LIKE YOU'VE BEEN DRAGGED THROUGH THE *MUD!* WHAT'S BEEN *HAPPENING* 'ROUND HERE?

YES--WHY DID YOU BRING US TO *EARTH-TWO** SO ABRUPTLY?

*EDITOR'S NOTE: AN ALMOST-DUPLICATE WORLD, OCCUPYING THE SAME SPACE AS OURS, BUT VIBRATING AT A DIFFERENT SPEED.

WE HAVE NEED OF *HELP,* AQUAMAN--THE SORT OF HELP ONLY YOU AND YOUR COLLEAGUES CAN GIVE!

COME--I WILL *SHOW* YOU WHAT I MEAN!

7

The *STELLAR SORCERER* STRIDES SLOWLY TO THE CENTER OF THE CHAMBER--SILENTLY MUTTERING INCANTATIONS LONG THOUGHT FORGOTTEN--AND VISIONS BLOSSOM IN THE DUSTY AIR BEFORE HIM...

THIS IS WHY I BROUGHT YOU HERE, *JUSTICE LEAGUE*... THE REASON MY MYSTIC POWERS SNATCHED YOU FROM ACROSS THE DIMENSIONAL BARRIERS!

LOOK UPON *THE HAND THAT HOLDS THE EARTH!*

TWICE HAVE WE TRIED TO RELEASE THAT EVIL *HAND'S* GRIP UPON OUR WORLD--AND TWICE HAVE WE *FAILED!*

WE ARE IN SORE NEED OF *HELP,* MY FRIENDS! *THAT* IS WHY WE TURN TO *YOU!*

I'M NOT CERTAIN *WE* COULD FARE ANY *BETTER, DR. FATE*--UNLESS WE KNOW *MORE* ABOUT THAT *HAND!* WHAT'S IT MADE OF? WHERE'S IT COME FROM?

WE'RE STILL TRYING TO PUZZLE OUT THOSE SAME QUESTIONS, *GREEN LANTERN!* ALL WE *DO* KNOW IS--IT BELONGS TO A MENACE WHO CALLS HIMSELF *THE IRON HAND!*

HE HAS GIVEN US 48 HOURS TO TURN SUPREME DOMINATION OF EARTH OVER TO HIM...

...OR THAT FANTASTIC FIST WILL *CLOSE*--AND CRUSH OUR PLANET TO ATOMS!

8

YOU SEE THEN OUR PREDICAMENT-- WE ARE CONFRONTED BY QUESTIONS THAT CRY OUT FOR ANSWERS--BUT THERE ARE NONE TO BE HAD!

IN DESPERATION, I TURNED TO MY MYSTIC CRYSTAL IN HOPES OF SOLUTION...

...BUT *THIS* IS ALL THAT WAS REVEALED TO ME!

HERE IN HONORED GLORY RESTS AN UNKNOWN SOLDIER OF VICTORY WHO DIED THAT HIS WORLD MIGHT LIVE

--A *GRAVE?*

THAT *INSCRIPTION*-- WHAT DOES IT *MEAN?*

AGAIN I KNOW NOT-- I COULD PIERCE THE CRYSTAL-VEIL NO FARTHER!

BUT WITH *YOUR* PRESENCE HERE, *ZATANNA,* THE SCALES MAY AT LAST BE TIPPED IN OUR FAVOR!

M-ME? WHAT CAN *I* DO THAT *DR. FATE* CAN'T?

SOMEWHERE BEYOND THE MISTS OF TIME- AND-SPACE EXISTS THE ENTITY KNOWN AS *ORACLE*--FROM WHOM *NO* SECRETS ARE WITHHELD! MY OWN ABILITIES ARE NOT POTENT ENOUGH TO PENETRATE THE BARRIER--*BUT*...

...WERE WE TO ADD *YOUR* POWERS, *ZATANNA*-- ALONG WITH THOSE OF *JOHNNY THUNDER'S* GENIE-LIKE SERVANT--TO MY OWN, WE MIGHT HAVE A *CHANCE!*

GOTCHA, DOC! OL' *THUNDERBOLT'LL* BE HERE IN TWO SHAKES!

SAY YOU!

AND, AMAZINGLY, AS *JOHNNY THUNDER* UTTERS THE ANCIENT *BAHDNISIAN* CHANT *CEI-U (SAY YOU)*...

YOU *RANG,* O MASTER OF THE *MUDDLED* AND *MUNDANE?*

T-BOLT! DOC FATE AND THE GANG NEED YOUR HELP!

THAT'S WHAT I'M *HERE* FOR, BRIGHT- EYES!

SOON, DARKNESS ENVELOPS THE ROOM, AN OVERPOWERING SHADOW TURNED AWAY ONLY BY THE GLOW OF BURNING EMBERS -- AND THE BLAZING VOICE OF *DOCTOR FATE* ...

ORACLE-- YOU WHO WALK WITH WORLDS AS YOUR STEPPING-STONES-- HEAR MY WORDS! WE--WHO SPEAK YOUR NAME IN THE MOST HUMBLE OF VOICES-- HAVE NEED OF YOU THIS DAY!

COME TO US, *ORACLE*--WE BESEECH THEE! *COME TO US!*

THERE IS A SINGING IN THE STYGIAN GLOOM -- THE VIBRANT SOUND OF WORLDS LONG GONE AND GALAXIES JUST ABORNING -- THE WILLFUL HUM OF ETERNITY AS IT SKIMS ACROSS THE FABRIC OF THE COSMOS--

-- AND THEN THERE COMES A PRESENCE TO THE *JUSTICE SOCIETY'S* HIDDEN SANCTUM ...

WHO DARES CALL ORACLE FROM THE REALM BEYOND?

I DARE, ORACLE! I--DOCTOR FATE-- WHO ASK NO MORE THAN A MOMENT'S INDULGENCE FROM ONE AS OMNIPOTENT AS *YOU!*

A MOMENT CAN BE AN ETERNITY TO SOME, IMPUDENT ONE -- BUT THE NAME OF *DOCTOR FATE* HAS REACHED MY EARS OFTEN, AND NAUGHT BUT GOOD HAS BEEN SAID!

SO *SPEAK* WHAT YOU WILL --AND ORACLE WILL *LISTEN!*

AFTER THE TALE HAS BEEN RETOLD ONCE MORE...

YOU SEEK SOLUTIONS, *DR. FATE*--BUT THAT IS ONE THING *ORACLE CANNOT* GIVE! YOUR DESTINY IS YOUR *OWN!* *ORACLE* CAN BUT RELATE WHAT *HAS* BEEN-- AND ALLOW YOU TO CHOOSE YOUR OWN COURSE OF ACTION! EVEN *HE* IS NOT PERMITTED TO REVEAL THE *FUTURE!*

WHERE'S THAT LEAVE US *NOW?* IF *ORACLE* CAN'T HELP US--*NOBODY* CAN!

YOU MIS-UNDERSTAND, *SANDMAN*--I DID NOT REFUSE TO HELP YOU!

COME--GAZE DEEPLY INTO THE EYES OF *ORACLE*--AND PERHAPS YOU WILL FIND WHAT YOU SEEK!

MANY OF YOUR YEARS AGO, A MENACE SIMILAR TO THE ONE YOU NOW FACE BESTRODE YOUR WORLD-- THE AWESOME, GIANT EARTHMAN-- THE *NEBULA-MAN!*

MANY OF YOUR PEOPLE FELL BEFORE THE MIGHT OF THIS BIZARRE CONQUEROR --UNTIL THERE WAS ONLY A HANDFUL WHO DARED STAND AGAINST HIM!

AT THE TOP OF YOUR WORLD THEY MET, THESE BOLD CHAMPIONS AND TERRIBLE TITAN-- AND THE EARTH RANG WITH THE SOUNDS OF THEIR SAVAGE BATTLE!

...UNTIL FINALLY THESE HEROES, TOO, FELL BEFORE THE COLOSSUS!

"BUT THESE VALIANT WARRIORS WERE NOT TO BE DEFEATED! AGAIN THEY ROSE IN COMBAT WITH A *NEW* WEAPON AT THEIR *COMMAND* --WITH ONE OF THEM SACRIFICING HIS LIFE TO USE THAT SECRET WEAPON TO FULL EFFECT..."

"SUCH WAS THE COURAGE OF--*THE SEVEN SOLDIERS OF VICTORY!*"

THEN *THAT* EXPLAINS THE GRAVE! THE DEAD *SOLDIER OF VICTORY* IS *BURIED* THERE!

SURE--THE *SEVEN SOLDIERS OF VICTORY!* WE SHOULD HAVE THOUGHT OF 'EM SOONER! THEY...THEY...

HEY, WAIT A SECOND! THERE'S SOMETHING *WRONG* HERE!

I CAN'T REMEMBER-- *WHO IN BLAZES ARE THE SEVEN SOLDIERS OF VICTORY?*

COME TO THINK OF IT-- *I* CAN'T REMEMBER, EITHER!

BEATS *ME*, CHUMS-- I'M STUMPED!

WELL, DON'T ASK *US!* NOBODY IN THE *JLA* REMEMBERS THE *SEVEN SOLDIERS* AT ALL!

OKAY, SPACE-FACE, YOU'VE HAD YOUR JOLLIES... NOW LET *US* IN ON YOUR LITTLE SECRET!

CURIOUS *YOU* SHOULD ASK, *GREEN ARROW*--FOR *YOU*, OF ALL WHO STAND HERE, HAVE THE GREATEST AFFINITY FOR SAID GROUP!

GAZE INTO THE EYES OF *ORACLE* ONCE MORE-- AND YOU SHALL SEE *WHY!*

WHO WERE THE SEVEN SOLDIERS OF VICTORY?

12

THE *SEVEN SOLDIERS OF VICTORY* WERE NOT UNLIKE YOURSELVES -- BOLD ADVENTURERS GATHERED TOGETHER IN THE NAME OF FREEDOM...

THE STAR-SPANGLED *KID* AND *STRIPESY* -- ACTUALLY, WEALTHY YOUNG *SYLVESTER PEMBERTON* AND HIS BODYGUARD-CHAUFFEUR, *PAT DUGAN* -- WHO BATTLED INJUSTICE IN THE ASTONISHING *STAR-ROCKET-RACER...*

THE *VIGILANTE* -- IN REALITY, *GREG SANDERS,* THE *"PRAIRIE TROUBADOUR"* -- WHO FOUGHT *CRIMES* OF THE *CITY* WITH THE *WEAPONS* OF THE *PLAINS...*

SIR JUSTIN, THE SHINING KNIGHT -- TIME-TOSSED PALADIN OF KING ARTHUR'S COURT -- WHO RODE THE FLYING STEED, *WINGED VICTORY,* AGAINST THE FORCES OF CORRUPTION...

THE *CRIMSON AVENGER* -- CRUSADING NEWSPAPER PUBLISHER *LEE TRAVIS* -- WHO, WITH THE HELP OF HIS ORIENTAL AIDE, *WING,* CARRIED HIS CAMPAIGN OF CRIME-PREVENTION INTO THE UNDERWORLD'S DARKEST HOLDS...

THE *GREEN ARROW* AND *SPEEDY* -- MILLIONAIRE FINANCIER *OLIVER QUEEN* AND HIS YOUNG WARD, *ROY HARPER* -- WHO BENT THEIR LONGBOWS TO PROTECT THE INNOCENT FROM THE GRASPING CLAW OF EVIL...

13

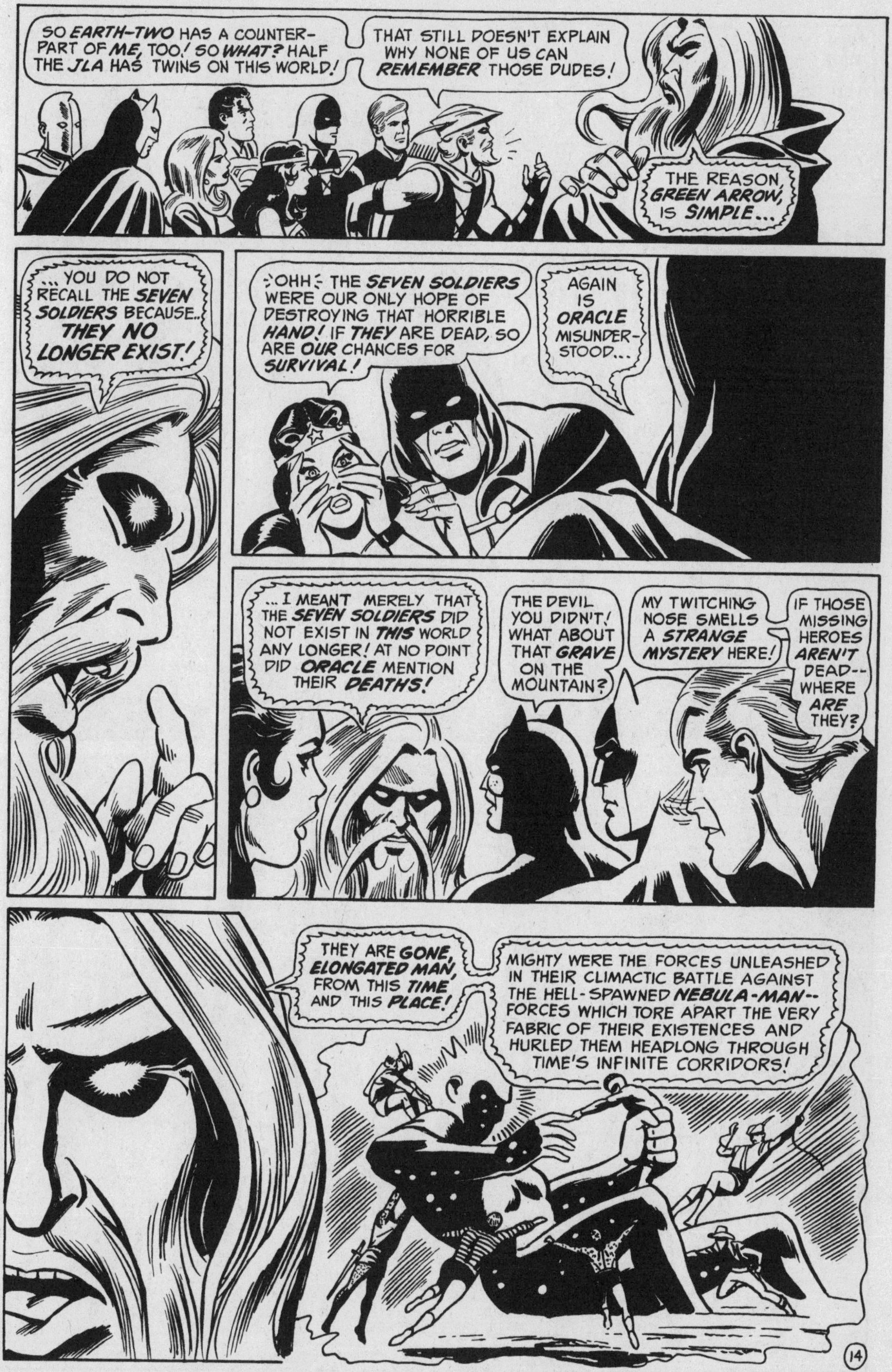
SO EARTH-TWO HAS A COUNTER-PART OF ME, TOO! SO WHAT? HALF THE JLA HAS TWINS ON THIS WORLD!
THAT STILL DOESN'T EXPLAIN WHY NONE OF US CAN REMEMBER THOSE DUDES!
THE REASON, GREEN ARROW, IS SIMPLE...
... YOU DO NOT RECALL THE SEVEN SOLDIERS BECAUSE... THEY NO LONGER EXIST!
OHH -- THE SEVEN SOLDIERS WERE OUR ONLY HOPE OF DESTROYING THAT HORRIBLE HAND! IF THEY ARE DEAD, SO ARE OUR CHANCES FOR SURVIVAL!
AGAIN IS ORACLE MISUNDER-STOOD...
... I MEANT MERELY THAT THE SEVEN SOLDIERS DID NOT EXIST IN THIS WORLD ANY LONGER! AT NO POINT DID ORACLE MENTION THEIR DEATHS!
THE DEVIL YOU DIDN'T! WHAT ABOUT THAT GRAVE ON THE MOUNTAIN?
MY TWITCHING NOSE SMELLS A STRANGE MYSTERY HERE!
IF THOSE MISSING HEROES AREN'T DEAD-- WHERE ARE THEY?
THEY ARE GONE, ELONGATED MAN, FROM THIS TIME AND THIS PLACE!
MIGHTY WERE THE FORCES UNLEASHED IN THEIR CLIMACTIC BATTLE AGAINST THE HELL-SPAWNED NEBULA-MAN-- FORCES WHICH TORE APART THE VERY FABRIC OF THEIR EXISTENCES AND HURLED THEM HEADLONG THROUGH TIME'S INFINITE CORRIDORS!
14

THEN THEY MIGHT JUST AS WELL BE DEAD FOR ALL THE *GOOD* THEY'LL DO US!

IF WHAT YOU SAY IS *TRUE*, FINDING THEM WILL BE LIKE LOOKING FOR SEVEN TINY NEEDLES IN A UNIVERSAL HAYSTACK! WE WOULDN'T STAND A COSMIC CHANCE--

YOURS ARE *DEFEATIST* MOUTHINGS, ATOM--AND YOU ARE *WRONG!*

JUST WHAT IS *THAT* SUPPOSED TO MEAN?

THOUGH THE GATES OF THE *FUTURE* ARE LOCKED, THE *PAST* IS ORACLE'S PROVINCE!

IF YOU WOULD *SEEK* THOSE SEVEN MISSING SENTINELS, *ORACLE* WILL POINT THE WAY FOR YOU!

HAVE WE ANY *ALTERNATIVE?* THE FUTURE OF OUR WORLD HANGS BY A SINGLE, FRAGILE THREAD!

WE *ACCEPT* YOUR GENEROUS OFFER, *ORACLE* --SHOW US THE WAY!

DOWN SEVEN OF TIME'S CORRIDORS MUST YOU WALK --SO DEPLOY YOUR FELLOWS CAREFULLY!

FOR THOSE YOU PURSUE MAY NO LONGER BE WHAT ONCE THEY WERE!

BENEATH *ORACLE'S* ETERNALLY-WATCHFUL GAZE, THE GREATEST HEROES OF TWO WORLDS SEPARATE INTO SEVEN GROUPS--SEVEN BOLD CHANCES FOR THE SALVATION OF A WORLD...

15

DIANA, HOW ABOUT COMING ALONG WITH *HOURMAN,* *STARMAN,* AND ME?

I'D LIKE TO, *BATMAN* --BUT I THINK I'LL STAY *HERE!*

THERE SHOULD BE SOMEBODY LEFT TO BRIEF ANYONE ELSE WHO MIGHT ARRIVE AFTER YOU'VE DEPARTED!

IF THAT'S THE WAY YOU *WANT* IT, *MISS PRINCE*-- BUT WE'D REALLY LIKE TO...

ENOUGH! IT IS TIME! THE POWER THAT IS *ORACLE* NOW OPENS THE *CHRONAL CORRIDORS* FOR YOU.

...AND SPEEDS YOU ON YOUR *QUEST!*

TAKE CARE OF THINGS, *DIANA*-- AND WISH US *LUCK*...

GOOD LUCK, *BATMAN!* I PRAY TO *APHRODITE* THAT YOU WON'T *NEED* IT!

BEYOND THE MEAGER BOUNDARIES OF REALITY, TWENTY-ONE COLORFUL FIGURES FLASH THROUGH THE ABSTRACT VOID...

ORACLE, FOR OUR SEARCH TO BE SUCCESSFUL, WE MUST KNOW *MORE* OF THOSE WE SEEK!

HOW DID THE *SEVEN SOLDIERS OF VICTORY* COME TO BE ?

16

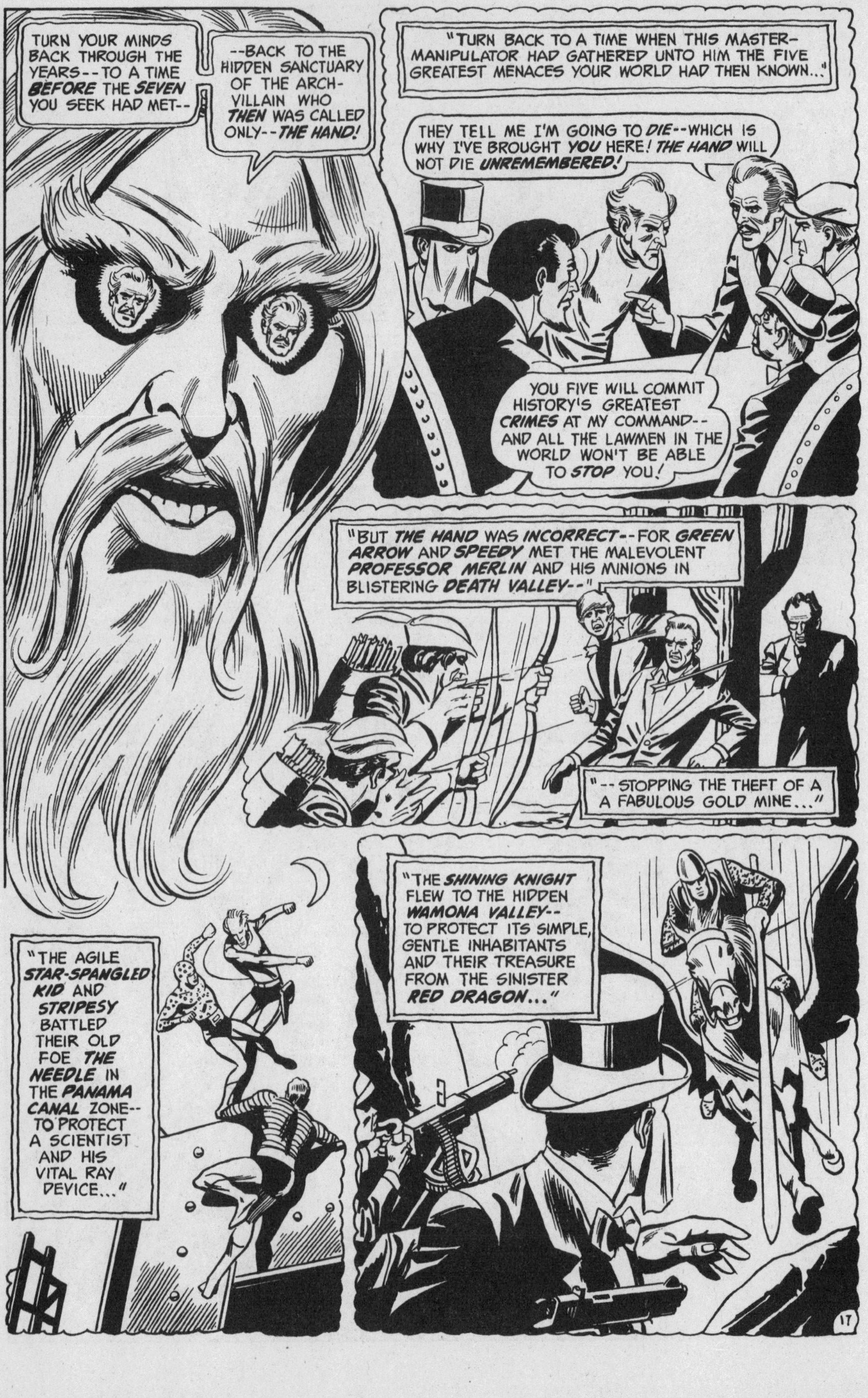
TURN YOUR MINDS BACK THROUGH THE YEARS--TO A TIME BEFORE THE SEVEN YOU SEEK HAD MET--
--BACK TO THE HIDDEN SANCTUARY OF THE ARCH-VILLAIN WHO THEN WAS CALLED ONLY--THE HAND!
"TURN BACK TO A TIME WHEN THIS MASTER-MANIPULATOR HAD GATHERED UNTO HIM THE FIVE GREATEST MENACES YOUR WORLD HAD THEN KNOWN..."
THEY TELL ME I'M GOING TO DIE--WHICH IS WHY I'VE BROUGHT YOU HERE! THE HAND WILL NOT DIE UNREMEMBERED!
YOU FIVE WILL COMMIT HISTORY'S GREATEST CRIMES AT MY COMMAND--AND ALL THE LAWMEN IN THE WORLD WON'T BE ABLE TO STOP YOU!
"BUT THE HAND WAS INCORRECT--FOR GREEN ARROW AND SPEEDY MET THE MALEVOLENT PROFESSOR MERLIN AND HIS MINIONS IN BLISTERING DEATH VALLEY--"
"--STOPPING THE THEFT OF A A FABULOUS GOLD MINE..."
"THE AGILE STAR-SPANGLED KID AND STRIPESY BATTLED THEIR OLD FOE THE NEEDLE IN THE PANAMA CANAL ZONE--TO PROTECT A SCIENTIST AND HIS VITAL RAY DEVICE..."
"THE SHINING KNIGHT FLEW TO THE HIDDEN WAMONA VALLEY--TO PROTECT ITS SIMPLE, GENTLE INHABITANTS AND THEIR TREASURE FROM THE SINISTER RED DRAGON..."
17

"THE *CRIMSON AVENGER* AND HIS ORIENTAL AIDE, *WING,* JOURNEYED TO TEEMING *TIMES SQUARE*--"

"AND *THE VIGILANTE* RACED TO *HOLLYWOOD*--TO SMASH A BIZARRE BLACKMAIL PLOT DEVISED BY THE DIABOLICAL *DUMMY*..."

"AT LAST, THE WINDING PATHS OF THOSE SEVEN BRAVE SENTINELS LED THEM TO THE HIDEAWAY OF *THE HAND* HIMSELF--AND INTO THE CENTER OF AN ELECTRONIC TRAP..."

"--TO STOP VICIOUS *BIG CAESAR* FROM CAUSING A POWER BLACKOUT THAT WOULD LEAVE *NEW YORK CITY* OPEN TO MASS ROBBERY..."

"BUT A WELL-PLACED BULLET FROM *THE VIGILANTE* SEVERED THE WEAPON'S SUPPORTS--AND ENDED *THE HAND'S* CRIMINAL CAREER--SEEMINGLY *FOREVER*..."

SO WELL DID THEY MESH TO DEFEAT THAT MONUMENTAL MENACE THAT THEY BANDED TOGETHER AT THE *SHINING KNIGHT'S* SUGGESTION--TO BECOME THE *SEVEN SOLDIERS OF VICTORY!*

AN AMAZING STORY, *ORACLE*--BUT TELL US MORE OF *THE HAND!*

WHY DID YOU SAY ONLY *"SEEMINGLY"* FOREVER?

ALL WILL BE REVEALED TO YOU IN TIME!

BUT *NOW, ORACLE* MUST SPEED YOU TO YOUR POINTS OF RENDEZVOUS--

--FOR THE QUEST HAS *BEGUN!*

18

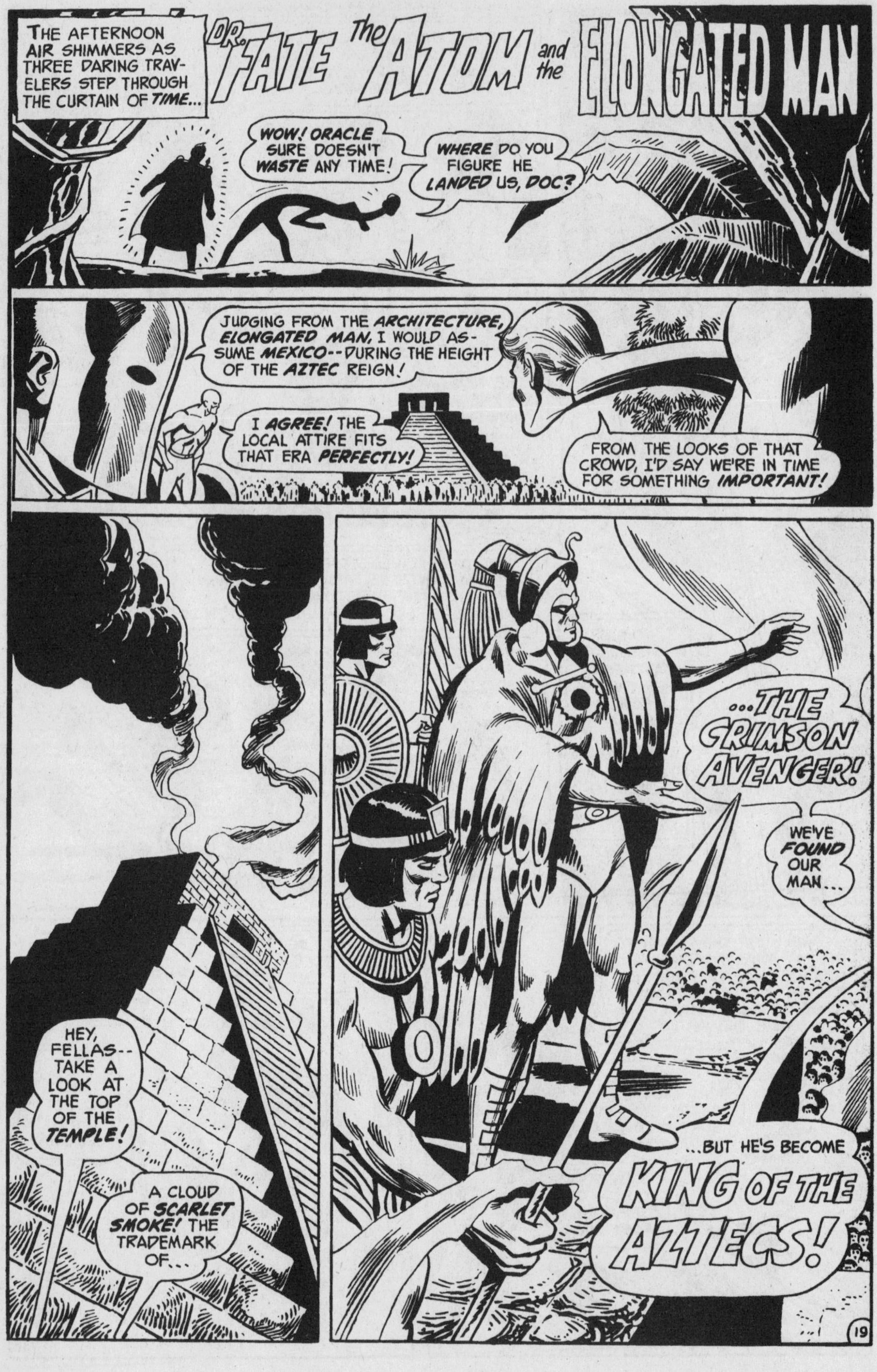
THE AFTERNOON AIR SHIMMERS AS THREE DARING TRAVELERS STEP THROUGH THE CURTAIN OF TIME...
DR. FATE The ATOM and the ELONGATED MAN
WOW! ORACLE SURE DOESN'T WASTE ANY TIME!
WHERE DO YOU FIGURE HE LANDED US, DOC?
JUDGING FROM THE ARCHITECTURE, ELONGATED MAN, I WOULD ASSUME MEXICO--DURING THE HEIGHT OF THE AZTEC REIGN!
I AGREE! THE LOCAL ATTIRE FITS THAT ERA PERFECTLY!
FROM THE LOOKS OF THAT CROWD, I'D SAY WE'RE IN TIME FOR SOMETHING IMPORTANT!
HEY, FELLAS--TAKE A LOOK AT THE TOP OF THE TEMPLE!
A CLOUD OF SCARLET SMOKE! THE TRADEMARK OF...
...THE CRIMSON AVENGER!
WE'VE FOUND OUR MAN...
...BUT HE'S BECOME KING OF THE AZTECS!
19

A SHORT WHILE LATER--WHEN THE TUMULTUOUS CROWD HAS FINALLY DISPERSED...

TREAD SOFTLY, FRIENDS!

WE'D BEST *FOLLOW* OUR CRIMSON QUARRY AND HIS COMPANIONS TO *QUIETER* QUARTERS--

--BEFORE WE TAKE ANY *ACTION!*

I'M WAY *AHEAD* OF YOU, DOC!

CAUTIOUSLY, THE COSTUMED TRIO APPROACHES THE GREAT EDIFICE--*DOCTOR FATE* MOUTHS A MYSTIC CHANT AND...

A TERRIFIC OPENING, DOC-- BUT IT'LL NEVER REPLACE THE *DOOR!*

THIS IS NO TIME FOR *HUMOR,* MR. DIBNY! THE *CRIMSON AVENGER* IS *WELL-GUARDED!*

WE'D BETTER ATTRACT HIS ATTENTION!

AND MOMENTS LATER...

PSST--AVENGER!-- KEEP *QUIET!*

WE'RE HERE TO HELP YOU *ESCAPE!*

WHAT--? INTRUDERS!

GUARDS, COME QUICKLY-- QUICKLY!

SOMETHING TELLS ME WE MADE A *BOO-BOO!*

LET'S GET THE HECK *OUTA* HERE!

YOU WILL BE GOING *NOWHERE,* STRANGE ONES-- TILL YOU ANSWER SOME *QUESTIONS!*

UUNNNHH!

20

WHEN THE *SOLDIERS THREE* COME TO...

WHAT DID THE *CRIMSON AVENGER* HIT US WITH--?

I FEEL LIKE A STRETCHED-OUT *RUBBER BAND!*

MY CONDITION IS NOT UNLIKE *YOURS,* FRIEND DIBNY--AND THESE *CHAINS* DO LITTLE TO *EASE* THE DISCOMFORT!

IS *THE ATOM* AWAKE YET?

SPRY AS A *SPRING,* DOC! I'M SO SMALL THE *AVENGER* AND HIS GOONS DIDN'T EVEN *NOTICE* ME!

SO, PRISONERS-- YOU ARE *AWAKE* AT LAST!

WHO SENT YOU TO *SPY* ON *HUITZILOPOCHTLI,* THE *SUN GOD?*

SUN GOD? YOU'RE *NO SUN GOD!*

YOU'RE THE *CRIMSON AVENGER*-- A HERO WE'VE JOURNEYED THROUGH THE CENTURIES TO *FIND!*

I *AM* A *GOD!* WHO ELSE COULD WIELD SUCH *POWER?*

--THE POWER GIVEN ME WHEN I FELL FROM OUT THE *SKY!*

APPARENTLY, MY FRIEND--YOU'RE SUFFERING FROM *DELUSIONS!*..

A CONDITION EASILY *CURED* ONCE WE GET YOU *AWAY* FROM THIS *TIME!*

WHAT *SORCERY*--? THEY *FREE* THEMSELVES!

GUARDS! GUARDS!

21

I WILL NOT BE SO LENIENT *AGAIN*! *THIS* TIME I WILL TURN YOU TO *ASHES*!

FORGIVE ME, MY *FRIEND*...

...BUT *THIS* TIME I FEAR I CANNOT *COOPERATE* SO READILY!

RASH *INTRUDERS*! YOU ARE *DOOMED*!

WHEREVER HIS POWERS STEM FROM, THEY ARE *AWESOME*!

I BARELY MANAGE TO *MAINTAIN* MY GROUND!

I'D SAY YOU GUYS HAD BEEN WATCHING TOO MANY OLD *PETER LORRE* MOVIES--

--EXCEPT FOR THE FACT THEY HAVEN'T INVENTED *TELEVISION* YET!

OOF!

UGH!

UNNH!

E-MAN IS HOLDING HIS OWN--BUT IT LOOKS LIKE *DOC FATE* IS IN TROUBLE!

I'D BETTER LEND MY *"TINY TALENTS"* TO THE GOOD *DOCTOR*--WHILE THERE'S STILL *TIME*!

THAT'S ASSUMING I DON'T GET *STEPPED* ON IN THE PROCESS!

≈WHEW≈--MADE *IT*!

THIS SWINGING SPEAR SHAFT'LL MAKE A DANDY LITTLE *CATAPULT*-- TO SEND ME TO THE *POINT* OF THE MATTER...

22

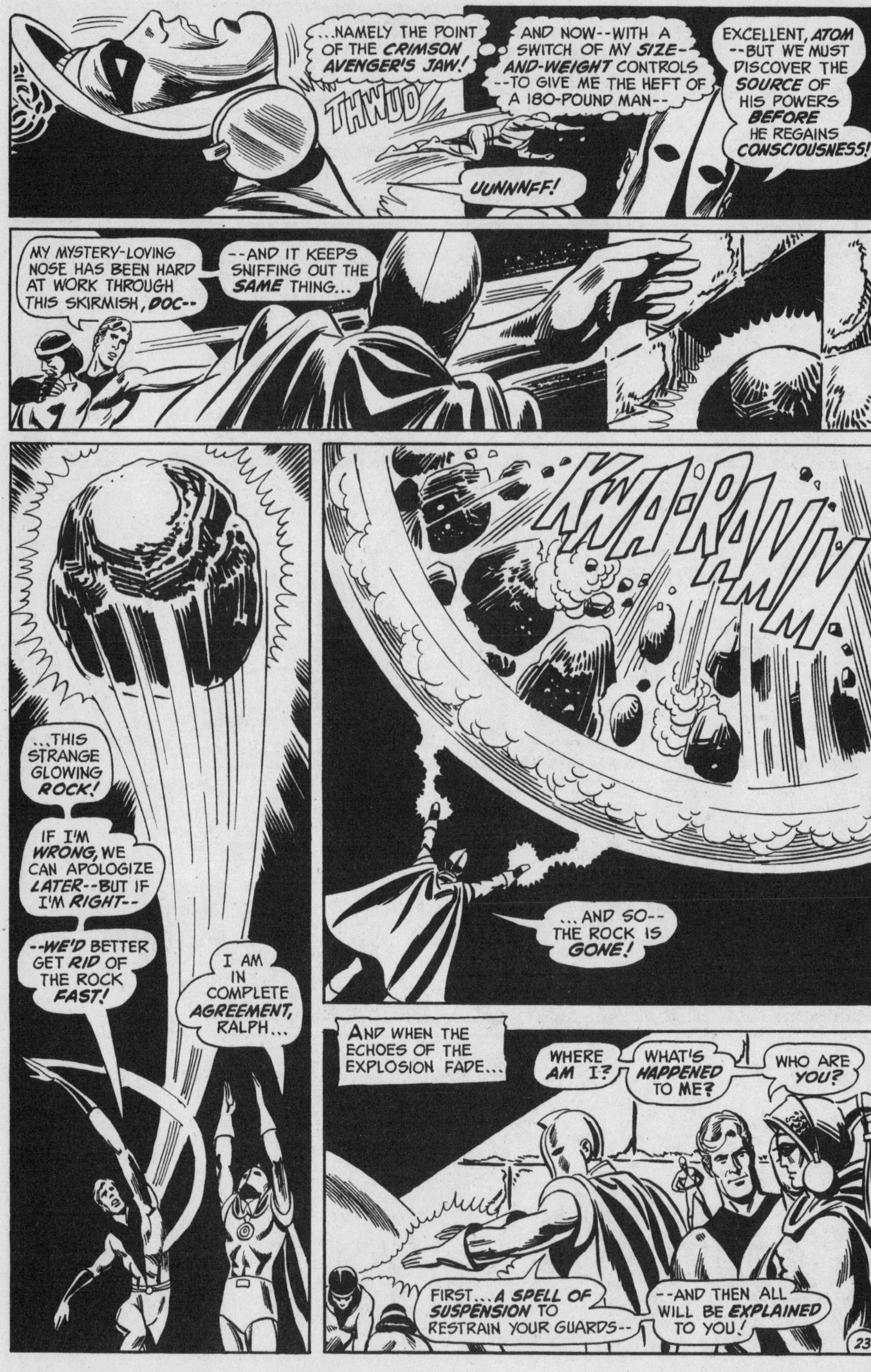

...NAMELY THE POINT OF THE CRIMSON AVENGER'S JAW!
AND NOW--WITH A SWITCH OF MY SIZE-AND-WEIGHT CONTROLS --TO GIVE ME THE HEFT OF A 180-POUND MAN--
EXCELLENT, ATOM --BUT WE MUST DISCOVER THE SOURCE OF HIS POWERS BEFORE HE REGAINS CONSCIOUSNESS!
THWUD
UUNNNFF!
MY MYSTERY-LOVING NOSE HAS BEEN HARD AT WORK THROUGH THIS SKIRMISH, DOC--
--AND IT KEEPS SNIFFING OUT THE SAME THING...
...THIS STRANGE GLOWING ROCK!
IF I'M WRONG, WE CAN APOLOGIZE LATER--BUT IF I'M RIGHT--
--WE'D BETTER GET RID OF THE ROCK FAST!
I AM IN COMPLETE AGREEMENT, RALPH...
KWA-RAMM
...AND SO--THE ROCK IS GONE!
AND WHEN THE ECHOES OF THE EXPLOSION FADE...
WHERE AM I?
WHAT'S HAPPENED TO ME?
WHO ARE YOU?
FIRST...A SPELL OF SUSPENSION TO RESTRAIN YOUR GUARDS--
--AND THEN ALL WILL BE EXPLAINED TO YOU!
23

AFTER EXPLANATIONS ARE MADE...

A *FANTASTIC* STORY! APPARENTLY WHEN I WAS HURLED THROUGH TIME, A CHUCK OF THE SHATTERED *NEBULA-MAN* WAS THROWN ALONG WITH ME --

--STEALING MY MEMORY-- AND IMBUING ME WITH THE *POWERS* YOU DESCRIBE!

SUDDENLY...

THAT *SMOKE--!* IT'S NOT CRIMSON LIKE MY OWN!

WHAT *IS* IT?

UNLESS I AM *MISTAKEN,* AVENGER-- IT IS OUR PASSPORT TO THE *FUTURE!*

ORACLE IS BRINGING US *HOME!*

YEAH--BUT IS HE BRINGING US HOME -- IN *TIME?*

AND IN A DARKENED LABORATORY IN ANOTHER PLANE OF EXISTENCE, THERE IS *ANOTHER* WHOSE THOUGHTS ARE CONCERNED WITH *TIME...*

THEY MOVE SO *SLOWLY,* THE HANDS OF THE *CLOCK--* ALMOST AS IF THEY WERE *TAUNTING* ME--

--TELLING ME I WILL NOT *SUCCEED!*

BUT THEY ARE *WRONG-- DEAD WRONG!*

THE EARTH WILL BOW BEFORE MY DEMANDS --

--AND THE *IRON HAND* WILL HOLD DOMINION OVER ALL!

NEXT ISSUE:

"*THE HAND THAT SHOOK THE WORLD!*"

THE END

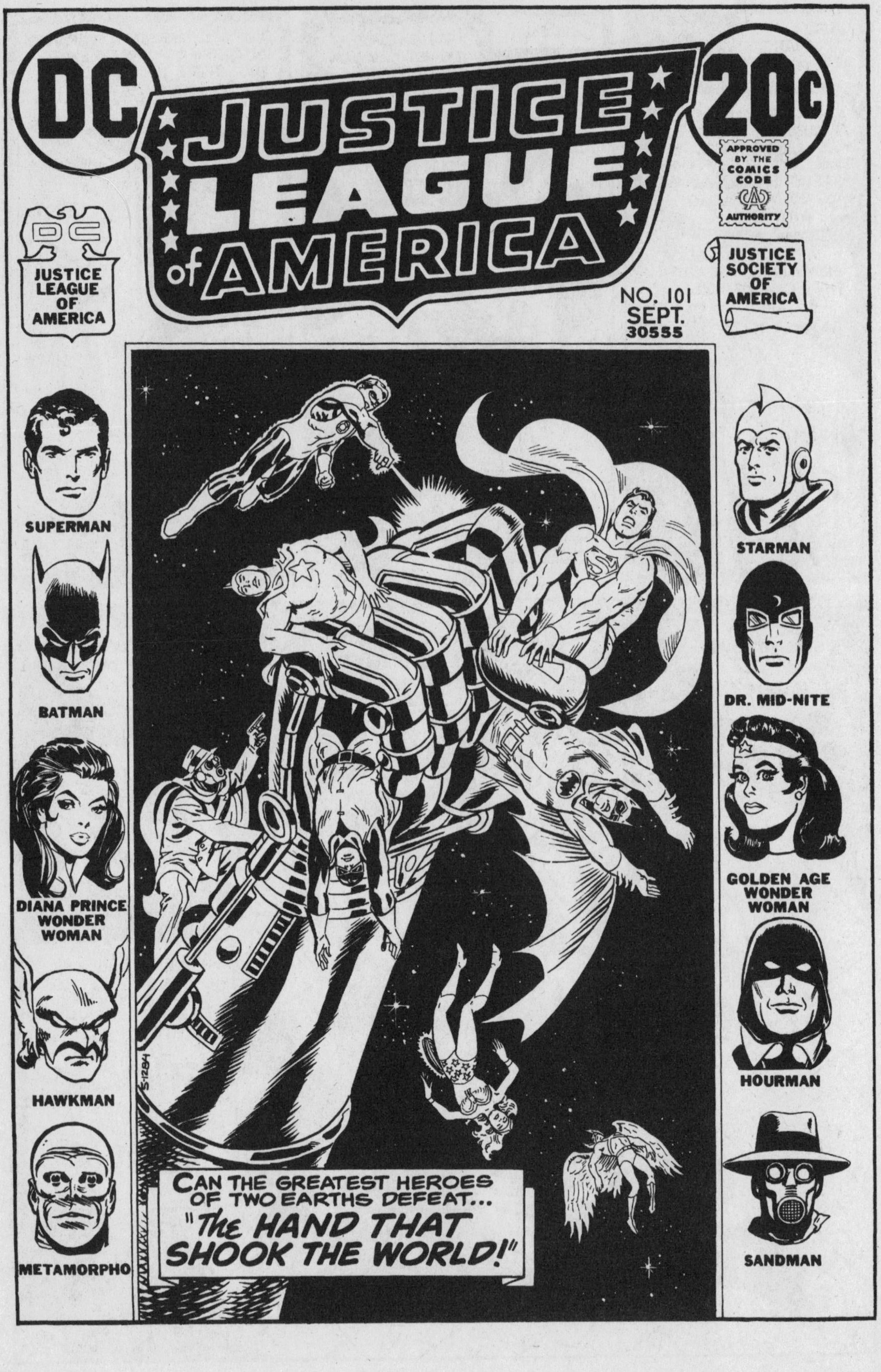
DC
JUSTICE LEAGUE of AMERICA
20¢
APPROVED BY THE COMICS CODE AUTHORITY
JUSTICE LEAGUE OF AMERICA
NO. 101
SEPT.
30555
JUSTICE SOCIETY OF AMERICA
SUPERMAN
BATMAN
DIANA PRINCE WONDER WOMAN
HAWKMAN
METAMORPHO
STARMAN
DR. MID-NITE
GOLDEN AGE WONDER WOMAN
HOURMAN
SANDMAN
CAN THE GREATEST HEROES OF TWO EARTHS DEFEAT...
"The HAND THAT SHOOK THE WORLD!"

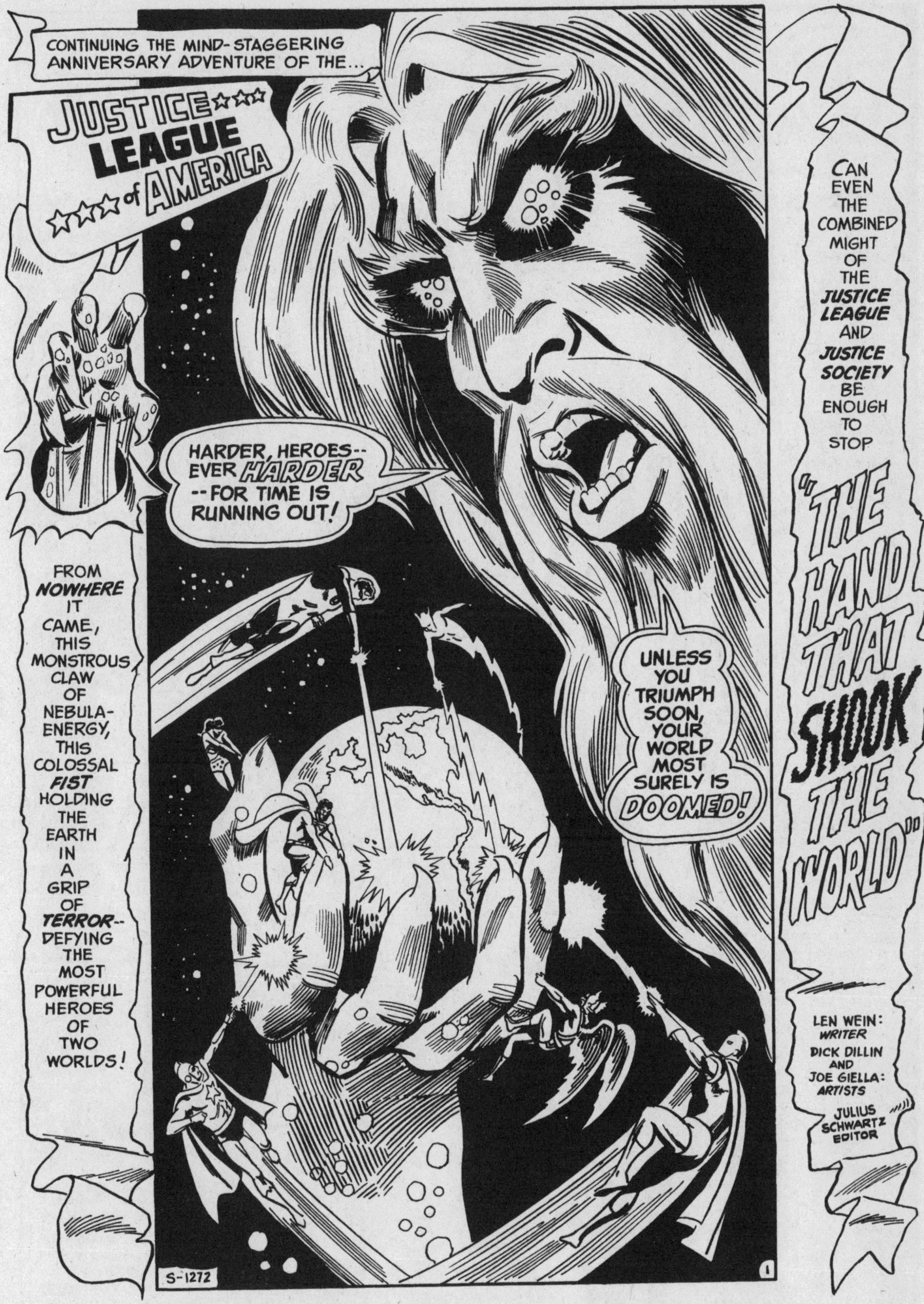
CONTINUING THE MIND-STAGGERING ANNIVERSARY ADVENTURE OF THE...
JUSTICE LEAGUE of AMERICA
HARDER, HEROES-- EVER HARDER --FOR TIME IS RUNNING OUT!
UNLESS YOU TRIUMPH SOON, YOUR WORLD MOST SURELY IS DOOMED!
FROM NOWHERE IT CAME, THIS MONSTROUS CLAW OF NEBULA-ENERGY, THIS COLOSSAL FIST HOLDING THE EARTH IN A GRIP OF TERROR-- DEFYING THE MOST POWERFUL HEROES OF TWO WORLDS!
CAN EVEN THE COMBINED MIGHT OF THE JUSTICE LEAGUE AND JUSTICE SOCIETY BE ENOUGH TO STOP
"THE HAND THAT SHOOK THE WORLD"
LEN WEIN: WRITER
DICK DILLIN AND JOE GIELLA: ARTISTS
JULIUS SCHWARTZ EDITOR
S-1272
1

TIME--THE ETERNAL ENIGMA--PASSES WITH DEPRESSING SLOWNESS IN THE SECLUDED SANCTUARY OF THE *JUSTICE SOCIETY OF AMERICA,* AS A SOLITARY FIGURE SITS-- AND *WAITS...*

...HOURS SINCE THEY ALL *VANISHED* INTO THE *PAST*-- AND NOT A *WORD!*

I'VE CHOSEN THE *HARDEST* TASK FOR MYSELF--

--WAITING!

AN *INTRUDER* IN OUR SECRET HEADQUARTERS!

WHO IN--?

OH, *GREEN LANTERN,* MR. *TERRIFIC--*

--YOU *STARTLED* ME!

INTRODUCE ME, FELLAS--!

ROBIN, MEET *DIANA PRINCE*-- THE *WONDER WOMAN* OF *EARTH-ONE!*

YOUR *GREEN LANTERN* TOLD ME OF THE *LOSS* OF YOUR *SUPER-POWERS,* DIANA ...

...I'M *SORRY!*

SO AM I--BUT THAT *DOESN'T* EXPLAIN WHAT SHE'S *DOING* HERE!

OUR WORLD'S IN MORTAL *DANGER*-- AND THE ENTIRE *JSA* IS *GONE!*

HE'S *RIGHT,* DIANA!

WHERE *IS* EVERYBODY?

THAT, FRIENDS, IS A *LONG* STORY!

FOLLOW ME-- AND SEE FOR YOURSELVES!

THIS--IS THE GRAVE OF THE *UNKNOWN SOLDIER OF VICTORY*-- HIDDEN DEEP IN THE *HIMALAYAS!*

DOCTOR FATE DISCOVERED IT WHILE SEEKING TO OVER-COME THE *HAND THAT HOLDS THE EARTH!*

WHAT DOES THE *GRAVE* SIGNIFY?

"THAT'S WHAT THE *OTHERS* ALSO WANTED TO KNOW--"

"-- SO DOCTOR FATE, ZATANNA, AND *JOHNNY THUNDER'S* MYSTIC *THUNDER-BOLT* COMBINED THEIR POWERS TO SUMMON THE COSMIC SEER, *ORACLE...*"

2

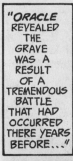

"ORACLE REVEALED THE GRAVE WAS A RESULT OF A TREMENDOUS BATTLE THAT HAD OCCURRED THERE YEARS BEFORE..."

"...A BATTLE BETWEEN THE TITANIC *NEBULA-MAN* AND THE *SEVEN SOLDIERS OF VICTORY*..."

WHO IN BLAZES ARE THE *SEVEN SOLDIERS OF VICTORY*?

I NEVER *HEARD* OF THEM!

I'M *OLDER* THAN YOU ARE, *ROBIN*-- BUT I'LL BE DARNED IF *I* CAN REMEMBER THEM EITHER!

WHAT'S *WRONG* WITH OUR MEMORIES?

ABSOLUTELY *NOTHING*!

NOBODY ON *EARTH* REMEMBERS THE *SEVEN SOLDIERS*--BECAUSE A *TIME-WARP* CREATED BY THE *NEBULA-MAN'S* DESTRUCTION HURLED THEM BACK THROUGH THE AGES!

GREEN ARROW AND *SPEEDY*, THE *SHINING KNIGHT*, THE *CRIMSON AVENGER*, THE *STAR-SPANGLED KID* AND *STRIPESY*, AND THE *VIGILANTE* NO LONGER *EXIST* IN YOUR WORLD...

"...BUT ONLY THESE *SEVEN* KNOW THE WAY TO *DESTROY* THE GALACTIC *HAND*!"

"THAT'S WHY *ORACLE* SENT THE COMBINED FORCES OF THE *JUSTICE LEAGUE* AND *JUSTICE SOCIETY* THROUGH TIME IN SEARCH OF THEM-- LEAVING ME BEHIND TO BRIEF OTHERS... SUCH AS *YOU*..."

THEN THE FATE OF *EARTH* RESTS IN THE HANDS OF OUR COLLEAGUES--

--AND THERE ISN'T A BLASTED *THING* WE CAN DO TO *HELP*!

3

EVEN AS *GREEN LANTERN* SPEAKS, THREE OF THOSE DARING DEFENDERS HAVE BEEN THRUST BACK INTO THE REALM OF REALITY...

SUPERMAN, SANDMAN and METAMORPHO THE ELEMENT MAN

WOW! *ORACLE* SURE HAS SOME *DELIVERY SERVICE!*

AYEEE! PRAISE *BUDDHA!* HE SENDS *WARRIORS* TO DEFEND US!

AN OLD CHINESE *MONK!* IT SEEMS WE'VE BEEN *EXPECTED!*

TELL ME, ANCIENT ONE-- *WHY* DO YOU NEED *WARRIORS* TO PROTECT YOU?

COME, PLEASE-- WHILE THIS HUMBLE ONE EXPLAINS AS BEST HE CAN!

WITHIN THESE POOR CHAMBERS RESTS THE *HERITAGE* OF MY PEOPLE--

--ALL THE BEAUTY AND HERITAGE OF OUR PAST, HIDDEN AWAY FROM THE EYES OF THE *INVADERS*...

...UNTIL *NOW!*

I GET IT--THEY'RE AFTER THIS *MUSEUM* OF YOURS!

WHO ARE THESE *INVADERS?*

THEY ARE AS MANY AS THE LEAVES OF THE FOREST!

ONCE THEIR LEADER WAS NAMED *TEMUJIN*--BUT NOW THEY CALL HIM THE "UNIVERSAL RULER"--

GENGHIS KHAN!

4

HIS LEGIONS ARE LED BY AN *ARMORED GOD* ON A *WINGED HORSE!* NOTHING CAN STAND AGAINST THEM!

ARMORED MAN--? WINGED HORSE--?

SOUNDS LIKE THE *SHINING KNIGHT!*

IT *DOES* SEEM *IMPOSSIBLE!*

YET... I *WONDER...*

NO NEED TO WONDER, *SUPES*-- WHEN WE CAN FIND OUT FOR *CERTAIN!*

NOBODY'S GONNA NOTICE A *HELIUM* BREEZE DRIFTING THROUGH THEIR CAMP--

--SO I CAN CHECK OUT OL' *GENGHIS'S* ARMY!

MERE MINUTES LATER...

THE ARMORED ONE IS STILL AT MY COMMAND, *SHAMAN!*

YOUR FIERY *GAZE* HAS SEARED HIM TO THE SOUL...

YOU HAVE SERVED ME *WELL!*

I LIVE FOR NOTHING ELSE, GREAT *KHAN!*

AND THAT IS AS IT *SHOULD* BE!

COME, WE MUST PREPARE FOR TOMORROW'S *ONSLAUGHT!*

THEN I'D BETTER SNATCH OUR *KNIGHT-ERRANT* OUT OF HERE *TONIGHT!*

ALL IT TAKES IS A STAINLESS *STEEL* SWORD TO PROVIDE A QUICK ENTRANCE AND...

SIR JUSTIN! YOU DON'T *KNOW* ME-- BUT I'M A *FRIEND!*

I'M HERE TO HELP YOU *ESCAPE...*

WHAT--? *INTRUDER! VARLET!*

NO ONE MAY DISTURB THE CHAMBERS OF MY *LIEGE,* KHAN--AND *LIVE* TO TELL THE TALE!

5

ZOUNDS! WHAT FOUL WIZARDRY IS *THIS*?

THE CREATURE DOTH EVADE MY EVERY *THRUST*!

'TIS AS ELUSIVE AS THE *WIND*!

--OR *FLUORINE GAS*, TO BE MORE PRECISE, PRINCE CHARMING!

NOW EITHER I PULL A QUICK *FADE*--OR I END UP SO MUCH *SCRAP METAL*!

AND SO...

...THAT'S THE SET-UP, CHUMS--

--*KHAN'S* WITCH-MAN HAS HOODOOED *SIR JUSTIN* INTO PLAYING *FIGUREHEAD* FOR HIS ARMY!

AND AS LONG AS THE *KNIGHT* KEEPS SLINGIN' THAT *SWORD* OF HIS, WE CAN'T GET CLOSE ENOUGH TO *CURE* HIM!

IN *THAT* CASE, ELEMENT MAN-- WE'LL LET *HIM* COME TO *US*!

TOMORROW MORNING, WHEN THE *MONGOLS* MOUNT THEIR ATTACK...

...WE'LL BE *WAITING*!

WHEN THE FIRST FINGERS OF DAWN STAB AT THE SKY, THREE STRANGELY-GARBED MEN WAIT ALONE-- TO MEET AN AWESOME *ARMY*...

HERE THEY COME--

OUTNUMBERING US FIVE-THOUSAND-TO-ONE!

YOU'RE DOING WONDERS FOR MY *MORALE*, SUPERMAN!

THIS IS POSITIVELY THE *LAST* TIME I LET YOU *VOLUNTEER* ME FOR *ANYTHING*!

6

YOU VOLUNTEERED YOURSELF, *ELEMENT MAN*--AND WITH NO REGRETS!

EITHER WE STAND AND *FIGHT*--OR THE HERITAGE OF A PEOPLE FALLS SHATTERED IN THE DUST!

YOU MIGHT NOT *HAVE* TO FIGHT AT ALL, FRIENDS!

I'LL BE RIGHT BACK!

ONWARD, MY FELLOWS--FOR YOUR NOBLE *LIEGE!*

VICTORY SHALL BE OURS!

I WOULDN'T *BET* ON THAT, *SIR JUSTIN!*

SO--MINE ENEMIES DO SEND *ANOTHER* STRANGE CREATURE TO DESTROY ME!

LIKE THE OTHER, IT SHALL GO DOWN IN *DEFEAT!*

THAT REMAINS TO BE SEEN, *SIR KNIGHT!* HAVE AT THEE!

IF I CAN BEAT THE *SHINING KNIGHT*, I MIGHT *ROUT* THE *MONGOLS* AS WELL!

*B*UT AS THE TWO CHAMPIONS MEET IN COMBAT...

THWAACK

≈*UUNNFF!*≈ NO CHANCE! SIR JUSTIN'S POWERS ARE *MAGICAL* IN ORIGIN!

HATE TO USE THAT OLD *"DISCRETION"* LINE--BUT RIGHT NOW IT SEEMS THE *SENSIBLE* THING TO DO!

OBSERVE, MY BRETHREN--THUS WILL YOUR WINGED GOD VANQUISH *ALL* WHO OPPOSE US!

ONWARD--TO *VICTORY!!*

AND INSTANTS LATER...

SUPERMAN--? WHAT HAPPENED OUT THERE?

NO TIME TO TALK!

YOU TWO HOLD OFF KHAN AND HIS CREW FOR A WHILE!

I'VE GOT SOMETHING IMPORTANT TO ATTEND TO!

HUH--? YOU GOTTA BE KIDDIN'!

YOUR SUPERMAN TAKES A LOT FOR GRANTED, METAMORPHO!

YEAH--YOU KNOW HOW IT IS WITH THOSE "ESTABLISHMENT-TYPES"!

STILL--IF WE'RE GONNA TAKE ON AN ARMY, I'D FEEL A LOT BETTER DOIN' IT AS A COBALT TANK!

C'MON, SANDMAN-- CLIMB ABOARD!

LIKE A GREAT TIDE OF SAVAGE HUMANITY, THE MONGOL HORDE SURGES ON-WARD--DRAWING EVER CLOSER TO THE TRANSFORMED METAMORPHO AND HIS CLOAKED PASSENGER --BUT SURPRISINGLY...

WE DRIVE OUR HORSES INTO THE GROUND WITH RUNNING--

...AND YET THAT ACCURSED VILLAGE REMAINS EVER BEYOND OUR GRASP!

BY THE GODS-- WHY?!

...CANNON SHELLS ARE FINISHED, SANDMAN--BUT IF THAT SLEEP-GAS FORMULA YOU GAVE ME IS INCORRECT--!

IT'S CORRECT, ELEMENT MAN-- I GUARANTEE IT!

NOW ADJUST YOUR CANNON AND GET THOSE SPARE ATOMS OF YOURS WORKING!

READY... AIM...

...FIRE!!

FWUMP

FWUMP

FWAMM

8

AND WHEN THE SMOKE OF BATTLE HAS CLEARED...

THIS CROWD WILL BE OUT FOR *HOURS!* LOOKS LIKE WE *SAVED* THAT VILLAGE!

SAVED *WHAT* VILLAGE, SANDMAN?

TAKE A LOOK-- AND TELL ME HOW AN ENTIRE *HILL* VANISHES?

NO BIG TRICK, *ELEMENT MAN...*

...I *MOVED* IT!

SUPERMAN!? SO *THAT'S* WHAT WAS SO *IMPORTANT!*

EXACTLY! RATHER THAN TAKE THE CHANCE THE *MONGOLS* MIGHT GET PAST US, I MOVED THE ENTIRE HILLSIDE TO A PLACE WHERE THEY'LL NEVER *FIND* IT!

I SEE YOU'VE GOT THINGS WELL IN HAND *HERE!*

--AS WELL AS CAN BE *EXPECTED!*

THE ANTIDOTE I GAVE *SIR JUSTIN* AND HIS STEED IS TAKING EFFECT!

SOON AS HE'S BACK TO *NORMAL,* WE'LL LEAVE--

YEAH-- HOW?

NOW THAT OUR TASK IS COMPLETE, I BET *ORACLE* KNOWS ABOUT IT--

--AND WILL BE *SENDING* FOR US!

IN THAT CASE, HOLD *SIR JUSTIN!*

THERE'S SOME- THING I WANT TO *DO!*

MOMENTS LATER...

YOU *PEGGED* IT, *SUPERMAN--* ORACLE'S PICK- UP SERVICE IS AS GOOD AS HIS *DELIVERY!*

WONDER WHAT SANDMAN DID TO OL' *GENGHIS?*

SOMETHING I HAVEN'T DONE IN YEARS!

--AND BELIEVE ME, IT FELT *GOOD!*

There is no land beyond the law
Where TYRANTS rule with unshakable power!
It's but a DREAM from which the evil wake,
To face their FATE...
Their terrifying hour!

THE SANDMAN

MEANWHILE-- THROUGH THE CENTURIES-- IN *JUSTICE SOCIETY* HEADQUARTERS...

...*ENOUGH!* THIS SITTING ON MY HANDS IS DRIVING ME *CRAZY!*

THERE MUST BE *SOME* ACTION TO TAKE...

...AND I'VE FIGURED OUT WHAT IT *IS!*

HOW ABOUT LETTING *US* IN ON THE SECRET, *GL?*

FAIR PLAY

THE GRAVE OF THE *UNKNOWN SOLDIER*--! *SOMEBODY* MUST HAVE PUT IT THERE--

--AND I'M HEADING FOR THE *HIMALAYAS* TO FIND OUT *WHO!*

NOT WITHOUT *US*, YOU AIN'T, *GL!*

HATE TO LEAVE YOU IN THE *LURCH* AGAIN, DIANA!

KEEP MINDING THE STORE!

AND WITHIN MINUTES...

HOW *DARK* THE SKY IS! ALMOST AS IF IT *RESENTS* THAT GHASTLY *HAND* INTRUDING INTO ITS SPACE!

I SENSE *MORE* THAN PHANTOM *FINGERS* IN THE AIR, *MR. TERRIFIC!*

--MORE LIKE AN...

FAIR PLAY

EARTHQUAKE!

YOU NEVER TOLD ME YOU WERE *PSYCHIC*, GL--

FAR FROM IT, *ROBIN!* I JUST...

GREAT SCOTT! THOSE *KIDS*--!

LIGHTNING REFLEXES SNAP INTO ACTION AND...

GOT 'EM-- WITH *NOTHING* TO SPARE!

GL'S *POWER RING* SAVES THE DAY AGAIN!

THE DAY'S NOT OVER YET, *ROBIN*...

10

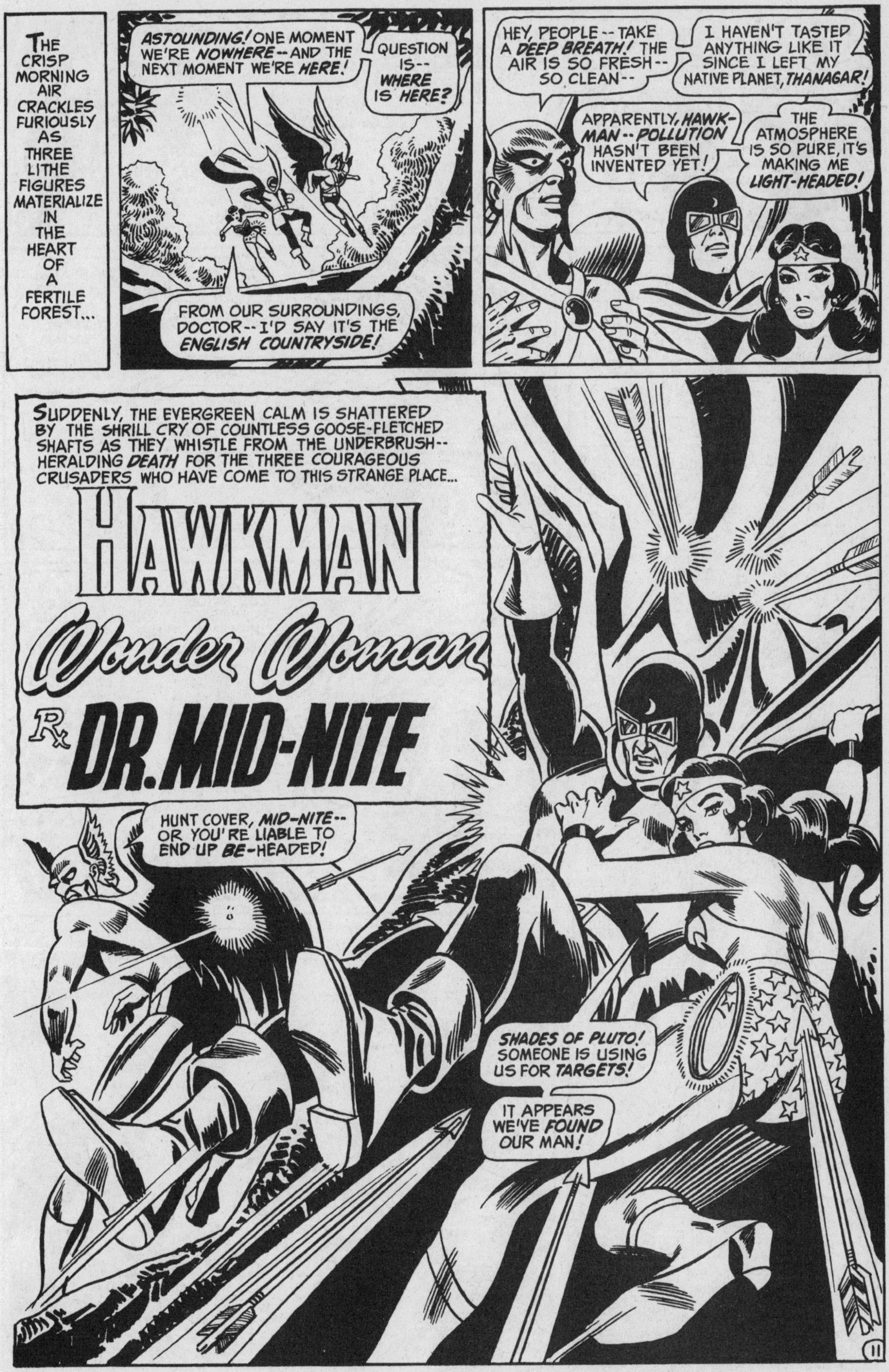
THE CRISP MORNING AIR CRACKLES FURIOUSLY AS THREE LITHE FIGURES MATERIALIZE IN THE HEART OF A FERTILE FOREST...
ASTOUNDING! ONE MOMENT WE'RE NOWHERE -- AND THE NEXT MOMENT WE'RE HERE!
QUESTION IS-- WHERE IS HERE?
FROM OUR SURROUNDINGS, DOCTOR -- I'D SAY IT'S THE ENGLISH COUNTRYSIDE!
HEY, PEOPLE -- TAKE A DEEP BREATH! THE AIR IS SO FRESH -- SO CLEAN --
I HAVEN'T TASTED ANYTHING LIKE IT SINCE I LEFT MY NATIVE PLANET, THANAGAR!
APPARENTLY, HAWK-MAN -- POLLUTION HASN'T BEEN INVENTED YET!
THE ATMOSPHERE IS SO PURE, IT'S MAKING ME LIGHT-HEADED!
SUDDENLY, THE EVERGREEN CALM IS SHATTERED BY THE SHRILL CRY OF COUNTLESS GOOSE-FLETCHED SHAFTS AS THEY WHISTLE FROM THE UNDERBRUSH-- HERALDING DEATH FOR THE THREE COURAGEOUS CRUSADERS WHO HAVE COME TO THIS STRANGE PLACE...
HAWKMAN
Wonder Woman
Rx DR. MID-NITE
HUNT COVER, MID-NITE -- OR YOU'RE LIABLE TO END UP BE-HEADED!
SHADES OF PLUTO! SOMEONE IS USING US FOR TARGETS!
IT APPEARS WE'VE FOUND OUR MAN!
11

MAYBE *NOT*, PRINCESS! I CAN SEE *SEVERAL* MEN OUT THERE--

AND THEY LOOK LIKE THEY'RE OUT FOR *BLOOD!*

WELL, THEY WON'T GET ANY OF MINE IF *I* CAN HELP IT--

--AND I *CAN* HELP IT!

IF *THIS* DOESN'T FLUSH OUT THOSE BLOODTHIRSTY BOWMEN--*NOTHING* WILL!

I'M BEATING MY WINGS HARD ENOUGH TO START A SMALL *HURRICANE!*

THAT'S IT, *HAWKMAN*--KEEP 'EM *FLYING!*

*I*NSTANTLY, THE AGILE *WONDER WOMAN*--BEAUTIFUL AS *APHRODITE*, WISE AS *ATHENA*, SWIFTER THAN *MERCURY*, AND STRONGER THAN *HERCULES*--LEAPS FROM CONCEALMENT AND...

GENTLEMEN, IF YOU'LL FOLLOW *ME*--

IT'S TIME WE BROUGHT THE BATTLE TO THE *ENEMY!*

RIGHT BEHIND YOU, PRINCESS!

JUST AS I THOUGHT! THESE MINOR-LEAGUE ARCHERS DON'T KNOW THE FIRST THING ABOUT *JIU-JITSU!*

WITHOUT THOSE LONG BOWS, THEY'RE SO MUCH *DEAD WOOD!*

*W*ITHIN MOMENTS--AS ABRUPTLY AS IT HAD BEGUN--THE CONFLICT IS OVER...

HOLD, STRANGE ONES...WE *SURRENDER*--FOR NOW! YOU CAN TELL THE SHERIFF OF NOTTINGHAM HE HAS WON THE *BATTLE*--

--BUT HE HAS YET TO WIN THE *WAR!*

SUFFERING SAPPHO! I THINK WE'VE MADE A--*MISTAKE!*

12

GOOD BOWMEN, WE'RE *NOT* AGENTS OF YOUR *SHERIFF!* OUR MISSION HERE IS A *PEACEFUL* ONE!

WE FOUGHT ONLY BECAUSE WE WERE *ATTACKED!*

Y-YOU'RE *RELEASING* US--? THEN WHAT YOU SAY IS *TRUTH!*

TELL ME-- HOW CAN THE MERRY MEN SERVE?

AND AFTER *HAWKMAN* HAS DESCRIBED THE ONE THEY SEEK...

I AM SORRY WE CANNOT HELP YOU, STRANGE ONES --BUT WE KNOW NOT ANY *GREEN ARROW!*

PERHAPS *ROBIN HOOD* COULD AID YOU WERE HE BUT HERE --FOR HE KNOWS *ALL* WHO BEND THEIR BOWS IN *NOTTINGHAMSHIRE...*

...BUT THE SHERIFF IS *HANGING* BRAVE *ROBIN* ON THE MORROW!

HANGING *ROBIN HOOD?!* ISN'T THERE ANYTHING YOU CAN DO TO *STOP* IT?

WOULD THERE WERE! THE *MERRY MEN* AND I SHALL LAY *SIEGE* TO *NOTTINGHAM CASTLE* ERE THE DAWN --BUT 'TIS ONLY A *FUTILE* GESTURE!

GOOD *ROBIN* SHALL SWAY IN THE BREEZE ERE WE CAN *BREACH* THOSE WALLS!

PERHAPS THAT WAS TRUE *BEFORE, LITTLE JOHN*-- BUT *NOT* ANY MORE!

WE'RE GOING TO HELP YOU *STORM* THAT CASTLE -- AND THERE ISN'T A BARRICADE STANDING THAT CAN STOP *US!*

13

DARK IT STANDS AND STONY-EYED, THIS ANGRY EDIFICE THAT JUTS FROM THE JADE-SHADOWED FOREST LIKE AN ACCUSING FINGER-- THIS UNFEELING FORTRESS THAT IS *NOTTINGHAM CASTLE...*

THEY'RE NOT GOING TO MAKE THIS *EASY* FOR US, ARE THEY?

HOW DO WE GET ACROSS THAT MOAT WITH THE *DRAWBRIDGE* UP?

IT SEEMS MOAT-FORDING IS *MY* DEPARTMENT, GENTLEMEN!

WAIT HERE TILL I'M DONE... AND THEN COME *RUNNING!*

SNAGGED THE BRIDGE ON THE *FIRST* TOSS! MY *MAGIC LASSO* NEVER *MISSES!*

NOW, I PRAY TO *ATHENA* MY *MUSCLES* ARE THE EQUAL OF MY TASK!

...YOUR ONLY RECOURSE IS TO BRING THE DRAWBRIDGE TO *YOU!*

AFTER ALL, IF YOU CAN'T GO TO THE *DRAWBRIDGE...*

FANTASTIC! SHE *DID* IT!

COME ON-- WE CAN'T LET HER EFFORTS GO TO *WASTE!*

KWA-WHRAM

14

BUT AS THE BRAVE BAND MOVES ACROSS THE FALLEN WALKWAY...

UH-OH-- WE HAVE *COMPANY* --

AND I DON'T THINK THEY WANT *TRESPASSERS!*

LEND ME YOUR *STAFF*, FRIEND!

I'D BETTER TEACH THE LOCAL *WELCOME WAGON* A LESSON IN *HOSPITALITY!*

PINIONS POUNDING, THE *FEATHERED FURY* HURTLES INTO THE MIDST OF THE ANGRY THRONG-- WITH DEVASTATING RESULTS...

MID-NITE-- WONDER WOMAN --THE *REST* OF YOU-- GET INTO THAT CASTLE AND *SCATTER!*

IF WE DON'T FIND *ROBIN HOOD* QUICKLY-- WE'RE LIABLE TO *SWING* RIGHT ALONGSIDE HIM IN THE MORNING!

AND MINUTES LATER, IN ONE OF THE CASTLE'S DEEPEST CORRIDORS...

JACKPOT! UNLESS THOSE GUARDS ARE STANDING THERE FOR *DECORATION*, I'VE *LOCATED* MY MAN!

ONCE MY HANDY *BLACKOUT BOMB* THROWS A LITTLE *DARK* ON THE SUBJECT, I'LL SEE WHAT I CAN DO TO *SPRING* HIM!

A FAINT HISS AS THE BLACKOUT BOMB HITS-- AND THE CORRIDOR IS FILLED WITH CLOUDS OF BILLOWING BLACK...

MY "*BLIND*" EYES CAN SEE AS *PERFECTLY* IN THE DARKNESS AS MY *INFRA-RED* LENSES HELP ME TO DO IN THE LIGHT--

--BUT MY TWO PLAY-MATES AREN'T QUITE AS *LUCKY!*

WITHIN MOMENTS, THE CELL DOOR SQUEALS OPEN TO REVEAL...

GREEN ARROW!?! WHAT ARE *YOU* DOING HERE IN *ROBIN HOOD'S* PLACE?

DR. MID-NITE! AM I GLAD TO SEE YOU!

I'LL EXPLAIN EVERYTHING AS SOON AS WE CAN *GET AWAY* FROM THIS RAT-HOLE!

15

OOPS! LOOKS LIKE *REINFORCE-MENTS* HAVE ARRIVED!

I'D BETTER GRAB ANOTHER *BLACKOUT BOMB!*

SAVE IT, DOC! THIS ONE'S ON *ME!*

THOSE CRUMBS SHOULDN'T HAVE LEFT MY *GEAR* WHERE I COULD GET MY HANDS ON IT!

IN ONE BLURRING MOTION, THE *ACE ARCHER* PULLS A SHAFT FROM HIS QUIVER--NOTCHES IT --AND LETS IT FLY...

THE OLD *NET ARROW* HASN'T FAILED ME YET!

THE GUARDS WON'T *UNRAVEL* THEMSELVES FOR DAYS!

IF THAT ARROW EVER *DOES* FAIL YOU, *G.A.*--YOU *WON'T* BE ALIVE TO *KNOW* IT!

C'MON--LET'S COLLECT THE OTHERS AND *GET OUT* OF HERE!

THE *OTHERS?*

LEAD ON, DOC-- NOW YOU'VE GOT ME *INTERESTED!*

AND AFTER THE VALIANT GROUP HAS BATTLED ITS WAY *OUT* OF THE CASTLE...

IT SEEMS WE RISKED OUR LIVES TO RESCUE THE *WRONG MAN!*

TELL US, KNAVE-- WHAT KNOWEST THOU OF *ROBIN HOOD?*

YOUR LEADER IS *SAFE, LITTLE JOHN*-- RECOVERING FROM WOUNDS IN THE LODGINGS OF A FRIENDLY FRIAR!

I DROVE OFF HIS *ATTACKERS*--AND *ROBIN* ASKED ME TO TAKE HIS PLACE!

I WAS COMING TO INFORM YOU MEN WHEN THE SHERIFF *CAPTURED* ME!

THEN OUR *GRATITUDE* IS YOURS, *GREEN ARROW!* WE...

W-WHAT *SORCERY* IS THIS? YOU *FADE* BEFORE OUR VERY EYES!

YOU'RE NOT THE *ONLY* ONE WONDERING, *LITTLE JOHN!*

WHAT *IS* HAPPENING?

OUR MISSION HERE IS *ACCOMPLISHED!*

ORACLE IS BRINGING US *HOME!*

16

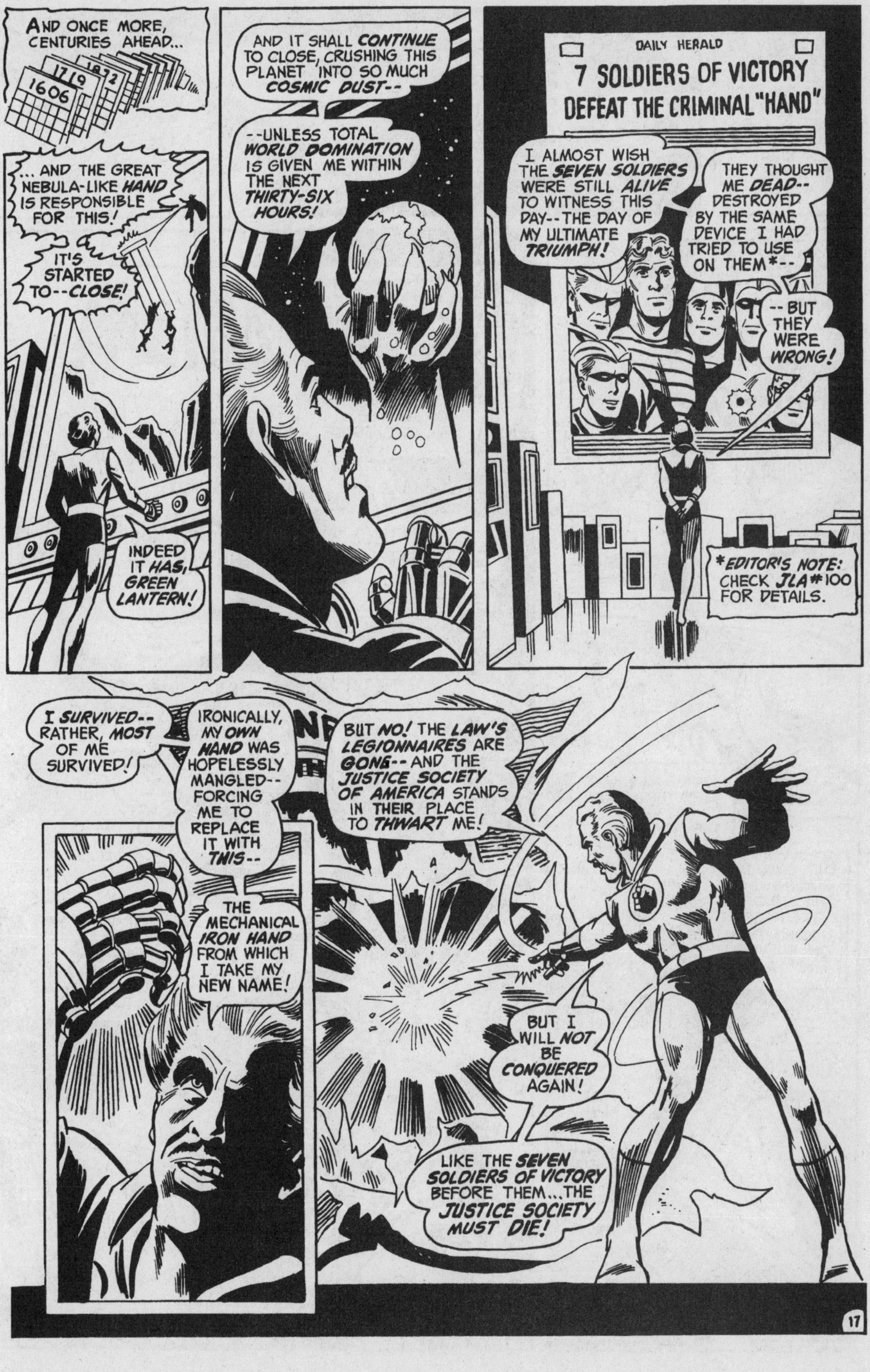
AND ONCE MORE, CENTURIES AHEAD...
1606
1719
1872
...AND THE GREAT NEBULA-LIKE HAND IS RESPONSIBLE FOR THIS!
IT'S STARTED TO--CLOSE!
INDEED IT HAS, GREEN LANTERN!
AND IT SHALL CONTINUE TO CLOSE, CRUSHING THIS PLANET INTO SO MUCH COSMIC DUST--
--UNLESS TOTAL WORLD DOMINATION IS GIVEN ME WITHIN THE NEXT THIRTY-SIX HOURS!
DAILY HERALD
7 SOLDIERS OF VICTORY DEFEAT THE CRIMINAL "HAND"
I ALMOST WISH THE SEVEN SOLDIERS WERE STILL ALIVE TO WITNESS THIS DAY--THE DAY OF MY ULTIMATE TRIUMPH!
THEY THOUGHT ME DEAD--DESTROYED BY THE SAME DEVICE I HAD TRIED TO USE ON THEM*--
--BUT THEY WERE WRONG!
*EDITOR'S NOTE: CHECK JLA#100 FOR DETAILS.
I SURVIVED--RATHER, MOST OF ME SURVIVED!
IRONICALLY, MY OWN HAND WAS HOPELESSLY MANGLED--FORCING ME TO REPLACE IT WITH THIS--
THE MECHANICAL IRON HAND FROM WHICH I TAKE MY NEW NAME!
BUT NO! THE LAW'S LEGIONNAIRES ARE GONE--AND THE JUSTICE SOCIETY OF AMERICA STANDS IN THEIR PLACE TO THWART ME!
BUT I WILL NOT BE CONQUERED AGAIN!
LIKE THE SEVEN SOLDIERS OF VICTORY BEFORE THEM...THE JUSTICE SOCIETY MUST DIE!
17

NIGHT DOES NOT COME EASILY TO THE BLISTERING DESERT--AND THOSE WHO TOIL ENDLESSLY BENEATH THE OMNIPOTENT *SUN* KNOW THIS FACT WELL...

LONG HAVE THEY LABORED TO COMPLETE THE TOWERING STRUCTURE THAT RISES FROM THE SHIFTING SANDS BEFORE THEM...

...AND *MANY* HAVE BEEN THE NUMBER TO PERISH IN THE TRYING...

BUT STILL THEY STRUGGLE ON, THE STING OF THE *WHIP* URGING THEM ON IF EVER THEY FALTER...

EACH MAN PRODUCES A FULL DAY'S *WORK*...

BUT THERE IS *ONE* WHO *ALONE* DOES THE WORK OF *MANY!*

AND THERE ARE THREE OTHERS WHO HAVE TRAVELED TO THIS ANTIQUE LAND IN SEARCH OF THAT SOLITARY ONE. THE SHADOWS OF *KHUFU'S TOMB* CLOAK THE MOVEMENTS OF...

BATMAN, STARMAN and HOURMAN

LOOKS LIKE WE'VE LOCATED *OUR* PARTICULAR SOLDIER!

LET'S GET HIM THE HECK *OUT* OF HERE!

NOT QUITE *YET,* HOURMAN! IT WOULD BE BETTER TO WAIT FOR *DARKNESS* TO FALL!

18

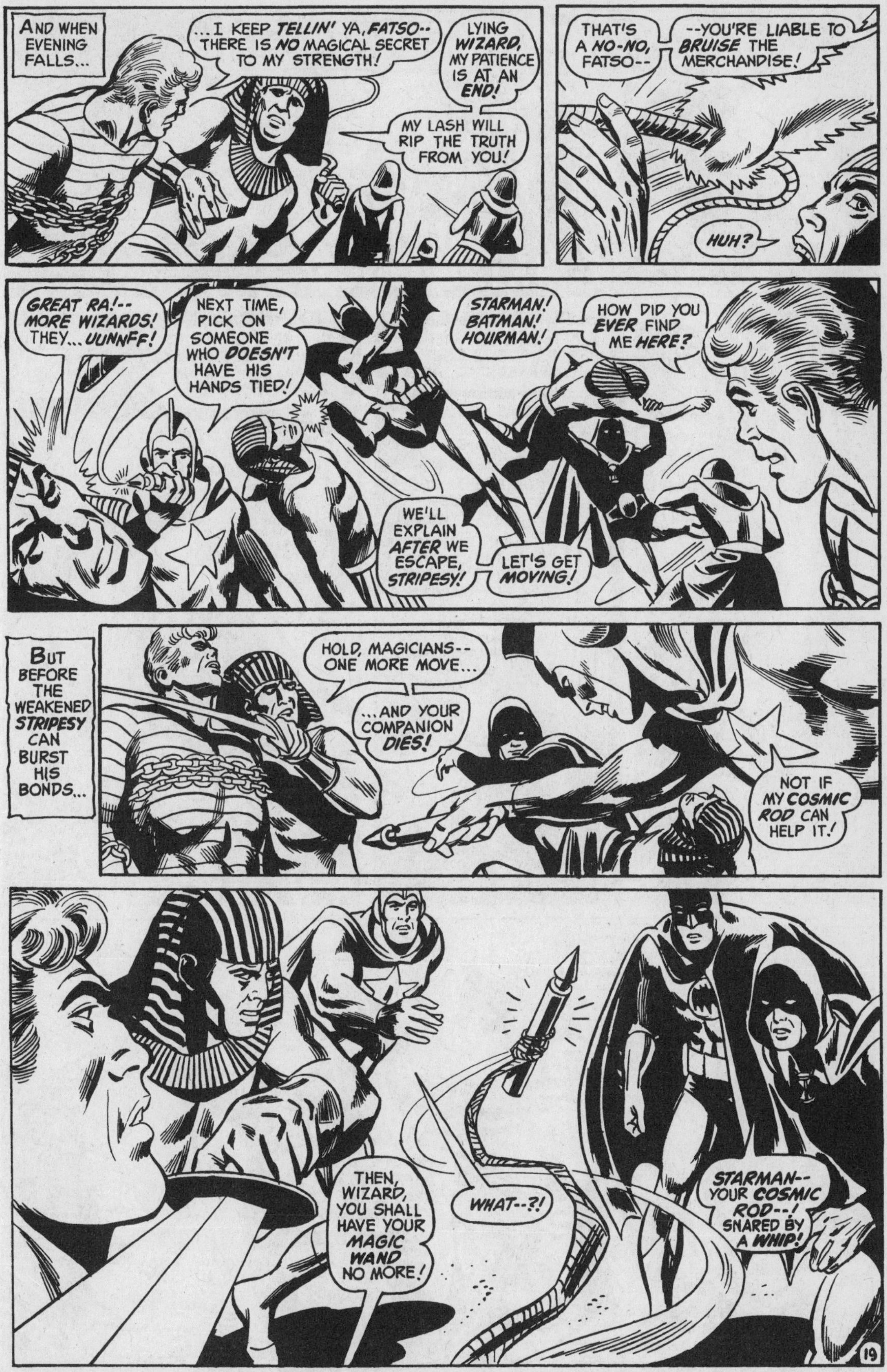
AND WHEN EVENING FALLS...
...I KEEP TELLIN' YA, FATSO-- THERE IS NO MAGICAL SECRET TO MY STRENGTH!
LYING WIZARD, MY PATIENCE IS AT AN END!
MY LASH WILL RIP THE TRUTH FROM YOU!
THAT'S A NO-NO, FATSO--
--YOU'RE LIABLE TO BRUISE THE MERCHANDISE!
HUH?
GREAT RA!-- MORE WIZARDS! THEY... UUNNFF!
NEXT TIME, PICK ON SOMEONE WHO DOESN'T HAVE HIS HANDS TIED!
STARMAN! BATMAN! HOURMAN!
HOW DID YOU EVER FIND ME HERE?
WE'LL EXPLAIN AFTER WE ESCAPE, STRIPESY!
LET'S GET MOVING!
BUT BEFORE THE WEAKENED STRIPESY CAN BURST HIS BONDS...
HOLD, MAGICIANS-- ONE MORE MOVE...
...AND YOUR COMPANION DIES!
NOT IF MY COSMIC ROD CAN HELP IT!
THEN, WIZARD, YOU SHALL HAVE YOUR MAGIC WAND NO MORE!
WHAT--?!
STARMAN-- YOUR COSMIC ROD--! SNARED BY A WHIP!
19

SORRY, *STRIPESY*-- GUESS *TURNABOUT* IS FAIR PLAY!

NO HARD FEELIN'S, FELLAS!

YOU DID YOUR *BEST!*

ENOUGH CHATTER, WIZARDS! DO YOU *SURRENDER?*

OR DOES MY *BLADE* TASTE HIS FLESH?

WHAT *CHOICE* DO WE HAVE?

YOU *WIN!*

THWACK THUNK

THOSE WHO SERVE THE *SON OF THE SUN* ALWAYS WIN!

¡UGH!

¡UNFF!

¡GGNN.!

AND WHEN THE THREE HEROES "CRAWL" OUT OF THE DARKNESS AT LAST...

MY *ACHING HEAD!* WHERE DID THOSE DUDES *DROP* US, ANYHOW?

UNLESS I MISS MY *GUESS*--

--WE'RE SMACK IN THE CENTER OF THE *PYRAMID,* HOURMAN--

--IN THE PHARAOH'S *BURIAL CHAMBER!*

I'VE BEEN TRYING TO BRING MY *COSMIC ROD* TO ME BY *MENTAL CONCENTRATION*--

BUT IT'S TOO FAR FROM ME!

AND MY SUPER- POWERED *HOUR* IS UP!

HOW ARE WE GONNA GET *OUT* OF THIS?

GIVE ME A MINUTE TO *THINK!*

FOR A TIME, *THE BATMAN* IS SILENT-- WHEN SUDDENLY...

WHAT THE HECK YOU *DOING?*

I'VE HAD THAT HOURGLASS FOR *YEARS!*

BETTER A NEW *TIMEPIECE* AND A NEW LEASE ON *LIFE,* HOURMAN!

JUST HANG ON A SECOND!

20

THERE! GRAB YOURSELVES A PIECE OF THE BROKEN *HOURGLASS--*

--AND START *CUTTING* THROUGH YOUR ROPES!

KRASSH

RIGHT ON, *BATMAN!*

I'LL SEND YOU A *BILL* FOR MY *EGG-TIMER!*

MOMENTS LATER...

DONE! NOW OUR PROBLEM IS FINDING A WAY *OUT* OF THIS JOINT!

AS I REMEMBER, THESE TOMBS WERE USUALLY BUILT WITH *MAZE*-LIKE PASSAGEWAYS--

--TO *CONFUSE* POTENTIAL LOOTERS!

-- AND US, STARMAN!

I'LL TAKE A *MIRACLO* PILL-- AND *PUNCH* US OUT AN *EXIT!*

HOLD IT, *HOURMAN--* THIS PLACE'LL BE AN HISTORIC *TREASURE* SOMEDAY!

NO-- THERE HAS TO BE A *BETTER* WAY--!

STARMAN--! MAYBE YOU *CAN'T* BRING YOUR *COSMIC ROD* HERE-- BUT YOU STILL *CONTROL* ITS *ATOMS!*

YOU'VE GOT TO *CONCENTRATE*-- LET THE *COSMIC ROD* SHOW US THE WAY OUT!

I'VE NEVER *ATTEMPTED* IT BEFORE-- BUT...

WELL, IT'S WORTH THE *TRY!*

AND TRY THE *ASTRAL AVENGER* DOES! HIS FACE CONTORTS INTO A MASK OF RAW COURAGE AND GRIM DETERMINATION-- UNTIL...

LOOK! THE FICKLE FINGER OF *FATE--* BECKONING US!

STARMAN DID IT!

LET'S GET *GOING!*

21

CAUTIOUSLY, THREE STRANGELY-GARBED CRUSADERS FOLLOW THE FLEETING ENERGY-TRAIL ALONG THE TWISTING PASSAGEWAYS-- AND SOON...

EASY, TEAM-- LOOKS LIKE WE'VE REACHED THE END OF THE TRAIL!

--AND THAT MUCH CLOSER TO MY COSMIC ROD!

WE'VE GOT INTERFERENCE OUT THERE!

NOT FOR LONG!

I'LL SHOW YOU A LITTLE TRICK!

SOME MENTAL MANIPULATION OF THE COSMIC ROD AND-- PRESTO!

SAVES A LOT OF WEAR AND TEAR ON MY UNIFORM!

TWHACK

THUNK

LET THAT BE A LESSON TO YOU BOYS--

--YOU SHOULDN'T TAKE SOME-THING THAT DOESN'T BELONG TO YOU!

WE'D BETTER FIND STRIPESY--

--BEFORE HIS CAPTORS DO SOMETHING HE'LL REGRET!

SHORTLY...

GREAT GALAXIES-- STRIPESY!

THEY'VE HUNG HIM OUT TO DRY-- LIKE AN ANIMAL HIDE!

THEN LET'S HIT THOSE GUARDS-- AND SKIN 'EM!

22

BATMAN-- STARMAN-- HOURMAN-- YOU ESCAPED--!

NATURALLY! WE'RE THE *GOOD GUYS!*

KEEP COOL, *STRIPESY!* WE'LL SET YOU FREE IN A SECOND!

NOT *THIS* TIME, PALS...

KWA RRR MP

...THIS TIME I FREE *MYSELF!!*

ACCKK!

NOW-- AS I RECOLLECT--

--I OWE YOU BUMS SOME *BRUISES!*

OOOFF!

UNNFF!

AND A BATTLE ROYAL LATER...

THOSE LUGS WERE REAL *QUITTERS--*

MY, MY! I WONDER WHY?

WOULDN'T GET UP AGAIN...AFTER ...THE FOURTH TIME I *SLUGGED* 'EM!

AND *I* WONDER HOW WE'RE GETTING BACK TO OUR OWN TIME-- NOW THAT OUR JOB HERE IS *DONE?*

THAT ANSWERS YOUR QUESTION, STARMAN!

ORACLE HAS *SENT* FOR US AGAIN!

WE'RE GOING *HOME...* TO 1972!

23

WHILE IN THAT YEAR OF 1972...
CAN'T BLAME GREEN LANTERN, ROBIN, AND MR. TERRIFIC FOR TAKING OFF AGAIN!
THIS WAITING IS ENOUGH TO DRIVE YOU OUT OF YOUR SKULL!
24
IT WOULDN'T BE SO BAD IF I HAD SOME COMPANY SOMEONE TO TALK TO--
--BUT THIS WAITING ALONE IS LIABLE TO KILL ME!
NEXT ISSUE: "...AND ONE OF US MUST DIE!"

JUSTICE LEAGUE of AMERICA

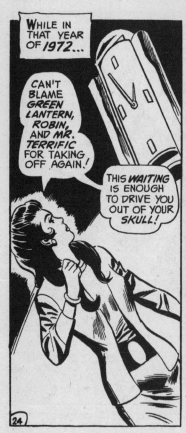

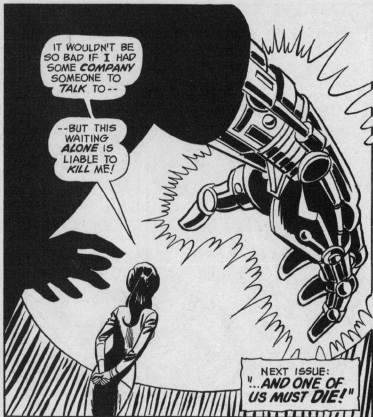

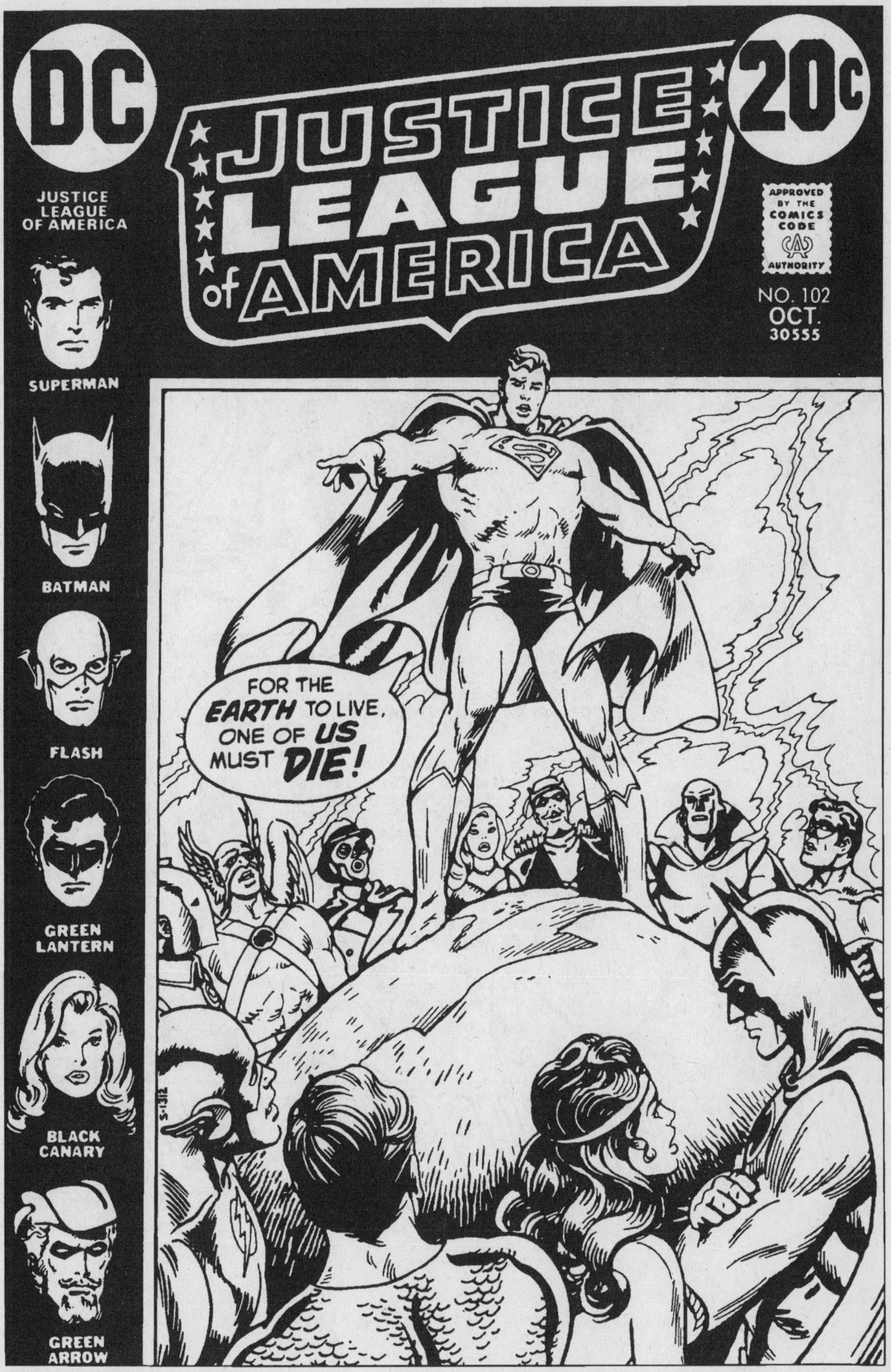
DC
JUSTICE LEAGUE of AMERICA
20¢
APPROVED BY THE COMICS CODE AUTHORITY
NO. 102
OCT.
30555
JUSTICE LEAGUE OF AMERICA
SUPERMAN
BATMAN
FLASH
GREEN LANTERN
BLACK CANARY
GREEN ARROW
FOR THE EARTH TO LIVE, ONE OF US MUST DIE!

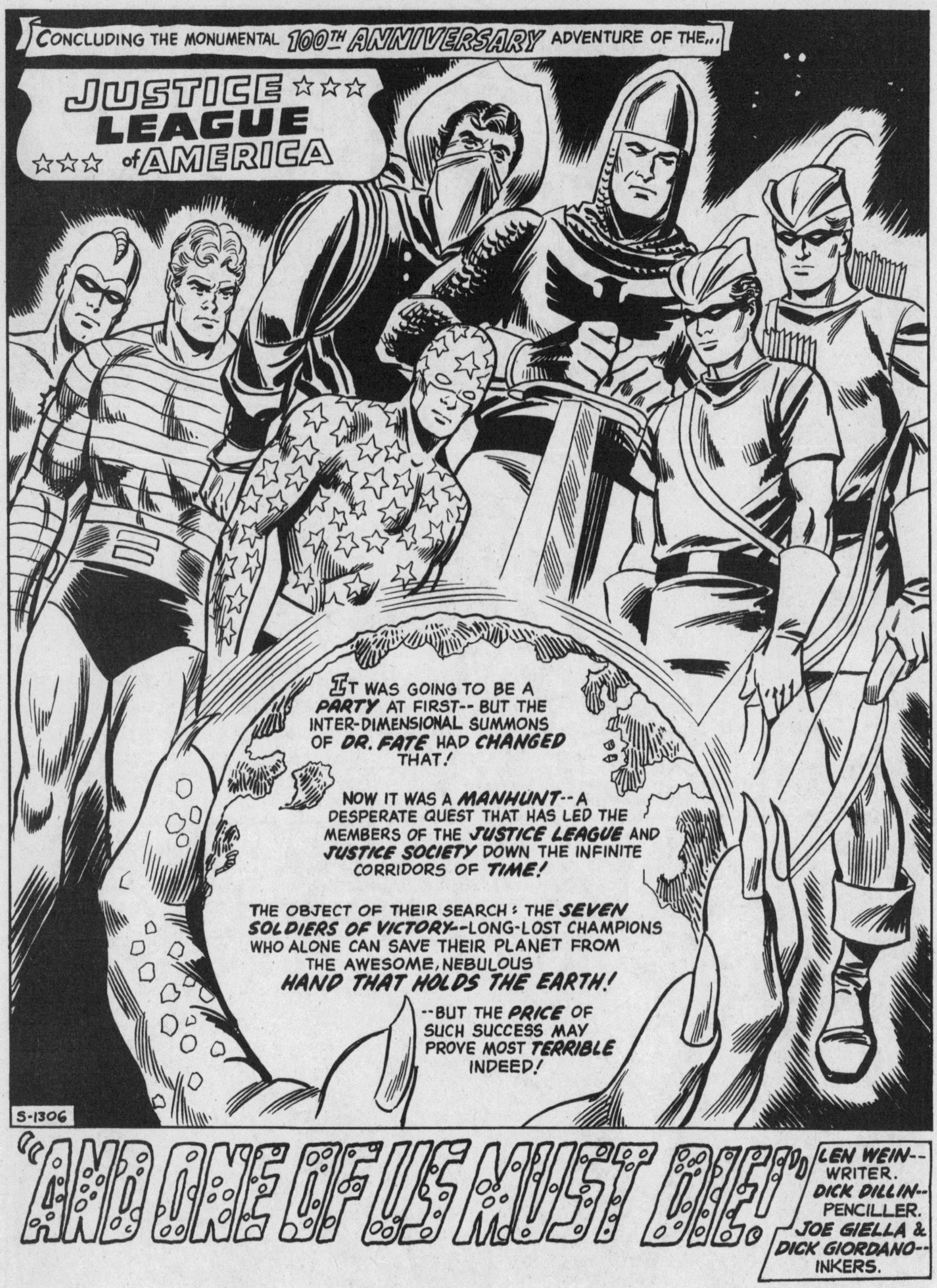
CONCLUDING THE MONUMENTAL 100TH ANNIVERSARY ADVENTURE OF THE...
JUSTICE LEAGUE of AMERICA
IT WAS GOING TO BE A PARTY AT FIRST-- BUT THE INTER-DIMENSIONAL SUMMONS OF DR. FATE HAD CHANGED THAT!
NOW IT WAS A MANHUNT--A DESPERATE QUEST THAT HAS LED THE MEMBERS OF THE JUSTICE LEAGUE AND JUSTICE SOCIETY DOWN THE INFINITE CORRIDORS OF TIME!
THE OBJECT OF THEIR SEARCH: THE SEVEN SOLDIERS OF VICTORY--LONG-LOST CHAMPIONS WHO ALONE CAN SAVE THEIR PLANET FROM THE AWESOME, NEBULOUS HAND THAT HOLDS THE EARTH!
--BUT THE PRICE OF SUCH SUCCESS MAY PROVE MOST TERRIBLE INDEED!
S-1306
"AND ONE OF US MUST DIE!"
LEN WEIN--WRITER.
DICK DILLIN--PENCILLER.
JOE GIELLA & DICK GIORDANO--INKERS.

IN A PLACE BEYOND PLACES HE SITS-- THIS ALL-KNOWING ENTITY NAMED *ORACLE!* HE SITS AND HE PONDERS...

...AND WEIGHS THE FATE OF A WORLD...

A STRANGE FEELING, THIS--

--FOR IT HAS BEEN LONG SINCE *ORACLE* LAST *CARED* ABOUT THE SURVIVAL OF-- A MERE *PLANET!*

BUT CARE I *DO*--AND I FIND THE SENSATION *PLEASANT!* PERHAPS WITH *GOOD* REASON--!

FOR WAS IT NOT I WHO SENT *EARTH'S* BOLDEST HEROES ON THEIR JOURNEY THROUGH TIME-AND-SPACE?

INDEED IT *WAS!*

BUT NOW I WOULD KNOW *MORE* OF THOSE WHO STAYED *BEHIND*--!

HOW, FOR INSTANCE, FARES *DIANA PRINCE*-- SHE WHO WAS ONCE CALLED *WONDER WOMAN*--?

NOT *WELL,* IT SEEMS--

--FOR SHE IS BESET BY THE *IRON HAND* WHOSE NEBULOID NAMESAKE IS THE CAUSE OF THE GREAT QUEST--

--AND SHE KNOWS NOT HER *DANGER!*

NOR DO THE *OTHER* HEROES WHO STRIVE TO PROTECT THEIR WORLD-- *GREEN LANTERN*-- *ROBIN*-- *MR. TERRIFIC!*

I COULD *END* THEIR PROBLEMS IN AN INSTANT--

--BUT I AM BOUND *NOT* TO *INTERFERE!*

IT IS DECIDED *MAN* MUST MAKE HIS *OWN* DESTINY--

--BUT IF, ON THIS BLEAK DAY, HE FALLS IN FINAL *DEFEAT*--

--A SMALL PART OF *ORACLE* SHALL DIE AS WELL!

2

AND EVEN AS *ORACLE* SPEAKS, THREE OF THOSE DESTINY-MAKERS SUDDENLY FIND THEMSELVES UPON THE SIDE OF A WOODED HILL...

GREEN ARROW

BLACK CANARY

AND THE INCOMPARABLE

JOHNNY THUNDER

DON'T KNOW WHERE *ORACLE* DUMPED US-- BUT THE MAN HAS *TASTE!*

SO I NOTICE-- BUT WE'D STILL BETTER START HUNTING FOR OUR... *EH?*

GREAT *IDEA*, *CANARY!* YOU AND ME'LL GO *THIS* WAY-- AND MEET UP WITH *GREEN ARROW* LATER ON!

HANG ON, *THUNDER--* THAT'S MY LADY YOU'RE BENDING!

YOUR LADY? I KNEW *BLACK CANARY* FOR MORE YEARS THAN YOU'VE GOT *ARROWS!*

WHAT--?!

I'VE GOT *NEWS* FOR YOU *CHAUVINISTS--*

--I HAPPEN TO BE *MY OWN* LADY--

--AND I INTEND TO SEE IT *STAYS* THAT WAY!

HUH--?

UUNNFF!

IF YOU WANT TO GO *HERO-HUNTING--* FINE!

BUT IF YOU WANT TO PLAY *TUG-OF-WAR*, FIND YOUR-SELVES A *NEW* ROPE!

HEY-- MAYBE WE *DON'T* HAVETA HUNT!

LOOK OVER *THERE--* SMOKE!

CAUTIOUSLY, THE TIME-TOSSED TRIO FOLLOWS THE CURLING COLUMN OF SMOKE-- UNTIL, AT LAST, THEY COME UPON...

AN *INDIAN VILLAGE--!*

WELL, AT LEAST WE KNOW WHERE WE *ARE* NOW--

--SOMEWHERE ON THE NORTH AMERICAN *PLAINS!*

ONLY QUESTION LEFT IS-- *WHO* ARE WE SEARCHING FOR?

3

OFFHAND, GREEN ARROW-- I WOULD SAY IT WAS *HIM!*

THE *VIGILANTE*-- A *PRISONER!* THEY'RE GOING TO *BURN* HIM AT THE STAKE!

TOO BAD THIS AIN'T THE *MOVIES*-- OR THE *CAVALRY* WOULD BE COMIN' TO THE *RESCUE* BY NOW!

THE *CAVALRY* HASN'T BEEN *INVENTED* YET, BRIGHT-EYES--

--SO I'M AFRAID OUR LONESOME COWBOY'LL JUST HAVE TO SETTLE FOR *US!*

MAYBE NOT, *GA!* I'LL CALL MY *MAGIC THUNDERBOLT*--

--AND HE CAN *CONJURE UP* A CAVALRY FOR US!

*SAY YOU!**

*EDITOR'S NOTE: CEI-U-- THE *BAHDNISIAN HEX* THAT GIVES JOHNNY CONTROL OF THE GENIE-LIKE *THUNDERBOLT!*

THE MYSTIC WORDS SPOKEN, *JOHNNY THUNDER* AWAITS THE ALMOST-INSTANTANEOUS APPEARANCE OF HIS SUPERNATURAL SERVANT....

...BUT AFTER SEVERAL LONG MINUTES....

THE *THUNDERBOLT* DIDN'T *SHOW!* THAT'S *NEVER* HAPPENED BEFORE!

THERE'S A *FIRST* TIME FOR EVERYTHING, PAL! HE PROBABLY GOT AS TIRED OF YOU AS *I* HAVE!

NOW, *COME ON*-- WE GOT US A *COWBOY* TO RESCUE!

THERE IS A FAINT RUSTLE OF THE TREE BRANCHES AS THE DARING TRIO MOVES FORWARD-- AND SUDDENLY....

WE'VE BEEN *DISCOVERED*--!

REALLY? I NEVER WOULD'VE *GUESSED*--!

THE BATTLE IS *SHORT*...

...AND NOT VERY *SWEET* AT ALL....

4

AND WHEN *GREEN ARROW, BLACK CANARY,* AND *JOHNNY THUNDER* FINALLY REGAIN CONSCIOUSNESS...

SO, WHITE-SKINS-- YOU *AWAKEN* AT LAST! YOU ARE *WEAK* ENEMIES, INDEED!

HATE TO *DISAPPOINT* YOU, DOC-- BUT WE CAME HERE IN *PEACE!*

THATS *RIGHT!* WE HAVE NO WISH TO *HARM* YOU!

YOU *LIE!* I HAVE SPOKEN TO THE *BUFFALO SPIRIT*--AND HE HAS TOLD ME YOU MUST *DIE*--

--OR *OTHER* WHITE-SKINS WILL ONE DAY COME-- TO *KILL* THE BUFFALO--

--AND *STEAL* AWAY OUR LAND!

GOTTA ADMIT YOU'VE GOT A *POWERFUL* ARGUMENT, FRIEND-- BUT I STILL WISH YOU'D *RECONSIDER*--!

NO-- THE SPIRITS HAVE *SPOKEN!* WHEN NEXT THE *MOON* IS FULL--

--YOU WILL *DIE!*

AS WILL DIE THE *OTHER* WHITE-SKINNED ONE-- *TONIGHT!*

AND MOMENTS *LATER*...

STILL TIME TO *CHANGE* YORE MIND, HOMBRE! I'M TELLIN' YUH--

--YUH GOT THE *WRONG* MAN!

SILENCE, WHITE-SKIN! WE KILL YOU ONLY IN OUR OWN *DEFENSE!*

IN THAT CASE, YOU WON'T MIND IF WE HAPPEN TO DEFEND *OURSELVES?!*

HIYEEE!

WELL, I'LL BE SWAGGERED--!

5

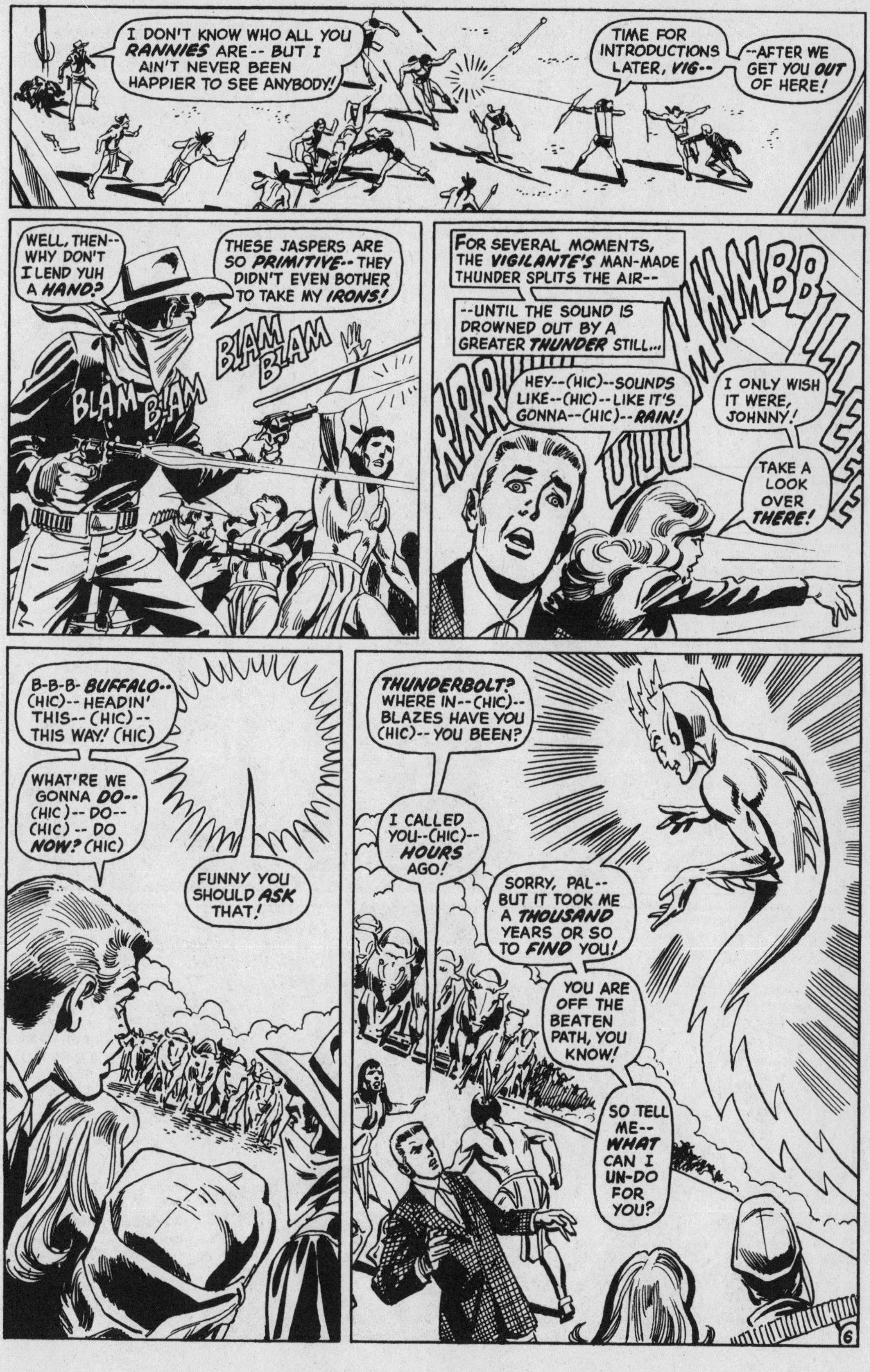
I DON'T KNOW WHO ALL YOU RANNIES ARE-- BUT I AIN'T NEVER BEEN HAPPIER TO SEE ANYBODY!
TIME FOR INTRODUCTIONS LATER, VIG--
--AFTER WE GET YOU OUT OF HERE!
WELL, THEN-- WHY DON'T I LEND YUH A HAND?
THESE JASPERS ARE SO PRIMITIVE-- THEY DIDN'T EVEN BOTHER TO TAKE MY IRONS!
BLAM BLAM
BLAM BLAM
FOR SEVERAL MOMENTS, THE VIGILANTE'S MAN-MADE THUNDER SPLITS THE AIR--
--UNTIL THE SOUND IS DROWNED OUT BY A GREATER THUNDER STILL...
HEY--(HIC)--SOUNDS LIKE--(HIC)--LIKE IT'S GONNA--(HIC)--RAIN!
I ONLY WISH IT WERE, JOHNNY!
TAKE A LOOK OVER THERE!
B-B-B- BUFFALO-- (HIC)-- HEADIN' THIS--(HIC)-- THIS WAY! (HIC)
WHAT'RE WE GONNA DO-- (HIC)-- DO-- (HIC) -- DO NOW? (HIC)
FUNNY YOU SHOULD ASK THAT!
THUNDERBOLT? WHERE IN--(HIC)-- BLAZES HAVE YOU (HIC)-- YOU BEEN?
I CALLED YOU--(HIC)-- HOURS AGO!
SORRY, PAL-- BUT IT TOOK ME A THOUSAND YEARS OR SO TO FIND YOU!
YOU ARE OFF THE BEATEN PATH, YOU KNOW!
SO TELL ME-- WHAT CAN I UN-DO FOR YOU?
6

THOSE-- (HIC)-- BUFFALO (HIC)--

--YOU'VE GOTTA-- (HIC)-- GOTTA-- (HIC)-- STOP 'EM!

YOUR WISH IS MY COMMAND-- --AS SOON AS YOU SAY THOSE TWO LI'L MAGIC WORDS!

BUT I CAN'T (HIC)-- CAN'T TALK! THAT WITCHMAN'S MAGIC-- (HIC)-- MAGIC DUST HAS GIVEN-- (HIC)-- GIVEN ME-- (HIC)-- HICCUPS!!

SORRY, O RULER OF THE RIDICULOUS-- --NO PASSWORDS-- NO MAGIC!

SAY, YOU IDIOT-- DO YOU-- (HIC)-- WANT THOSE MONSTERS TO (HIC)-- TRAMPLE US INTO-- (HIC)-- CORNMASH?

DO SOMETHIN'!

THEM WAS THE WORDS, CHIEF!

THE BEMUSED THUNDERBOLT STUDIES THE ONRUSHING HERD--

--THEN, WITH A CASUAL WAVE OF HIS HAND, HE TURNS THEM INTO....

--BUTTERFLIES!? YOU GOTTA BE KIDDIN'!

LOOK-- I DON'T TELL YOU HOW TO RUN YOUR BUSINESS, DO I?

BESIDES-- THOSE BISON WILL CHANGE BACK TO NORMAL-- WHEN THEY'VE CALMED DOWN!

MEBBE SO-- BUT WHAT'RE WE GONNA DO ABOUT THEM?

UH, THAT CREW--! I'LL JUST...

SMOKE--? WE'RE FADIN' AWAY!

THUNDERBOLT, IS THIS YOUR DOING?

SORRY, PRETTY LADY-- BUT I CAN'T TAKE CREDIT FOR THIS ONE!

THEN IT MUST BE ORACLE! OUR MISSION HERE IS FINISHED--

--AND HE'S BRINGING US-- HOME!

7

MEANWHILE-- CENTURIES AWAY-- THREE MORE STRANGELY-GARBED MEN HURTLE THROUGH THE MISTY SKY, THEIR EYES CAREFULLY SCANNING THE PREHISTORIC TERRAIN BELOW...

AQUAMAN WILDCAT and GREEN LANTERN

STILL NO HINT OF WHERE WE'VE ENDED UP, WILDCAT?

'FRAID *NOT*, AQUAMAN! YOU CAN'T TELL ONE *ROCK* FROM ANOTHER DOWN THERE!

HEY--! LOOKS LIKE THERE'S *MORE* THAN A RAMBLING ROCK-GARDEN BELOW US!

CAVEMEN-- CRO-MAGNON-- FROM THE LOOKS OF 'EM!

WELL--AT LEAST WE KNOW *WHEN* WE ARE!... *50,000 YEARS IN THE PAST!*

APPEARS THEY'VE CORNERED SOME WILD ANIMAL IN THAT CAVE!

THAT'S NO *WILD ANIMAL*, LANTERN--

IT'S *THE STAR-SPANGLED KID!*

8

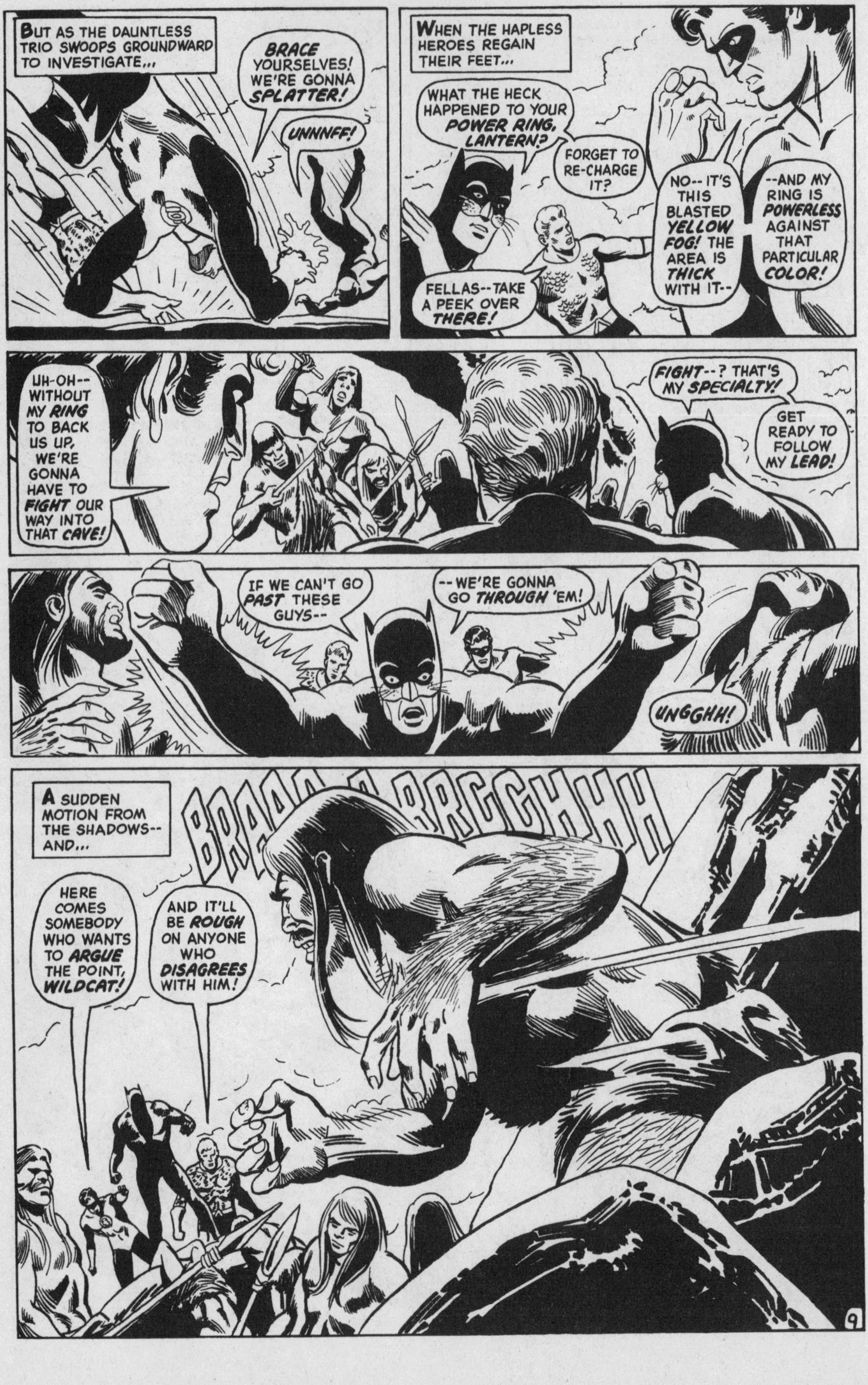
BUT AS THE DAUNTLESS TRIO SWOOPS GROUNDWARD TO INVESTIGATE...
BRACE YOURSELVES! WE'RE GONNA SPLATTER!
UNNNFF!
WHEN THE HAPLESS HEROES REGAIN THEIR FEET...
WHAT THE HECK HAPPENED TO YOUR POWER RING, LANTERN?
FORGET TO RE-CHARGE IT?
NO-- IT'S THIS BLASTED YELLOW FOG! THE AREA IS THICK WITH IT--
--AND MY RING IS POWERLESS AGAINST THAT PARTICULAR COLOR!
FELLAS--TAKE A PEEK OVER THERE!
UH-OH-- WITHOUT MY RING TO BACK US UP, WE'RE GONNA HAVE TO FIGHT OUR WAY INTO THAT CAVE!
FIGHT--? THAT'S MY SPECIALTY!
GET READY TO FOLLOW MY LEAD!
IF WE CAN'T GO PAST THESE GUYS--
--WE'RE GONNA GO THROUGH 'EM!
UNGGHH!
A SUDDEN MOTION FROM THE SHADOWS-- AND...
BRAAA-A-RRGGHHH
HERE COMES SOMEBODY WHO WANTS TO ARGUE THE POINT, WILDCAT!
AND IT'LL BE ROUGH ON ANYONE WHO DISAGREES WITH HIM!
9

RRRAAAGGH

WELL, I DISAGREE WITH HIM--

--AND I WANT TO KNOW HOW HIS ARGUMENTS STAND UP AGAINST COLD, HARD *FACTS!*

UNNFF!

THUD

FACT ONE: THIS PREHISTORIC *GOLIATH* MOVES LIKE A WEEK'S SUPPLY OF *EXHAUSTED MOLASSES!*

KKRUNCHH

FACT TWO: HE'S ARGUING WITH THE *EX-HEAVY-WEIGHT CHAMPION* OF THE WHOLE WIDE WORLD--

--AND I DON'T LIKE TO *LOSE* AN ARGUMENT!

HEY--WHERE'S EVERYBODY *GOING?* I THOUGHT THEY WANTED TO *FIGHT!*

OKAY, *WILDCAT--* YOU MADE YOUR *POINT!*

NOW SUPPOSE WE START SEARCHING FOR THE *STAR-SPANGLED KID?*

WHY *NOT?* IT'S BEGINNING TO *RAIN* OUT HERE ANYWAY!

10

MOMENTS LATER-- WITHIN THE GREAT STONE CHAMBER...

SO *THAT'S* HOW THE *KID* MANAGED THAT ILLUSION--!

A PRIMITIVE *PROJECTOR*-- MADE OF *QUARTZ* AND *SCRAP MATERIAL!*

INGENIOUS! BUT *WHERE* IS THE *KID* HIMSELF!

HIDING IN ONE OF THOSE *SIDE TUNNELS*, I BET!

YOU'RE PROBABLY *RIGHT!* THE QUESTION IS-- *WHY?*

WE FIND THE ANSWER TO *THAT* WHEN WE FIND THE *STAR-SPANGLED KID!*

CHECKING THIS MAZE OUT COULD TAKE *FOREVER!*

LET'S EACH TAKE A *DIFFERENT* TUNNEL-- AND MEET BACK HERE WHEN WE'VE MADE THE ROUNDS!

LONG MINUTES PASS-- AS THE THREE ADVENTURERS SCOUR THE CAVERN'S COUNTLESS CORRIDORS...

...UNTIL, AT LAST, THE *SEA KING* SPIES...

SOMETHING IN THE SHADOWS UP AHEAD--!

--THE *STAR-SPANGLED KID!*

WHO--? THANK THE *STARS*-- A FELLOW *HUMAN BEING!*

BUT *HOW*-- HOW'D YOU *FIND* ME HERE?

I'LL EXPLAIN THAT *LATER!* WHAT I WANT TO KNOW *NOW* IS--

--*WHY* HAVE YOU BEEN HIDING IN THIS *CAVE?*

TO PROTECT THE *FUTURE* OF THE HUMAN RACE!

I'VE GOT A TERRIBLE CASE OF *FLU!* IF EVEN *ONE* OF THOSE PRIMITIVE ANCESTORS OF OURS WERE TO *CATCH* THE DISEASE FROM ME AND *DIE*--

--IT COULD *ALTER* THE COURSE OF *HISTORY!*

RRRRRRMMMM

SHHHHSSSHH! THAT *RUMBLING* NOISE--

SOUNDS LIKE...

11

RRROOOAAAARRR

"A FLOOD!

WHEN IT *RAINS* IN THIS PREHISTORIC WORLD-- IT *POURS!*

WITHIN INSTANTS, THE RAGING TORRENT FILLS THE ROUGH-HEWN CHAMBER...

THE WATER'S IMPACT HAS KNOCKED THE *KID* COLDER THAN A *PENGUIN'S NOSE!*

BETTER GET HIM OUT OF HERE BEFORE HE *DROWNS--*

--THEN COME BACK FOR *GL* AND *WILDCAT!*

LIKE A SALMON RETURNING TO THE SPAWNING GROUND, THE *UNDER-WATER WONDER* PITS HIS MIGHTY SINEWS AGAINST THE SURGING FLOODTIDE AND...

DIFFICULT TO MAKE ANY HEADWAY AGAINST THIS CURRENT--!

FOR ANYONE ELSE IT WOULD BE *IMPOSSIBLE!*

HOPE MY PARTNERS-IN-PERIL CAN HOLD OUT TILL I CAN *GET* THEM!

WHEN SUDDENLY...

WHAT--? A GREAT GREEN *GOLDFISH BOWL*-- ENCLOSING US IN A BUBBLE OF *AIR!*

SEEMS I *UNDERESTIMATED* MY COLLEAGUES!

SWIFTLY, THE GLOWING GLOBE MANEUVERS ITS WAY THROUGH THE FLOOD WATERS....

...BRINGING *AQUAMAN* AND THE *STAR-SPANGLED KID* INTO THE COMPANY OF...

GREEN LANTERN! BUT YOU SAID THE YELLOW FOG DISRUPTED YOUR *POWER RING--!*

IT *DID*-- BUT THE DRIVING *RAIN WASHED* THE FOG AWAY!

HEY-- I SEE YOU *FOUND* OUR PINT-SIZED *PRIZE PACKAGE!*

THEN WE'VE *DONE* ALL WE SET OUT TO DO *HERE!*

ALL THAT REMAINS *NOW* IS FOR *ORACLE* TO BRING US BACK AGAIN!

INSTANTLY, A GREAT CLOUD OF *SMOKE* SWIRLS AROUND THE FOUR STRANGE FIGURES-- AND THEY ARE *GONE!*

12

LET US ADJUST THE CURTAIN OF TIME-AND-SPACE TO FOCUS ON THREE MORE OF OUR CENTURY-SPANNING SEARCHERS AS THEY STEP BACK ONTO THE PLANE OF REALITY...

THE FLASH, ZATANNA, THE MAGICIAN, and THE RED TORNADO

WOW--THAT WAS QUITE A RIDE!

WHERE DID ORACLE DEPOSIT US?

MY RELATIVITY-SENSORS INDICATE WE'VE LANDED ON A SMALL MEDITERRANEAN ISLAND, ZATANNA!

IN THAT CASE, IT SHOULDN'T TAKE ME MORE THAN A FEW SECONDS TO CHECK THE ISLAND FOR OUR MISSING SOLDIER!

WAIT HERE-- I'LL BE RIGHT BACK!

WHAT-- AND MISS ALL THE FUN?

HANG ON, FLASH-- WE'RE COMING WITH YOU!

CIGAM TEPRAC RAEPPA!*

* EDITOR'S NOTE: READ ZATANNA'S MYSTIC COMMANDS BACKWARDS!

AND A SUPER-SPEED SCRUTINY OF THE SMALL ISLE REVEALS....

LOOK! ON THE CREST OF THAT HILL----THE OBJECT OF OUR QUEST!

RIGHT, RED TORNADO-- THAT'S OUR BOY!

SPEEDY! HEY--SPEEDY--OVER HERE! YOU'VE GOT COMPANY!

BUT AS THE BOY BOWMAN MOVES TOWARD HIS THREE FRIENDLY PURSUERS....

EEEEEK! S-SOMETHING'S HAPPENED TO HIM! HE... HE'S...

--SPEEDY HAS BECOME A CENTAUR!

13

WHAT *SORCERY* COULD HAVE CAUSED SUCH A..?

HEADS UP, *ZATANNA*-- OR YOU MAY NOT *LIVE* LONG ENOUGH TO FIND OUT!

CEASE! WHO DARES TRESPASS UPON THE ISLE OF *AEAEA?*

WHAT--?!

I AM THE SORCERESS-- *CIRCE*--

--AND THESE ARE MY FAITHFUL *SERVANTS!*

OF COURSE! ACCORDING TO GREEK LEGEND, *CIRCE* HAD THE POWER TO TURN ORDINARY MEN INTO *HYBRID ANIMALS!*

THAT'S WHAT YOU'VE DONE TO *SPEEDY!*

QUITE *CORRECT,* WENCH-- HE IS FAR MORE *MANAGEABLE* THIS WAY!

BUT *WHAT* DO *YOU* WANT HERE ON *CIRCE'S ISLE?*

WE HAVE COME FOR *HIM,* SORCERESS-- THE *CENTAUR* WHO STANDS BESIDE YOU!

RETURN HIM TO HIS *NORMAL* STATE-- AND WE WILL LEAVE YOU IN *PEACE!*

CERTAINLY, *SPAWN OF MERCURY!* IF YOU WANT YOUR FRIEND'S COMPANION-SHIP SO DEARLY, YOU SHALL *HAVE* IT,...

...BY JOINING HIM IN MY *MENAGERIE!*

BRACE YOURSELVES, GROUP-- SHE'S PLANNING SOMETHING *TRICKY!*

INDEED I *AM!* I'VE *ENCHANTED* THE YOUNG BOWMAN'S SHAFTS!

SHOULD AN ARROW SO MUCH AS TOUCH *YOU*-- YOU SHALL BECOME THAT WHICH IS MOST *REPUGNANT* TO YOU!

SHE *MEANS* IT!

EVERYONE-- *SCATTER! SPEEDY* CAN'T HIT *ALL* OF US!

14

AND THREE TWANGS OF A LONG BOW LATER...

THAT GLOWING ARROW'S *ENCHANTED!* NO MATTER HOW I DODGE AND WEAVE, IT FOLLOWS RIGHT ALONG BEHIND ME--

--AND STARTING TO *CATCH UP!*

BETTER POUR ON THE *SUPER-SPEED*--

BUT EVEN BEFORE THE *CRIMSON COMET* CAN COMPLETE HIS THOUGHT, THE BLUNT-TIPPED SHAFT STRIKES HIM SQUARELY AND...

GOOD LORD! MY WIFE *IRIS* USED TO CALL ME "*THE SLOWEST MAN ALIVE*"-- AND HOW RIGHT SHE *NOW* IS!

I'VE BECOME... *HALF-SNAIL!*

WHILE HALF-WAY ACROSS THE ISLAND...

THAT *BRICK WALL* I CONJURED UP ISN'T SLOWING THE ARROW DOWN!

UNLESS I QUICKLY COME UP WITH THE PROPER SPELL, IT'LL BE...

THOK!

...*TOO LATE!*

THE ARROW TURNED ME INTO A *HUMMINGBIRD!*

TO MAKE MATTERS *WORSE*-- IT'S FROZEN MY *VOCAL CORDS!*

I CAN'T UTTER A *COUNTER-ACTING* SPELL!

AS FOR THE THIRD "TARGET"...

SPEEDY'S ARROW IS LIKE A *HEAT-SEEKING MISSILE*--FOLLOWING ME WHEREVER I GO!

EH--? I SEE *FLASH'S* ARROW HAS CAUGHT UP TO HIM! GOT TO *HELP!*

BUT AS THE *RED TORNADO* STORMS TO *FLASH'S* SIDE...

THE *DIVERSION* LET THE *MAGICAL ARROW* OVERTAKE ME....HIT ME....

...GIVE ME THE BODY OF A *MOLE!*

WELCOME TO THE *CLUB, REDDY!*

YOU TRY SPINNING *NOW*--AND YOU'LL *DRILL* YOURSELF INTO THE GROUND!

A FITTING *FATE*--IS IT NOT, *FLEET ONE?*

15

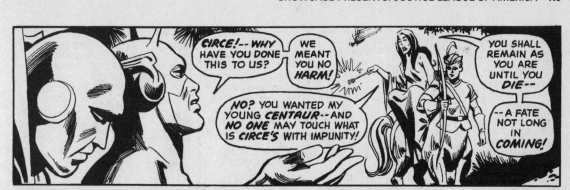

CIRCE!-- WHY HAVE YOU DONE THIS TO US?

WE MEANT YOU NO *HARM!*

NO? YOU WANTED MY YOUNG *CENTAUR*--AND *NO ONE* MAY TOUCH WHAT IS *CIRCE'S* WITH IMPUNITY!

YOU SHALL REMAIN AS YOU ARE UNTIL YOU *DIE--*

--A FATE NOT LONG IN *COMING!*

UNDER MY ENCHANT-MENT, YOU TWO SHALL BATTLE UNTO *DEATH--*

--AS A LESSON TO OTHERS WHO WOULD SEEK TO ANNOY *CIRCE!*

C-CAN'T *HELP* M-MYSELF!

CIRCE IS F-FORCING ME TO *OBEY!*

IT SHOULD BE A *SPLENDID SUPER-SPEED STRUGGLE!* WOULD THAT I COULD REMAIN TO *WITNESS* IT--

--BUT THERE ARE *OTHER* MATTERS THAT DEMAND *CIRCE'S* ATTENTION *IMMEDIATELY!*

THE SORCERESS GALLOPS OFF INTO THE DISTANCE, LEAVING BEHIND TWO STRUGGLING VICTIMS OF HER MAGIC--

--AND ONE ALMOST FORGOTTEN IN THE HEAT OF THE MOMENT...

GOT TO FIND A WAY TO *STOP* THEM BEFORE THEY *KILL* EACH OTHER!

THE WINDS THEY'RE CREATING ARE KNOCKING ME AROUND LIKE A *PING-PONG BALL!*

HMMMMMM

WAITAMINNIT! THAT *HUMMING!*

MY *WINGS*--VIBRATING AT THIS INCREDIBLE SPEED--CREATE A *SOUND!*

IF I CAN *CONTROL* THAT NOISE, I MIGHT BE ABLE TO *DUPLICATE* THE SOUND OF MY *VOICE*--

--AND COUNTER-ACT *CIRCE'S* SPELL!

DESPERATELY, THE MISTRESS OF THE OCCULT EXPERIMENTS WITH HER NEWLY-GAINED PINIONS--

UUNNGGGG

RRORRR

HUMMMMMM

WWWHRRR

--PERFORMING COUNTLESS DIFFER-ENT MANEUVERS IN AN ATTEMPT TO ACHIEVE A VARIETY OF SOUNDS...

16

UNTIL AT LAST...

CIGAM FO ECRIC ENOGEB!

THANK THE STARS-- IT'S *WORKING!*

FLASH AND RED TORNADO ARE RETURNING TO *NORMAL!*

AND AS *CIRCE'S* MAGIC WEARS OFF *ZATANNA* HERSELF...

THANKS FOR THE *HANDY NET,* FLASH! IT'S DIFFICULT STAYING ALOFT WITHOUT *WINGS!*

SO I NOTICED! DO ME A *FAVOR,* ZATANNA?

NEXT TIME YOU CANCEL AN ENCHANT-MENT--MAKE SURE YOU'RE STANDING ON THE *GROUND!*

NEED I REMIND YOU-- WE STILL HAVE *SPEEDY* TO RESCUE!

I HAVEN'T *FORGOTTEN,* TORNADO! IN FACT, I'VE FIGURED OUT *HOW* TO DO IT!

A SHORT WHILE LATER-- IN THE GRACIOUS TEMPLE THAT IS THE ISLAND'S SOLE STRUCTURE...

I'VE COME BACK FOR MY *FRIEND,* CIRCE--AND THIS TIME I'M *TAKING* HIM!

'TIS *YOU* AGAIN, SCARLET ONE? YOU LEARN YOUR LESSONS *HARD!*

FOR YOUR INSOLENCE, I WILL TURN YOU INTO A *LOWLY EARTHWORM!*

I WOULDN'T *DO* THAT, SORCERESS-- HIS *WIFE* WOULDN'T LIKE IT!

AND I'LL TAKE YOUR *WAND--* YOU'RE TOO *DANGEROUS* TO HAVE A LOADED WEAPON!

NO-- IT CANNOT BE--?

WHY SAY THAT, *CIRCE--* WHEN IT OBVIOUSLY *IS?*

ECRIC EMOCEB DEZYLARAP!

AT ZATANNA'S COMMAND, *CIRCE* BECOMES MOTIONLESS-- AND ALMOST INSTANTLY....

WHERE *AM* I? WH--WHAT'S *HAPPENED?*

WHO--*WHO* ARE *YOU?*

IT'S A LONG STORY, *SPEEDY--* WE'LL FILL YOU IN LATER!

RIGHT NOW, WE HAVE TO DISPOSE OF *CIRCE!*

I'VE TAKEN CARE OF THAT, *FLASH!*

WITHOUT HER *WAND,* SHE IS *POWERLESS!*

17

WITH HER WAND NO MORE, *CIRCE'S* "PETS" ARE REGAINING THEIR TRUE FORMS!

THERE'S NOTHING LEFT TO *KEEP* US HERE...

...EXCEPT FOR THE PROBLEM HOW TO FIND OUR WAY BACK *HOME!*

SUDDENLY...

LOOKS LIKE *ORACLE* SOLVED THAT PROBLEM FOR US-- WE'RE *FADING OUT!*

HEY!...WHAT'S *GOING ON* HERE? I DON'T UNDERSTAND *ANY* OF THIS!

YOU *WILL,* YOUNGSTER-- ASSUMING WE RETURN TO OUR WORLD-- IN *TIME!*

IN THE HANDS OF ALL-KNOWING *ORACLE,* TIME IS A *CELESTIAL CLAY* TO BE SCULPTURED AS HE SEES FIT...

NOW HE FOLDS THE CLAY IN UPON ITSELF, GATHERING THE SCATTERED EDGES-- BRINGING THE GREATEST ASSORTMENT OF SUPER-BEINGS EVER RECORDED TO THE *JUSTICE SOCIETY'S* SANCTUARY...

ALL PRESENT AND ACCOUNTED FOR!

THE *SEVEN SOLDIERS OF VICTORY* TOGETHER ONCE AGAIN!

BUT-- IF THE *SEVEN SOLDIERS* ARE ALL *HERE*--

--WHO IS BURIED IN THE *UNKNOWN SOLDIER'S TOMB?*

18

WE CAN ANSWER *THAT,* JOHNNY!

GREEN LANTERN-- ROBIN-- MR. TERRIFIC--! WHERE HAVE *YOU* BEEN?

TO THE TOP OF THE *HIMALAYAS*-- WHERE WE *DISCOVERED...*

NO, FRIEND-- --LET *ME* TELL EVERYONE WHAT YOU FOUND!

THE *UNKNOWN SOLDIER OF VICTORY* IS MY AIDE AND COMPANION-- *WING!*

IT WAS *HE* WHO *DIED* TO DEFEAT THE *NEBULA-MAN*--

--AND IF THERE IS ANY *JUSTICE* IN THIS WORLD, HE WAS BURIED WHERE HE FELL -- WITH *HONORS!*

HE *WAS*, INDEED, CRIMSON AVENGER!

HOLY MEN FROM A NEARBY TEMPLE WITNESSED THE BATTLE--AND LAID YOUR FRIEND TO REST WHEN IT WAS *OVER!*

HE WAS AS *BRAVE* A MAN AS EVER LIVED! YOU'VE A RIGHT TO BE *PROUD* OF HIM!

NOBODY'LL *LIVE* LONG ENOUGH TO BE PROUD--UNLESS WE GET TO WORK *REBUILDING* THE *WEAPON* THAT *WING* USED TO DEFEAT THE *NEBULA-MAN!*

YOU'LL DO *NOTHING*, FRIENDS--

--IF YOU *VALUE* THIS PRETTY LADY'S *LIFE!*

WHO?

19

DIANA--?

AND THE *IRON HAND*-- OUR OLD ARCH-ENEMY!

BUT THAT *JASPER'S* S'POSED T'BE *DEAD!*

NOT DEAD, *VIGILANTE*-- MERELY *DAMAGED*-- WITH AN *IRON HAND* AS PROOF!

WHOM PFF

AN *IRON HAND* THAT SHALL *SCATTER* DIANA PRINCE ALL OVER THE COUNTRYSIDE--

--IF ANYONE HERE IS SO *FOOLISH* AS TO MAKE A *THREATENING* MOVE TOWARDS ME--!

AND IN CASE YOU *DOUBT* MY *HAND'S* POWER--!

P-PLEASE... YOU *WOULDN'T*--!

OHHH-- I THINK I'M GOING TO-- *FAINT*--!

HUH?

FOR AN INSTANT THE *IRON HAND* IS DISTRACTED...

...AND THAT INSTANT IS ALL *DIANA (WONDER WOMAN) PRINCE* NEEDS...

M-MY *MECHANICAL HAND*--! YOU'VE *SEVERED* IT!

WHOM

KZZATT

CONSIDER YOURSELF *LUCKY!* I COULD HAVE DONE THAT TO YOUR *NECK!*

TARRRRG

20

COSTUMED OR NOT, YOU'RE STILL A *WONDER,* DIANA!

SAVE THE *COMPLIMENTS* FOR LATER, *BATMAN!* RIGHT NOW WE NEED *INFORMATION!*

TALK, *IRON MOUTH* --TELL US HOW TO *STOP* THAT *COLOSSAL HAND* OF YOURS--

--OR I'LL TAKE YOU APART A *BONE* AT A TIME!

DO WHAT YOU *WANT,* LADY-- IT MAKES *NO* DIFFERENCE-- *NOW!*

THE CONTROLS WERE IN MY *SHATTERED HAND!* I COULDN'T DEACTIVATE MY CREATION NOW-- EVEN IF I *WANTED* TO!

WE'RE *DOOMED,* YOU BLOODY FOOLS-- EVERYONE IS *DOOMED!*

PERHAPS *NOT,* VILLAIN--

--IF THE *SEVEN SOLDIERS* CAN RECREATE THE *WEAPON* THEY BUILT TO DESTROY YOUR *EARLIER* MENACE-- THE *NEBULA-MAN!*

WHAT *SAY* YOU, SOLDIERS--CAN IT BE DONE?

IT'S A QUESTION OF *TIME!*

THE WEAPON ITSELF IS A *LIGHTNING ROD* OF SORTS-- GATHERING *NEBULOID-ENERGY* FROM SPACE-- THEN CHANNELING IT AGAINST THE *OPPOSING NEBULA THREAT--*

--BUT IT TAKES *TIME* TO CHARGE COMPLETELY-- *MORE* TIME THAN WE HAVE!

YOU JUST *BUILD* THE *NEBULA-ROD, KID!*

LET *US* WORRY ABOUT *CHARGING* IT!

IT'S A *DEAL!* I'LL GET YOU A LIST OF THE *MATERIALS* WE'LL NEED!

21

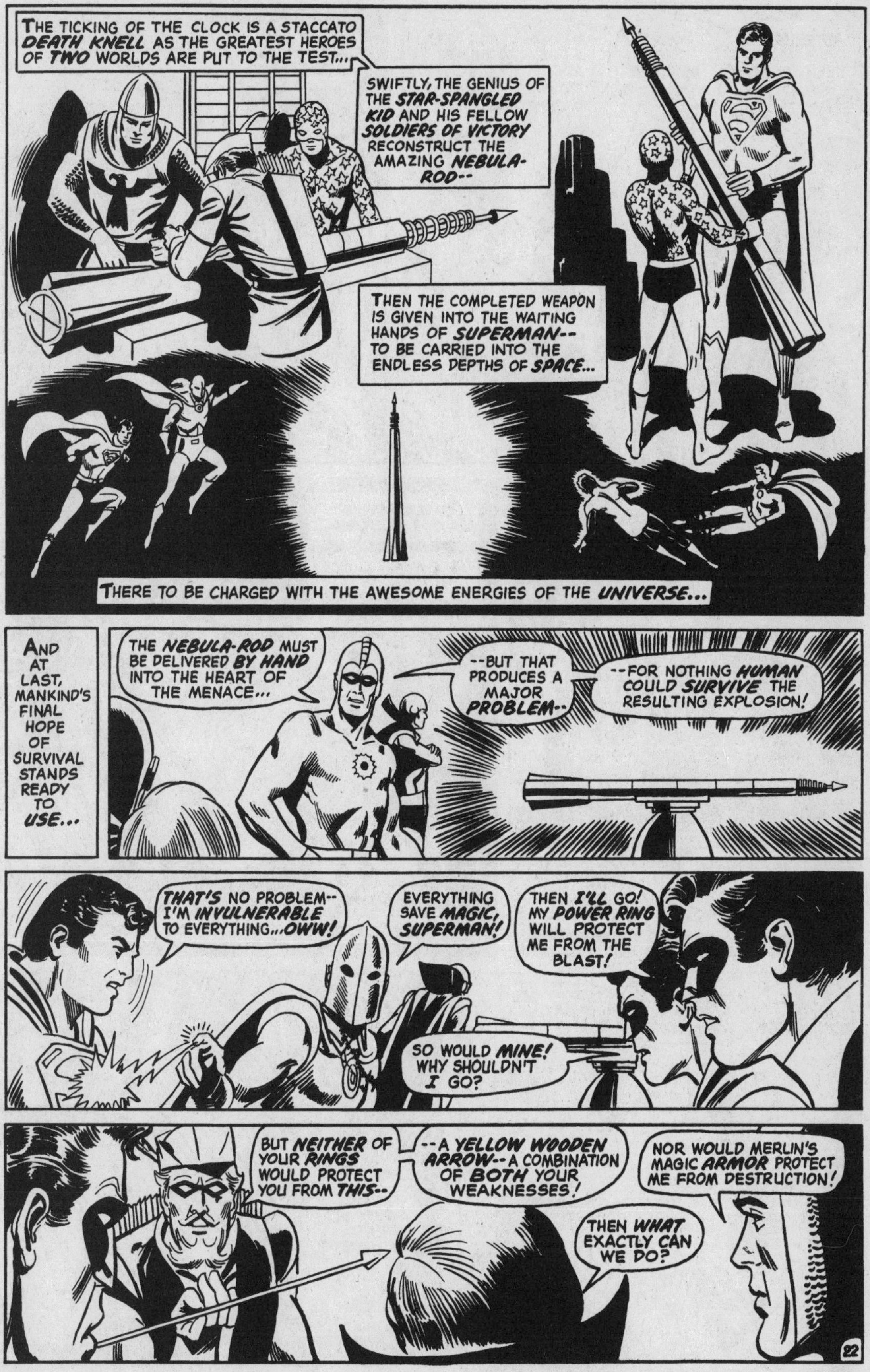
THE TICKING OF THE CLOCK IS A STACCATO DEATH KNELL AS THE GREATEST HEROES OF TWO WORLDS ARE PUT TO THE TEST...
SWIFTLY, THE GENIUS OF THE STAR-SPANGLED KID AND HIS FELLOW SOLDIERS OF VICTORY RECONSTRUCT THE AMAZING NEBULA-ROD--
THEN THE COMPLETED WEAPON IS GIVEN INTO THE WAITING HANDS OF SUPERMAN-- TO BE CARRIED INTO THE ENDLESS DEPTHS OF SPACE...
THERE TO BE CHARGED WITH THE AWESOME ENERGIES OF THE UNIVERSE...
AND AT LAST, MANKIND'S FINAL HOPE OF SURVIVAL STANDS READY TO USE...
THE NEBULA-ROD MUST BE DELIVERED BY HAND INTO THE HEART OF THE MENACE...
--BUT THAT PRODUCES A MAJOR PROBLEM--
--FOR NOTHING HUMAN COULD SURVIVE THE RESULTING EXPLOSION!
THAT'S NO PROBLEM-- I'M INVULNERABLE TO EVERYTHING...OWW!
EVERYTHING SAVE MAGIC, SUPERMAN!
THEN I'LL GO! MY POWER RING WILL PROTECT ME FROM THE BLAST!
SO WOULD MINE! WHY SHOULDN'T I GO?
BUT NEITHER OF YOUR RINGS WOULD PROTECT YOU FROM THIS--
--A YELLOW WOODEN ARROW--A COMBINATION OF BOTH YOUR WEAKNESSES!
NOR WOULD MERLIN'S MAGIC ARMOR PROTECT ME FROM DESTRUCTION!
THEN WHAT EXACTLY CAN WE DO?
22

NOTHING! THE PROBLEM HAS BEEN *SOLVED* FOR US.

WHAT--? THE NEBULA-ROD IS *GONE*--

--AND SO IS THE *RED TORNADO!*

OH, NO! HE--HE *COULDN'T* HAVE--!

BUT HE *DID!* HE TOOK THE NEBULA-ROD--

--AND LEFT THIS *NOTE* IN ITS PLACE!

WHAT DOES IT SAY, *BATMAN?*

"MY FRIENDS... WHEN YOU READ THIS... IT WILL BE *TOO LATE* TO STOP ME..."

"I HAVE TAKEN THE *NEBULA-ROD*...AND GONE TO FACE MY *DESTINY... ALONE!*"

"YOU SAID NOTHING *HUMAN* COULD DO WHAT MUST BE DONE...AND *SURVIVE*..."

"THEN PERHAPS I HAVE A *BETTER CHANCE* THAN MOST..."

"AN *ANDROID* IS NOT HUMAN..."

"IF I PERISH... ALL THAT WILL BE LOST IS SOME *CIRCUITRY AND GEARS*..."

"IF I AM *SUCCESSFUL*... I WILL SEE YOU ALL SOON..."

"IF I AM *NOT*... REMEMBER ME..."

"*YOUR FRIEND* ... RED TORNADO!"

THAT'S *ALL* IT SAYS...

M-MAYBE IT'S *NOT* TOO LATE--! MAYBE THERE'S *STILL* TIME TO *HELP* HIM--

KW-A-RA-RA- RA-A- ROOOOM

AND THE SOUNDS OF MUFFLED WEEPING ARE LOST AMID THE ECHOES OF THE BLAST!

I'M AFRAID... *NOTHING* CAN HELP HIM *NOW!*

23

AND A SHORT WHILE LATER...
HOW DID IT GO UP THERE?
THEY'VE VANISHED--BOTH OF THEM! THE NEBULOID HAND--AND RED TORNADO!
THE FORCE OF THE EXPLOSION MUST HAVE TORN EACH OF THEM TO ATOMS!
ALL THE TIMES I PUT HIM DOWN--CONSIDERED HIM JUST A MACHINE!
HE WAS MORE OF A MAN THAN ANY OF US!
I KNOW HOW YOU FEEL, HOURMAN--
I LOST A GOOD FRIEND, TOO!
AND SOMEWHERE--SOMEHOW--RED TORNADO AND WING BOTH KNOW HOW WE FEEL!
24

JUSTICE LEAGUE of AMERICA

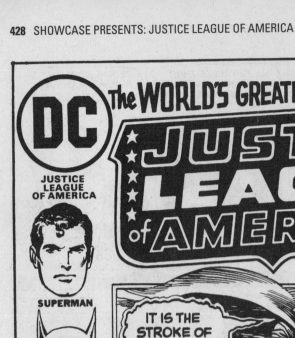

SUPERMAN

BATMAN

FLASH

GREEN
LANTERN

HAWKMAN

GREEN ARROW

WHAT MAKES A MAN A *CHAMPION?* IS IT POWERS AND ABILITIES FAR *BEYOND* THOSE OF OTHER MORTALS--

OR IS IT THE KNOWLEDGE THAT THE *CAUSE* ONE FIGHTS FOR IS *RIGHTEOUS* AND *JUST?*

MEN CALL ME THE *PHANTOM STRANGER* -- AND I COME THIS TIME TO SEEK AN *ANSWER!*

ARE TRUE CHAMPIONS *BORN*... OR ARE THEY *MADE?*

S-1327

A LATE OCTOBER NIGHTTIDE-- ON A SHADOWED CROSSROADS OUTSIDE QUIET *RUTLAND, VERMONT--*

--AS A CURIOUS CROWD MILLS ABOUT IMPATIENTLY...

I'M STILL NOT SURE WHY YOU *DRAGGED* ME OUT HERE, TOM!

HANG ON A MINUTE, MARTY-- AND YOU *WILL!* THE *CEREMONY* IS ABOUT TO *START!*

WHEN THE OLD CLOCK TOWER TOLLS MIDNIGHT, 'TIS SAID, OLD *MISTRESS SARAH* SPEAKS TO THE *SPIRITS* -- AND THEY TELL HER DARK *SECRETS* IN RETURN...

...THE NAMES OF THOSE WHO ARE TO *DIE* -- WITHIN *TWENTY-FOUR HOURS!*

THEN, AS IT HAS FOR YEARS, THE RITUAL BEGINS!

WITH EACH CHILLING PEAL OF THE CLOCK, A *NAME* IS CHANTED --A WARRANT OF *DEATH* THAT IS LOST IN THE MIND...

BONG! SUPERMAN! BONG! FLASH! BONG! HAWKMAN! BONG! BATMAN! BONG! GREEN LANTERN! BONG! GREEN ARROW!

WITH EACH BELL TOLLED, THESE NAMES I SAY, OF THOSE WHO'LL *DIE* BY END OF DAY!

1

AND WHAT OF THOSE SIX MEN *CONDEMNED* BY A *WHISPER?* THOSE SIX STAUNCH DEFENDERS WHO FORM THE BACKBONE OF THE WORLD'S GREATEST CRIME-FIGHTING ORGANIZATION?

LET'S SHIFT OUR ATTENTION TO A GLEAMING SATELLITE WHIRLING 22,300 MILES ABOVE EARTH'S EMERALD FACE-- AND *SEE...*

ABOUT *TIME* YOU GOT HERE, *BATMAN!*

THE *REST* OF US HAVE BEEN WAITING AN *HOUR!*

SORRY, *GREEN ARROW--*

--BUT I WAS WRAPPING UP A *"JUNK-DEALING"* RING -- AND TOOK LONGER THAN I FIGURED!

WELL -- SINCE THE *OTHER* MEMBERS ARE STILL ON *EARTH-TWO* -- HELPING THE *SEVEN SOLDIERS OF VICTORY* ADJUST TO THE WORLD OF THE *PRESENT* --

--I CALL THIS *EMERGENCY MEETING* TO *ORDER!*

WHY DID YOU *SUMMON* US HERE, *BATMAN?*

*EDITOR'S NOTE: FOR COMPLETE DETAILS CHECK JLA #100-102!

M-ME? I DIDN'T SUMMON ANYONE!

I THOUGHT *ONE* OF YOU DID!

NONE OF US! SINCE YOU ARRIVED *LATE,* WE JUST NATURALLY *ASSUMED...*

--BUT YOU ASSUMED *INCORRECTLY,* GREEN LATERN!

THE *BATMAN* DID NOT SUMMON YOU ALL HERE...

...I *DID!!*

WHO--?!

2

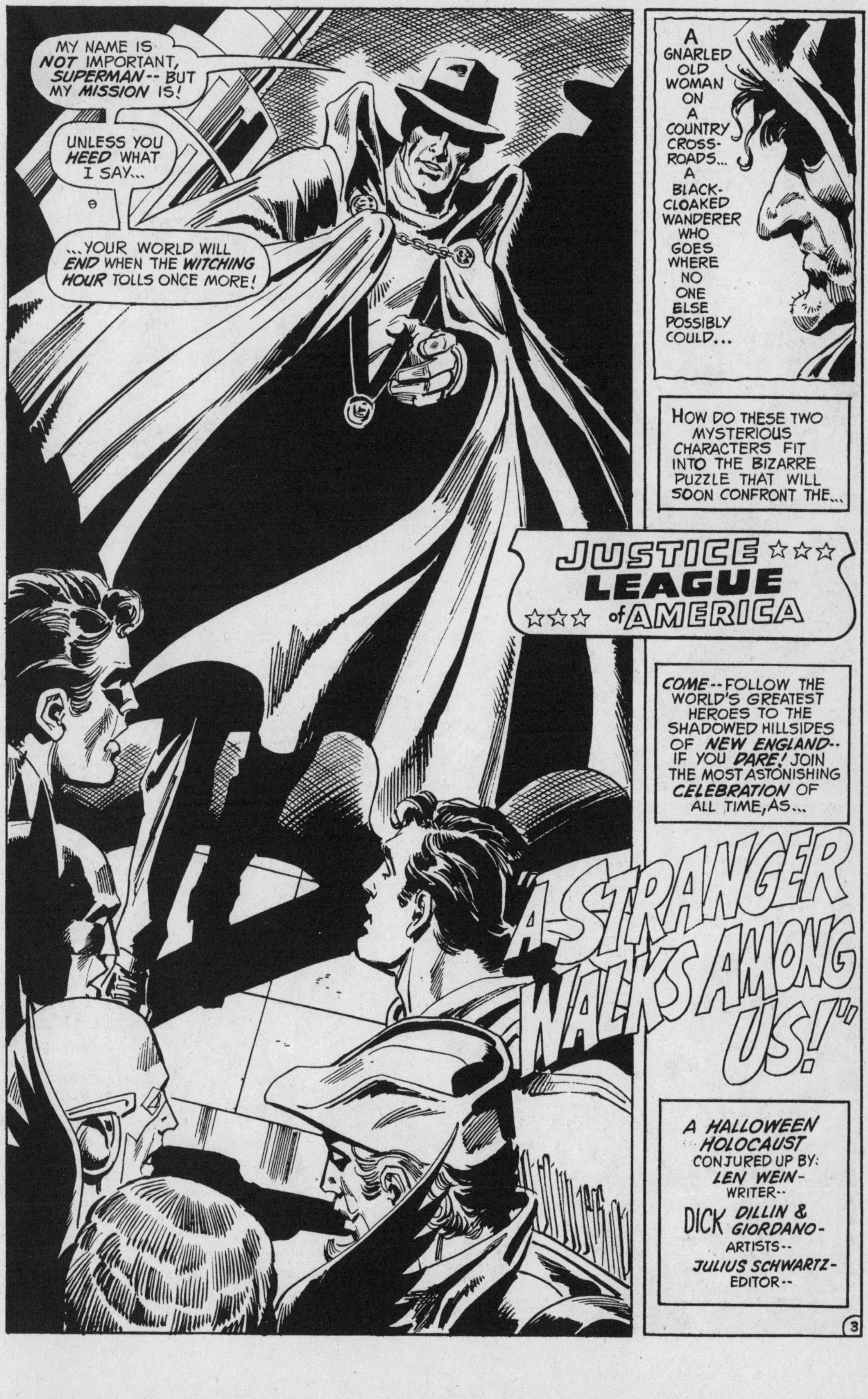
MY NAME IS NOT IMPORTANT, SUPERMAN -- BUT MY MISSION IS!
UNLESS YOU HEED WHAT I SAY...
...YOUR WORLD WILL END WHEN THE WITCHING HOUR TOLLS ONCE MORE!
A GNARLED OLD WOMAN ON A COUNTRY CROSS-ROADS... A BLACK-CLOAKED WANDERER WHO GOES WHERE NO ONE ELSE POSSIBLY COULD...
HOW DO THESE TWO MYSTERIOUS CHARACTERS FIT INTO THE BIZARRE PUZZLE THAT WILL SOON CONFRONT THE...
JUSTICE LEAGUE of AMERICA
COME -- FOLLOW THE WORLD'S GREATEST HEROES TO THE SHADOWED HILLSIDES OF NEW ENGLAND -- IF YOU DARE! JOIN THE MOST ASTONISHING CELEBRATION OF ALL TIME, AS...
"A STRANGER WALKS AMONG US!"
A HALLOWEEN HOLOCAUST CONJURED UP BY: LEN WEIN - WRITER -- DICK DILLIN & GIORDANO - ARTISTS -- JULIUS SCHWARTZ - EDITOR --
3

LOOK--I DON'T KNOW HOW YOU *BREACHED* OUR *SECURITY DEVICES*, PAL--

BUT YOU AND YOUR *"GHOST STORY"* ARE GOING OUT OF HERE ON YOUR...

HOLD ON, G.A. -- I *KNOW* THIS... MAN!

WE'D BETTER *LISTEN* TO WHAT HE HAS TO SAY!

OKAY, DOOMSAYER-- *THE BATMAN* JUST BOUGHT YOU *THREE MINUTES*--!

YOU'D BETTER USE 'EM *WELL*!

QUIET, ARCHER --LET THE MAN *SPEAK*!

THANK YOU, *HAWKMAN*-- I'LL BE *BRIEF*!

I'VE COME HERE TO DO SOMETHING I FIND MOST *UNUSUAL*, GENTLEMEN--

I'VE COME TO ASK FOR YOUR *HELP*!

THERE IS AN *EVIL* AFOOT ON THE LAND --SO *AWESOME* --SO *OVERPOWERING* --THAT I FEAR I CANNOT COMBAT IT --*ALONE*!

TODAY IS *OCTOBER THIRTY-FIRST*-- HALLOWEEN-- A DAY FOR *DARK THINGS* TO WANDER THE EARTH--

--AND IT IS *HERE*, IN THE CITY CALLED *RUTLAND, VERMONT* --THAT THOSE *UNHOLY* ENTITIES WILL CROSS THE BLACK GATE --AND GAIN *LIFE* ONCE MORE!

CANADA Montreal

VT.

WATERTOWN

NEW YORK RUTLAND

N.H.

MASS.

ATLANTIC OCEAN

SOUNDS *HEAVY*-- BUT JUST *HOW* DO THOSE GHOSTIES FIGURE TO SNEAK ACROSS--?

SOMEBODY SLIP 'EM A *PASSKEY*?

IN A MANNER OF SPEAKING, *GREEN ARROW*, SOMEBODY *WILL*!

THEY'RE BEING *SUMMONED* TO *EARTH* AS *SERVANTS* OF ONE YOU KNOW QUITE *WELL*...

FELIX FAUST!

4

FAUST?! BUT HE'S STILL IN *PRISON!* I PUT HIM THERE *MYSELF!*

THE CELL HOLDS ONLY AN *ETHEREAL ILLUSION,* SUPERMAN-- A SIMPLE TRICK FOR ONE WITH FAUST'S *MYSTIC SKILLS!*

AND *NOW,* GENTLEMEN-- SINCE YOU KNOW ALL YOU *NEED* TO KNOW-- I WILL TAKE MY *LEAVE*--!

ONE MINUTE, FRIEND-- WE'RE NOT *DONE* WITH YOU YET!

A *POWER-RING* PRISON WILL DELAY YOUR DEPARTURE UNTIL WE *ARE* DONE!

I WOULDN'T BE TOO SURE OF THAT, GL!

WHAT IS *THAT* SUPPOSED TO MEAN, *BATMAN?*

TAKE A PEEK UNDER THAT *ICE-CREAM CONE* OF YOURS-- --AND SEE FOR *YOURSELF!*

WHA--? H-HE'S *GONE!* BUT-- HOW--?!

NOBODY CAN GET *IN* OR *OUT* OF THIS SATELLITE-- WITHOUT PASSING MORE SECURITY PRECAUTIONS THAN THEY HAVE AT *FORT KNOX!*

HE CAN! MAYBE THAT'S WHY HE'S KNOWN AS-- *THE PHANTOM STRANGER!*

SO *DARK EYES* IS A *SPOOK*--SO *WHAT?* WHERE DOES THAT LEAVE *US?*

AS LONG AS YOU KEEP EXERCISING YOUR *MOUTH,* ARCHER-- IT LEAVES US *NOWHERE!*

HAWKMAN'S *RIGHT*-- WE'D BETTER *CONSIDER* OUR ACTIONS!

WHAT'S TO *CONSIDER?* WHERE *FELIX FAUST* IS-- WE'D BETTER BE, TOO!

FELLAS-- I THINK WE'LL DO OUR *TRICK-OR-TREATING* IN *RUTLAND* THIS YEAR!

NEW YORK

VERMONT

RUTLAND

LAKE

LAKE ONTARIO

SYRACUSE

ROCHESTER

LAKE ERIE

⑤

THE *STAGE* IS SET-- BUT OUR *CAST* IS NOT YET COMPLETE...

...WE FIND THE REMAINING FOUR *PLAYERS* ON A LONELY *VERMONT* ROADSIDE LATE THIS SAME AFTERNOON...

I DON'T *BELIEVE* IT! THE WHOLE FREAKIN' *MUFFLER* FELL OFF!

STEVE -- I *TOLD* YOU THIS CRATE WOULDN'T LAST ALL THE WAY TO *RUTLAND!*

IT'S THE *STORY* OF MY *LIFE!* WE'LL NEVER GET TO *FAGAN'S* ON TIME AT *THIS* RATE!

I'M STILL NOT SURE I EVEN *WANT* TO GO TO *FAGAN'S, LEN!* AFTER ALL THE HASSLES I HAD AT THE PARTY THERE *LAST* YEAR*--!

*EDITOR'S NOTE: *"NIGHT OF THE REAPER"*-- BATMAN #237!*

GARBAGE! IF YOU DIDN'T *WANT* TO COME *GERRY* -- YOU WOULDN'T *BE* HERE!

BESIDES -- YOU'RE THE ONE WHO CONVINCED *US* WHAT A GREAT TIME WE'D HAVE!

WAITAMINNIT! SQUABBLING ISN'T GONNA GET US *ANYWHERE!* SAVE YOUR ENERGY FOR THE PARADE, *GLYNIS*--

--CONSIDERING THE *SUPERGIRL* COSTUME YOU'LL BE WEARING-- YOU'LL NEED ALL THE *ENERGY* YOU GET-- TO KEEP *WARM!*

HEY-- *DON'T* HASSLE MY CAR, PEOPLE! IT'S *TRYING* TO GET US TO THE *PARADE!*

--AND IT *WILL*-- IF WE DON'T LET IT *SIT* TOO LONG!

BBRRAAKKK WRROOMM BBLLLATTTT KAKK KAKK

BOY, WILL *TOM FAGAN* BE *SURPRISED* WHEN HE SEES *US!*

6

THE AFTERNOON DWINDLES SWIFTLY-- AS THE WORLD'S GREATEST HEROES SCOUR THE PLACID *VERMONT* COUNTRYSIDE...

...IN SEARCH OF THINGS UNWORLDLY... AND *INHUMAN*...

...UNTIL, AS *DUSK* BEGINS TO FALL...

STRUCK OUT, DIDN'T YOU?

...LIKE ROOKIES IN THE *LITTLE LEAGUE,* G.A.!

HOW *COULD* WE SUCCEED-- WHEN WE'RE NOT EVEN SURE WHAT WE'RE *SEARCHING* FOR?

I'M NOT SURE I'D RECOGNIZE A *DEMON* IF I *TRIPPED* OVER ONE!

FLASH IS *RIGHT!* IF THERE *IS* SOMETHING HAUNTING THIS AREA--

--OUR *SUPER-POWERS* CAN'T *DETECT* IT!

I *AGREE, SUPERMAN!* WHAT WE *NEED* HERE-- IS A *BASE OF OPERATIONS*--

--A PLACE WE CAN USE TO *PLAN* OUR NEXT MOVES!

--AND I THINK I KNOW JUST THE *SPOT!*

FOLLOW ME, CHUMS-- YOU'RE IN FOR A *SURPRISE!*

⑦

SEVERAL MILES DISTANT-- ON THE OUTSKIRTS OF THE TOWN...

SOME MORE *LATE* ARRIVALS! IT'S...

HEY--*LEN*--*GLYNIS*-- *GERRY*--*STEVE*-- HOW *ARE* YOU? GLAD YOU COULD MAKE IT!

SO ARE *WE*, TOM!

STEVE'S CAR IS *FALLING APART* BY DEGREES--BUT WE'D HAVE BEEN HERE IF WE HAD TO COME BY *OX-CART!*

--WHICH WOULD PROBABLY HAVE BEEN MORE *COMFORTABLE*, ANYWAY!

I *KNOW* WHAT YOU MEAN! STILL-- I'M PLEASED YOU *ACCEPTED* MY *INVITATION!*

DOES THAT INVITATION HOLD FOR *US*, TOM?

WHO--?

OH... MY... *GOSH!*

HAPPY HALLOWEEN, TOM--IT'S GOOD TO *SEE* YOU AGAIN!

SAVE THE *SALUTATIONS*, PAL--AND ASK THE MAN THE *QUESTION!*

WHAT *GREEN ARROW* IS TRYING TO GET ACROSS IN HIS OWN *INEPT* WAY IS--

--CAN WE STICK AROUND HERE FOR A LITTLE WHILE?

A-A *LITTLE WHILE?* YOU CAN STAY HERE *FOREVER* IF YOU WANT--

--BUT SINCE YOU *ARE* HERE --WELL, THERE'S A FAVOR *WE'D* LIKE TO ASK--

JUST *NAME* IT, TOM-- AND IF IT'S WITHIN OUR POWER...

JULIE WILL *NEVER* BELIEVE ME WHEN I TELL HIM ABOUT *THIS!*

YOU SEE-- WE HAVE THIS *PARADE* EVERY YEAR-- WHERE WE *HONOR* YOU GUYS--

--AND-- WELL-- SINCE YOU'RE HERE IN THE *FLESH*-- WE THOUGHT --THAT MAYBE YOU'D-- WELL--

I THINK I CATCH YOUR *DRIFT*, TOM-- AND I THINK I KNOW WHAT OUR *ANSWER* IS--!

8

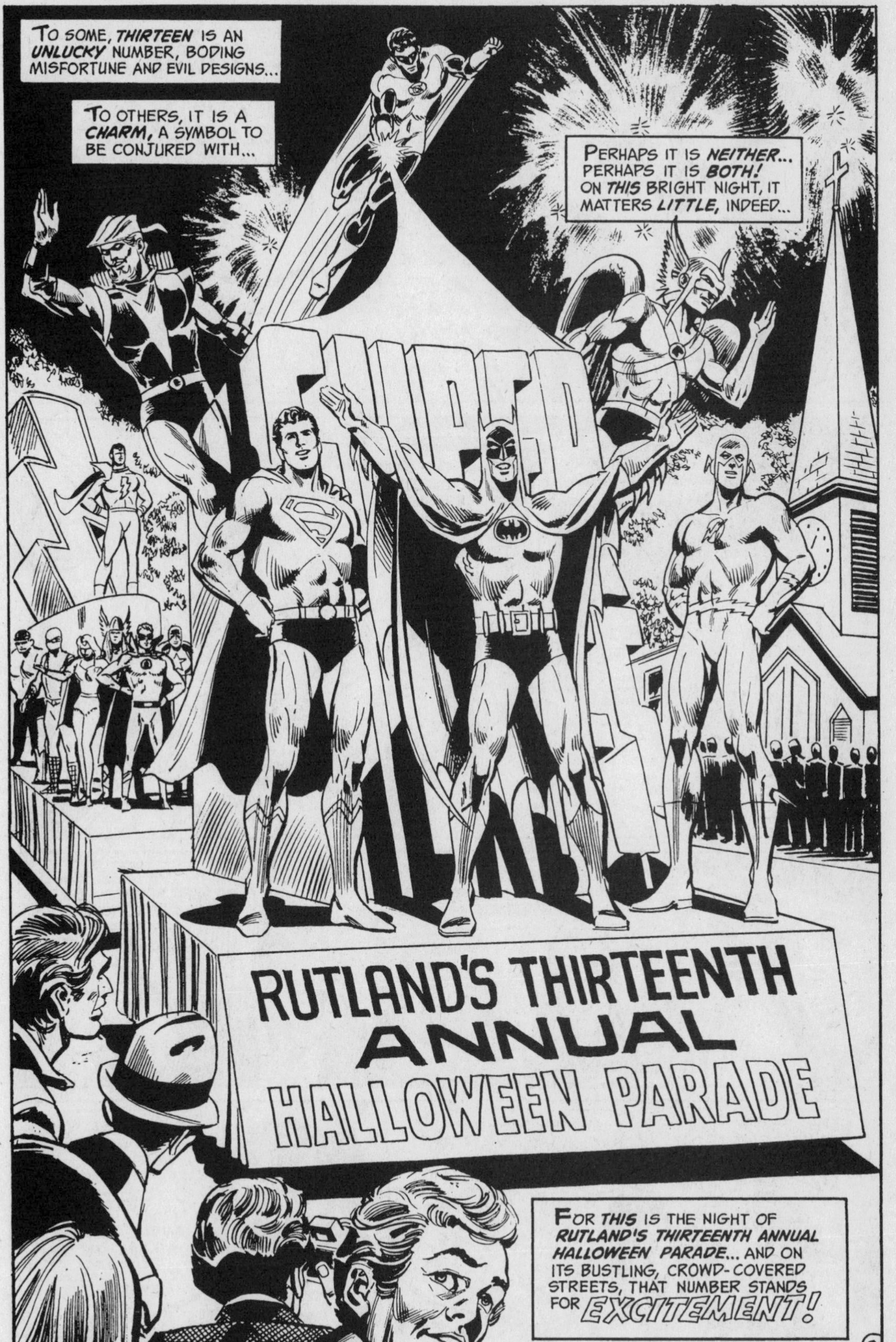

TO SOME, THIRTEEN IS AN UNLUCKY NUMBER, BODING MISFORTUNE AND EVIL DESIGNS...
TO OTHERS, IT IS A CHARM, A SYMBOL TO BE CONJURED WITH...
PERHAPS IT IS NEITHER... PERHAPS IT IS BOTH! ON THIS BRIGHT NIGHT, IT MATTERS LITTLE, INDEED...
RUTLAND'S THIRTEENTH ANNUAL HALLOWEEN PARADE
FOR THIS IS THE NIGHT OF RUTLAND'S THIRTEENTH ANNUAL HALLOWEEN PARADE... AND ON ITS BUSTLING, CROWD-COVERED STREETS, THAT NUMBER STANDS FOR EXCITEMENT!
9

AS THE CHEERFUL PROCESSION WINDS ITS WAY THROUGH TOWN...

QUITE A *FEELING,* ISN'T IT, *BATMAN*-- TO KNOW SO MANY PEOPLE *RESPECT* AND *ADMIRE* YOU?

MAYBE--BUT I'M NEVER SURE IF IT'S *RESPECT* THEY FEEL FOR ME--

--OR *FEAR!*

HEY-- DO YOU FELLOWS HEAR SOMETHING *ODD?* MAYBE IT'S MY *IMAGINATION* BUT--

BLISTERING BUZZARDS! LOOK *BEHIND* US!

THE OTHER *FLOATS*--THEY'RE *GONE!*--VANISHED!

BUT THE *CROWD*-- STILL CHEERING AS IF *NOTHING* HAD HAPPENED!

WELL-- WE WERE *LOOKING* FOR SOMETHING *STRANGE*--

--AND BY *GOD!*--WE'VE *FOUND* IT!

AMAZING! THE ENTIRE ASSEMBLAGE IS COMPLETELY *ENTRANCED!*

FAUST'S HANDIWORK, NO DOUBT!

MAN-- I'VE SEEN PEOPLE *STONED* BEFORE-- BUT THIS IS *RIDICULOUS!*

ARCHER, YOUR SENSE OF "*HUMOR*" IS-- *SICKENING!*

LISTEN, FEATHER-FACE-- I'VE HAD JUST ABOUT *ENOUGH* OF YOU--!

EASY, *ARROW*-- WE HAVE MORE *IMPORTANT* THINGS TO DEAL WITH RIGHT NOW!

I SUGGEST WE *SPLIT UP*--AND *SCOUR* THE COUNTRYSIDE!

WE'LL FIND OUR *ANSWERS* WHEN WE FIND THOSE *FLOATS!*

10

MOMENTS LATER, TWO SWIFTLY-MOVING FIGURES SCOUT THE DENSE *VERMONT* WOODLAND...

FRIEND TO FRIEND, *KATAR**--WHY DO YOU KEEP PUTTING *GREEN ARROW DOWN* THE WAY YOU DO?

I REALLY WISH I *KNEW*, FLASH! THERE'S JUST SOMETHING ABOUT THE MAN THAT *IRRITATES* ME! HE...

* EDITOR'S NOTE: KATAR HOL--HAWKMAN'S NAME ON HIS NATIVE PLANET, THANAGAR!

HANG ON, *HAWKMAN*-- I *HEAR* SOMETHING!

I'LL GO ON *AHEAD*-- CHECK IT OUT!

HEY-- *WAIT* FOR ME!

BUT THE *SCARLET SPEEDSTER* IS ALREADY OUT OF HEARING RANGE--THREADING HIS WAY THROUGH THE BRUSH BLINDING VELOCITY-- UNTIL...

SSFWWNISSHH

UUNNFF!

BA ANG

THE *MODERN MERCURY* STAGGERS TO HIS FEET TO FIND HIMSELF FACING...

THREE OF THE PARADE-GOERS--DRESSED AS *SUPERGIRL*-- *ADAM STRANGE*-- AND--

--COMMANDO AMERICA-- AT YOUR SERVICE!

QUICKLY, FRIENDS--WE MUST DO AS OUR *MASTER* COMMANDS--

FLASH AND HAWKMAN MUST BE *DESTROYED*!

BATMAN WAS *RIGHT*-- WE'VE *FOUND* OUR ANSWERS!

11

APPARENTLY, *FAUST'S DEMONS* HAVE TO INHABIT THE BODIES OF OTHERS TO *SURVIVE* IN OUR WORLD!

--AND THEIR *MAGIC* CAN MAKE THESE *COSTUMED HOST-BODIES* AS *POWERFUL* AS THE HEROES THEY PORTRAY!

RIGHT NOW, SPECULATION ISN'T GONNA GET ME ANYTHING BUT *DEAD!*

THAT RAY-GUN MAY BE A *TOY*--BUT THOSE *ENERGY-BLASTS* ARE FOR *REAL!*

IF I DON'T MOVE TO *STOP* HIM *FAST*--I MAY *NEVER* MOVE AGAIN!

SUDDENLY, THE *WIZARD OF WHIZ* SKIDS TO A *HALT*--

--AND WITH ONE WHIRLING, BLINDING MOTION...

THWUNK

UUFF!

THROWING A *PUNCH* AT THIS SPEED PUTS A STREAM OF *COMPRESSED AIR* IN FRONT OF IT--THAT ALLOWS ME TO *FLATTEN* MY FOE FROM A *DISTANCE!*

NOW I'D BETTER SEE IF *HAWKMAN* NEEDS *HELP!*

BUT AS *THE FLASH* SPRINTS FORWARD, ANOTHER GAUDILY-GARBED FIGURE MOVES WITH ALMOST-EQUAL SPEED...

WE HAVE BEEN GIVEN THE *COMMAND*--

DEATH TO THE JUSTICE LEAGUE!

BTANNG

FLASH IS *DOWN*--AND I'VE GOT MY HANDS FULL TRYING TO OUTFLY THIS *DEMON SUPERGIRL!*

MAYBE *THANAGARIAN RULES OF CHIVALRY* WON'T ALLOW ME TO DEAL PROPERLY WITH *HER*--

BUT THERE *IS* SOMETHING I CAN DO ABOUT THAT *STAR-SPANGLED ASSASSIN* DOWN THERE!

12

AT THE *WINGED WONDER'S* COMMAND, THE AIR IS SUDDENLY ALIVE WITH THE SOUND OF FEATHERED FURY...

÷WHEET!÷ ÷WHEET!÷ PROTECT *FLASH* FROM THE *EVIL ONE*, MY FRIENDS!

WHAT MANNER OF MADNESS--?

BUT AS *HAWKMAN* COMMANDS HIS AVIAN ARMY...

THE *MASTER* SAYS YOU MUST *DIE!*

WHAT--?

FOOL! I LET MYSELF BECOME *DISTRACTED!* IF "SUPERGIRL" DAMAGES MY *WING-CONTROLS*, I'LL...

...FALL!

RRRIPP

WE HAVE DONE AS COMMANDED! NOW WE RETURN TO THE *MASTER!*

TH-THEY'RE *FADING AWAY*-- AND I'M TOO WEAK TO *STOP* THEM!

CAN'T *MOVE*-- FEEL *WEAK*--! SOMETHING'S *WRONG*-- WE NEED *HELP!*

WE *HAVE* HELP, HAWKMAN... LOOK!

THE-- *PHANTOM STRANGER!*

OVER *HERE*, FRIEND-- QUICKLY! WE *NEED* YOU!

13

BUT, AMAZINGLY, THE BLACK-CLOAKED WANDERER *IGNORES* THE TWO SPRAWLED HEROES--

--PAUSES FOR ONLY AN INSTANT TO RE-TRIEVE SOMETHING FROM THE MATTED FOREST FLOOR...

STRANGER-- *HELP* US-- PLEASE--

-- THEN IS *GONE* AGAIN INTO THE SHADOWS!

HELP-- US--!

AND SOON--ALL IS *SILENT!*

WHILE ELSEWHERE...

SPLENDID! THINGS GO ACCORDING TO SCHEDULE-- *EXACTLY!*

TWO *JUSTICE LEAGUERS DOWN*-- AND *FOUR* MORE TO GO!

THIS WILL BE A MOST *ENJOYABLE* EVENING, INDEED!

AND MILES FROM WHERE HIS TWO COMPANIONS FELL, *THE BATMAN* FINDS HIMSELF ENGAGED IN SHOCKINGLY-SIMILAR COMBAT...

THIS BARGAIN-BASEMENT *WEB-SLINGER* HAS ALL THE POWERS OF THE *REAL THING!*

IF HE SNARES ME IN THAT STICKY *NETTING*-- I'M *FINISHED!*

14

FOOL! IT WILL AVAIL YOU *LITTLE* TO DEFY ME! YOU MERELY PROLONG THE *INEVITABLE!*

MY *BATARANG*-- LOST IN THE TREES! BETTER COME UP WITH SOMETHING ELSE... *FAST!*

SSHWWIICCKKT

SO I'D BETTER GIVE HIM SOMETHING *ELSE* TO WORRY ABOUT!

HOLD STILL, BATMAN-- THE *MASTER* HAS DECREED...

HUH?

LOOKS LIKE YOU COULD USE A *HAND*, OLD FRIEND!

ONLY IF IT COMES WITHOUT THE *GAG-LINE!*

THAT WAS A PUN WORTHY OF *ROBIN!*

GREEN LANTERN!? THEN MY TASK IS *TWICE* AS VITAL...

...FOR I MUST *DESTROY* YOU *BOTH!*

WHA--? CAUGHT MY *FREE HAND* IN THAT *GLOP!*

BETTER SWAT HIM DOWN--BEFORE HE MESSES UP THE WHOLE *UNIFORM!*

THE *GUARDIANS* HATE TO *REPLACE* THE THINGS!

HEY--IT APPEARS *WEB-HEAD* HAS *FRIENDS!*

15

JUDGING BY THE COSTUME, WE'RE FACING A POOR MAN'S VERSION OF THE *NORSE THUNDERGOD!*

AND SOMETHING TELLS ME HE USES THAT HAMMER FOR *MORE* THAN DRIVING *NAILS!*

STILL-- A POWER-RING *CAGE* SHOULD TAKE HIM OUT OF *ACTION!*

BUT AS THE *EMERALD GLADIATOR* MOVES TO CAPTURE HIS FOE...

HUH? THE *HAMMER*--! SMASHING THROUGH THE CAGE--! *THWID*

UUNNFF!

GL IS OUT! GOT TO *FLATTEN* THE "*THUNDER GOD*"--

--BEFORE HE DOES THE SAME TO *ME!*

GREAT GOING, *BATMAN!* ANYTHING I CAN DO TO *HELP?*

WHO--?

WHOK

UUNNHH!

ANYTHING I CAN DO TO HELP...THE *MASTER*, THAT IS!? HA HA HA HA!

ROBIN--? YOU--!

16

HAUNTING LAUGHTER STILL ON THEIR LIPS, THE DEMON-INFESTED FORMS FADE SWIFTLY AWAY-- AND THEN...

HELP US--! I--FEEL SO-- WEAK--!

SOMETHING-- DRAINING MY LIFE-FORCE--! YOU MUST-- HELP--! P-PLEASE...

FOUR HAVE FALLEN-- AND LITTLE TIME REMAINS!

UNLESS ALL SIX JUSTICE LEAGUERS PERISH AT THE STROKE OF MIDNIGHT-- MY OUT-WORLD DEMONS WILL BE FORCED TO RETURN WHENCE THEY CAME!

AND I WOULDN'T WANT THAT TO HAPPEN...

NO, I WOULDN'T LIKE THAT AT ALL!

ELSEWHERE-- THREE RECENTLY-ENTRANCED VISITORS TO THE GREEN MOUNTAIN STATE PAUSE FOR THE BRIEFEST OF MOMENTS...

I CAN'T UNDERSTAND WHERE GLYNIS DISAPPEARED TO--

DON'T LOOK AT ME, LEN! THAT'S SOME STRANGE LADY YOU GOT!

SHE'S OBVIOUSLY NOT IN TOWN! LET'S HEAD BACK TO FAGAN'S PLACE!

MAYBE SHE WANDERED OVER THERE!

17

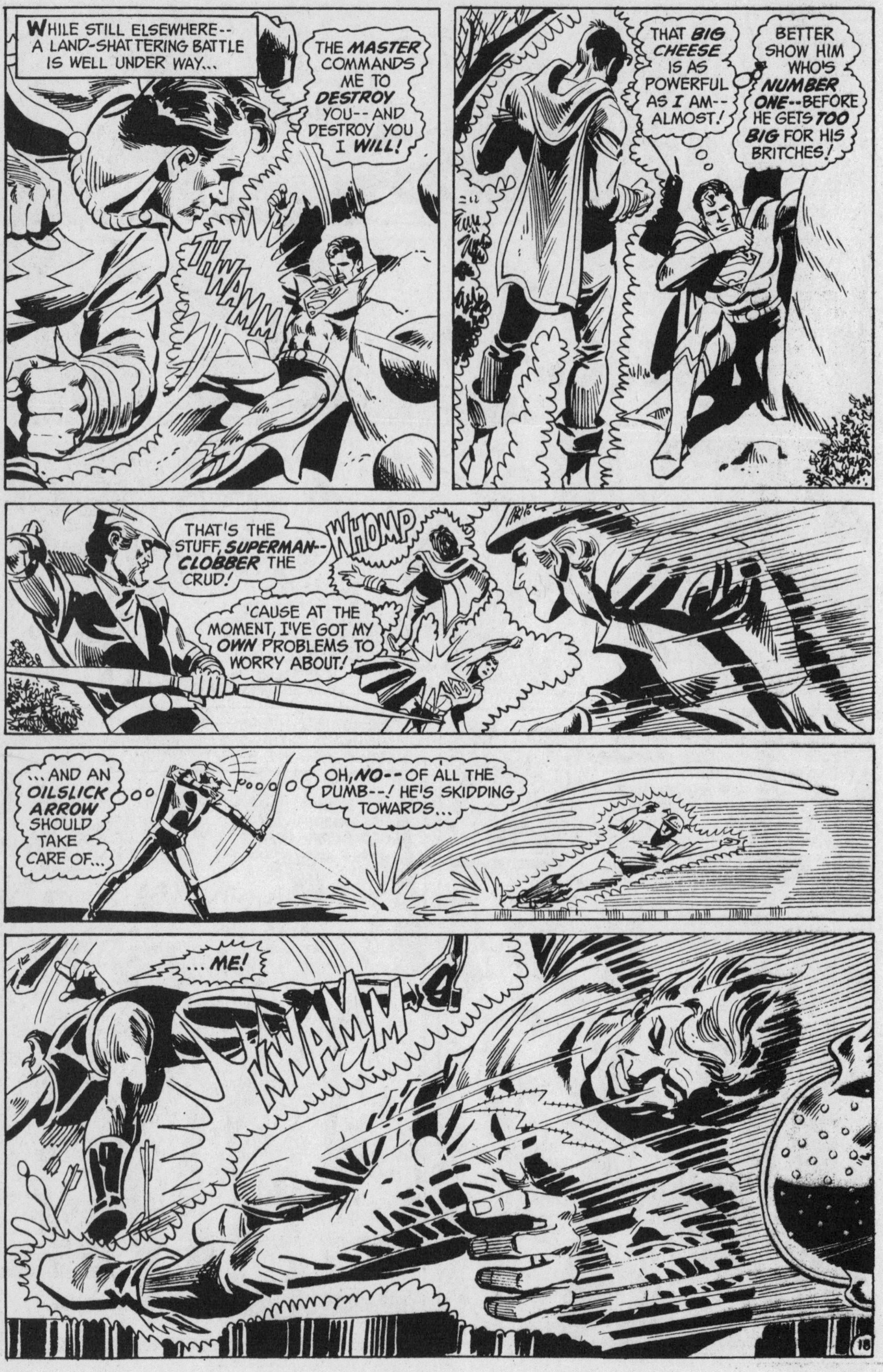
WHILE STILL ELSEWHERE-- A LAND-SHATTERING BATTLE IS WELL UNDER WAY...
THE MASTER COMMANDS ME TO DESTROY YOU-- AND DESTROY YOU I WILL!
THWAMM
THAT BIG CHEESE IS AS POWERFUL AS I AM-- ALMOST!
BETTER SHOW HIM WHO'S NUMBER ONE--BEFORE HE GETS TOO BIG FOR HIS BRITCHES!
THAT'S THE STUFF, SUPERMAN-- CLOBBER THE CRUD!
WHOMP
'CAUSE AT THE MOMENT, I'VE GOT MY OWN PROBLEMS TO WORRY ABOUT!
...AND AN OILSLICK ARROW SHOULD TAKE CARE OF...
OH, NO-- OF ALL THE DUMB--! HE'S SKIDDING TOWARDS...
...ME!
KWAMM
18

G.A. AND HIS OPPONENT ARE *BOTH* FLAT ON THEIR BACKS-- AND THERE'S *NOTHING* I CAN *DO* ABOUT IT!

BIG RED IS AS STRONG AS I AM-- AND NEITHER OF US CAN GAIN AN INCH AGAINST THE OTHER!

THERE MUST BE *SOME* WAY TO END THIS STALEMATE-- BUT *WHAT?*

LOOK CLOSELY AT YOUR ADVERSARY'S LIPS, *SUPERMAN*, AND YOU WILL *DISCOVER* THE WAY...

...AS THE RED-GARBED FIGURE MUTTERS AN ENCHANTMENT THAT WAS OLD WHEN THE EARTH WAS YOUNG...

...AND DRAWS A BOLT OF *MAGIC ENERGY* OUT OF THE BLACKENED SKY...

UUNNHH!

THE *MAN OF STEEL* PLUMMETS TO EARTH LIKE A WOUNDED EAGLE-- TO LIE SPRAWLED AND UNCONSCIOUS AT HIS COMPANION'S SIDE...

...AND THE TWO GLOWING FORMS WHO BROUGHT THEM TO THIS FATE FADE QUIETLY FROM SIGHT...

...LEAVING AN EQUALLY MYSTERIOUS FIGURE STANDING IN THEIR PLACE...

19

ALL SIX ARE *DOWN!* THE MIGHTY *JUSTICE LEAGUE* HAS *FALLEN*--

--AND FROM THE ASHES OF THEIR *DEFEAT* SHALL RISE THE CORNERSTONE OF A *NEW* EMPIRE...

THE GLORIOUS EMPIRE OF-- *FELIX FAUST!*

...ALMOST LIKE *GLYNIS* VANISHED-- LIKE SHE WAS SWALLOWED UP BY SOME *MALEVOLENT FORCE!*

YOU KNOW--YOU *TALK* JUST LIKE YOU *WRITE!*

YEAH! C'MON, MAN--THIS IS A *BIG* HOUSE! YOUR LADY COULD BE *ANYWHERE!*

THERE'RE STILL PLENTY OF ROOMS *UPSTAIRS* WE HAVEN'T CHECKED!

ONE QUEST CONTINUES-- AS ANOTHER NEARS ITS END...

RETURN WITH US TO THAT QUIET RUTLAND CROSSROADS ONCE AGAIN-- AS THE *WITCHING HOUR* DRAWS NIGH...

...AND A SILENT, INK-GARBED WANDERER PREPARES HIMSELF FOR THE URGENT TASK THAT LIES AHEAD...

ONCE MORE THE *MIDNIGHT* COMES-- AND THE OLD TOWER BELLS MOURN ITS PASSING WITH THEIR RINGING SONG...

...WITH EACH CLANGING NOTE, A *NAME* ESCAPES THE DARK-EYED STRANGER'S LIPS--AND A CAREFULLY PILFERED *POSSESSION* IS THROWN TO THE CURLING WIND...

BONG GREEN LANTERN

BONG GREEN ARROW

BONG

BATMAN

BONG! FLASH

BONG SUPERMAN

BONG HAWKMAN

20

AT LAST, THE CLANGOR DWINDLES TO A SIGH...

...AND THERE IS SUDDEN MOVEMENT AT THE ROADWAY'S EDGE...

WHA-WHAT *HAPPENED* TO US? WHAT'S *HE* DOING HERE?

YOU--*STRANGER!* I THOUGHT YOU WERE A *FRIEND!* BUT YOU *BETRAYED* US--!

NO, *BATMAN--* I *SAVED* YOU--

--FROM THE *MYSTIC MACHINATIONS* OF *FELIX FAUST!*

YOU HAD BEEN *ENCHANTED--* THE SIX OF YOU -- BY A SPELL OF IMMINENT *DEATH!*

TO *COUNTERACT* THE SPELL, I REQUIRED A *PERSONAL POSSESSION* FROM EACH OF YOU--BUT IT COULD *NOT* BE AN ITEM *FREELY* GIVEN!

SINCE *FAUST'S* MAGIC HAD CONDEMNED YOUR *DEMON-BATTLE* TO *FAILURE,* I DEVOTED MY EFFORTS TO THE ULTIMATE *SALVATION* OF YOUR *LIVES--*

--AND YOU DEFINITELY *SUCCEEDED!*

WITH YOUR *REVIVAL--* AND THE REGAINING OF YOUR *LIFE-ENERGIES--* FAUST'S MINIONS CANNOT REMAIN WITHIN THEIR HOST-BODIES FOR *LONG!*

AND AS PROOF OF THE *PHANTOM STRANGER'S* WORDS...

WHAT--? SOMETHING'S GONE *WRONG!* THE DEMONS ARE *FLEEING* THEIR HOSTS!

THERE IS ONLY *ONE* POSSIBLE REASON FOR *THAT!*

THE *JUSTICE LEAGUE OF AMERICA* STILL LIVES!

THEY'LL BE COMING *AFTER* ME NOW! GOT TO GET AWAY BEFORE...

SLAM

MISTER--*DON'T!* WHATEVER YOUR *PROBLEM* IS... THERE HAS TO BE A *BETTER* WAY--

PLEASE-- DON'T KILL YOURSELF!

21

BUT AS THE TRIO LUNGES FORWARD TO STOP THE INTENDED "SUICIDE"...

TOO LATE! HE *JUMPED*--!

AND LOOK WHERE HE *JUMPED* TO!

MY *CAR*--! THAT *DUDE* IS STEALING MY *CAR*!

MY MAGIC ENERGIES ARE ALMOST *DRAINED*! I'D BEST LEAVE BY THE MOST *INCONSPICUOUS* MEANS POSSIBLE!

WITH HIS LAST IOTA OF SUPERNATURAL STRENGTH, THE *SINISTER SORCERER* JUMPS THE CAR'S IGNITION--AND...

WE *BLEW* IT! HE'S *GETTING AWAY*--MUFFLER AND ALL!

MY *CAR*--! MY POOR, FREAKIN' *CAR*--!

HEY--IT'S 12:02 A.M.! WHAT A *LOUSY* WAY TO START A *NEW DAY*!

AND AS THE DUSTY OLD HEAP RUMBLES AWAY DOWN THE ROAD...

MY POOR *HEAD*--! W-WHAT'S BEEN *GOING ON* AROUND HERE?

GLYNIS!?! SWEETHEART! WE'VE BEEN LOOKING ALL OVER FOR YOU!

--AND WEARING OUR *FEET* OFF!

WHERE IN BLAZES HAVE YOU *BEEN*?

I-I DON'T *KNOW*--! I JUST SUDDENLY FOUND MYSELF WANDERING THROUGH THAT CLEARING OVER THERE...

...AND I COULD SWEAR I SAW A... A *BATTLE* RAGING!

A *BATTLE*? NO--MORE LIKE A *WAR*...

...AS THE FORCES OF ORDER AND CHAOS CLASH ON THE VERDANT VERMONT COUNTRYSIDE--WITH PURE *PANDEMONIUM* THE RESULT!

CRASH

SPLAT

THWUDD

BLAMM

22

WHILE, ON A NEARBY *RUTLAND* STREET, ANOTHER PLAN OF ACTION HAS BEEN VENTURED... AND *LOST*...

ALL RIGHT, BUDDY-- PULL THIS MUSEUM- PIECE OVER TO THE SIDE OF THE *ROAD*!

MY SUPERNATURAL POWERS... TOTALLY *EXHAUSTED*! NO WAY TO *FIGHT BACK*!

ONLY ONE THING TO *DO*--!

OKAY, OFFICERS-- I'M *YOURS*! PUT THE *'CUFFS* ON!

I JUST CAN'T FIGURE OUT WHAT TIPPED YOU OFF TO ME!

I DON'T KNOW WHAT YOU'RE *TALKIN'* ABOUT!

YA GOT A FAULTY *MUFFLER* ON THIS THING AND WE JUST PULLED YOU OVER TO CHECK IT OUT!

HA HA HA HA HA HA HA

MOMENTS LATER...

GONE-- ALL OF THEM...

...AND *GREEN LANTERN* SEALED THE DIMENSIONAL PORTAL BEHIND THEM!

GENTLEMEN, IT APPEARS YOU FARED *WELL*!

THE *PHANTOM STRANGER*--! JUST THE MAN WE WANT TO SEE!

WE'VE BEEN TALKING IT OVER AMONG OURSELVES--AND--WELL-- WE'D LIKE YOU TO *JOIN* THE *JUSTICE LEAGUE*!

AN *HONOR*, SUPERMAN-- ONE I'M NOT ENTIRELY CERTAIN I *DESERVE*!

YOU LET *US* DECIDE THAT, PAL!

WE'RE GOING TO *VOTE* ON IT NOW!

THERE IS A MOMENT OF FURIOUS DISCUSSION...

...AND WITHIN SECONDS...

WE'VE *DECIDED*! PHANTOM STRANGER, YOU ARE NOW A *MEMBER* OF THE...

SOMEHOW I THINK HE *KNOWS*, SUPERMAN... AND THAT WE'LL SEE HIM *AGAIN*...

WELL, CAN YOU *BEAT* THAT? HE'S *GONE*-- DIDN'T EVEN WAIT AROUND LONG ENOUGH TO FIND OUT IF HE *MADE* IT!

...IF *EVER* WE *NEED* HIM!

23

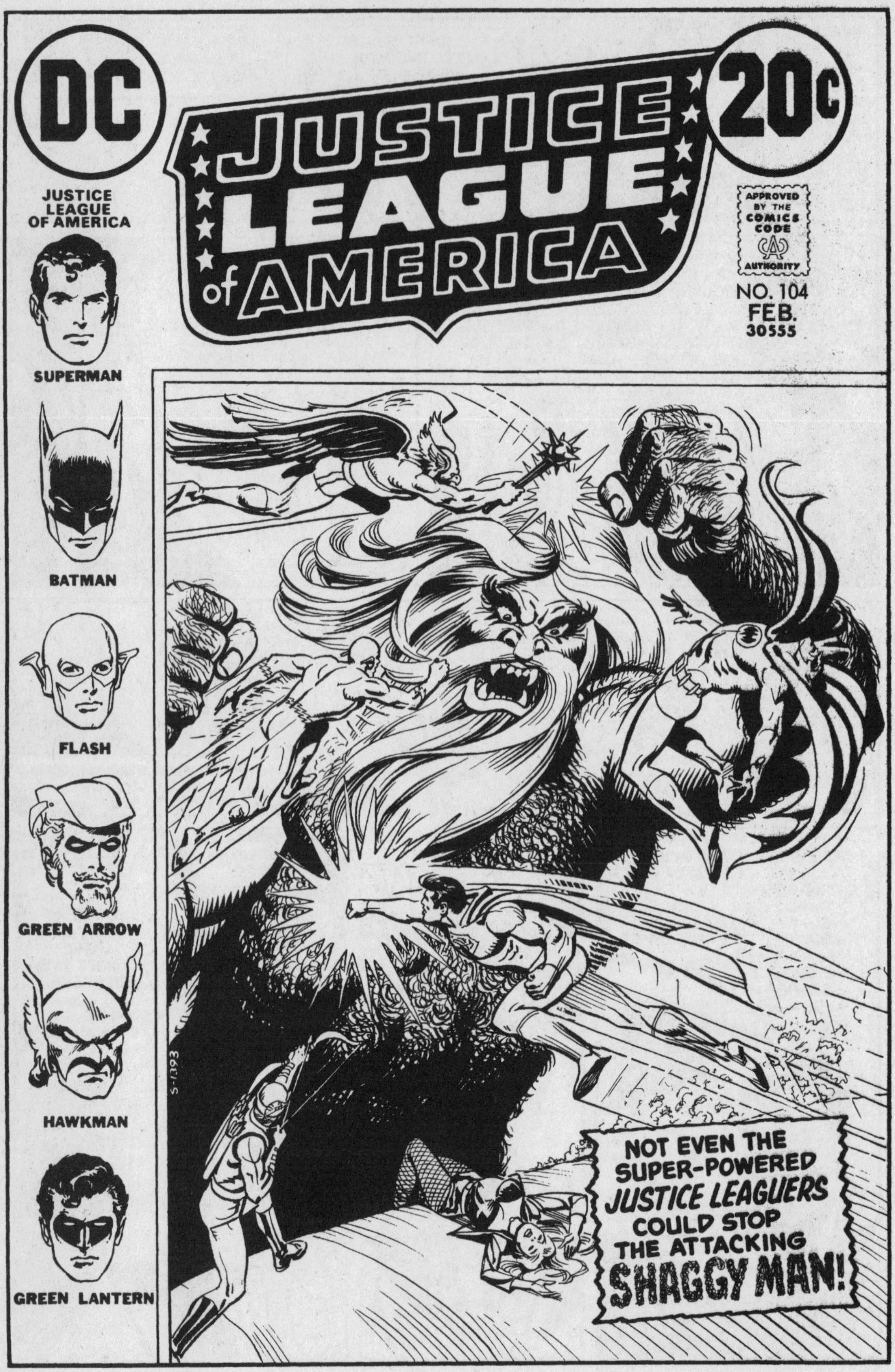
DC
JUSTICE LEAGUE of AMERICA
20¢
JUSTICE LEAGUE OF AMERICA
SUPERMAN
BATMAN
FLASH
GREEN ARROW
HAWKMAN
GREEN LANTERN
APPROVED BY THE COMICS CODE AUTHORITY
NO. 104
FEB.
30555
NOT EVEN THE SUPER-POWERED JUSTICE LEAGUERS COULD STOP THE ATTACKING SHAGGY MAN!

IMMORTALITY: HOW DOES ONE PASS THE TIME?

FOR ETERNALLY IMMOBILE *HECTOR HAMMOND,* ARCH-FOE OF *GREEN LANTERN,* THE TIME IS SPENT--*WORLD-TRAVELING...*

...*FOR* THE PRISON CELL THAT HOLDS HIS IMMOBILE *BODY* IS HELPLESS TO CONTAIN HIS *FUTURE-EVOLVED MIND...*

CAIRO...   PARIS...

MOSCOW...

...THE MOST SCENIC SPOTS ON EARTH ARE HIS TO "VISIT"...

...INCLUDING ONE PARTICULAR SPOT ORBITING 22,300 MILES *ABOVE* THE EARTH...

S-1362

...THE GLEAMING SATELLITE HEADQUARTERS OF THE...

JUSTICE ☆☆☆ LEAGUE ☆☆☆ of AMERICA

...AND IF THERE IS NOTHING FURTHER TO *DISCUSS,* LET'S GET DOWN TO THE *MATTER AT HAND...*

EVERYONE PRESENT-- *EXCEPT* THE ONE I HATE MOST--

--*THE GREEN LANTERN!* THERE *MUST* BE A WAY TO *DESTROY* HIM--

--AND PERHAPS I CAN *FIND* IT IN THE MOST *UN-LIKELY* PLACE OF ALL...

1

...THE *JUSTICE LEAGUE'S* OWN *LIBRARY!*

CONTAINED HERE ARE THE *DETAILS* OF EVERY *CASE* THEY'VE BEEN INVOLVED IN--EVERY *VILLAIN* THEY'VE *FOUGHT*...

...*DESPERO...KANJAR RO...AMOS FORTUNE... AMAZO...THE KEY...* THE *JLA* HAS DEFFATED THEM AGAIN AND AGAIN...

...BUT THERE IS *ONE* --ONE VERY *SPECIAL* ONE--WHO COULD *SUCCEED* WHERE THE OTHERS ALL *FAILED*...

...*PROVIDED* HE HAS THE *PROPER* GUIDANCE!

THE TUNDRA LAND OF NORTHERN *CHILE,* BLEAK, UNRELENTING-- BARREN OF ANY *LIVING THING*...

...SAVE FOR A *BIZARRE MENTAL IMAGE* THAT FLOATS ABOVE THE CRUEL TERRAIN...

THE GROUND *TREMBLES*--! HE'S *HERE,* ALL RIGHT-- I'M *CERTAIN* OF IT--

--AND A LITTLE *MENTAL MANIPULATION* WILL *PROVE* IT!

KWAMM

KRUMMP

2

*E*ARTHQUAKE: A RENDING AND SHIFTING OF THE PLANET'S CRUST -- MOTHER NATURE *CHANGING* HER MIND...

...BUT DON'T BLAME THE GOOD LADY FOR *THIS* UPHEAVAL -- BLAME INSTEAD THE TWO GREAT BROWN-TUFTED *HANDS* THAT THRUST UP OUT OF THE DARK SOIL AS IF CLAWING FOR THE LIGHT...

...FOLLOWED BY AN EQUALLY AWESOME *FIGURE* THAT SHATTERS THE LANDSCAPE LIKE THE CHEAPEST *PARCHMENT*...

PERFECT! THE CREATURE IS ABSOLUTELY *PERFECT!*

...A FIGURE WHOSE ONLY THOUGHT IS *SLAUGHTER!*

BEWARE, YE OF THE *JUSTICE LEAGUE*...

"THE SHAGGY MAN WILL GET YOU IF YOU DON'T WATCH OUT!"

REDISCOVER A FANTASTIC FOE WITH *LEN WEIN* - WRITER *DICK DILLIN & DICK GIORDANO* - ARTISTS *JULIUS SCHWARTZ* - EDITOR

③

HECTOR HAMMOND STUDIES THE MISSHAPEN MONSTROSITY THAT STANDS CONFUSED, UNSURE OF ITS SURROUNDINGS--

--AND HIS COMPUTER-SWIFT MIND RE-EXAMINES HIS LIBRARY FINDINGS...

HE "SEES" SCIENCE GONE WILD--AS AN INVENTOR ATTEMPTS TO CREATE A LIVING PLASTIC ORGANISM--AND PRODUCES A MONSTER INSTEAD...

...AN ALMOST MINDLESS MONSTER WHOSE ONLY IMPULSE IS TO DESTROY ANYTHING THAT MOVES...

...AN IMPULSE THAT LEADS TO INEVITABLE CONFLICT WITH THE JUSTICE LEAGUE --AND FINAL IMPRISONMENT IN A SPECIALLY-PREPARED PIT IN NORTHERN CHILE...

BUT THE IMMORTAL ONE'S RECOLLECTIONS ARE QUICKLY DISRUPTED AS...

GURRRRKK.!

WHA--? MY PAWN'S BEEN DISTRACTED-- BY THE MOTION OF THAT PASSING BIRD--!

I'D BEST PROCEED WITH MY PLAN--BEFORE I LOSE CONTROL OF HIM!

FOR A MOMENT, THE MENTAL IMAGE KNITS ITS BROW IN CONCENTRATION--THEN ...

GONE! I'VE SPED MY "SPECIAL DELIVERY PACKAGE" ON ITS WAY! PHASE ONE OF MY PLAN IS COMPLETE!

NOW THE FUN BEGINS!

4

WHILE, IN THE *JUSTICE LEAGUE* SANCTUARY, HARDLY A MINUTE HAS PASSED...

...A GOOD *CLEAN-UP!* AQUAMAN-- CANARY--YOU'LL TAKE THE *TROPHY ROOM!* FLASH WILL DUST UP WITHIN THE OUTER *RIM!*

GREEN ARROW-- HAWKMAN-- YOU CAN TEND TO THE *LIFE-SUPPORT SYSTEMS*-- WHILE *SUPERMAN* SCRUBS UP *OUT-SIDE* THE SATELLITE!

ATOM AND I WILL ATTEND TO THE *GYM!*

LOOKS LIKE I HAVE IT *EASIER* THAN EVERYONE ELSE--

--I'VE BEEN TEAMED UP WITH A *FEATHER-DUSTER!*

NO COMMENT!

MOMENTS LATER...

FASCINATING! I'VE BEEN WANTING TO *BROWSE* THROUGH THIS ROOM SINCE JOINING THE JLA--BUT NEVER REALLY HAD THE *CHANCE!*

THEN PERMIT ME TO TAKE YOU ON *AQUAMAN'S HANDY-DANDY, SUPER-SPECTACU-LAR, TOTALLY-PORTABLE, TROPHY ROOM TOUR!*

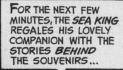

FOR THE NEXT FEW MINUTES, THE *SEA KING* REGALES HIS LOVELY COMPANION WITH THE STORIES *BEHIND* THE SOUVENIRS...

...THE ADVENTURES WITH *PROF. FORTUNE'S* WHEEL OF MISFORTUNE...THE *"ATOM"* BOMB...DR. LIGHT'S LIGHT-WAVE WEAPON... AMAZO... KANJAR RO'S AWESOME GAMMA GONG...

UNTIL FINALLY...

...AND *THIS* IS THE *SHAGGY MAN!* I WASN'T IN ON *THAT* ONE--BUT THE REST OF THE GANG TOLD ME ALL *ABOUT* IT! THEY BATTLED HIM DOWN IN...

WAITAMINNIT! SOMETHING'S VERY *WRONG* HERE--!

--WE *NEVER* HAD A *STATUE* OF THE SHAGGY MAN!

5

GRUGGHH!

THWAK

THAT REPLICA'S *ALIVE*-- AND *KICKING!*

BETTER PUT IT *OUT OF ACTION*-- *FAST!*

BUT AS THE *BLACK CANARY* LAUNCHES A POWERHOUSE KICK TOWARDS THE HAIRY HEAD...

UUNNHH--THAT *SHAGGY* THING MOVES *FASTER* THAN I THOUGHT--

--AND IT HAS A *GRIP* LIKE *GREEN ARROW!*

THE CANARY'S IN *TROUBLE!* THAT BRUTE WILL *BREAK* HER LEGS--

--UNLESS *I* CAN BREAK ITS *HOLD* ON HER!

KFNAMM

BULL'S-EYE! THAT HAIRY HORROR HAS *DROPPED* THE *CANARY!*

--BUT NOW IT'S COMING AFTER *ME* AGAIN!

THE *SHAGGY MAN* HAS US OUTCLASSED--*PHYSICALLY!* WHAT WE NEED NOW IS A--*WEAPON!*

--AND THIS ROOM IS JUST THE PLACE TO *FIND* ONE!

6

CRISP BLUE EYES DARTING SWIFTLY ABOUT THE CHAMBER, THE *BLACK CANARY* SUDDENLY SPIES...

--THE *RADIATION-RIFLE* USED BY *THE KEY!* MAYBE *THIS* WILL SINGE HIS BEARD!

GURRRKK!

KRASSHH

DESPERATELY, THE *BLONDE BOMBSHELL* TRIGGERS THE BIZARRE WEAPON, BUT...

NO GOOD! THE RADIATION DOESN'T EVEN *FAZE* HIM!

BUT I THINK I SEE SOMETHING THAT *WILL!*

--THE *LIGHT-WAVE WEAPON!* IF I CAN MANAGE TO *ACTIVATE* IT, IT WILL TELEPORT THE *SHAGGY MAN* TO SOME FAR-DISTANT *PLANET!*

KEEP HIM *OCCUPIED,* BLACK CANARY--WHILE I FIGURE OUT HOW THIS CONTRAPTION *WORKS!*

RIGHT--BUT *DON'T* TAKE YOUR TIME!

BLAST! AQUAMAN IS LIABLE TO *SUCCEED* WITH THAT CURSED DEVICE--

--UNLESS *I* TAKE A HAND TO *STOP* HIM!

NOW, *CANARY*--LURE HIM OVER *HERE!* I'VE GOT THE MACHINE WARMED UP--AND READY TO *FIRE!*

JUST GET HIM WITHIN *RANGE* AND...

7

BUT BEFORE THE *SEA KING* CAN COMPLETE HIS URGENT CRY, A *SOUND* COMES TO THE ROOM...

--A SOUND THAT IS MORE LIKE *MURDER* THAN MELODY...

THE *GAMMA-GONG--!* SOMEONE'S TOLLED THE *GAMMA GONG--*

--AND THE *VIBRATIONS* ARE TEARING ME APART!

AT LAST, THE SOUND *FADES*--TAKING THE CONSCIOUSNESS OF *AQUAMAN* AND THE *BLACK CANARY* WITH IT AS IT GOES...

I MENTALLY ALTERED THE GONG'S *PITCH* TO BRING *UN-CONSCIOUSNESS* RATHER THAN *IMMOBILITY!*

TOO BAD I COULD NOT TOLL IT *LOUD* ENOUGH TO EFFECT THE *OTHERS*--BUT THAT MIGHT HAVE AFFECTED THE *SHAGGY MAN* AS WELL!

MOVE ON, SHAGGY ONE--THERE IS NOTHING MORE FOR YOU *HERE--*

--AND YOU HAVE *OTHER* BATTLES TO FIGHT!

WHILE, IN THE *JLA'S* GYMNASIUM...

LOOK AT THE *DUST* IN THIS PLACE--! CAN'T IMAGINE WHERE IT CAME FROM!

BUT THIS IS PROBABLY THE *LEAST-USED* ROOM IN THE ENTIRE SATELLITE!

YEAH--WHO HAS TIME TO WORK OUT *HERE*--WHEN WE GET SO MUCH PRACTICE *IN THE FIELD?*

WELL, ATOM--NOW'S AS GOOD A TIME AS ANY TO *START!*

HEY--WAIT FOR *ME!*

BUT BEFORE THE *TINY TITAN* CAN JOIN HIS CAPED COMPANION...

WHAT--?!

LOOKS LIKE WE'VE GOT *COMPANY!*

8

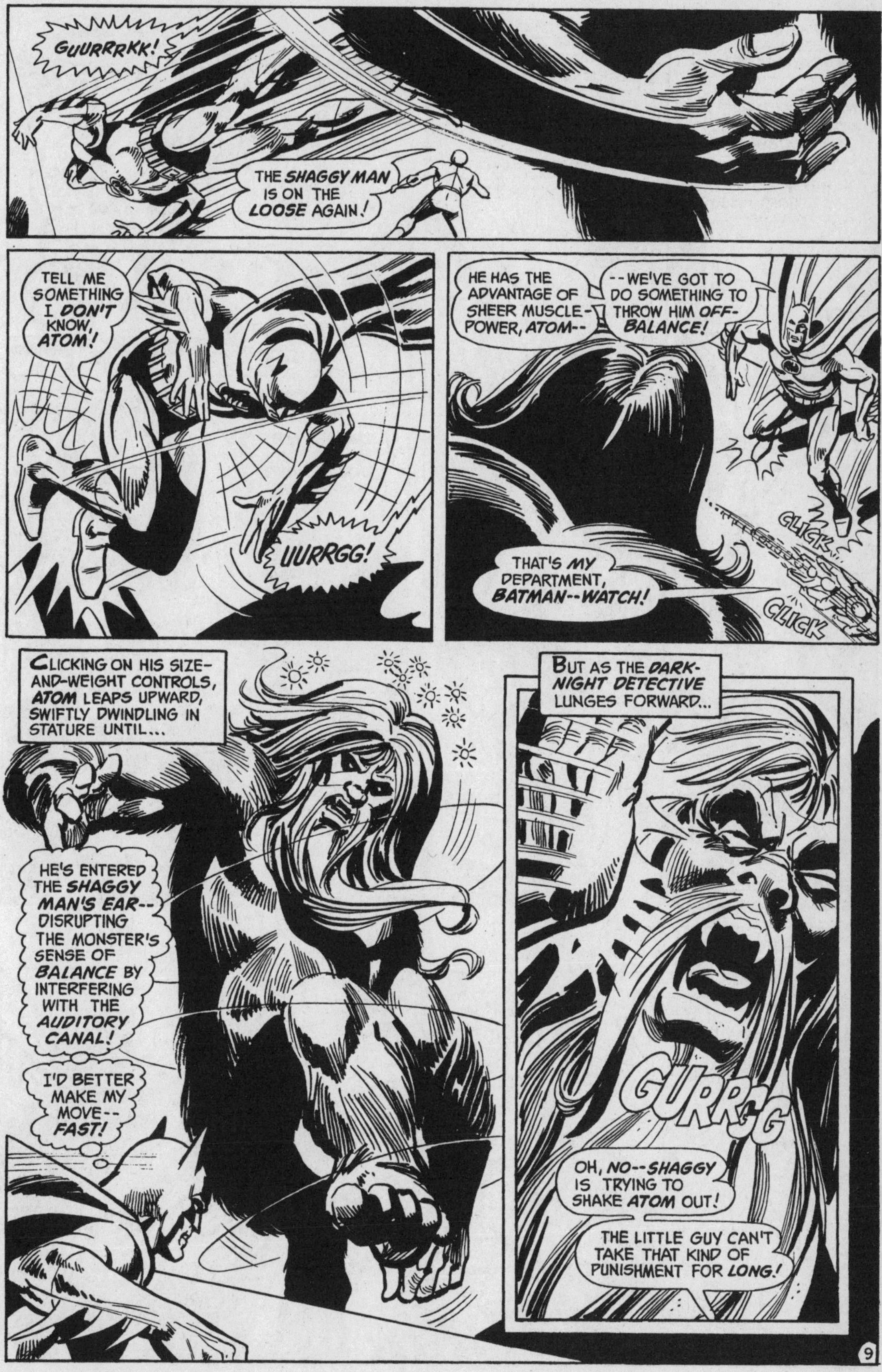
GUURRRKK!
THE SHAGGY MAN IS ON THE LOOSE AGAIN!
TELL ME SOMETHING I DON'T KNOW, ATOM!
UURRGG!
HE HAS THE ADVANTAGE OF SHEER MUSCLE-POWER, ATOM--
--WE'VE GOT TO DO SOMETHING TO THROW HIM OFF-BALANCE!
CLICK
THAT'S MY DEPARTMENT, BATMAN--WATCH!
CLICK
CLICKING ON HIS SIZE-AND-WEIGHT CONTROLS, ATOM LEAPS UPWARD, SWIFTLY DWINDLING IN STATURE UNTIL...
HE'S ENTERED THE SHAGGY MAN'S EAR--DISRUPTING THE MONSTER'S SENSE OF BALANCE BY INTERFERING WITH THE AUDITORY CANAL!
I'D BETTER MAKE MY MOVE--FAST!
BUT AS THE DARK-NIGHT DETECTIVE LUNGES FORWARD...
GURRGG
OH, NO--SHAGGY IS TRYING TO SHAKE ATOM OUT!
THE LITTLE GUY CAN'T TAKE THAT KIND OF PUNISHMENT FOR LONG!
9

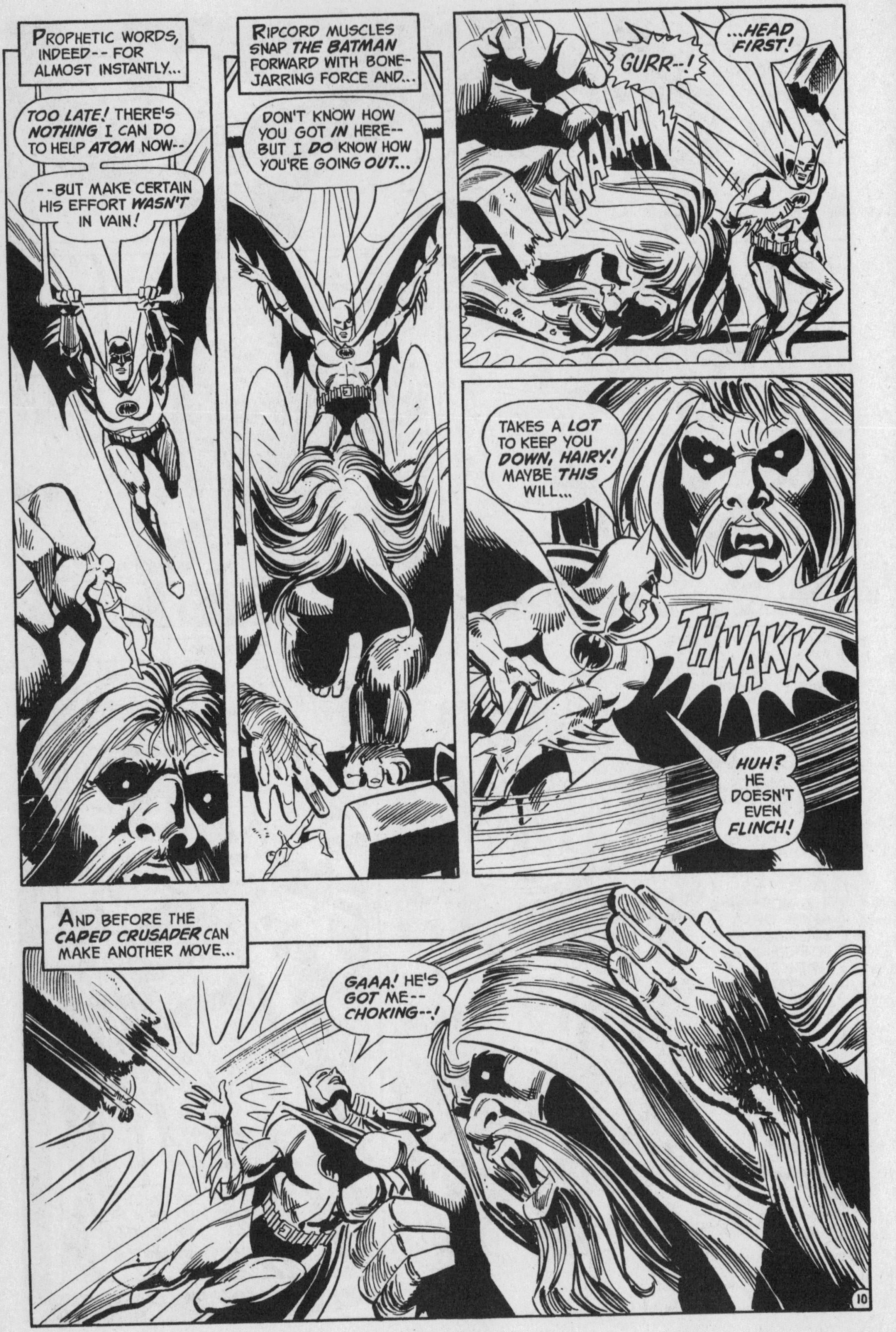
PROPHETIC WORDS, INDEED-- FOR ALMOST INSTANTLY...
TOO LATE! THERE'S NOTHING I CAN DO TO HELP ATOM NOW--
--BUT MAKE CERTAIN HIS EFFORT WASN'T IN VAIN!
RIPCORD MUSCLES SNAP THE BATMAN FORWARD WITH BONE-JARRING FORCE AND...
DON'T KNOW HOW YOU GOT IN HERE-- BUT I DO KNOW HOW YOU'RE GOING OUT...
...HEAD FIRST!
GURR--!
KWAMM
TAKES A LOT TO KEEP YOU DOWN, HAIRY! MAYBE THIS WILL...
THWAKK
HUH? HE DOESN'T EVEN FLINCH!
AND BEFORE THE CAPED CRUSADER CAN MAKE ANOTHER MOVE...
GAAA! HE'S GOT ME-- CHOKING--!
10

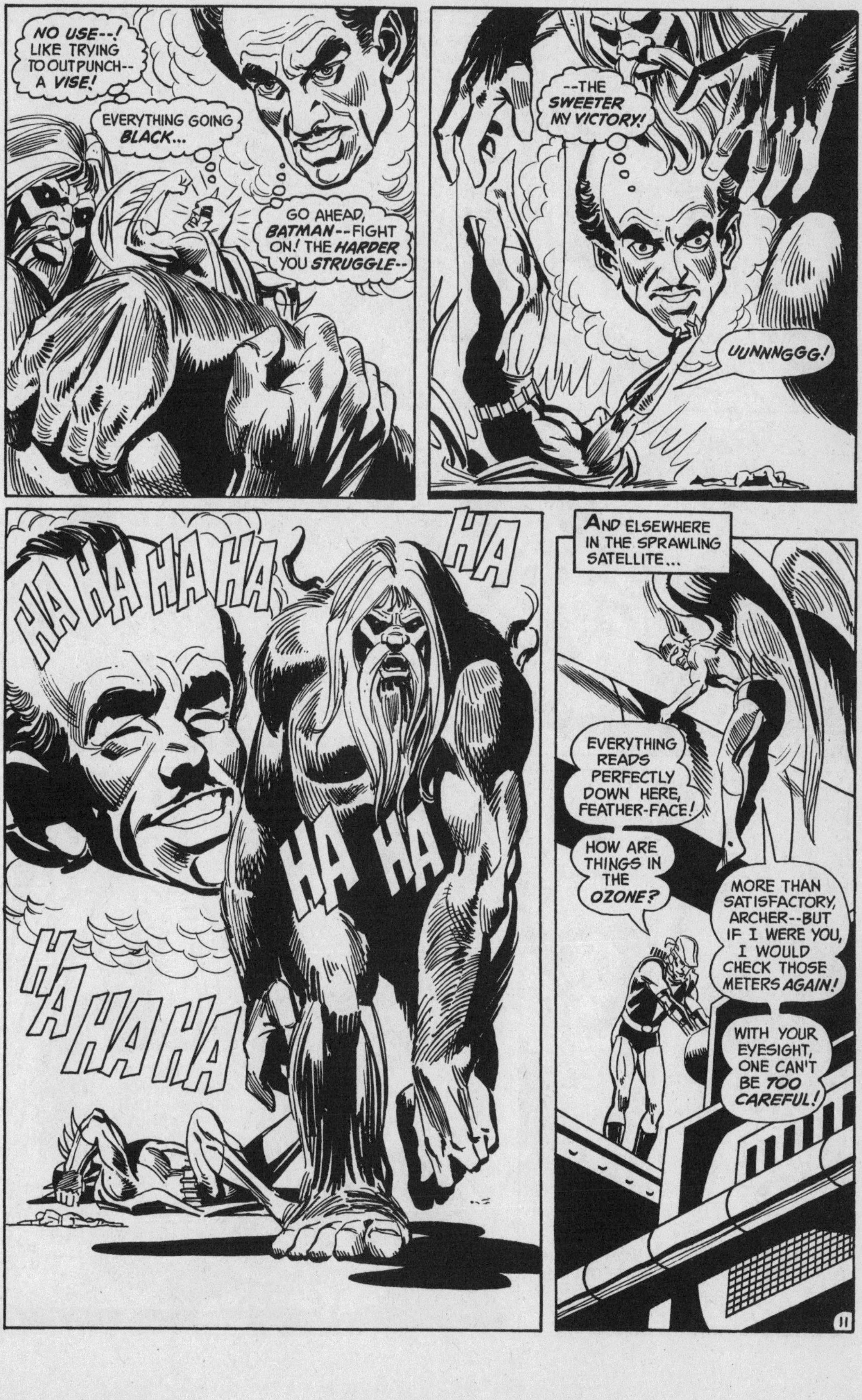
NO USE--! LIKE TRYING TO OUTPUNCH-- A VISE!
EVERYTHING GOING BLACK...
GO AHEAD, BATMAN--FIGHT ON! THE HARDER YOU STRUGGLE--
--THE SWEETER MY VICTORY!
UUNNNGGG!
HA HA HA HA HA HA
HA HA
HA HA HA HA HA
AND ELSEWHERE IN THE SPRAWLING SATELLITE...
EVERYTHING READS PERFECTLY DOWN HERE, FEATHER-FACE!
HOW ARE THINGS IN THE OZONE?
MORE THAN SATISFACTORY, ARCHER--BUT IF I WERE YOU, I WOULD CHECK THOSE METERS AGAIN!
WITH YOUR EYESIGHT, ONE CAN'T BE TOO CAREFUL!
11

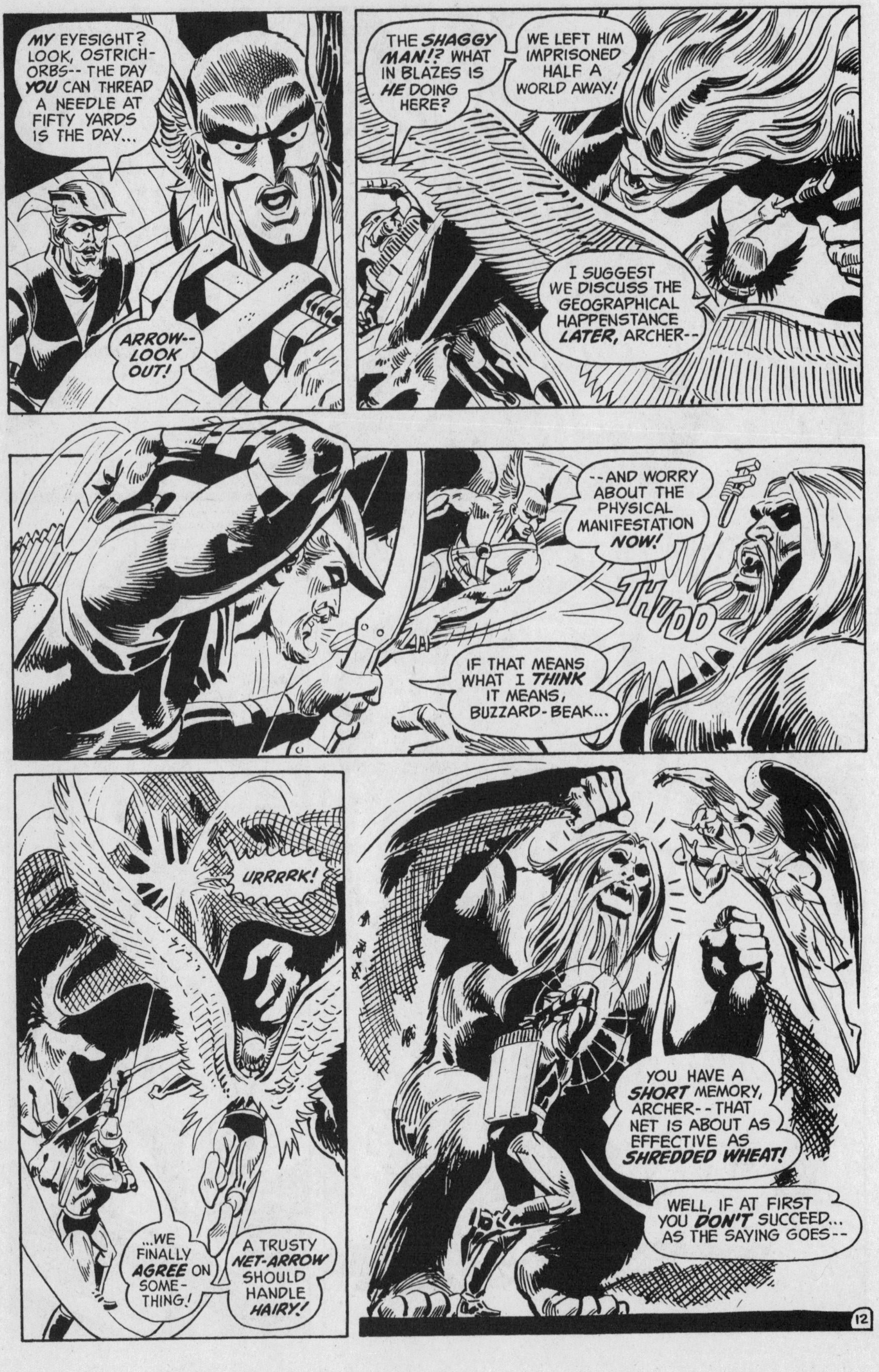
MY EYESIGHT? LOOK, OSTRICH-ORBS-- THE DAY YOU CAN THREAD A NEEDLE AT FIFTY YARDS IS THE DAY...
ARROW-- LOOK OUT!
THE SHAGGY MAN!? WHAT IN BLAZES IS HE DOING HERE?
WE LEFT HIM IMPRISONED HALF A WORLD AWAY!
I SUGGEST WE DISCUSS THE GEOGRAPHICAL HAPPENSTANCE LATER, ARCHER--
--AND WORRY ABOUT THE PHYSICAL MANIFESTATION NOW!
THUDD
IF THAT MEANS WHAT I THINK IT MEANS, BUZZARD-BEAK...
URRRRK!
...WE FINALLY AGREE ON SOME-THING!
A TRUSTY NET-ARROW SHOULD HANDLE HAIRY!
YOU HAVE A SHORT MEMORY, ARCHER--THAT NET IS ABOUT AS EFFECTIVE AS SHREDDED WHEAT!
WELL, IF AT FIRST YOU DON'T SUCCEED... AS THE SAYING GOES--
12

NO *SECOND* CHANCES, ARCHER--A POWERHOUSE PUNCH OF WING-GENERATED *AIR PRESSURE* SHOULD RUFFLE HIS FUR!

NO-- DON'T--! YOU'LL INTERFERE WITH MY...

SWARANMM

...EXPLOSIVE ARROW--!

THE MOST *NOBLE* EFFORT YET! *HAWKMAN* AND *GREEN ARROW* ACTUALLY MANAGED TO OVERCOME THE CREATURE... *TEMPORARILY!*

...FOR I DID NOT CHOOSE THIS *PARTICULAR AGENT* WITHOUT *REASON...*

...AND RAPID *TISSUE REGENERA-TION* IS AMPLE REASON INDEED!

WITHIN MOMENTS, THE *SHAGGY MAN* WILL HAVE GROWN A *NEW* BODY...

...AND THE BATTLE WILL BEGIN *ANEW!*

13

WHILE IN THE *STORAGE ROOM,* RIMMING THE SATELLITE...

AT *SUPER-SPEED,* I COULD CLEAN THIS ENTIRE SATELLITE IN *HALF* THE TIME IT WILL TAKE THE OTHERS *COMBINED...*

-- BUT *THIS* WAY, THERE'S A SENSE OF *GROUP PARTICIPATION!*

WAITAMINNIT!.. EITHER I'M CONFRONTED BY A *RUNAWAY MOP...*

--OR THE *SHAGGY MAN* HAS INVADED OUR HEAD-QUARTERS!

I'M HEADING RIGHT *FOR* HIM--AND THERE'S *NO* WAY I CAN STOP IN TIME!

OF COURSE, WHEN YOU CAN MOVE AS FAST AS *I* CAN-- YOU DON'T NECESSARILY *HAVE* TO STOP...

...IT'S MERELY *EASY COME... EASY GO!...*

GRAGGH!

ROCKETING AROUND THE *HAIRY HUMANOID* AT ASTONISHING SPEED, *THE FLASH* BECOMES A ONE-MAN *ARMY--* RAINING COUNTLESS BLOWS UPON HIS FOE IN A MATTER OF INSTANTS-- BUT...

NO EFFECT! HE'S GOT A HIDE LIKE A *CAST-IRON RUG!*

⑭

WELL, MAYBE I CAN'T *OUTFIGHT* HIM--BUT I SURE CAN *OUTSMART* HIM!

A LITTLE HIGH-SPEED *ACTION*--USING THE SPARE EQUIPMENT WE KEEP STORED IN THE RIM TO *BOX* OLD *SHAGGY* INTO A *CORNER!*

*F*ASTER THAN ANY EYE CAN FOLLOW, THE *MODERN MERCURY* PUTS HIS UNIQUE TALENTS TO THE TEST...

GOT TO *SURROUND* HIM WITH THIS STUFF-- BEFORE HE HAS A CHANCE TO *MOVE!*

*R*ACING AROUND THE RIM SO SWIFTLY THAT HE APPEARS TO BE ON *BOTH* SIDES OF THE *SHAGGY MAN* AT ONCE, THE *SCARLET SPEEDSTER* ERECTS A PAIR OF MAKESHIFT *WALLS* TO IMPRISON HIS *FOLLICLED FOE...*

...THEN APPLIES SUPER-SPEED *VIBRATIONS* TO FUSE THE CELL *AIRTIGHT...*

S-SOMETHING MUST BE WRONG WITH THE *VENTILATING SYSTEM!* GETTING HARD TO *BREATHE* IN HERE--!

SOMETHING *IS* WRONG! LIGHTS GROWING *DIMMER*--! THE *LIFE-SUPPORT SYSTEM* IS GOING *HAYWIRE!*

BUT THAT WAS *HAWKMAN* AND *GREEN ARROW'S* DETAIL--!

WHAT *HAPPENED* TO-- *UNNNH*--!

WHAT HAPPENED TO THE *AIR* HERE? I'M WONDERING THAT MYSELF, *FLASH!*

15

AND WITH *HECTOR HAMMOND,* ANSWERS COME INSTANTANEOUSLY...

SO *THAT'S* IT! *GREEN ARROW'S* EXPLOSIVE *RUINED* THE SATELLITE'S SUPPORT-MECHANISMS!

THIS ISN'T AT ALL WHAT I HAD *PLANNED!*

DANGER

WHILE OUTSIDE THE SATELLITE ITSELF...

SHOULD SMOOTH THE LAST OF THESE *METEOR-DENTS* OUT OF THE SHIP'S HULL IN A FEW SECONDS!

THEN I CAN *POLISH* HER UP-- GET HER SHINING LIKE A ...

HUH?

UUNNFF--

I'VE NEVER *MET* THIS CHARACTER BEFORE-- BUT I'VE HEARD ENOUGH ABOUT HIM!

HOW DID THE *SHAGGY MAN* GET ABOARD OUR SATELLITE?

RIGHT NOW, THE *ANSWER* TO THAT QUESTION HAS PROBLEMS OF HIS OWN...

THE SATELLITE'S *ORBIT* HAS BEGUN TO *DECAY--* AND THERE'S *NOTHING* I CAN DO ABOUT IT!

16

THIS MONSTER'S NOT REALLY *ALIVE*-- SO THERE'S NOTHING TO KEEP ME FROM *HITTING* IT WITH ALL...

GREAT SCOTT! IT'S COMING APART AT THE *SEAMS!*

HE'S GROWING A WHOLE NEW *BODY!*

I'D FORGOTTEN ABOUT THAT PECULIAR *TALENT* OF HIS!

--BUT I GUARANTEE I WON'T MAKE THAT MISTAKE *AGAIN!*

--*USELESS!* MY *MIND-OVER-MATTER* POWERS ARE SIMPLY NOT *STRONG* ENOUGH TO HOLD THE SATELLITE IN PLACE!

DANGER

WITHIN *SECONDS*, IT WILL STRIKE THE *ATMOSPHERE*--AND MOMENTS AFTER THAT-- IT WILL BE *GONE!*

CAN'T LET *FUZZY* GET HIS HANDS ON ME AGAIN!

ALL THE KING'S HORSES AND ANYONE ELSE WHO FEELS INCLINED WON'T BE ABLE TO PUT HIM BACK TOGETHER AFTER *THIS* SHOT!

17

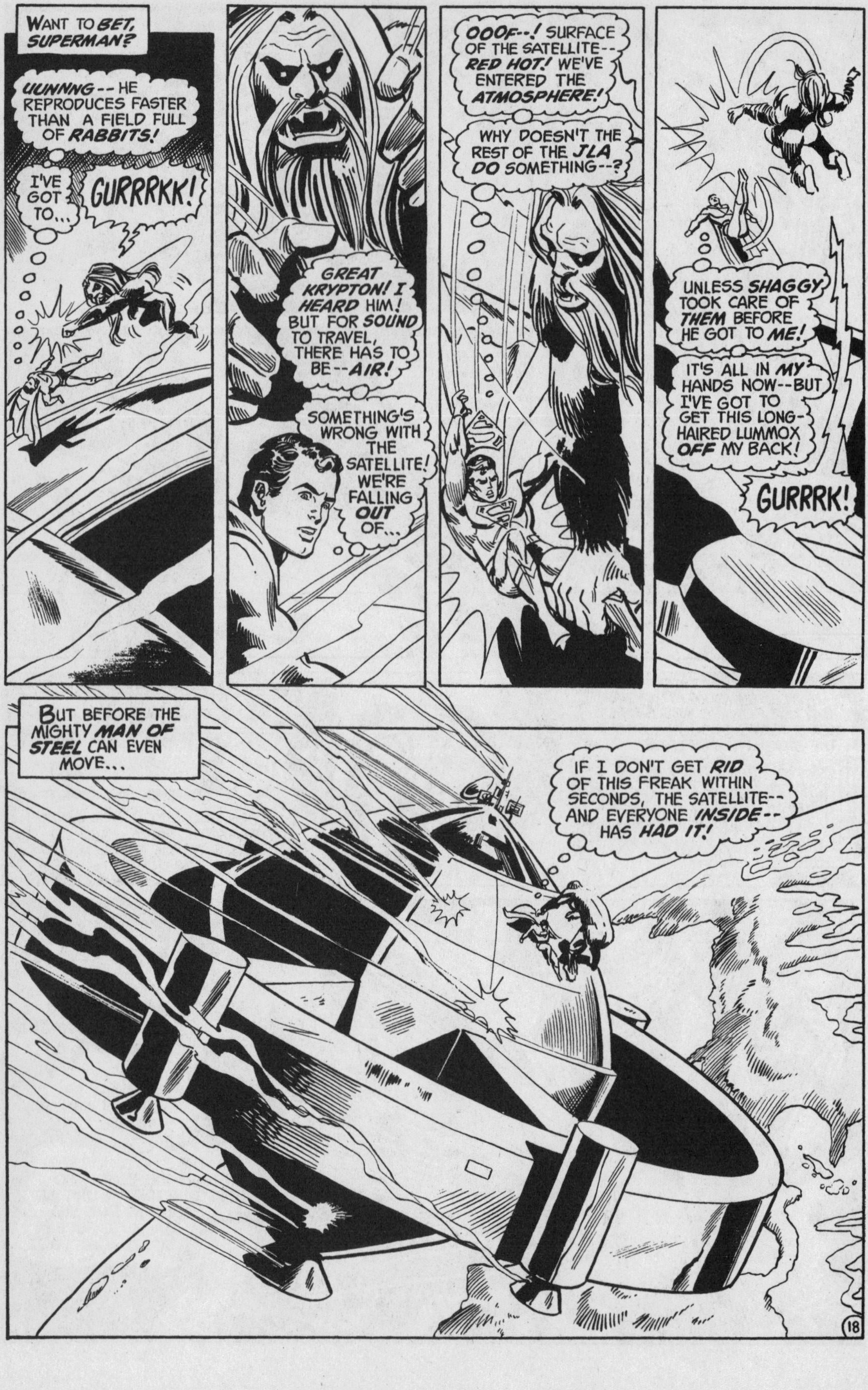
WANT TO BET, SUPERMAN?
UUNNNG--HE REPRODUCES FASTER THAN A FIELD FULL OF RABBITS!
I'VE GOT TO...
GURRRKK!
GREAT KRYPTON! I HEARD HIM! BUT FOR SOUND TO TRAVEL, THERE HAS TO BE--AIR!
SOMETHING'S WRONG WITH THE SATELLITE! WE'RE FALLING OUT OF...
OOOF--! SURFACE OF THE SATELLITE--RED HOT! WE'VE ENTERED THE ATMOSPHERE!
WHY DOESN'T THE REST OF THE JLA DO SOMETHING--?
UNLESS SHAGGY TOOK CARE OF THEM BEFORE HE GOT TO ME!
IT'S ALL IN MY HANDS NOW--BUT I'VE GOT TO GET THIS LONG-HAIRED LUMMOX OFF MY BACK!
GURRRK!
BUT BEFORE THE MIGHTY MAN OF STEEL CAN EVEN MOVE...
IF I DON'T GET RID OF THIS FREAK WITHIN SECONDS, THE SATELLITE--AND EVERYONE INSIDE--HAS HAD IT!
18

THE STREETS OF *METROPOLIS* ARE TANGLED WITH TRAFFIC-- AS CROWDS OF BUSY PEDESTRIANS PAUSE IN THEIR HUSTLE TO STARE SKYWARD WITH HORRIFIED EYES...

TERROR FALLS FROM THAT SKY THIS DAY-- A FLAME-LICKED MASS OF GLEAMING METAL THAT ONCE WAS CALLED *SENTINEL*-- BUT NOW IS ONLY *MENACE*...

LOOK-- UP IN THE SKY--!

IT'S A *BIRD!*

IT'S A *PLANE!*

HECK! IT'S ONE 'A THEM *SATTERLIGHTS!* I'D KNOW'D THEY WAS GONNA *COME FALLIN'* ON US SOONER 'R LATER!

BUT AS THE SATELLITE HURLS EARTHWARD, THE SKY IS FILLED WITH A BLAZING EMERALD LIGHT AND...

A SUDDEN *STOP* WOULD TEAR THE SATELLITE *APART!* THIS *CHUTE* HAD BETTER WORK ON THE *FIRST* TRY!

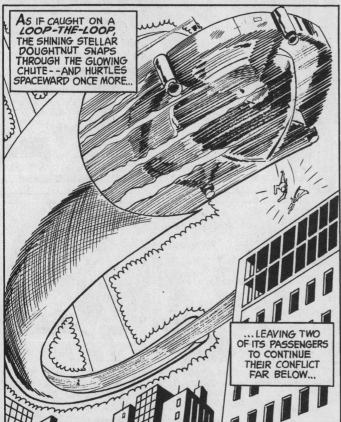

AS IF CAUGHT ON A *LOOP-THE-LOOP,* THE SHINING STELLAR DOUGHNUT SNAPS THROUGH THE GLOWING CHUTE--AND HURTLES SPACEWARD ONCE MORE...

...LEAVING TWO OF ITS PASSENGERS TO CONTINUE THEIR CONFLICT FAR BELOW...

SUPERMAN CAN DEAL WITH *SHAGGY* WHILE I PUT THE SATELLITE BACK INTO *ORBIT*-- AND FIND OUT WHAT HAPPENED TO THE *OTHERS!*

THEY NEED MY HELP *MORE* THAN THE *MAN OF STEEL* DOES RIGHT NOW!

BUT YOU MIGHT CHANGE YOUR MIND, *GREEN LANTERN,* IF YOU'D BOTHER TO STUDY THE COMBAT BELOW YOU A TRIFLE MORE CLOSELY...

IT'S NOT WORTH *SMASHING* HIM ANY *MORE!* HE'S LIKE THE MYTHICAL *HYDRA!*

A *NEW HEAD* GROWS BACK TO REPLACE EACH ONE I *KNOCK OFF!*

KWRAIMM

I ONCE WONDERED HOW *I* MIGHT HAVE FARED BATTLING THE *SHAGGY MAN*--BUT AFTER A FEW MINUTES WITH THIS *MADMAN...*

...I'M SORRY I--UGH--ASKED!

THUMPK

KRUMMT

ALL I CAN DO IS KEEP HIM OFF-BALANCE AND CONFUSED--TILL I CAN THINK OF SOMETHING *BETTER!*

THEN, AS THE *ACTION ACE* FOLLOWS HIS MAD-MANED ADVERSARY INTO THE STREET...

SHAGGY'S OUT OF WHAT LITTLE MIND HE HAS WITH *ANGER!* LOOKS LIKE IT'S TIME FOR A *SHOWDOWN!*

ANYTHING *WE* CAN DO TO *HELP?*

WHAT--? THANK THE STARS-- YOU'RE ALL *ALIVE!*

JUST *BARELY, SUPES!* THAT OVERGROWN *TOUPEE* YOU'RE FIGHTING IS *NOT* AT ALL *FRIENDLY!*

IF *GREEN LANTERN* HADN'T *REVIVED* US--

WE CAN TALK ABOUT THAT *LATER, CANARY*--AFTER WE'VE *FINISHED* THE *SHAGGY MAN!*

20

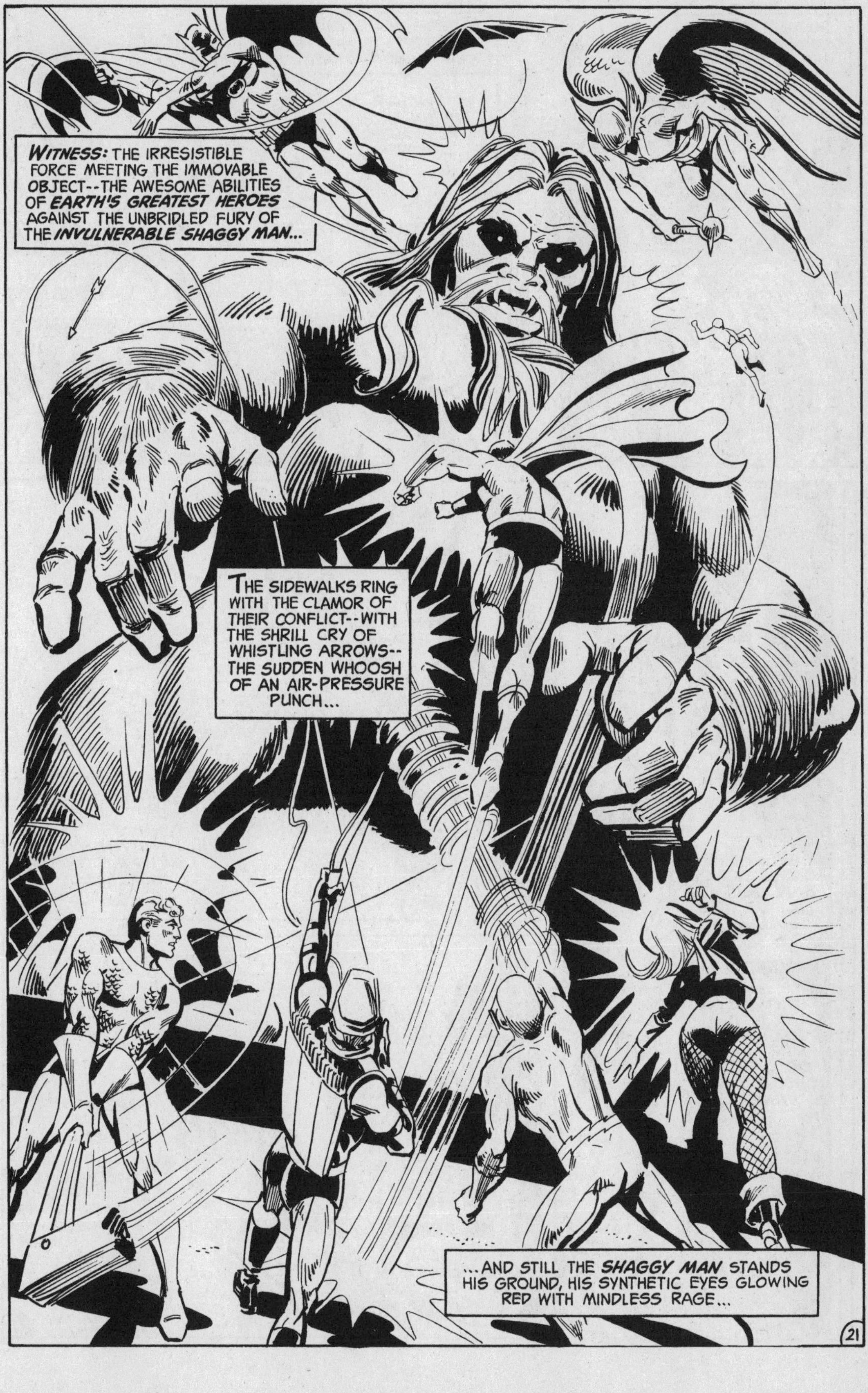
WITNESS: THE IRRESISTIBLE FORCE MEETING THE IMMOVABLE OBJECT--THE AWESOME ABILITIES OF EARTH'S GREATEST HEROES AGAINST THE UNBRIDLED FURY OF THE INVULNERABLE SHAGGY MAN...
THE SIDEWALKS RING WITH THE CLAMOR OF THEIR CONFLICT--WITH THE SHRILL CRY OF WHISTLING ARROWS--THE SUDDEN WHOOSH OF AN AIR-PRESSURE PUNCH...
...AND STILL THE SHAGGY MAN STANDS HIS GROUND, HIS SYNTHETIC EYES GLOWING RED WITH MINDLESS RAGE...
21

...UNTIL, LIKE A DOG SHAKING WATER OFF ITS BACK...

NO USE! WE'RE ONLY *ANNOYING* HIM!

THEN HOW DO WE *STOP* HIM?

GGURRKK

BUT THE *BLACK CANARY'S* ONLY REPLY IS *ACTION,* SWIFT--AND *SUDDEN*...

WHA--? *BRUSH-FACE* HAS GRABBED *DINAH*--!

HE'S REVIVING THE OLD *"KING KONG"* BIT!

GRRAHHH!

WELL, WE'RE FRESH OUT OF *BI-PLANES*--BUT I'M SURE WE'LL *MANAGE* ON OUR OWN!

WE'LL BE *ON* HIM IN A SECOND--BUT WHAT CAN WE *DO* WHILE HE'S HOLDING THE *CANARY?*

IF *THAT'S* YOUR ONLY PROBLEM--CONSIDER IT *SOLVED!*

GREEN LANTERN--! THEN THE *SATELLITE--?*

IN *100%* WORKING ORDER, SUPERMAN--!

NOW, IF YOU'LL BE SO KIND AS TO TEND TO THE *BLACK CANARY*--

--I HAVE SOME *OTHER* BUSINESS TO TAKE CARE OF!

GOOD LUCK, *GREEN LANTERN*--I'M AFRAID YOU'RE GOING TO *NEED* IT!

22

ONE GOOD *POWER-RING BLAST*-- AND THEY'LL BE ABLE TO *STUFF SHAGGY* AND *MOUNT* HIM ON A WALL!

GRU--!

FOR A MOMENT, THE EMERALD ENERGY HOLDS THE FOLLICLED FURY MOTIONLESS--BUT THEN...

GRAARGG!

HE'S BREAKING *LOOSE!* HAVE TO *CONCENTRATE* --PUT MORE *WILL POWER* INTO THE NEXT BLAST--!

AND AS THE *EMERALD GLADIATOR* FOCUSES HIS WILL, AN UNSEEN SPECTATOR ENTERS THE PLAY...

AT LAST THE ONE ALL THIS WAS *PLANNED* FOR ARRIVES --AND I FIND I'VE *EXHAUSTED* MY MENTAL POWERS WHILE STRUGGLING TO REPAIR THAT SATELLITE!

SHAGGY MUST FIGHT *THIS* BATTLE *ALONE!*

BUT IT APPEARS HE DOES NOT *NEED* MY HELP!

HE WAS INDEED THE *PROPER* CHOICE TO MAKE!

CAN'T GET ENOUGH *POWER* BEHIND THE RING TO *DO* ANYTHING! HAIRY SEEMS TO HAVE A NATURAL *RESISTANCE* TO IT--!

A FEW MORE STEPS AND HE'LL BE ALL OVER ME!

HAVE TO KEEP *COOL*-- *CONCENTRATE*-- FOCUS EVERY GUT-LEVEL *IMPULSE* INTO ONE *FINAL* SHOT--

--*NOW!!*

...AND IT IS *DONE!*

NO! WHAT *HAPPENED?* WHERE HAS THE *SHAGGY MAN GONE?*

23

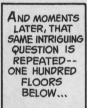

AND MOMENTS LATER, THAT SAME INTRIGUING QUESTION IS REPEATED-- ONE HUNDRED FLOORS BELOW...

GREEN LANTERN? YOU ALL RIGHT? WHAT HAPPENED UP THERE?

YEAH--DID HAIRY-HIDE GIVE YOU THE SLIP?

NO, G.A.,--I MERELY REMOVED HIM--

--TO SOMEPLACE WHERE WE CAN KEEP AN EYE ON HIM!

GURRRKKK!

NOW, GANG-- I BELIEVE WE HAVE A BUILDING TO REPAIR!

NEXT ISSUE ON SALE ON OR ABOUT FEB. 1ST

AND COUNTLESS MILES AWAY...

DEFEATED AGAIN-- BY THE ONE I HATE MOST-- BUT THERE'S NO NEED TO DESPAIR!

IF IT TAKES FOREVER, I'LL FIND A WAY TO DESTROY GREEN LANTERN--

...AND FOREVER IS EXACTLY WHAT I HAVE!

NEXT ISSUE: A NEW JUSTICE LEAGUER AND... "THE SPECTER IN THE SHADOWS"!

24

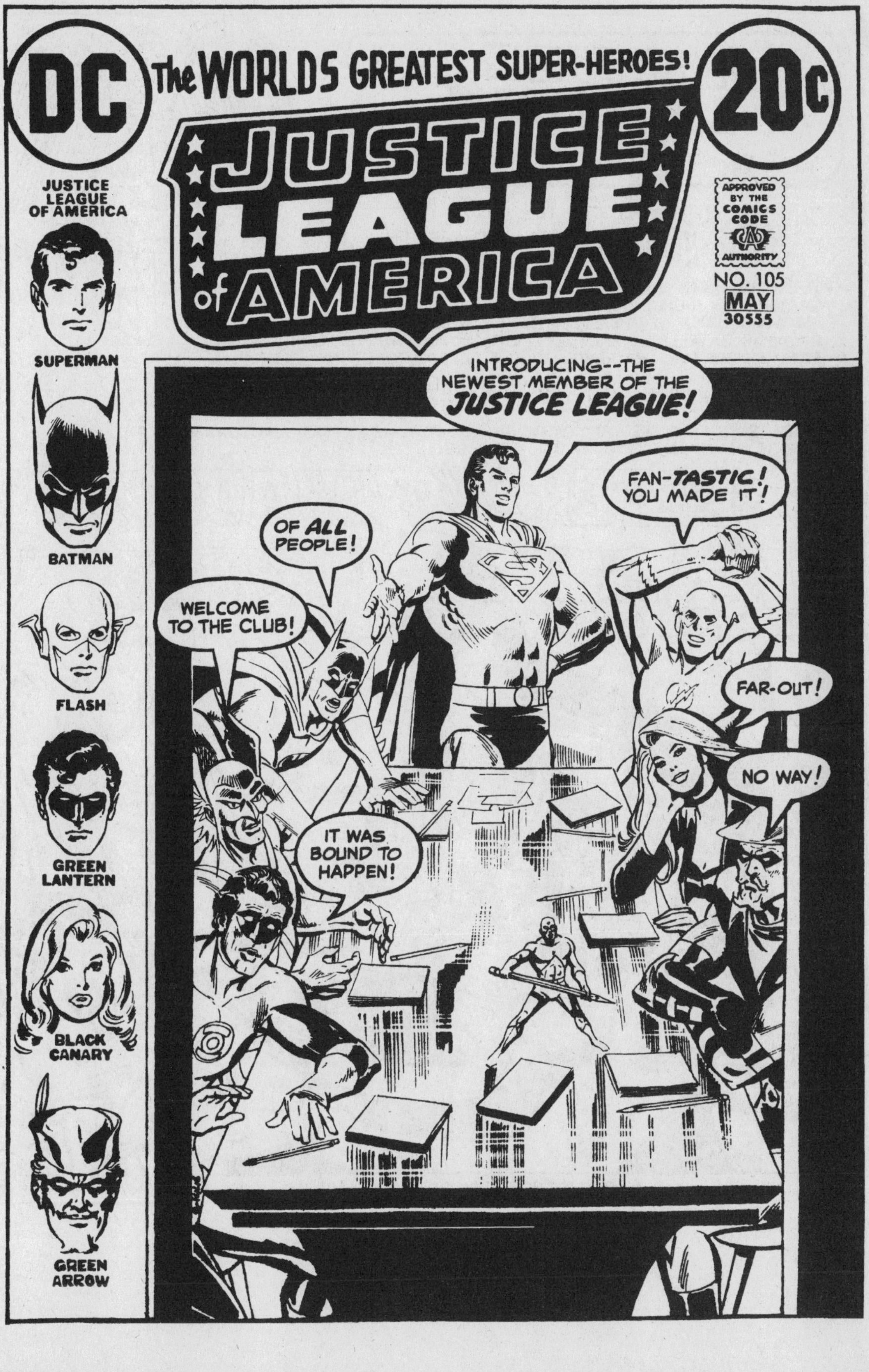
DC
The WORLDS GREATEST SUPER-HEROES!
20¢
JUSTICE LEAGUE of AMERICA
APPROVED BY THE COMICS CODE AUTHORITY
NO. 105
MAY
30555
JUSTICE LEAGUE OF AMERICA
SUPERMAN
BATMAN
FLASH
GREEN LANTERN
BLACK CANARY
GREEN ARROW
INTRODUCING--THE NEWEST MEMBER OF THE JUSTICE LEAGUE!
FAN-TASTIC! YOU MADE IT!
OF ALL PEOPLE!
WELCOME TO THE CLUB!
FAR-OUT!
NO WAY!
IT WAS BOUND TO HAPPEN!

JUSTICE ★★★ LEAGUE ★★★ of AMERICA

HEREBY ELECTS THE

ELONGATED MAN

TO MEMBERSHIP FOR LIFE -- WITH ALL PRIVILEGES AND GRATUITIES, INCLUDING THE WEARING OF THE SIGNAL DEVICE AND POSSESSION OF THE SPECIAL KEY WHICH PERMITS ENTRY INTO THE SATELLITE-SANCTUARY, ITS LIBRARY AND SOUVENIR ROOMS. IT IS HEREBY FURTHER RESOLVED AND ACTED UPON, THAT THE

ELONGATED MAN

SHALL RECEIVE A SPECIAL COMMENDATION FOR HIS EXPERT ASSISTANCE IN THE CASE WE HAVE ENTITLED ON OUR SCROLLS...

"SPECTER in the SHADOWS!"

THE ROLL CALL

ATOM
BLACK CANARY
FLASH
GREEN ARROW
GREEN LANTERN
SUPERMAN
AND AT LONG LAST...
THE ELONGATED MAN!

WELCOME TO THE *JUSTICE LEAGUE, ELONGATED MAN!*

LEN WEIN: WRITER   DICK DILLIN & DICK GIORDANO: ARTISTS   JULIUS SCHWARTZ: EDITOR

A BALMY SPRING AFTERNOON-- AS TWO SURPRISINGLY FAMILIAR PEOPLE BROWSE LEISURELY THROUGH A PROMINENT ART MUSEUM...

HOW *BEAUTIFUL!* RALPH, DON'T YOU JUST ADORE *VAN GOGH?*

OH, I DON'T KNOW, SUE-- GIVE ME *GAUGUIN* ANY DAY!

ALL THOSE PAINTINGS OF TROPIC ISLANDS-- LOVELY *SOUTH SEA GIRLS...*

MR. DIBNY-- I'D CHOOSE MY *NEXT* PHRASE VERY *CAREFULLY!*

REMEMBER--YOU'RE A *HAPPILY MARRIED MAN*--AND IF YOU'D LIKE TO *STAY* THAT WAY...

...YOU'LL *WATCH* WHAT YOU...

SPLURSHH

STUNNED, *SUE DIBNY* STAGGERS BACK-- AS A HANDFUL OF HUMANOID FORMS ERUPTS INTO ACTION...

DON'T KNOW *WHAT* THOSE CREATURES ARE--BUT THEY'RE OBVIOUSLY NOT HERE TO *ADMIRE* THE DECOR--!

--AND IF *THAT* ISN'T A CUE FOR THE *ELONGATED MAN* TO TAKE AN *ELASTIC HAND,* I DON'T KNOW *WHAT* IS!

2

UH-UH, LUMPY--THAT'S WHAT YOU CALL YOUR NO-NO!

THE SIGNS SAY "PLEASE DO NOT TOUCH!"

SPLAT

BUT THOSE SIGNS *DON'T* APPLY TO *MY* TOUCHING *YOU*... HUH?

MY FIST--SINKING IN--AS IF THIS LUNATIC LOOTER WAS MADE OF *BREAD-DOUGH!*

SPLURPT

NO--CHANGE THAT TO *SILLY PUTTY!*

THESE CREATURES REACT TO A PUNCH LIKE *NOTHING* I'VE EVER SEEN--!

FOR HEAVEN'S SAKE, RALPH *-- LOOK OUT!

*EDITOR'S NOTE: *E-MAN*, THE *ONLY* HERO TO PUBLICLY REVEAL HIS DUAL IDENTITY, GAINS HIS STRETCHING POWERS BY DRINKING AN ELIXIR DISTILLED FROM THE JUICE OF A TROPICAL FRUIT-- *GINGOLD!*

BUT BEFORE THE *DUCTILE DETECTIVE* CAN RESPOND TO HIS WIFE'S ANGUISHED SHOUT...

÷ UUNNNFF THESE THINGS MAY *LOOK* SILLY--BUT THEY *MOVE* AS FAST AS *THE FLASH!*

RESTRAINING MY ARMS AND LEGS--MAKING IT ALMOST *IMPOSSIBLE* FOR ME--TO *STRETCH*--!

HELPLESS IN THE SEMI-HUMANOIDS' GOOEY GRASP, THE *STRETCHABLE SLEUTH* IS BATTERED ABOUT MERCILESSLY...

--UNTIL HIS DARING LADY LEAPS TO HIS... *RESCUE?*

LET *GO* OF HIM, YOU LITTLE MONSTERS -- *LET GO!* HARM ONE *HAIR* OF HIS PRECIOUS HEAD AND I'LL... OOOOHHHH...

3

MOMENTS LATER, THE *ELONGATED MAN* IS SENT SPRAWLING TO THE FLOOR-- AND THE PUTTY-MEN RETURN TO THEIR INTERRUPTED CRIME!

THEN, WITH SMASHING SUDDENNESS...

TH-THEY'RE LEAPING OUT THE *WINDOW*--

--BUT... IT'S *FIVE* STORIES DOWN--!

G-GOT TO *STOP* THEM-- FROM *ESCAPING*--!

BUT BY THE TIME THE DAZED DETECTIVE CAN STRETCH TO THE SHATTERED WINDOW...

WHAT--? THEY'VE FORMED THEMSELVES INTO ONE BIG *BALL*-- BOUNCING AWAY FROM HERE *FASTER* THAN I COULD HOPE TO *FOLLOW*--!

AND SECONDS LATER...

OH, RALPH-- YOU *ALL RIGHT?* HOW DO YOU *FEEL?*

EMBARRASSED, MOSTLY! HOW DO I EXPLAIN BEING PUNCHED OUT BY A HALF-DOZEN GOOEY GUMDROPS?

BUT *THAT'S* NOT WHAT REALLY *BOTHERS* ME--!

WHAT *I* WANT TO KNOW IS-- *WHY* DID THOSE CHARACTERS LEAVE ALL THESE PRICELESS *PAINTINGS* LYING AROUND AND STEAL ONLY THE *FRAMES?*

AND FROM THE WAY YOUR MYSTERY-LOVING *NOSE* IS TWITCHING, YOU WON'T REST UNTIL YOU *FIND OUT!*

NO, SUE-- I HAVE A FEELING THIS CASE IS *TOO BIG* FOR ME ALONE...

THIS IS A JOB FOR-- *THE JUSTICE LEAGUE OF AMERICA!*

WHAT'S THAT YOU SAY, GENTLE READER? *WHAT* IS THE *ELONGATED MAN* DOING WITH A *JUSTICE LEAGUE SIGNAL DEVICE*..?

4

FOR THE *ANSWER* TO THAT QUESTION, WE MUST TURN TIME BACK ONE BRIEF WEEK--TO A ROLLING COUNTRY ROAD ENJOYING THE REBIRTH OF SPRING--

--AND A SLEEK SPORTS CAR, LEAPING TO THE COMMAND OF A CONTENTED *RALPH DIBNY*...

WHAT A *GLORIOUS* DAY, SUE! AIR'S SO *FRESH* IT MAKES ME FEEL LIKE...

GREEN LANTERN!? W-WHAT ARE YOU DOING HERE?

FORGIVE THE SUDDEN *INTRUSION*, RALPH--BUT I HAVE A VERY SPECIAL *INVITATION* TO EXTEND--!

AND MINUTES LATER, IN A SPECIAL SATELLITE ORBITING 22,300 MILES ABOVE THE EMERALD EARTH...

SINCE THE *MARTIAN MANHUNTER'S* RESIGNATION, THE JLA HAS BEEN OPERATING AT *LESS* THAN FULL STRENGTH! IT'S HIGH TIME WE VOTED IN A *NEW* MEMBER--

--AND *YOU*--RALPH *(ELONGATED MAN)* DIBNY--ARE *IT!*

WELCOME TO THE *JUSTICE LEAGUE,* E-MAN--CONGRATULATIONS!

I--I'M *STUNNED--SPEECHLESS--!* FOR THE FIRST TIME IN MY LIFE, I *DON'T* KNOW WHAT TO SAY--!

WELL, ALL I CAN SAY IS--IT'S *ABOUT TIME!*

SUE--YOU'RE EMBARRASSING ME! THAT'S A *TERRIBLE* THING TO SAY!

WHY? ISN'T A GIRL ENTITLED TO A LITTLE *WIFELY PRIDE* RIGHT ABOUT NOW?

NOW, BE STILL, SILLY-- AND LET EVERYONE *CONGRATULATE* YOU!

SMMACK

THAT'S THE WAY IT WAS ONE WEEK AGO--BUT THE ATMOSPHERE THAT PERVADES THE JLA'S SATELLITE SANCTUARY *NOW* IS HEAVIER INDEED...

... AND THAT'S THE WHOLE *STORY*, GANG! I USUALLY HANDLE THIS KIND OF CRAZY CASE BY *MYSELF*--

--BUT THOSE FLUBBER-FREAKS HAVE ME *OUT-MATCHED* PHYSICALLY!

YOU CAN COUNT ON US TO *HELP*, RALPH--BUT I'M NOT SURE WHAT *SORT* OF HELP WE CAN GIVE!

OUR BEST CHANCE OF *FINDING* THOSE CREATURES IS--WAIT UNTIL THEY STRIKE *AGAIN*--BUT THAT'S...

PING PING PING PING

SOMETHING'S COMING IN ON THE *EARTH-MONITOR*!

AND WHEN THE INFORMATION HAS BEEN FULLY RECORDED...

THOSE PUTTY-PEOPLE *HAVE* STRUCK AGAIN--

IN *MOTOR CITY*--ON AN OIL RIG OFF THE *CALIFORNIA COAST*--AND IN THE SMALL NORTHEASTERN TOWN OF *DESOLATION*!

THEN WHAT ARE WE *WAITING* FOR? LET'S GET *AFTER* THEM!

MOTION CARRIED *UNANIMOUSLY*! SUPERMAN, WHY DON'T YOU AND I TAKE A QUICK TRIP TO *MOTOR CITY*?

CALIFORNIA'S *MY* OLD STOMPING GROUND, RALPH! SUPPOSE THE TWO OF US TACKLE *THAT* END?

WE'RE ALL THAT'S *LEFT*, GUYS--SO I GUESS *OUR* ASSIGNMENT IS *DESOLATION*--AND, BELIEVE ME--

--THERE WAS NEVER A PLACE MORE *APTLY* NAMED!

6

"SPECTER IN THE SHADOWS!" CHAPTER 2

DESOLATION: AN *APTLY* NAMED TOWN, INDEED! LIFE IS MORE THAN *HARD* HERE--IT IS A NEVER-ENDING STRUGGLE AGAINST THE VERY *EARTH* ITSELF--TO PULL SOMETHING OF *VALUE* FROM ITS COLD, UNFEELING *HEART*...

INTO THIS UNSIGHTLY LITTLE SCAB ON THE LAND RACE THREE OF THE *JUSTICE LEAGUE'S* FINEST...

The FLASH

The ATOM

THE GREEN ARROW

AS THE SAYING GOES, GENTLEMEN-- THIS *MUST* BE THE PLACE!

THIS IS THE PLACE, ALL RIGHT-- I LOSE MY APPETITE JUST *LOOKING* AT IT!

BUT WE'RE HERE TO DO *MORE* THAN LOOKING, G.A.!

LET'S *SPLIT UP*-- HIT THOSE SILLY PUTTY-MEN FROM *THREE* SIDES!

OKAY BY *ME*, FLASH-- IF *GREEN ARROW* WILL GIVE ME A *LIFT*!

THEN HANG ON TO YOUR *HAIRLINE*, HALF-PINT-- I HAVEN'T HAD TIME TO INSTALL *SEAT-BELTS* ON THIS THING!

THWANGG

I'LL SEND YOU A *POST CARD* FROM PUTTY-LAND, ARCHER!

SOUND: A SHRILL WHISTLE AS *GREEN ARROW'S* GOOSE-FLETCHED SHAFT SLICES THE VALLEY AIR --

--THEN A SICKENING *SQUISH* AS 180 POUNDS OF 6-INCH *ATOM* SINK DEEP INTO A QUASI-HUMAN HIDE...

E-MAN WAS *RIGHT*! THESE THINGS *ARE* MADE OF *PUTTY*!

⑦

BUT THAT LITTLE PIECE OF *KNOWLEDGE* ISN'T GOING TO DO ME A FAT LOT OF *GOOD* RIGHT NOW!

MY *SIZE-AND-WEIGHT CONTROLS* MADE ME *HEAVY* ENOUGH TO GET *INTO* THIS MESS--LET'S *SEE* IF THEY CAN GET ME OUT OF IT!

THE *TINY TITAN* CLOSES HIS FISTS, CAREFULLY MANIPULATING THE CONTROL MECHANISMS HIDDEN IN THE PALMS OF HIS GLOVES--THEN...

CLICK CLICK CLICK

IT'S *WORKING!* INCREASING MY *SIZE* IS SQUEEZING ME OUT OF THE PUTTY-MAN'S BODY LIKE SOAP FROM A LATHERED FIST!

WONDER HOW THE *OTHERS* ARE DOING?

WELL, AT LEAST *ONE* OF THE "OTHERS" HAS FOUND HIMSELF IN A STICKINGLY SIMILAR SITUATION...

I FEEL LIKE *BR'ER RABBIT* AND THE *TAR BABY!* MY ARM'S *STUCK FAST* TO THIS CREEPY-LOOKING CREATURE!

HARD AS I TRY, I CAN'T PULL IT BACK OUT!

SO...IF I CAN'T GO *BACK,* I MIGHT JUST AS WELL GO *FORWARD*--

--*VIBRATING* AT SUCH SUPER-SPEED THAT I PASS RIGHT *THROUGH* THIS *PLAY-DOH*-LIKE PEST!

AND WHAT OF *GREEN ARROW?* LET'S SWIVEL TO A SPOT ACROSS THE STREET--AND *SEE...*

THAT IDIOT ARMY'S TURNED TAIL--RUNNING BACK INTO THE *MINE!*

I'LL FINISH THINGS QUICKLY--WITH AN *EXPLOSIVE-ARROW!*

8

WHAT THE--?

YOU *FIRE* THAT CONTRAPTION, *ARROW*--AN' YOU'LL FINISH *EVERYTHING*!

THERE'S POCKETS OF *COAL GAS* IN THAT MINE! ONE *SPARK*--AN' THEY'LL BE SCRAPIN' UP *PIECES* OF THIS TOWN FOR MONTHS!

THAT MIGHT NOT BE TOO *BAD* AN IDEA-- *CONSIDERING*--

--BUT I GUESS I'M GONNA HAVE TO HANDLE THIS THE *HARD* WAY--!

IT'S TIME I JOINED MY BUDDIES IN THE *MINE*!

MUSCLES FLEXING, THE *EMERALD ARCHER* SPRINTS ACROSS THE DUSTY STREET-- AND INTO THE GAPING MAW OF THE RUN-DOWN MINE...

...WHILE A SOMBER, TOP-COATED FIGURE STEPS SOUNDLESSLY FROM THE SHADOWS...

WELL--IT'S ABOUT *TIME* YOU GOT HERE, *G.A.*! WHAT *KEPT* YOU?

SORRY, SMALL FRY! WOULD YOU BELIEVE I GOT STOPPED FOR *JAY-WALKING*--?

ANYWAY, I'M HERE TO MAKE UP FOR *LOST* TIME!

MAYBE I CAN'T USE MY *ARROWS* IN HERE--

--BUT LET'S SEE WHAT A HUNK OF PLAIN, UNADORNED *WOOD* WILL DO TO--!

N-O-T-H-I-N-G!

COAL GAS: NOXIOUS FUMES OF ACRID *METHANE*, RELEASED BY THE HURTLING SHARD OF WOOD, BILLOW INTO THE STALE MINE AIR-- FILLING THE ROUGH-HEWN CHAMBER WITH RIPPLING CLOUDS OF-- *DEATH!*

HSSSSSSSS SSS

PLUNKT!

9

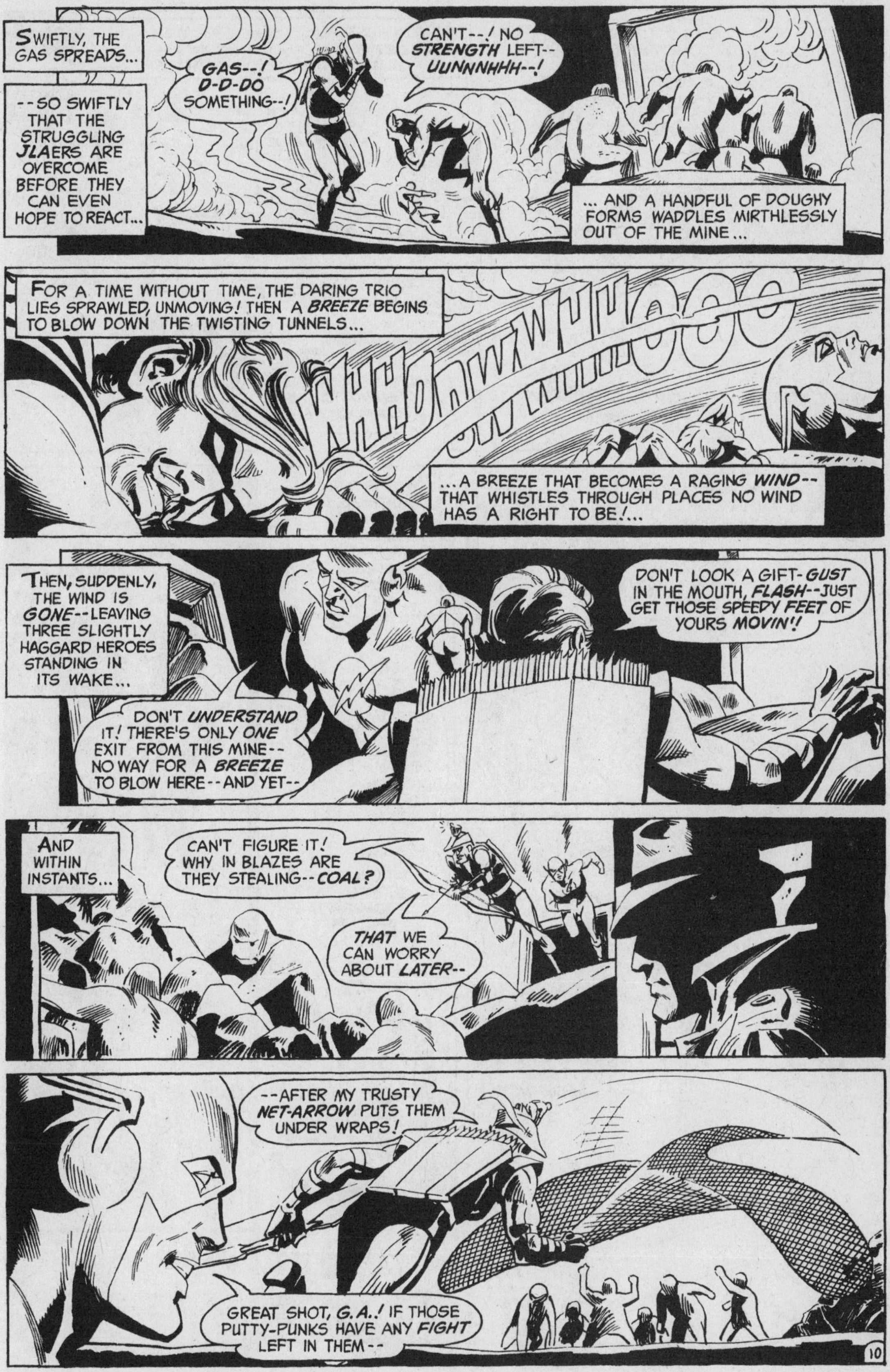
SWIFTLY, THE GAS SPREADS...
--SO SWIFTLY THAT THE STRUGGLING JLAERS ARE OVERCOME BEFORE THEY CAN EVEN HOPE TO REACT...
GAS--! D-D-DO SOMETHING--!
CAN'T--! NO STRENGTH LEFT-- UUNNNHHH--!
... AND A HANDFUL OF DOUGHY FORMS WADDLES MIRTHLESSLY OUT OF THE MINE ...
FOR A TIME WITHOUT TIME, THE DARING TRIO LIES SPRAWLED, UNMOVING! THEN A BREEZE BEGINS TO BLOW DOWN THE TWISTING TUNNELS...
WHHOOWWHHOOO
...A BREEZE THAT BECOMES A RAGING WIND-- THAT WHISTLES THROUGH PLACES NO WIND HAS A RIGHT TO BE!...
THEN, SUDDENLY, THE WIND IS GONE--LEAVING THREE SLIGHTLY HAGGARD HEROES STANDING IN ITS WAKE...
DON'T LOOK A GIFT-GUST IN THE MOUTH, FLASH--JUST GET THOSE SPEEDY FEET OF YOURS MOVIN'!
DON'T UNDERSTAND IT! THERE'S ONLY ONE EXIT FROM THIS MINE-- NO WAY FOR A BREEZE TO BLOW HERE--AND YET--
AND WITHIN INSTANTS...
CAN'T FIGURE IT! WHY IN BLAZES ARE THEY STEALING--COAL?
THAT WE CAN WORRY ABOUT LATER--
--AFTER MY TRUSTY NET-ARROW PUTS THEM UNDER WRAPS!
GREAT SHOT, G.A.! IF THOSE PUTTY-PUNKS HAVE ANY FIGHT LEFT IN THEM--
10

--A LITTLE SUPER-COMPRESSED *AIR-PRESSURE* SHOULD SQUEEZE IT RIGHT *OUT* OF THEM!

AT BLINDING SPEED, THE *MODERN MERCURY* WHIRLS AROUND HIS NETTED FOES-- ALMOST OBSCURING THEM FROM SIGHT...

C'MON, *ARROW*-- LET'S GET IN ON THE *FINISH* OF THIS!

WAIT! SOMETHING'S *HAPPENING* TO THE *PUTTY-MEN--!*

SUDDENLY, THE BOUNDS OF *FLASH'S* SUPER-SPEED PRISON ARE SHATTERED--

--AS A GREAT BULBOUS SHAPE TAKES TO THE AZURE SKY...

HUH? THEY'VE TURNED INTO AN OLD-FASHIONED *BALLOON!*

USING MY *NET* TO CONTAIN THEMSELVES--

--AND MY *AIR-PRESSURE* TO GIVE THEM *BUOYANCY!*

WITH STUNNING SWIFTNESS, A FISTFUL OF GREEN-FLETCHED ARROWS IS LAUNCHED HEAVENWARD-- BUT...

FORGET IT, *G.A.*-- THEY'RE ALREADY OUT OF *RANGE!* NO WAY TO *CATCH* THEM NOW!

AT LEAST WE STOPPED THEM FROM *GETTING* WHAT THEY CAME FOR!

BY *WHY* WERE THEY SWIPING *COAL?* WHO COULD POSSIBLY HAVE *SENT* THEM?

AND AS THE *SCARLET SPEEDSTER* SPEAKS, A CERTAIN TOP-COATED FORM TURNS GRIMLY-- AND STEALS ONCE MORE INTO THE SHADOWS...

11

"SPECTER IN THE SHADOWS!" CHAPTER 3

MOTOR CITY: AUTOMOTIVE CAPITAL OF A GREAT NATION. *DREAMS* ARE CONCEIVED HERE--SLEEK METALLIC FANTASIES THAT PULSE THROUGH THE COUNTRY'S CONCRETE ARTERIES--THE HALLMARKS OF A LIFE-STYLE...

INTO THE CITY'S LARGEST CAR FACTORY BURST THE *MAN OF STEEL* AND THE *BLONDE BOMBSHELL*...

SUPERMAN *and the* BLACK CANARY

THERE ARE THE *PUTTY-MEN*, BIRD-LADY, RIGHT WHERE MY *TELESCOPIC VISION* SPOTTED THEM--

--IN THE ACT OF STEALING... *TIRES?!*

OURS NOT TO REASON *WHY*, SUPERMAN--

--OURS BUT TO *WIN*-- OR *TRY!*

HEY--THESE THINGS REALLY *DO* STRETCH LIKE *TAFFY!*

SSKKWWWURSSHH

TWISTING HER LITHE BODY, THE *BLACK CANARY* LANDS ON HER FEET AND...

TAFFY--MEET *TIRE!* WOULDN'T BE SURPRISED IF YOU TWO WERE DISTANTLY *RELATED!*

BUT THE SMILE SWIFTLY FADES FROM THE *CANARY'S* LOVELY FACE AS...

THWUNGG

UUNNGHH--PUTTY-MAN'S STRETCHING HIS BODY-- SNAPPING THE TIRES *BACK* AT ME--!

AND HARDLY MORE THAN A WHISPER ESCAPES THE *GIRL GLADIATOR'S* LIPS-- AS SHE SINKS INTO OBLIVION...

÷SIGH÷

THWUMPA

THWUMPA

12

AND ELSEWHERE IN THE SPRAWLING PLANT...

TOO BAD *BATMAN* ISN'T HERE! THIS IS THE KIND OF ACTION HE *THRIVES* ON!

STILL--*BLACK CANARY* MAKES A RATHER *ATTRACTIVE* SUBSTITUTE!

WONDER HOW SHE'S *DOING?*

A SHORT DISTANCE AWAY, THE SUBJECT OF *SUPERMAN'S* THOUGHTS LIES SENSELESS, MOVING SLOWLY, INEXORABLY, TOWARDS AN "IMPRESSIVE" FINISH...

...WHILE THE *ONLY BEING* WHO MIGHT POSSIBLY *SAVE* HER MEETS WITH AN UNEXPECTED *DELAY...*

THEY'RE *DOWN*-- BUT NOT *OUT!*

DROPPING EMPTY AUTO BODIES ON ME!

...OR *IS* HE THE "ONLY BEING"?

A MANUFACTURING PLANT IS A COMPLEX CONSTRUCTION OF CONCRETE AND STEEL, COMPLETELY ENCLOSED FROM THE OUTSIDE WORLD...

HOW, THEN, DOES ONE EXPLAIN THE SUDDEN *WIND* THAT WHISTLES THROUGH THE STRUCTURE, SNATCHING A "SLEEPING BEAUTY" FROM THE POUNDING JAWS OF *DEATH?...*

13

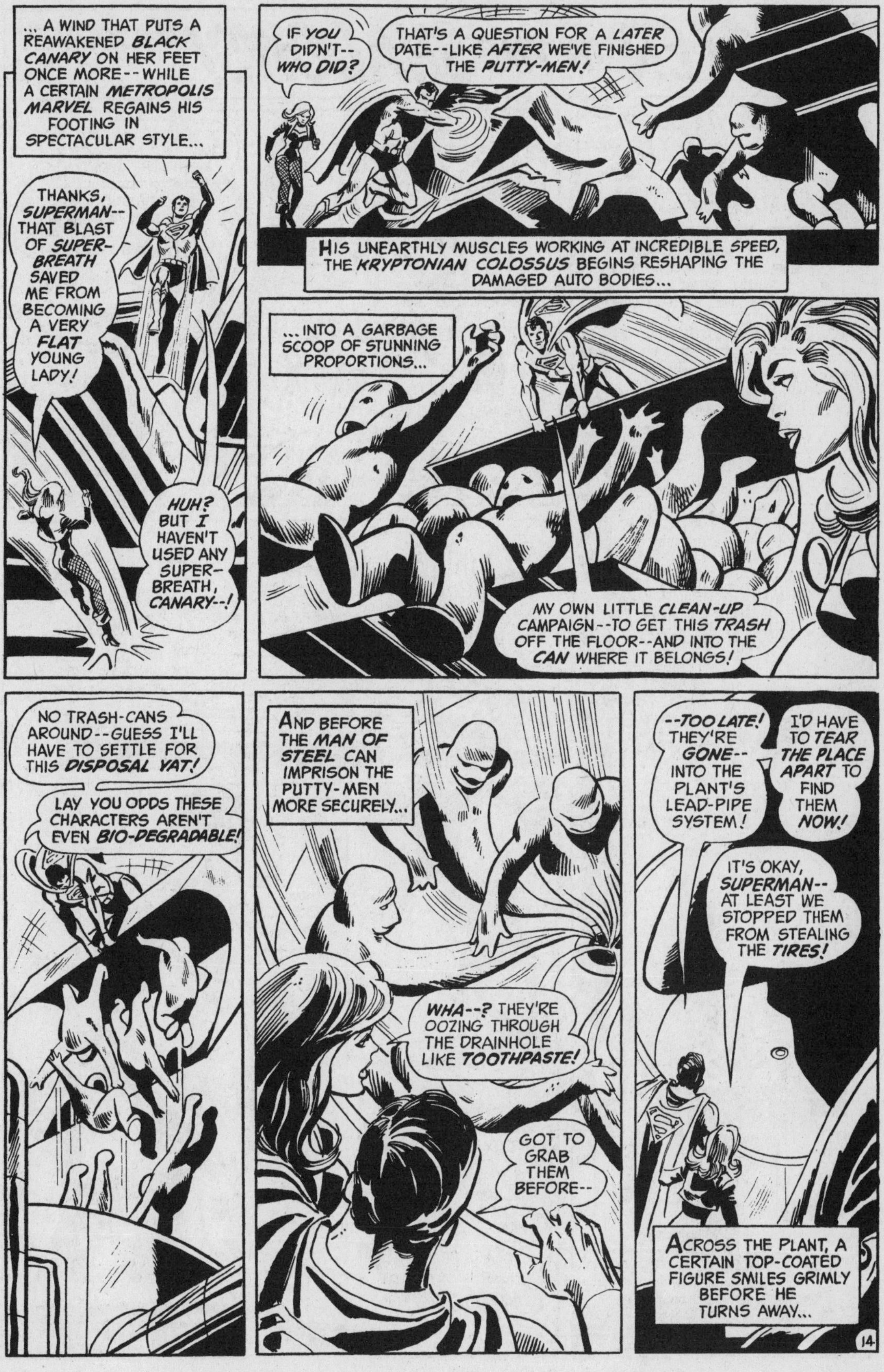
... A WIND THAT PUTS A REAWAKENED BLACK CANARY ON HER FEET ONCE MORE--WHILE A CERTAIN METROPOLIS MARVEL REGAINS HIS FOOTING IN SPECTACULAR STYLE...
THANKS, SUPERMAN--THAT BLAST OF SUPER-BREATH SAVED ME FROM BECOMING A VERY FLAT YOUNG LADY!
HUH? BUT I HAVEN'T USED ANY SUPER-BREATH, CANARY--!
IF YOU DIDN'T--WHO DID?
THAT'S A QUESTION FOR A LATER DATE--LIKE AFTER WE'VE FINISHED THE PUTTY-MEN!
HIS UNEARTHLY MUSCLES WORKING AT INCREDIBLE SPEED, THE KRYPTONIAN COLOSSUS BEGINS RESHAPING THE DAMAGED AUTO BODIES...
... INTO A GARBAGE SCOOP OF STUNNING PROPORTIONS...
MY OWN LITTLE CLEAN-UP CAMPAIGN--TO GET THIS TRASH OFF THE FLOOR--AND INTO THE CAN WHERE IT BELONGS!
NO TRASH-CANS AROUND--GUESS I'LL HAVE TO SETTLE FOR THIS DISPOSAL VAT!
LAY YOU ODDS THESE CHARACTERS AREN'T EVEN BIO-DEGRADABLE!
AND BEFORE THE MAN OF STEEL CAN IMPRISON THE PUTTY-MEN MORE SECURELY...
WHA--? THEY'RE OOZING THROUGH THE DRAINHOLE LIKE TOOTHPASTE!
GOT TO GRAB THEM BEFORE--
--TOO LATE! THEY'RE GONE--INTO THE PLANT'S LEAD-PIPE SYSTEM!
I'D HAVE TO TEAR THE PLACE APART TO FIND THEM NOW!
IT'S OKAY, SUPERMAN--AT LEAST WE STOPPED THEM FROM STEALING THE TIRES!
ACROSS THE PLANT, A CERTAIN TOP-COATED FIGURE SMILES GRIMLY BEFORE HE TURNS AWAY...
14

"SPECTER IN THE SHADOWS!" CHAPTER 4

THE *CALIFORNIA COAST:* 840 MILES OF LOW, SANDY BEACHES AND ROCK-DIRT HEADLANDS, DOTTED BY A HANDFUL OF NATURAL ISLANDS--AND A COUPLE OF *MAN-MADE* ONES.

HERE AND THERE, GREAT *OIL DRILLS* PUMP A MURKY BLACK FLUID FROM THE DEPTHS OF THE SUN-STREAKED SEA--THE LIFE-BLOOD OF A NATION.

A GLEAM OF JADE-LIGHT-- AND TWO FORMS COME SLICING THROUGH THE HUMID PACIFIC SKY...

GREEN LANTERN and The ELONGATED MAN

JACKPOT, RALPH --WE'VE *FOUND* 'EM!

I CLAIM *FIRST LICKS,* GL!

I *OWE* THESE CHARACTERS *PLENTY* FROM THE *LAST* TIME WE TANGLED!

IN YOUR CASE, PAL-- *TANGLED* IS EXACTLY THE RIGHT WORD!

BLAST! SHOULD'VE KNOWN MY *POWER RING* WOULDN'T AFFECT PASTY- *YELLOW* PUTTY-MEN--!

THWA—SHH

STILL, THERE'S *EFFECT*--AND THERE'S *CAUSE*--

--AND THE *RING* CAN DEFINITELY *CAUSE* THESE OIL DRUMS TO *POUND* MY POINT HOME!

THAT SHOULD HOLD 'EM FOR A FEW SECONDS! HOW *YOU* MAKING OUT--?

RALPH--? RALPH--?!

NO-OOOH!

GO GET HIM, *JUSTICE LEAGUER!*

15

TIME STANDS STILL AS AN ANXIOUS *GREEN LANTERN* PEERS DOWN INTO THE VIOLENTLY FROTHING WATERS--

--WAITING-- WAITING...

...UNTIL A SIMPLE DOUGHY FORM BURSTS FROM THE INKY DEPTHS--*ALONE*...

GREAT GUARDIANS! RALPH'S STILL *DOWN* THERE!

GOT TO GO *AFTER* HIM--

--AND PRAY I'M NOT *TOO LATE!*

LIKE A JADE JAVELIN, THE *POWER-RINGED PALADIN* PLUNGES BENEATH THE WAVES--

--LEAVING A SHADOWY SPECTATOR TO CONTINUE HIS SILENT VIGIL...

NO *TRACE* OF HIM-- BUT THE RIP-TIDES ARE *STRONG* HERE!

COULD THEY HAVE *CARRIED AWAY* RALPH'S BODY...?

HUH? A FIELD OF *GOLDEN SEAWEED*-- AND I *STUMBLED BLINDLY* INTO IT--!

16

THIS *YELLOW* MENACE *TIGHTENING* AROUND ME--

SEARING VELVET FILLS THE SPACES BEHIND THE *GREEN GLADIATOR'S* EYES AS THE WRITING VEGETATION TIGHTENS ITS EMBRACE--

THE UNDERSEA CURRENT RIPPLES AND ROLLS--

--AND SUDDENLY COMES *ALIVE!*...

...BUT IT IS A LIFE WHICH *GIVES* LIFE--

--AS THE SWIFTLY-SWIRLING MAELSTROM PULLS *GREEN LANTERN* FREE OF THE GREEDILY GRASPING GROWTH...

...AND HURLS HIM TO THE SURFACE ONCE MORE!...

PUTTY-MEN *GONE*--NOT A CHANCE OF TRACKING THEM *NOW*--!

I COULDN'T EVEN GET *THAT* RIGHT!

POOR *RALPH*-- ALL THIS POWER AT MY COMMAND-- AND I STILL COULDN'T *SAVE* HIM--!

WHO'D HAVE THOUGHT THE *ELONGATED MAN'S FIRST* CASE WITH THE *JUSTICE LEAGUE* WOULD ALSO BE HIS *LAST?*

HOW WILL I BREAK THIS TO THE *OTHERS?*

IN A MOMENT, THE *EMERALD CRUSADER* IS GONE--AND THE MYSTERIOUS FIGURE WHO HAS BEEN WATCHING FROM THE SHADOWS TURNS AWAY AS WELL...

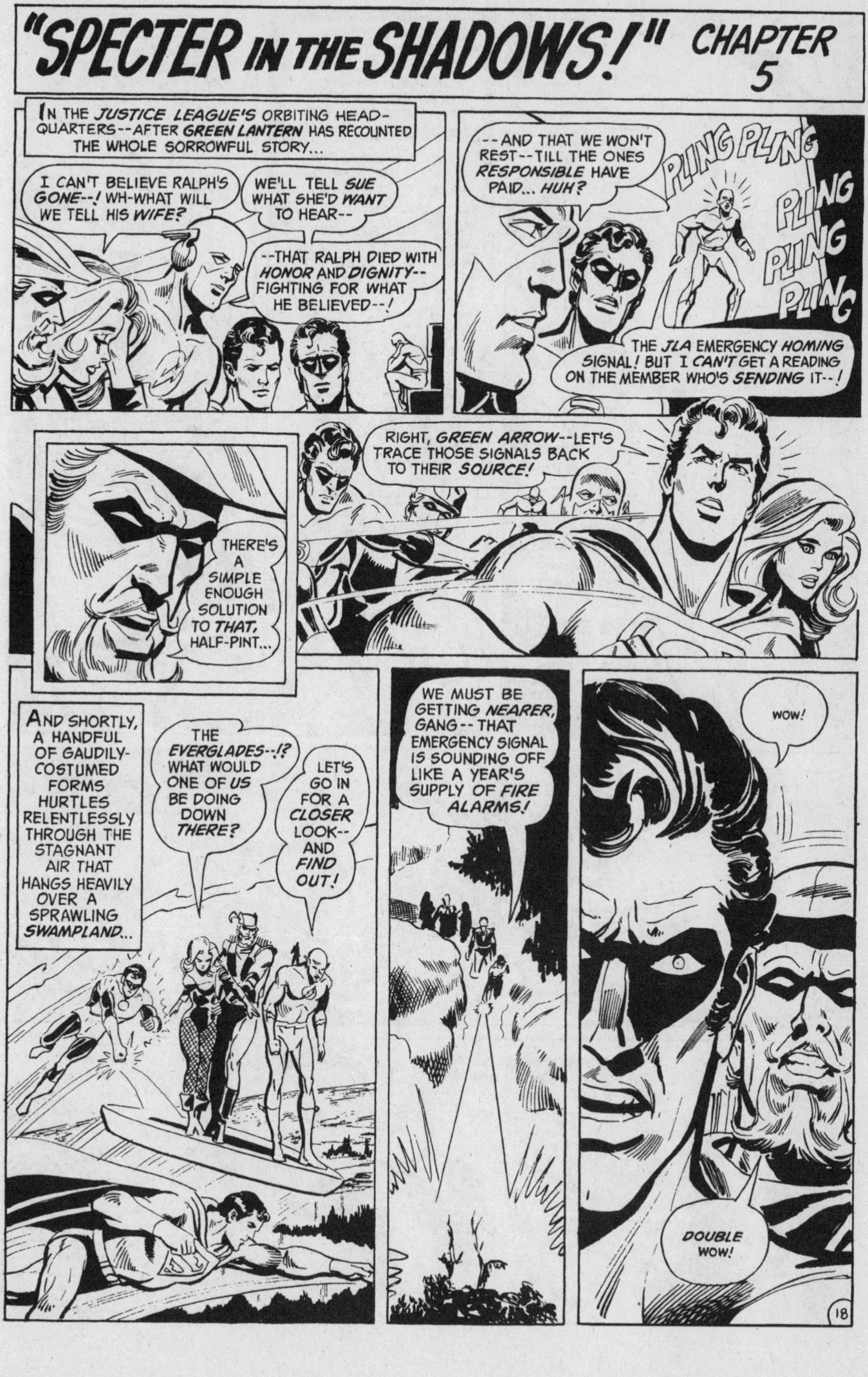
"SPECTER IN THE SHADOWS!" CHAPTER 5
IN THE JUSTICE LEAGUE'S ORBITING HEADQUARTERS--AFTER GREEN LANTERN HAS RECOUNTED THE WHOLE SORROWFUL STORY...
I CAN'T BELIEVE RALPH'S GONE--! WH-WHAT WILL WE TELL HIS WIFE?
WE'LL TELL SUE WHAT SHE'D WANT TO HEAR--
--THAT RALPH DIED WITH HONOR AND DIGNITY--FIGHTING FOR WHAT HE BELIEVED--!
--AND THAT WE WON'T REST--TILL THE ONES RESPONSIBLE HAVE PAID... HUH?
PLING PLING PLING PLING PLING
THE JLA EMERGENCY HOMING SIGNAL! BUT I CAN'T GET A READING ON THE MEMBER WHO'S SENDING IT--!
THERE'S A SIMPLE ENOUGH SOLUTION TO THAT, HALF-PINT...
RIGHT, GREEN ARROW--LET'S TRACE THOSE SIGNALS BACK TO THEIR SOURCE!
AND SHORTLY, A HANDFUL OF GAUDILY-COSTUMED FORMS HURTLES RELENTLESSLY THROUGH THE STAGNANT AIR THAT HANGS HEAVILY OVER A SPRAWLING SWAMPLAND...
THE EVERGLADES--!? WHAT WOULD ONE OF US BE DOING DOWN THERE?
LET'S GO IN FOR A CLOSER LOOK--AND FIND OUT!
WE MUST BE GETTING NEARER, GANG--THAT EMERGENCY SIGNAL IS SOUNDING OFF LIKE A YEAR'S SUPPLY OF FIRE ALARMS!
WOW!
DOUBLE WOW!
18

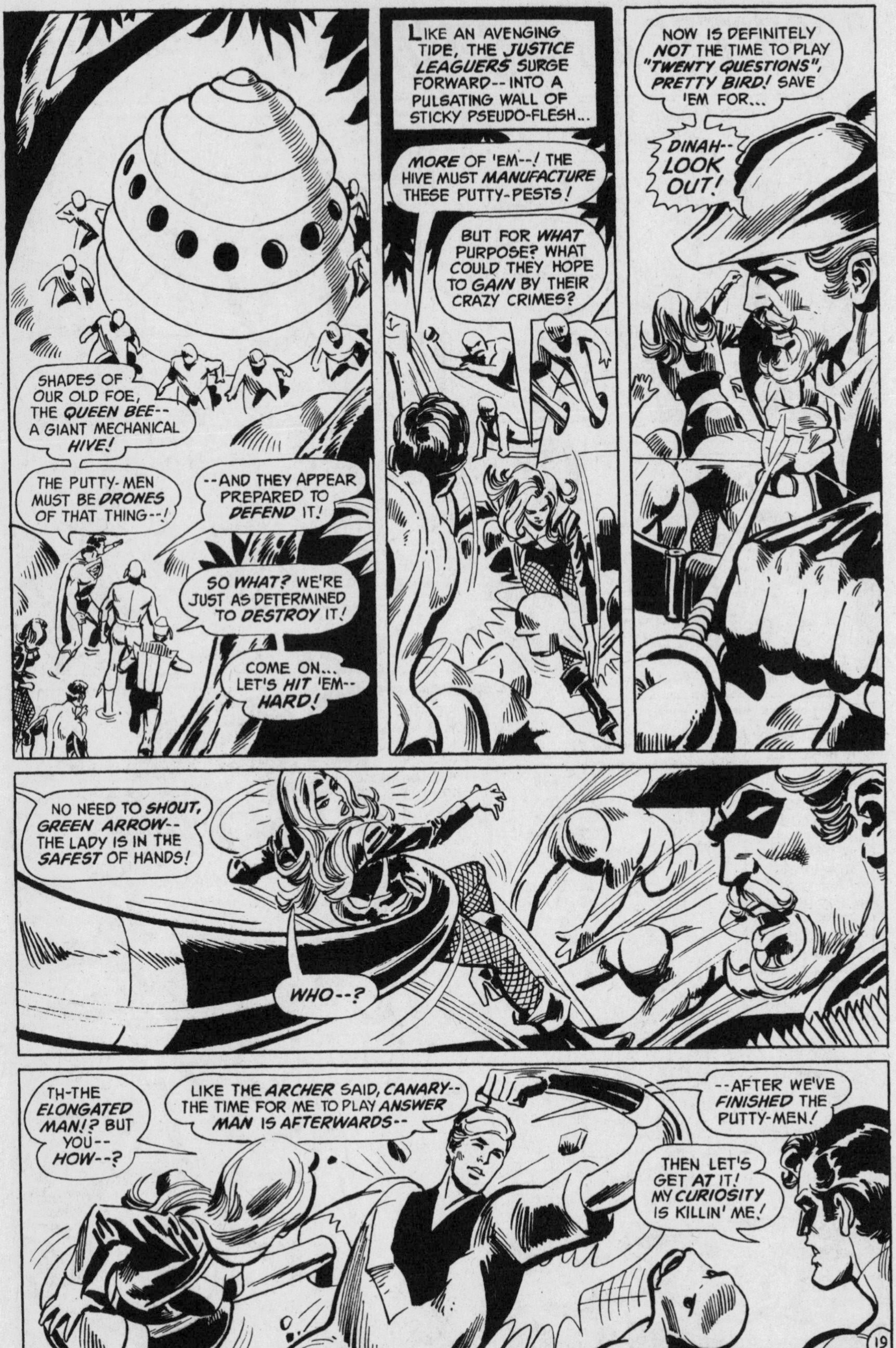
SHADES OF OUR OLD FOE, THE QUEEN BEE-- A GIANT MECHANICAL HIVE!
THE PUTTY-MEN MUST BE DRONES OF THAT THING--!
--AND THEY APPEAR PREPARED TO DEFEND IT!
SO WHAT? WE'RE JUST AS DETERMINED TO DESTROY IT!
COME ON... LET'S HIT 'EM-- HARD!
LIKE AN AVENGING TIDE, THE JUSTICE LEAGUERS SURGE FORWARD-- INTO A PULSATING WALL OF STICKY PSEUDO-FLESH...
MORE OF 'EM--! THE HIVE MUST MANUFACTURE THESE PUTTY-PESTS!
BUT FOR WHAT PURPOSE? WHAT COULD THEY HOPE TO GAIN BY THEIR CRAZY CRIMES?
NOW IS DEFINITELY NOT THE TIME TO PLAY "TWENTY QUESTIONS", PRETTY BIRD! SAVE 'EM FOR...
DINAH-- LOOK OUT!
NO NEED TO SHOUT, GREEN ARROW-- THE LADY IS IN THE SAFEST OF HANDS!
WHO--?
TH-THE ELONGATED MAN!? BUT YOU-- HOW--?
LIKE THE ARCHER SAID, CANARY-- THE TIME FOR ME TO PLAY ANSWER MAN IS AFTERWARDS--
--AFTER WE'VE FINISHED THE PUTTY-MEN!
THEN LET'S GET AT IT! MY CURIOSITY IS KILLIN' ME!
19

A STUDY IN *TEAMWORK:* THE REMARKABLE POWERS OF *EARTH'S GREATEST HEROES* PUT TO EXTRAORDINARY USE...

...AS AWESOME *EMERALD ENERGY* CARVES A YAWNING *PIT* INTO THE MARSHLAND FLOOR...

...A PIT SWIFTLY FILLED TO CAPACITY AT THE IRRESISTIBLE URGING OF THE *FASTEST MAN ALIVE*...

...AND FUSED FOREVER SHUT BY THE *MAN OF STEEL'S* SEARING HEAT VISION...

THEN--AND *ONLY* THEN-- IS THERE TIME FOR QUESTIONS--AND-ANSWERS...

WHY DIDN'T YOU LET *US* IN ON YOUR PUTTY-MAN MASQUERADE, RALPH--?

WE WERE *BROKEN-HEARTED*--!

SORRY, GANG-- BUT THERE WASN'T *TIME*!

THE IDEA DIDN'T OCCUR TO ME TILL I HAD ONE OF THOSE CHARACTERS UNDER-WATER--!

IT WAS THE ONLY WAY I COULD THINK OF TO *DISCOVER* THEIR HIDE-OUT--

HUMMM MMMM MM

HUH? WHAT IN BLAZES IS *THAT?*

I'M NO *EXPERT* ON THAT HIVE--BUT I *HAVE* LEARNED A LITTLE BIT!

THE SOUND YOU HEAR IS THE *ACTIVATION* OF THE HIVE'S SELF-DESTRUCT MECHANISM!

A MATTER OF MOMENTS --AND THIS WHOLE NEIGHBORHOOD WILL BE IN ITTY-BITTY *PIECES*!

HUMMM MMMM

20

THE ONLY WAY TO **PREVENT** THE EXPLOSION IS TO **DEFUSE** THE DETONATOR--BUT...

SKIP THE **BUTS!** LET'S TAKE THAT BIG GOLD BLISTER APART AT THE SEAMS!

BUT AS THE DARING DEFENDERS BULLDOZE FORWARD...

UNNF! THERE'S AN INVISIBLE **FORCE-FIELD** SURROUNDING IT--STRONGER THAN EVEN **I** CAN PENETRATE!

THAT'S WHAT I WAS TRYING TO **TELL** YOU! THERE'S **NO WAY** INTO THAT GIZMO!

BELIEVE ME--I'VE **TRIED!**

MAYBE **YOU** TRIED, RALPH-- BUT YOU DIDN'T HAVE **HELP** THEN!

I BETCHA OUR COMBINED POWER CONCENTRATED ON A SINGLE SPOT WILL **CRACK** THAT FIELD!

BUT EVEN SO-- THE PASSAGEWAYS IN THERE ARE TOO **SMALL** FOR ANYONE TO MOVE THROUGH!

BOY, RALPH--DO **YOU** HAVE THINGS TO **LEARN!**

AND THE **ELONGATED MAN'S** NEXT LESSON IS QUICKLY TAUGHT--AS HIS FELLOW JLAERS COMBINE THEIR AMAZING ABILITIES IN A DESPERATE EFFORT TO BREACH THE HIVE'S DEFENSES--

-- AND TO A SMALL DEGREE **SUCCEED**...

THAT'S MY **CUE!** SEE YOU SOON!

THEN--DEEP WITHIN THE MECHANICAL LABYRINTH...

HUMMING'S GROWING **LOUDER**-- MUST BE GETTING CLOSER TO MY GOAL!

SUDDENLY...

WHA--? MUST'VE STUMBLED INTO ONE OF THE PUTTY-MAN PRODUCTION CENTERS!

STUFF'S WRAPPING AROUND ME--MESSING UP MY SIZE-AND-WEIGHT CONTROLS!

I'M **TRAPPED!**

21

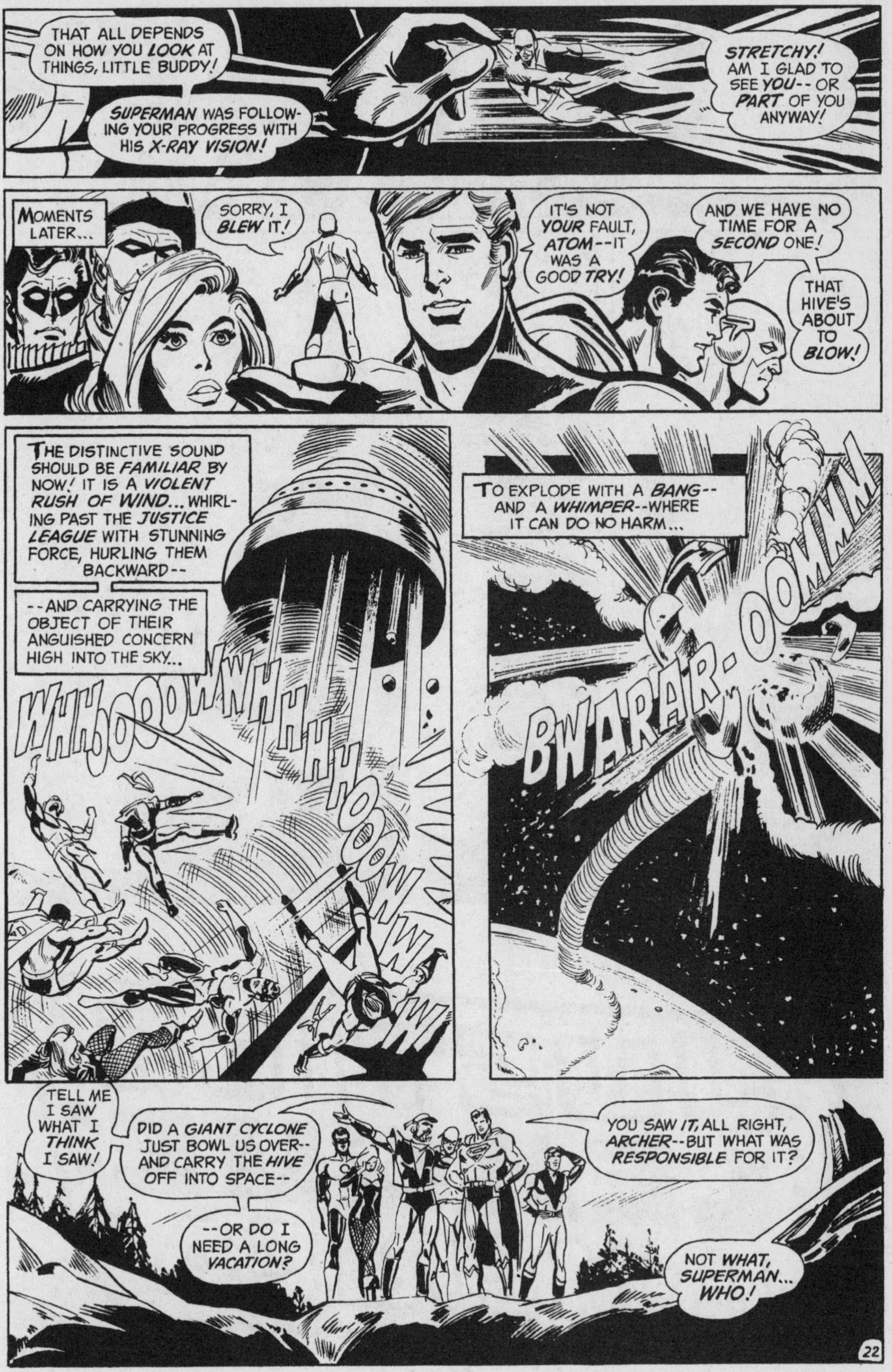
THAT ALL DEPENDS ON HOW YOU LOOK AT THINGS, LITTLE BUDDY!
SUPERMAN WAS FOLLOWING YOUR PROGRESS WITH HIS X-RAY VISION!
STRETCHY! AM I GLAD TO SEE YOU-- OR PART OF YOU ANYWAY!
MOMENTS LATER...
SORRY, I BLEW IT!
IT'S NOT YOUR FAULT, ATOM--IT WAS A GOOD TRY!
AND WE HAVE NO TIME FOR A SECOND ONE!
THAT HIVE'S ABOUT TO BLOW!
THE DISTINCTIVE SOUND SHOULD BE FAMILIAR BY NOW! IT IS A VIOLENT RUSH OF WIND... WHIRLING PAST THE JUSTICE LEAGUE WITH STUNNING FORCE, HURLING THEM BACKWARD--
--AND CARRYING THE OBJECT OF THEIR ANGUISHED CONCERN HIGH INTO THE SKY...
WHHOOOOWWNHHHHHHOOOWWW
TO EXPLODE WITH A BANG--AND A WHIMPER--WHERE IT CAN DO NO HARM...
BWARAR-OOMMM
TELL ME I SAW WHAT I THINK I SAW!
DID A GIANT CYCLONE JUST BOWL US OVER--AND CARRY THE HIVE OFF INTO SPACE--
--OR DO I NEED A LONG VACATION?
YOU SAW IT, ALL RIGHT, ARCHER--BUT WHAT WAS RESPONSIBLE FOR IT?
NOT WHAT, SUPERMAN... WHO!
22

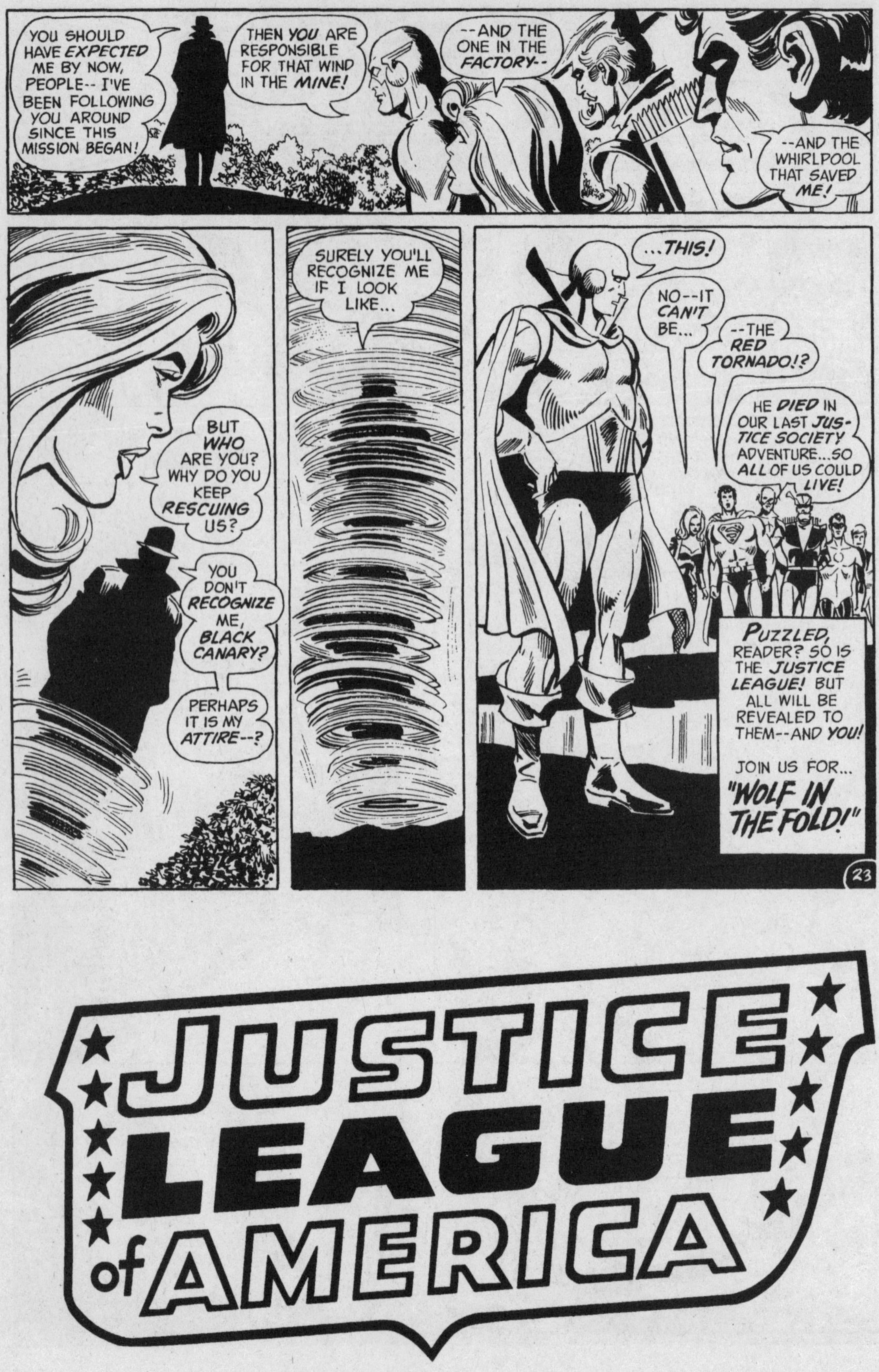
YOU SHOULD HAVE EXPECTED ME BY NOW, PEOPLE-- I'VE BEEN FOLLOWING YOU AROUND SINCE THIS MISSION BEGAN!
THEN YOU ARE RESPONSIBLE FOR THAT WIND IN THE MINE!
--AND THE ONE IN THE FACTORY--
--AND THE WHIRLPOOL THAT SAVED ME!
BUT WHO ARE YOU? WHY DO YOU KEEP RESCUING US?
YOU DON'T RECOGNIZE ME, BLACK CANARY?
PERHAPS IT IS MY ATTIRE--?
SURELY YOU'LL RECOGNIZE ME IF I LOOK LIKE...
...THIS!
NO--IT CAN'T BE...
--THE RED TORNADO!?
HE DIED IN OUR LAST JUSTICE SOCIETY ADVENTURE...SO ALL OF US COULD LIVE!
PUZZLED, READER? SO IS THE JUSTICE LEAGUE! BUT ALL WILL BE REVEALED TO THEM--AND YOU!
JOIN US FOR...
"WOLF IN THE FOLD!"
23

JUSTICE LEAGUE of AMERICA

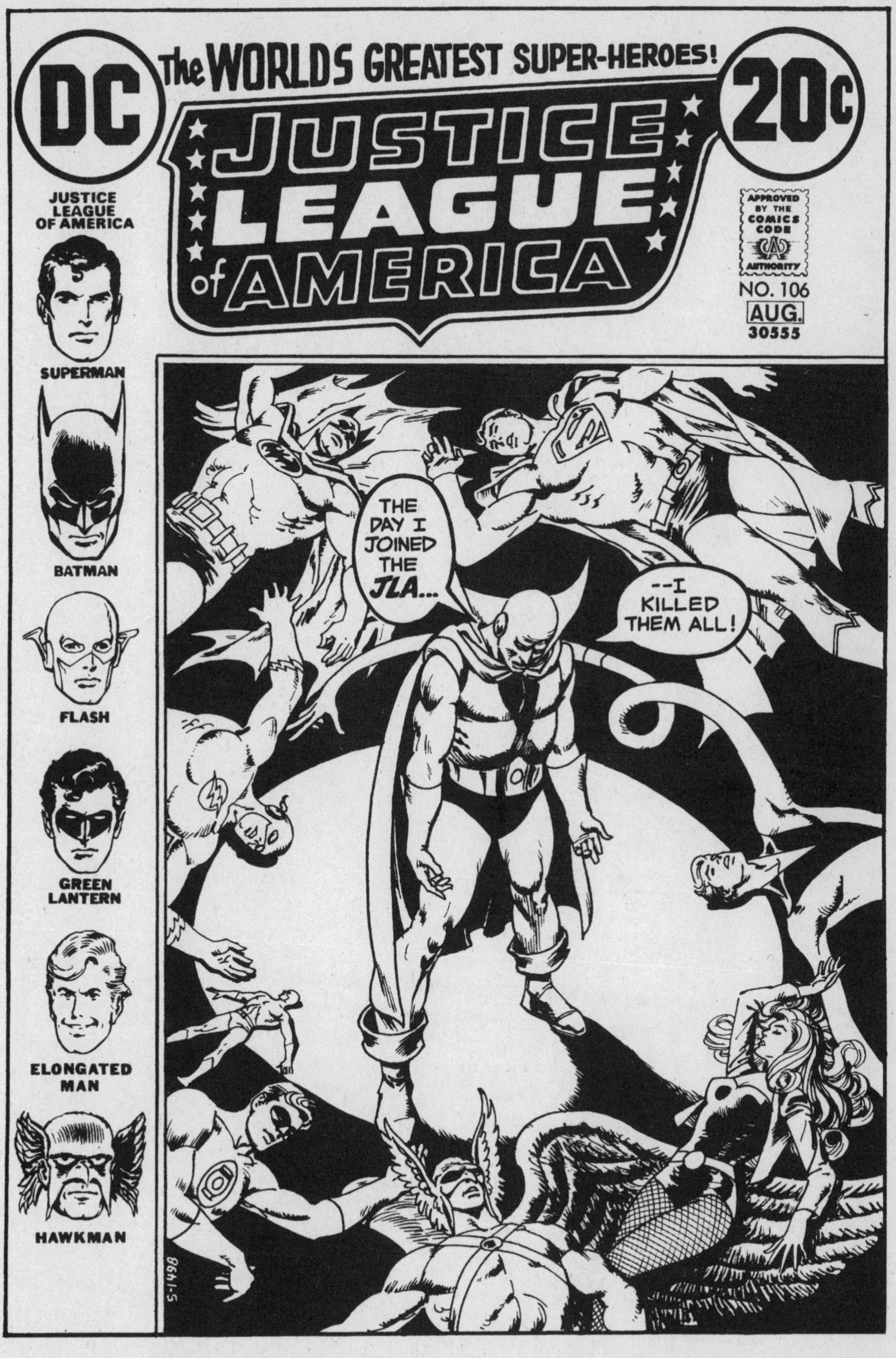
DC
The WORLDS GREATEST SUPER-HEROES!
20¢
JUSTICE LEAGUE of AMERICA
APPROVED BY THE COMICS CODE AUTHORITY
NO. 106
AUG.
30555
JUSTICE LEAGUE OF AMERICA
SUPERMAN
BATMAN
FLASH
GREEN LANTERN
ELONGATED MAN
HAWKMAN
THE DAY I JOINED THE JLA...
--I KILLED THEM ALL!
S-1498

THE TIME: *TODAY*...

THE PLACE: A GIGANTIC *SATELLITE* WHIRLING IN STATIONARY ORBIT 22,300 MILES ABOVE THE SURFACE OF THE *EARTH*...

THE OCCASION: A HASTILY-CALLED EMERGENCY MEETING OF THE...

JUSTICE ☆☆☆ LEAGUE ☆☆☆ of AMERICA

FOR THOSE WHO CAME IN LATE: SEVEN OF OUR STALWARTS HAVE JUST RETURNED FROM THE FLORIDA EVERGLADES, FOLLOWING THEIR OFF-BEAT BATTLE WITH THE PLIABLE *PUTTY-MEN*...

...A BATTLE TURNED IN THEIR FAVOR BY THE LAST-MINUTE APPEARANCE OF THE STORMY *RED TORNADO* -- A HERO THEY ALL THOUGHT *DEAD!*

WE'LL FILL IN ANY *DETAILS* AS WE GO ALONG...

LET'S KEEP THIS BRIEFING SHORT AND SWEET!

RED TORNADO -- CONSIDERING THE CIRCUMSTANCES -- WHAT DO YOU HAVE TO *SAY* FOR YOURSELF?

NOT MUCH CAN I SAY, GREEN LANTERN--THERE'S NOT A GREAT DEAL I KNOW!

COME ON, PAL--WE ALL WATCHED YOU DIE!

HOW DID YOU PULL YOUR LAZARUS BIT--AND WHEN DID YOU GROW A FACE?

YOU JEST, GREEN ARROW--BUT THIS IS NOT A LAUGHING MATTER!

MY MEMORY CIRCUITS ARE UNCLEAR ON THE SUBJECT--MOSTLY PROJECTION AND CONCLUSION--

--BUT I WILL ENLIGHTEN YOU AS BEST I CAN!

"AS YOU REMEMBER, I STOLE THE NEBULA-ROD WHEN YOU AND THE JUSTICE SOCIETY COMBINED FORCES AGAINST THE HAND THAT HELD THE EARTH..."

"THE EXPLOSION OCCURRED AS EXPECTED--AND YOU THOUGHT ME DESTROYED!"

"OBVIOUSLY, I WAS NOT!"

"...IN THE HOPE THAT MY ANDROID BODY MIGHT SURVIVE THE ERUPTING INTERSTELLAR ENERGIES WHERE YOUR HUMAN FORMS WOULD NOT..."

"INSTEAD, IN A ONE-IN-A-BILLION CHANCE, THE ERUPTION TORE A HOLE IN THE DIMENSIONAL FABRIC--AND HURLED ME FROM MY EARTH INTO YOURS..."

"HOW LONG I LAY AS ONE DEAD I DO NOT KNOW--BUT EVENTUALLY, MY DAMAGED BODY WAS DISCOVERED..."

"...BY A BLIND SCULPTOR LIVING ALONE DEEP IN YOUR ROCKY MOUNTAINS..."

2

"THE OLD MAN TOOK ME INTO HIS HOME-- TENDED ME..."

"...AND WHAT PROMPTED HIM TO SCULPT *FEATURES* UPON MY *EMPTY ANDROID* FACE I WILL NEVER KNOW..."

"EVENTUALLY, MY INTERNAL REPAIR MECHANISMS RETURNED ME TO *CONSCIOUSNESS*..."

WHERE... *AM* I? WHAT HAS ...*HAPPENED* TO ME?

BE *CALM*, FRIEND-- *RELAX!* YOU ARE IN *SAFE* HANDS!

"CONVERSATIONS WITH THE OLD MAN DURING MY *RECOVERY* CONVINCED ME I WAS ON THE *WRONG EARTH!*"

"WHEN I WAS *WELL* ENOUGH, I THANKED MY *BLIND* FRIEND--AND SET ABOUT TO *CORRECT* THE SITUATION..."

"BUT THAT WAS EASIER *PLANNED* THAN *ACCOMPLISHED!*"

"TO MY SURPRISE, I FOUND I COULD NOT *PIERCE* THE DIMENSIONAL BARRIER..."

"SOME SIDE EFFECT OF THE *NEBULOID* DESTRUCTION PREVENTED ME FROM EVER *RETURNING* TO MY HOME WORLD!"

I CAME SEARCHING FOR *YOU* THEN--BUT KNOWING YOUR *LOW* OPINION OF ME-- I HELPED YOUR CAUSE IN *SECRET*--

--DECIDING THAT THE *SOONER* YOU DEFEATED THE *PUTTY-MEN*, THE *SOONER* YOU'D HAVE TIME FOR *ME!*

TORNADO, THAT'S NOT *FAIR!* JUST BECAUSE WE FAILED TO LISTEN TO YOU *ONCE*--

YES--AND THAT FAILURE CAUSED THE *DEATH* OF *BLACK CANARY'S HUSBAND!* BUT *ENOUGH* OF SUCH GRIM THINGS!

SUFFICE IT THAT I *DESTROYED* THE *PUTTY-MAN-PRODUCING HIVE-DEVICE*--AND YOU FINALLY BROUGHT ME *HERE!*

3

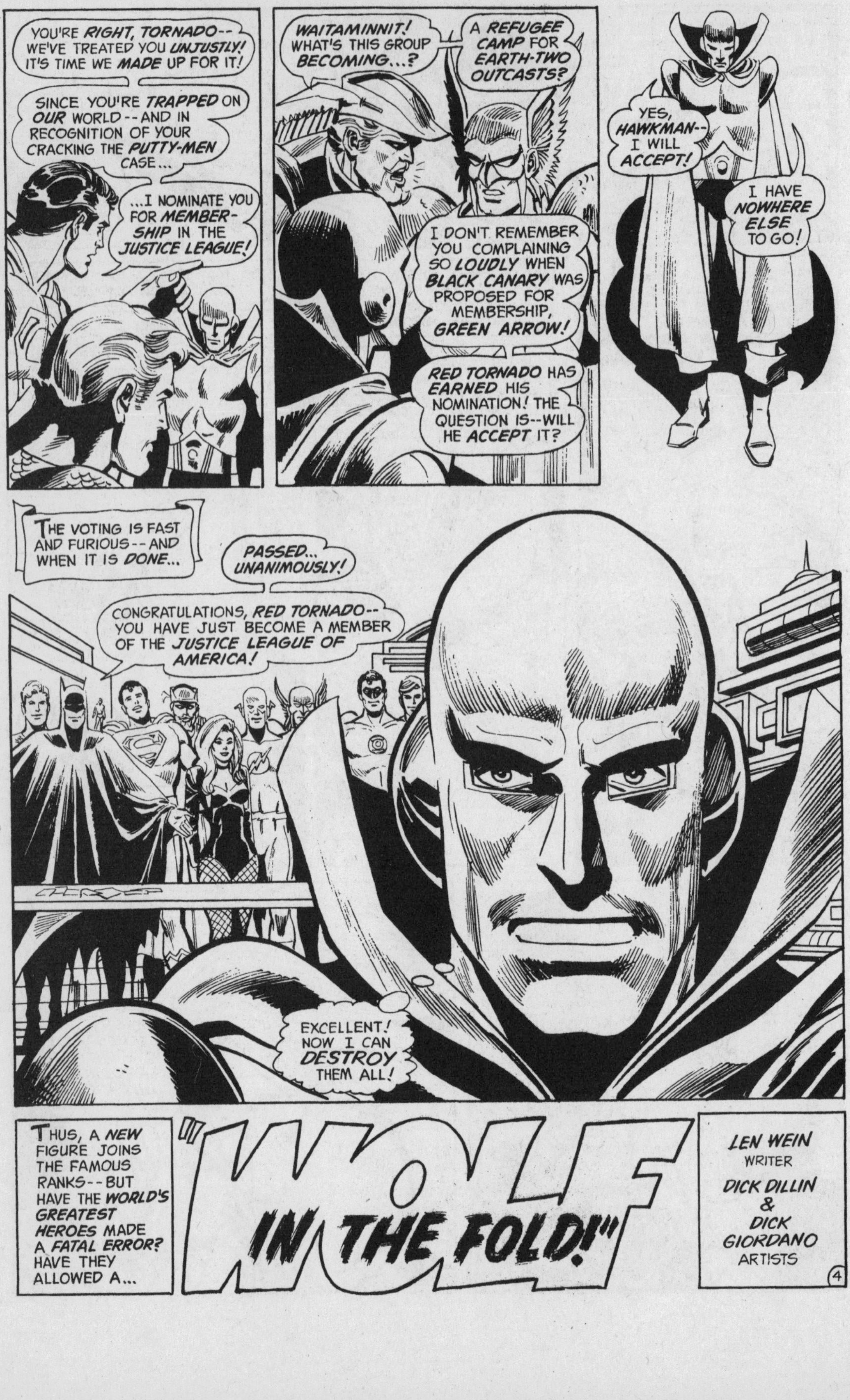
YOU'RE RIGHT, TORNADO-- WE'VE TREATED YOU UNJUSTLY! IT'S TIME WE MADE UP FOR IT!
SINCE YOU'RE TRAPPED ON OUR WORLD--AND IN RECOGNITION OF YOUR CRACKING THE PUTTY-MEN CASE...
...I NOMINATE YOU FOR MEMBERSHIP IN THE JUSTICE LEAGUE!
WAITAMINNIT! WHAT'S THIS GROUP BECOMING...?
A REFUGEE CAMP FOR EARTH-TWO OUTCASTS?
I DON'T REMEMBER YOU COMPLAINING SO LOUDLY WHEN BLACK CANARY WAS PROPOSED FOR MEMBERSHIP, GREEN ARROW!
RED TORNADO HAS EARNED HIS NOMINATION! THE QUESTION IS--WILL HE ACCEPT IT?
YES, HAWKMAN-- I WILL ACCEPT!
I HAVE NOWHERE ELSE TO GO!
THE VOTING IS FAST AND FURIOUS--AND WHEN IT IS DONE...
PASSED... UNANIMOUSLY!
CONGRATULATIONS, RED TORNADO-- YOU HAVE JUST BECOME A MEMBER OF THE JUSTICE LEAGUE OF AMERICA!
EXCELLENT! NOW I CAN DESTROY THEM ALL!
THUS, A NEW FIGURE JOINS THE FAMOUS RANKS--BUT HAVE THE WORLD'S GREATEST HEROES MADE A FATAL ERROR? HAVE THEY ALLOWED A...
"WOLF IN THE FOLD!"
LEN WEIN WRITER
DICK DILLIN & DICK GIORDANO ARTISTS
4

FOR *PART* OF THE ANSWER, LET US TURN *ELSEWHERE*-- TO A HIDDEN *LABORATORY* DEEP IN THE *ROCKY MOUNTAINS*...

--AND THE *ORIGINATOR* OF THE *RED TORNADO'S* MURDER-FILLED THOUGHT...

EXCELLENT! NOW I CAN *DESTROY* THEM ALL!

HIS NAME IS *MORROW, THOMAS OSCAR*--BUT HIS FRIENDS, IF HE HAD ANY, WOULD CALL HIM *TOMORROW*...

T.O. MORROW--WHO, INSPIRED BY HIS NAME, HAS DEDICATED HIMSELF TO DELVING INTO THE WORLD OF THE *FUTURE*...

T.O. MORROW--HE WHO *FIRST* *CREATED* THE *AMAZING RED TORNADO*...

...ONLY TO HAVE HIS *CREATION* TURN *AGAINST* HIM IN THE CAUSE OF *JUSTICE!*

T.O. MORROW-- WHO PAUSES IN HIS BUSINESS TO *GLOAT*...

MY TEMPORARY *CONTROL* OVER THE *TORNADO* IS GONE-- BUT IT NO LONGER *MATTERS!*

SOON THE *JUSTICE LEAGUE* WILL BE *FINISHED*-- AND I'LL SLEEP *PEACEFULLY* AT LAST!

NOT THAT I HOLD ANY *GRUDGES* AGAINST THEM! THEY DO *THEIR* THING--I DO *MINE!* IT'S JUST A MATTER OF *SELF-PRESERVATION!*

IF MY COMPUTER HADN'T MADE THIS *PREDICTION*, I'D PROBABLY HAVE LEFT THEM *ALONE!*

IN PRECISELY 28 DAYS, THE COSMIC BALANCE WILL SHIFT-- AND EITHER T.O. MORROW OR THE JUSTICE LEAGUE OF AMERICA WILL CEASE TO EXIST

THE CHOICE, OF COURSE, WAS *OBVIOUS!* THE PROBLEM WAS-- HOW TO DISPOSE OF THE *JLA* BEFORE THE *DEADLINE!*

AND THE OLD COMPUTER CAME THROUGH *AGAIN!*

FOR THE JUSTICE LEAGUE TO BE DESTROYED A NEW MEMBER MUST BE ADDED TO ITS RANKS...

AND I HAD JUST THE *ONE!* FOR FATE HAD DROPPED THE *RED TORNADO* RIGHT BACK IN MY *LAP!*

5

I *REPAIRED* HIM--GAVE HIM HIS NEW *FACE*--THEN *ALTERED* HIS MEMORY CIRCUITS TO *REMEMBER* ME AS A *BLIND OLD MAN!*

THAT ACCOMPLISHED *PART* OF IT--BUT I STILL HAD TO GIVE HIM *CAUSE* TO *JOIN* THE *JUSTICE LEAGUE!*

MY MONITORS HAD DISCOVERED THE *QUEEN BEE'S* HIDDEN *HIVE!* I *ACTIVATED* IT-- INVOLVED THE *JLA* WITH ITS *PUTTY-DRONES*--

--AND *ARRANGED* THE SITUATION SO THE *RED TORNADO* WOULD COME OUT LOOKING *GOOD!*

YOU *SAY* SOMETHIN', BOSS?

NO, ROSCOE-- JUST CHECKING TO BE CERTAIN EVERYTHING IS *SET!*

IT'S ALL *READY*, BOSS-- JUST LIKE YOU *SAID!*

WE'LL TAKE THESE *FUTURE-WEAPONS* AND *USE* 'EM WHERE THE *RED TORNADO* IS CERTAIN TO *SEE!*

SPLENDID! ANYTHING AT ALL TO MAKE HIM USE HIS NEWLY-GAINED *JLA SIGNAL DEVICE!*

FOR I'VE PLANTED A SMALL *MECHANISM* INSIDE THE *TORNADO'S* BODY THAT *ALTERS* THE DEVICE'S *FREQUENCY!*

THE *FIRST* TIME HE *PRESSES* THAT TRANSMITTER--

--THE *JUSTICE LEAGUE OF AMERICA* WILL *DIE!*

6

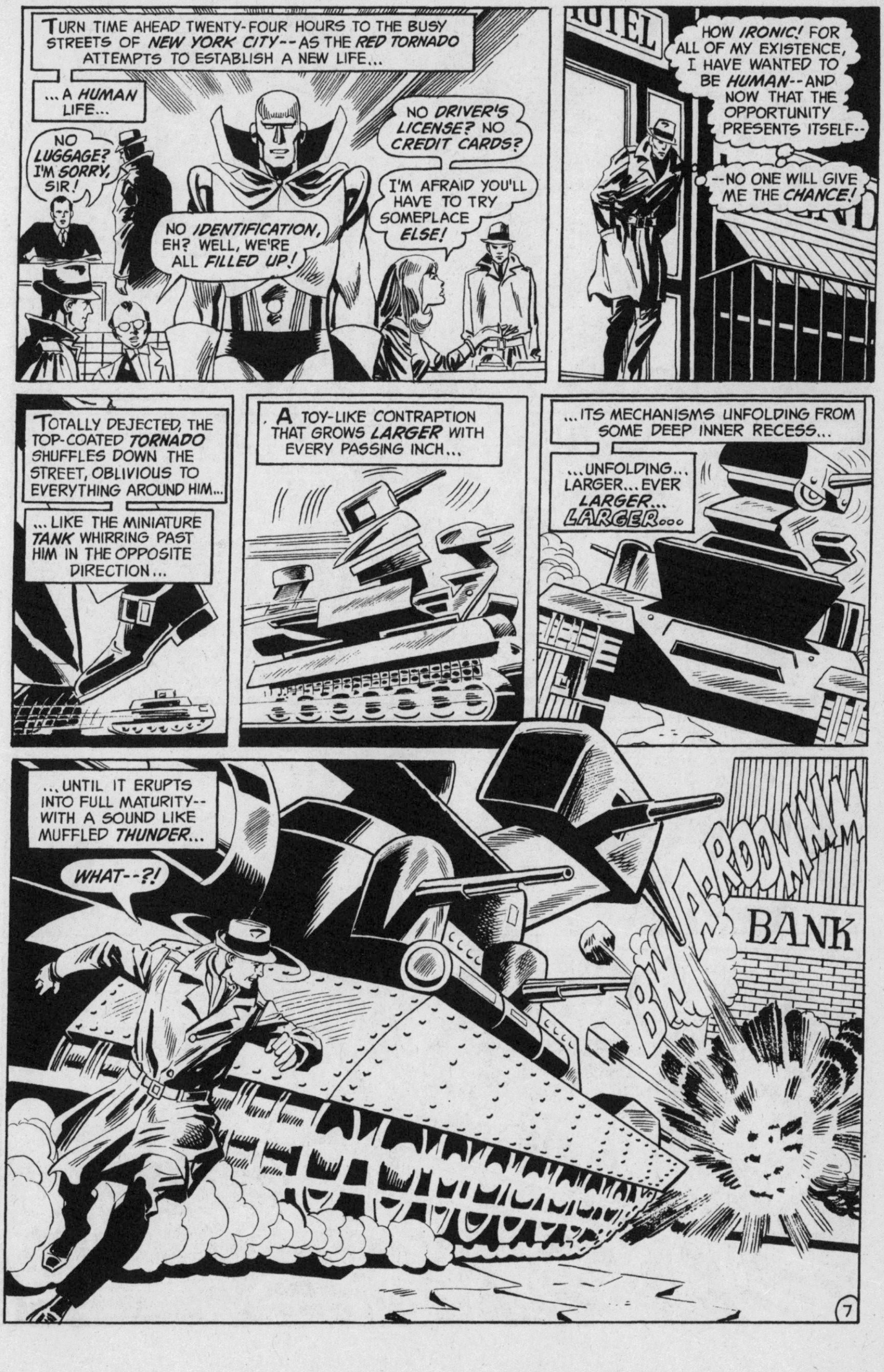
TURN TIME AHEAD TWENTY-FOUR HOURS TO THE BUSY STREETS OF NEW YORK CITY--AS THE RED TORNADO ATTEMPTS TO ESTABLISH A NEW LIFE...
...A HUMAN LIFE...
NO LUGGAGE? I'M SORRY, SIR!
NO IDENTIFICATION, EH? WELL, WE'RE ALL FILLED UP!
NO DRIVER'S LICENSE? NO CREDIT CARDS?
I'M AFRAID YOU'LL HAVE TO TRY SOMEPLACE ELSE!
HOW IRONIC! FOR ALL OF MY EXISTENCE, I HAVE WANTED TO BE HUMAN--AND NOW THAT THE OPPORTUNITY PRESENTS ITSELF--
--NO ONE WILL GIVE ME THE CHANCE!
TOTALLY DEJECTED, THE TOP-COATED TORNADO SHUFFLES DOWN THE STREET, OBLIVIOUS TO EVERYTHING AROUND HIM...
...LIKE THE MINIATURE TANK WHIRRING PAST HIM IN THE OPPOSITE DIRECTION...
A TOY-LIKE CONTRAPTION THAT GROWS LARGER WITH EVERY PASSING INCH...
...ITS MECHANISMS UNFOLDING FROM SOME DEEP INNER RECESS...
...UNFOLDING... LARGER... EVER LARGER... LARGER...
...UNTIL IT ERUPTS INTO FULL MATURITY--WITH A SOUND LIKE MUFFLED THUNDER...
WHAT--?!
BANK
BWA-A-ROOMMM
7

TO BORROW A LINE FROM ONE OF MY NEWLY-GAINED *PARTNERS*...

THIS IS A JOB...

...FOR...

...RED TORNADO!

HIS ALREADY-ANGUISHED MIND RAGING FOR BATTLE, THE *CRIMSON CYCLONE* WHIRLS ACROSS THE STREET...

YOU ARE ALL *UNDER ARREST!* SURRENDER QUIETLY-- AND YOU WILL NOT BE *HURT!*

WHO IN BLAZES IS *THAT?!*

BEATS *ME*-- BUT IT SURE AIN'T *SUPERMAN!*

YOU WILL LEARN, FELONS-- MUCH TO YOUR CHAGRIN--THAT ONE NEED NOT BE A *MAN OF STEEL*--

--TO CONQUER MEN OF *TIN!*

YOUR SUPER-STRENGTH-GIVING *EXOSKELETONS* WILL AVAIL YOU *NOTHING*--

--IF YOU CANNOT *UNTANGLE* YOURSELVES TO *USE* THEM!

8

WE DON'T NEED *MUSCLE* TO FINISH *YOU* OFF, WHIRLY-BIRD!

THIS HERE *ENERGY-TRANSVERTER* OUGHT'A DO THE JOB UP *FINE!*

APPARENTLY, I DID NOT CLEARLY MAKE MY *POINT...*

BUT BEFORE THE *WHIRLWIND WONDER* CAN COMPLETE HIS SENTENCE...

THAT *DEVICE*-- TURNING MY POWERS *AGAINST* ME!

I'M *CAUGHT*-- A *PRISONER* OF MY OWN TORNADO!

I HATE TO *DO* THIS-- HATE TO PROVE THAT THE *JLA* WAS *RIGHT*--

--THAT I *AM* INCAPABLE OF HANDLING THINGS ON MY OWN--

--BUT THE TRIUMPH OF GOOD OVER EVIL IS THE *LEAGUE'S* PRIMARY CONCERN, SO...

FANTASTIC! IN ONE MORE MOMENT, *RED TORNADO* WILL *PRESS* HIS SIGNAL--AND MY WORRIES --AND THE *JUSTICE LEAGUE'S* -- WILL BE *OVER!*

ONLY *THEIRS* WILL BE OVER-- *PERMANENTLY!*

BUT AS THE *RUBY REVOLVER'S* FINGER STREAKS TO HIS BELT-BUCKLE....

UH UH UH-- DON'T TOUCH THAT *DIAL!*

WHO--?

9

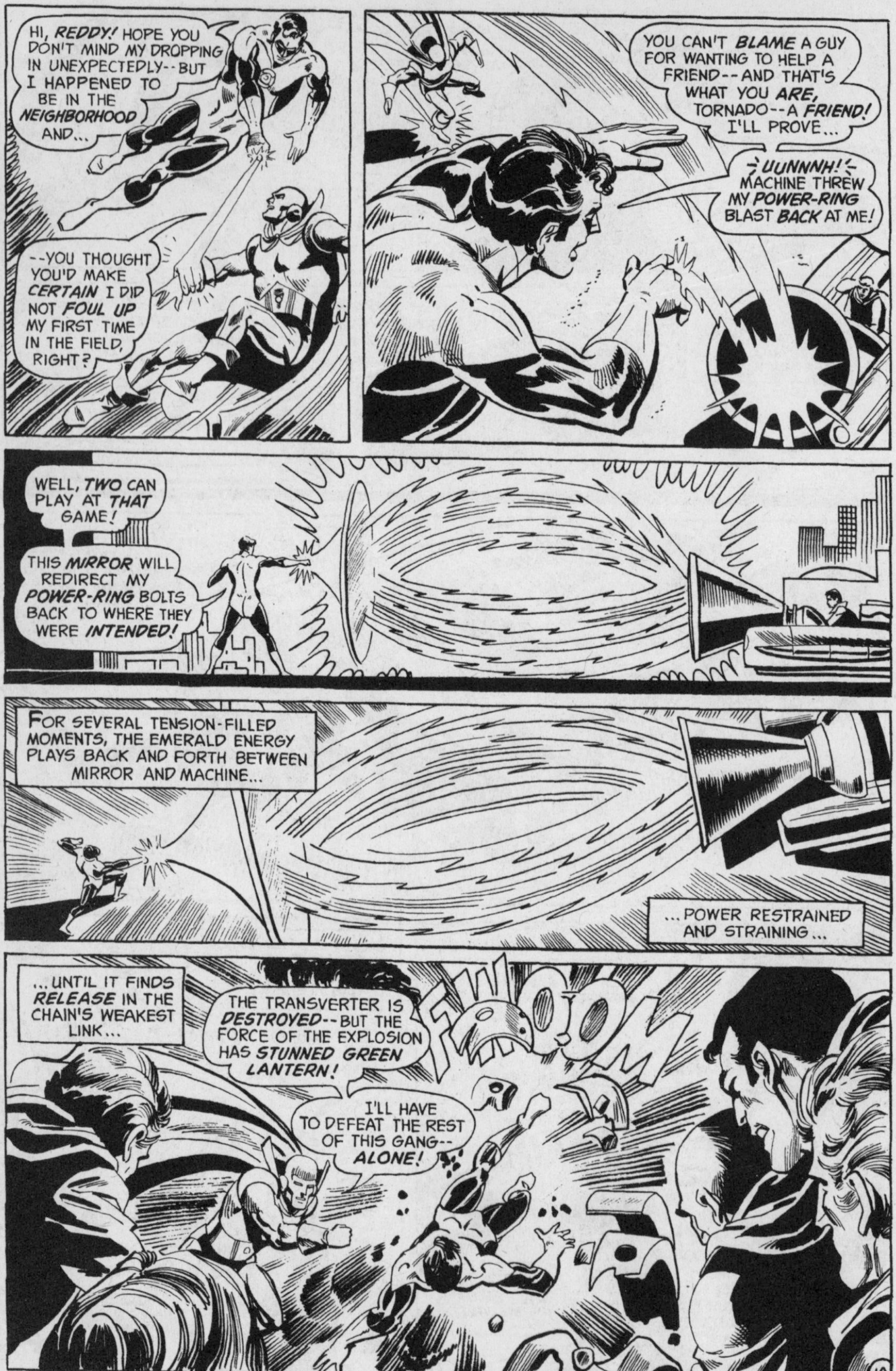
HI, REDDY! HOPE YOU DON'T MIND MY DROPPING IN UNEXPECTEDLY--BUT I HAPPENED TO BE IN THE NEIGHBORHOOD AND...
--YOU THOUGHT YOU'D MAKE CERTAIN I DID NOT FOUL UP MY FIRST TIME IN THE FIELD, RIGHT?
YOU CAN'T BLAME A GUY FOR WANTING TO HELP A FRIEND--AND THAT'S WHAT YOU ARE, TORNADO--A FRIEND! I'LL PROVE...
UUNNNH! MACHINE THREW MY POWER-RING BLAST BACK AT ME!
WELL, TWO CAN PLAY AT THAT GAME!
THIS MIRROR WILL REDIRECT MY POWER-RING BOLTS BACK TO WHERE THEY WERE INTENDED!
FOR SEVERAL TENSION-FILLED MOMENTS, THE EMERALD ENERGY PLAYS BACK AND FORTH BETWEEN MIRROR AND MACHINE...
...POWER RESTRAINED AND STRAINING...
...UNTIL IT FINDS RELEASE IN THE CHAIN'S WEAKEST LINK...
THE TRANSVERTER IS DESTROYED--BUT THE FORCE OF THE EXPLOSION HAS STUNNED GREEN LANTERN!
FWOOOM
I'LL HAVE TO DEFEAT THE REST OF THIS GANG--ALONE!
10

REDDY! ONE OF THE FIRST THINGS YOU'LL HAVE TO *LEARN* IS--

THWAK

--YOU ARE *NEVER* ALONE IN THE *JUSTICE LEAGUE!*

BATMAN! FLASH! DON'T TELL ME *YOU* CAME TO "VISIT," TOO?

GL DOESN'T HAVE A *MONOPOLY* ON FRIENDSHIP, *TORNADO!* WE *ALL* OWE YOU SOMETHING--

--AND WE USUALLY *REPAY* OUR DEBTS!

YOU GUYS TAKE CARE OF THINGS *HERE!* I'LL HANDLE THE *TANK!*

SHOK

AND A SPLIT-INSTANT LATER...

THIS WAR-MACHINE IS CONSTRUCTED ON A *FOURTH-DIMENSIONAL* PRINCIPLE, UTILIZING *NEGATIVE-SPACE* TO CONTAIN MOST OF ITS BULK!

I'D HOPED SOME *SUPER-VIBRATIONS* WOULD REVEAL A CRITICAL *STRESS POINT--* BUT NO SUCH LUCK!

TIME I CALLED FOR *REINFORCEMENTS!*

TORNADO-- COME QUICKLY! I'M GONNA NEED YOUR *HELP!*

WITH MIND-STUNNING SPEED, THE *SCARLET SWIRLER* REACHES *FLASH'S* SIDE--AND *SOON...*

CIRCLING THE TANK COUNTER TO THE *SPEEDSTER'S* PATH-- FOCUSING ALL MY *VIBRATIONS* ON IT AS INSTRUCTED!

BUT WHAT DOES *FLASH* HOPE TO *ACCOMPLISH?*

11

WHILE, ACROSS THE STREET, A CERTAIN *CAPED CRIME-BUSTER* IS ACCOMPLISHING *PLENTY*...

HOPE THE *TORNADO* DOESN'T *RESENT* OUR PRESENCE-- BUT HE'D *NEVER* HAVE BEEN ABLE TO CONTROL THIS SITUATION BY *HIMSELF!*

EVEN *GREEN LANTERN* COULDN'T HANDLE IT *SOLO!*

THWRACK

BATMAN!--I'M *SURPRISED* AT YOU! THE NUMBER ONE RULE IN THE *SUPER-HERO* BUSINESS IS--*ALWAYS WATCH YOUR BACK!*

I *WAS* WATCHING, GL--BUT I DECIDED TO LEAVE THE LAST ONE FOR *YOU!*

REMIND ME TO RETURN THE "FAVOR" SOME DAY!

SO--I SEE YOU PEOPLE HAVE TIED UP THINGS ON *YOUR* END!

NATURALLY, *FLASH*-- WE ONLY...

HEY--WHAT HAPPENED TO THE *TANK?*

OH, *THAT*-- A *SIMPLE* THING, REALLY!

RED TORNADO AND I JUST KEPT BOMBARDING IT WITH *CONFLICTING* VIBRATIONS TILL WE HIT THE PRIME STRESS POINT--

--AND *REVERSED* THE EXPANSION PROCESS!

WOULD ANYONE CARE FOR A VERY *DEADLY* WIND-UP TOY?

BLAST! I WAS *SO CLOSE*--!

TIME IS RUNNING *OUT*-- BUT I STILL HAVE A FEW GAMBITS LEFT TO *PLAY!*

12

SOON AFTER, IN *JLA* HEADQUARTERS...

GREEN LANTERN, I *RESENT* YOUR INTRUSION IN MY BATTLE! I DEMAND TO BE TREATED AS AN *EQUAL* MEMBER OF THE *JUSTICE LEAGUE,* OR...

AWW...COME ON, *TORNADO*-- YOU WERE JUST ABOUT TO *CALL* US WHEN WE SHOWED!

THAT IS A MISTAKE I WILL *NOT* MAKE AGAIN!

ENOUGH *BICKERING!* WE HAVE A PROBLEM BEFORE US THAT NEEDS A *SOLUTION!*

THE *UNIFORMS* THEY WORE WERE *FAMILIAR!* IF ONLY...

GOT IT!--*T.O. MORROW!* HIS FACELESS MINIONS WORE THAT OUTFIT THE *FIRST* TIME WE MET...

--THE *RED TORNADO!* INTERESTING THAT BOTH HE AND *MORROW* SHOULD REAPPEAR AT THE *SAME* TIME! SORT OF MAKES ONE *WONDER*--!

WHAT--!?

ENOUGH! I HAVE *BETTER* THINGS TO DO THAN STAND HERE AND TOLERATE YOUR VEILED *ACCUSATIONS!*

TORNADO --WAIT! WE DIDN'T *MEAN*...

NO, *FLASH*-- LET HIM *GO!* IT'S *SIMPLER* THIS WAY!

I HAVE MATTERS TO DISCUSS THAT ARE *NOT* FOR THE *RED TORNADO'S* EARS!

13

BY MORNING, THE AWESOME ANDROID'S ANGER HAS FADED--TO BE REPLACED BY LONELINESS-- AND *SELF-DOUBT*...

I *DISLIKE* DOING THIS--BUT SINCE I CAN'T FIND *ACCOMMODATIONS* WITHOUT FIRST FINDING *EMPLOYMENT*...

NEW YORK JOB OPPORTUNITIES, INC.

NEXT, PLEASE!

SILENTLY, THE *RED TORNADO* TAKES HIS SEAT--THE INEVITABLE FORMS ARE PRODUCED AND...

NAME?

UH... *SMITH!* *JOHN* SMITH!

ADDRESS?

GENERAL DELIVERY!

UH-HUH! *AGE?*

AT THE MOMENT I FEEL LIKE THE *OLDEST* MAN ALIVE!

PLEASE--JUST ANSWER THE QUESTIONS! *PREVIOUS EMPLOYMENT?*

FREE-LANCE LAW OFFICER!

FREE-LANCE...? ER--*REASON* FOR APPLICATION?

SURVIVAL!

HEY--ARE YOU *PUTTING ME ON*, MISTER... SMITH--?

NO, YOU'RE *NOT*, ARE YOU? I CAN SEE IT IN YOUR *EYES!*

TELL ME, SIR-- WHEN WAS THE *LAST* TIME YOU HAD A DECENT MEAL?

WHY, I...

NEVER MIND--I CAN *IMAGINE!* C'MON--I'LL TREAT YOU TO *LUNCH!*

BUT--!

NO *BUTS!* THE NAME'S *KATHY SUTTON*-- GIRL-SAMARITAN--AND I HAVEN'T *LOST* A CLIENT YET!

14

SHORTLY...

FOR A GUY WHO HASN'T *EATEN* LATELY, YOU SURE DON'T SEEM *HUNGRY!*

SOMETHING *WRONG?*

NO--I WAS MERELY WONDERING WHY YOU ARE SO *GENEROUS* TO A *STRANGER!*

YOU'RE NO STRANGER, SMITH--I SEE YOUR TYPE EVERY DAY! NEW TO THE BIG CITY--FULL OF *DREAMS--IDEALS--* BUT WITH NO *MONEY--*NO PLACE TO *STAY!*

HECK--I WAS LIKE THAT *MYSELF* ONCE!

YOU'RE QUITE A *WOMAN,* KATHY SUTTON!

SURE--THE LAST OF THE SOFT TOUCHES, THAT'S *ME!*

STILL--IF YOU NEED A PLACE TO *STAY--*I THINK I CAN *FIND* YOU ONE!

THAT WOULD BE *APPRECIATED!*

IT'S A *NICE* ROOM, MR. SMITH--YOU'LL *LIKE* IT! NEVER WOULD'VE RENTED IT TO A *STRANGER* IF MISS SUTTON HADN'T PUT IN A GOOD WORD FOR YA--

--AND *ADVANCED* ME THE FIRST WEEK'S *RENT!*

SHE'S A *DARLIN'* GIRL, KATHY IS!

YES--SHE'S A *"DARLIN'"* GIRL, INDEED!

15

IN THE DAYS THAT FOLLOW, THE BOND OF *FRIENDSHIP* GROWS STRONGER BETWEEN THE VIBRANT *KATHY SUTTON* AND THE SOMBER-FACED ANDROID WHO CALLS HIMSELF *JOHN SMITH*...

...FOR IT IS A BOND FORGED OF MUTUAL ENJOYMENT AND PERHAPS, THE FIRST SAD, STINGING FLAMES OF--*LOVE*...

BUT, MILES AWAY, A SINISTER, WHITE-GARBED FIGURE CONSIDERS THAT BOND THE *WEAKEST* LINK IN A FAR MORE *DANGEROUS* CHAIN...

SO--THE *RED TORNADO* HAS FOUND HIMSELF A *GIRL FRIEND!* DIDN'T THINK HE HAD IT *IN* HIM!

NO MATTER, THOUGH-- FOR HE'S PROVIDED ME WITH NUMEROUS NEW POSSIBILITIES--

--AND TIME IS *RUNNING OUT* FOR ME!

AND THE FOLLOWING MORNING...

JOHN! JOHN-- I'VE *GOT* SOMETHING FOR YOU--!

I'VE FOUND YOU A *JOB!*

THAT'S *SPLENDID,* KATHY!

WELL...IT'S NOT *MUCH* OF A JOB, REALLY--JUST A *LAB ASSISTANT* TO A DOCTOR *GORDON*-- BUT...

KATHY--DO YOU HEAR AN ODD *SOUND?*

16

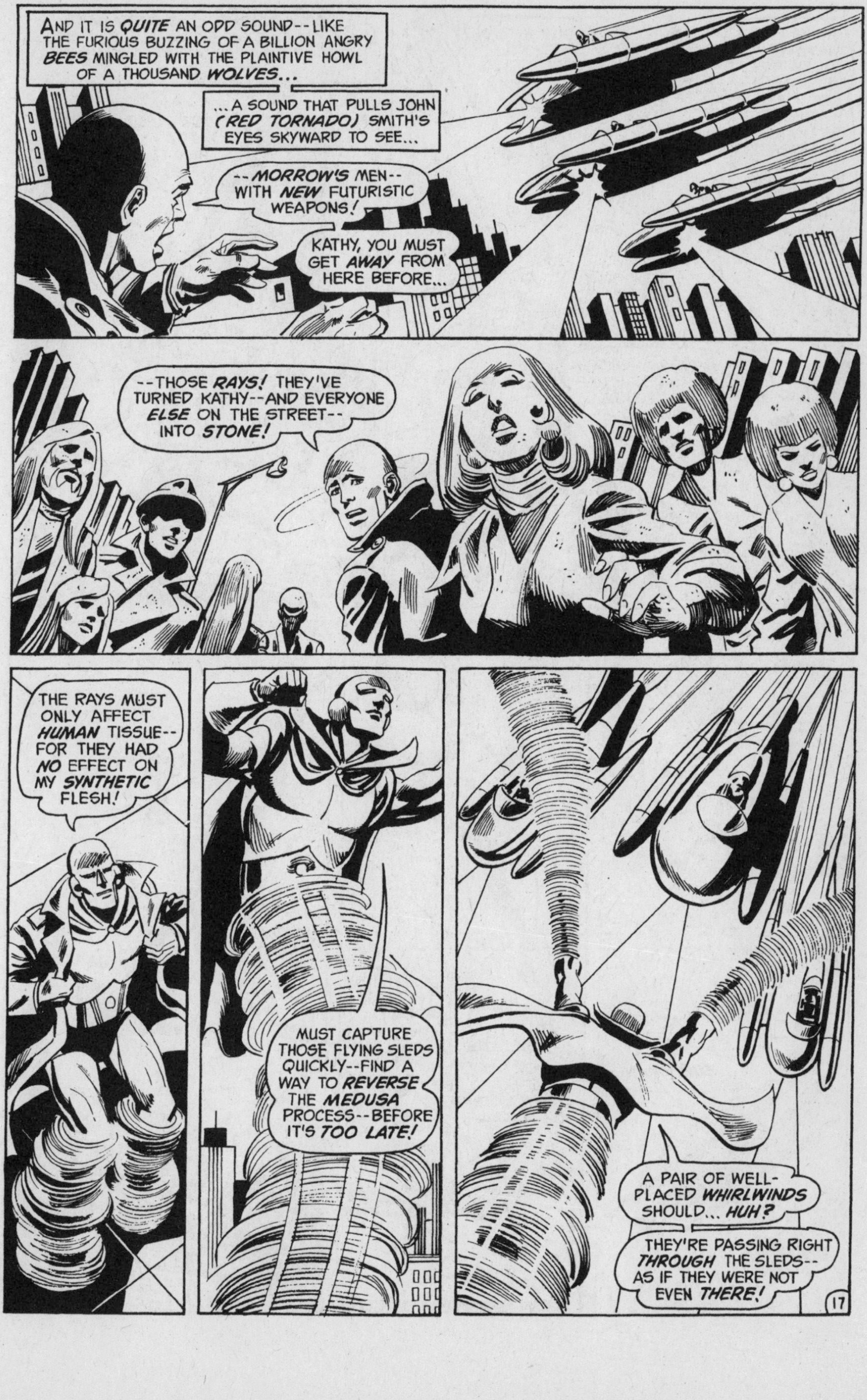
AND IT IS QUITE AN ODD SOUND--LIKE THE FURIOUS BUZZING OF A BILLION ANGRY BEES MINGLED WITH THE PLAINTIVE HOWL OF A THOUSAND WOLVES...
...A SOUND THAT PULLS JOHN (RED TORNADO) SMITH'S EYES SKYWARD TO SEE...
--MORROW'S MEN--WITH NEW FUTURISTIC WEAPONS!
KATHY, YOU MUST GET AWAY FROM HERE BEFORE...
--THOSE RAYS! THEY'VE TURNED KATHY--AND EVERYONE ELSE ON THE STREET--INTO STONE!
THE RAYS MUST ONLY AFFECT HUMAN TISSUE--FOR THEY HAD NO EFFECT ON MY SYNTHETIC FLESH!
MUST CAPTURE THOSE FLYING SLEDS QUICKLY--FIND A WAY TO REVERSE THE MEDUSA PROCESS--BEFORE IT'S TOO LATE!
A PAIR OF WELL-PLACED WHIRLWINDS SHOULD... HUH?
THEY'RE PASSING RIGHT THROUGH THE SLEDS--AS IF THEY WERE NOT EVEN THERE!
17

THAT'S 'CAUSE WE *WEREN'T* THERE, WISE GUY! THESE SHIPS ARE PROTECTED BY *IMAGE-DISTORTERS*-- LITTLE DODADS THAT MAKE YA SEE US WHERE WE *AIN'T*!

BUT WE CAN SEE *YOU* PERFECT-LIKE!

UUHHNN-- ENERGY BOLTS DISRUPTING MY CIRCUITS! CAN'T *MOVE*--!

B B B ZZAATT

BUT THE SCARLET-CLAD FORM HAS SCARCELY HIT THE SIDEWALK WHEN ANOTHER POWERFUL FORM STREAKS IN TO TAKE ITS PLACE...

EASY, *TORNADO!* I'LL HANDLE THIS!

SUPERMAN!

I'VE HEARD OF MAKING *LARGE* WITHDRAWALS-- BUT THERE'S A *LIMIT*--

LET GO OF THAT *BANK, SUPERMAN*--

-- OR WOULD'JA LIKE US TO DROP *HER* INSTEAD?

YOU WOULDN'T *DARE*--!

WOULDN'T WE?

KATHY-- NOOOOO!

NO!

18

HANG ON TO YOUR PROPELLER-BEANIE, *TORNADO*-- THE LADY IS IN *GOOD* HANDS!

WHO IN--?

THE *ELONGATED MAN!* HAVE *YOU* BEEN TRAILING ME, TOO?

ANYTHING FOR A *PAL,* PAL! RALPH-- ONCE-AN- *OUTFIELDER* ALWAYS-AN-*OUTFIELDER*-- DIBNY, AT YOUR SERVICE--

--AND I *DIDN'T* COME ALONE!

HAWKMAN! BUT THAT *MACE* WILL DO HIM NO GOOD! HE CANNOT ATTACK SOMETHING THAT IS *NOT* WHERE ONE SEES IT!

THOSE DEVICES AREN'T REALLY *INVISIBLE!* THEY JUST DEFLECT THEIR IMAGES AGAINST AN EMPTY SKY!

BUT WHAT IF THAT SKY WERE *NOT* EMPTY?

WHEET WHEET

SUDDENLY, THE AIR IS ALIVE WITH THE BEATING OF WINGS-- AS AN AVIAN ARMY RESPONDS TO *HAWKMAN'S* WHISTLED CALL...

♪WHEET!♪ ♪WHEET!♪ FILL THE SKY, MY BROTHERS! TURN IT BLACK AS *NIGHT!*

WITHIN INSTANTS...

I'VE *"FOULED UP"* THE AIR-SPACE SO MUCH, WE CAN MAKE OUT THE *TRUE* LOCATIONS OF THE THREE FLYERS AS OPPOSED TO THE *PROJECTED* IMAGES!

ENOUGH *EXPLANATION,* HAWKMAN! LET'S *HIT* 'EM!

19

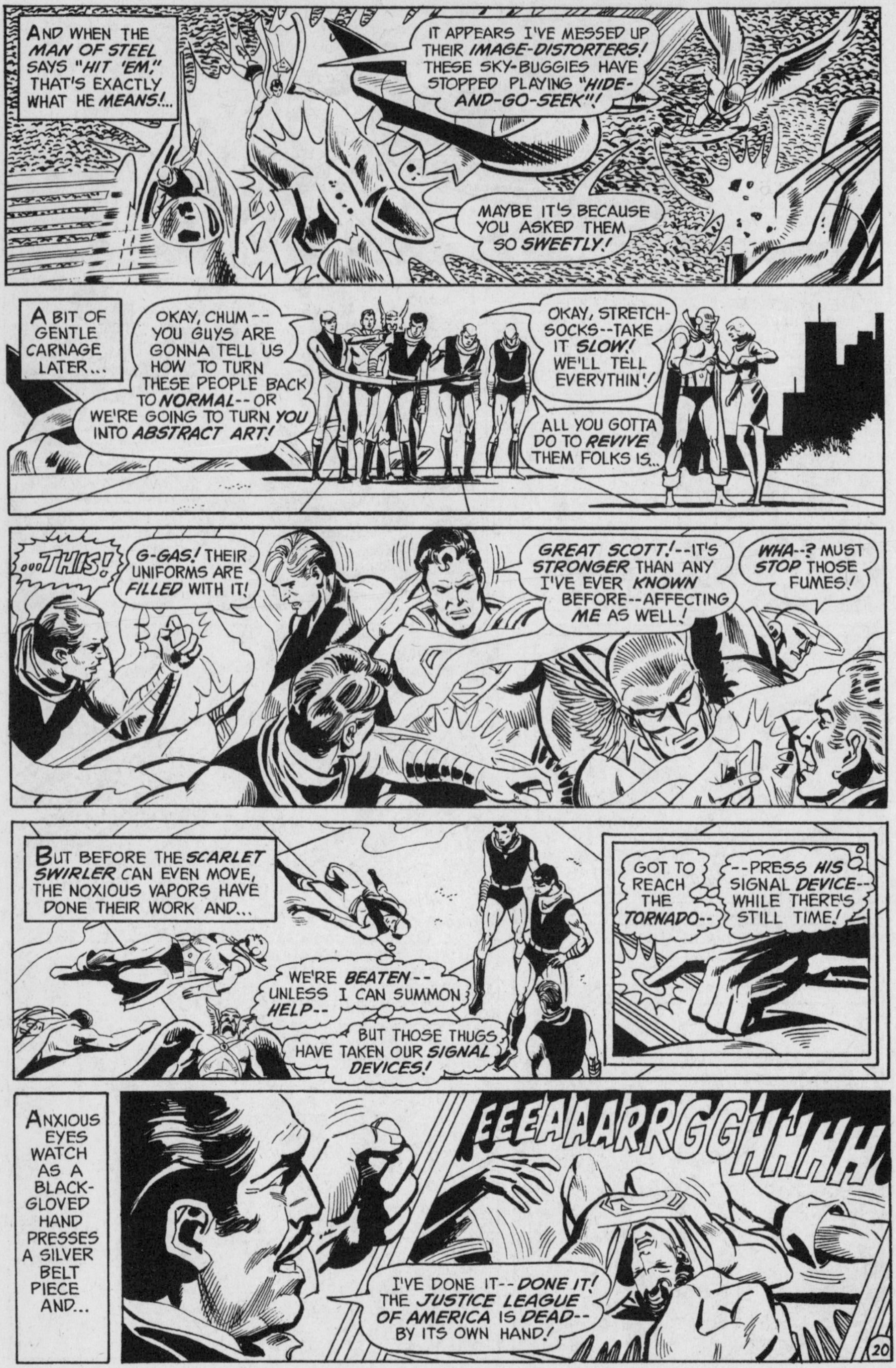
AND WHEN THE MAN OF STEEL SAYS "HIT 'EM," THAT'S EXACTLY WHAT HE MEANS!...
IT APPEARS I'VE MESSED UP THEIR IMAGE-DISTORTERS! THESE SKY-BUGGIES HAVE STOPPED PLAYING "HIDE-AND-GO-SEEK"!
MAYBE IT'S BECAUSE YOU ASKED THEM SO SWEETLY!
A BIT OF GENTLE CARNAGE LATER...
OKAY, CHUM-- YOU GUYS ARE GONNA TELL US HOW TO TURN THESE PEOPLE BACK TO NORMAL--OR WE'RE GOING TO TURN YOU INTO ABSTRACT ART!
OKAY, STRETCH-SOCKS--TAKE IT SLOW! WE'LL TELL EVERYTHIN'!
ALL YOU GOTTA DO TO REVIVE THEM FOLKS IS...
...THIS!
G-GAS! THEIR UNIFORMS ARE FILLED WITH IT!
GREAT SCOTT!--IT'S STRONGER THAN ANY I'VE EVER KNOWN BEFORE--AFFECTING ME AS WELL!
WHA--? MUST STOP THOSE FUMES!
BUT BEFORE THE SCARLET SWIRLER CAN EVEN MOVE, THE NOXIOUS VAPORS HAVE DONE THEIR WORK AND...
WE'RE BEATEN-- UNLESS I CAN SUMMON HELP--
BUT THOSE THUGS HAVE TAKEN OUR SIGNAL DEVICES!
GOT TO REACH THE TORNADO--
--PRESS HIS SIGNAL DEVICE-- WHILE THERE'S STILL TIME!
ANXIOUS EYES WATCH AS A BLACK-GLOVED HAND PRESSES A SILVER BELT PIECE AND...
EEEAAARRGGHHHH
I'VE DONE IT--DONE IT! THE JUSTICE LEAGUE OF AMERICA IS DEAD-- BY ITS OWN HAND!
20

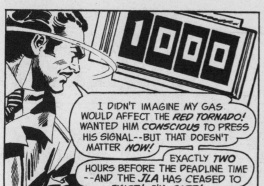

I DIDN'T IMAGINE MY GAS WOULD AFFECT THE *RED TORNADO!* WANTED HIM *CONSCIOUS* TO PRESS HIS SIGNAL--BUT THAT DOESN'T MATTER *NOW!*

EXACTLY *TWO* HOURS BEFORE THE DEADLINE TIME --AND THE *JLA* HAS CEASED TO *EXIST!* I'M *SAFE!*

I'VE BEEN COOPED UP IN THIS LAB FOR ALMOST A *MONTH!* TIME I WENT TO GET SOME *FRESH AIR*-- AND *CELEBRATE!*

GOING SOMEWHERE, *T.O. MORROW?*

NO! IT CAN'T BE!

YOU'RE *DEAD*-- YOU'RE *ALL DEAD!!*

A GROSS *EXAGGERATION,* MORROW! *NONE* OF US IS DEAD! WE JUST WANTED TO MAKE YOU *THINK* SO!

RIGHT! *SUPERMAN* DISCOVERED THAT *EXTRA* CIRCUIT INSIDE *R.T.* DAYS AGO-- AND BURNED IT OUT WITH HIS *SUPER-VISION!*

BUT WHAT I SAW ON MY *SCREEN*--?!

JUST A LITTLE *SHOW* PUT ON FOR YOUR BENEFIT--WITH THE HELP OF MY *POWER RING!*

WE WANTED TO MAKE SURE YOU HAD NO *OTHER* HOLD ON THE *TORNADO* THAT WE *DIDN'T* KNOW ABOUT!

21

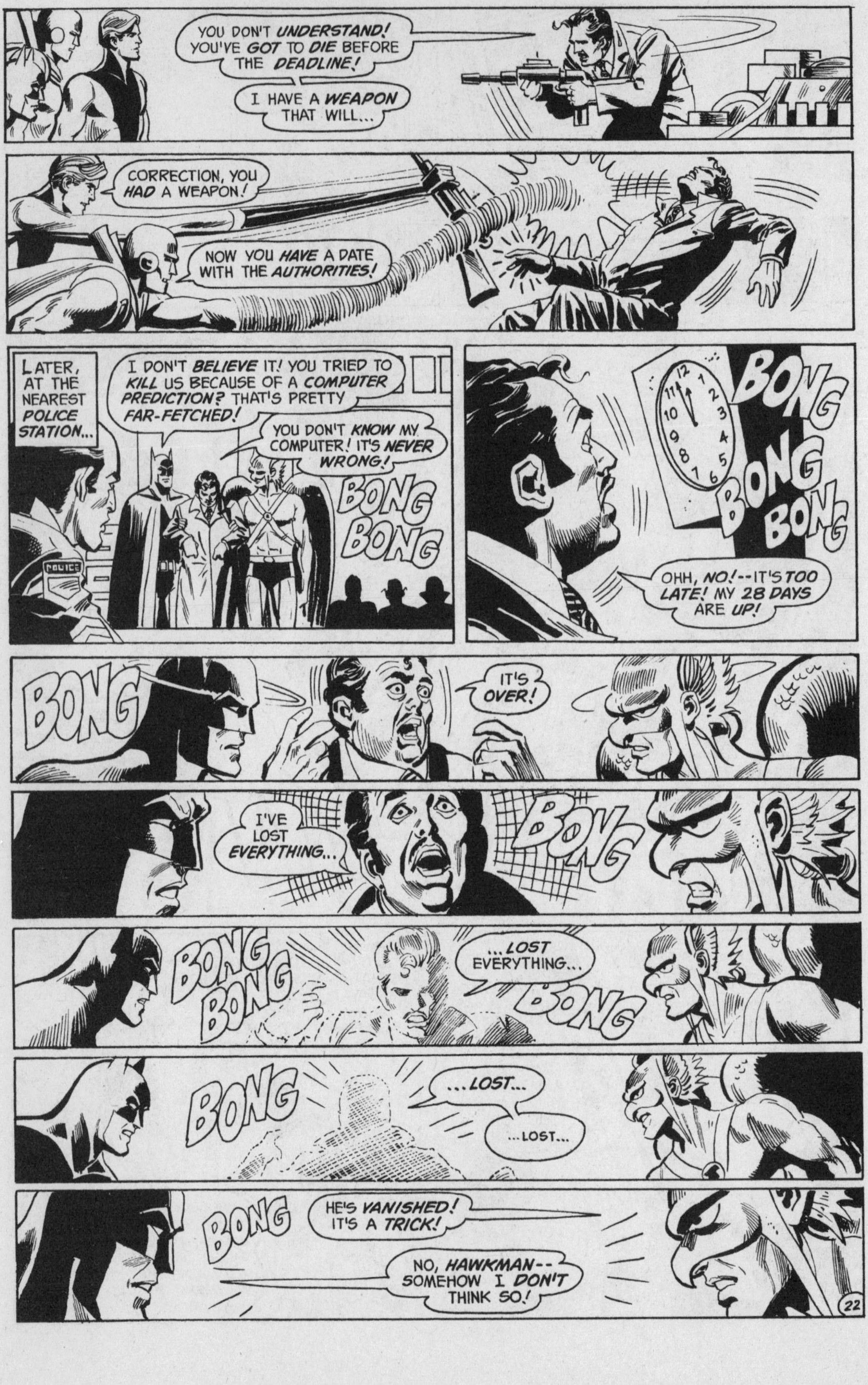
YOU DON'T UNDERSTAND! YOU'VE GOT TO DIE BEFORE THE DEADLINE!
I HAVE A WEAPON THAT WILL...
CORRECTION, YOU HAD A WEAPON!
NOW YOU HAVE A DATE WITH THE AUTHORITIES!
LATER, AT THE NEAREST POLICE STATION...
I DON'T BELIEVE IT! YOU TRIED TO KILL US BECAUSE OF A COMPUTER PREDICTION? THAT'S PRETTY FAR-FETCHED!
YOU DON'T KNOW MY COMPUTER! IT'S NEVER WRONG!
BONG BONG
POLICE
BONG BONG BONG
OHH, NO!--IT'S TOO LATE! MY 28 DAYS ARE UP!
BONG
IT'S OVER!
I'VE LOST EVERYTHING...
BONG
BONG BONG
...LOST EVERYTHING...
BONG
BONG
...LOST...
...LOST...
BONG
HE'S VANISHED! IT'S A TRICK!
NO, HAWKMAN-- SOMEHOW I DON'T THINK SO!
22

IN *JLA HQ.,* AFTER *MORROW'S* UNDERLINGS HAVE BEEN JAILED-- AND THEIR VICTIMS REVIVED...

SORRY IF WE SEEMED TO *USE* YOU, *TORNADO*-- BUT WE HAD *NO* IDEA HOW MUCH *CONTROL* *MORROW* HAD OVER YOU!

AN *UNDERSTANDABLE* REACTION, *BATMAN*-- WHEN THE PERSON YOU ARE DEALING WITH IS A--*MACHINE!*

BUT YOU'RE *NOT* A MACHINE, *TORNADO*-- JUST A BIT MORE *VULNERABLE* TO CERTAIN THINGS THAN *MOST* PEOPLE ARE!

MY OWN THOUGHTS EXACTLY, *GREEN LANTERN!* NOW-- IF YOU FELLOWS WILL *EXCUSE* ME--?

RED TORNADO, WHERE ARE YOU *GOING?* IS IT SOMETHING WE *SAID?*

IN A WAY, *RALPH DIBNY...* *IN A WAY!*

I'M GOING TO DISCOVER IF AN ANDROID IS VUNERABLE TO-- *LOVE!*

THE END

SHOWCASE
PRESENTS

LOOK FOR THESE OTHER TITLES FEATURING CLASSIC TALES OF THE MEMBERS OF THE JUSTICE LEAGUE OF AMERICA!

SHOWCASE

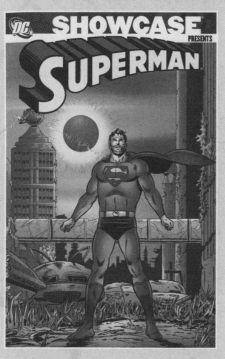
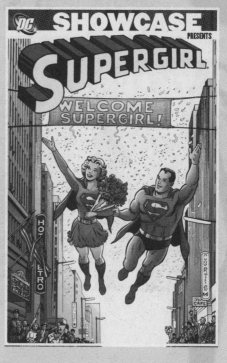

SHOWCASE
PRESENTS

LOOK FOR THESE OTHER TITLES FEATURING
CLASSIC TALES OF THE DARK KNIGHT!

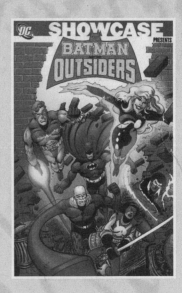